Generative Approaches to
Finnic and Saami Linguistics

Generative Approaches to Finnic and Saami Linguistics

edited by

Diane Nelson
Satu Manninen

CSLI PUBLICATIONS
Center for the Study of
Language and Information
Stanford, California

CSLI Publications
Center for the Study of Language and Information
Leland Stanford Junior University
Printed in the United States
07 06 05 04 03 5 4 3 2 1

Library of Congress Cataloging-in-Publication Data

Generative approaches to Finnic and Saami linguistics /
edited by Diane Nelson and Satu Manninen.
p. cm. (CSLI lecture notes ; no. 148)
Includes bibliographical references and index.

ISBN 1-57586-412-6 (pbk. : alk. paper)
ISBN 1-57586-411-8 (hardback : alk. paper)

1. Finnic languages–Grammar, Generative.
I. Nelson, Diane Carlita, 1968-
II. Manninen, Satu, 1968-
III. Series.
PH93.G46 2003
494′.54–dc21 2003005481
CIP

∞ The acid-free paper used in this book meets the minimum requirements of the American National Standard for Information Sciences—Permanence of Paper for Printed Library Materials, ANSI Z39.48-1984.

CSLI was founded in 1983 by researchers from Stanford University, SRI International, and Xerox PARC to further the research and development of integrated theories of language, information, and computation. CSLI headquarters and CSLI Publications are located on the campus of Stanford University.

CSLI Publications reports new developments in the study of language, information, and computation. In addition to lecture notes, our publications include monographs, working papers, revised dissertations, and conference proceedings. Our aim is to make new results, ideas, and approaches available as quickly as possible. Please visit our web site at
http://cslipublications.stanford.edu/
for comments on this and other titles, as well as for changes and corrections by the author and publisher.

Contents

Contributors

ASH ASUDEH: Department of Linguistics, Stanford University, Margaret Jacks Hall, Bldg. 460, Stanford CA 94305-2150, USA.
asudeh@csli.stanford.edu

KERSTI BÖRJARS: Department of Linguistics, University of Manchester, Manchester M13 9PL, UK.
kersti.borjars@man.ac.uk

MARTIN EHALA: Department of General and Applied Linguistics, Tallinn Pedagogical University, Narva Rd 25, Tallinn EE 101 20, Estonia.
ehala@tpu.ee

VIVIENNE FONG: Department of English Language and Literature, National University of Singapore, Blk AS5, 7 Arts Link, Singapore 117570, and Department of Linguistics, New York University, 719 Broadway, 4th Floor, New York, NY 10003, USA.
ellfongf@nus.edu.sg

HELI HARRIKARI: Institute of General and Theoretical Linguistics, University of Tübingen, Wilhelmstaße 113, 72 074 Tübingen, Germany.
heli_harrikari@uni-tuebingen.de

KATRIN HIIETAM: Department of Linguistics, University of Manchester, Manchester M13 9PL, UK.
katrin.hiietam@stud.man.ac.uk

MARIT JULIEN: Department of Linguistics, University of Tromsø, 9037 Tromsø, Norway.
marit.julien@hum.uit.no

ELSI KAISER: Department of Linguistics, University of Pennsylvania, 619 Williams Hall, 36th and Spruce Street, Philadelphia, PA 19104-6305, USA.
ekaiser@babel.ling.upenn.edu

PAUL KIPARSKY: Department of Linguistics, Stanford University, Margaret Jacks Hall, Bldg. 460, Stanford CA 94305-2150, USA.
kiparsky@csli.stanford.edu

SATU MANNINEN: Department of English, University of Lund, Helgonabacken 14, 223 62 Lund, Sweden.
satu.manninen@englund.lu.se

DIANE NELSON: Department of Linguistics and Phonetics, University of Leeds, Leeds LS2 9JT, UK.
d.c.nelson@leeds.ac.uk

MIKAEL SVONNI: Department of Archeology and Sami Studies, University of Umeå, 901 87 Umeå, Sweden.
mikael.svonni@samiska.umu.se

IDA TOIVONEN: Linguistics Department, University of Canterbury, Private Bag 4800, Christchurch, New Zealand.
ida.toivonen@canterbury.ac.nz

ANNE VAINIKKA: Department of Cognitive Science, The Johns Hopkins University, 243 Krieger Hall, 3400 N. Charles St, Baltimore, MD 21218-2685, USA.
avainikka@vonneumann.cog.jhu.edu

MIKAEL VINKA: Department of Linguistics, McGill University, 1001 Sherbrooke Street W, Montreal PQ H3A 1G5, Canada.
evinka@PO-Box.McGill.CA

1

Introduction

SATU MANNINEN AND DIANE NELSON

1 Preliminary Remarks

The idea for this volume was born in August 1999.[1] A number of young linguists working on Finnish and related languages within the generative frameworks met at a conference in Helsinki, and we realised that most of us were currently living outside of Finland and knew very little of each other's work or existence. One important aim of this volume is therefore to bring together younger researchers working on the syntax, semantics, and phonology of the Finnic and Saami languages from a current generative perspective, and to provide a forum where work on these languages can be presented. A further goal is to familiarise researchers working within the generative frameworks with the specific properties of Finnic and Saami, and to encourage further work on these languages within these frameworks. As most of the languages in this family have only a few hundred elderly speakers each, it is of utmost importance to raise awareness of their structure and properties before they die out completely.[2]

[1] The authors gratefully acknowledge financial support from the British Academy Joint Activities Fund towards work in editing this volume. We would also like to thank the reviewers, Katrin Hiietam for help with the Estonian data in this chapter, Marit Julien for help with the Saami data and Arto Anttila for comments on a draft.

[2] The original goal was to include papers on a number of Finnic and Saami languages. It soon became clear, however, that little or no work exists on most of these languages within the

Generative Approaches to Finnic and Saami Linguistics.
Diane Nelson and Satu Manninen (eds.).

This introduction is intended to provide a background to the chapters that follow. In section 2 we outline the historical and current geographical situation of Finnic and Saami. In section 3 we discuss the morphology and syntax of this group of languages. Our aim is to give the reader a general idea of the form of these languages, and to help those readers who have little or no previous knowledge of the languages to decipher morphologically complex examples throughout the volume.[3] In section 4 we discuss the most important phonological properties of Finnic and Saami, and in section 5 we introduce the individual papers. In each section, the emphasis will be on those areas with which the papers in this volume are concerned. Throughout the discussion, we will also give references to previous (often non-generative) work done on the morphology, syntax, and phonology of Finnic and Saami.

2 An Overview of the Finnic and Saami Languages

Finnic and Saami belong to the Finno-Ugrian sub-group of the Uralic languages. The Finnic languages and dialects, also often called the *Baltic-*Finnic languages and dialects, comprise Finnish, Karelian, Veps, Ingrian, Ludian, Votic (Votian), Estonian, and Livonian, while the Saami languages and dialects comprise the Eastern, Central, and Southern Saami language groups. More distant relatives of Finnic and Saami include the Volgan languages Mordvin and Mari. The Permic languages, Udmurt and Komi, and the Ugrian languages Mansi, Khanty, and Hungarian are also related (e.g. Karlsson 1982; Leino 1989; Lehikoinen 1995; Price 1998; Kulonen 1999; Laakso 1999; Lehtinen 2000, and the references cited there):

generative frameworks. The articles in this volume therefore mainly focus on the structure and properties of the larger languages Finnish and Estonian, as well as on the Saami group, which has recently started to receive more attention. We hope that this volume will stimulate further work on the lesser-studied languages in this group.

3 Special abbreviations in this chapter include: ALL=allative case; ABESS=abessive case; ADESS=adessive case; ABL=ablative case; INESS=inessive case; PART=partitive case; PCP=participle; PX=possessive affix.

Finnic	**Saami**	**Volgan**	**Permic**	**Ugrian**	**Samoyed**
Finnish	Eastern	Mordvin	Udmurt	Mansi	Nenets
Karelian	Central	Mari	Komi	Khanty	Enets
Veps	Southern			Hungarian	Nganasan
Ingrian					Selkup
Ludian					
Votic					
Estonian					
Livonian					
		Finno-Ugric group			**Uralic group**

→

Distance to Finnic increases

Table 1: The relatives of Finnic and Saami

The Finnic languages have developed from a common proto-language, so-called early proto-Finnic, which was spoken by groups of people living in the areas surrounding the Gulf of Finland about 1,000 BC. Although the origin of the Saami group has been subject of much debate in the past, the generally accepted current view is that they, too, are an offspring of early proto-Finnic see (see e.g. Posti 1953; Korhonen 1981; Koivulehto 1988; Price 1998; Sammallahti 1998a, 1998b; Kulonen 1999; Laakso 1999; Lehtinen 2000, and the references given therein). The Saami languages were the first to diverge from early proto-Finnic, forming a common proto-Lappic language around 1,000 BC – 700 AD. Proto-Lappic then developed into the various modern Saami languages and dialects. The relation between Finnic and Saami can be illustrated as follows:

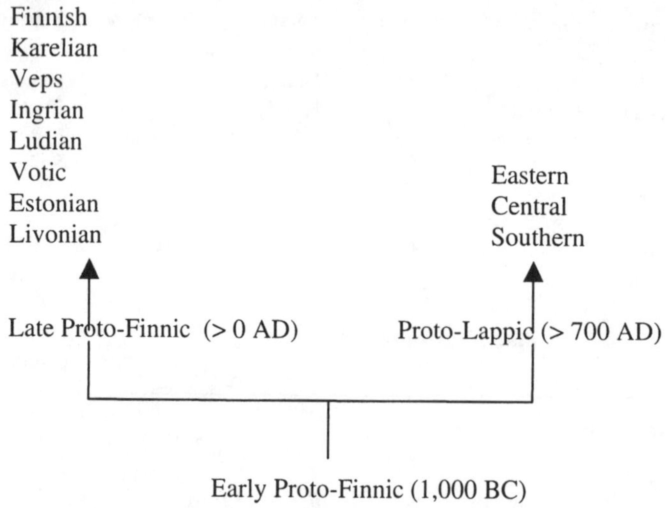

Figure 1: The relation between Finnic and Saami

The Finnic languages can be divided further into (i) the northern and eastern languages and dialects, and (ii) the southern languages and dialects. The northern varieties include Finnish, which is the national language of Finland and is spoken by around 5 million people living in Finland and the adjacent areas. The eastern varieties include Karelian, Ingrian, Ludian, Veps, and Votic, spoken in the north-western parts of Russia, in the area stretching from the Kola peninsula in the north to the Gulf of Finland in the south (see the map in Figure 2 below). The largest of the eastern varieties, Karelian, is spoken by 40,000-100,000 people. Ludian and Veps have about 5,000-6,000 speakers each, while the estimates for the number of people speaking Ingrian and Votic vary from 300-800 for Ingrian to less than 50 elderly speakers for Votic. [4]

The southern Finnic languages include Estonian and Livonian. Estonian is the national language of Estonia and currently has about 1 million speakers, most of whom live in Estonia, Russia, Finland and Sweden. Livonian,

[4] These are the most recent estimates given by the Department of Finno-Ugrian Studies of the University of Helsinki in 1998 (http://www.helsinki.fi/~tasalmin/fu.html). The estimates vary greatly because it is not always clear whether the people in question have listed themselves as being only of ethnic Finnic minority origin, or whether they are also actual speakers of these languages. For example, some sources estimate that only about 10% of the people living in the Karelian Republic in Russia speak Karelian as their mother tongue.

the once dominant language of the coastal areas of Latvia (the so-called Līvõd Rānda, or Livonian Coast, surrounding the Gulf of Riga) is currently on the brink of extinction, with less than a dozen elderly speakers. The close relationship of the Finnic languages in terms of their basic vocabulary can be observed from Table 2, which lists the numerals from 1 to 10 in Finnish, Veps, Votic, Estonian, and Livonian:

	Finnish	Veps	Votic	Estonian	Livonian
1	yksi	üks'	uhsi	üks	ikš
2	kaksi	kaks'	kahsi	kaks	kakš
3	kolme	koume	kőlmőd	kolm	kuolm
4	neljä	nel'l'	nellä	neli	neel'a
5	viisi	viž	viisi	viis	viiž
6	kuusi	kuź	kuusi	kuus	kuuž
7	seitsemän	siičmen	seitsee	seitse	seis
8	kahdeksan	kahcan	kahősa	kaheksa	kaadőks
9	yhdeksän	ühcan	uhesää	üheksa	iidőks
10	kymmenen	kümńen	tšümmee	kümme	kim

Table 2: Numerals 1-10 in some Finnic languages

While the status of Finnish and Estonian as distinct languages is uncontroversial, the status of the other varieties is less clear. Rather than being a separate language, Votic is sometimes considered an offshoot of Estonian, while Ingrian and Ludian are sometimes thought to be just remote branches of Karelian (see e.g. Laakso 1999). Although we will adopt here the view that Finnish, Karelian, Ingrian, Ludian, Veps, Votic, Estonian, and Livonian are all separate languages, we will assume the existence of a language/dialect continuum where the northernmost dialects of Karelian are so close to the dialects spoken in eastern Finland that they are often mutually intelligible, and where the southernmost Karelian dialects closely resemble Veps, Ingrian and Ludian. The map below illustrates the distibution of the Finnic languages (based on data from Laakso 1999 and Viitso 1998):

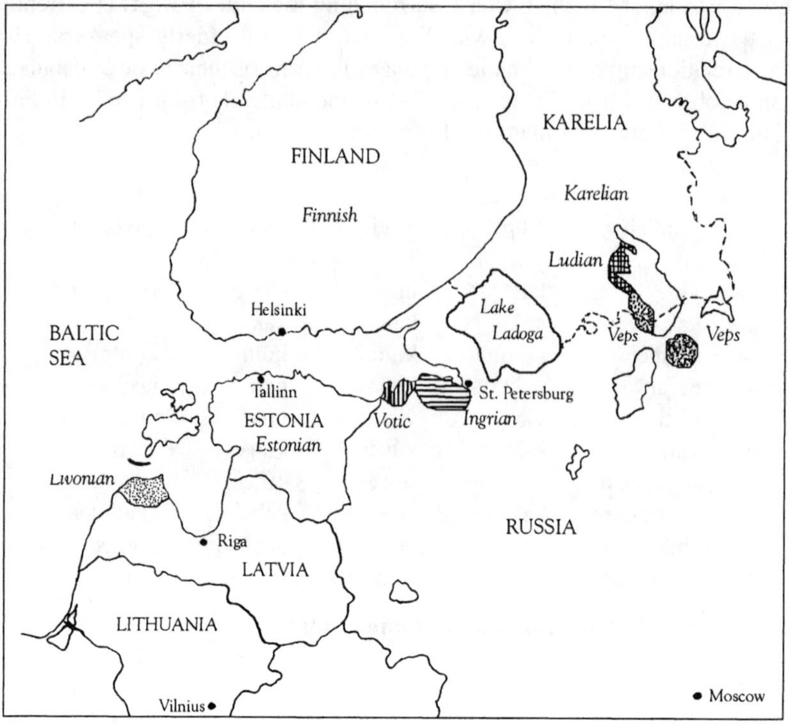

Figure 2: Map showing the distribution of the Finnic languages

The Saami languages are spoken by the Saami (Sámi; Sápmi), a minority indigenous people living in northern and central Norway, northern parts of Sweden and Finland, and in the north-western parts of Russia (the Kola peninsula). The areas where Saami languages are spoken are illustrated below (based on data from Sammallahti 1998b):

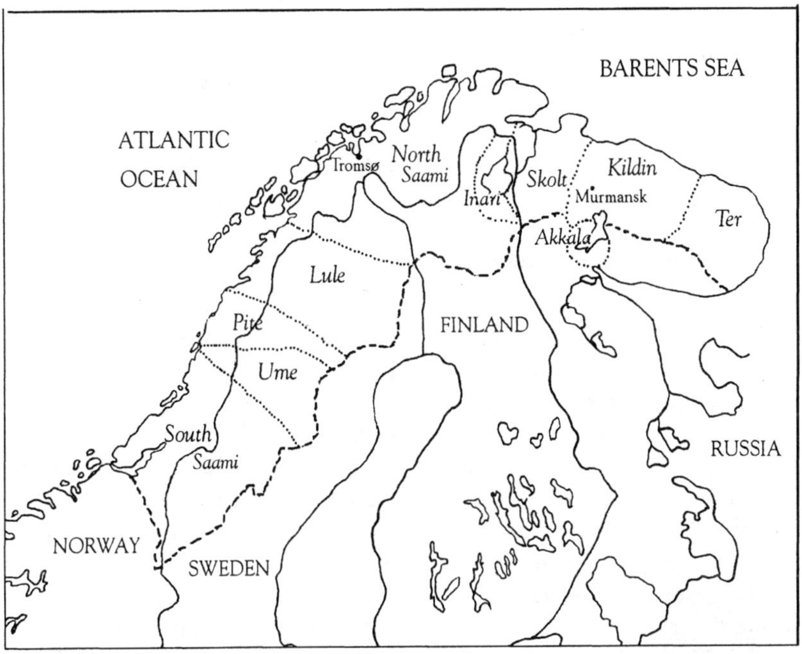

Figure 3: Map showing the distribution of the Saami languages

The Saami languages are divided into three main groups: Eastern Saami, Central Saami, and Southern Saami. As all of these have considerable differences in their grammar and lexicon and are mutually incomprehensible, they are usually classified as separate languages. The three main varieties of Saami can be divided further into ten (surviving) main linguistic areas. Again, although the main varieties are mutually unintelligible, the ten dialectal areas form a continuum where the adjacent varieties are closely related and speech in a neighbouring language is normally intelligible:[5]

[5] Sammallahti (1998a) divides the Saami languages into just two main groups: the western varieties include South Saami, Ume Saami, Pite Saami, Lule Saami, and North Saami, while the eastern varieties include Inari Saami, Skolt Saami, Akkala Saami, and Kola Saami.

Southern Saami	**Central Saami**	**Eastern Saami**
South Saami	Pite Saami	Inari Saami
Ume Saami	Lule Saami	Skolt (Kolta) Saami
	North Saami	Akkala Saami
		Kola Saami:
		Kildin Saami
		Ter (Turja) Saami

Table 3: The Saami languages and dialects

While the estimates for the overall number of Saami speakers vary from 50,000 to as many as 100,000, the different ways in which census data are collected and presented in the different countries make it virtually impossible to give any reliable estimates as to the number of speakers each language has. For example, while North Saami is thought to be spoken by about 80% of all Saami speakers, about 20-30,000 people, estimates for the number of Ter Saami speakers vary from 500 to just 6. All sources agree, however, that most Saami languages are nowadays spoken by only a few hundred elderly speakers, and are thus on the verge of becoming extinct within the next hundred years unless language preservation efforts are successful. Many, like the eastern Kemi Saami, have already disappeared (see e.g. Korhonen 1981; Lehikoinen 1995; Sammallahti 1998a and 1998b; Laakso 1999).

3 Morphological and Syntactic Properties of Finnic and Saami

In this section, we provide an introduction to the most central properties of Finnic and Saami: the emphasis will be on those areas of morphology and syntax with which papers in this volume are concerned.

The Finnic and Saami languages are all highly agglutinating, with large numbers of derivational and inflectional affixes (for discussion on the agglutinating nature of these languages, see e.g. Metslang 1994 and Grünthal 2000). The stem morphemes are often divided into three categories (nominals, verbs, and particles) on the basis of the types of inflectional morphemes that they take. We will discuss each category in more detail below.

3.1 Nominal Inflection

Finnic and Saami nominals consist of the word classes of nouns, adjectives, numerals, pronouns and some non-finite verbs. These normally take affixes for case, number and possession.

Case

The common proto-Uralic language had six morphological cases: nominative, genitive, accusative, locative, ablative, and lative (see e.g. Lehikoinen 1995: 66; Lehtinen 2000: 49). In modern Finnish, nominals can take inflectional affixes for about 15, in Estonian for about 14 and in Saami for 7-9 different cases. In Finnish and Estonian, the number of cases varies depending on the grammarians' classification of some of the less frequent cases; in Saami, the number of cases varies from language to language. Below, we give examples of the Finnish, Estonian, and Inari Saami structural cases for the singular noun 'dog':

	Finnish	**Estonian**	**Saami (Inari)**
Nominative	koira	koer	peenuv
Genitive	koiran	koera	pennuu
Accusative	koiran	—	pennuu
Partitive	koiraa	koera	penuvid[6]

Table 4: Examples of Finnish, Estonian and Inari Saami structural cases for singular *koira*, *koer* and *peenuv* 'dog'

The nominative is the basic form of the noun, while the genitive is used to express ownership, as in the Finnish *koiran pentu* and Estonian *koera kutsikas* 'a/the puppy of the dog'. The genitive is also used in postpositional phrases, such as the Finnish and Estonian *koiran edessä* and *koera ees* 'in front of a/the dog' - for more discussion of prepositional and postpositional phrases, see Manninen's contribution to this volume. Although in Finnish the accusative and genitive case forms have undergone syncretism in the singular, the distinction between these cases is still visible in the pronoun system. We will return to this briefly:

---

[6] This form has variants including *pennâgid*, *pennud* and *peenuvid* (Sammallahti and Morottaja 1993: 128).

	Nouns: *koira*, 'dog'	3s pronoun, *hän*, 'he/she'
Genitive sg	koiran	hänen
Accusative sg	koiran	hänet

Table 5: The genitive-accusative contrast in Finnish

One of the most widely-discussed features of Finnish is the fact that the accusative and partitive object cases are used to distinguish between bounded and unbounded predicate aspect, as well as to signal NP properties such as in/definiteness, specificity and mass/count; see e.g. de Hoop (1996), Heinämäki (1984), Rigler (1992), Vainikka (1989), Vainikka and Maling (1996), Kiparsky (1998), Nelson (1998a), and Askonen (2001):

(1) a. Hän luk-i kirja-n.
S/he read-PAST.3SG book-ACC
'S/he read the book.'

b. Hän luk-i kirja-a.
S/he read-PAST.3SG book-PART
'S/he was reading the/a book' / 'S/he read a book.'

(2) a. Hän sö-i voileivä-t.
S/he eat-PAST.3SG sandwich-PL.ACC
'S/he ate (all the) sandwiches.'

b. Hän sö-i voileip-i-ä.
S/he eat-PAST.3SG sandwich-PL-PART
'S/he ate (some) sandwiches/She was eating sandwiches.'

Because Estonian lacks accusative case, a similar alternation is signalled by the genitive and partitive cases. Some grammarians, including Blake (1994), have proposed that even in Estonian bounded vs unbounded predicate aspect is expressed by means of alternating the case of the direct object, while others suggest the alternation might be linked more closely to telicity:[7]

[7] Thanks to Katrin Hiietam for discussing the Estonian data. Although we will assume here that alternation between genitive and partitive case is associated with predicate aspect in Esto-

(3) a. Ta luges raamatu (läbi).
S/he read.PAST.3SG book.GEN (through)
'S/he read a book.'

b. Ta luges raamatu-t.
S/he read.PAST.3SG book-PART
'S/he was reading a book.'

(4) a. Ta sõi võileiba-de.
S/he eat.PAST.3SG sandwich-PL.GEN
'S/he ate the sandwiches.'

b. Ta sõi võileibu.
S/he eat.PAST.3SG sandwich.PL.PART
'S/he ate (some) sandwiches/She was eating sandwiches.'

In Saami, no equivalent of the Finnish and Estonian accusative/genitive-partitive case contrast occurs to mark boundedness or perfectivity, but certain aspectual contrasts are signalled via verbal morphology. Some examples (from North Saami) are given below (data from Sammallahti 1998a: 88):

(5) a. vuodjit 'to drive'
b. vuojašit 'to keep driving'
c. vuojęstit 'to drive a little'

Let us now turn to look at Finnic and Saami locative cases. These can be divided further into the abstract, inner, and outer locative cases; as is clear from Table 6, the Saami languages do not have as rich a system of locative cases as Finnish and Estonian:

---

nian, not everyone agrees. Some discussion on Estonian object case can be found in Nemvalts (1996), Erelt et al (1997), Metslang (1994, 1997), and Grünthal (2000). Estonian also often uses a large number of particles (e.g. *läbi* 'through' and *ära* 'away') to ensure that the distinction between bounded and unbounded predicate aspect is made. This is particularly common in nouns where the genitive and partitive forms are identical: *Ta sõi kala ära* 'S/he ate (all the) fish' vs. *Ta sõi kala* 'S/he ate (some) fish'.

	Finnish[8]	**Estonian**	**Saami (Inari)**[9]
Abstract locatives			
Translative	koira-ksi	koera-ks	-
Essive	koira-na	koera-na	penuv-in
Inner locatives			
Inessive	koira-ssa	koera-s	-
Elative	koira-sta	koera-st	pennu-st (locative)
Illative	koira-an	koera-sse	pennu(u)v-ân
Outer locatives			
Adessive	koira-lla	koera-l	-
Ablative	koira-lta	koera-lt	-
Allative	koira-lle	koera-le	-

Table 6: The locative cases in Finnish, Estonian and Inari Saami for singular *koira*, *koer* and *peenuv* 'dog'

The translative case is often used with change of state verbs, to indicate that something changes into something else ('into a dog'), while the essive case occurs with stative verbs and describes properties ('as/like a dog') – these cases are discussed in Fong's contribution to this volume. The inner locative cases are used to indicate that something is located inside of something else (inessive: 'in a dog'), or that something moves outside (elative: 'out of a dog') or inside (illative: 'into a dog') of something else. The outer locative cases are used to indicate that something is located on top of something else (adessive: 'on a dog'), or moves away from (ablative: 'from a dog') or on top of (allative: 'to a dog') something else. In Saami, these directional meanings are represented by illative and locative cases only. Each of these locative cases has also other uses: the Finnish and Estonian adessive, as well as the Saami locative, are frequently used to express pos-

8 For more detailed discussions of the Finnish locative cases, see Nikanne (1991, 1993), Manninen (this volume), and Löbel (1994).

9 All of the inflected forms given in this table have variants, listed in Sammallahti and Morottaja (1993: 128).

session (see the examples in (6) below) and manner meaning, for example, while the allative case is frequently found on indirect objects of ditransitive predicates (see (7)):

(6) a. Koira-lla on nälkä. (Finnish)
Dog-ADESS be.3SG hunger.NOM
'The dog is hungry.'

b. Koera-l on nälg. (Estonian)
Dog-ADESS be.3SG hunger.NOM
'The dog is hungry.'

c. Mu-ste laa kuttâ poccuu. (Inari Saami)
I-LOC be.3PL six reindeer.SG/ACC
'I have six reindeer.'

(7) a. Matti anto-i Maija-lle omena-n. (Finnish)
Matti give-PAST.3SG Maija-ALL apple-ACC
'Matti gave Maija an apple.'

b. Mati andi-s Mari-le õuna. (Estonian)
Mati give-PAST.3SG Mari-ALL apple.GEN
'Mati gave Mari an apple.'

Let us now look briefly the Finnic and Saami marginal cases. Note that some of these can only appear with plural nouns:

	Finnish	Estonian	Saami (Inari)
Abessive	koira-tta	koera-ta	pennuu-ttáá
Comitative	koir-i-ne-en (pl)	koera-ga	pennu(u)-in[10]
Instructive	koir-i-n (pl)	—	—
Terminative	—	koera-ni	—

Table 7: The marginal cases in Finnish, Estonian and Inari Saami for singular *koira*, *koer* and *peenuv* 'dog'

The abessive case is usually used to indicate that something is lacking ('without a dog'), while the comitative case indicates that something is pre-

[10] Sammallahti and Morottaja (1993: 128) give *pennâgááin* as a variant form.

sent ('with a dog'). The instructive is used to indicate that something is performed with (the help of) something else ('with the help of a dog'). The Estonian terminative indicates how far something moves ('up to the dog').

The core structural cases in Finnish

As mentioned above, the accusative-partitive case alternation in Finnish reflects semantic contrasts related to NP semantics (quantizedness, definiteness, specificity and mass/count) and VP-semantics (telicity and boundedness). Another aspect of Finnish syntax which has attracted attention in the generative literature is the distribution of the core structural cases, nominative, accusative, and genitive (see e.g. Vainikka 1989; Nelson 1998a, 1998b; Mitchell 1991b; Milsark 1985; Kiparsky 2001; Askonen 2001, as well as many of the contributions in Holmberg and Nikanne 1993).

The central facts may be viewed from a syntactic or a morphological standpoint, or both. As illustrated above in Table 5, the Finnish case affixes have undergone syncretism in the singular genitive and accusative NPs (*-n*), but retain a distinct affix for plural NPs and pronouns (*-t*) in both nominative and accusative. In other words, a singular NP in its unmarked lexical form appears to be unambiguously nominative, but one marked with the affix (*-n*) is ambiguously genitive or accusative. A pronoun marked with (-*t*) is unambiguously accusative, but a plural NP marked with (*-t*) is ambiguously nominative or accusative. This level of morphosyntactic ambiguity becomes particularly relevant in certain syntactic environments, where singular NPs appear to "passivize" but pronouns do not. These environments include imperatives, possessor locative constructions, certain infinitival constructions which license non-nominative subjects, and impersonal passives. Some examples are given in (8):

(8) a. Aili to-i heidä-**t** / lauku-**n** asema-lta.
Aili bring-PAST.3S them-ACC / bag-ACC/GEN station-ABL
'Aili brought them / the bag from the station.'

b. Heidä-**t** / laukku tuo-tiin asema-lta.
them-ACC / bag-NOM bring-PASS.PAST station-ABL
'They / the bag was brought from the station.'

Previous explanations for these patterns include conflation of genitive and accusative case features in the singular (Vainikka 1989); double case assignment to the single argument in passives and related constructions (Nelson 1998a, 1998b); or a paradigm in which no accusative case affix is specified for nouns, only for pronouns (Kiparsky 2001). Both Vainikka and

Asudeh address this issue and propose alternate analyses in the current volume.

Number

The common Uralic proto-language distinguished between three different numbers: singular, dual and plural (e.g. Lehikoinen 1995:65; Lehtinen 2000:48). While the Saami languages have retained this three-way distinction, modern Finnish and Estonian only distinguish between the singular and plural number. In Finnish, the plural number is signalled by *–t* in the nominative and accusative case, and by *-i/j-* in all other cases. In Estonian, nominative plurals are formed by adding *-d,* partitive plurals by adding *-id, -sid* or a vowel to the genitive singular form. The plural of other cases is formed by adding either *-de* or *-te* to the genitive singular form (see e.g. Erelt et al 1997 for discussion and examples of each situation). In Saami, the realisation of the plural varies from one language or dialect to another, and is conditioned by factors such as case and noun class. However, some Saami forms are clearly related to the two distinct types of markers found in Finnish and Estonian:

	Finnish	**Estonian**	**Saami (North)**
Nominative sg	koira	koer	beana
Nominative pl	koira-t	koera-d	beatnaga-t
Genitive sg	koira-n	koer-a	beatnaga
Genitive pl	koir-i-en	koera-de	beatnagi-i-d
Inessive sg	koira-ssa	koera-s	beatnagi-s
Inessive pl	koir-i-ssa	koera-de-s	beatnagi-i-n

Table 8: Examples of Finnish, Estonian and Saami plural affixes for 'dog'

Case and number agreement in NPs

In Finnish and most Estonian NPs, attributive adjectives show case and number agreement with the head N that they modify. In the Estonian essive, abessive (illustrated below), comitative and terminative cases, however, the adjectives are in the genitive case, while the head N alone inflects for the other case:

	Finnish	**Estonian**
Nominative sg	musta koira 'black dog'	must koer 'black dog'
Nominative pl	mustat koirat	mustad koerad
Genitive sg	mustan koiran	musta koera
Genitive pl	mustien koirien	mustade koerade
Inessive sg	mustassa koirassa	mustas koeras
Inessive pl	mustissa koirissa	mustades koerades
Abessive sg	mustatta koiratta	musta koerata
Abessive pl	mustitta koiritta	mustade koeradeta

Table 9: Examples of case and number agreement in Finnish and Estonian NPs

The Saami languages have a complex adjectival system, where many adjectives have separate forms for attributive and predicative uses. Below, we give two examples from North Saami (from Sammallahti 1998a:62):

(9) a. Duojár lea **čeahppi**.
craftsman is skillful

b. **čeahpẹs** duojár
skillful craftsman

Unlike their Finnish and Estonian counterparts, attributive adjectives in Saami show irregular morphology, and not all adjectives have special attributive forms; further research is needed to throw light on the details of this system.

Number agreement in copular constructions

In Saami, Finnish and Estonian, predicative adjectives and nominals show number agreement with the subject NP. Finnish predicative adjectives and nominals inflect for nominative or partitive case, while the subject NP inflects for nominative case - see e.g. Hakulinen and Karlsson (1979), Vilkuna (1996), and Vainikka's contribution to this volume. In Estonian, predicative adjectives and nominals usually only inflect for nominative case. Note also that in both Finnish and Estonian, there is subject-verb agreement between the subject NP and the finite verb:[11]

(10) a. Matto on uusi. (Finnish)
rug.SG.NOM be.3SG new.SG.NOM
'The rug is new'

b. Mato-t ovat uude-t.
rug-PL.NOM be.3PL new-PL.NOM
'The rugs are new.'

c. Mato-t ovat uus-i-a.
rug-PL.NOM be.3PL new-PL-PART
'The rugs are new.'

(11) a. Vaip on uus. (Estonian)
rug.SG.NOM be.3SG new-SG.NOM
'The rug is new.'

b. Vaibad on uued.
rug.PL.NOM be.3PL new.PL.NOM
'The rugs are new.'

c. *Vaibad on uusi
rug.PL.NOM be.3PL new.PL.PART

---

[11] Some grammarians, including Vilkuna (1996), have pointed out that Finnish predicative nominals can also inflect for genitive case, and there is no number agreement between the subject NP and the predicative nominal:

(i) Talo on minu-n.
house.SG.NOM be.3SG my-GEN.SG
'The house is mine.'

Talo-t ovat minu-n.
house-.PL.NOM be.3PL my-GEN.SG
'The houses are mine.'

One could argue, though, that in constructions of this kind, there is an empty N head showing number agreement, and the possessive pronoun (in the genitive case) occupies the specifier position of this NP. The empty head position can be filled by the overt N *oma* 'own':

(ii) Talo on minun (oma-ni).
house.SG.NOM be.3SG my own-SG.NOM.1PX
'The house is my own.'

Talo-t ovat minun (om-i-a-ni).
house-PL.NOM be.3PL my own-PL.PART.1PX
'The houses are my own.'

In Estonian, the head N must be filled by *oma* 'own' – omission of this pronoun creates strong emphasis on the possessive pronoun (e.g. Grünthal 2000: 52):

(iii) Majad on minu *(omad).
house.PL.NOM be.3PL I.GEN own.PL.NOM

The examples above show that the partitive case has a different distribution in predicative constructions in Finnish and Estonian.

Possessive agreement

In Finnish and Saami, possession is expressed by means of both genitive personal pronouns and possessive agreement suffixes on the head noun (Finnish has pronouns and suffixes for 1st, 2nd, and 3rd person singular and plural, Saami for 1st, 2nd, and 3rd person singular, dual, and plural - see e.g. Sammallahti 1998a:63ff). In Finnish and Saami, the pronouns either co-occur with the suffixes and there is agreement between them, or the suffixes occur alone. In Estonian, on the other hand, possession is usually expressed by means of genitive personal pronouns only. Table 10 lists the forms for the noun (nominative case form of) 'house/hut':[12]

[12] Estonian personal pronouns have both a long form (e.g. in Table 10 the long genitive forms would be *minu, sinu, tema, meie, teie, nende* while the short forms as *mu, su, ta, me, te, nende*). Although the long forms are often understood to be more focussed than the short forms, both forms are used frequently in present day Estonian. In this Introduction, we use the short forms only. Some Finnish pronouns also have long and short forms (*e.g. minun-mun* 'my/mine' and *sinun-sun* 'your/yours'). The short forms are only used in colloquial spoken Finnish.

	Finnish	**Estonian**	**Saami (North)**
1st singular	(minun) talo-ni '(my) house'	mu maja 'my house'	goaht-án 'my house'
2nd singular	(sinun) talo-si	su maja	goaht-át
3rd singular	(hänen) talo-nsa	ta maja	goaht-is
1st dual			goaht-áme
2nd dual			goaht-áde
3rd dual			goaht-iska
1st plural	(meidän) talo-mme	me maja	goaht-amet
2nd plural	(teidän) talo-nne	te maja	goaht-adet
3rd plural	(heidän) talo-nsa	nende maja	goaht-iset

Table 10: Possessive pronouns and possessive suffixes in Finnic and Saami (nominative)

In Finnish, the third person possessive affix may either be bound locally or non-locally, resulting in different interpretations of the third person possessor:[13]

(12) a. Maija mö-i talo-**nsa**.
Maija sell-PAST.3S house-ACC.3PX
'Maija$_i$ sold her$_i$ house'

b. Maija mö-i **hänen** talo-**nsa**.
Maija sell-PAST.3S his/her house-ACC.3PX
'Maija$_i$ sold his/her$_j$ house'

Because Estonian lacks possessive suffixes on the head noun, the contrast between one's own and someone else's house is expressed by means of adding the pronoun *oma* 'own' or an appropriate possessive pronoun:

---

[13] Since the first and second person affixes do not function anaphorically, this has led to an ongoing debate in the literature as to the morphological status of the possessive paradigm. For discussion and analyses see e.g. Pierrehumbert (1980), Nevis (1984), Kanerva (1987), Trosterud (1993), Nelson (1998a), and Toivonen (2000). Possessive constructions are discussed in Kaiser's contribution to this volume.

(13) a. Mari müüs **oma** maja.
Mari sell.PAST.3S own house.GEN
'Mari$_i$ sold her$_i$ house.'

b. Mari müüs **ta** maja.
Mari sell.PAST.3S his/her house.GEN
'Mari$_i$ sold his/her$_j$ house.'

Affix order
Throughout Finnic and Saami, the basic ordering of affixes for inflectional nominal morphology is as follows:

nominal stem – number – case – possessive affix

(14) a. talo-i-ssa-si
house-pl-iness-2sPx 'in your houses' (Finnish)

b. maja-de-s (Estonian)
house-pl-iness 'in (the) houses'

c. goađi-sta-n
hut-sg-loc-1sPx 'in my hut' (North Saami)

Comrie (1980) notes that the ordering of case with respect to possessive suffixes varies across the Uralic language family as a whole, and proposes an analysis for the development for the ordering seen in Finnic and Saami.

Final remarks
Apart from a few derivational affixes referring only to females, the Finnic and Saami languages lack all gender distinctions: although the Finnish *kirjailija-tar* 'writer-ess' and its Estonian equivalent *kirjutaja-tar* can only be used to refer to female writers, it is equally common to use the words *kirjailija* 'writer' and *kirjutaja* of both male and female writers. Finnic and Saami do not even distinguish between genders in their use of personal pronouns: the same pronouns *hän* 'she/he' (Finnish) *tema/ta* (Estonian) and *son* (Saami) can be used to refer to men, women and children alike. A further property of Finnic and Saami is that they lack indefinite and definite articles. However, in some languages and dialects (such as Finnish and Estonian) demonstrative pronouns are now taking over the functions of defi-

nite articles – this change is discussed in Börjars and Hiietam's contribution to the volume.

3.2 Verbal Inflection

An important property of Finnic and Saami finite verbs (both auxiliaries and lexical verbs) is that they show person and number agreement with the subject. Below we give the forms for the verbs *sit* and *go* (the North Saami data is from Sammallahti 1998a: 221):

	Finnish	**Estonian**	**Saami (North)**
Pres 1sg	(minä) istun 'I sit'	(ma) istun 'I sit'	manan 'I go'
Pres 2sg	(sinä) istut	(sa) istud	manat
Pres 3sg	*(hän) istuu	(ta) istub	manná
Pres 1dual			manne
Pres 2dual			mannabeahtti
Pres 3dual			mannaba
Pres 1pl	(me) istumme	(me) istume	mannat
Pres 2pl	(te) istutte	(te) istute	mannabēhtet
Pres 3pl	*(he) istuvat	(nad) istuvad	mannet
Past 1sg	(minä) istuin	(ma) istusin	mannen
Past 2sg	(sinä) istuit	(sa) istusid	mannet
Past3sg	*(hän) istui	(ta) istus	manai
Past 1dual			manaime
Past 2dual			manaide
Past 3dual			manaiga
Past 1pl	(me) istuimme	(me) istusime	manaimet
Past 2pl	(te) istuitte	(te) istusite	manaidet
Past 3pl	*(he) istuivat	(nad) istusid	manne

Table 11: The Finnic and Saami present and past tense forms for 'sit' and 'go'

As shown in Table 11, the Finnish past tense is signalled by *-i-*. In Estonian, past tense is signalled by either *-s-* or *-si-* (there are also some changes in form of the agreement morphemes), and in Saami, by a variety of markers, many of which include the vowels *-i-* or *-e-* (see e.g. Korhonen 1967; Sammallahti 1998 for a more detailed discussion and examples). As is also shown by Table 11, Finnish is a partial pro-drop language: all 1st and 2nd person subjects may be omitted without causing ungrammaticality. The Saami languages also allow pro-drop in most environments. In Estonian, 1st, 2nd and even 3rd person subjects may be omitted, but only in affirmative sentences. This is because in Estonian, the negative verbal element *ei* fails to inflect for subject-verb agreement. We will return to this shortly.

Present and past perfect tenses

In Finnish and Estonian present and past perfect tenses, the auxiliary *be* inflects for agreement and for tense/mood, the lexical verb being participial (see e.g. Hakulinen and Karlsson 1979; Karlsson 1982; Leino 1989; Vilkuna 1996; Erelt et al 1997). In Saami, the present and past perfect tenses are often formed in the same way, by combining the auxiliary be with a past participial form of the main verb (see e.g. Korhonen 1967; Trosterud 1994; Sammallahti 1998a and 1998b; Julien 2001; see also Julien's contribution to this volume):[14]

[14] Finnish and Estonian distinguish between indicative, imperative and conditional moods. Finnish also has potential mood, while Estonian has a separate mood for indirect speech (see e.g. Hakulinen and Karlsson 1979; Leino 1989; Holmberg and Nikanne 1993; Vilkuna 1996 for Finnish, and Erelt et al 1997 for Estonian. Some discussion on the origins of the Finnic potential can also be found in Forsberg 2000). Saami moods include conditional, imperative and potential (Sammallahti 1998a:76). As the overt realisation of mood is closely related to tense, Holmberg et al (1993) have proposed that tense is a subcategory of mood in these languages, and that tense and mood are associated with one and the same clausal functional projection. This view contrasts with the one presented in e.g. Cinque (1999) who argues that there exist various (combinations of) categories of tense and mood, each of which heads its own functional projection. For more discussion, the reader is referred to the literature.

Finnish	**Estonian**	**Saami (Inari)**
(minä) ole-n istu-nut. I be-1SG sit-PCP 'I have sat.'	(ma) ole-n istu-nud. I be-1SG sit-PCP 'I have sat.'	(mun) lam čokká-m. I.SG be.PRES.1SG sit-PCP 'I have sat.'
(sinä) ole-t istu-nut. you be-2SG sit-PCP 'You have sat.'	(sa) ole-t istu-nud. I be-2SG sit-PCP 'You have sat.'	(tun) lah čokká-m. you be.PRES.2SG sit-PCP 'You have sat.'
(minä) ol-i-n istu-nut. I be-PAST-1SG sit-PCP 'I had sat.'	(ma) ol-i-n istu-nud. I be-PAST-1SG sit-PCP 'I had sat.'	(mun) lijjim čokká-m. I.SG be.PAST.1SG sit-PCP 'I had sat.'
(sinä) ol-i-t istu-nut. you be-PAST-2SG sit-PCP 'You had sat.'	(sa) ol-i-t istu-nud. you be-PAST-2SG sit-PCP 'You had sat.'	(tun) lijjih čokká-m. you be.PAST.2SG sit-PCP 'You had sat.'

Table 12: Examples of Finnic and Saami present and past perfect tenses for the verb *sit*

Besides *be*, Finnic and Saami have a number of other verbs that can be used as auxiliaries. Many of these verbs, which are followed by infinitival forms of other verbs, express futurity, possibility, probability, necessity, and obligation. For more discussion and examples, see e.g. Hakulinen and Karlsson (1979), Vilkuna (1996) for Finnish, Metslang (1994) and Erelt et al (1997) for Estonian, and Magga (1986), Sammallahti (1998) for the Saami group.

Negative sentences

Let us now turn to Finnic and Saami negative sentences. One of the distinctive features of the Uralic language family as a whole is that negation is realised as an inflected verbal element. In Lule and South Saami negation hosts both tense and agreement (e.g. Korhonen 1973, 1981; Trosterud 1994; Sammallahti 1998a; Julien, this volume; Korhonen and Trosterud mention that some southern Estonian dialects and Livonian may also belong to this group). In Finnish and in North and Ter Saami, on the other hand, negation inflects only for subject-verb agreement, while the auxiliary *be* or the lexical verb inflects for tense/mood (see e.g. Cannellin 1930; Savijärvi 1977 for Finnish). In standard Estonian, the negative element *ei* usually fails to show any subject-verb agreement, and the following auxiliary or lexical verb only inflects for tense/mood (e.g. Erelt et al 1997):[15]

Finnish	Estonian	Saami (Lule)
(Minä) e-n istu. I NEG-1SG sit 'I do not sit.'	Ma ei istu. I NEG sit 'I do not sit.'	I-v tjále. NEG-1S write 'I do not write.'
(Minä) e-n istunut. I NEG-1SG sit.PCP 'I did not sit.'	Ma ei istunud. I NEG sit.PCP 'I do not sit.'	I-ttji-v tjále. NEG-PAST-1S write 'I did not write.'
(Minä) e-n ole istunut. I NEG-1SG be.PRES sit.PCP 'I have not sat.'	Ma ei ole istunud. I NEG be.PRES sit.PCP 'I have not sat.'	
(Minä) e-n ollut istunut. I NEG-1SG be.PAST sit.PCP 'I had not sat.'	Ma ei olnud istunud. I NEG be.PCP sit.PCP 'I had not sat.'	
(Sinä) e-t istu. you NEG-2SG sit 'You do not sit.'	Sa ei istu. you NEG sit 'You do not sit.'	
(Sinä) e-t ole istunut. you NEG-2SG be sit.PCP 'You have not sat.'	Sa ei ole istunud. you NEG be.PRES sit.PCP 'You have not sat.'	

Table 13: Negative sentences in Finnic and Saami

[15] In line with Holmberg et al (1993) and Julien (this volume), we take the negated present tense constructions to contain a present tense form of the lexical verb, while the negated past tense constructions contain a past tense form of this verb. Note, though, that while Holmberg et al assume the verb to have features for both tense *and mood*, Julien argues that it only has features for tense. We return to this briefly.

Although in the Finnish and Estonian past tense, the lexical verb *istunut/istunud* is identical to the past participial verb *istunut/istunud* found in the present and past perfect tenses, Holmberg et al (1993), Holmberg and Nikanne (1994), and Vilkuna (1996), among others, have adopted the view that in the former construction, the morpheme *-nut/-nud* is a past tense morpheme associated with both tense and mood features, while in the latter construction it is a past participial morpheme which is only associated with tense features. Julien (this volume) contests this view: in her diachronic study of the Finnic and Saami tense system she shows how both participial forms can be analysed uniformly as representing exactly the same feature combination (for non-finite tense).

It is interesting to note that the Saami languages seem to incorporate several morphologically distinct verbs into their negative paradigm. Below is the negation paradigm from Inari Saami:

(15) a. *Negation in Inari Saami*

1sg	jiem
2sg	jieh
3sg	ij
1du	iän
2du	eppee
3du	iävá
1pl	ep
2pl	eppeδ
3pl	iä

b. Jos **jiem** ličči vaibâm, te sárnuččim âânnâp.
if neg.1s be.cond tired, then speak.cond.1s more
'If I weren't tired, I would speak more.'

Passives

Let us now look briefly at passive sentences in Finnic and Saami. Saami passive paradigms show full subject agreement with passivized arguments. Finnic passives, however, may be classified as impersonal passives because (a) they lack full subject agreement paradigms, (b) they usually disallow agent by-phrases, and (c) they target both transitive and intransitive verbs:[16]

[16] Manninen and Nelson (2002) show however that in Finnish, the agent by-phrase can sometimes have the form of a postpositional phrase.

(16) North Saami (from Sammallahti 1998a: 84):
Dat dolv-ojuv'vui buohccevīssui.
(s)he/it.NOM take-PASS.3S.PRET hospital.ILL
'S/he / it was taken to hospital.'

(17) Finnish
Juhla-ssa tanssi-ttiin / *miehi-ltä.
party-INESS dance-PASS.PAST /men-ABL
'At the party it was danced /*by the men' (i.e. there was dancing)

As shown by Table 14 below, Finnish passives are formed by means of *-ta/-ttu*. In affirmative present and past tenses, the passive affix is followed by a *-Vn* affix. Mitchell (1991a) has argued that this affix is an affirmative marker, appearing in the same functional projection as the negative verbal element *ei*; others have treated it as a kind of agreement marker (see e.g. Vilkuna 1996, Manninen 1999, Manninen and Nelson 2002). In Estonian, passives are usually formed by *-dakse/-takse* (present tense), *-da/-ta* (past tense), and *-dud/-tud* (present/past perfect):[17]

	Finnish	**Estonian**
present	istu-ta-an	istu-takse
past	istu-tt-i-in	istu-ti
present perfect	o-n istu-ttu	o-n istu-tud
past perfect	ol-i istu-ttu	ol-i istu-tud
present, neg	ei istu-ta	ei istu-ta
past, neg	ei istu-ttu	ei istu-tud
present perfect, neg	ei ole istu-ttu	ei ole istu-tud
past perfect, neg	ei ol-lut istu-ttu	ei ol-nud istu-tud

Table 14: Examples of Finnic passives for 'sit'

The Saami languages do not all have such complete paradigms for the passive compared to other types of verbal inflection; in some Saami lan-

[17] It is sometimes suggested that Estonian lacks a passive construction - see e.g. Torn (2000) and Hiietam and Vihman (2002). Similar ideas have been proposed for Finnish - e.g. by Shore (1986, 1988) and Tommola (1993). For a contrasting view, see Manninen and Nelson (2002).

guages, for example Inari Saami, the passive takes the form of the affix *–um* but is used only infrequently.

Non-finite verbs

Finnic and Saami non-finite verbs do not inflect for finite subject-verb agreement, although some gerunds and other nominalised stems can host nominal agreement (possessive) affixes. Some can also inflect for (present or past) tense - see Holmberg et al (1993) and Julien (2001; this volume) for some discussion. Non-finite verbs can be divided further into infinitivals and participials.

Finnish has four different infinitival forms (these are often referred to as the *-ta, -te, -ma* and *-minen* infinitives or infinitives I-IV), while Estonian has two (the so-called *-da-* and *-ma* infinitives). The infinitives can usually only appear with a limited number of case and other nominal affixes: for a list of these affixes, the reader is referred to the literature, e.g. Hakulinen and Karlsson (1979), Vilkuna (1996) for Finnish, and Erelt et al (1997) for Estonian:

(18) a. Maija on luke-ma-ssa (Finnish)
Maija be-pres.3sg read-inf-iness
'Maija is reading'

b. Maija on luge-ma-s (Estonian)
Maija be-pres-3gs read-inf-iness
'Maija is reading'

Finnic participles take a much wider range of case and other nominal morphemes than do infinitivals. Grammarians have often distinguished between the present and past participial forms, and the so-called negative participial:

(19) a. sula-va suklaa (Finnish)
melt-PCP.NOM chocolate.NOM
'chocolate that is melting'

b. sula-nut suklaa
melt-PCP.NOM chocolate.NOM
'chocolate that has melted'

c. sula-maton suklaa
melt-PCP.NOM chocolate.NOM
'chocolate that will not melt/that has not melted'

(20) a. sula-v šokolaad (Estonian)
melt-PCP.NOM chocolate.NOM
'chocolate that is melting'

b. sula-nud šokolaad
melt-PCP.NOM chocolate.NOM
'chocolate that has melted'

c. sula-matu šokolaad
melt-PCP.NOM chocolate.NOM
'chocolate that will not melt/that has not melted'

The Saami languages also have a large number of non-finite verbal forms, many of which can appear with the paradigm of possessive affixes to mark non-finite agreement. In North Saami, for example, infinitival forms may appear in complement clauses (21a) and as gerunds with abessive case (21b) (Sammallahti 1998a: 85-7):

(21) a. Dat doaivvūi mū boahtit.
s/he thought.3S I.ACC come.INF
'S/he thought that I would come.'

b. Dagai dan mū dieđe-keahttá.
did.3S it.ACC I.GEN know-GER.ABESS
'S/he did it so that I did not know.'

3.3 Particles

The most important feature distinguishing particles from nominal and verbal stems is that they can usually only be followed by (a limited number of) clitics.[18] Originally many Finnic and Saami particles had the form of normal productive nominal or verbal stems which were followed by normal productive nominal or verbal inflectional affixes (e.g. the Finnish *siellä/sieltä* and Estonian *seal/sealt* 'there/from there'). In the modern languages, either because the stems have lost most of their nominal or verbal properties (e.g. they are only able to appear with a limited number of affixes) or because the inflectional affixes have lost their productivity so that they are only able to appear with a limited number of stem morphemes, particles are usually taken to form a class of their own.

[18] In Finnic and Saami, clitics often have an emphasizing function, or they can be used to turn statements into questions. We will return to clitics briefly.

Syntactically and semantically, Finnic and Saami particles consist of prepositions and postpositions, adverbs, conjunctions and interjections (the equivalents of *ouch!* and *eek!*). In all these languages, postpositions are more frequent than prepositions – this is attributed to the fact that Finnic has developed from and SOV language into an SVO language.[19] Table 15 gives examples of typical pre- and postpositions, adverbs, and conjunctions in Finnic and Saami:

	Finnish	**Estonian**	**Saami (North)**
Adverbs	kauni**isti** 'beautifully' (kaunis = beautiful)	ilusa**sti** 'beautifully' (ilusa = beautiful)	čeahpi**t** 'skillfully' (čeahppi = skillful)
	viisaa**sti** 'wisely' (viisas = wise)	targa**lt** 'wisely' (targa = wise)	garrasi**t** 'hard' (garas = hard)
Postpositions	kanssa 'with' edessä 'in front of'	ühes 'with' ees 'in front of'	mielde 'with' duohken 'behind'
Conjunctions	ja 'and' tai 'or' mutta 'but'	ja 'and' või 'or' aga 'but'	ja 'and' dahję 'or' muhtǫ 'but'

Table 15: Examples of Finnic and Saami particles

In Finnish, adverbs are often derived from the base form of adjectives with the affix *-sti*, while the Estonian adverbs are derived from the genitive form of adjectives, using the affixes *-sti* and *-lt*. There are also other affixes which turn adjectival or noun stems into adverbs - see e.g. Ahlman (1933), Tuomikoski (1973), Hakulinen and Karlsson (1979), Manninen (1999; 2000) for a discussion of Finnish, and Erelt et al (1997) for Estonian. In Saami, the affix for turning adjectives into adverbs is usually *-t;* Sammallahti (1998: 93f., 107f.) points out, though, that this affix is usually only used

[19] See e.g. Lehikoinen (1995) and Lehtinen (2000). For more discussion on postpositional phrases, see e.g. Hakulinen and Karlsson (1979), Jaakola (1997), and Manninen (this volume) for Finnish, Erelt et al (1997) for Estonian, Sammallahti (1998) for the Saami group, and Tikka (1998) some other Finnic languages (especially Veps).

to form manner adverbs, and the other types of adverbs (e.g. spatial and temporal adverbs) are formed by other means.[20]

Clitics

Before closing off this sub-section, let us look briefly at the types of clitics found in Finnic and Saami. As already pointed out, many clitics have a discourse or emphasizing function - here are some examples from Finnish and Estonian:

(22) a. Maija-han tul-i. (Finnish)
Maija-CL come-PAST.3SG
'Maija did come, you know.'

b. Minä-kin tul-i-n.
I-CL come-PAST.1SG
'I came too.'

c. Minä tul-i-n-kin
I come-PAST-1SG-CL
'I DID come/I came after all.'

(23) a. Minu-l-gi on nälg. (Estonian)
I-ADESS-CL be.1SG hungry
'I am hungry too.'

b. Minul on-gi nälg.
I.ADESS be.1sg-CL hungry
'I AM hungry.'

In both Finnish and Saami, clitics can also be used to turn declarative sentences into yes/no questions:

(24) a. Nä-i-n Peka-n. (Finnish)
see-PAST-1SG Pekka-ACC
'I saw Pekka.'

20 Besides adverbs, normal case-inflected nouns and adjectives can also function as adverbials in Finnic and Saami - for discussion and examples, see e.g. Huumo (1996) and Manninen (1999; 2000).

b. Nä-i-t-kö Peka-n?
see-PAST-2SG-CL Pekka-ACC
'Did you see Pekka?'

(25) a. Oidnen Biera. (North Saami)
see-PAST.1SG Peter-ACC
'I saw Peter.'

b. Oidnet-go Biera?
see.PAST.2SG-CL Peter-ACC
'Did you see Peter?'

Rather than clitics attaching to finite verbs, Estonian tends to use a separate question word, *kas*, to form yes/no questions:[21]

(26) a. Sa eläd Tallinnas.
you live.PRES.2SG Tallinn.INESS
'You live in Tallinn.'

b. Kas sa eläd Tallinnas?
Q you live.PRES.2SG Tallinn.INESS
'Do you live in Tallinn?'

c. Sa tuled.
You come.PRES.2SG
'You are coming.'

d. Kas sa tuled?
Q you come.PRES.2SG
'Are you coming?'

After these introductory remarks on particles and clitics, let us now move on to discuss word order in Finnic and Saami.

3.4 Word Order

Although the common proto-Uralic language had SOV word order (see e.g. Lehikoinen 1995; Lehtinen 2000 for some discussion), most modern Finnic

[21] In spoken Estonian, questions are sometimes formed without *kas*: such constructions have normal word order but rising intonation. Sometimes questions are also formed by inverting the finite verb and the subject: *Tuled sa?* 'Are you coming'. The same phenomenon can also be observed in colloquial spoken Finnish: *Tulet sä? / Tuut sä?* 'Are you coming'.

and Saami languages and dialects have SVO word order (the North Saami data in (27c) is from Sammallahti (1998: 95)):

(27) a. Pekka näk-i sude-n. (Finnish)
Pekka see-PAST.3SG wolf-ACC
'Pekka saw a/the wolf.'

b. Pekka nägi hundi. (Estonian)
Pekka see.PAST.3SG wolf.ACC
'Pekka saw a/the wolf.'

c. Áhčči ōinnii Niillasa. (North Saami)
father see.PAST.3SG Nils.ACC
'Father saw Nils.'

Unlike in Finnish and Estonian, in Saami infinitival and participial constructions can also have SOV order. In South Saami, SOV is the normal word order even in finite main clauses (data from Sammallahti 1998a: 95):

(28) a. Ii diktán mū dan oaidnit. (North Saami)
neg.3SG let.PAST I.ACC it.ACC see.PCP
'(He/she) did not let me see it.'

b. Dah maanah utnieh. (South Saami)
they child.PL.ACC have
'They have children.'

Although the neutral unmarked word order for modern Finnic and Saami is SVO, under appropriate discourse conditions the word ordering of these languages can be very free. Given a simple transitive sentence, all word orders are potentially possible; note, however, that only the topmost sentences would be appropriate as answers to questions like 'What happened?' For more discussion and examples, see e.g. Vainikka (1989) and especially Vilkuna (1989, 1995) for Finnish, Erelt et al (1997) for Estonian, and Sammallahti (1998: 95) for the Saami group:

Finnish	**Estonian**
Minä sö-i-n omena-a. I eat-PAST-1SG apple-PART 'I was eating an apple.'	Ma sõ-i-n õun-a. I eat-PAST-1SG apple-PART 'I was eating an apple.'
Minä omenaa söin. 'It was I who was eating an apple.'	Ma õuna sõin.
Omenaa minä söin. 'It was an apple that I was eating.'	Õuna ma sõin.
Omenaa söin minä. 'I was the one eating an apple.'	Õuna sõin ma.
Söin minä omenaa. 'I WAS eating an apple.'	Sõin ma õuna.
?Söin omenaa minä. 'Eating an apple, indeed I was.'	Sõin õuna ma.

Table 17: Word order variation in Finnish and Estonian

4 Some Phonological Properties

In this section we discuss briefly some relevant phonological features of Finnic and Saami. We begin by discussing the properties of vowel sounds, and turn then to the properties of consonants. The emphasis will again be on those phonological properties with which the papers in this volume are concerned.

Within the Finnic and Saami languages, Finnish and South Saami display vowel harmony. This means that all vowels in a word must be either front vowels (e.g. Finnish *y* [y], *ö* [ø], *ä* [æ]) or back vowels (*a* [ɑ], *u* [u], *o* [o]). The Finnish front vowels *i* and *e* are special in that they are neutral with respect to vowel harmony (see e.g. Laaksonen and Lieko 1992). In inflected forms, the vowels of the stem always determine the quality of the vowels in the affixes. Stems containing only close front vowels take front vowel suffixes as a default (28d-e):

(29) a. köyhä /*köyha
'poor'

b. kauha /*kauhä
'ladle, scoop'

c. suo-ss**a** /*-ss**ä**
swamp-iness
'in a/the swamp'

d. järve-ss**ä** /*-ss**a**
lake-iness
'in a/the lake'

e. kive-ll**ä** /*-ll**a**
stone-adess
'with a stone'

There are certain exceptions to this generalisation for Finnish, however. Compounds, and words containing the negative prefix *epä-*, for example, are exempt from vowel harmony:

(30) a.	metsä=mansikka	'forest strawberry'
b.	löyly=huone	'steam room'
c.	epä=toivo	'despair'

Finnic and Saami languages also have a rich array of phonological alternations which affect stem-final vowels in connection with suffixation: sometimes the vowels disappear completely, and sometimes they change in quality or length - for a more detailed discussion, see e.g. Laaksonen and Lieko (1992) and Anttila (2002) for Finnish, and Sammallahti (1998) for the Saami group. The examples in (32)-(34) are from Finnish:

(31) a.	maa earth, ground	→	ma-i-ssa earth-PL-INESS
b.	pää head	→	pä-i-ssä head-PL-INESS
(32) a.	lapsi child	→	lapse-n child-GEN

b.	apina monkey	→	apino-i-lle monkey-PL-ALLAT
(33) a.	suo bog	→	so-i-lla bog-PL-ADESS
b.	tie road	→	te-i-llä road-PL-ADESS

In the Finnic and Saami languages, both consonants and vowels are contrastive for quantity. Finnish has a two-way length contrast (short vs. long) in both vowels and consonants (see e.g. Laaksonen and Lieko 1992). Estonian, on the other hand, has a three-way length contrast (short vs. long vs. overlong) in both vowels and consonants (see e.g. Bye 1997, Hint 1997 - see also Ehala's contribution to this volume). Most Saami languages also have a three-way system of quantity for consonants, where Q3 represents overlong, similar to Estonian. However, Inari Saami has a distinct system: the long-overlong contrast in Q2 and Q3 has been replaced by a contrast between long and half-long consonant quantities (Bye 2000). See Sammallahti (1998) for a detailed discussion of Saami phonology.

The quantity contrasts come into play in the Finnic and Saami languages with the phenomenon known as *consonant gradation*. This is an alternation process in which consonants undergo weakening in determined environments (such as the onsets of closed syllables). In Finnish, for example, the geminates *kk*, *pp* and *tt* (strong grade) alternate with the single consonants *k*, *p*, *t* (weak grade), and the single consonants *k*, *p*, and *t* (strong grade) alternate with zero or another consonant (weak grade). Some examples of Finnish consonant gradation are given in Table 17 - the first forms are nominative singular, the second nominative plural forms of nouns. For more examples and discussion, see e.g. Laaksonen and Lieko (1992) or Harrikari (1999a, 1999b). See also Harrikari's contribution in this volume.:[22]

[22] Not all affixes trigger consonant gradation in Finnish. The paradigm of possessive affixes (discussed in section 3.1) is one example; see Nevis (1986, 1987) for further discussion.

Quantitative alternation

	Strong grade	*Weak grade*
kk ~ k	ta**k.k**i 'coat'	ta.**k**it
tt ~ t	ta**t.t**i 'mushroom'	ta.**t**it
pp ~ p	ti**p.p**a 'drop'	ti.**p**at

Qualitative alternation

	Strong grade	*Weak grade*
p ~ v	pa.**p**u 'bean'	pa.**v**ut
t ~ d	ma.**t**o 'worm'	ma.**d**ot
k ~ Ø	la.**k**i 'law'	la.Øit
mp ~ mm	ka**m.p**a 'comb'	ka**m.m**at
nt ~ nn	ra**n.t**a 'shore'	ra**n.n**at
ŋk ~ ŋŋ	ken.kä 'shoe'	ken.gät
	(ke**ŋ.k**ä)	(ke**ŋ.ŋ**ät)
lt~ ll	ku**l.t**a 'gold'	ku**l.l**at
rt ~ rr	pa**r.t**a 'beard'	pa**r.r**at

Table 17: Examples of consonant gradation in Finnish

As the examples in Table 17 show, the strong grade typically appears at the beginning of an open syllable, the weak grade at the beginning of a closed syllable.

In Estonian, consonant gradation is a more complex phenomenon than in Finnish, and a detailed discussion is beyond this introductory chapter - see e.g. Hint (1973; 1997a) for more discussion and examples. It is worth mentioning here, though, that Estonian has quantitative alternation between short, long, and overlong consonant sounds. There is also qualitative alternation between single consonant sounds and zero or another consonant. In Table 18, we give some examples of consonant gradation in Estonian. In the quantitative alternation, the first examples are partitive singular, the second genitive singular forms of nouns. In the qualitative alternation, the first examples are nominative singular, the second genitive singular forms of nouns:[23]

Quantitative alternation

	Strong grade	*Weak grade*
Q3 ~ Q2	lu**kk**u 'lock'	lu**k**u
	ko**tt**i 'bag'	ko**t**i
	ka**pp**i 'cupboard'	ka**p**i
	pal**k**a 'salary'	pal**g**a
	kau**p**a 'shop'	kau**b**a

Qualitative alternation

	Strong grade	*Weak grade*
b ~ v	lei**b** 'bread'	lei**v**a
b ~ Ø	lu**b**a 'permission'	loa
d ~ j	sõ**d**a 'war'	sõ**j**a
ld ~ ll	sil**d** 'bridge'	si**ll**a
rg ~ rj	mä**rg** 'wet'	mä**rj**a

Table 18: Consonant gradation in Estonian

Saami morphophonology is more complex than either Finnish or Estonian. Morphological paradigms in the Saami languages frequently contain *morphologized* alternations, where gradation is no longer triggered by the original phonological environment (e.g. the closing of a syllable), but is conditioned instead by the identity of the stem or affix itself. These processes often affect adjacent vowels and include strengthening, lengthening, shortening, and changes in the position of syllable boundaries (Sammallahti

[23] The distinction between Q1, Q2, and Q3 is not always reflected orthographically in Estonian. The written letters *g*, *d* and *b* often correspond to short (Q1) unvoiced consonant sounds (i.e. /k/, /p/ and /t/) but in some environments, they can also correspond to long (Q2) unvoiced sounds. An orthographic geminate (e.g. *-tt-*) usually corresponds to an overlong sound (Q3, as in the word *katta* 'to cover'), but overlong sounds can also be represented by single consonants which follow long vowels, diphthongs or some specific voiced consonants (e.g. *võita* 'to win' and *kaupa* 'shop-part.sg').

1998a). Some examples are given below from North Saami (34) and Inari Saami (35-6):

North Saami (Eastern Eanodat dialect; Sammalahti 1998:50):

(34) a.	vuol**'k**aan[24]	'having left'
b.	vuo**'lk**a	'he leaves'
c.	vuo**lkk**a	'departure'
d.	vuo**lk'k**aan	'I leave'

Inari Saami

(35) a.	láásáš	small island
b.	lásáá	small island.gen.sg
c.	lássááh	small island.pl.nom

(36) a.	**okk**o	~	**oh**o	~	**ooh**oid (half-long h)
	week.nom		week.acc/gen		week. pl.acc
b.	nj**une** (half-long n)	~	nj**une**	~	nj**uun**ijn
	nose.nom		nose.acc/gen		nose.pl.loc

More research is needed in this area of Saami phonetics and phonology in order to identify exactly how these variations in quantity are realised and perceived by speakers.

5 The Papers

In this section we give a brief summary to the papers in this volume. The papers are organised into four main sections: phonology, syntax (case), syntax (other topics), and language change.

5.1 Phonology: Ehala, Harrikari, Kiparsky

In his paper *Estonian Quantity: Implications for Moraic Theory* Martin Ehala addresses the problem of quantity in Estonian. As is widely known, Estonian has a three-way length contrast in both vowels and consonants, and there are restrictions on the occurrence of Q2 (long) and Q3 (over-long) elements. The claims made in Ehala's paper are, first, that quantity in Estonian is independent of segment quantity and, consequently, the mora cannot

24 Sammallahti uses the prime symbol (') to mark the presence of what he describes as an extra subglottal pulse in the preceding syllable.

be used for both simultaneously. Finally, the treatment of Q2 as light but long and Q3 as heavy and long simplifies the description of stress in Estonian.

Heli Harrikari's paper *Opaque Consonant Gradation in Finnish – A Recourse to IO-OO Correspondence* discusses the problem of opacity in Optimality Theory. On the basis of Finnish consonant gradation data she shows how a fully parallel OT succeeds in explaining opaque patterns without utilising derivational tools. Essentially, she argues for the effective use of both input-output and output-output correspondence as solutions to the problem of surface opacity. In addition to the use of the two types of correspondence as separate faithfulness mechanisms she shows how the effects of IO and OO correspondence might be combined through constraint conjunction: as a result of this conjunction, she argues, simultaneous access can be established to various faithfulness relations, a mechanism which is necessary for explaining certain types of opacity. In the last sections of her paper, Harrikari compares her system to the derivational LPM-OT and shows how this latter system crucially fails to account for the Finnish consonant gradation data.

Paul Kiparsky's paper *Finnish Noun Inflection* examines stem and affix alternations in Finnish noun morphology. Kiparsky first examines the systems of stress and syllable structure which condition nominal inflection, and then adopts a set of ranked constraints for Finnish. He then proposes a stratal OT solution to the problem of stress in polysyllables: in this approach, fixed polysyllables have an obligatory fixed secondary stress at the stem level, while movable polysyllables do not. Kiparsky shows that the data lend support to stratal OT approaches in favor of parallel approaches, including analyses which invoke Turbidity theory.

5.2 Syntax (Case): Fong, Asudeh, Vainikka

Vivienne Fong's paper *Resultatives and Depictives in Finnish* ties in with current research on the relationship between syntax and event structure (Tenny 1994; Rappaport Hovav and Levin 1995; Butt and Geuder 1998). Fong identifies two cases in Finnish, the essive and the translative, which at first blush appear to denote, respectively, BE (state) and BECOME (change of state) in secondary predicates. Based on evidence from resultatives and depictives, she notes an apparent mismatch between case and events: in certain cases, the translative case is unexpectedly associated with predicates where no overt change of state occurs. Fong proposes a solution to this problem that involves a new typology of event structures. The translative case morpheme, she argues, occurs when the event denoted by the predicate is *diphasic*; in other words, it contains two subparts, one which asserts a prior state of affairs and one which presupposes a change of state. It is this presupposition of change, rather than the change itself, that governs the distribution of this case. The essive case on the other hand is argued to be the unmarked default case, as it occurs without this presupposition. Fong's analysis elegantly shows that the distribution of these cases is indeed predictable from predicate semantics.

Ash Asudeh's paper *A Licensing Theory for Finnish* represents a critique of Kiparsky's recent Optimality-Theoretic analysis of Finnish case morphology (Kiparsky 2001) in favour of a reformulation of his original model for licensing based on feature unification (Kiparsky 1996). Licensing in this sense captures the relation between syntactic position, abstract case and morphological case. Focusing on the distribution of the core grammatical cases in Finnish, nominative, accusative, genitive and partitive, Asudeh develops an analysis which treats nominative as a default, and which avoids positing specific features to license nouns versus pronouns; instead, accusative case is simply not available to nouns in his system. This more restrictive approach to feature unification invokes fewer constraints than Kiparsky's OT analysis, while capturing additional generalisations about the distribution of genitive case.

Anne Vainikka looks at similar data from a different approach in *Postverbal Case Realization in Finnish*. Building on her previous work on case, Vainikka presents new data from four construction types (simple transitives with "thematic objects", copular predicates, existential sentences and the possessive construction) in order to identify the status of the postverbal argument in each case. She concludes that despite having superficial nominative case morphology, all are in complement position where partitive case is the default. Accusative case, she argues, may only be assigned to complements in the presence of the features [+COMPLETED] or [+SPECIFIC]. Finally, she applies the same set of diagnostics to case-marked adverbials, but concludes that some apparently accusative expressions are actually genitive and occur in a different structural position from other complements.

5.3 Syntax (other topics): Kaiser, Manninen, Nelson and Toivonen, Svonni and Vinka

In her paper *Encoding (Non)Locality in Anaphoric Relations*, Elsi Kaiser presents an analysis the semantics of the Finnish possessive construction. As we have seen, possession in Finnish is expressed by means of a possessive suffix (Px) which can co-occur with an overt possessive pronoun (see e.g. Hakulinen and Karlsson 1979; van Steenbergen 1989; Trosterud 1993; Toivonen 2000, and the references cited therein). Kaiser argues that the presence or absence of the possessive pronoun is governed by a locality constraint at work in two realms of the grammar: in (pragmatic) discourse anaphora resolution, and in semantic variable binding. In the latter situation, Kaiser claims, the absence or presence of the third person possessive pronoun visibly encodes the difference between binding and covaluation (see also Reinhart 1997; Heim 1993). Kaiser then extends this analysis to regular pronouns in Finnish, showing that they are governed by the same locality constraints.

In *Finnish PPs and the Phase Impenetrability Condition*, Satu Manninen takes a Minimalist approach to the underlying structure of prepositions and postpositions in Finnish. PPs in Finnish display differing properties both with respect to word order and to case: in postpositional phrases nouns appear in genitive case, while in prepositional phrases they appear in partitive. Manninen argues that both structures are underlyingly right-branching, but an EPP feature in the postpositional head triggers movement of the DP to a position preceding P in the surface word order. Manninen then presents new data from extraction out of PPs to show that postpositional phrases in Finnish are strong phases and therefore subject to the Phase Impenetrability Condition, a constraint on operations proposed in Chomsky (2000).

In their paper *Counting and the Grammar: Case and Numerals in Inari Saami* Diane Nelson and Ida Toivonen re-evaluate the idea that grammar cannot involve "counting," and that lexical entries are not organised in any kind of numerical order or linear string. In Inari Saami, nominals following numerals seven and higher are assigned partitive case by default, while the numbers from two to six override this case marking lexically. They propose that the numerals from two to six assign a special kind of accusative case, direct case, which accounts for the patterns of interaction between numerals, nouns and locative cases assigned by a governing verb. Based on recent evidence from cognitive science about the representation and acquisition of numerals, they suggest that the Inari Saami does involve "counting" in the sense that the case assignment feature for numerals 2-6 is acquired in a way that is sensitive to the value of numerals in a string. However, this mapping of numerals to values is itself dependent on children reaching a certain stage in their cognitive development.

In *Constraints on Productive Morphological Causatives in the Torne dialect of North Sámi*, Mikael Svonni and Mikael Vinka examine the properties of North Saami morphological causatives from a cross-linguistic perspective. Their paper represents an attempt to classify Saami causative structures as Faire-Infinitive or Faire Par causatives (Kayne 1975). Based on the data relating to case, passivisation and other syntactic features of the causee in particular, they reject an FI analysis partly because Saami causatives are typologically ambiguous, sharing syntactic properties of the two FI subclasses. Svonni and Vinka show that because the causee argument may be missing in the syntax, and because they select agentive base verbs, Saami causatives are best analysed as FP causatives, where the overt causee is analyzed as an applied object.

5.4 Language Change: Hiietam and Börjars, Julien

Estonian is often given an example of a language that lacks a pure definiteness marker (such as a definite article). In *The Emergence of a Definite Article in Estonian*, Katrin Hiietam and Kersti Börjars claim that in modern Estonian, the demonstrative element *see* is developing into a non-contrastive definiteness marker and that it might be on its way to becoming a definite article. The paper begins with a discussion of definiteness and demonstrativeness, and of Greenberg's and Diessel's typological studies of the development of definitess markers from demonstrative elements. After reviewing the evidence that a similar phenomenon is underway for the Finnish element *se*, the authors present data from Estonian in support of their claim that *see* is also used to indicate definiteness. This represents an important finding in Finnic syntax, as it shows that both Finnic and Estonian are independently undergoing a similar syntactic change.

In many Finnic and Saami languages, the past participial form is used in both present and past perfect constructions, and in the negated past tense. In her paper *On the Negated Past in Finnic and Saami,* Marit Julien discusses the diachronic development of the negated past tense construction in these languages (cf. Korhonen 1973; Holmberg et al 1993; Trosterud 1994). Julien argues that in most Finnic and Saami languages, the old Uralic negated past tense construction, where agreement and tense were marked solely on negation, has been replaced by the old negated present perfect construction, where agreement was marked on negation, tense on the participial. This change took place after the introduction of the auxiliary *be* into the present perfect construction: assuming that present perfect is always the result of combining a matrix present tense with an embedded relative past tense (see e.g. Stowell 1995, 1996; Zagona 1995; Giorgi and Pianesi 1997; Demirdache and Uribe-Etxebarria 2000 and the references given therein), Julien argues that in the older negated present perfect forms, the participial form was used to signal both the presence of a null finite present tense and a non-finite past tense in the construction. In the newer negated forms, where finite present tense was already overtly marked on the auxiliary, the participial was only needed to signal non-finite past tense. The old negated present perfect, lacking the copula, could then be reanalysed as contrasting minimally with the negated present tense form, creating a situation where agreement is marked on negation, while the (non-finite) present or past tense is marked on the following lexical verb.

References

Abondolo, D. (ed). 1998. *The Uralic Languages*. London: Routledge.

Ahlman, E. 1933. Adverbeista. *Virittäjä* 1933:137-159.

Anttila, A. 2002. Morphologically Conditioned Phonological Alternations. *Natural Language and Linguistic Theory* 20:1-42.

Askonen, E. 2001. *Objektin aspektuaalinen sijanvalinta.* (Suomen ja saamen kielen ja logopedian laitoksen julkaisuja, 19.) Oulu: The University of Oulu.

Blake, B. 1994. *Case.* Cambridge: Cambridge University Press.

Butt, M. and Geuder, W. (eds). 1998. *The Projection of Arguments. Lexical and Compositional Factors*. Stanford: CSLI Publications.

Bye, P. 1997. A Generative Perspective on 'Overlength' in Estonian and Saami. *Estonian Prosody: Papers From a Symposium*, ed. I. Lehiste and J. Ross, 36-67. Tallinn: Eesti Keele Instituut.

Bye, P. 2000. Opacity in the Alternation of Grade and Quantity in Saami: A Sympathy-Theoretic approach. Doctoral dissertation, University of Tromsø.

Cannellin, K. 1930. Kielteisyyden ilmaiseminen suomen kielessä. *Virittäjä* 34:238-244.

Chomsky, N. 2000. Minimalist Inquiries. *Step by Step*, eds. R. Martin, D. Michaels and J. Uriagereka, 89-155. Cambridge, Mass.: The MIT Press.

Cinque, G. 1999. *Adverbs and Functional Heads: A Cross-linguistic Perspective.* Oxford: Oxford University Press.

Comrie, B. 1980. The Ordering of Case and Possessive Suffixes in the Uralic Languages: An Approach to the Comparative-Historical Problem. *Lingua Posnaniensis* 23:81-86.

Demirdache, H. and Uribe-Etxebarria, M. 2000. The Primitives of Temporal Relations. *Step by Step*, eds. R. Martin, D. Michaels and J. Uriagereka, 157-187. Cambridge, Mass.: The MIT Press.

Erelt, M. Erelt, T. and Ross, K. 1997. *Eesti keele käsiraamat.* Tallinn: Eesti keele sihtasutus.

Forsberg, H. 2000. The Finnic Potential Mood and the Potential of Finnic. *Facing Finnic. Some Challenges to Historical and Contact Linguistics.* (Castrenianumin toimitteita, 59.), ed. J. Laakso, 9-30. Helsinki: Finno-Ugrian Society.

Giorgi, A. and Pianesi, F. 1997. *Tense and Aspect: From Semantics to Morphosyntax.* Oxford: Oxford University Press.

Grünthal, R. 2000. Typological Characteristics of the Finnic Languages: a Reappraisal. *Facing Finnic. Some Challenges to Historical and Contact Linguistics.*

(Castrenianumin toimitteita, 59.), ed. J. Laakso, 31-63. Helsinki: Finno-Ugrian Society.

Hakulinen, A. and Karlsson, F. 1979. *Nykysuomen lauseoppia.* Helsinki: Suomalaisen kirjallisuuden seura.

Harrikari, H. 1999a. Epenthesis, Geminates, and the OCP in Finnish. *Nordic Journal of Linguistics* 22:3-26.

Harrikari, H. 1999b. A Constraint-Based Approach to Finnish CV Spoonerisms. *Nordic Journal of Linguistics* 22:111-136.

Heim, I. 1993. Anaphora and Semantic Interpretation: A Reinterpretation of Reinhart's Approach. Ms., MIT.

Heinämäki, O. 1984. Aspect in Finnish. *Aspect Bound,* eds. C. de Groot and H. Tommola, 153-177. Dordrecht: Foris.

Hint, M. 1973. *Eesti keele sõnafonoloogia I.* Tallinn: Keele ja Kirjanduse Instituut.

Hint, M. 1997a. *Eesti keele astmevahelduse ja prosoodiasüsteemi tüpoloogilised probleemid* [Typological Problems of the Estonian Grade Alternation and Prosodic System]. Tallinn and Helsinki: Eesti keele sihtasutus.

Hint, M. (1997b) The Estonian Quantity Degrees in Prosody and Morphophonology. *Estonian Prosody: Papers from a Symposium,* eds. I. Lehiste and J. Ross, 125-135. Tallinn: Eesti Keele Instituut.

Holmberg, A. and Nikanne, U. (eds.) 1993. *Case and Other Functional Categories in Finnish Syntax.* Berlin: Mouton.

Holmberg, A., Nikanne, U., Oraviita, I., Reime, H. and Trosterud, T. 1993. The Structure of INFL and the Finite Clause in Finnish. *Case and Other Functional Categories in Finnish Syntax,* eds. A. Holmberg and U. Nikanne, 177-206. Berlin: Mouton.

Holmberg, A. and Nikanne, U. 1994. Expletives and Subject Positions in Finnish. *NELS 24: Proceedings of the North East Linguistics Society, Vol One,* ed. M. Gonzàlez. Amherst, Mass.: University of Massachusetts.

de Hoop, H. 1996. *Case Configuration and Noun Phrase Interpretation.* New York: Garland.

Huumo, T. 1996. *Ajan, omistajan, paikan ja tilan adverbiaaien keskinäiset suhteet suomen kielessä.* Doctoral dissertation, University of Turku.

Jaakola, M. 1997. Genetiivin kanssa esiintyvien adpositioiden kieliopillistumisesta. *Kieli. Tapaustutkimuksia suomesta,* eds. T. Lehtinen and L. Laitinen, 121-156. Helsinki: Helsingin yliopiston suomen kielen laitos.

Julien, M. 2001. The Syntax of Complex Tenses. *The Linguistic Review* 18:125-67.

Kanerva, J. 1987. Morphological Integrity and Syntax. *Language* 63:498-521.

Karlsson, F. 1982. *Suomen peruskielioppi.* Helsinki: Suomalaisen Kirjallisuuden Seura.

Kayne, R. 1975. *French Syntax: The Transformational Cycle.* Cambridge, Mass.: The MIT Press.

Kiparsky, P. 1998. Partitive Case and Aspect. *The Projection of Arguments: Lexical and Compositional Factors*, eds. Butt, M. and W. Geuder, 265-307. Stanford: CSLI Publications.

Kiparsky, P. 2001. Structural Case in Finnish. *Lingua* 111:315-376.

Koivulehto, J. 1988. Lapin ja itämerensuomen suhteesta. *Virittäjä* 92:26-51.

Korhonen, M. 1967. *Die Konjugation im Lappischen. Morphologisch-historische Untersuchung I: Die finiten Formkategorien.* (Mémoires de la Société Finno-Ougrienne, 143.) Helsinki: The Finno-Ugrian Society.

Korhonen, M. 1973. Zur Geschichte des negativen Präteritums und Perfekts im Ostseefinnischen und Lappischen. *Commentationes Fenno-Ugricae in Honorem Erkki Itkonen*, 174-184. Helsinki: The Finno-Ugrian Society.

Korhonen, M. 1981. *Johdatus lapin kielen historiaan.* Helsinki: Suomalaisen Kirjallisuuden Seura.

Kulonen, U. 1999. The Origins of Finnish and Related Languages. Available at http://virtual.finland.fi/finfo/english/langua.html.

Laakso, J. 1999. *Karhunkieli.* Helsinki: Suomalaisen Kirjallisuuden Seura.

Laakso, J. (ed.) 2000. *Facing Finnic. Some Challenges to Historical and Contact Linguistics.* (Castrenianumin toimitteita, 59.) Helsinki: The Finno-Ugrian Society.

Laaksonen, K. and Lieko, A. 1992. *Suomen kielen äänne- ja muoto-oppi.* Helsinki: Finn Lectura.

Lehikoinen, L. 1995. *Suomea ennen ja nyt.* Helsinki: Finn Lectura.

Lehtinen, T. 2000. *Suomen kielen tausta.* Helsinki: Department of Finnish, University of Helsinki.

Leino, P. 1989. *Suomen kielioppi.* Helsinki: Otava.

Leskinen, H. 1969. Eräs 3. p:n possessiivisuffiksin viitaussuhde. *Virittäjä* 73:432-4.

Levin, B. and Rappaport Hovav, M. 1995. *Unaccusativity.* Cambridge, Mass.: The MIT Press.

Löbel, E. 1994. KP/DP Syntax: Interaction of Case Marking with Referential and Nominal Features. *Theoretical Linguistics* 20:37-70.

Magga, O. 1986. *Studier I samisk infinitivsyntaks. Del I: Infinitivsetning. Akkusativ og infinitiv.* Sami Instituhtta/ Nordisk samisk institutt/ Pohjoismainen saamelaisinstituutti.

Manninen, S. 1999. Manner Adverbials and the Structure of Finnish Sentences: A Minimalist Approach. Doctoral dissertation, University of Edinburgh.

Manninen, S. 2000. Why 'Adverb' is a Lexical Case: Evidence from Finnish. *Adverbs and Adjunction*, eds. A. Alexiadou and P. Svenonius, 133-154. Linguistics in Potsdam 6.

Manninen, S. and Nelson, D. 2002. The Finnish Passive is Really a Passive. *Leeds Working Papers in Linguistics and Phonetics,* Vol 9, ed. D. Nelson. Leeds: University of Leeds.

Milsark, G. 1985. Case Theory and the Grammar of Finnish. *Proceedings of the New England Linguistics Society* XV:319-331.

Metslang, H. 1994. *Temporal Relations in the Predicate and the Grammatical System.* (Oulun yliopiston suomen ja saamen kielen laitoksen tutkimusraportteja, 39.) Oulu: University of Oulu.

Metslang, H. 1997. Eesti prefiksaaladverbist *ära* soome keele taustal. *Lähivertailuja* 9. (Castrenianumin toimitteita, 53.), eds. R. Grünthal and R. Kasik, 31-46. Helsinki: The Finno-Ugrian Society.

Mitchell, E. 1991a. Evidence from Finnish for Pollock's Theory of IP. *Linguistic Inquiry* 22:373-79.

Mitchell, E. 1991b. Case and the Finnish Object. *Cornell Working Papers in Linguistics* 9:193-228.

Nelson, D. 1998a. *Grammatical Case Assignment in Finnish.* New York: Garland.

Nelson, D. 1998b. Case Competition in Finnish. *Nordic Journal of Linguistics* 21:145-78.

Nemvalts, P. 1996. *Case Marking of Subject Phrases in Modern Standard Estonian.* (Studia Uralica Upsaliensia, 25) Uppsala: Acta Universitatis Upsaliensis.

Nevis, J. 1984. Five Morphemes in Finnish: Possessive Suffixes or Anaphoric Clitics? *Ohio State University Working Papers in Linguistics 29*:174-207.

Nevis, J. 1986. Finnish Particle Clitics and General Clitic Theory. *Ohio State University Working Papers in Linguistics* 33.

Nevis, J. 1987. Clitics and Semi-clitics in Finnish. *The Nordic Languages and Modern Linguistics 6*, eds. P. Lilius and M. Saari, 251-263. Helsinki: Helsinki University Press.

Nikanne, U. 1991. *Zones and Tiers: A Study of Thematic Structure.* Helsinki: Suomalaisen Kirjallisuuden Seura.

Nikanne, U. 1993. On Assigning Semantic Cases in Finnish. *Case and Other Functional Categories in Finnish Syntax*, eds. A. Holmberg and U. Nikanne, 75-88. Berlin: Mouton.

Pierrehumbert, J. 1980. The Finnish Possessive Suffixes. *Language* 56: 603-21.

Posti, L. 1953. From Pre-Finnic to Late Proto-Finnic. *Finnisch-Ugrische Forschungen* 31:1-91.

Price, G. (ed.) 1998. *Encyclopedia of the Languages of Europe.* Oxford: Blackwell.

Reinhart, T. 1997. *Strategies of Anaphora Resolution.* Paper delivered at Interface Strategies conference, Amsterdam, 9/97. To appear as OTS Working Paper TL97-007.

Rigler, E. 1992. Morphological, Grammatical and Semantic Cases in Finnish. Ms, University of Edinburgh.

Savijärvi, I. 1977. *Itämerensuomalaisten kielten kieltoverbi.* Joensuu: Suomalaisen Kirjallisuuden Seura.

Sammallahti, P. 1998a. *The Saami Languages.* Kárášjohka: Davvi Girji OS.

Sammallahti, P. 1998b. Saamic. *The Uralic Languages,* ed. D. Abondolo, 43-95. London: Routledge.

Sammallahti, P. and Morottaja, M. 1993. *Säämi-suomâ sänikirje. Inarinsaamelais-suomalainen sanakirja.* Ohcejohka: Girjegiisá.

Shore, S. 1986. *Onko suomessa passiivia.* Helsinki: Suomalaisen kirjallisuuden seura.

Shore, S. 1988. On the So-Called Finnish Passive. *Word* 39: 151-176.

Van Steenbergen, M. 1989. Finnish: Configurational or Not? *Configurationality: The Typology of Asymmetries*, ed. L. Marácz and P. Muysken, 143-157. Dordrecht: Foris.

Stowell, T. 1995. What Do Present and Past Tenses Mean? *Temporal Reference, Aspect and Actionality, Vol 1: Semantic and Syntactic Perspectives*, eds. P. Bertinetto, V. Bianchi, J. Higginbotham and M. Squartini, 381-396. Torino: Rosenberg and Sellier.

Stowell, T. 1996. The Phrase Structure of Tense. *Phrase Structure and the Lexicon*, eds. J. Rooryck and L. Zaering, 277-291. Dordrecht: Kluwer.

Tenny, C. 1994. *Aspectual Roles and the Syntax-Semantics Interface*. Dordrecht: Kluwer.

Tikka, T. 1998. *Vepsän suffiksoituneet postpositiot.* (Studia Uralica Uppsaliensia, 22) Uppsala: Acta Universitatis Uppsaliensis.

Tommola, H. 1993. Ambipersoonainen suppressiivi: diateesista suomessa ja virossa. *Studia Comparativa Linguarum Orbis Maris Baltici* 1, ed. V. Yli-Vakkuri, 41-93, University of Turku.

Torn, R. 2000. The Status of the Passive in English and Estonian. *Working Papers in English and Applied Linguistics,* Vol 7, 105-149. Research Centre for English and Applied Linguistics, University of Cambridge.

Trosterud, T. 1993. Anaphors and Binding Domains in Finnish. *Case and Other Functional Categories in Finnish*, eds. A. Holmberg and U. Nikanne, 225-243. Berlin: Mouton.

Trosterud, T. 1994. Auxiliaries, Negative Verbs and Word Order in the Sami and Finnic Langauges. *Minor Uralic Languages: Structure and Development*, ed A. Künnap, 173-181. Tartu: University of Tartu.

Toivonen, I. 2000. The Morphosyntax of Finnish Possessives. *Natural Language and Linguistic Theory* 18:579-609.

Tuomikoski, R. 1973. Adjecktiivin ja adverbin erosta. *Virittäjä* 1973/3: 199-213.

Vainikka, A. 1989. Deriving Syntactic Representations in Finnish. Doctoral dissertation, University of Massachusetts at Amherst.

Vainikka, A. and J. Maling. 1996. Is Partitive Case Inherent or Structural? *Partitives*, ed. J. Hoeksema, 179-208. Berlin: Mouton.

Vihman, V. and Hiietam, K. 2002. The Personal Passive in Estonian. Paper presented at the Linguistics Association of Great Britain meeting, UMIST, Sept. 19, 2002.

Viitso, T-R. 1998. Fennic. *The Uralic Languages,* ed. D. Abondolo, 96-114. London: Routledge.

Vilkuna, M. 1989. *Free Word Order in Finnish.* Helsinki: Suomalaisen Kirjallisuuden Seura.

Vilkuna, M. 1995. Discourse Configurationality in Finnish. *Discourse Configurational Languages,*. ed. K. Kiss, 244-268. Oxford: Oxford University Press.

Vilkuna, M. 1996. *Suomen lauseopin perusteet.* Helsinki: Edita.

Zagona, K. 1995. Temporal Argument Structure: Configurational Elements of Construal. *Temporal Reference, Aspect and Actionality, Vol 1: Semantic and Syntactic Perspectives,* eds. P. Bertinetto, V. Bianchi, J. Higginbotham and M. Squartini, 397-410. Torino: Rosenberg and Sellier.

Part I

Phonology

2

Estonian Quantity: Implications for Moraic Theory

MARTIN EHALA

1 Introduction[1]

Estonian distinguishes three degrees of quantity: short (Q1), long (Q2) and overlong (Q3). Q1 occurs in short stressed syllables (CV) like the first syllable of *koli* 'trash', and Q2 in long stressed syllables (CVV and CVC) as, for example, the first syllable of *kooli* 'school' g. sg., and *kolli* 'ghost' g. sg. Q3, like Q2, occurs also in long stressed syllables, but with an extra prosodic quantity – the so-called "overlength" – added. This "overlength" is traditionally transcribed by a lengthening sign after the segment that carries its peak: *koo:li* 'school' p. sg., or *kol:li* 'ghost' p. sg. As the minimal triplets *koli – kooli – koo:li* and *koli – kolli – kol:li* show, all three quantity degrees are phonologically distinctive.

Furthermore, in Estonian, quantity also influences the stress placement: a Q3 syllable can form a monosyllabic foot of its own, in which case the secondary stress immediately follows the main stress: *sóo:làsele* 'inhabitant of swamp', sg. abl. Neither Q1 nor Q2 can show this pattern: a stressed Q1

[1] I would like to thank Matti Leiwo, Pirjo Turunen, Anthony Fox and two anonymous reviewers for their comments and criticism, as well as CIMO for a research grant at the University of Jyväskylä that enabled me to undertake this research.

Generative Approaches to Finnic and Saami Linguistics.
Diane Nelson and Satu Manninen (eds.).

or Q2 syllable must be followed by at least one unstressed syllable as seen in *élusàle* 'alive', sg. abl. (Q1), and *sóolasèle* 'salty', sg. abl. (Q2).

Phonologically, the ternary pattern of Estonian quantity has been explained by various means. The majority of accounts have characterised overlength either in moraic terms as lengthening in the Q3 syllables (Bye 1997, Eek and Meister 1997), or in metrical terms as the ability of Q3 syllables to exhaust a foot (Prince 1980, Kager 1994). Both approaches have their problems – moraic accounts lead to excessive use of moras (3 or even 4 moras per syllable), metrical accounts retain representational binarity, but at the cost of recursive foot structure.

However, these problems could be avoided if the marked member of the Estonian quantity system is considered Q2 rather than Q3. As I am going to argue in this paper, such a revision is well motivated both on empirical and theoretical grounds as well as by the evidence from the historical evolution of the Estonian quantity system. Besides this, the Estonian quantity system also provides support for the hypothesis that syllable weight is not a linear function of segmental length. This has direct implications to Moraic Theory (Hayes 1989, 1995) which uses the notion of mora to encode both length and weight distinctions.

2 Phonetic Properties of Estonian Quantity

More than a half century of experimental phonetic research on Estonian quantity has proved that it is impossible to derive the Estonian three quantity degrees from the corresponding durational differences of sounds (see Lehiste 1997). Perception experiments have also shown that the acoustic information contained in a single syllable is not sufficient to distinguish the three quantity degrees. Eek and Meister (1997) conducted an experiment to study whether listeners are able to identity the quantity degree of the first syllable of a disyllabic word without the information of the second syllable vowel. The listeners were able to identify the short quantity (Q1), but were not able to differentiate between Q2 and Q3. Only when the listeners were presented information about the quantity of the second syllable vowel were they able to identify Q2 and Q3.

This suggests that the durational ratio of the syllables in a disyllabic foot is the main indicator of quantity in Estonian. However, as Ilse Lehiste (1997) reports, the duration ratios alone are not sufficient to distinguish Q2 and Q3. In a perception experiment, listeners were presented "disyllabic" noise bursts which corresponded in their durational ratios to disyllabic Q1 (2:3), Q2 (3:2) and Q3 (2:1) sequences. For the sake of symmetry 1:2 sequence stimuli were also included. The subjects were able to distinguish the short-long (1:2 and 2:3) sequences from long-short (2:1 and 3:2) sequences, but were unable to differentiate further 1:2 sequences from 2:3 sequences and 2:1 from 3:2. The experiment was replicated by synthesised disyllabic nonsense word stimuli. The results were similar to the previous experiment.

One of the features differentiating the Estonian Q2 and Q3 feet is the fundamental frequency curve (Lehiste 1997, Eek and Meister 1997). In a Q2 disyllabic foot, F0 curve reaches its peak on the end of the first syllable vowel and starts to fall on the second syllable vowel, but the fall starts higher than in Q3 feet. In Q3 feet, the F0 peak is achieved in the first third of the first syllable vowel and is followed by a steady fall that continues also on the second syllable. However, the difference in the F0 curve is insufficient to distinguish between Q2 and Q3 syllables, if the second syllable is not present.

This has lead phoneticians to a conclusion that Estonian quantity degrees are perceptually identified in the domain of a disyllabic foot by a number of interrelated phonetic cues, the most important of which are the durational ratios of syllables in the foot and the fundamental frequency curve. I have represented the patterns of Estonian three quantity degrees in (1) where the length of the lines marks the durational ratio of syllables in the foot and the curves above them indicate the contour of F0. As the Estonian disyllabic feet strive to isochrony, I have represented all of them as durationally equal, though the Q1 foot is the shortest, Q2 foot (surprisingly) the longest and Q3 in between, closer to Q2 than Q1. The durational differences of different foot types, however, are smaller than the durational differences between intra-feet segments (Eek and Meister 1997).

(1)

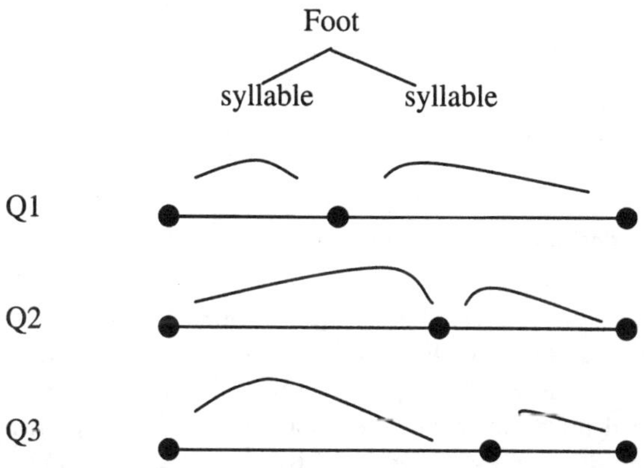

3 Phonological Accounts of Estonian Quantity

The oldest theory of Estonian quantity comes from Veske (1879). He argued that all Estonian phonemes have three distinctive degrees of length. This theory was dominating in Estonian linguistics about a hundred years, but has gradually lost its currency as experimental phonetic research has made it apparent that the Estonian quantity degrees do not correspond to durational differences of speech sounds. Currently, most of the linguists agree that the Q2-Q3 distinction is a prosodic one. However, there is quite a wide range of opinions about what is the domain of Q2-Q3 distinction and how to express it phonologically.

As a ternary opposition of quantity is typologically rare and theoretically unwelcome, the most common phonological solution has been to separate the three-way distinction to two binary oppositions: segmental length distinguishes between short (Q1) and long (Q2) quantity, and an extra prosodic quantity distinguishes overlong (Q3) from Q2. This is most clearly expressed in (Hint 1997a: 133), repeated here as (2):

(2)

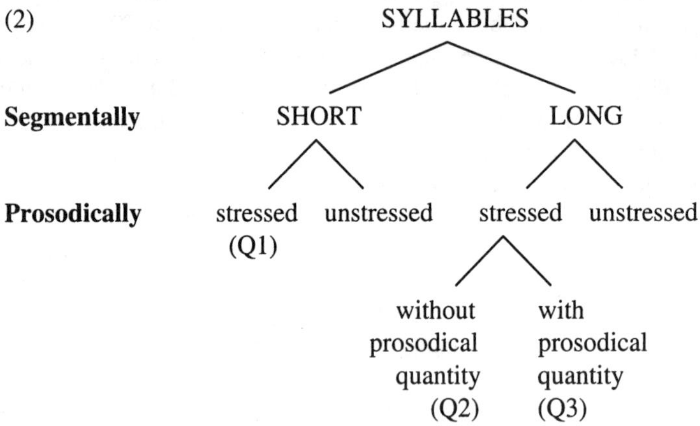

This hypothesis defines the Estonian quantity opposition as a syllabic phenomenon.

Alternatively, it is suggested that Estonian quantity must be interpreted phonologically as a feature of the whole foot (Eek and Meister 1997): Q1 and Q2 feet are balanced, and Q3 feet are unbalanced. The terms balanced/unbalanced refer directly to the phonetic differences of feet: the articulatory energy appears more evenly distributed in Q1 and Q2 disyllabic feet than in Q3 feet (see (1)). Schematically this can be presented as (3):

(3)

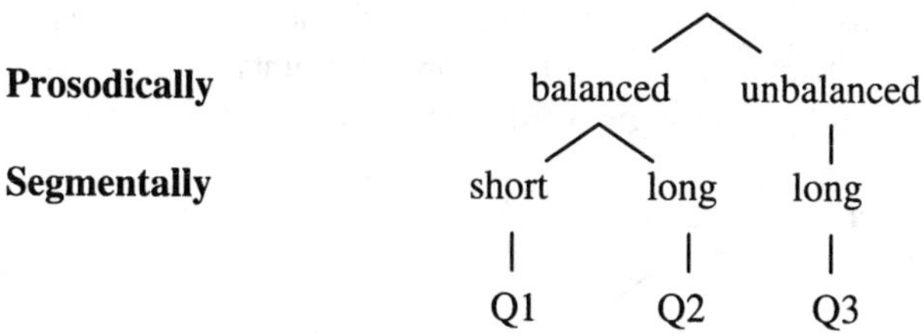

The difference between (2) and (3) lies in the prosodic domain where Q3 is to be phonologically represented. In (2) it is the syllable, in (3) it is the foot. It should be noted that the difference between balanced and unbalanced feet have been so far expressed only by moraic means (Eek and Meister 1997), not much different from those which use moras to represent overlength in syllabic terms (for example Bye 1997). Thus, so far there is no precise representational difference between the syllable-based and foot-based accounts of Estonian quantity.

What is common to these approaches is that both of them assume that Q3 is the marked member of the Estonian quantity system. In moraic terms, this is commonly represented by an extra mora assigned to the syllable, making Q3 syllables trimoraic (/koμμμ.liμ/ 'school' sg. p.). To avoid theoretically unwelcome trimoraic syllables, some authors (Bye 1997, Eek and Meister 1997) have suggested that overlength is to be represented either as a free mora or a degenerate syllable.

Though both of the approaches (2 and 3) manage to account for the patterns of Estonian quantity at the prosodic level of representation, their problems become apparent at the intersection of segmental and prosodic quantity. I will give two short examples based on the analyses of Bye (1997) and Eek and Meister (1997) to demonstrate this.

According to Bye (1997), overlength in Q3 syllables is variably expressed either by a degenerate syllable or a free mora. This allows him to explain why Q3 syllables may constitute feet of their own (*káu:kèle* – /[kau:][ke.le]/ 'far'), but need not (*káu:kele* – /[kau:.ke]le/). If Q3 forms a foot of its own, it is represented as a sequence of a syllable and a degenerate syllable (4a); if not, the overlength is expressed by an unassociated mora (4b):

(4) a. $\sigma_{\mu\mu}+\sigma_{\mu}^{degen}$
b. $\sigma_{\mu\mu}+\mu$

Bye (1997) does not specify, how the moras should be connected to the segments, but he assumes that the third mora is connected to the Q3 centre (indicated by lengthening sign ':' in traditional accounts). Thus, I suppose that the two representations for the word *kau:kele* would look like this:

(5)

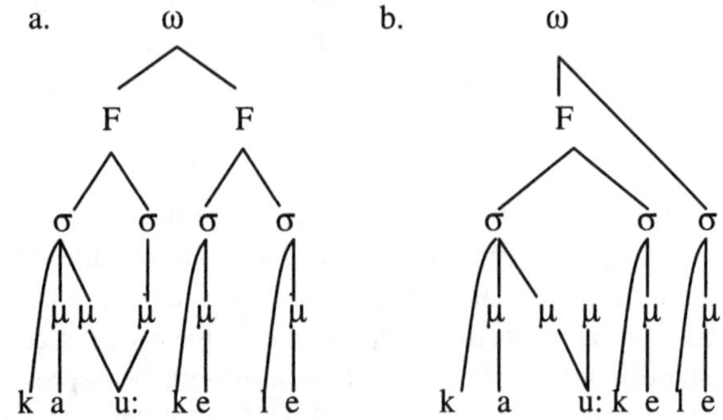

In (5a), the degenerate syllable analysis enables parsing the first syllable and the degenerate syllable as a foot, which allows secondary stress to fall on the second syllable: *káu:kèle*. As the free mora on (5b) is not associated to a syllable node, monosyllabic foot is not possible, which leads to a stress pattern *káu:kele*.

This analysis is correct for most of the cases. However, the question is whether degenerate syllables and free moras are indeed theoretically more welcome than trimoraic syllables. They might, provided that one can dispense trimoraic syllables altogether, but under the conventions of Moraic Theory (Hayes 1989, 1995), the description of Estonian would still require trimoraic syllables, even if Q3 is represented by a degenerate syllable or a free mora. Let us consider two forms: Q2 *aitta* (a name) and Q3 *ait:ta* ('barn' sg. p.). If geminate consonants and short vowels are underlyingly monomoraic (Hayes 1989), the representation of the name *aitta* (Q2) would require three moras in the first syllable (/aμiμtμ.taμ/) though it does not have overlength. Provided that the third mora could be analysed as a degenerate syllable (/aμiμ.tμ.taμ/), this would lead to an unattested stress pattern in trisyllabic forms of this word, such as **áittàle* sg. abl. Furthermore, the Q3 form *ait:ta* ('barn' sg. p.) would then require an additional, fourth mora /aμiμtμ**μ**.taμ/ to distinguish it from Q2 name *aitta* that already has three moras in the first syllable. There is no satisfactory answer, how to accommodate quadrimoraic syllables with the analysis proposed by Bye (1997). Of course, one might also adopt the principle of mora-splitting (Maddieson 1993), but the three devices together (degenerate syllables, free moras and splitting) would seriously reduce the attractiveness of the theory allowing for far more possible combinations than there are attested syllable types.

Eek and Meister (1997) have tried to solve the problem without the notions of degenerate syllables and free moras, just relying on the concept of mora splitting. In their interpretation, all disyllabic feet contain three moras which are distributed to replicate as close as possible the phonetic patterns of Q1, Q2 and Q3 disyllabic feet (see (1)). This would necessarily require splitting moras between the syllables:

(6)

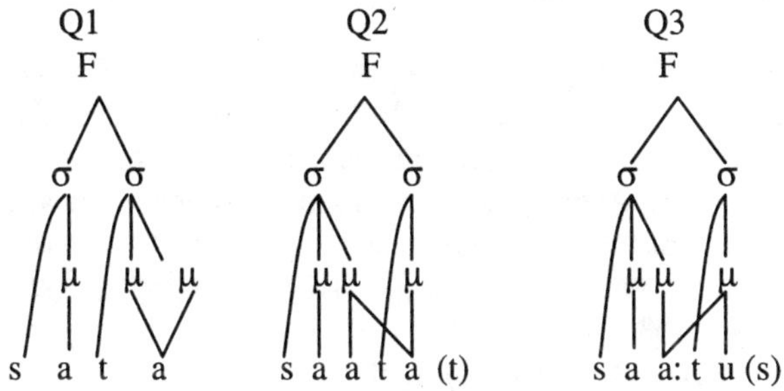

The examples in (6), taken from Eek and Meister (1997: 94) show the representation of Q1 word *sata* 'hundred', Q2 word *saatat* 'you escort' and Q3 word *saa:tus* 'product'. The phonetically half-long vowel in the second syllable of Q1 feet is represented as bimoraic, the difference between long *saatat* and overlong *saa:tus* is expressed by different splitting patterns: in Q2 feet, the first syllable gives some of its weight to the second syllable, and in Q3 vice versa. This correctly expresses the phonetic facts that in Q2 feet, the second syllable vowel is often half-long and in Q3 feet it is extra-short. However, the whole analysis is unacceptable due to crossing association lines.

It might be argued that the problems of combining prosodic and segmental quantity in moraic accounts of Estonian overlength are due to the principles of Moraic Theory, but one should admit that other approaches do not do better.

For example in treatments of Prince (1980) and Kager (1994), overlength is accounted for by the ability of Q3 syllables to form a monosyllabic foot of their own. In these accounts Q3 syllables differ from Q2 ones by their ability to exhaust two metrical grid positions (s w for Prince (1980), x x for Kager (1994)), while Q2 and Q1 can exhaust only one grid position. This explanation would be perfect, if Q3 would always constitute a foot. However, as already mentioned, Q3 syllables may, but need not to form a monosyllabic foot. The two stress patterns of the word *kau:kele* illustrate this behaviour well: in *káu:kèle* (/[kau:.][ke.le]/) Q3 is a foot, in *káu:kele*

(/[kau:.ke.]le/) it is not. If the only defining feature of Q3 is its ability to exhaust a foot, the description of forms like *kâu:kele* would require recursive foot structure: /[[kau:.]ke.]le/, to avoid two extrametrical syllables. Such a treatment is at odds with the principle of Prosodic Hierarchy (Selkirk 1984, McCarthy and Prince 1986), according to which feet cannot be comprised of feet. Hayes (1995) who adopts essentially the analysis of Prince (1980) overcomes this by stating that trimoraic syllables may optionally be treated as disyllabic sequences. As in his analysis Q3 syllables are trimoraic, the foot exhaustion feature is not defining for Q3 and need not be absolute.

Above I have shortly overviewed some accounts of Estonian quantity, none of which is fully satisfactory. The problems of all these explanations stem from a common assumption that the marked member of the opposition is the overlong Q3. Actually, as we will see in Section 5, the analysis of the historical evolution of the phenomenon suggests that the ternary quantity opposition has not emerged due to over-lengthening of the Q2, but instead by shortening of Q3.

This is the crucial point of my analysis. Provided that the marked member of the opposition is Q2 (historically shortened Q3), one could consider Q1 a normal short and light (monomoraic) quantity and Q3 a normal long and heavy (bimoraic) quantity. Q2 would be something in between: segmentally long, but light by weight (monomoraic). According to this hypothesis, the examples in (6) would have a representation as in (7):

(7)

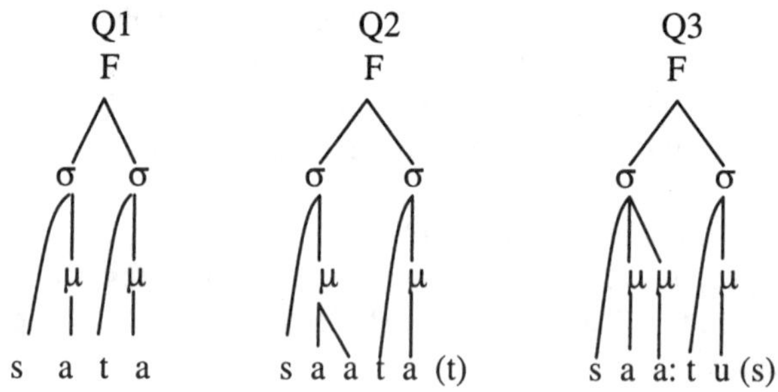

As we will see in Sections 6 and 7, this analysis would significantly simplify the treatment of both the Estonian quantity as well as the stress system. However, the same analysis would run counter to one of the main principles of the Moraic Theory, namely that syllabic quantity is a linear function of segmental length (shortly discussed in the next Section). The main theoretical argument of the paper is that the representation of weight and segmental length should be separated. This will be discussed in detail in Section 8.

4 Segmental Length and Syllable Weight in Moraic Theory

In the Moraic Theory (Hayes 1989, 1995), the notion of mora has a dual role: it is the basic unit of syllable weight and, at the same time, it is used to express segmental length distinctions. The last is achieved by the following set of conventions:

(8) a) short vowels have one mora
b) long vowels have two moras
c) short consonants are moraless
d) long consonants and geminates have one mora
e) glides are moraless
f) segments in syllable onsets are moraless

From such conventions, it follows that syllable weight is a linear function of segmental length. This means that CV syllables are always light (i.e. monomoraic) and CVV syllables always heavy (bimoraic). CVC syllables are light by default, but in languages where CVC counts as heavy, the coda consonant is assigned a mora by the rule of Weight by Position (Hayes 1989).

For the description of most languages, the double role of moras (to express both weight and length) does not constitute problems. However, complications arise in languages that have geminate consonants, but count CVC syllables as light (see Tranel 1991). If geminate consonants are underlyingly moraic, the CVC syllables closed by geminates are necessarily heavy (bimoraic) while the rest of CVC syllables are light. One possibility to solve the controversy is to separate the representation of segmental length from that of weight, as suggested by Tranel (1991) or to use an extra tier of moras (Hayes 1995).

Complications arise also in languages where syllable weight is not a linear function of segmental length, such as Estonian. As already mentioned, in Estonian, syllabic quantity is not calculated from the moraicity of its constituents (except Q1). For example Q2 syllable *sep* in *seppa* ('smith' sg. g.) is bimoraic according to (8), but Q2 syllable *ait* as in *aitta* (a name) is trimoraic. Interestingly, Q3 syllable *ait:* in *ait:ta* ('barn' sg. p.) is also trimoraic, but Q3 syllable *sep:* as in *sep:pa* ('smith' sg. p.) is bimoraic following (8). This problem could also be solved if weight is to be represented differently from that of length.

The conventions in (8) create also unnecessary superfluity in phonological descriptions. If syllable weight is calculated on the basis of segmental length, all languages that have a distinction of segmental length should also have a distinction of syllable weight. This needs not necessarily be so. Consider an analogy of tones: tones are usually represented in phonological descriptions of these languages that make use of them. The languages that do not use tones do not have a tonal tier. Why should languages that do not use syllable weight, have weight obligatorily expressed in their phonological representations? Certainly it would be more appropriate to express weight distinctions only in these languages where it is relevant. This could be done if encoding the length distinctions could be separated from encoding the weight distinctions.

There are several proposals for how to do it. The most common of these is the original proposal of Heinrich Hock (1985) to use CV-tier to express length distinctions and μ-tier for weight distinctions. Tranel (1991) and others repeat the same proposal. Recently Fox (1998) has suggested to adopt a separate Q-tier which is to be placed between the syllable and foot levels.

The main argument against all these solutions is that this would require an extra representational grid, which would make the theory too unrestricted. This objection can be eliminated if we abandon the CV-tier and represent length distinctions by counting the root nodes (Selkirk 1990). According to her proposal, geminates and long vowels have one set of feature values that are linked to two root nodes, the feature values of single segments are linked to one root node.

It is often argued against separating weight from length, since it would allow more association combinations between segmental length and syllable weight than actually attested, such as bimoraic short segments and monomoraic long segments (Hayes 1989: 293). I think these worries are slightly exaggerated. Concerning bimoraic short segments, I leave the discussion for time being. As about the possibility of monomoraic long segments, these are attested in some languages and the strongest evidence for them comes from Estonian, where they occur in Q2 syllables. This claim is supported by the evidence from the historical evolution of the Estonian quantity system to which I turn below.

5 Historical Evolution of the Estonian Quantity System

There are several hypothesises concerning the historical evolution of Estonian quantity (for an overview, see Tauli 1954). The most widely accepted of them is the Veske-Collinder's theory (Veske 1879, Collinder 1929) which explains the emergence of Q3 by compensatory lengthening after syncopy and apocopy in about XIII–XV century.

In the course of syncopy and apocopy in Estonian, short vowels were lost under certain conditions in the word final position and in the middle of the word. The conditions were as follows:

1. The short vowel was lost from the unstressed open syllable if the preceding stressed syllable was long. Under this condition, short vowels were lost both in the absolute end of disyllabic words (*jal:k* < **jalka* 'foot') and in second syllables of longer words (*tüt:ret* < **tüttäret* 'daughters', *an:tnut* < **antanut* 'given').
2. The word final short vowel in trisyllabic words was lost regardless of the weight of preceding syllables (*orav* < **orava* 'squirrel', *raamatt* < **raamattu* 'book').
3. The word final short vowel in disyllabic words was not lost, if the first syllable was short (*pesa* < **pesa* 'nest').
4. The syncopy and apocopy were not triggered if the syllable concerned was closed (*laulu* < **laulun* <**laulun* 'song' g. sg., *oravat* < **oravat* 'squirrels').
5. Parallel to the syncopy and apocopy, there was also shortening of long vowels and diphthongs in unstressed syllables both in closed as well as in open ones (*met:sa* < **met:san* < **metsaan* 'forest' ill. sg., *met:sa* < **metsaa* 'forest' p. sg.).

Hint (1980) has summarised these conditions elegantly in terms of moras: the vowel of unstressed open syllables was lost, if it was on the distance of two moras from the nearest preceding stress.

According to Veske (1879) and Collinder (1929), the changes mentioned above were accompanied by compensatory lengthening in the immediately preceding stressed heavy syllable. As a result, these syllables acquired overlength whereas the rest of the stressed heavy syllables remained in their original quantity which in the present Estonian system equals to Q2. Thus, overlength evolved in cases like *jal:k* < **jalka*, *tüt:ret* < **tüttäret*, *an:tnut* < **antanut*, *met:sa* < **metsaa*, whereas no compensatory lengthening occurred, if the immediately preceding syllable was stressless (*orav* < **orava*, *raamatt* < **raamattu*).

Thought the correlation between the vowel loss or shortening and the modern Q3 in the preceding syllable is quite high, it does not necessarily mean that there was compensatory lengthening involved. First there are a few morphological types where no vowel loss occurred, but the preceding stressed syllables are Q3 nevertheless. One of these types includes verbs of weakening grade alternation such as *γp:pima* 'to study'. This type has about 2000 stems which make up nearly one fifth of Estonian verb stems. In these verbs the short vowel from the second open syllable has not been lost, though the first syllable is heavy. Accordingly, there could not have occurred compensatory lengthening, either. Contrary to expectations, the first syllables of these verbs are still Q3 (*γp:pima*, *kam:mima* 'to comb', *hoo:lima* 'to care about'). This deviation is commonly explained by analogy with verbs of the type of *tun:tuma* 'to seem' where the Q3 could have emerged by compensatory lengthening (*tun:tuma* < *_tuntuuma_, see Kettunen 1929). The problem with this explanation is that the *γp:pima*-type is more than twice as numerous than the *tun:tuma*-type that has only about 900 stems. First, it is unlikely that the smaller type has provided the basis for analogy to the larger type. Second, analogical levelling usually does not spread to all cases where it could, but in Estonian there are no verbs of appropriate structure that have escaped this alleged analogy. Thirdly, and most importantly, the *tun:tuma*-type does not have grade alternation: all its forms are in Q3 (*tun:tuma* : *tun:tup* 's/he/it seems'), whereas *γp:pima*-verbs have the regular grade alternation pattern, Q2 occurring in forms where the second syllable was historically closed (*γppib* 's/he/it studies', Q2), and Q3 where the second syllable was open (*γp:pima* 'to study', Q3). If the *tun:tuma* type really had influenced the *γp:pima* type, the last would certainly have no grade alternation.

There is a similar problem with the nouns of strengthening grade alternation (*hammas* 'tooth'). This type has Q3 in plural forms, though the original diphthong in the second syllable has not shortened: *ham:pait* < *_hampait_ 'tooth' p. pl. In this case, it is not possible to appeal to analogy, either, since there is no type that could serve as the basis for it. The question then arises, how could these forms have overlength if no compensatory lengthening has taken place.

Though just two types that do not conform to the compensatory lengthening pattern might not be enough to falsify the theory, I will show later that there is alternative analysis that is able to account also for these deviant types, and is therefore superior to the compensatory lengthening hypothesis.

However, the problems of the Veske-Collinder theory do not end here. While compensatory lengthening after the loss of the vowel is easily modeled in Moraic Theory (Hayes 1989), it is not the case after shortening of the long vowel. The reason is that the syllable node cannot be eroded by Parasitic Delinking (Hayes 1989: 268), since it still contains an overt nuclear segment (8b). And consequently, the loose mora could not acquire a new association without crossing the association lines (8c):

(9)

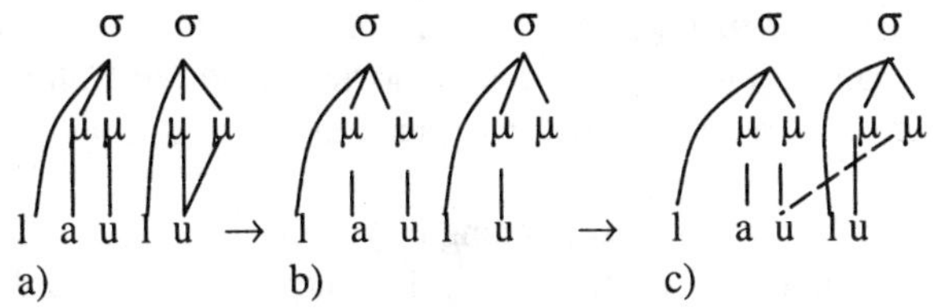

Of course, it would always be possible to find a way to avoid crossing the lines, but the question is whether it is indeed reasonable to modify the theory to accommodate a type of change for which there is only hypothetical evidence from one language. It is much more reasonable to ask whether the suggested compensatory lengthening took place at all. And there is evidence that it did not.

Let us compare Estonian and Finnish. The languages are closely related, and though they are not mutually intelligible, there are many words that sound and mean the same in both languages. The quantity system of Finnish differs from that of Estonian by lacking the three degrees of quantity that Estonian has developed after the Proto Baltic-Finnic has broken down to separate languages. Instead, Finnish has retained the binary short-long opposition of length which is generally believed to resemble the quantity system of Proto Baltic-Finnic. According to Veske-Collinder hypothesis, this difference between Finnish and Estonian quantity can be explained by the lack of syncopy and apocopy in Finnish – the change that created Estonian Q3 through compensatory lengthening.

If this is the case, then the Estonian Q1 forms should be quantitatively close to Finnish short quantity and the Q2 forms to the long one. The Q3, on the other hand, should be different from that of the Finnish long quantity. While the Finnish short quantity and Q1 are quite close, the Finnish long quantity corresponds perceptually and articulatorly to Q3 rather than to Q2 (see Pajusalu 1994 for details). Similar findings are also reported by Eek and Help (1986: 12–13): "... in contemporary Finnish ... the duration of a long vowel or a long ambisyllabic consonant in the main stressed syllable is approximate or even exceeds the duration of the Estonian main stressed syllable with the grave accent (the so-called Q3) ..." The results of the phonetic research is supported by the fact that Finnish learners of Estonian do not have difficulties with articulating and perceiving Q1 and Q3, but do find it hard to replicate Q2. All these facts are certainly incompatible with the hypothesis that it is the Q3 that is the late development of Estonian.

This controversy was not unknown to Collinder, either. To explain it, he suggested that there has been an across-the-board lengthening in Finnish long syllables that turned them phonetically similar to Estonian Q3 (see

Ariste 1947 for discussion). This is obviously an *ad hoc* explanation that does not have any independent motivation from the history of Finnish.

Above I pointed out three shortcomings in the Veske-Collinder's theory, for which there is no satisfactory explanation:

1. The lack of vowel loss or shortening in *γp:pima-* and *hammas*-types.
2. The impossibility of compensatory lengthening after shorthening of long vowels in the next syllable.
3. Phonetic closedness of Finnish long quantity and Estonian Q3.

Next I will outline an alternative explanation to the emergence of the Estonian quantity system, an explanation which is also able to cope in a natural way with the above mentioned deviations.

This explanation was first suggested by the last century Finnish scholar Emil Nestor Setälä (1896). He argued that the Estonian quantity system dates back to Proto Finno-Ugric and is a part of Lappish and Baltic-Finnic grade alternation. Certainly, Setälä's dating of Estonian quantity alternation so early has raised justified doubts, and at present, his theory has completely lost its currency. However, connecting the origin of the Estonian quantity opposition to the Baltic-Finnic grade alternation has its appeal, and some linguists have also attempted it in the 20th century.

The change which led to the emergence of the Baltic-Finnic grade alternation is believed to have started under Proto-Germanic influence in II millenium BC (see Posti 1953–54). The nature and the conditions of the change were similar to that of the Verner's Law: the second syllable initial stop was weakened if the syllable was closed; if it was open, the stop remained unchanged. As the second syllable was closed in some forms of the stem (such as genitive case) and open in others (partitive), the change created an alternation which in contemporary Baltic-Finnic languages is known as consonant gradation or grade alternation:

(10)	Genitive	Partitive
a.	*jal^{k}an > *jalan > jala (Q1)	*jalkata > *jalkaa > jalka (Q3)
b.	*tark^{k}an > *tarkan > tarka (Q2)	*tarkkata > *tarkkaa > tarkka (Q3)
c.	*sep^{p}an > *sep^{p}an > sep^{p}a (Q2)	*seppata > *seppaa > seppa (Q3)

Above, the stops in genitive case forms weakened, since the second syllable was closed by the genitive ending *-n*. In cases like (9 a and b) the weakening lead to total loss of the stop, in (9c) the geminate was just weakened. (Note that in modern Finnish, the cognate of (14c) has evolved to a full loss of the geminate (Fn *sepän* 'smith' sg.g.), exactly like the cognates of (14 a and b) *jalan* 'foot' sg.g. and *tarkan* 'precice' sg.g.). At a later stage,

Estonian lost *n* in a word final position, which lead to a contemporary genitive forms *jala* 'foot', *tarka* 'clever' and *seppa* 'smith'. These are the weak grade forms. In partitive forms, there was no weakening, since the second syllable was open. At the later stage the partitive ending *-ta* shortened to *-a*, and was eventually lost altogether in the course of apocopy. The resulting partitive forms *jalka*, *tarkka* and *seppa* are called the strong grade.

In Finnish, the grade alternation only involves stops; in Estonian, it also includes quantity alternation: Q2 forms are the weak grade and Q3 forms the strong grade. Ariste (1947) has suggested that the Estonian quantity alternation (and the ternary quantity opposition as a whole) has emerged on the analogy of Baltic-Finnic consonant gradation. He argues that the weakening in cases like (9b) and (9c) spread first to words with other geminate consonants (10a) and consonant clusters (10b), and thereafter also to words with long vowels (10c) and diphthongs (10d):

(11)	Genitive	Partitive
a.	*konnan > ko^{n}nan > ko^{n}na (Q2)	*konnata > konnaa > konna (Q3)
b.	*metsan > me^{t}san > me^{t}sa (Q2)	*metsata > metsaa > metsa (Q3)
c.	*looman > lo^{o}man > lo^{o}ma (Q2)	*loomata > loomaa > looma (Q3)
d.	*laulun > la^{u}lun > la^{u}lu (Q2)	*lauluta > laulua > laulu (Q3)

After this had happened, the initially weakly expressed prosodic alternation strove to become more salient. In this process, both the weak grade weakened even more and the strong one started to lengthen. This lengthening process, as Ariste (1947) claims, caused the loss of partitive case ending *-a*. When this happened, case differences (partitive *versus* genitive) become to be expressed solely by means of quantity alternation. In a sense, Ariste (1947) argues that the quantity alternation emerged due to the system's pressure to find a use for a phonetic variation that has accidentally entered into language.

Hint (1981, 1997) agrees with Ariste (1947) that the consonant loss in the weak grade was accompanied by a prosodic weakening, and that this pattern was taken over to types in (11) by analogy. However, in his opinion it happened much later, in about XVI century, after Estonian has lost its genitive and partitive case endings. After the case endings were lost, the forms of genitive and partitive became homophonic in cases like (11) whereas the forms in (10) were kept apart by the means of consonant gradation. To avoid ambiguity, the prosodic alternation, accompanying grade alternation was taken over as the sole means of differentiating the otherwise homophonous case forms in (11).

Tauli (1954) argues that the weakening in cases like (11) did not emerge due to analogy, but as a part and parcel with the consonant gradation, i.e. as an expansion of the Verner's Law from stops to other segments, too. Though the quantity alternation is not known in other Baltic-Finnic languages (except for some signs of it in Livonian), I agree with Tauli (1954) that it was caused by the same processes responsible for the consonant gradation. There is a good argument for such an interpretation.

First, there is evidence from Finnish dialects that the first consonant in a consonant cluster between the first and second syllable is shorter when the second syllable is closed, than when it is open (Laurosela 1922). The same tendency can be noticed in some varieties of spoken Finnish, and the data in a thorough study of Finnish quantity by Lehtonen (1970: 126–129) indicate that the weakening appears also in standard language though only in case of intervocalic geminates (CVC_GC_GVC). Of course, this weakening in Finnish is by no means phonemic, but just a phonetic particular which is left unnoticed by native speakers. But still, it suggests that the processes that once caused grade alternation (Verner's Law) are still somewhat active in present Finnish. And this can be seen also in present Estonian, for example in the derivational system.

If a disyllabic Q3 stem like *vää:ra* 'wrong' or *pär:li* 'pearl' is added a derivational suffix which closes the second syllable (*-nt*, *-nk*, *-kkas*, *-ntama* etc), Q3 weakens to Q2: *väärant* 'bastard', *pärlentama* 'to shine like a pearl'. Morphologically neither of these stems has quantity alternation, all their forms are in Q3. Even stems which have grade alternation (*anne* : *an:te* 'gift' n. and g. sg.) do not occur with these affixes in their weak grade form (**annekkas*, Q2), but instead in a weakened (Q2) strong grade form (*antekkas* 'gifted'). The norms of the standard Estonian prescribe Q3 in these derived forms (*an:tekkas*), but even efforts of the mother tongue teachers at schools have not had any success in correcting the usage.

These facts suggest that the quantity alternation might well have emerged first as a phonetic phenomenon together with the consonant gradation in Proto Baltic-Finnic, but it only turned phonemic in Estonian after several sound changes caused some vital case endings to be lost, as argued by Hint (1980, 1997). In other Baltic-Finnic languages the alternation was largely levelled out.

Where I do not agree with Tauli (1954) is the emergence of Q3. He argues for a phonetic lengthening in Q3 after the syncopy and apocopy, but not for a compensatory lengthening of the phonemic nature. The existence of a purely phonetic historical change is, however, very hard to disprove. Still, the fact that Finnish long quantity and Estonian Q3 are very close both articulatorly and perceptionally suggests rather that there has been no significant lengthening involved in the emergence of Estonian Q3 syllables.

Assuming that Q2 emerged through weakening rather than Q3 through compensatory lengthening allows us to explain the irregular pattern where

Q3 is not accompanied by apocopy or syncopy (*γp:pima-* and *hammas*-type). First, as I do not assume any lengthening in Q3, I do not assume any causal connection between syncopy/apocopy and the emergence of Q3. Thus, neither the lack of vowel loss or shortening in certain cases or presence of them in other cases should not have had any consequences to the quantity of the preceding syllable: these syllables retained their initial quantity (long = Q3) either cases. And that seems to be so: Q3 occurs invariably in forms that were not weakened under Verner's Law (i.e. in forms where the second syllable was open) regardless of the syncopy or apocopy that might or might not happen in this syllable at the later stage. It is only an historical accident that the syncopy and apocopy later happened in the same environment (in the open second syllable if the preceding stressed syllable was long).

What is more important is that Q2 occurs invariably in forms that were weakened under Verner's Law (i.e. where the second syllable was closed). And this explains why *γp:pima* and *hammas* type still have the regular pattern of quantity alternation, despite the lack of vowel loss or shortening after Q3 syllables: it is not lengthening in Q3 (strong grade) which caused quantity alternation, but weakening in Q2 (weak grade). The fact that *γ p:pima* and *hammas* type have the weak grade regularly in forms where the following syllable was closed, and strong case elsewhere notwithstanding of vowel loss, gives a strong support to this hypothesis. This is also the crucial fact that Veske-Collinder's theory of compensatory lengthening is unable to account for: in *γp:pima* type, the occurrence of Q3 could be explained by analogy to *tun:tuma* type, but not the presence of quantity alternation, since the *tun:tuma* type does not have one.

6 Estonian Quantity Reconsidered

The historical evidence, presented above has direct consequences to the synchronic theory of Estonian quantity. The most prominent phonological accounts of Estonian quantity assume that its essence is connected to the notion of overlength, and that it is Q3 which is the marked member in this ternary opposition. However, the evidence from historical evolution of Estonian quantity suggests that it is Q2 that is the marked member of the opposition, whereas Q1 and Q3 remain more or less identical to the Proto Baltic-Finnic short and long quantities respectively. If this is correct, the Estonian quantity system could be analysed without the help of any unusual theoretical concepts such as degenerate syllables or recursive foot structure.

Let us consider first the emergence of Q2 in moraic terms. I assume, following Ariste (1948), Tauli (1956) and Hint (1981, 1997) that the consonant loss in the weak grade of grade alternating words (*tark^{k}an >

*tarkan > tarka 'clever' sg. g.) was accompanied by a prosodic weakening. Actually, in Moraic Theory (Hayes 1988, 1995) this change is essentially prosodic, since the only feature that distinquishes geminates from single consonants is their moraicity:

(12)

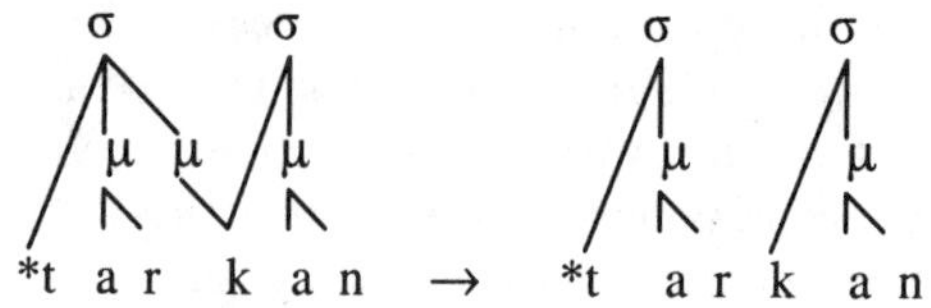

Together with this change, weakening of the first syllable also affected words with other geminates, consonant clusters, long vowels and diphthongs. However, unlike the cases with stops (12), the other types of weakening were purely prosodic, without any segmental losses:

(13)

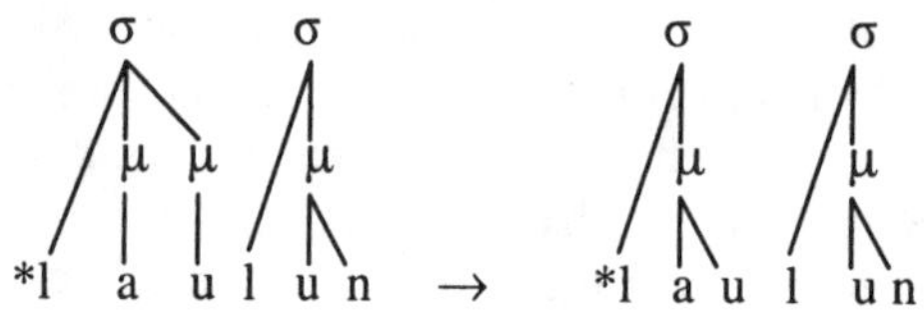

If the difference between Q2 and Q3 is to be analysed as difference in their moraic count as argued above, one is forced to conclude that the quantity alternation which emerged in cases like (13) made syllable weight phonologically distinctive in Estonian. This becomes apparent if we compare the genitive and partitive forms of the same word *lau:l* 'song'. These forms are distinquished solely by their prosodic difference, partitive *lau:lu* is in a strong grade (Q3), genitive *laulu* in a weak grade (Q2). In moraic terms, it can be expressed as follows:

(14) Partitive (Q3) Genitive (Q2)

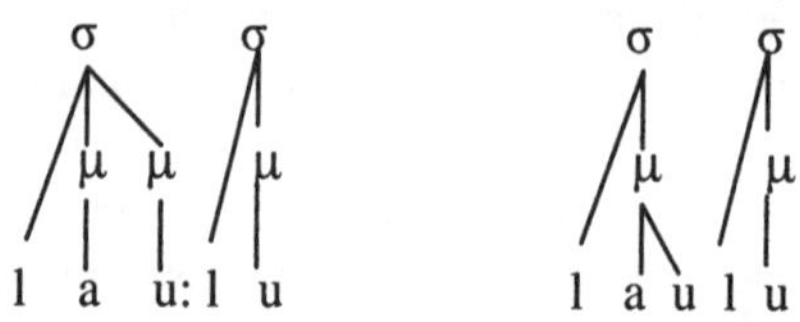

Here it should be noted that the lengthening sign in the transcription of Q3 forms is a convention based on the hypothesis of compensatory lengthening in these forms. As the current analysis is based on the opposite hypothesis, it should need a different transcription: Q2 indicated by a shortening sign, for example, *laŭlu*, Q3 without diacritics: *laulu*. However, for the sake of consistency, I will not change the transcription in the middle of the paper.

As the only means that differentiates the case forms in (14) is the weight of the first syllable, it should be concluded, that Estonian has a distinctive syllable weight. Schematically it can be summarised as follows:

(15)

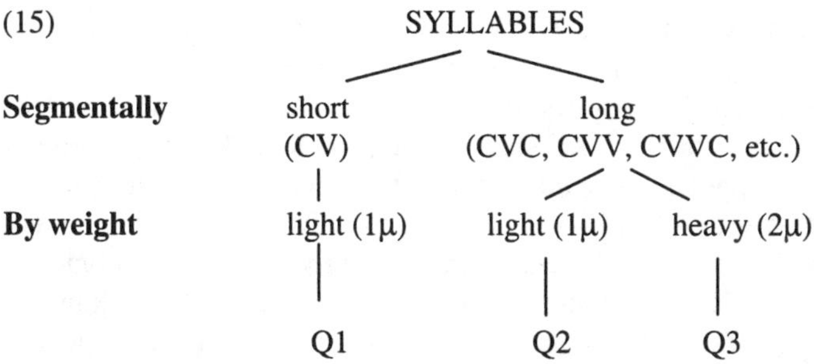

The notion of distinctive syllable weight may appear unusual, but actually it is unavoidable in any phonological accounts of Estonian quantity that describe it in moraic terms. The reason is that it does not matter whether Q2 is treated as light and Q3 as heavy or Q2 as heavy and Q3 as superheavy, the difference between *laulu* g. sg and *lau:lu* p. sg. boils down to the difference in syllable weight.

This interpretation also requires counting long syllables with the same segmental structure sometimes bimoraic and sometimes monomoraic, ie. it requires the acceptance of monomoraic long vowels and diphthongs as well as moraless geminate consonants. This claim is easier to accept if we bear in mind that monomoraic long syllables (Q2) are durationally shorter than corresponding Q3 syllables (see Pajusalu 1994).

Furthermore, there appear also to be other languages that, for stress purposes, count syllables with the same segmental structure sometimes light and sometimes heavy. For example, Hayes (1995: 242) argues, on the basis of the data by Woodbury (1987), that in Norton Sound, a dialect of Central Alaskan Yupik, CVC syllables are heavy only if they are in the initial position in the word. The same phenomenon occurs also in Pacific Yupik (Hayes 1995: 333–334). In Kashmiri, CVC syllable is heavy only if it is the best potentially stressable syllable in the word, otherwise it is light (Morén 1998). In Latin, the CVC syllables are counted as heavy, unless they appear in a weak position in the foot. This can be observed in Latin quantitative verse, as show the following cases provided by Allen (1973: 182–83): ***úter**vostró:rum*, *dé**dit**dó:rno:*, *gú**ber**ná:bunt* (light CVC syllables are presented in boldface). Hayes (1995: 120) accounts for this by a rule of Iambic Shortening which deletes a mora from a heavy syllable if it appears in a weak position in the foot. This rule applies equally to CVV and CVC syllables. In CVV syllables it causes the long vowel to shorten, in CVC syllables no segmental changes follow the mora deletion.

So far we have seen that CVC syllables allow their weight to vary without changes in their segmental structure. Fijian provides examples where this happens also to diphthongs in CVV syllables. Fijian has a rule that shortens long vowels in the penultimate syllable, if the final vowel is short. The same rule also applies to diphthongs. Such diphthongs become phonetically shorter than normal ones and their first components undergo a greater degree of phonetic assimilation with the following segment (Schütz 1985: 545). Hayes (1995: 145–46) calls this rule Trochaic Shortening and treats it as loss of mora. If this rule applies to long vowels they become ordinary short vowels, but diphthongs become monomoraic. For example, addition of the suffix *ða* to the stem *rai* 'see' leads to *răiða* 'see it' with a monomoraic diphthong. Hayes (1995: 145) represents this case as follows:

(16)

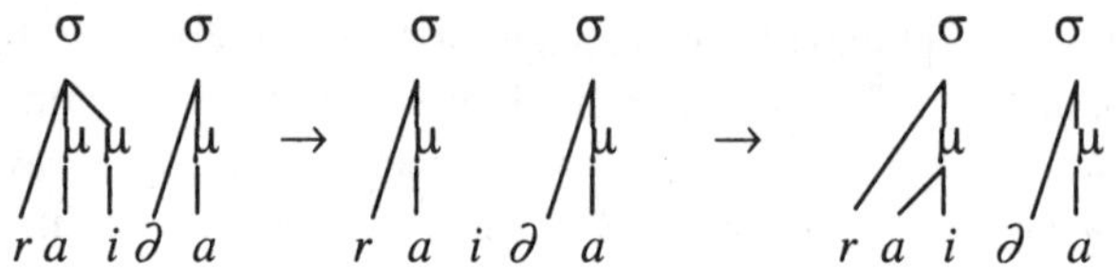

In all of these languages, the occurrence of monomoraic long syllables is structurally conditioned, their exceptional quantity is due to the quantity of neighbouring syllables or by their position in respect to the word boundary. Interestingly, there appears to be at least one language besides Estonian that makes use of distinctive syllable weight. It is Cahuilla (see Seiler 1977). In this language, there is a morphophonological rule that intensifies the first syllable in stems beginning with CVCV or CVCCV. In CVCV sequences it manifests as gemination (17a), in CVCCV sequences as lengthening of the coda consonant (17b, examples from Hayes 1995: 139):

(17)	a. *čéxivèn*	'clear'	b. *wélnet*	'mean one'
	čéxxìven	'it is very clear'	*wéllnèt*	'very mean one'

Normally CVC syllables are light in Cahuilla, the intensified ones, however, count as heavy. This can be seen from the secondary stress, which is moved to the second syllable in the intensified forms. Both Seiler (1977) and Hayes (1995) analyse this as mora insertion to the first syllable.

A similar stress pattern is also characteristic to Estonian: weight distinction between Q2 and Q3 syllables is relevant for Estonian stress assignment. As secondary stress can fall to the immediately following syllable, if the preceding syllable is Q3, but cannot, if it is Q2 or Q1, treating Q3 as heavy and Q2 and Q1 as light also simplifies the description of Estonian stress system significantly.

7 Implications for the Estonian Stress System

In Estonian, main stress is generally on the first syllable and secondary stresses follow on a binary or ternary intervals:

(18) *téravàmaltt* or *téravamàltt*

At the end of the word only CVV, CVCC or CVVC syllables can bear a stress, but not CV and CVC syllables. Thus, ternary stress interval is not permitted in cases like **téravamàl* and **sóoyemattèl*. This could be accounted for by assuming consonant extrametricality at the end of a phonological word (Hayes 1995: 322). There is also a tendency to avoid ternary stress if the third syllable in the ternary interval is long. The tendency is the strongest for CVV syllables with diphthongs (long vowels are allowed only in the syllable bearing the main stress), thus *élavàileki* is correct while **élavailèki* is not. If the third syllable is CVC, ternary stress can be used (*válusattèle*), though binary stress is more common in such cases (*válusáttele*).

Estonian stress pattern is further complicated by the fact that Q3 syllables can exhaust a foot. This means that a Q3 syllable may be followed by a secondary stress on the next syllable (*káu:kéle*). However, the requirement to exhaust a foot is not obligatory for Q3, as seen in *káukele*.

The most widely accepted account of Estonian stress is Prince (1980). In his analysis Q3 syllables are assigned two grid positions (strong and weak), all other syllables only one. Since two grid positions exhaust the foot, it allows Prince (1980) to define Q3 structurally as foot.

This gives an elegant account of the stress pattern where a Q3 syllable is followed by a secondary stress on second (19 a) or third syllable (19 b):

(19) a) [káu:][kèle]ki 'far away, too'
[júl:][késse]ki 'bold, too', ill. sg.
[jál:][kàte][lèki] 'foot, too', g. pl
b) [káu:]ke[lèki]
[júl:]kes[séki]
[jál:]ka[tèle]ki

However, in Estonian, secondary stress may fall also to the fourth syllable, like *jál:kadelèki*. Such cases are critical to the analysis of Prince (1980), since they would require two extrametrical syllables between the main and secondary stress: [jál:]kate[lèki]. To account for this and to maintain his claim that the defining property of Q3 is its ability to exhaust a foot, Prince (1980) employs the notion of recursive foot: [[jál:]ka]te[lèki]. This notion has not found independent motivation and is at present abandoned on theoretical grounds.

Hayes's (1995: 316–329) account of Estonian stress adopts essentially the analysis of Prince (1980), but he does not claim that Q3 must always be a foot. Instead he defines Q3 as being trimoraic, and allows trimoraic syllables optionally to be treated as disyllabic sequences. As a disyllabic sequence can constitute a foot, this accounts correctly for the cases like (19 a, b). If the Q3 syllable is not treated as a disyllabic sequence, it makes it possible to account for cases like *jál:katelèki* without the use of recursive foot structure: [jál:ka]te[lèki]. Thus, in Hayes (1995), the correct result is achieved by trading the recursive foot structure for trimoraic syllables and their property to act as disyllabic sequences.

If we treat Q3 syllables as heavy and all other syllables as light, as argued in this paper, it would allow us to adopt the analysis of Prince (1980) without the need for recursive foot structure. The argument is based on the assumption that foot is binary either on moraic or syllabic basis (Prince 1980: 534):

(20) $F \rightarrow u\ u$ (where $u = \sigma, \mu$)

In Estonian, stress is calculated variably on syllabic or moraic basis. This position is well motivated by the fact that Estonian, if it ever has been fully weight sensitive, is shifting back to a syllable-counting stress system. This can clearly seen from the changes in progress in the Estonian morphological system.

In Estonian, affix allomorphy is conditioned by the stress pattern of the word (see Hint 1980, Kager 1995). For example the partitive pl. ending *–it* is possible only in stems where the secondary stress falls on it: *soolase-it* 'salty' p. pl. ([sóola][sèit]), *pae:se-it* 'limestony' p. pl. ([páe:][sèit]). This is due to a phonotactic constraint of Estonian that prohibits diphthongs and long vowels from unstressed syllables. In the word final syllable could not have a secondary stress, partitive plural is formed by vowel alternation: *vallalise* ⟶ *vallalisi* 'single', pl. p. ([válla][lìsi]).

About a half a century ago, trisyllabic words with Q3 in initial syllable allowed only one pattern: *suu:lise* ⟶ *suu:lisi* 'oral' p. pl. ([súu:][lìsi]). Increasingly, such words started to be used with the *–it* ending *suu:liseit* ([súu:li][sèit]), and at present both variants are allowed in literary language. This change can be explained by assuming that stress assignment has shifted from the moraic basis to the syllabic one: in older forms the Q3 syllable was obligatorily a foot, which made the final syllable unstressable, since the second syllable already had a secondary stress ([súu:][lìsi]). In innovative forms, Q3 syllables are treated as any other syllables, i.e. stress placement has become syllabic. This makes the final syllable stressable, as the second syllable does not have one ([súu:li][sèit]). Since this innovation is spreading to another morphological type, there is enough ground to believe that at present, Estonian allows both moraic and syllabic basis for stress assignment.

If this is the case, the critical cases like *jál:kàtelèki*, *jál:katèleki*, and *jál:katelèki* could be accounted for as [jál:][kàte][lèki] (moraic stress assignment), [jál:ka][tèle]ki (syllabic stress) and [jál:ka]te[lèki] (syllabic stress with a ternary stress pattern) respectively.

Assuming that Q3 is heavy and Q2 and Q1 are light makes it possible to do without the use of recursive foot structure, trimoraic syllables or optional disyllabicity of Q3. The reason is that Q3 is not treated as the marked member in the Estonian quantity system, and consequently, does not need to be defined anything else, but a heavy syllable. Following (24), a heavy syllable constitutes a foot on moraic basis, but not on syllabic basis. Since Q2 syllables are treated as light, it explains why they are not able to constitute a monosyllabic foot.

8 Implications for Moraic Theory

In section 3, I outlined some problems that arise from the principle of the Moraic Theory that syllable weight is a linear function of segmental length. To avoid these problems, it is necessary to separate these two phonological domains. A strong support for this comes from the Estonian quantity system: the distinction between Q2 and Q3 is independent of segmental length distinctions.

However, it might be argued that the question is not about length and weight, but weight and syllable prominence. The distinction between weight and prominence is made on the basis of length as opposed to a raw prominence of perceptual salience that is usually due to high tone, low vowels or heaviness of the syllable (see Hayes 1995: 270–76). Thus, it might be argued that the distinction between Q2 and Q3 is also one of prominence rather than quantity: the phonetic cues differentiating between Q2 and Q3 are not solely durational, but include also difference in pitch contour. However, Hayes (1995) argues at length that syllable prominence does not influence foot construction that is based solely on weight properties. Thus, prominence can guide the main stress placement amongst eligible candidates, but not determine the foot size and boundaries. Yet Estonian quantity degrees are namely those that are relevant for constructing the foot structure of words: the possibility of monosyllabic feet is determined by Q3. Provided that Hayes's (1995) distinction between weight and prominence is correct, The Estonian quantity must be treated as a distinction of weight, not that of the prominence.

The other possibility to solve the problem is to use a dual distinction of weight (Hayes 1995). In this case, there are two moraic grids in the prosodic representation. The lower moraic grid represents length contrasts, calculated using the conventions in (8), the higher layers are constructed according to the sonority of the segment involved: the more sonorous a segment is the higher the column of moras it is associated to. Such a double notation allows representing weight contrasts relevant for stress assignment on the higher level and length contrasts on the lower level. For example, the representation of a light CVC syllable, closed by the first half of a geminate would be as follows:

(21)

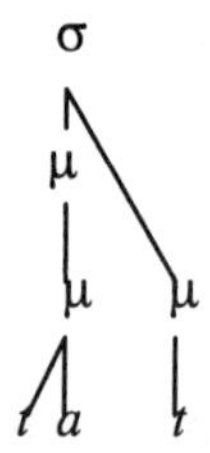

This representation captures the fact that CVC syllable counts as light in this language (upper grid) while retaining the convention that geminates are underlyingly moraic (lower grid).

The descriptive power of this notation is constrained by the Continuous Column Constraint (Prince 1983: 33, Hayes 1995: 34), which prohibits gaps in the column, i.e the situation where a segment has a mora on the higher level, but not on the lower level. This constraint captures the fact that bimoraic short vowels are not attested typologically: as they would require one mora on the lover level, but two on the higher one, they would violate the constraint. On the other hand, the notation allows for monomoraic long vowels and diphthongs, and there is indeed evidence for the existence of these.

Though the possibility of dual weight can account for the discrepancies between segmental length and syllable weight, it does not separate the notion of length from that of weight. The need for this arises in languages that make the distinction of segmental length, but not the one of weight. Provided that length is expressed by moras, all languages having length must also have weight. This must not be so if the theory strives to descriptive adequacy.

This feature, as well as the ones described above can be accounted for by the two-root theory of length (Selkirk 1990) that encodes length by counting root nodes and weight by counting moras. This means that moras need not to be underlyingly expressed and weight can be defined in the course of derivation just like syllable boundaries.

This is well motivated since underlying representations should not contain information that could be provided by rules (or constraints). Furthermore, this allows for the variation between weight-sensitive and weight-insensitive languages: if a language has a weight distinction, moras are assigned to appropriate segments, if weight distinction is not employed, no moras are assigned. This can be elegantly expressed in terms of Optimality Theory.

The distinction between weight-sensitive and weight-insensitive languages is achieved by ranking faithfulness constraint FAITHμ relative to the family of mora-assigning constraints ASSIGNμ. If FAITHμ >>ASSIGNμ, no moras are allowed (since they are missing underlyingly) and language surfaces as weight-insensitive. If ASSIGNμ >> FAITHμ, the candidates with moras attached will win over moraless candidates. Languages having this ranking are weight-sensitive. However, some languages, such as Estonian, use distinctive syllable weight, and this means that for Estonian moras cannot be assigned in the course of derivation, but need to be specified in underlying representations. These languages would need the ranking FAITHμ >>ASSIGNμ, to prevent changes in moraic tier.

Let us now look more closely how the constraint rankings account for attested variation in syllable weight. For this, it is necessary to specify the more precicely the constraint family ASSIGNμ. I suggest it include 4 constraints, listed in (22):

(22)	Vμ	- vowels are moraic
	$*\sigma_{\mu\mu\mu}$	- trimoraic syllables are prohibited
	WxP	- postpeak material must be mora-bearing
	*Cμ	- consonants must not be moraic

These four constraints may have the following rankings: Vμ and *$\sigma_{\mu\mu\mu}$ are unordered and universally top ranked within the family ASSIGNμ. The ranking of WxP and *Cμ varies across languages, which gives us two possible rankings:

(23) a) Vμ, *$\sigma_{\mu\mu\mu}$ >> WxP >> *Cμ
b) Vμ, *$\sigma_{\mu\mu\mu}$ >> *Cμ >> WxP

Ranking in (23a) gives us the possible weight combinations for a language where CVC syllable counts as heavy (see the typology in Table 1). First two types, presented in Table 1, are grammatical since they do not violate any ASSIGNμ constraints. The third type (CVμVμC) violates WxP, but it is still grammatical, since it does it to satisfy higher ranking *$\sigma_{\mu\mu\mu}$ and Vμ. The fourth type (CVμCμ) violates the lowest ranking *Cμ to satisfy WxP, and is therefore grammatical. All other possible combinations are ungrammatical, as they would in some or other way violate against high-ranking constraints. For example, the fifth example violates WxP, and as this violation is not forced by higher-ranking constraints, it is the fatal one. The sixth example violates the lowest ranking *Cμ, but since it is not to satisfy any higher-ranking constraints, it is fatal. The rest of the examples in Table 1 are not acceptable, since they violate highest-ranking constraints Vμ and *$\sigma_{\mu\mu\mu}$.

		Vμ	*$\sigma_{\mu\mu\mu}$	WxP	*Cμ
1	CVμ				
2	CVμVμ				
3	CVμVμC			*	
4	CVμCμ				*
5	*CVμC			*!	
6	*CμVμ				*!
7	*CVCμ	*!			*
8	*CVμCμC μ		*!		**

Table 1

If the language uses ranking order (23b) as in Table 2, most of the possible syllable types are the same as presented in Table 1 (types 1–3). The difference concerns the type CVC which surfaces as light, because of the *Cμ

which ranks higher than WxP. The last candidate in Tableau 2 is not acceptable, since it has an unforced *Cμ violation.

		Vμ	$*\sigma_{\mu\mu\mu}$	*Cμ	WxP
1	CVμ				
2	CVμVμ				
3	CVμVμC				*
4	CVμC				*
5	*CVμCμ			*!	

Table 2

As seen, the ranking orders in (23) summarise the widely attested cross-linguistic variation of weight in CVC syllables. Surely, the constraints presented above are quite unspecified yet, and work perfectly only in cases where codas have only one consonant. If the coda contains two or more consonants, the constraints as presented in (22), do not specify which one of the consonants receives a mora which one does not. Second, the constraints predict that for CVVC syllables, codas should be weightless. It is not clear yet whether this prediction is empirically correct. Though this syllable type is rare cross-linguistically, Estonian has it and a further study is needed to test this prediction.

9 Conclusion

The evidence, presented in this paper suggests that syllable weight is comparatively autonomous from the segmental (root) tier, and in some languages, it is not even in a direct correlation with segmental length. Weight seems to be autosegmental just like other prosodic features such as, for example, tones. Moraic theory, as presented in Hayes (1988, 1995), however, treats weight as totally dependent on segmental structure, i. e. it has also a duty to represent segmental length. As there are more combinations of segmental length than attested possibilities of syllable weight, it is one of the main reasons why there is yet no satisfactory theory of calculating syllable weight from the segmental structure of syllable. If mora were freed from the duty of expressing segmental length, several desirable consequences would follow:

1. Weight need not be underlying, which means that segmental length would not create unattested weight values.

2. The rule of Weight by Position would become redundant, as different constraint interactions would assign moras according to a general principle.
3. The account of Estonian quantity would become significantly simplified.

Surely, the constraints for weight assignment need to be specified further, and Estonian with its complex length and weight combinations is a good testing ground for elaborating the Moraic Theory.

References

Allen, S. 1973. *Accent and Rhythm.* Cambridge Studies in Linguistics 12. Cambridge: Cambridge University Press.

Ariste, P. 1947. *Foneetilisi probleeme eesti keele alalt.* Tartu: Teaduslik Kirjandus.

Bye, P. 1997. A Generative Perspective on 'Overlength' in Estonian and Saami. In *Estonian Prosody: Papers from a Symposium*, ed. I. Lehiste and J. Ross, 36–68. Tallinn: Eesti Keele Instituut.

Collinder, B. 1929. *Über den finnisch-lappischen Quantitätswechsel.* Uppsala.

Eek, A. 1986. Problems of Estonian Word Prosody. *Estonian Papers of Phonetics* 1984–1985:13–66.

Eek, A. and T. Help. 1986. *Rütminihked eesti keele kujunemisloos.* Tallinn: Eesti NSV Teaduste Akadeemia.

Eek, A. and E. Meister. 1997. Simple Perception Experiments on Estonian Word Prosody: Foot Structure vs. Segmental Quantity. In *Estonian Prosody: Papers from a Symposium*, ed. I. Lehiste and J. Ross, 71–99. Tallinn: Eesti Keele Instituut.

Fox, A. 1988. The Mora, Compensatory Lengthening, and a Two-Tier Theory of Quantity. *Leeds Working Papers in Linguistics and Phonetics* 6: 40–67.

Hayes, B. 1989. Compensatory Lengthening in Moraic Phonology. *Linguistic Inquiry* 20: 253–306.

Hayes, B. 1995. *Metrical stress theory: Principles and case studies.* Chicago: University of Chicago Press.

Hint, M. 1973. *Eesti keele sõnafonoloogia I.* Tallinn: Keele ja Kirjanduse Instituut.

Hint M. 1980. Minevikuline ja tulevikuline aines keelesüsteemis. Prosoodiatüübi nihked ja selle tagajärjed. *Keel ja Kirjandus* 24: 215–223, 270–278, 349–355.

Hint, M. 1997. *Eesti keele astmevahelduse ja prosoodiasüsteemi tüpoloogilised probleemid. Typological problems of Estonian grade alternation and prosodical system. Viron kielen astevaihtelun ja prosodian typologiset ongelmat.* Tallinn-Helsinki: Eesti Keele Sihtasutus.

Hint, M. 1997a. The Estonian Quantity Degrees in Prosody and Morphophonology, In *Estonian Prosody: Papers from a Symposium*, ed. I. Lehiste and J. Ross, 125–135. Tallinn: Eesti Keele Instituut.

Hock, H. H. 1986. Compensatory Lengthening: In Defence of the Concept 'Mora'. *Folia Linguistica* 2:431–460.

Kager, R. 1994. *Ternary Rhythm in Alignment Theory*. Manuscript, University of Utrecht.

Kager, R. 1995. On Affix Allomorphy and Syllable Counting. Paper presented at *Conference on interfaces in phonology*, Berlin, March 23–25, 1995. [Accessible at http://ruccs.rutgers.edu/roa.htm].

Kettunen, L. 1929. *Eestin kielen äännehistoria*. Helsinki.

Laurosela, J. 1922. *Foneettinen tutkimus Etelä-Pohjanmaan murteesta*. Helsinki.

Lehiste, I. 1997. Search for Phonetic Correlates in Estonian Prosody. In *Estonian Prosody: Papers from a Symposium*, ed. I. Lehiste and J. Ross, 11–35. Tallinn: Eesti Keele Instituut.

Maddieson, I. 1993. Splitting the Mora. *UCLA Working Papers in Phonetics* 83: 9–18.

McCarthy, J. and A. S. Prince. 1986. *Prosodic Morphology*. Manuscript, University of Brandeis.

Morén, B. 1998. *The Puzzle of Kashmiri Stress: Implications for Weight Theory*. Ms, Rutgers University. [Accessible at http://ruccs.rutgers.edu/roa.htm].

Odden, D. 1997. Some Theoretical Issues in Estonian Prosody. In *Estonian Prosody: Papers from a Symposium*, ed. I. Lehiste and J. Ross, 165–193. Tallinn: Eesti Keele Instituut.

Pajusalu, K. 1994. Kuidas soomlased õpivad kuulma eesti keele välteid. In *Lähivertailua 7*, ed. Karl Pajusalu and Valma Yli-Vakkuri, 75–88. Turku: Turun Yliopisto.

Posti, L. 1953–54. From Pre-Finnic to Late-Proto-Finnic. Studies on the Development of the Consonantal System. *Finnisch-Ugrische Forschungen* 31: 1–91.

Prince, A. S. 1980. A Metrical Theory for Estonian Quantity. *Linguistic Inquiry* 11: 511–562.

Prince, A. S. 1983. Relating to the Grid. *Linguistic Inquiry* 14: 19–100.

Schütz, A. J. 1985. *The Fijian Language*. Honolulu: University of Hawaii Press.

Seiler, H. 1977. *Cahuilla Grammar*. California: Malki Museum Press.

Selkirk, E. 1984. *Phonology and Syntax: The Relation between Sound and Structure*. Cambridge, Massachusetts: MIT Press.

Selkirk, E. 1990. A Two Root Theory of Length. *University of Massachusetts Occasional Papers in Linguistics* 14.

Setälä, E. N. 1896. Über Quantitätswechsel im Finnisch-ugrischen. *Journal de la Société Finno-ougrienne* 14.

Tauli, V. 1954. The Origin of the Quantitative System in Estonian. *Journal de la Société Finno-Ougrienne* 57: 1–19.

Tranel, B. 1991. CVC Light Syllables, Geminates and Moraic Theory. *Phonology* 8: 291–302.

Vanoverbergh, M. 1955. *Iloko Grammar*. Detroit: Cellar Book Shop.

Veske, M. 1879. *Eesti keele healte õpetus ja kirjutuse viis*. Tartu.

Woodbury, A. 1987. Meaningful Phonological Processes: A Consideration of Central Alaskan Yupik Eskimo Prosody. *Language* 63: 685–740.

3

Opaque Consonant Gradation in Finnish – A Recourse to IO–OO Correspondence

HELI HARRIKARI

1 Introduction*

Let us assume that language X contains the rule in (1).

(1) $A \rightarrow B / \_C$

This derivational rule, which converts element A to element B in the context of element C, ensures that sequence AC never occurs in this language[1]. Let us further assume the existence of another rule, which quarantees that C never precedes D, but it is regularly converted to E, as a result of the rule in (2).

* I am grateful to John McCarthy for guiding through the early stages of this research. Thanks are also due to the participants of LIN 751 at UMass Amherst in Spring 1999, the audience of WCCFL 19 at UCLA in Spring 2000, especially Bruce Hayes, and the audience of the Doctoral Seminar at the University of Helsinki in Spring 2000 for helpful questions and suggestions. Excerpts of this study have been published as Harrikari (2000b).

[1] This claim implies that under no circumstances the interaction of other rules results in sequence AC.

Generative Approaches to Finnic and Saami Linguistics.
Diane Nelson and Satu Manninen (eds.).

(2) $C \rightarrow E / \_D$

Both rules are simple as such; however, the assumption that they exist in the same language has further consequences. It might happen that element C, which forms the crucial environment for rule (1), will be lost because of rule (2). Rule (1) outputs sequence BC, and then via morpheme concatenation, for example, D is attached to C, resulting in BCD. Rule (2), however, ensures that no such sequence surfaces, but instead BED appears. This leads to the situation where the appearance of B is no longer transparently motivated, as the triggering element C is lost. Such a pattern represents *opacity*, more specifically, *overapplication*. Under the definition of overapplication, the motivation for a phonological or morphological operation is no longer apparent. The opposite to overapplication is *underapplication* where an operation unexpectedly fails to occur, despite the presence of the triggering environment. In traditional derivational frameworks, opaque patterns have been captured by assuming ordering of rules, and also by different levels of derivation that are motivated by morphology, syntax, and semantics. The example above is thus accounted for by assuming that rule (1) necessarily precedes rule (2), as element C must be present when rule (1) is executed. Once rule (1) has taken place, element C might be lost, but the result of rule (1) is correctly retained.

Since the introduction of Optimality Theory (OT, Prince & Smolensky 1993, McCarthy & Prince 1993a) to the field of theoretical phonology and morphology, a large part of research has been directed towards the treatment of opacity. The reason for this is clear: New tools for opacity should be developed, since the derivational methods, such as different levels of derivation and rule ordering, are no longer available in parallelist, output-oriented OT. It is thus no surprise that opacity has been widely discussed in OT, for example, in Prince & Smolensky 1993, McCarthy & Prince 1993b, Benua 1995, 1997, Cho 1995, Archangeli & Suzuki 1996, 1997, Goldsmith 1996, McCarthy 1996, 1997, 1999ab, Burzio 1997ab, Booij 1997, Halle & Idsardi 1997, Kager 1997, 2000, Kiparsky 1997, 1998, 1999abc, Paradis 1997, Roca 1997, Rubach 1997, and Hermans & van Oostendorp 2000, to take a few examples.

Attempts to account for opacity in OT without derivationality do exist. Two of these suggestions have received wide attention, namely Output-Output Correspondence (OO, Benua 1995, 1997, Burzio 1997ab) and Sympathy Theory (McCarthy 1997, 1999ab, Itô & Mester 1997). The basic idea of both proposals is to extend correspondence relations in OT – that were first built to handle input-output (IO) relations – to concern also relations between the outputs of the same paradigm, or alternatively between the optimal output and a designated failed candidate. Through extended correspondence relations, both OO correspondence and Sympathy Theory aim to offer reasons for patterns that lack surface motivation. Essentially, both approaches maintain strict parallelism, avoiding any kind of derivation. A rather different solution for opacity is suggested by Kiparsky (1997, 1998, 1999abc). His LPM-OT is a fusion of derivational Lexical Phonology and Morphology (LPM, Kiparsky 1982, 1985) and OT. The approach maintains the derivationality of LPM by retaining different levels of derivation, but simultaneously adopts the idea of parallel constraint interaction of OT. Thus, contrary to OO correspondence and Sympathy Theory, LPM-OT assumes that in order to solve the problem of opacity, a certain degree of derivationality must necessarily be maintained.

This paper participates in the discussion on OT and opacity by presenting a case study of Finnish Consonant Gradation (CG). Through CG, I will show how parallel OT explains opaque patterns without utilizing derivational tools. Essentially, the analyses will show the effective use of both IO and OO correspondence as solutions for opacity. In addition to the two types of correspondence, the paper also demonstrates how the effects of IO and OO correspondence might be combined through constraint conjunction (Smolensky 1993, 1995, 1997). Conjunction enables a simultaneous access to various faithfulness relations, a mechanism that is necessary for explaining certain types of opacity. Furthermore, as a comparison, I will illustrate solutions that LPM-OT provides for the patterns of Finnish CG. The derivational analyses will demonstrate that despite capturing certain patterns, LPM-OT crucially fails to account for others. The paper will show how the failure is due to the fundamental derivational characteristics of the theory.

The remainder of the paper is organized as follows. Section 2 introduces the data, both the basic idea of CG and the three opaque patterns. In Section 3, I will develop fully parallel analyses for the problems, while the purpose of Section 4 is to show the accounts offered by LPM-OT. Finally, Section 5 summarizes the analyses and discusses further theoretical implications.

2 Data Description

2.1 Basics of CG

CG is an alternation process where consonants undergo weakening in certain environments, as exemplified in (3). Numerous attempts have been made to account for the basic patterns, both in derivational theories, such as LPM (Kiparsky 1982, 1985) (e.g. Kiparsky 1993, 1997), as well as in non-derivational frameworks, most importantly in OT (e.g. Dolbey & Sprouse 1996, Bye 1998, McCartney 1998).

(3) Quantitative and qualitative gradation[2]

	Strong grade	Gloss	Weak grade	Gloss
kk–k	[ta**k**.**ki**]	'coat'	[ta.**kin**]	'of a coat'
tt–t	[ka**t**.**to**]	'roof'	[ka.**tol**.la]	'on a roof'
pp–p	[hy**p**.**pi**.ä]	'to jump,	[hy.**pin**]	'I jump
freq.'				
k–Ø	[ruo.**ka**]	'food'	[ruo.Øas.sa][3]	'in food'
t–d	[pi.**tää**]	'to like'	[pi.**din**]	'I liked'
p–v	[lu.**pa**]	'permit'	[lu.**van**]	'of a permit'
nt–nn	[**an**.taa]	'to give'	[**an**.**nam**.me]	'we give'
lt–ll	[va**l**.**ta**]	'power'	[va**l**.**las**.sa]	'in power'
rt–rr	[pa**r**.**ta**]	'beard'	[pa**r**.**ran**]	'of a beard'
ŋk–ŋŋ	[kaŋ.**ki**]	'pry bar'	[kaŋ.ŋes.ta]	'from/of a pry bar'
mp–mm	[**am**.**pu**.a]	'to shoot'	[**am**.**mut**]	'you shoot'
uku–uvu	[pu.**ku**]	'suit'	[pu.**vus**.sa]	'in a suit'
k–j	[jäl.**ki**]	'trace'	[jäl.**jen**]	'of a trace'

CG consists of both quantitative and qualitative alternations. The generalizations of both types of gradation are however identical: The strong grade appears at the beginning of an open syllable, while the weak grade is the property of closed syllables. The strong grade is the default, since the appearance of the weak grade can be predicted[4].

[2] The grapheme <ä> indicates the low, front, unrounded vowel, and <y> the high, front, rounded one. I follow Finnish orthography and thus indicate long segments with two identical graphemes. Both vowel length and consonant length are phonological in Finnish.

[3] An alternative output form is [ruu.Øas.sa].

[4] For so-called reverse CG, see for example Karlsson (1983), Keyser and Kiparsky (1984).

2.2 Opaque CG

The opaque instances of CG discussed in this paper are underapplication, overapplication, and the so-called unexpected regular gradation. The common factor between the three cases is that all of them are related to the behavior of CG in the context of possessive suffixes[5].

The possessive suffixes of nouns, unlike inflectional suffixes, do not trigger CG, despite the fact that certain possessive suffixes create an environment for CG (i.e. for the weak grade) by closing the syllable. This causes opacity as illustrated in (4)[6]. Examples demonstrating the different impact of the inflectional suffixes on CG are also shown in (4)

(4) Possessive suffixes (singular and plural): no CG

Sg. 1. person	-ni	[ka.**tu**.-ni]	'my street(s)'
Sg. 2. person	-si	[ka.**tu**.-si]	'your street(s)'
Sg. 3. person	-nsa,/Vn	[ka.**tu**-n.sa]	'his/her street(s)'
		*[ka.**du**-n.sa]	
Pl. 1. person	-mme	[ka.**tu**-m.me]	'our street(s)'
		*[ka.**du**-m.me]	
Pl. 2. person	-nne	[ka.**tu**-n.ne]	'your street(s)'
		*[ka.**du**-n.ne]	
Pl. 3. person	-nsa/Vn	[ka.**tu**-n.sa]	'their street(s)'
		*[ka.**du**-n.sa]	

Inflectional suffixes: regular CG

[ka.**du**-s.sa]	'in a street (inessive)'
[ka.**du**-s.ta]	'from a street (elative)'
[ka.**du**-l.la]	'on a street (adessive)'
[ka.**du**-l.le]	'to a street (allative)'
[ka.**tu**.-na]	'as a street (essive)'
[ka.**tu**.-a]	'of a street (partitive)'

As the data in (4) illustrate, the strong grade appears in all forms containing a possessive suffix. This is expected in the 1. and 2. singular forms, as the suffix has no effect on the syllable structure of the root. In contrary, in the rest of the forms with possessive suffixes, the suffix closes the final syllable

[5] These opaque problems from the viewpoint of OT and LPM-OT were identified by Kiparsky (1997).

[6] The alternating consonants – /t/ and /d/ in the case of /katu/ 'street, nominative, sg.' – are boldfaced, while possessive suffixes are indicated by underlining.

of the root, resulting in the environment for the weak grade, which however does not appear. This represents the underapplication of CG, the first target of this paper.

The presence of possessive suffixes affects the behavior of inflectional suffixes, as the final consonant of an inflectional suffix fails to surface when followed by a possessive suffix, as illustrated in (5).

(5) Stem + Case
huo.nee.-see**n** 'into a room (illative)'
hat.tu-i.-hi**n** 'into hats (illative) '
ta.lo.-j-e**n** 'of houses (genitive)'

Stem + Case + Poss. suffix
huo.nee.-see∅.-si 'into your room (illative)'
hat.tu-i.-hi∅.-ni 'into my hats (illative)'
ta.lo.-j-e∅.-si 'of your houses (genitive)'

The examples in (6) further show how the deletion of the suffix-final consonant sometimes leads to opaque CG, since the deleted consonant serves as the trigger of CG. Despite the consonant deletion, the weak grade is retained, a pattern that represents overapplication. This is the second problem analyzed in this paper.

(6) Stem + Case[7]
pe.ru.no-i.-**de**n 'of potatoes (genitive)'
(< peruna-i-ten)
ta.va.ro-i.-**de**n 'of things (genitive)'
(< tavara-i.-ten)

Stem + Case + Poss. Suffix
pe.ru.no-i.-**de**∅.-si 'of your potatoes (genitive)'
*pe.ru.no-i.**te**∅.si
ta.va.ro-i.-**de**∅.-ni 'of my things (genitive)'
*ta.va.ro-i.**te**∅.si

The third pattern is reminiscent of the case of overapplication. The examples in (7) resemble those in (6), since the deletion of the coda has simi-

---

[7] Alternative forms encountered are [perunoitten] and [tavaroitten]. Similarly, the forms with possessive suffixes might alternatively appear as [perunoittesi] and [tavaroittesi]. The analysis here, however, does not attempt to account for these cases, but they might be considered as dialectal variations.

larly occurred. The data in (7) however contain no overapplication, but instead the regular strong grade appears.

(7) [ka.**tu**-∅̲.-ni] 'of my street(s) (genitive)'
(< *ka.**du**-n̲.-ni < /ka.**tu**-n̲.-ni/)
[ha**t**.**tu**-∅̲.-ni] 'of my hat(s) (genitive)'
(< *ha.**tu**-n̲.-ni < /ha**t**.**tu**-n̲.-ni/)
[hy**p**.**py**-∅̲.-ni] 'of my jump(s) (genitive)'
(< *hy.**py**-n̲.-ni < /hy**p**.**py**-n̲.-ni/)

The coda deletion creates an open syllable, and following the pattern of overapplication in (6), the weak grade is expected in (7). However, the strong grade surfaces in (7), thus making the pattern crucially different from the one illustrated in (6). It should also be pointed out that the examples in (7) are not opaque as such, since they clearly follow the regular CG pattern. Only in the light of the case of overapplication, does the pattern in (7) become unexpected.

The examples above have illustrated three problems with respect to opaque CG: underapplication, overapplication, and unexpected regular gradation. I will now turn to the accounts which parallelist OT and derivational LPM-OT offer for the phenomena. I will begin the discussion with the analyses provided by OT. The first problem to be discussed is the case of overapplication, followed by unexpected regular gradation, and underapplication. The reader is assumed to be familiar with the theories discussed, and consequently, I will not review the basics of the approaches, but the paper concentrates on the relevant core analyses only.

3 Parallelist OT

3.1 Overapplication

3.1.1 Basic analysis

Let us now begin the analysis of overapplication. Recall that this is the case where the deletion of the suffix-final consonant – the trigger of CG – has led to the situation where the weak grade is no longer transparently motivated. The key of an OT analysis is thus to seek for a way of expressing the relationship between the weak grade and the deleted consonant. The first task is to identify the relevant constraints.

The constraints concerned with CG are introduced in (8). CG is to be understood as a cover constraint, the purpose of which is simply to show where in the constraint hierarchy CG must be obeyed. The nature of the constraint is not explanatory; it does not attempt to explain the reasons for CG. The faithfulness constraint violated by CG is IDENT-IO(voice)[8].

(8) CG
Consonant gradation must be obeyed.

IDENT-IO(voice) (McCarthy & Prince 1995)
Output correspondents of an input [γvoice] segment are also [γvoice].

Furthermore, due to the coda deletion, two other constraints are required, shown in (9).

(9) $*C]_\sigma$ + POSS
Do not have a sequence of a coda and a possessive suffix.

MAX-C (McCarthy & Prince 1995)
Every consonant in the input has a correspondent in the output.

The descriptive constraint $*C]_\sigma$ + POSS simply prohibits coda consonants before possessive suffixes without aiming for an explanation for the restriction. The obedience to $*C]_\sigma$ + POSS causes the violation of the faithfulness constraint MAX-C. Crucial rankings between the four constraints must also be established: In both pairs markedness dominates faithfulness. The dominant position of CG over IDENT-IO(voice) is determined by the existence of the gradation pattern, whereas the dominance of $*C]_\sigma$ + POSS over MAX-C has its basis in the coda deletion. No evidence for other crucial rankings exist at this point. Let us now see the predictions that the four constraints make about the overapplication. The tableau in (10) illustrates the evaluation of [tavaroideni] 'of my things'.

[8] The quantitative gradation naturally requires another type of faithfulness constraint, such as WT-IDENT (McCarthy 1995).

(10) [tavaroideni] 'of my things'
$*C]_\sigma$ + POSS >> MAX-C, CG >> IDENT-IO(voice)

/tavarai-ten-ni/[9]	$*C]_\sigma$ + POSS	MAX-C	CG[10]	IDENT-IO (voice)
a. ta.va.roi.ten.ni	*!		*	
b. ta.va.roi.den.ni	*!			*
☜c. ta.va.roi.te.ni		*		
☞d. ta.va.roi.de.ni		*		*!

The evaluation in (10) shows how the ranking makes incorrect predictions. It selects the candidate with the strong grade (i.e. the regular CG pattern) as the winner, despite the fact that the attested output is the one with overapplication. Clearly, it seems as the parallel analysis has no means of capturing the relationship between CG and the triggering coda. The reranking of constraints is of no help either, as under all circumstances, the attested output causes an additional violation when compared to the incorrectly selected form. The question now arises whether the existence of overapplication can be captured without invoking derivation. I suggest that a solution *does* exist, and the name of the solution is OO correspondence.

3.1.2 OO Correspondence

OO correspondence – an extension of IO correspondence (McCarthy & Prince 1995) – is a mechanism that aims at explaining surface opacity by establishing correspondence relations between outputs of a single paradigm. The core idea is that phonological operations unexpectedly occur (or fail to occur) due to the attempt to retain similarity between outputs in the paradigm. This might lead to opacity. OO correspondence has been widely discussed, and also variations of the basic idea have been proposed, the best known of which are those by Benua (1995, 1997) and Burzio (1997ab). According to Benua, OO correspondence can hold only between an output and a less complex free-standing base of the same paradigm, while Burzio's model allows wider correspondence relations.

I adopt the idea of OO correspondence, and propose that the case of overapplication is captured by a parallel analysis if we assume certain cor-

9 The root-final /a/ appears as [o] in the output. I do not attempt to capture this alternation, since it shows no relevance in the analysis. For analyses of this vowel alternation, see Harrikari (2000a) and Anttila (2002).

10 The constraint CG is violated only when the strong grade appears in a closed syllable. The weak grade in open syllables thus does not incur a violation of CG.

respondence relations between outputs. Essentially, a relationship holds between the form with overapplication, [tavaroi-de-ni] 'of my things', and the less complex form, the one without possessive suffix, [tavaro-i-den] 'of things'[11]. The latter output is crucial, since there the weak grade is transparently motivated through the surface representation of the triggering coda. By assuming correspondence between the two forms, it might be suggested that the weak grade is maintained even after the coda deletion in order to retain the similarity of the forms. The two outputs are close to each other and clearly in correspondence with respect to many parameters; however, the relevant type of correspondence is the one expressed by the constraint in (11). The constraint is restricted to concern forms containing clitics, a group that also includes possessive suffixes but correctly excludes inflectional ones[12].

(11) OO_{Clitic}-IDENT(voice)[13]
Output correspondents of [γvoice] segments of the base to which the clitic is attached are also [γvoice].

According to the constraint in (11), the voicing specification of every output segment in the base to which a clitic is attached must be identical to that of the corresponding segment in the less complex form. Consequently, the voicing features of the base in [tavaroi-de-ni] 'of my things' (i.e. [tavaroide-]) must be identical to that of [tavaro-i-den] 'of things'. The effects of the OO constraint are shown in (12). Since the OO constraint crucially concerns the correspondence between the evaluated outputs and the less complex form of the paradigm, [tavaro-i-den] 'of things', the outputs are compared to the free-standing base in the case of the OO constraint.

---

[11] Another approach to opacity in OT, Sympathy Theory (McCarthy 1997, 1999ab) is also able to offer a parallel account by suggesting that the required correspondence relation holds between the attested output and a designated failed candidate.

[12] See Kanerva (1987) for an alternative view on the distinction between affixes and clitics in Finnish, particularly concerning possessive suffixes.

[13] The existence of OO_{Clitic}-IDENT(voice) implies a parallel constraint for inflectional suffixes. The constraint is, however, lower-ranked, and thus has no impact in the evaluation here.

(12) [tavaroideni] 'of my things'
$*C]_\sigma$ + POSS >> MAX-C, CG >> OO_{Clitic}-IDENT(voice) >> IDENT-IO(voice)

OO base: [tavaroiden] 'of things'

/tavarai-ten-ni/	$*C]_\sigma$ + POSS	MAX-C	CG	OO_{Clitic}-IDENT (voice)	IDENT-IO (voice)
a. ta.va.roi.ten.ni	*!		*	*	
b. ta.va.roi.den.ni	*!				*
c. ta.va.roi.te.ni		*		*!	
☞d. ta.va.roi.de.ni		*			*

The evaluation shows how the dominating position of OO_{Clitic}-IDENT(voice) over IDENT-IO(voice) correctly selects candidate (d), the one with the overapplication pattern, as the optimal form. This is attributed to the fact that the affix of candidate (c) contains the segment [t], thus crucially violating OO_{Clitic}-IDENT(voice), whereas the corresponding segment is [d] in output (d), therefore being identical to that of the free-standing base.

It can thus be concluded that by employing OO correspondence and by assuming the dominant position of OO over IO faithfulness, the pattern of overapplication is captured. Through the OO constraint, the required relationship between the attested output and the less complex form is expressed. Consequently, the unexpected weak grade in the optimal output is motivated through the correspondence to the form with the transparent reason for the gradation.

3.2 Unexpected Regular Gradation

I will now move to the second opaque phenomenon, namely the appearance of unexpected regular gradation. Recall that the pattern shows no opacity as such, since the strong grade correctly surfaces in open syllables, as in [katuni] 'of my street(s)' (i.e. [ka.tu-<u>∅</u>.-ni] from [*ka.du-<u>n</u>.-ni] from /ka.tu-<u>n</u>.-ni/). In the light of overapplication analyzed above, however, the strong grade is not expected, but the weak counterpart should occur in this case as well.

The first task is to investigate the effects of the constraint ranking constructed above. The tableau in (13) shows the evaluation of [katuni] 'of my street(s)'. The free-standing base for the OO constraint is [kadun] 'of street', the output without the possessive suffix.

(13) [katuni] 'of my street(s)'
OO base: [kadun] 'of street'

/katu-n-ni/	$*C]_\sigma$ + POSS	MAX-C	CG	OO_{clitic}-IDENT (voice)	IDENT-IO(voice)
a. ka.tun.ni	*!		*		
b. ka.dun.ni	*!				*
☞c. ka.tu.ni		*		*!	
☜d. ka.du.ni		*			*

The tableau in (13) shows the failure of candidates (a) and (b) under $*C]_\sigma$ + POSS, a result that leaves candidates (c) and (d) to continue the competition. The decision between the two outputs is made by the interface of IO and OO correspondence. The interaction of the two, however, incorrectly results in the selection of candidate (c). The ranking is clearly not able to differentiate between the two cases of opaque CG, but predicts the overapplication also in contexts where it does not occur, a pattern that must be attributed to the dominant position of OO correspondence. On the other hand, the incorrect prediction is not surprising, as the constraint hierarchy was specifically constructed overapplication in mind. The relevant task now is to identify the crucial difference between the case of overapplication and that of unexpected regular gradation, and find a way of expressing the difference in the constraint hierarchy.

I suggest a solution based on the so-called positional faithfulness (Beckman 1998). The purpose of positional faithfulness is to assign a special status through faithfulness for certain linguistic positions, which show privileged status over others. To take a few examples, positions and elements such as roots, stressed syllables, root-initial syllables, and syllable onsets are superior over affixes, unstressed syllables, syllables in non-initial positions in roots, and finally syllable codas. The case of unexpected regular gradation is also an instance of such a status dichotomy. More specifically, the crucial division is made between roots and affixes here. Let us now further entertain this idea.

The unexpected regular appearance of the strong grade concerns the segments of a root, whereas the case of overapplication is a property of affixal segments. Following the reasoning based on positional faithfulness, one might suggest that the retention of the strong grade is more important in privileged roots than in affixes. Consequently, the strong grade surfaces in roots whenever possible, in other words, when no transparent reason for the weak grade can be identified. This also explains the unexpected appearance of the strong grade in [katu-ni] 'of my street(s). In order to formally capture this idea, I propose the positional faithfulness constraint defined in (14), which requires the retention of the voicing specification of the segments in roots, without interfering affixal segments.

(14) IDENT-IO(voice)$_{\text{ROOT}}$ (based on McCarthy & Prince 1995, Beckman 1998)
Output correspondents of an input [γvoice] segment of the root are also [γvoice].

Recall that the dominant position of OO correspondence over IO correspondence was the source of the incorrect prediction above. It follows that in order to show its effects, the positional faithfulness constraint must dominate the OO constraint. This is shown in the tableau in (15), which reevaluates the example [katuni] 'of my street(s)'.

(15) $*C]_{\sigma}$ + POSS >> MAX-C, CG >> IDENT-IO(voice)$_{\text{ROOT}}$ >> OO$_{\text{clitic}}$-IDENT(voice) >> IDENT-IO(voice)

OO base: [kadun] 'of street'

/katu-n-ni/	$*C]_{\sigma}$ + POSS	MAX-C	CG	IDENT-IO (voice)$_{\text{ROOT}}$	OO$_{\text{clitic}}$-IDENT (voice)	IDENT-IO(voice)
a. ka.tun.ni	*!				*	
b. ka.dun.ni	*!			*		*
☞c. ka.tu.ni		*			*	
d. ka.du.ni		*		*!		*

The analysis in (15) shows how the effects of OO correspondence remain masked, due to the higher-ranking positional faithfulness. Consequently, the constraint ranking correctly selects the output with the regular gradation. The revised ranking also continues to make adequate predictions in the case of overapplication, as the positional faithfulness constraint has no impact on [tavaroideni] 'of my things'.

In summary, this section has shown how the fully parallel analysis is able to account for the unexpected appearance of the regular gradation in [katuni] 'of my street(s)' by introducing the concept of positional faithfulness into the constraint hierarchy. Most importantly, no need for derivational tools has emerged.

3.3 Underapplication

3.3.1 The basic analysis

The final problem of opaque CG to be discussed is the case of underapplication. Recall that contrary to inflectional suffixes, CG takes no place in the presence of possessive suffixes only, as exemplified by [ka.tu-m.me] 'our street(s)' (i.e. *[ka.du-m.me]. The question is, of course, why the regular CG pattern is unacceptable in the context of possessive suffixes. This implies seeking for an explanation for the minimal pair [katu-mme] 'our street(s)' (from /katu-mme/) and [kadu-mme] 'we regret' (from /katu-mme/).

Let us begin by illustrating the predictions that the constraint hierarchy makes about the minimal pair. The tableau in (16) demonstrates the evaluation of the two forms; the upper part of the tableau shows the evaluation of the form with the inflectional suffix, while the lower example concentrates on the form with the possessive suffix. The less complex free-standing base in the case of the OO constraint is the nominative singular [katu].

(16) OO: [katu] 'street, sg. nominative'

/katu-mme/ (infl.)	*C]$_\sigma$ + POSS	MAX-C	CG	IDENT-IO (voice)$_{ROOT}$	OO$_{Clitic}$-IDENT (voice)	IDENT-IO (voice)
a. ka.tum.me			*!			
☞ b. ka.dum.me				*		*
/katu-mme/ (poss.)						
☞ a. ka.tum.me			*!			
☜ b. ka.dum.me				*	*	*

The evaluations in (16) show the relevance of the interaction of two constraints: CG and IDENT-IO(voice)$_{ROOT}$. In both cases, the decision is made under CG, which selects the form with the regular gradation (i.e. the weak grade) as the optimal solution. This is the correct prediction in the case of inflection but not in the case of possessive suffixes. The analysis thus clearly cannot predict the regular gradation in one context, simultaneously retaining the strong grade in another. While seeking for a solution for this problem, I will concentrate on the underapplication example, [katu-mme] 'our street(s)'; the regular gradation pattern in the context of inflection requires no further actions, since it is already correctly captured by the dominant position of CG over IDENT-IO(voice)$_{ROOT}$.

3.3.2 Constraint conjunction

The essential question is how to account for the strong grade in the output with the possessive suffix, i.e., why the regular weak grade is a less optimal solution. The task is to find the force behind the appearance of underapplication: We have to discover a constraint that crucially masks the effects of CG in the case of possessive suffixes. From another point of view, this means that the analysis must be able to express the idea that selecting the form with the regular gradation is a worse choice that choosing the output with overapplication.

The output with the possessive suffix is reminiscent of other outputs of the same paradigm, such as the nominative singular [katu] 'street', a fact expressed by the OO constraint OO$_{Clitic}$-IDENT(voice). The same relationship is, however, also expressed by the lowest-ranking IO constraint IDENT-IO(voice), as this constraint also requires similar faithfulness with respect to the voicing specification of segments. The only difference between the constraints is the target of the comparison: In the case of OO correspondence, it is another output of the same paradigm, while IO correspondence requires a comparison to the input. The intriguing observation is that the target with respect to both types of correspondence is identical, in other words, [katu] 'street, nominative, sg'.

I suggest that since IO and OO correspondence clearly aim for the same result, their forces must be joined in this case. More specifically, when deciding on the gradation in the case of possessive suffixes, IO and OO correspondence should not be evaluated as separate tools only, but also a simultaneous recourse to them must be made. This goal is achieved through a mechanism called constraint conjunction (Smolensky 1993, 1995, 1997)[14]. In conjunction, two constraints are conjoined, and the conjunction is violated only if both conjuncts are violated. The violation of one of the conjuncts thus does not result in the violation of the conjunction. In the case of underapplication, the constraints to be conjoined are already identified as IDENT-IO(voice) and OO$_{Clitic}$-IDENT(voice)[15].

Let us now illustrate the effects that the conjunction has on the hierarchy. Crucially, the conjunction must dominate CG, as shown in (17). For

[14] The concept of constraint conjunction has also been utilized, for example, in order to explain chain shifts in OT (Kirchner 1996, Harrikari 2000a).

[15] For an overview of the conjunctions of different constraint types and the typological predictions that they make, see for example McCarthy (2002).

simplicity, I do not show the higher-ranking constraints $*C]_\sigma$ + POSS and MAX-C.

(17) IDENT-IO(voice) & OO_{Clitic}-IDENT(voice) >> CG >> IDENT-IO(voice)$_{ROOT}$ >> OO_{Clitic}-IDENT(voice) >> IDENT-IO(voice)

OO: [katu] 'street, sg. nominative'

/katu-mme/ (infl.)	IDENT-IO (voice) & OO_{Clitic}-IDENT (voice)	CG	IDENT-IO (voice)$_{ROOT}$	OO_{Clitic}-IDENT (voice)	IDENT-IO (voice)
a. ka.tum.me		*!			
☞ b. ka.dum.me			*		*
/katu-mme/ (poss.)					
☞ a. ka.tum.me					
b. ka.dum.me	*!		*	*	*

First, the evaluation in (17) shows how the conjunction has no effects on the output with the inflectional suffix. This is due to the fact that OO_{Clitic}-IDENT(voice) can never be violated by this output. It follows that the conjunction is never violated, and the decision is made under the basic ranking of CG over IDENT-IO(voice)$_{ROOT}$, resulting in the regular gradation. Second, and most importantly, the tableau shows that in the case of the possessive suffix, the form containing the weak grade violates both IDENT-IO(voice) and OO_{Clitic}-IDENT(voice), and consequently, the conjunction is violated, making the candidate with the strong grade optimal. In conclusion, the introduction of the constraint conjunction to the hierarchy provides a way of capturing the fact that possessive suffixes do not trigger CG, while inflectional suffixes regularly do so. Again, no need for derivational tools has been observed.

4 Derivational LPM-OT

I will begin the analyses of the three opaque patterns in the framework of derivational LPM-OT by first assessing the phenomenon just discussed, namely underapplication. Underapplication will then be followed by overapplication, and finally, the appearance of unexpected regular gradation will be discussed. This is the most logical order of analyses in this framework. Solutions provided by LPM-OT will be preceded by an account offered by the predecessor of the theory, i.e. LPM, which helps to understand the current properties of LPM-OT in more detail.

4.1 Underapplication

Recall that the essential task in the case of underapplication is to account for the minimal pair [katu-mme] 'our street(s)' (from /katu-mme/) and [kadu-mme] 'we regret' (from /katu-mme/), in other words, why CG is triggered by inflectional suffixes, but not by possessive suffixes. The pattern receives a natural analysis in traditional LPM. The idea is that inflectional suffixes are attached before CG occurs, whereas possessive suffixes do not appear until after CG has taken place. It is thus assumed that derivation first creates the form with inflection, which is correctly affected by CG. The derivation then moves to the next level and creates the form with possession, which correctly fails to obey CG, as shown in the simplified derivation in (18).

(18)	[katumme] 'our street(s)'	[kadumme] 'we regret'
	[katu]	[katu]
Level I		
Syllabification	ka.tu	ka.tu
Inflection	------	[ka.tu]mme
Resyllabification	------	ka.tum.me
CG	------	ka.dum.me
Level II		
Poss. suffixes	[ka.tu]mme	------
Resyllabification	ka.tum.me	------
Final output	[katumme]	[kadumme]

The derivation in (18) demonstrates how the appearance of possessive suffixes has no effect on CG, as the consonant alternation occurs before the stage of possession. This results in correct predictions.

LPM-OT follows the derivational idea of LPM and assumes that inflectional suffixes are attached on a different level than possessive suffixes. Before presenting the solution provided by LPM-OT, few basic tenets of the theory need to be mentioned. First, three levels of derivation are assumed – stem-level, word-level, and postlexical level. LPM-OT, however, employs the idea of parallelist OT, as each level of derivation consists of an OT grammar, i.e. of a parallel constraint hierarchy. Second, the derivational aspect of the theory continues to be reflected by the assumption that the optimal output of one level serves as the input to the next level. Finally, the grammars of the three levels differ from each other only with respect to the ranking of faithfulness; faithfulness constraints can be promoted or demoted, while the rest of the hierarchy is retained throughout derivation.

LPM-OT suggests that inflectional suffixes are attached on the stem-level, while the attachment of possessive suffixes is a phenomenon of the word-level. Markedness (CG) crucially dominates faithfulness (IDENT-IO(voice) on the stem-level, which results in the regular gradation. The ranking of markedness and faithfulness is, however, reverse on the word-level, leading to the situation where the effects of CG are masked. First, the stem-level analysis is shown in (19).

(19) Stem-level: [kadumme] 'we regret'
CG >> IDENT-IO(voice)

/katu-mme/	CG	IDENT-IO(voice)
a. ka.tum.me	*!	
☞b. ka.dum.me		*

The evaluation in (19) shows how CG correctly occurs, making candidate (b) optimal. No more additions take place after the stem-level operations, and consequently, the optimal output of the tableau (19) is also the final form. Next, the tableau in (20) illustrates the word-level evaluation, the stage of derivation where possessive suffixes are added. The ranking of constraints is now reverse.

(20) Word-level: [katumme] 'our street(s)'
IDENT-IO(voice) >> CG

/katu-mme/	IDENT-IO(voice)	CG
☞a. ka.tum.me		*
b. ka.dum.me	*!	

As the tableau (20) shows the assumption that IDENT-IO(voice) dominates CG results in neglecting the effects of CG, and consequently in the preference for the output with the strong grade.

In summary, both traditional, derivational LPM and more recent LPM-OT are able to capture the case of underapplication. In both approaches, the effects of CG are blocked on the later level of derivation, causing opacity. Only the mechanisms through which the goal is achieved are different: In LPM, the tool is level ordering, whereas LPM-OT relies on the reranking of constraints.

4.2 Overapplication

The next issue to be discussed is the case of overapplication. Recall that the crucial question is how to express the relationship between CG and the coda consonant that serves as the trigger of CG but which, however, has no output correspondent. In the parallel OT analysis, the tool employed was OO correspondence through which the appearance of the opaque weak grade was motivated. LPM and consequently LPM-OT suggest that the overapplication is captured by rule ordering, the different levels of derivation, and constraint reranking.

According to LPM, the analysis of [tavaroideni] 'of my things' (< *[tavaroiden-ni] requires CG to occur before the coda deletion. Consequently, CG cannot be affected by the deletion of the coda, but the weak grade – originally triggered by the deleted coda – is maintained. The derivation is shown in (21).

(21) [tavaroideni] 'of my street(s)'

	[tavaro-i]
Level I	
Syllabification	ta.va.roi
Inflection	[ta.va.roi] ten
CG[16]	ta.va.roi.den
Level II	
Poss. suffixes	[ta.va.roi.den] ni
Coda deletion	ta.va.roi.de ni
Resyllabification	ta.va.roi.de.ni
Final output	[tavaroideni]

[16] One might suggest that traditional derivations shown in the analyses here are inconsistent due to the fact that CG, for example, sometimes appears as an operation of Level I, but as a pattern of Level II under other circumstances. The derivations here are, however, must be understood as relative. The purpose of them is simply to demonstrate the order of operations with respect to each other.

LPM-OT offers an account that relies on the varying position of CG on the various levels of derivation. CG dominates faithfulness on the stem-level, the stage of derivation where inflectional suffixes are attached. The effects of CG are then blocked by the reranking of markedness and faithfulness on the word-level, in which possessive suffixes are added. More important than the reranking of constraints is, however, the assumption that the optimal output of one level functions as the input to the next one. This results in obligatory faithfulness to the previous level of derivation, through which the results of the earlier levels are maintained despite the operations of the later levels. I show this reasoning in the tableaux in (22) and (23). First, the inflectional suffix is added at the stem-level.

(22) Stem-level: [tavaroiden] 'of things'
CG >> IDENT-IO(voice)

/tavara-i-ten/	CG	IDENT-IO(voice)
a. ta.va.roi.ten	*!	
☞b. ta.va.roi.den		*

The analysis in (22) illustrates how CG is correctly predicted to occur at the stem-level. The evaluation next proceeds to the word-level, which is the stage of derivation of three relevant components: the attachment of possessive suffixes, the coda deletion, and the blockage of CG. The tableau in (23) shows the analysis of the word-level where the ranking of constraints is reverse and the winner of the stem-level serves as the input.

(23) Word-level: [tavaroideni] 'of my things'
$*C]_\sigma$ + POSS, IDENT-IO(VOICE) >> CG, MAX-C

/tavaroiden-ni/	$*C]_\sigma$+ POSS	IDENT-IO(voice)	CG	MAX-C
a. ta.va.roi.den.ni	*!			
b. ta.va.roi.ten.ni	*!	*	*	
☞c. ta.va.roi.de.ni				*
d. ta.va.roi.te.ni		*!		*

As the evaluation shows, the candidate with overapplication is correctly selected as optimal. This is attributed to the fact that the input contains the weak grade, which is then maintained through the faithfulness constraint IDENT-IO(voice).

To summarize this section, both LPM and LPM-OT are able to capture the case of overapplication. Traditional LPM employs rule ordering, which assumes CG to occur before the triggering environment for CG is lost through the coda deletion. LPM-OT expresses the same idea by obligatory faithfulness to the earlier levels of derivation, by assuming that the optimal output of the stem-level must be the input of the word-level.

4.3 Unexpected Regular Gradation

I will finally turn to the third problem of opacity, the case of unexpected regular gradation. Recall that this is an instance of opacity only in the light of the overapplication analysis. Overapplication would be expected also in this case instead of the regular strong grade.

The predictions which LPM makes about the example [ka.tu-∅.-ni] (< *ka.du-n.-ni < /ka.tu-n.-ni/) 'of my street(s)' are first shown in (24).

(24) [katuni] 'of my street(s)'

	[katu]	
Level I		
Syllabification	ka.tu	
Inflection	[ka.tu]n	
CG	ka.dun	
Resyllabification	ka.dun	
Level II		
Poss. suffixes	[ka.dun]ni	
Coda deletion	ka.du.ni	
Resyllabification	ka.du.ni	
Final output	*[kaduni]	[attested: katuni]

The derivation in (24) correctly expresses the idea that CG crucially takes place on the earlier level of derivation, as was the case in the analysis of underapplication as well as that of overapplication. It thus follows that the coda deletion has no effect on CG, but the weak grade appears, again similar to the overapplication pattern. The resulting output is not, however, the attested one. It thus seems as LPM fails to capture the existence of unexpected regular gradation. The reformulation of the steps of derivation is not available either, as the analysis presented here is the one required by the two other instances of opaque CG.

How about LPM-OT? The analysis below demonstrates the evaluation of [ka.tu.ni] 'of my street(s)', based on the analysis developed for the overapplication pattern. Let us look at the evaluation of the stem-level first, as shown in (25).

(25) Stem-level: [kadun] 'of street'
CG >> IDENT-IO(voice)

/katu-n/	CG	IDENT-IO(voice)
a. ka.tun	*!	
☞b. ka.dun		*

The tableau in (25) shows how CG correctly takes place because of the dominant position of markedness over faithfulness. The ranking of the constraints is then reverse at the word-level, and the winner of the stem-level functions as the input, as shown in (26).

(26) Word-level: [katuni] 'of my street'
$*C]_\sigma$ + POSS, IDENT-IO(voice) >> CG, MAX-C

/kadun-ni/	$*C]_\sigma$+ POSS	IDENT-IO(voice)	CG	MAX-C
a. ka.tun.ni	*!	*	*	
b. ka.dun.ni	*!			
☞c. ka.tu.ni		*!		*
☜d. ka.du.ni				*

The evaluation in (26) clearly shows how the analysis follows the lines of LPM in the sense that the overapplication is incorrectly predicted to occur also here. The failure is attributed to the assumption that the optimal output of the stem-level, the one with the weak grade, is necessarily the input of the word-level. In other words, the obligatory faithfulness to the intermediate level of derivation is a problem, which cannot be solved here. It should be further pointed out that the solution provided by the parallel analysis, positional faithfulness, is of no use either. It requires faithfulness to the input, suggesting preference for the weak grade. It thus must be concluded that neither LPM nor LPM-OT is able to solve the problem of unexpected regular gradation.

5 Summary and Further Implications

This paper has presented the analyses that fully parallel OT and derivational LPM-OT are able to offer for three instances of opaque consonant gradation in Finnish. The main purpose of this study has been to demonstrate that opacity is captured by a parallelist approach without necessarily invoking derivational tools.

The analyses by the parallel OT require the utilization of tools such as OO correspondence, positional faithfulness, and constraint conjunction. They are all mechanisms which have been widely used in the recent phonological and morphological literature. Through these additional tools, the appearance of such opaque patterns as underapplication, overapplication and unexpected regular gradation receive their motivation. LPM-OT and its predecessor, LPM, are shown to rely on rule ordering, the different levels of derivation and the reranking of constraints. These mechanisms are able to provide a natural explanation for the existence of underapplication as well as that of overapplication; however, the case of unexpected regular gradation necessarily remains without solution in these frameworks.

Let us finally briefly discuss reasons for the failure by LPM-OT and also further theoretical implications of the analyses presented. The constraint conjunction employed in the parallel OT analysis plays a central role when considering theoretical issues raised by the analyses. What are the further implications of the conjunction? What type of information does it actually extract from the structure of various outputs of the same paradigm? What is the relationship between the conjunction and the failure encountered by LPM-OT in the case of unexpected regular gradation?

As mentioned, the constraints of the conjunction concern two types of correspondence relations with respect to the outputs evaluated. First, the IO constraint provides a link to the input, in other words, to the very initial part of the evaluation. One might also compare this to the initial stage of derivation. Second, the OO constraint serves as a means of extracting information from other outputs of the same paradigm, more specifically, from the less complex free-standing base. This might be compared to the intermediate stage of derivation. When the two instances of correspondence are combined through constraint conjunction, a mechanism results, which is able to simultaneously access both the information contained in the input as well as the information about the output. To put it in derivational terms, information from the initial stage and the intermediate stage is simultaneously available. This is a mechanism that is not available in LPM-OT. The derivational approach does not have an access further back, only to the immediately preceding level. To take a concrete example, when consonant gradation has once taken place, the fact that the earlier levels of derivation might have contained forms without the effects of the gradation remains unexpressed in derivational models. Once consonant gradation has occurred, no traces of the opposite situation can be observed. This causes problems such as the one encountered by LPM and LPM-OT in the case of unexpected regular gradation. It thus seems as in order to explain certain linguistic patterns, simultaneous information from various sources must be retrieved.

Furthermore, I would like to point out that the discussion on the simultaneous access to the various levels of the analysis is reminiscent of the phenomenon called Bracket Erasure, which is well-known in traditional derivational models. A detailed description of the phenomenon is out of the scope of this paper. The main idea is, however, that through Bracket Erasure, certain information about the elements in the earlier levels of derivation is lost. Consequently, no access is necessarily available to the structural properties of the earlier levels. This is parallel to the problem encountered in LPM-OT; the theory contains no mechanism, which would make the information of the earlier levels accessible.

After reading this paper one might be under the impression that only the differences between the parallelist and derivational approaches are emphasized. This is true. This also leads to the impression that no connections between the two might be found. This is not true. When the theories are closely compared, one might observe striking similarities in them. To take an example, it might be claimed that the OO constraints of parallelist OT often have the same effects as the IO constraints of the word-level in LPM-OT. OO constraints require the employment of a particular OO base to which the evaluated outputs are compared. It seems, however, that this base is often identical to the winner of the stem-level in LPM-OT, the correspondence to which is then expressed by IO correspondence of the word-level. The basic idea of the required correspondence is similar, only the mechanisms employed differ remarkably. Connections such as this are issues that should be looked at in the future research.

References

Anttila, A. 2002. Morphologically Conditioned Phonological Alternations. *Natural Language and Linguistic Theory* 20:1-42. [Rutgers Optimality Archive, http://ruccs.rutgers. edu/roa.html.]

Archangeli, D. and K. Suzuki. 1996. Yokuts Templates: Correspondence to Neither Input nor Output. *UCI Working Papers in Linguistics 2: Proceedings of the South Western Optimality Theory Workshop*, ed. B. Agbayani & N. Harada, 17–28. Irvine, CA: Irvine Linguistics Students Association.

Archangeli, D. & K. Suzuki. 1997. The Yokuts Challenge. *Derivations and Constraints in Phonology*, ed. Iggy Roca, 197–226. Oxford: Clarendon Press.

Beckman, J. 1998. Positional Faithfulness. Doctoral dissertation. University of Massachusetts, Amherst. [Rutgers Optimality Archive, http://ruccs.rutgers. edu/roa.html.]

Benua, L. 1995. Identity Effects in Morphological Truncation. *University of Massachusetts Occasional Papers in Linguistics 18: Papers in Optimality Theory*, ed. J. Beckman, L. Walsh Dickey and S. Urbanczyk, 77–136. Amherst, MA: GLSA.

Benua, L. 1997. Transderivational Identity: Phonological Relations between Words. Doctoral dissertation, University of Massachusetts, Amherst. [Rutgers Optimality Archive, http:// ruccs.rutgers.edu/roa.html.]

Burzio, L. 1997a. Cycles, Non-derived-environment Blocking and Correspondence. Ms. Johns Hopkins University. [Rutgers Optimality Archive, http:// ruccs.rutgers.edu/ roa. html.]

Burzio, L. 1997b. Italian Participial Morphology and Correspondence Theory. *Proceedings of the First Mediterranean Conference of Morphology*, ed. G. Booij, A. Ralli and S. Scalise, 42–53. Mytilene, Greece.

Booij, G. 1997. Non-derivational Phonology Meets Lexical Phonology. *Derivations and Constraints in Phonology*, ed. I. Roca, 261–288. Oxford: Clarendon Press.

Bye, P. 1998. Coherence in Finnish Consonant Gradation: Towards a Theory of Phonological Lenition. *The Main Session. Chicago Linguistic Society* 32, eds. Wysocki, Tamra et al, 39-54.

Cho, Y.-m Y. 1995. Rule Ordering and Constraint Interaction in OT. *Berkeley Linguistic Society* 21:336–350.

Dolbey, A. and R. Sprouse. 1996. A Unified Approach to Finnish Consonant Gradation. Handout distributed at TREND.

Goldsmith, J. 1996. Tone in Mituku: How a Floating Tone Nailed Down an Intermediate Level. *Current Trends in Phonology: Models and Methods*, ed. J. Durand and B. Laks, 267–280. Salford: ESRI.

Halle, M. and W. Idsardi. 1997. R, Hypercorrection, and the Elsewhere Condition. *Derivations and Constraints in Phonology*, ed. I. Roca, 331–348. Oxford: Clarendon Press.

Harrikari, H. 2000a. The Inalterability of Long Vowels in Finnish. *Proceedings of Nanzan GLOW 99*, 97–114. Nanzan University, Nagoya. Reprinted in H. Harrikari 2000. *Segmental Length in Finnish – Studies within a Constraint-Based Approach.* Doctoral dissertation. Publications of the Department of General Linguistics 33. University of Helsinki.

Harrikari, H. 2000b. Opaque Consonant Gradation in Finnish: The Case of Possessive Suffixes. In *Proceedings of the West Coast Conference on Formal Linguistics 19*, ed. Billerey and Lillehaugen, 191-203. Somerville, MA: Cascadilla Press.

Hermans, B. and M. van Oostendorp. 2000. *The Derivational Residue in Phonological Optimality Theory*. Amsterdam: Benjamins.

Idsardi, W. 1997. Phonological Derivations and Historical Changes in Hebrew Spirantization. *Derivations and Constraints in Phonology*, ed. I. Roca, 367–392. Oxford: Clarendon Press.

Idsardi, W. 1998. Tiberian Hebrew Spirantization and Phonological Derivations. *Linguistic Inquiry* 29:37–73.

Itô, J. and A. Mester. 1997. Sympathy Theory and German Truncations. *University of Maryland Working Papers in Linguistics* 5. Proceedings of the Hopkins Optimality Workshop / Maryland Mayfest 1997, ed. V. Miglio and B. Morén. University of Maryland.

Kager, R. 1997. Rhythmic Vowel Deletion in Optimality Theory. *Derivations and Constraints in Phonology*, ed. I. Roca, 463–499. Oxford: Clarendon Press.

Kager, R. 2000. Surface Opacity of Metrical Structure in Optimality Theory. *The Derivational Residue in Phonological Optimality Theory*, ed. B. Hermans and M. van Oostendorp, 207-245. Amsterdam: Benjamins.

Kanerva, J. M. 1987. Morphological Integrity and Syntax: The Evidence from Finnish Possessive Suffixes. *Language* 63:498–521.

Karlsson, F. 1983. *Suomen kielen äänne- ja muotorakenne*. [Structure of Finnish Phonology and Morphology]. Juva: WSOY.

Keyser, S. J. and P. Kiparsky. 1984. Syllable Structure in Finnish Phonology. *Language Sound Structure*, ed. M. Aronoff and R. T. Oehrle. Cambridge: MIT Press.

Kiparsky, P. 1982. Lexical Morphology and Phonology. *Linguistics in the Morning Calm*, ed. The Linguistics Society of Korea. Seoul: Hanshin Publishing Co.

Kiparsky, P. 1985. Some Consequences of Lexical Phonology. *Phonology Yearbook* 2. ed. C. Ewen & E. Kaisse, 83–138. Cambridge: Cambridge University Press.

Kiparsky P. 1993. Blocking in Non-Derived Environments. *Studies in Lexical Phonology*, ed. S. Hargus & E. Kaisse. San Diego, California: Academic Press.

Kiparsky, P. 1997. Scandinavian Summer School in Generative Phonology, Hvalfjarðarströnd, Iceland. Class notes.

Kiparsky, P. 1998. Paradigm Effects and Opacity. Ms. Stanford University. CSLI.

Kiparsky, P. 1999a. Opacity and Cyclicity. Paper presented at the West Coast Conference of Formal Linguistics 18, University of Arizona, Tucson.

Kiparsky, P. 1999b. The Non-existence of Base-Output Constraints. Paper presented at SWOT, University of California, San Diego.

Kiparsky, P. 1999c. Quantity in Finland Swedish. Ms. Stanford University.

Kirchner, R. 1996. Synchronic Chain Shifts in Optimality Theory. *Linguistic Inquiry* 27:341–350.

McCarthy, J. 1995. Faithfulness in Prosodic Morphology and Phonology: Rotuman Revisited. Ms. University of Massachusetts, Amherst.

McCarthy, J. 1996. Remarks on Phonological Opacity in Optimality Theory. *Studies in Afroasiatic Grammar: Papers from the 2nd Conference on Afroasiatic Linguistics*, ed. J. Lecarme, J. Lowenstamm & U. Shlonsky, 215–243. Sophia Antipolis, 1994. The Hague: Holland Academic Graphics.

McCarthy, J. 1997. Sympathy & Phonological Opacity. Handout, Hopkins Optimality Workshop / Maryland, Mayfest 1997.

McCarthy, J. 1999a. Sympathy & Phonological Opacity. *Phonology* 16:331–399.

McCarthy, J. 1999b. Sympathy, Cumulativity, and the Duke-of-York Gambit. Ms. University of Massachusetts, Amherst.

McCarthy, J. 2002. *A Thematic Guide to Optimality Theory*. Research Surveys in Linguistics. Cambridge: Cambridge University Press.

McCarthy, J & A. Prince. 1993a. Prosodic Morphology I: Constraint Interaction and Satisfaction. Ms. University of Massachusetts, Amherst and Rutgers University.

McCarthy J. & A. Prince. 1993b. Generalized Alignment. In *Yearbook of Morphology 1993*, ed. G. Booij and J. van Marle. Dordrecht: Kluwer. [Rutgers Optimality Archive, http:// ruccs.rutgers.edu/roa.html.]

McCarthy, J. & A. Prince. 1995. Faithfulness and Reduplicative Identity. In *University of Massachusetts Occasional Papers in Linguistics 18: Papers in Optimality Theory*, ed. J. Beckman, L. Walsh Dickey & S. Urbanczyk. Amherst, MA: GLSA. [Rutgers Optimality Archive, http://ruccs.rutgers. edu/roa.html.]

McCartney, S. 1998. Opacity and Sympathy in Finnish Consonant Gradation. Ms. University of Texas, Austin / University of Helsinki.

Paradis, C. 1997. Non-transparent Constraint Effects in Gere: From Cycles to Derivations. *Derivations and Constraints in Phonology*, ed. I. Roca, 529–550. Oxford: Clarendon Press.

Prince, A. and P. Smolensky. 1993. Optimality Theory: Constraint Interaction in Generative Grammar. Ms., Rutgers University, New Brunswick, and University of Colorado, Boulder, RuCCS-TR-2.

Roca, I. 1997. Derivations or Constraints, or Derivations and Constraints? *Derivations and Constraints in Phonology*, ed. I. Roca, 3–41. Oxford: Clarendon Press.

Rubach, J. 1997. Extrasyllabic Consonants in Polish: Derivational Optimality Theory. *Derivations and Constraints in Phonology*, ed. I. Roca, 551–581. Oxford: Clarendon Press.

Smolensky, P. 1993. Harmony, Markedness, and Phonological Activity. Paper presented at Rutgers Optimality Workshop-1 at Rutgers University, New Brunswick, NJ. [Rutgers Optimality Archive, http://ruccs.rutgers.edu/roa .html.]

Smolensky, P. 1995. On the Internal Structure of the Constraint Component of UG. Colloquium presented at University of California, Los Angeles. [Rutgers Optimality Archive, http:// ruccs.rutgers.edu/roa.html.]

Smolensky, P. 1997. Constraint Interaction in Generative Grammar II: Local Conjunction or Random Rules in Universal Grammar. Paper presented at Hopkins Optimality Theory Workshop / Maryland Mayfest '97. Baltimore, MD.

4

Finnish Noun Inflection

PAUL KIPARSKY

1 Introduction

Inflected words in Finnish show a range of interdependent stem and suffix alternations which are conditioned by syllable structure and stress. In a penetrating study, Anttila (1997) shows how the statistical preferences among optional alternants of the Genitive Plural can be derived from free constraint ranking. I propose an analysis which covers the rest of the nominal morphology and spells out the phonological constraints that interact to produce the alternations, and show how it supports a stratal version of OT phonology.[1]

In the model of stratal OT that I will be assuming, stems, words, and phrases are subject to distinct parallel constraint systems, which may differ in the ranking of constraints. These levels interface serially: the output of the stem morphology and phonology is the input to the word morphology and phonology, and the output of the word morphology and phonology is the input to the syntax and postlexical phonology.

[1] I am deeply indebted to Arto Anttila for discussing this material with me over many years, and for commenting on this latest effort of mine to make sense of it.

Generative Approaches to Finnic and Saami Linguistics.
Diane Nelson and Satu Manninen (eds.).

(1)

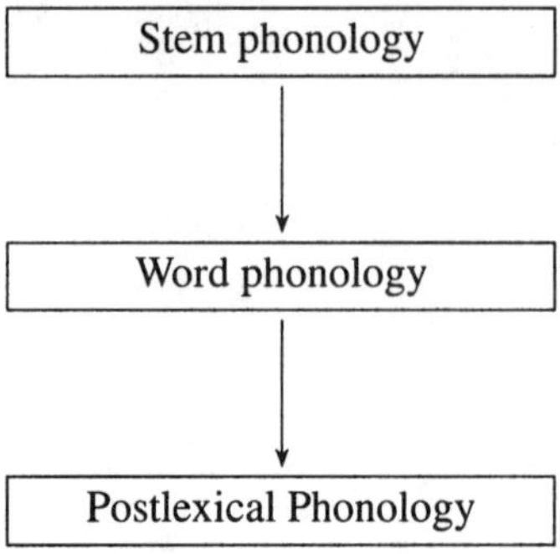

I assume that the constraint system of level $n+1$ may differ in ranking from constraint system of level n by promotion of one or more constraints to undominated status. These may be faithfulness constraints as well as markedness constraints. No crucial ranking among the promoted constraints is required, at least in the cases studied so far.

The stem phonology corresponds to Lexical Phonology's level 1 and the word phonology corresponds to Lexical Phonology's level 2; together they constitute what is traditionally called the lexical phonology. The Finnish data to be examined mostly have to do with word-internal phonological processes, so it is the distinction between the stem and word levels within the lexical phonology which will carry the explanatory burden.

Diverging from previous approaches to level-ordering, I will assume three types of affixes:

(2)
a. Stem-to-stem affixes: [[X]$_{\text{Stem}}$ + Affix]$_{\text{Stem}}$
b. Stem-to-word affixes: [[X]$_{\text{Stem}}$ + Affix]$_{\text{Word}}$
c. Word-to-word affixes (lexical clitics): [[X]$_{\text{Word}}$ + Affix]$_{\text{Word}}$

Stems must satisfy the stem phonology, and words must satisfy the word phonology. The levels and categories are assumed to be universal, but the allocation of morphemes to them is not predictable, and not all languages necessarily have all types. For example, inflectional endings are attached to words in English, but to stems in Finnish.

Opacity effects (counterfeeding and counterbleeding) result from masking of the constraint system of one level by the constraint system of a later level. Therefore, stratal OT entails the following restrictions on the interaction of processes:

(3)
- Constraints are transparent, except that
- postlexical processes can mask stem-level and word-level processes, and
- word-level processes can mask stem-level processes.

2 Stress

2.1 The Finnish stress system

The descriptive generalizations. Speaking for the moment in derivational terms, Finnish stress is assigned by laying down binary feet from left to right. Final syllables are not stressed if they are light, and only optionally if they are heavy. An important phenomenon is the LH̀ EFFECT: when the left-to-right scansion encounters a Light-Heavy sequence, the light syllable is skipped, with the result that a ternary foot is formed. At the left edge of a word, the LH̀ effect is superseded by the inviolable requirement that a word must have initial stress.

The basic alternating stress pattern is shown in (4):

[4] a. *(ká.las)(tè.let)* 'you're fishing'
b. *(ká.las)(tè.le)(mì.nen)* 'fishing'
c. *(í́l.moit)(tàu.tu)(mì.nen)* 'registering'
d. *(jǽr.jes)(tè.le)(mæ̀t.tö)(mỳy.des)(tæ̀n.sä)* 'from his lack of systematization'

The ternary feet resulting from the LH̀ effect are seen in (5) (the relevant LH sequences in boldface):

[5] a. X́ X L H̀ X: *(ká.las.**te**)(**lèm**.me)* 'we're fishing'
b. X́ X X̀ X L H̀ X: *(íl.moit)(tàu.tu.**mi**)(**sès**.ta)* 'registering' (Elat. Sg.)
c. X́ X X̀ X L H̀ X X̀ X: *(jǽr.jes)(tèl.mäl.**li**)(**sỳy**.del)(læ̀ni)* 'my systematicity' (Adess.Sg.)
d. X́ X X̀ X X̀ X L H̀ X: *(jǽr.jes)(tèl.mäl)(lìs.tä.**mä**)(**tæ̀n**.tä)* 'unsystematized' (Prt.Sg.)
e. X́ X L H̀ X L H̀ X: *(vói.mis.**te**)(**lùt**.te.**le**)(**màs**.ta)* 'having caused to do gymnastics' (Elat.Sg.)

The constraints. In constraint-based terms, Finnish can be characterized by the system in (6) (building on Hanson & Kiparsky 1996 and on Elenbaas & Kager 1999, which should be consulted for more detailed information and references).

[6] a. *CLASH: No stresses on adjacent syllables.
b. LEFT-HEADEDNESS: The stressed syllable is initial in the foot.
c. ALIGN(PRWD, LEFT; FT, LEFT) ("The left edge of every Prosodic Word coincides with the left edge of a foot.") Abbreviated as ALIGN-LEFT.
d. FOOT-BIN: Feet are minimally bimoraic and maximally disyllabic.
e. *LAPSE: Every unstressed syllable must be adjacent to a stressed

syllable or to the word edge (Elenbaas and Kager 1999).

f. NON-FINAL: The final syllable is not stressed.

g. STRESS-TO-WEIGHT: Stressed syllables are heavy.

h. LICENSE-σ: Syllables are parsed into feet.

i. ALIGN(FOOT, LEFT; PRWD, LEFT) ("The left edge of every foot coincides with the left edge of some Prosodic Word".) Abbreviated as ALL-FT-LEFT.

The LH̀ effect is here taken to be a manifestation of STRESS-TO-WEIGHT: a light syllable rejects a secondary stress if it can be placed on the following heavy syllable instead (without violating the higher-ranked *CLASH and *LAPSE, of course).[2]

[7]

	*CLASH	ALIGN-L	*LAPSE	NON-FINAL	STRESS-TO-WEIGHT	LICENSE-σ	ALL-FT-LEFT
Input: /opiskelija/							
1a. ☞ (ó.pis)(kè.li)ja					**	*	2
1b. (ó.pis)ke(lì.ja)					**	*	3
1c. o(pís.ke)(lì.ja)		*			*	*	1,3
1d. (ó.pis)ke.li.ja			*		*	***	
1e. (ó)(pís)(kè.li).ja	*				**	*	1,3
Input: /opetta-ma-ssa/							
2a. ☞ (ó.pet)ta(màs.sa)					*	*	3
2b. (ó.pet)(tà.mas)sa					**		2
Input: /kalastele-t/							
3a. (ká.las)te(lèt)				*	*	*	3
3b. ☞ (ká.las)(tè.let)					**		2
3c. (ká.las)te.let			*		*	**	

[2] Some light inflectional endings, such as Essive Singular *-na* and the possessive suffixes (e.g. *-ni* 'my') are preaccenting, as though they made the preceding syllable heavy. The *CLASH constraint then blocks secondary stress on the syllable before it, e.g. /opetta-ja-na/ *(ó.pet.ta)(jà.na)* 'teacher' (Ess.Sg.). When two such preaccenting suffixes occur in a row, the regular phonological pattern reappears, e.g. /opetta-ja-na-ni/ *(ó.pet)(tà.ja)(nà.ni)* 'my teacher' (Ess.Sg.). On the proposed analysis, *CLASH prevents both preaccents from appearing, and FOOT-BIN together with LICENSE-σ decide in favor of the second.

Tableau (7) shows how ternary feet result from the interaction of (6g-i).[3]

Final heavy syllables can optionally be stressed. See Elenbaas and Kager 1999:305 for an account of the basic option in terms of free constrant ranking. The frequency of this alternative seems to be proportional to the heaviness of the syllable, e.g. *(rá.vin)to(làt)* $\prec$ *(rá.vin)to(làa)* $\prec$ *(rá.vin)to(làan)*.

2.2 Lexical vs. rhythmic secondary stress

Long stems and the LH̀ effect. Polysyllabic stems in Finnish fall into two accentual types, MOVABLE and FIXED. They are most clearly distinguishable by the morphological and morphophonological properties that we shall investigate below, but there are also more direct, albeit somewhat elusive, phonological differences between them. Movable polysyllables have a rhythmic secondary stress which oscillates between the third or fourth syllable, normally according to the weight of those syllables, in line with the LH̀ effect. Fixed polysyllables have a lexical secondary stress which is invariant on a given syllable of the stem. Although the nominative singulars of movable and fixed stems have the same output stress pattern, their inflected forms (Inessive and Ablative Singulars, in these examples) diverge as follows.

(8) Movable stress (LH̀ effect in inflection):

a. *Kálevàla* ?**Kálevàlassa* *Kálevalàssa* 'Kalevala'
b. *Ámerìkka* ?**Ámerìkassa* *Ámerikàssa* 'America'
c. *ártikkèli* ?**ártikkèlissa* *ártikkelìssa* 'article'
d. *ápteekkàri* ?**ápteekkàrilla* *ápteekkarìlla* 'pharmacist'

(9) Fixed stress (no LH̀ effect):

a. *Álabàma* *Álabàmassa* ?**Álabamàssa* 'Alabama'
b. *pálsternàkka* *pálsternàkassa* ?**pálsternakàssa* 'parsnip'
c. *ésplanàdi* *ésplanàdilla* ?**ésplanadìlla* 'esplanade'

Marking stem-level stress with the IPA accent mark (ˈ), we have /ˈalaˈbama/, /ˈpalsterˈnakka/ etc.

Other examples of this stress contrast in polysyllabic loanwords are given in (10).

(10) a. Stems with fixed penult stress (inflected like disyllabic stems):

1. Four syllables: *barrikadi, paragrafi, portugali, serenadi, aladobi, sarkofagi, ortopedi, privilegi, kalomeli, kapitteli, filosofi, etanoli, ekonomi, megafoni, makaroni, invalidi, pyramidi, melaniini, margariini, molekyyli, mannekiini,*

[3]The undominated foot-wellformedness constraints LEFT-HEADEDNESS and FOOT-BIN are omitted from the tableau. Violations of ALIGN(FOOT, LEFT; PRWD, LEFT) are assessed, as usual, by toting up the number of syllables that separate each foot from the left edge of the word; almost any other method would do as well.

amatööri, pulituuri

2. Five syllables: *adrenaliini, antropologi, kolesteroli, konkvistadori, magnetofoni, pyramidoni, asetyleeni*

b. Movable stems (inflected like trisyllabic stems):

1. Four syllables: *asessori, hantlankari, salpietari, triangeli, artikkeli, partikkeli, monokkeli, tuberkkeli, konstaapeli, meanderi, kalenteri, silinteri, sylinteri, oraakkeli, korridori, makrospori, professori, senaattori*
2. Five syllables: *alabasteri, gladiaattori, plagiaattori, provokaattori, oleanteri*

Six-syllable stems normally break down into three feet, e.g. Prt.Pl. *íntellèktuèlleja* (not **íntellèktuèlleita*) 'intellectuals', Gen.Pl. *éksistèntialìstien* (not **éksistèntialìsteiden*) 'existentialist', unless the LH̀ effect dictates a trisyllabic first foot, e.g. *kátalysàattori* 'catalyst', in which case the word inflects like a three-syllable word.

The essential distinction between rhythmic and lexical stress is that the rhythmic stress is invisible to the morphology and to the stem-level (morpho)-phonology, while lexical stress is visible. It is not a matter of distinctiveness or predictability; in fact, Anttila (1997 and p.c.) has shown that the distribution of lexical secondary stresses is largely predictable from weight and sonority, although there seems to be a residue of variation. Most heavy penults in long stems are lexically stressed, with movable stems like *Amerikka* being the exception. Light penults tend to be lexically unstressed, but there is a substantial class of lexically stressed light penults in "learned" loanwords.[4] Anttila (p.c.) points out that vowel quality, and even the weight and quality of the preceding and following syllables, determine the place of the stress. His generalization is roughly that if the second stem syllable is light, the third syllable is lexically stressed even if it is light, unless it is followed by a syllable with a more sonorous vowel.

Vowel harmony. Another phonological criterion for distinguishing between rhythmic and lexical secondary stress comes from the harmonic alternation between front vowels *ä,ö,ü* and back vowels *a,o,u* in suffixes. Stems containing only neutral vowels regularly take front vowels, while words containing a mix of back vowels and the neutral vowels *i, e* regularly take back vowels. However, *lexical* secondary stress may optionally initiate a new domain of vowel harmony: if such a secondary stress falls on a neutral vowel, and all following stem vowels are neutral, the ending may have front harmony, as if

---

[4]Many of them used to have long vowels, but this is considered incorrect now, perhaps because it looks like Swedish influence. Examples of such older, now disreputable spellings, still common in pronunciation, are *barrikaadi, esplanaadi, serenaadi, filosoofi, invaliidi, pyramiidi.*

the entire stem contained *only* neutral vowels. In other words, harmony then takes its cue only from the second half of the stem, beginning with the lexically accented syllable. For example, *arkkitehdi-lla* 'architect' (Adess.Sg.) has a fully acceptable alternant *arkkitehdi-llä*, comparable to an all-neutral word like *lehdi-llä* 'leaves' (Adess.Pl.) (see Ringen and Heinämäki 1999).[5]

(11) a. Lexical stress often initiates a vowel harmony domain:

árkkitèhdilta	*árkkitèhdiltä*	'architect' (Ablat.Sg.)
bólševìkilla	*bólševìkillä*	'bolshevik' (Adess.Sg.)
káramèlleja	*káramèllejä*	'candy' (Prt.Pl.)
pýramìdista	*pýramìdistä*	'pyramid' (Elat.Sg.)

b. Rhythmic stress very seldom initiates a vowel harmony domain:

ártikkelìlla	?**ártikkelìllä*	'article' (Adess.Sg.)
prófessorèita	?**prófessorèitä*	'professor' (Prt.Pl.)
strátegisèsta	?**strátegisèstä*	'strategic' (Elat.Sg.)
kálenterìsta	?**kálenterìstä*	'calendar' (Elat.Sg.)

On the basis of their harmonic behavior, fixed stems have often been analyzed as QUASI-COMPOUNDS, i.e. as compounds from the prosodic point of view, though not from the morphological point of view.[6] The quasi-compound analysis can be linked to the above observations about stress, though I believe the connection is a somewhat indirect one, in the following sense. Since compounds consist of at least two phonological words or stems, each of which must have a stress, stems are good candidates for reanalysis as prosodic compounds if they contain two stem-level stresses. That is why fixed polysyllables are much more likely to be analyzed as compounds than movable polysyllables. However, the double stress merely *invites* the compound reanalysis, it does not force it. Fixed polysyllables *can* very well be treated as single prosodic words, as their harmonic variation confirms.

The mediating role of morphology is supported by two further points. *Trisyllabic* words are never treated as quasi-compounds, presumably because a single syllable could never be mistaken for one half of a compound. Their four-syllable inflected forms are also as a rule treated like single words for

[5]These judgments are based on the data cited in Ringen and Heinämäki 1999 and Välimaa-Blum 1999, as well as on a corpus of words occurring in the 1987 issues of the magazine *Suomen Kuvalehti*, approximately 1,3 million words. The corpus is available on the University of Helsinki Language Corpus Server, Department of General Linguistics, University of Helsinki.

[6]The idea is traditional, though I am not sure who originated it. For discussion see e.g. Kiparsky 1993, and most recently Ringen and Heinämäki 1999 and Välimaa-Blum 1999.

purposes of vowel harmony.[7]

(12) Stem-final rhythmic stress never initiates a vowel harmony domain

/paperi-i-ssa/	*páperèissa*	**páperèissä*	'paper' (Iness.Pl.)
/kaveri-lla/	*káverìlla*	**káverìllä*	'guy' (Adess.Sg.)

Secondly, polysyllabic words which are transparently composed of a stem plus a derivational suffix (such as ″*iitti* '-ite', ″*iivi* '-ive', and especially the suffix ″*isti* '-ist', which is productive in Finnish) are unlikely quasi-compounds for morphological reasons, even though they have a lexical secondary stress. They too are almost always treated as single words for purposes of vowel harmony:

(13) Lexical suffix stress very seldom initiates a vowel harmony domain

a.	*vókatìivi-lla*	*?*nóminatìivi-llä*	'vocative' (Adess.Sg.)
b.	*áteìsti-lla*	*?*áteìsti-llä*	'atheist' (Adess.Sg.)
c.	*kápitalìsti-lla*	*?*kápitalìsti-llä*	'capitalist' (Adess.Sg.)
d.	*háitarìsti-lla*	**háitarìsti-llä*	'accordionist' (Adess.Sg.)

If the form is built on a free stem, as (13d) *háitarìsti* from *haitari* 'accordion', front harmony is totally out of the question. The explanation is that the quasi-compound analysis **haita-risti-llä* is so obviously contraindicated by the morphology.

In sum: variation in vowel harmony shows that stems with fixed stress can be treated like compounds to the extent that they otherwise look like them in the stem-level phonological representation. Their output phonological shape is not what counts. This provides an independent argument for lexical secondary stress.

3 Segmental alternations

3.1 Stop Deletion and Consonant Gradation

The distribution of stops. Two central morphophonological processes govern the distribution of its single stops *p,t,k* and geminated stops *pp,tt,kk*. They are stated in informal processual terms in (14) (where $\mathring{V}$ represents an unstressed vowel).

(14) a. STOP DELETION: $t \rightarrow \emptyset \;/\; \mathring{V}\_\_V$

b. CONSONANT GRADATION: $\left\{ \begin{matrix} tt,pp,kk \rightarrow t,p,k \\ t,p,k \rightarrow d,v,\emptyset \end{matrix} \right\} \;/\; [+son]\_\_VC$

Stop Deletion (called *t*-Deletion in Keyser & Kiparsky 1984) deletes single intervocalic stops after a light unstressed syllable. Consonant Gradation re-

[7] For a possible special case, see fn. 22 below.

duces geminate voiceless stops to single voiceless stops, and single voiceless stops to voiced stops (under certain conditions to voiced fricatives and to zero) when a vowel or sonorant consonant precedes and a branching (VC) rhyme follows. (Here I will only be considering the degemination branch of the Consonant Gradation process.) For example, affixes of the form -CCV and -C regularly trigger Consonant Gradation under these conditions. (15) illustrates the operation of Stop Deletion and Consonant Gradation with forms from the declensional paradigm of *lakko* 'strike'.[8]

[15]					
	a.	/lakko/	*lak.ko*	Nom.Sg.	
	b.	/lakko-na/	*lak.ko.na*	Ess.Sg.	
	c.	/lakko-ta/	*lak.ko.a*	Prt.Sg.	(Stop Del.)
	d.	/lakko-i-ta/	*lak.ko.ja*	Prt.Pl.	(Stop Del., G.F.)
	e.	/lakko-n/	*la.kon*	Gen.Sg.	(Cons.Grad.)
	f.	/lakko-ssa/	*la.kos.sa*	Iness.Sg.	(Cons.Grad.)

Both processes apply almost without exception in derived environments.[9] But, as Anttila 1994 notes, the processes also characterize the structure of native *stems*: even in underived environments, violations are practically confined to unassimilated loans and names, such as:

[16] a. Stem-internal exceptions to Stop Deletion: *senorita, vibrato, inkognito, Kimito*

b. Stem-internal exceptions to Consonant Gradation: *pikkelsi* 'pickle', *okkulttinen* 'occult', *opportunismi* 'opportunism', *appelsiini* 'orange', *rottinki* 'rattan'

The distribution of stops in stems shows that the constraint behind Stop Deletion applies also to *p* and *k*. Although actual alternations only involve /t/, sequences of the form [V̊kV] and [V̊pV], like [V̊tV], are essentially restricted to unassimilated loanwords and names such as (17a). Most loanwords accommodate to the constraint, and they do so by geminating the obstruent, not by deleting it, as the examples in (17b) illustrate.[10]

[8]Examples are cited in Finnish orthography, with stress and syllabification added where necessary. Syllables ending in short vowels (-V) are light, syllables ending in -VC, -VV, -VVC are heavy. The vowel sequences *ei, äi, yi, öi, ai, ui, oi, au, ou, eu, iu, ey, äy, öy, ie, yö, uo, iy* are diphthongs. Other vowel sequences, such as *ia, ua, ea, oa*, are disyllabic.

[9]There is no Consonant Gradation before the ending *-is*, because this ending imposes templatic expressive gemination, superseding the Consonant Gradation constraint, e.g. *julkkis* 'celebrity, public figure', from *julkinen* 'public'. A systematic class of exceptions to Consonant Gradation are certain stems in /-s(e)/, which furnish the oblique stems of words whose nominative ends in *-nen*, e.g. *Kekkonen*, Prt.Sg. *Kekkos-ta*.

[10]Presumably in order to minimize the difference between the Finnish and original pronunciations. A related gemination process applies in Fenno-Swedish (Kiparsky, to appear).

(17) a. *judoka* 'judo practitioner', *paprika* 'bell pepper, paprika', *karakteristika* 'characteristic' (in mathematics), *rokokoo* 'rococo', *Aleko, Alepa, heteka* 'a type of bed'

b. *profeetta* 'prophet', *mammutti* 'mammoth', *apotti* 'abbot', *Eurooppa* 'Europe', *sinappi* 'mustard'

Stop Deletion, then, reflects a broad distributional restriction on $\mathring{\breve{V}}$[p,t,k]V sequences, although, because no suffixes begin with a single /p/ or /k/, the alternations it governs all happen to be of the form /t/ $\sim$ $\emptyset$. This said, I will continue to use the term Stop Deletion to refer to its processual effects.

Examples. Numerous stems and endings alternate in accord with Stop Deletion and/or Consonant Gradation (CG), often interacting with other process, as the examples in (18)-(22) illustrate for a variety of inflectional and derivational suffixes.[11]

(18) Partitive Singular /-ta/

a.	/puu-ta/	*puu.ta*	'tree'	
b.	/voi-ta/	*voi.ta*	'butter'	
c.	/si-tä/	*si.tä*	'that'	
d.	/palttoo-ta/	*palt.too.ta*	'overcoat'	
e.	/puku-ta/	*pu.ku.a*	'suit'	(Stop Del.)
f.	/katiska-ta/	*ka.tis.kaa*	'fish trap'	(Stop Del., V-Contr.)

(19) Partitive Plural /-i-ta/

a.	/puu-i-ta/	*pui.ta*	'trees'	
b.	/he-i-tä/	*hei.tä*	'them'	
c.	/palttoo-i-ta/	*palt.toi.ta*	'overcoats'	
d.	/puku-i-ta/	*pu.ku.ja*	'suits'	(Stop Del., G.F.)
e.	/katiska-i-ta/	*ka.tis.ko.ja*	'fish traps'	(Stop Del., G.F.)

(20) Genitive Plural /-i-ten/

a.	/puu-i-ten/	*pui.den*	'trees'	(Cons.Grad.)
b.	/voi-i-ten/	*voi.den*	'butter'	(Cons.Grad.)
c.	/nuo-i-ten/	*noi.den*	'those'	(Cons.Grad.)
d.	/palttoo-i-ten/	*palt.toi.den*	'overcoats'	(Cons.Grad.)
e.	/puku-i-ten/	*pu.ku.jen*	'suits'	(Stop Del., G.F.)
f.	/katiska-i-ten/	*ka.tis.ko.jen*	'fish traps'	(Stop Del., G.F.)

(21) Infinitive /taC/

[11]For simplicity I incorporate vowel harmony into the underlying representations.

a.	/nouse-taC/	*nous.taC*	'rise'	(Cons.Grad.)
b.	/tuo-taC/	*tuo.daC*	'bring'	(Cons.Grad.)
c.	/hakk-at-taC/	*ha.ka.taC*	'to chop'	(Cons.Grad.)
d.	/tule-taC/	*tul.laC*	'to come'	(Cons.Grad., Assim.)
e.	/mene-täC/	*men.näC*	'to go'	(Cons.Grad., Assim.)
f.	/laula-taC/	*lau.laaC*	'to sing'	(Stop Del., V-Contr.)

(22) Verbalizer /-at/

a.	/hakk-at-kaa/	*ha.kat.kaa*	'chop!' (2Pl.)	(Cons.Grad.)
b.	/hakk-at-taC/	*ha.ka.taC*	'chop' (Inf.)	(Cons.Grad., twice)
c.	/hakk-at-a/	*hak.kaa*	'chops' (3Sg.)	(Stop Del., V-Contr.)
d.	/hakk-at-u/	*hak.kuu*	'chopping' (N.)	(Stop Del., V-Contr.)

The ghost consonant. A comment is in order about the final /-C/ in (21) and (22b), an underlying consonantal element with no segmental melody of its own. The evidence for this "ghost" segment is extensive, but a few of the main points may be summarized here. First, it regularly triggers Consonant Gradation, e.g. /liikkeC/ *liike* 'movement, shop' (see also (21b-e), (22b)). Secondly, it blocks the regular raising of word-final *e* to *i*, e.g. Nom.Sg. /kuore/ *kuori* 'rind', but /liikkeC/ *liike*, not **liiki* or **liikki*. Third, it blocks Stop Deletion, e.g. Prt.Sg. /liikkeC-tä/ *liikettä*, not **liikkeä*. Fourth, it triggers stem-final -*e* epenthesis before all -CCV and -C endings, as well as a subset of -CV endings, e.g. Iness.Sg. /liikkeC-ssä/ *liikkeessä*, Gen.Sg. /liikkeC-n/ *liikkeen*, Ess.Sg. /liikkeC-nä/ *liikkeenä*.[12] Fifth, when the next segment is a consonant, the -C materializes as a copy of it. This happens before those -CV endings which retain the unepenthesized -C stem,[13] as in Prt.Sg. /liikkeC-tä/ *liikettä* as well as before clitics such as *-ko/-kö* (e.g. *liike[kk]ö* 'the shop?'), in compounds (e.g. *liike[kk]atu* 'shopping street'), and in external sandhi as long as there is close contact between the words (e.g. *liike[mm]enestyi* 'the shop flourished'). The examples in (23) show how words ending in /-C/ contrast with words ending in vowels.

(23)
a. /ei se tuo-tta-C voi-ta/ *ei se tuota[v v]oita* 'it does not produce butter'
b. /ei se tuo-ta voitta-C/ *ei se tuota voita* 'it won't beat THAT ONE'
c. /ei se voitta-C tuo-ta/ *ei se voita[t t]uota* 'it won't beat that one'
d. /ei se voi-ta tuo-tta-C/ *ei se voita tuota* 'it does not produce BUTTER'

[12] Ultimately, the *-e* is probably part of the underlying form, for the empirical reasons presented in in Keyser & Kiparsky 1984. Thus, the "ghost consonant" is really a "ghost syllable", in conformity with the constraint that all Finnish stems end in vowels (the Stem Constraint motivated in section 5).

[13] Or, if we adopt the analysis of fn. 12, before those -CV endings which allow stem-final *-e* to be deleted.

3.2 Optionality and complementarity

Movable polysyllabic stems. A stem-final vowel combines with the plural suffix /i/ into a diphthong.[14] After underlying diphthongs, Stop Deletion is always blocked: e.g. *lauantai-ta* 'Saturday' (Prt.Sg.). After morphologically derived diphthongs, stops are optionally deleted in a subclass of polysyllabic stems, and the second half of the diphthong becomes an onset, taking the place of the deleted stop. This is exactly the class of stems we have already identified through their stress and vowel harmony behavior as MOVABLE POLYSYLLABLES.

(24) Diphthongs optionally trigger Stop Deletion in movable polysyllables:

a.	/korjaamo-i-ta/	*kór.jaa.mò.ja* *kór.jaa.mòi.ta*	'repair shops' (Prt.Pl.)
b.	/kalevala-i-ta/	*Ká.le.và.lo.ja* *Ká.le.va.lòi.ta*	'Kalevalas' (Prt.Pl.)
c.	/professori-i-ta/	*pró.fes.sò.re.ja*[15] *pró.fes.so.rèi.ta*	'professors' (Prt.Pl.)
d.	/artikkeli-i-ta/	*ár.tik.kè.le.ja* *ár.tik.ke.lèi.ta*	'articles' (Prt.Pl.)

(In this section I mark primary and secondary word stress, for reasons which will soon become apparent.)

In movable polysyllables, the diphthong formed by combining the stem-final vowel with the plural suffix /i/ has another unexpected property. It optionally triggers Consonant Gradation of its onset stop, as in the essive and illative plurals in (25).

(25) Diphthongs optionally trigger Consonant Gradation in movable polysyllables:

a.	/ullakko-i-na/	*úl.lak.kòi.na* *úl.la.kòi.na*	'attic' (Ess.Pl.)
b.	/ullakko-i-hin/	*úl.lak.kòi.hin* *úl.la.kòi.hin*	'attic' (Ill.Pl.)
d.	/amerikka-i-na/	*Á.me.rìk.koi.na* *Á.me.ri.kòi.na*	'America' (Ess.Pl.)
e.	/amerikka-i-hin/	*Á.me.rìk.koi.hin* *Á.me.ri.kòi.hin*	'America' (Ill.Pl.)

[14] Under certain conditions the stem-final vowel is deleted instead, e.g. /matala-i-ta/ *matalia* 'low' (Prt.Sg.); see Anttila 1997.

[15] Note the lowering of /-i/ to *-e* in (24c,d). When Stop Deletion applies in the genitive plural, stem-final /-i/ and /-e/ instead appear as /-i/, and the glide is absorbed, e.g. /professori-i-ten/ *professorien* ∼ *professoreiden*.

In contrast, Consonant Gradation never applies before a derived diphthong in the second syllable of disyllabic stems.

(26) Diphthongs do not trigger Consonant Gradation in disyllabic stems:

a.	/lakko-i-na/	*lák.koi.na*	**lá.koi.na*	'strike' (Ess.Pl.)
b.	/lakko-i-hin/	*lák.koi.hin*	**lá.koi.hin*	'strike' (Ill.Pl.)

When the diphthong is followed by a tautosyllabic consonant, as in (27a-c), Consonant Gradation is obligatory regardless of the syllable count. And, of course, Consonant Gradation is obligatory before a simple VC rhyme, whatever the length of the stem, e.g. (27d).

(27) Obligatory Consonant Gradation:

a.	*lá.koi.ssa*	**lák.koi.ssa*	'strike' (Ins.Pl.)
b.	*Á.me.ri.kòis.sa*	**Á.me.rìk.kois.sa*	'America' (Ins.Pl.)
c.	*úlla.kòis.sa*	**úllak.kòis.sa*	'attic' (Ins.Pl.)
d.	*úlla.kòs.sa*	**úllak.kòs.sa*	'attic' (Ins.Sg.)

The problem, then, is why the systematic variation in (24) and (25) occurs, and why precisely with diphthongs in a subclass of polysyllabic stems.

Fixed polysyllabic stems. FIXED POLYSYLLABLES do not show variation in either Consonant Gradation or Stop Deletion (cf. Anttila 1997:20).

(28) Diphthongs trigger Stop Deletion in fixed polysyllables:

a.	*ká.ra.mèl.le.ja*	**ká.ra.mèl.lei.ta*	'candy' (Prt.Pl.)
b.	*ká.ra.mèl.li.en*	**ká.ra.mèl.lei.den*	'candy' (Gen.Pl.)
c.	*Á.la.bà.mo.ja*	**Á.la.ba.mòi.ta*	'Alabama' (Prt.Pl.)
d.	*Á.la.bà.mo.jen*	**Á.la.ba.mòi.den*	'Alabama' (Gen.Pl.)

(29) Diphthongs do not trigger Consonant Gradation in fixed polysyllables:

a.	*páls.ter.nàk.koi.na*	**páls.ter.nà.koi.na*	'parsnips' (Ess.Pl.)
b.	*páls.ter.nàk.koi.hin*	**páls.ter.nà.koi.hin*	'parsnips' (Ill.Pl.)
c.	*ból.še.vìk.kei.na*	**ból.še.vìk.ei.na*	'bolsheviks' (Ess.Pl.)
d.	*ból.še.vì.kei.hin*	**ból.še.vì.kei.hin*	'bolsheviks' (Ill.Pl.)

In fact, fixed polysyllabic stems pattern just like disyllabic stems; compare (28) and (29) with (30):

(30)	a.	/sama-i-ta/	*sá.mo.ja*	**sá.moi.ta*	'same' (Prt.Pl.)
	b.	/sama-i-ten/	*sá.mo.jen*	**sá.moi.den*	'same' (Gen.Pl.)
	c.	/lakko-i-na/	*lák.koi.na*	**lá.koi.na*	'strike' (Ess.Pl.)
	d.	/lakko-i-hin/	*lák.koi.hin*	**lá.koi.hin*	'strike' (Ill.Pl.)

So we have a second mystery compounding the first: why do stems of four or more syllables stems fall into two different types, movable (patterning like trisyllables) and fixed (patterning like disyllables)?

Complementarity of Stop Deletion and Consonant Gradation. The two alternations of Stop Deletion and Consonant Gradation are strictly COMPLEMENTARY: when the conditions for both are present, one or the other must apply, but both may not. Thus, when a movable potentially gradating stem is combined with a suffix in *-t*, there are always only two forms, never four:

(31) Complementarity of Stop Deletion and Consonant Gradation:

a.	/ullakko-i-ta/	*úl.lak.kò.ja*	*úl.la.kòi.ta*
		**úl.lak.kòi.ta*	**úl.la.kò.ja*
b.	/amerikka-i-ten/	*Á.me.rìk.ko.jen*	*Á.me.ri.kòi.den*
		**Á.me.rìk.koi.den*	**Á.me.rì.ko.jen*

And when a fixed potentially gradating stem, such as *papiljotti*, is combined with a suffix in *-t*, there is always only one form, never two.

(32) /papiljotti-i-ta/ *pápiljòtteja* **pápiljòteita* 'hair curlers' (Prt.Pl.)
**pápiljòteja* **pápiljotèita*

This is remarkable considering that each process on its own is optional (e.g. *ullakoina* ∼ *ullakkoina*, *korjaamoja* ∼ *korjaamoita*).

So we have two more mysteries: when both Stop Deletion and Consonant Gradation are applicable, why must at least one of them take effect? And why do both of them never take effect together?

3.3 Another systematically opaque context

Diphthong shortening. As already stated, long vowels trigger neither Consonant Gradation before them (see (33)), nor Stop Deletion after them (see (34)).

(33)	a.	/palttoo-ssa/	*palt.toos.sa*	**pal.toos.sa*	'overcoat' (Ins.Sg.)
	b.	/hakkatV-u-n/	*hak.kuun*	**ha.kuun*	'chopping' (Gen.Sg.)
	c.	/rakkasV-lla/	*rak.kaal.la*	**ra.kaal.la*	'dear' (Ads.Sg.)

(34)	a.	/palttoo-ta/	*palt.too.ta*	**palt.too.a*	'overcoat' (Prt.Sg.)
	b.	/hakkatV-u-ta/	*hak.kuu.ta*	**hak.kuu.a*	'chopping' (Prt.Sg.)
	c.	/suklaa-ta/	*suk.laa.ta*	**suk.laa.a*	'chocolate' (Prt.Sg.)

Superheavy (three-mora) diphthongs are categorically excluded in Finnish, and when they arise in the morphology they are always shortened, as when the plural /-i/ is added to /-VV/ stems:

(35)	a.	/puu-i-ssa/	*puis.sa*	**puuis.sa*	'tree' (Ins.Pl.)
	b.	/voi-i-ssa/	*vois.sa*	**voiis.sa*	'butter' (Ins.Pl.)
	c.	/suklaa-i-ssa/	*suk.lais.sa*	**suk.laais.sa*	'chocolate' (Ins.Pl.)

The behavior of shortened diphthongs. The shortened diphthongs are pronounced like original short diphthongs. Still, a following tautosyllabic consonant triggers no Consonant Gradation before them, and a following single stop does not undergo Stop Deletion after them.

(36) a. /palttoo-i-ssa/ *palt.tois.sa* **pal.tois.sa* 'overcoats' (Ins.Pl.)
b. /hakkat-u-i-ssa/ *hak.kuis.sa* **ha.kuis.sa* 'choppings' (Ins.Pl.)
c. /rakkasV-i-lla/ *rak.kail.la* **ra.kail.la* 'dear' (Ad.Pl.)

(37) a. /palttoo-i-ta/ *palt.toi.ta* **pal.toi.ta* 'overcoats' (Prt.Pl.)
b. /hakkat-u-i-ta/ *hak.kui.ta* **ha.kui.ta* 'choppings' (Prt.Pl.)
c. /rakkasV-i-ta/ *rak.kai.ta* **ra.kai.ta* 'dear' (Prt.Pl.)

This contrasts with ordinary diphthongs formed with a short vowel plus a plural *i*. For example, the retained geminates in (36) are in exactly the same output environments as the degeminated ones in (38), and the retained stops in (37) are in exactly the same output environments as the deleted stops in (39) .

(38) a. /taltta-i-ssa/ *tal.tois.sa* **tal.ttois.sa* 'chisels' (Ins.Pl.)
b. /akku-i-ssa/ *a.kuis.sa* **ak.kuis.sa* 'batteries' (Ins.Pl.)
c. /lakko-i-lla/ *la.koil.la* **lak.koil.la* 'strikes' (Ad.Pl.)

(39) a. /taltta-i-ta/ *tal.tto.ja* **talt.toi.ta* 'chisels' (Prt.Pl.)
b. /akku-i-ta/ *a.kku.ja* **ak.kui.ta* 'batteries' (Prt.Pl.)
c. /lakko-i-ta/ *la.ko.ja* **lak.koi.ta* 'strikes' (Prt.Pl.)

This gives mystery number five: why are Stop Deletion and Consonant Gradation opaquely conditioned? Why do shortened diphthongs block these processes, in contexts phonetically indistinguishable from those that otherwise trigger them?

A stratal OT solution. We concluded first that polysyllabic stems in Finnish fall into two subclasses, fixed stems such as *palsternakka*, and movable stems such as *Amerikka*. Fixed polysyllables always keep their secondary stress on that syllable. Movable polysyllables receive a rhythmic secondary stress on the third or fourth syllable, depending on syllable weight in accord with the LH̀ effect. Now we have seen that the two types of polysyllables differ with respect to two other core processes of the stem phonology: Stop Deletion and Consonant Gradation. Fixed stems display no optionality with respect to these processes, whereas movable stems show systematic optionality with respect to both.

The analysis proposed here is that fixed polysyllables differ from movable polysyllables in having an obligatory fixed secondary stress at the stem level. All the differences between the two types of polysyllables follow from this basic stress difference. Some of them are conditioned by stress directly, others indirectly via syllable structure. The key point is that rhythmic secondary stress by (6) is assigned optionally (subject to certain weight constraints) in the stem phonology, and obligatorily (regardless of syllable weight) in the word phonology. Stop Deletion and Consonant Gradation are conditioned by *stem-level* stress and by *stem-level* syllable structure. In the output, stem-level stresses and stem-level syllabification are masked by word-level rhythmic stress and resyllabification, which are irrelevant to Stop Deletion and Consonant Gradation. These conclusions translate directly into evidence for stratal OT and against parallelism, for the separation between stem-level and word phonology on which the analysis depends is not available in fully parallel OT.

In sum, word-initial stress and fixed medial stress always assigned at the stem level, while movable medial stress may be assigned either at the stem level or at the word level. It would be desirable to base this generalization on some principle (rather than simply on the data of the language). Distinctiveness is irrelevant: initial primary stress, visible in the stem phonology, is as predictable as rhythmic secondary stress, which is not. One reason why initial main stress is obligatorily assigned in the stem phonology may be that prosodic phonology requires a word to consist of at least a foot, which is its prosodic head (peak). This is a very common and perhaps universal prosodic licensing requirement. On the other hand, many languages (for example, Cairene Arabic) reportedly do *not* require that words be parsed into binary feet by secondary stresses ("conflation", Hayes 1995:119). The option lies precisely in whether Finnish imposes this requirement at the stem level, or not. Formally, the variation results from free ranking in the stem phonology of the constraint that prohibits secondary stress with a constraint demanding alternating stress. For present purposes, let us assume that the constraint against secondary stress is simply *STRESS (for more sophisticated alternatives, see Crowhurst 1996 and de Lacy 1998). The antagonistic constraint that forces a full metrical parse of the word is presumably *LAPSE (or LICENSE-σ, in concert with undominated FOOT-BIN). In the word phonology, the ranking is fixed so that alternating rhythmic stress is obligatory.

Additional differences between the stem phonology and the word phonology will emerge as we go on to develop the constraint system behind these descriptive generalizations.

3.4 Stress and syllable structure

Stress-to-Weight. In the stem phonology, STRESS-TO-WEIGHT ("stressed syllables are heavy") dominates the constraints that assign alternating secondary stress. They are themselves dominated by the constraint that requires the word-initial syllable to bear primary stress. They are also dominated by *CLASH and by the Faithfulness constraint MAX(Stress).

(40) *CLASH, LEFT-HEADEDNESS, ALIGN-LEFT, MAX(Stress) $\gg$ STRESS-TO-WEIGHT

The ranking in (40) has important corollaries, to which I now turn.

The dominant status of STRESS-TO-WEIGHT precludes light syllables from getting rhythmic stress in the stem phonology (except in initial position, where ALIGN-LEFT forces it). Being always word-level, the rhythmic stress of light syllables is invisible to stem phonology, and so cannot block Stop Deletion. That is why Stop Deletion is obligatory after short vowels even if they bear rhythmic secondary stress:[16]

(41)	a.	/paperi-ta/	*paperia*	**paperita*	'paper' (Prt.Sg.)
	b.	/ullakko-ta/	*ullakkoa*	**ullakkota*	'attic' (Prt.Sg.)
	c.	/salama-ta/	*salamaa*	**salamata*	'lightning' (Prt.Sg.)

When a stem-final short vowel is combined with the plural marker *-i*, a diphthong results, which is eligible to bear stress. Optional assignment of rhythmic stress in the stem-level phonology then generates the systematic alternation treated above, and illustrated again in (42), where the optional Stop Deletion reflects the stress option.

(42) /ullakko-i-ta/ *ullakkoja* *ullakoita* 'attic' (Prt.Pl.)

We have now uncovered yet another difference between lexical and rhythmic secondary stress. Rhythmic stress is assigned in the stem phonology only to heavy syllables, because of high-ranking STRESS-TO-WEIGHT. Lexical stress, however, can be lexically marked on light syllables as well, as in (10a), in consequence of the ranking MAX(Stress) $\gg$ STRESS-TO-WEIGHT.[17]

WEIGHT-TO-STRESS and the structure of nuclei. As for the complementary constraint WEIGHT-TO-STRESS, its high rank in the stem-level phonology excludes unstressed long nuclei in the stem phonology. Somewhat shockingly, it turns out that apparent unstressed diphthongs in Finnish are phonologically monomoraic, and apparent unstressed long vowels are phonologically disyllabic sequences. This is the key to understanding the complementarity between Stop Deletion and Consonant Gradation.

Recall that the output of /mellakka-i-ta/ is either *mellakkoja*, with Stop Deletion, or *mellakoita*, with Consonant Gradation, but not **mellakoja* or **mellakkoita*. When both processes have scope, one of them must apply, but both cannot apply together — even in environments where each is otherwise optional. The reason is that both processes are obligatory, but require incompatible structural conditions, whose presence is itself subject to variation. The

[16]The statement in the text holds strictly for contemporary standard Finnish. In certain dialects and sometimes in the standard language of the 19th century and earlier, *-t* is retained after polysyllabic stems in /-a/ and /-ä/, e.g. *salamata*, but not **paperita, *ullakkota*. Since *a, ä* are the most sonorous of the vowels, this dialectal variation adds support for our analysis which ties the blocking of Stop Deletion to stem-level stress controlled by STRESS-TO-WEIGHT.

[17]Of course, light *final* syllables cannot have lexical stress because NON-FINAL is undominated, so that no monomoraic feet are permitted anywhere in Finnish.

parameter of variation was identified in Wiik 1967 as the syllabification of the stem-final diphthong, which (in line with the phonological theory of the time) he represented as *oi* and *oj*, respectively. In Keyser & Kiparsky 1984 these alternative syllabifications were analyzed in terms of rhyme structure, itself derived from the independently motivated variation in secondary stress described above. Specifically, we argued that stressed diphthongs (Wiik's *oi*) have two moras, while unstressed diphthongs (Wiik's *oj*) have one mora, and we showed that this structural difference explains the incidence of Consonant Gradation and Stop Deletion.

Monosyllabic and disyllabic stems exhibit no variation because their stress pattern is fixed. The initial (or only) syllable of a word always bears main stress, so a diphthong in the *first* syllable of a word is always bimoraic. Because of *CLASH, the second syllable is always unstressed, so a diphthong in the second syllable is always monomoraic. This determines the shape of both the onset and of the following desinence. As stated in (14), Consonant Gradation takes place before branching (VC) rhymes, and Stop Deletion takes place after light unstressed syllables. An unstressed diphthong, forming a simple rhyme, does not trigger Consonant Gradation by itself (see (43a,b,e,f)). Of course, if it is followed in the rhyme by a consonant which closes the syllable, Consonant Gradation takes place (see (43c,d,g,h)). By the same token, an unstressed diphthong obligatorily triggers Stop Deletion (see (43i,j)):

(43)					
	a.	/lakko-i-na/	*lák.koi.na*	(No C.G.)	'strikes' (Ess.Pl.)
	b.	/lakko-i-hin/	*lák.koi.hin*	(No C.G.)	'strikes' (Ill.Pl.)
	c.	/lakko-i-n/	*lá.koin*	(C.G.)	'strikes' (Instr.Pl.)
	d.	/lakko-i-ssa/	*lá.kois.sa*	(C.G.)	'strikes' (Iness.Pl.)
	e.	/sattu-i/	*sát.tui*	(No C.G.)	'happened' (3.Sg.)
	f.	/sattu-i-vat/	*sát.tui.vat*	(No C.G.)	'happened' (3.Pl.)
	g.	/sattu-i-t/	*sá.tuit*	(C.G.)	'happened' (2.Sg.)
	h.	/sattu-i-mme/	*sá.tuim.me*	(C.G.)	'happened' (1.Pl.)
	i.	/lakko-i-ta/	*lák.ko.ja*	(Stop Del.)	'strikes' (Prt.Pl.)
	j.	/lakko-i-ten/	*lák.ko.jen*	(Stop Del.)	'strikes' (Gen.Pl.)

The behavior of polysyllabic stems is also predicted. Polysyllabic stems with fixed lexical stress on the penult syllable function exactly like disyllabic stems with respect to Consonant Gradation and Stop Deletion, as was already documented in (28) and (29). Polysyllabic stems of the movable type have a one-mora or two-mora final diphthong in the stem phonology, depending on whether rhythmic stress is assigned in the stem phonology or not, an option which yields the respective structures in (44).

(44) a. Stressed diphthong, two moras: mél.la.k[$\grave{o}_\mu i_\mu$]-

b. Unstressed diphthong, one mora: mél.lak.k[oi]$_\mu$-

On the stress option (44a), diphthongs trigger Consonant Gradation (e.g. Prt.Pl. *méllakòita*). On the no-stress option (44b) they trigger Stop Deletion (e.g. Prt.Pl. *méllakkòja*). Since these are the only two options, one of the two processes must apply: the reason there are not two more partitive plurals (**méllakkòita*, **méllakòja*) is that stress obligatorily determines syllable structure and the syllabic conditions on Consonant Gradation and *i*-Deletion are mutually incompatible. Both their apparent optionality, and their complementarity, are thus explained.

To complete the story, it remains to show how exactly WEIGHT-TO-STRESS governs syllable structure, and to generalize the analysis from diphthongs to long vowels.

Deriving the syllable structure of diphthongs and long vowels. The generalization that stressed noninitial diphthongs in Finnish have two moras and unstressed diphthongs have one mora in the stem phonology is a consequence of a constraint which prohibits unstressed bimoraic nuclei, a special case of WEIGHT-TO-STRESS.

(45) WEIGHT-TO-STRESS

$$*\mathrm{Nuc}_w \\ \wedge \\ \mu\ \mu$$

(where Nuc_w denotes an unstressed syllable nucleus)

The stem-level prohibition of unstressed two-mora nuclei is enforced for long vowels as well. However, there it is implemented in a different way. Whereas unstressed diphthongs are compressed into short nuclei, long vowels are *expanded into two syllables.*[18]

(46) The implementation of WEIGHT-TO-STRESS

a. Unstressed diphthongs Stressed diphthongs

b. Unstressed long vowels Stressed long vowels

Why are unstressed diphthongs accommodated to (45) by becoming monomoraic, whereas unstressed long vowels are accommodated to (45) by becoming disyllabic? Because the bimoraicity of long vowels is distinctive, being the defining property of length itself. A "monomoraic long vowel" is a contradiction in terms. Bimoraicity is not a defining property of diphthongs, however. In most languages diphthongs are redundantly bimoraic, and some languages have "monomoraic diphthongs", short vocalic nuclei affiliated with two melodies, e.g. English (Harris 1994:278), Icelandic (Árnason 1992), and Gere (Paradis 1997:532). Therefore, the constraint MAX-Vμ, which postulates that an input vocalic mora must be have an output correspondent, prevents long vowels and long diphthongs from shortening, but it does not

[18]The splitting of long vowels into two syllables under the compulsion of metrical constraints is familiar from Southern Paiute and other languages.

prevent regular diphthongs from being realized as monomoraic. This is the desired outcome.

In sum: in the stem-level syllabification of Finnish, all unstressed diphthongs are monomoraic, and all stressed diphthongs are bimoraic, in satisfaction of WEIGHT-TO-STRESS and STRESS-TO-WEIGHT. These constraints are however dominated by MAX-Vμ. The only way unstressed long vowels can satisfy WEIGHT-TO-STRESS without violating MAX-Vμ is by being split into two short syllables, even though this incurs an ONSET violation. Diphthongs, on the other hand, can be reconciled with the constraints simply by being assigned one mora rather than two.[19]

Thus, the structure of unstressed syllables is given by the three constraints in (47), where (47a,b) $\gg$ (47c).[20]

(47) a. WEIGHT-TO-STRESS
A heavy nucleus must be stressed.

b. MAX-Vμ
An input vocalic mora must be realized in the output.

c. ONSET
A syllable must have an onset.

Unstressed diphthongs, long vowels, and long diphthongs (the latter two specified as bimoraic in the input), are respectively syllabified as in (48).

[19]Note that the diphthongs we are concerned here are derived from a stem-final vowel plus the plural affix *-i-*. Diphthongs formed by stem-final vowels plus the past tense affix *-i-*, and underlying diphthongs, behave differently, as we will see below.

[20]The pairs of representations (a) and (b) (where α is a set of features defining a segment) are assumed to be indistinguishable (OCP):

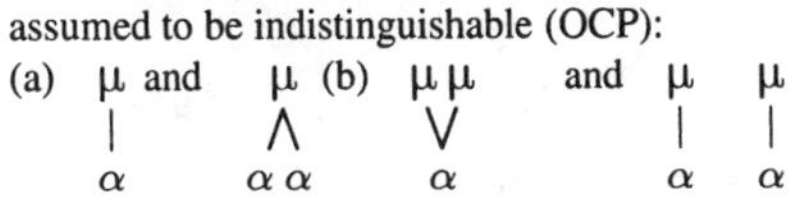

(48)

Diphthongs: /oi/	WT-TO-STR	MAX-Vμ	ONSET
a. ☞ 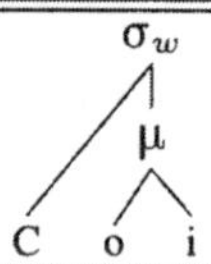			
b. 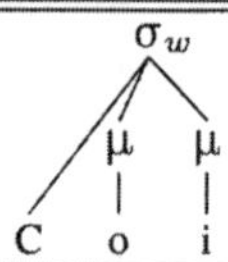	*		
c. 			*

Long vowels: /oo/	WT-TO-STR	MAX-Vμ	ONSET
a. 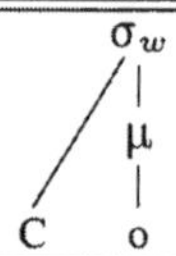		*	
b. 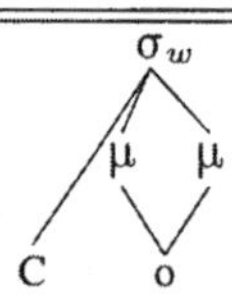	*		
c. ☞ 			*

Long diphthongs: /ooi/	WT-TO-STR	MAX-Vμ	ONSET
a. 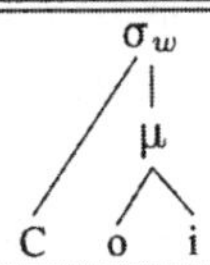		*	
b. 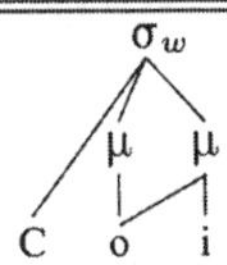	*		
c. ☞ 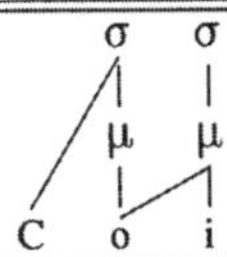			*

Consonant Gradation reformulated. The above result has another immediate payoff. It explains all seemingly arbitrary properties of Consonant Gradation. The opaque conditioning in (36) and (38), which brings about surface contrasts such as *palttoissa* vs. *taltoissa*, is due to the fact that Consonant Gradation is defined on the *stem-level* syllabification. In the stem-level syllabification, unstressed long diphthongs form separate short nuclei, and consequently do not trigger Consonant Gradation, even when followed by a syllable-closing consonant. For example, the cited examples are respectively syllabified as *palt.to.ois.sa* and *tal.tois.sa* at the stem level, so that the environment of Consonant Gradation is satisfied only in the latter.

In fact, we can now clean up the right context of Consonant Gradation and remove the arbitrary stipulations from it. Instead of the previous messy context (49a), we now have simply (49b).

(49) a. *Old formulation:* In the onset of a syllable whose rhyme ends in a consonant, except if it has a long vowel or a shortened diphthong, or which consists of a diphthong with lexical stress, and optionally in the onset of a syllable whose rhyme consists of a diphthong with rhythmic stress.
b. *New formulation:* In the onset of a heavy syllable.

Defined at the stem level, (49b) captures the exact conditions under which the process applies. It is no longer necessary to exclude long vowels from the triggering environment of Consonant Gradation, or to list the contexts in which diphthongs trigger it.

So simplified, Consonant Gradation (at least the degemination part of it) can be seen to be a special case of the quantititive dissimilation constraint *HH, which is proposed, and extensively motivated for Finnish, by Anttila

1997.

Stop Deletion reformulated. The context of Stop Deletion also becomes simpler and more natural. Instead of the messy formulation (50a) we can have (50b).

(50) a. *Old formulation:* Between an unstressed short vowel and a vowel, or between an unstressed underlying short diphthong and a vowel, and optionally between a short diphthong with rhythmic stress and a vowel.

b. *New formulation: (i)* Between a short unstressed vowel and a vowel. (Or even: *(ii)* Between short unstressed vowels.)

Further simplifications are probably possible. The reason the preceding vowel must be short is that onsetless syllables are excluded after long syllables in Finnish stems (as Anttila points out). For example, Stop Deletion applies in /puku-ta/ *pu.ku.a* but not in /puu-ta/ *puu.ta* (see (18)) because *pu.ku.a* conforms to the canonical shape of stems (e.g. *saippua* 'soap', *pors.tu.a* 'porch', while **puua* is not a possible stem.

3.5 Interim summary

The analysis in outline. The distinction between stem stress and word stress is essential to understanding Finnish morphophonology. Initial main stress and fixed secondary stress are always visible in the stem-level phonology, while rhythmic secondary stress is optionally visible in the stem phonology, and then only on heavy syllables, because of high-ranking STRESS-TO-WEIGHT. Optional rhythmic stress in the stem phonology results from movable ranking of LICENSE-σ. In addition to triggering the LH̀ effect, the constraints STRESS-TO-WEIGHT and WEIGHT-TO-STRESS cause unstressed diphthongs to be parsed as single Vs, and unstressed long vowels to be parsed as disyllables. In the word phonology, rhythmic stress is obligatory because *LAPSE dominates *STRESS.

Consonant Gradation *(pp, tt, kk → p, t, k,* and *p, t, k → v, d, ∅)* applies in the onset of a heavy syllable. E.g. /lakko+n/ → *la.kon*, /méllakkò-i-na/ → *mél.la.kòi.na* (*oi* is stressed, therefore bimoraic) but /lákko-i-na/ → *lákkoina* (*oi* is unstressed, therefore monomoraic by WEIGHT-TO-STRESS, so gradation fails).

Stop Deletion applies after a short unstressed nucleus. E.g. /lakko+ta/ → *lakkoa*. Prt.Pl. /méllakkò-i-ta/ → *mél.la.kòi.ta* (*oi* is stressed, so Stop Deletion fails) but /lákko-i-ta/ → *lakkoja* (*oi* is unstressed, and parsed into a single V slot, so Stop Deletion applies).

We derive the variability of Consonant Gradation and Stop Deletion from the optionality of secondary stress via syllable structure, and explain their complementarity by the fact that they require inconsistent syllable structures.

Functionally, lexical secondary stresses pattern with predictable word-initial primary stresses in being obligatorily visible in the stem phonology and morphology. Rhythmic secondary stress stands apart in being optionally visible in the stem-level phonology and morphology, due to the free ranking of *LAPSE and *STRESS.

Illustrative tableaux. (51) shows the invariant patterning of disyllabic words and of fixed polysyllabic stems, on the (convenient but nonessential) assumption that the latter have an underlying lexically marked stress. How the free ranking generates variation in movable polysyllables is seen in (52) and (53) (where the two freely ranked constraints are boldfaced). Keep in mind that (in observance of the constraints in (47), omitted from the tableaux), unstressed diphthongs are monomoraic and stressed diphthongs are bimoraic.

(51) Derivation of *lakkojen* 'strikes' (Gen.Pl.) and *almanakkojen* 'almanacs' (Gen.Pl.) under the ranking ***STRESS** ≫ ***LAPSE**:

Stem-Level		*CLASH	ALIGN-L	MAX-STRESS	UNI-PK	***STRESS**	***LAPSE**	CONSGRAD	STOPDEL	STR-TO-WT	MAX-SEG	ALL-FT-L	MAX-Cμ
Input: lakko-i-ten													
1a.	lák.kòi.den	*				**		*				1	
1b.	lá.kòi.den	*				**				*		1	*
1c.	lák.kò.jen	*				**					*	1	
1d.	lá.kò.jen	*				**				*	*	1	*
1e.	lák.koi.den					*			*				
1f.	lá.koi.den					*			*	*			*
1g. ☞	lák.ko.jen					*					*		
1h.	lá.ko.jen					*				*	*		*
Input: almanákka-i-ten													
2a.	ál.ma.nàk.koi.den					**			*			2	
2b.	ál.ma.nà.koi.den					**			*	*		2	*
2c. ☞	ál.ma.nàk.ko.jen					**					*	2	
2d.	ál.ma.nà.ko.jen					**				*	*	2	*
2e.	ál.ma.nàk.kòi.den	*				***		*				2,3	
2f.	ál.ma.nà.kòi.den	*				***				*		2,3	*
2g.	ál.ma.nàk.kò.jen	*				***				*	*	2,3	
2h.	ál.ma.nà.kò.jen	*				***				**	*	2,3	*
2i.	ál.ma.nak.koi.den			*		*	*	*	*				
2j.	ál.ma.na.koi.den			*		*	*	*	*				*
2k.	ál.ma.nak.ko.jen			*		*	*	*			*		
2l.	ál.ma.na.ko.jen			*		*	*	*			*		*
2m.	ál.ma.nak.kòi.den			*		**		*				3	
2n.	ál.ma.na.kòi.den			*		**						3	*
2o.	ál.ma.nak.kò.jen			*		**				*	*	3	
2p.	ál.ma.na.kò.jen			*		**				*	*	3	*
2q.	al.ma.nák.ko.jen		*			**					*	2	
2r.	ál.ma.nák.ko.jen				*	**					*	2	

In this case, the opposite ranking ***LAPSE** ≫ ***STRESS** would yield the same result. In other word types, the ranking of these constraints makes a difference, as the next tableaux show.

(52) Derivation of *mellakkojen* 'riots' (Gen.Pl.) and *Amerikkojen* 'Americas' (Gen.Pl.) under the ranking *STRESS ≫ *LAPSE:

Stem-level		*CLASH	ALIGN-L	MAX-STRESS	UNI-PK	*STRESS	*LAPSE	CONSGRAD	STOPDEL	STR-TO-WT	MAX-SEG	ALL-FT-L	MAX-Cμ
Input: mellakka-i-ten													
3a.	mél.lak.kòi.den					**		*				2	
3b.	mél.la.kòi.den					**						2	*
3c.	mél.lak.kò.jen					**				*	*	2	
3d.	mél.la.kò.jen					**				*	*	2	*
3e.	mél.lak.koi.den					*	*		*				
3f.	mél.la.koi.den					*	*		*				*
3g. ☞	mél.lak.ko.jen					*	*				*		
3h.	mél.la.ko.jen					*	*				*		*
Input: amerikka-i-ten													
4a.	á.me.rik.kòi.den					**		*		*		3	
4b.	á.me.ri.kòi.den					**				*		3	*
4c.	á.me.rìk.koi.den					**			*	*		2	
4d.	á.me.rì.koi.den					**			*	**		2	*
4e.	á.me.rìk.ko.jen					**				*	*	2	
4f.	á.me.rì.ko.jen					**				**	*	2	*
4g.	á.me.rik.kò.jen					**				**		3	
4h.	á.me.ri.kò.jen					**				**	*	3	*
4i.	á.me.rik.koi.den					*	*		*	*			
4j.	á.me.ri.koi.den					*	*		*	*			*
4k. ☞	á.me.rik.ko.jen					*	*			*	*		
4l.	á.me.ri.ko.jen					*	*			*	*		*

(53) Derivation of *mellakoiden* 'riots' (Gen.Pl.) and *Amerikoiden* 'Americas' (Gen.Pl.) under the ranking ***LAPSE** ≫ ***STRESS**:

Stem-level		*CLASH	ALIGN-L	MAX-STRESS	UNI-PK	***LAPSE**	***STRESS**	CONSGRAD	STOPDEL	STR-TO-WT	MAX-SEG	ALL-FT-L	MAX-Cμ
Input: mellakka-i-ten													
3a.	mél.lak.kòi.den						**	*				2	
3b. ☞	mél.la.kòi.den						**					2	*
3c.	mél.lak.kò.jen						**			*	*	2	
3d.	mél.la.kò.jen						**			*	*	2	*
3e.	mél.lak.koi.den					*	*		*				
3f.	mél.la.koi.den					*	*		*				*
3g.	mél.lak.ko.jen					*	*				*		
3h.	mél.la.ko.jen					*	*				*		*
Input: amerikka-i-ten													
4a.	á.me.rik.kòi.den						**	*		*		3	
4b. ☞	á.me.ri.kòi.den						**			*		3	*
4c.	á.me.rìk.koi.den						**		*	*		2	
4d.	á.me.rì.koi.den						**		*	**		2	*
4e.	á.me.rìk.ko.jen						**			*	*	2	
4f.	á.me.rì.ko.jen						**			**	*	2	*
4g.	á.me.rik.kò.jen						**			**		3	
4h.	á.me.ri.kò.jen						**			**	*	3	*
4i.	á.me.rik.koi.den					*	*		*	**			
4j.	á.me.ri.koi.den					*	*		*	*			*
4k.	á.me.rik.ko.jen					*	*			*	*		
4l.	á.me.ri.ko.jen					*	*			*	*		*

Conclusion. The upshot is that the core alternations seen in Finnish inflection are governed by phonological constraints relating to stress and syllable structure. The data already show clearly that they are located specifically in the stem phonology, but in the next section I add two pieces of evidence that should remove any lingering doubt on this score. The first is that stem-level secondary stress conditions what is unquestionably an allomorphic alternation. The second is that it is sensitive to the morphological composition of the affected diphthong.

3.6 Morphological and lexical evidence

Stress-conditioned illative allomorphy. The illative case ending displays a distribution of allomorphs which independently confirms the above analysis of stress. There are two basic forms, the short form (the elsewhere allomorph), and the long form. The short form is /-hVn/, with a variant /-Vn/ due to phonological deletion of *h* after unstressed simple vowels. Chameleon-like, the short form's V always matches the color of the preceding vowel. The long form is /-sVVn/, where V matches a preceding /i/, else is /e/. This distribution is illustrated by the Illative Singular forms in (54).

(54) Short form of the Illative: *-hVn*, *-Vn*

a. *maa-han* 'land', *puu-hun* 'tree', *tee-hen* 'tea', *tie-hen* 'road', *hai-hin* 'shark'
b. *mi-hin* 'into what', *tä-hän* 'into this'
c. *sama-an* 'same', *latu-un* 'ski trail', *talo-on* 'house', *salama-an* 'lightning', *ullakko-on* 'attic', *Amerikka-an* 'America'

The long form of the illative appears after "contracted stems", that is, stems whose output form ends in a long unstressed vowel, which as shown in 3.4 is a disyllabic sequence in the stem-level phonology. It has two morphologically conditioned allomorphs, /-seen/ in the singular and /-siin/ in the plural.

(55) Long form of the Illative: *-seen*, *-siin*

a. Sg. /-VV-seen/: *vapaaseen* 'free', *terveeseen* 'healthy', *palttooseen* 'overcoat'
b. Pl. /-VV-i-siin/: *vapaisiin* 'free', *terveisiin* 'healthy', *palttoisiin* 'overcoats'

In view of the stem-level disyllabicity of unstressed vowels, we can say that the long form is selected after two syllables which are affiliated with the same vowel melody, and the short form is selected elsewhere. Considering the fact that the short form's vowel is obligatorily affiliated with the stem's vowel melody, the basis of this distribution seems to be a constraint which prohibits the configuration

(56)

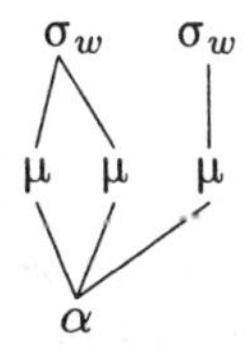

where α is a feature complex defining a vowel. Whatever the formulation, the descriptive generalization is in any case not in doubt. It is independently motivated by the allomorphy of the third person possessive suffix. The suffix has two allomorphs, *-nsa* and *-(h)Vn*. In the latter, just as in the short form of the illative, *h* is deleted except after primary stress, and *V* is a copy of the preceding vowel. The form *-nsa* occurs in all contexts, and *-(h)Vn* occurs as an optional variant after case endings ending in vowels, e.g. *talo-ssa-nsa* ~ *talo-ssa-an* 'in his/her/their house' (but not after bare stems, e.g. *kissa-nsa, *kissa-an* 'his/her/their cat'). The point of interest is that, just like the *-(h)Vn* allomorph of the illative, the *-(h)Vn* allomorph of the 3.Sg. possessive also does not appear after an unstressed long vowel (even if the second mora of the long vowel is a case ending). For example, the 3.Sg. possessive form of /tupa-ta/ *tupaa* can only be *tupaansa*, not **tupaahan* or **tupaaan*. This is another instantiation of the constraint (56).

Moreover, the distribution of the long and short forms of the illative is sensitive to a stylistic vowel contraction process, exemplified by the free variants in (57a) (Anttila 1999). As (57b) shows, case allomorphy obligatorily depends on the stem's output form.

(57) a. *kor.ke.a* (three syllables) ~ *kor.kee* (two syllables) 'high', *le.ve.ä* ~ *le.vee* 'broad' (Nom.Sg.)
b. *kor.ke.a-an* ~ *kor.kee.-seen* 'high', *le.ve.ä-än* ~ *le.vee.-seen* 'broad' (Ill.Sg.)

The Illative Plural. After diphthongs formed by the combination of stem-final vowels with plural *-i*, the distribution of *-hin* and *-siin* is reveals the effect of optional rhythmic stress in the stem phonology. After stressed diphthongs and after short unstressed diphthongs, the form *-hin* is obligatory (see (58a,b)). But after long diphthongs, /-siin/ and /-hin/ are both possible (see (58c)).

(58) Illative plurals:
a. /CVV-i-/: /puu-i-hin/ *puihin* 'trees', /tie-i-hin/ *teihin* 'roads', /tee-i-hin/ *teihin* 'teas', /hai-i-hin/ *haihin* 'sharks'
b. /-CV-i-/: /tapa-i-hin/ *tapoihin* 'customs', similarly *latuihin* 'ski trails', *taloihin* 'houses', *korjaamoihin* 'repair shops'
c. /-VV-i-/: /vapaa-i-hin/ ~ /vapaa-i-siin/ *vapaihin* ~ *vapaisiin* 'free', similarly *terveihin* ~ *terveisiin* 'healthy', *palttoihin* ~ *palttoisiin* 'overcoats' (contracted -VV stems)

The pattern in (58) is exactly what is predicted by our proposal about secondary stress. Consider *vapaaseen* and its plural variants *vapaihin* ~ *vapaisiin*. Underlying /vapaa/ receives initial stress; /-paa/ cannot be a stressed syllable because of *CLASH, and it cannot be an unstressed syllable because of WEIGHT-TO-STRESS. So it must be two syllables, both of them unstressed by STRESS-TO-WEIGHT (see (46)), the former also by *CLASH. Thus the output of the stem phonology is *vá.pa.a*. This is an instance of the context that requires the long illative /-sVVn/. The respective nominative and illative singular forms surface in the word phonology as *vá.paa*, *vá.paa.seen*.

In the plural, the affix /-i/ combines with the third syllable of the stem *vá.pa.a-* into a diphthong *-ai-*, which according to the constraint system developed above receives optional secondary stress in the stem phonology. the resulting plural stem is either *vá.pa.ai-* (CV́.CV.V-, a context requiring the long illative) or *vá.pa.ài-* (CV́.CV.V̀V-, a context requiring the short illative). The respective illative plural output forms are *vá.pai.siin* and *vá.pai.hin*.

The data in (59) epitomize the illative pattern discussed in the preceding paragraphs with the Illatives of *vapaa* 'free', *raitis* 'sober', and *maa* 'land'.

(59)	Illative Singular		Illative Plural	
a.	**vapaahan*	*vapaaseen*	*vapaihin*	*vapaisiin*
b.	**raittiihin*	*raittiiseen*	*raittiihin*	*raittiisiin*
a.	*maahan*	**maaseen*	*maihin*	**maisiin*

Inherently heavy nuclei. Certain stems ending in unstressed long vowels or diphthongs, mostly non-native, behave like stems ending in stressed long vowels or diphthongs. The data in (60) demonstrate their behavior with respect to illative allomorphy. The stems *rokokoo* 'rococo', *revyy* 'revue', and *blinii* 'pancake' in (60a,b,c)) show this pattern obligatorily, and the stems *kamee* 'cameo', *veesee* 'toilet', and *suklaa* 'chocolate' in in (60d,e,f) show it optionally.

(60)	Illative Singular		Illative Plural	
a.	*rokokoohon*	**rokokooseen*	*rokokoihin*	**rokokoisiin*
b.	*revyyhyn*	**revyyseen*	*revyihin*	**revyisiin*
c.	*bliniihin*	**bliniiseen*	*bliniihin*	**bliniisiin*
d.	*kameehen*	*kameeseen*	*kameihin*	*kameisiin*
e.	*veeseehen*	*veeseeseen*	*veeseihin*	*veeseisiin*
f.	*suklaahan*	*suklaaseen*	*suklaihin*	*suklaisiin*

The stems *Tokoi* (name), *Petroskoi* 'Petrozavodsk', *samurai* 'samurai', *lauantai* 'Saturday', and *maumau* 'maumau' in (61) show that stem-final underlying diphthongs behave consistently like heavy syllables.

(61)	Partitive Singular		Genitive Plural	
a.	*Tokoita*	**Tokoja*	*Tokoiden*	**Tokojen*
b.	*Petroskoita*	**Petroskoja*	*Petroskoiden*	**Petroskojen*
c.	*samuraita*	**samuraja*	*samuraiden*	**samurajen*
d.	*lauantaita*	**lauantaja*	*lauantaiden*	**lauantajen*
e	*maumauta*	**maumaua*	**maumauiden*	**maumaujen*[21]

[21]For phonological reasons, stems that end in a -Vu diphthong, such as (61e), have no plural forms at all. This is the case even if the diphthong is stressed; for example, there is no such form as **tiuissa* for the Inessive Plural of *tiu* 'a collection of 20'.

Such word-final long vowels and diphthongs must be lexically marked as bimoraic, either directly, or indirectly by a lexical stress.[22]

Invariant short diphthongs. In verb inflection, diphthongs always count as short nuclei, triggering Consonant Gradation only when the syllable is closed by a consonant.

(62)	a. /suuttu-i-mme/	*suutuimme*	'we got angry'
	b. /suuttu-i-vat/	*suuttuivat*	'(they) got angry'
	c. /katu-i-mme/	*kaduimme*	'we repented'
	d. /katu-i-vat/	*katuivat*	'(they) repented'
	e. /ase-ttu-i-mme/	*asetuimme*	'we placed ourselves'
	f. /ase-ttu-i-vat/	*asettuivat*	'(they) placed themselves'
	g. /rankaise-ta/	*rangaista*	'to punish'
	h. /rankaise-vat/	*rankaisevat*	'(they) punish'

The past tense ending *-i* thus differs from the homonymous plural ending in being obligatorily nonmoraic.

4 Variation: trends and preferences

4.1 The trend to word-level rhythmic stress

One of the most remarkable aspects of the variation in Finnish noun inflection is the fine-grained pattern of preferences among the options, first explored by Itkonen 1957, and analyzed in greater depth in OT terms on the basis of massive corpus data by Anttila 1997. The preferences depend on several factors, including the height of the stem-final vowel, the place of articulation of the preceding consonant, and, most of all, the penult's weight. These preferences interact with a global trend that cuts across all categories, which disfavors stem-level assignment of rhythmic stress. That is, the "conflation" system is gaining ground in the stem phonology.

The shift away from stem-level rhythmic stress is manifest in a historical drift of the preferences among the variant plurals. In Standard Finnish usage, this drift has been uniform at least over the last century or so (Itkonen 1957, Paunonen 1974a, 1974b).

---

[22]Positing a lexical stress on a disyllable such as *Tokoi* (a surname) would of course require the ranking MAXSTRESS ≫ *CLASH in the stem-level constraint system. This ranking would also allow a straightforward treatment of a strange group of loanwords which have primary stress on the second syllable in the donor language (usually Swedish) and behave as though they had a latent lexical accent on the that syllable. This is shown (among other things) in that they occasionally initiate a harmonic domain in the second syllable (see p. 114 for the relation of harmony and lexical stress). For example, in addition to the expected Prt.Pl. *kónfliktèja* 'conflicts', the SK corpus also attests *?kónfliktèjä*.

(63)

		Innovating type	Older type	
a.	Prt.Pl.	*kórjaamòja*	*kórjaamòita*	'repair shops'
b.	Gen.Pl.	*kórjaamòjen*	*kórjaamòiden*	'repair shops'
c.	Ess.Pl.	*méllakkòina*	*méllakòina*	'riots'
d.	Short Ill.Pl.	*méllakkòihin*	*méllakòihin*	'riots'
e.	Long Ill.Pl.	*vápaisiin*	*vápaihin*	'free'

The innovating forms are those that, according to the analysis proposed here, are derived when rhythmic stress is deferred to the word phonology. Thus, the unifying theme behind (63a-e) is that the ranking *STRESS ≫ *LAPSE is gaining ground at the stem level. As rhythmic stress gradually becomes a purely word-level phenomenon, it ceases to interact with morphophonology and allomorphy. My interpretation of the change differs fom the traditional view, according to which the drift in (63) is heterogeneous. That view holds that (63a-d) originate in interparadigmatic analogy which transfers the inflection of disyllabic stems to polysyllabic stems (e.g. Prt.Pl. *méllakkòja* on the analogy of Prt.Pl. *lákkoja*), whereas (63e) originates in *intraparadigmatic* analogy which transfers the singular inflection to the plural (e.g. Ill.Pl. *vá.pai.siin* on the analogy of Ill.Sg. *vá.paa.seen*). Our analysis provides a welcome unification of these changes as effects of the loss of stem-level rhythmic stress. If our interpretation of the historical change is correct, it adds a measure of support for the synchronic analysis, and with it for stratal OT.

The next question is *why* the changes go in this direction, and not in the other. An answer will be proposed in section 5.

4.2 The preference for alternating weight

(63) is about a trend, not about a preference. Although many instances of the expanding types in (63) are more frequent than their recessive counterparts in the modern language, by no means all of them are. But all of them have been steadily gaining favor in modern literary usage. The actual frequencies of particular instances of the expanding and receding types in discourse varies widely depending on the other factors. One of these factors is the weight of the second syllable, just as in the longer words we discussed earlier in section 2.2.

In trisyllabic stems, when the penult is light, the diphthong formed by the stem-final vowel with plural *i* is usually treated as bimoraic, i.e. as bearing a stem-level stress according to our analysis.[23] That is, it represents the option

[23]When the onset of the third syllable is a single consonant, it is usually a sonorant, as the examples in (64a) show. This has to do with Finnish morpheme structure (a reflex of the process we are referring to as Stop Deletion, in fact). The rare stems with obstruents in this position, represented by *judoka* 'judoka' in the sample, pattern the same way in their inflection. A native word of this type would be *heteka* 'a type of bed with a frame of tubular steel' would also have the preferred partitive plural *hetekoita* rather than ?*hetekoja*.

whereby rhythmic stress may be assigned at the stem level. In (64a) I substantiate this claim with a list of the partitive plurals of such stems that I was able to extract from the *Suomen Kuvalehti* corpus (fn. 5). The incidence of Stop Deletion shows whether stress is assigned.

(64) XLL trisyllabic stems:

a. Stem-level rhythmic stress (bimoraic syllabification, no Stop Deletion):
akanoita ansioita anturoita apinoita asioita askeleita astioita aukioita avaroita bageleita brokereita dealereita dekkareita demareita dollareita duunareita enkeleitä förareita faveloita fictioneita funktioita gangstereita hamstereita henkseleitä heteroita himmeleitä hokkareita hummereita huviloita ideoita ikkunoita jääkäreitä jännäreitä judokoita julmureita jumppareita kaapeleita kaappareita kaloreita kameleita kappeleita kapseleita kavereita keisareita kiikareita kikujuita kiskureita kondareita konkareita konttoreita kortteleita lääkäreitä makkaroita manteleita markkinoita meisseleitä mestareita mongoleita moottoreita muskeleita muusikoita neekereitä olioita oscareita palsameita panssareita papereita penikoita pettureita pilareita pillereitä porkkanoita porvareita puhveleita ryaneita sektoreita sipuleita tarinoita titteleitä tohveleita tovereita voimaloita

b. Word-level rhythmic stress (monomoraic syllabification, Stop Deletion):
aplodeja arabeja arkadeja atomeja diplomeja dylaneja fasadeja gallupeja graffiteja idoleja kondomeja metodeja muslimeja neuroneja preludeja tamileja

c. Variation:
arveluita∼arveluja kollegoja∼kollegoita mitaleja∼mitaleita palveluita∼palveluja sopuleja∼sopuleita symboleja∼symboleita

The preference for the weak stem is actually even stronger than it appears, for in many of the words in (64c) and in a few of the words in (64b) the light penult may be only apparent. They are often pronounced with long vowels, and used to be so spelled (and still sometimes are, though this is considered incorrect now).[24] So pronounced, these words really belong in the XHL stems in (65.) Nevertheless, the monomoraic treatment is always a live option for XLL stems, and in a few subtypes perhaps even preferred (for example,

[24]Examples of such variant pronunciations and spellings of the words in (64b,c) are e.g. *aploodeja, arkaadeja, diploomeja, idooleja, kolleegoja, metoodeja, neurooneja, symbooleja.* Also, a word like *gallupeja* 'gallups' (Prt.Pl.) would typically be pronounced with a geminate [pp].

palveluja 'services' seems to be at least as good as *palveluita*).

In stems with an underlying *heavy* penult, however, the monomoraic forms are regularly preferred. For example, a form like *arkistoja* 'archives' is preferred to *arkistoita*, and *kranaatteja* 'grenades' is strongly preferred to *kranaateita*. The following data comes from the same corpus as before.

(65) XHL trisyllabic stems:

a. Stem-Level rhythmic stress (bimoraic syllabification, no Stop Deletion):
armeijoita maneereita mysteereitä turbiineita

b. Word-Level rhythmic stress (monomoraic syllabification, Stop Deletion):
abortteja abstrakteja absurdeja adresseja agentteja aktiiveja akuutteja arkistoja artisteja aspekteja asuntoja atleetteja aurinkoja banaaneja barrancoja brosyyrejä bulvaaneja desantteja duelleja efektejä eksakteja esansseja experttejä fasisteja fossiileja futuureja galakseja haupitseja hotelleja humaaneja immuuneja infarkteja instansseja intiaaneja jonglöörejä jumperseja juristeja kanaaleja kanootteja kapriiseja kapteeneja katiskoja kaupunkeja kemistejä keraameja kersantteja kirjastoja kirurgeja kolumneja kommentteja kompasseja komplekseja konfliktejä konflikteja kongresseja konsertteja konsultteja kontakteja korrekteja kranaatteja kristalleja kritiikkejä kuponkeja meriittejä normaaleja paraateja pistooleja poliiseja reliikkejä reliktejä reseptejä sellistejä spontaaneja tekniikoita triviaaleja tulppaaneja urbaaneja vahinkoja vokaaleja

c. Variation:
bakteereja∼bakteereita hehtaareja∼hehtaareita kenraaleja∼ kenraaleita kulttuureja∼ kulttuureita kiväärejä∼kivääreitä kokeiluita∼kokeiluja kriteerejä∼kriteereitä romaaneja∼romaaneita signaaleja ∼signaaleita upseereja∼upseereita

The preference for monomoraic treatment after heavy penults, reflecting the absence of rhythmic stress in the stem phonology, is quite strong. Yet the disfavored variants, again, are unquestionably grammatical.

This usage profile reveals a preference for *weight dissimilation*: two successive light syllables and two successive heavy syllables are avoided, and a light-heavy and heavy-light alternation is preferred. For example, compare the words *logiikka* 'logic' and *heteka* 'a type of bed'. In the partitive plural, *logiikkoja* (-HL-) is favored over *logiikoita* (-HH-), and *hetekoita* (-LH-) is favored over *hetekoja* (-LL-). Anttila 1997 provides an OT analysis of these effects using constraints that impose alternating weight on adjacent syllables (*HH, *LL). I adopt this idea provisionally here, although it may need to be reformulated as a direct weight-stress relation in the light of the patterning of the lexical stress in longer words (section 2.2).

4.3 The preference for word-level rhythmic stress

The data in (64) and (65) show that adjacent syllables preferably have alternating weight (weight dissimilation). The data summarized in (63) suggests a historical trend towards word-level rhythmic stress. To test whether this trend also corresponds to a synchronic preference, we can isolate cases where weight dissimilation is not at stake.

The test cases we need are those where the diphthong is preceded by a geminate stop. The bimoraic treatment resulting from stem-level assignment of rhythmic stress entails Consonant Gradation, with an output that satisfies the weight alternation just as well as the monomoraic treatment resulting from word-level assignment of rhythmic stress. Consider the word *loogikko* 'logician'. In the partitive plural, the choice is between *loogikkoja* (-HL-, monomoraic) and *loogikoita* (-LH-, bimoraic), with an equally favored quantitative pattern. Similarly in the genitive plural, e.g. *mellakkojen* and *mellakoiden* 'riots'. Here, where the preference for weight alternation is neutralized, other preferences should decide the issue. If avoidance of stem-level rhythmic stress is a preference, it should manifest itself here. The expectation is that the bimoraic type *loogikoita* should be disfavored, and the monomoraic type *loogikkoja*, with rhythmic stress deferred to the word level, should be preferred. The corpus data show that this is the case. The frequency profile of the trisyllabic stems in /-kkV, -ttV/ shown in (66) is similar to that of (65), not to that of (64), although, as expected, the trend is not quite so strong.

(66) a. *allakoita dirikoita graafikoita penikoita teknikoita*
b. *aavikkoja ammatteja budjetteja ennakkoja hamletteja harvikkoja kadetteja kajakkeja kasetteja kasvatteja kulakkeja lemmikkejä otsikkoja paketteja poletteja taktikkoja whipettejä*
c. *fyysikkoja~fyysikoita klassikkoja~klassikoita muusikoita~muusikkoja*

Forms in /-ppV/, though accidentally missing in the corpus, conform to the generalization. For example, *sinappeja* 'mustards', *anoppeja* 'mothers-in-law' are preferred to *sinapeita, anopeita.* These findings are summarized in (67), where the preferred variants are boldfaced.

(67)	a.	/paperi/	***pá.pe.rèi.ta*** (-LH-)	*pá.pe.rè.ja* (-LL-)	'paper'
	b.	/raketti/	*rá.ke.tèi.ta* (-LH-)	***rá.ket.tè.ja*** (-HL-)	'rocket'
	c.	/trapetsi/	?**trá.pet.sèi.ta* (-HH-)	***trá.pet.sè.ja*** (-HL-)	'trapeze'

The variation is generated by the subsystem of constraints that includes (at least) Anttila's *HH and *LL (weight dissimilation), *STRESS (conflation), and *LAPSE. The ranking shown below is one which generates the favored variants in (67).

(68)

Stem Level	*HH	*LL	*LAPSE	*STRESS
Input: /paperi-i-ta/				
1a. ☞ pá.pe.rèi.ta		*		*
1b. pá.pe.re.ja		**	*	
Input: /raketti-i-ta/				
2a. rá.ke.tèi.ta		*		*
2b. ☞ rá.ket.te.ja		*	*	
Input: /trapetsi-i-ta/				
3a. trá.pet.sèi.ta	*			*
3b. ☞ trá.pet.se.ja		*	*	

Other rankings deliver the rest of the options, in proportion to their observed frequency of occurrence. We know already from (51)–(53) that the ranking of *STRESS and *LAPSE is free. The desired profile of variation emerges on the assumption that *all* the rankings are free, excepting only that *HH dominates *LL. This leaves 12 constraint rankings out of the possible total of 24. A third of them favor *papereja*, half of them favor *raketteja*, and three quarters favor *trapetseja*. Namely:

- *papereja* is the optimal output if *STRESS ≫ *LL and *LAPSE (four rankings)
- *raketteja* is the optimal output if *STRESS ≫ *LAPSE (six rankings)
- *trapetseja* is the optimal output if *STRESS or *HH ≫ *LAPSE (nine rankings).

Assuming all rankings are equiprobable, this corresponds to the observed relative frequency of the three types, in line with Anttila's theory of variation.

Note that in the stratal OT model, as in parallel OT, the pattern in (66) cannot simply be assimilated to the pattern in (65) on the basis of its *underlying* geminate (cf. Anttila 1997:18, fn. 9). Once a stem suffixed with plural *-i* undergoes Consonant Gradation, the underlying geminate is no longer visible when secondary stress is assigned on subsequent cycles, and cannot be recovered.

Conclusion: the opacity of stress-conditioned processes. Because the two kinds of secondary stress, lexical and rhythmic, differ so radically in their phonological and morphological effects, opacity is rampant in Finnish phonology. Movable polysyllables, though lacking lexical stress, do bear an obligatory secondary stress phonetically: as detailed above, all words of more than three syllables in Finnish have, in addition to their initial primary stress, a secondary stress on their third syllable (or, by the LH̀ effect, on their fourth if it is heavy and the third is light).[25] In the output, the rhythmic secondary stresses motivated by *LAPSE are not audibly different from the lexical secondary stresses.[26] Moreover, both kinds of secondary stresses, rhythmic and lexical, count in metrical verse. The following pentameter line contains an example of a rhythmic secondary stress in metrical strong position:

s s s s s
(69) himmein ruusuin, enkelien siivin 'with translucent roses, on angels' wings'
(Saima Harmaja, *Tähti*)

The third syllable of *én.ke.lì.en* 'angels' (Gen.Pl.) is lexically unstressed. Being unstressed, it reduces to *-i-* (see below), and triggers Stop Deletion in the following ending /-ten/. (The option of assigning stress st the stem level gives the variant *én.ke.lèi.den.*) Nevertheless, it occupies a strong position in the cited verse, and such positions are reserved for stressed syllables in Finnish (Kiparsky and Hanson 1996). This an important datum because Finnish versification is, in general, a highly reliable indicator of stress.

5 The stem constraint

Now let's return to the question why the options reflecting the monomoraic treatment of diphthongs are spreading historically. I propose that this is because they comply with a general constraint that stems must end in -V, which I call the STEM CONSTRAINT.

Finnish *words* can end either in a vowel, or in a coronal consonant:

(70) *avaime-n* 'of the key', *avaime-t* 'the keys', *alas* 'down', *kuin* 'as, like', *mars!* 'go!'.

Stems, however, must end in a vowel at the point of affixation. Before an affix (including the zero case affix), stem-final *-e* is deleted subject to metrical and syllabic constraints. To a first approximation, the descriptive generalization is that *-e* is deleted when the stem is polysyllabic and the preceding consonants form a permissible coda, or can be reduced to one (Keyser & Kiparsky 1984). These restrictions are seen in (71b).[27]

(71) a. /olute-ta/ *olutta* 'beer', /hampase-ta/ *hammasta* 'tooth', /avaime-ta/ *avainta* 'key' (Prt.Sg.), /tuhante/ *tuhat* '1000', /varikse/ *varis* 'crow' (Nom.Sg.).

[25] With the proviso that in final position, light syllables cannot be stressed at all, and the stress on heavy syllables is optional, as mentioned above.

[26] At least to my ear. Experimental work on this question would be welcome.

[27] Any vowel is however subject to deletion in word-internal hiatus: /rinta-ukse/ *rinnus* 'lapel', /korkea-uinen/ *korkuinen* 'high', /isä-uute/ *isyys* 'fatherhood'. Word-finally, /-e/ is raised to *-i*.

b. /siipe-tä/ *siipeä* 'wing', /suve-ta/ *suvea* 'summer', /kive/ *kivi* 'stone', /sorme/ *sormi* 'finger' (*e*-deletion would produce impossible clusters), /vete-tä/ *vettä* 'water' (Prt.Sg.), but /vete/ *vesi* 'water' (**vet* is prosodically subminimal), /ikkuna-ta/ *ikkunaa* 'window' (Prt. Sg.), *leikkisä* 'playful' (Nom.Sg.) (only *-e* is freely deleted).

I assume that Strict Layering forces recursive prosodic integration of stem-level affixes:

(72) $[\,[\,X\,]_\alpha\ \mathrm{Af}\,]_\alpha \rightarrow [\,X + \mathrm{Af}\,]_\alpha$

For example, affixing /-ta/ to the stem $[\text{avaime}]_\alpha$ yields a new stem, which can undergo *-e* deletion without violating the Stem Constraint, e.g. $[\text{avainta}]_\alpha$.

Function words (non-inflected words in general) can end in -C, but if they are monosyllabic they must be heavy in deference to prosodic minimality:[28]

(73) /joss/ *jos* 'if', *taas* 'again', /kunn/ *kun* 'when', *vain* 'only', /nytt/ *nyt* 'now'

Casual (and poetic) speech allows apocope of other vowels, especially in suffixes. This process too respects the coda constraints just mentioned; contrast (74a) and (74b):[29]

(74) a. *olisi* → *olis, ois* 'would be', *parissa* → *paris* 'in the company of', *sulta* → *sult* 'from you', *onkos* → *onks* 'is?'
b. *onko* ↛ **onk* 'is?', *oliko* ↛ **olik* 'was?', *olipa* ↛ **olip* 'was!'

Borrowed words adopt to the Stem Constraint by epenthesis. Interestingly, the epenthetic vowel is usually *-i*, not the deleting vowel *-e* which might have been expected to be the most unmarked element of the language.

(75) Swedish *proféssor* > *professori*, *biff* > *pihvi* 'steak', *rom* [romm] > *rommi* 'rum', *kurs* [kOrss] > *kurssi* 'course', Russian *car'* > *tsaari* 'czar', *kon'* > *koni* 'nag', English *gin* > *gini* [tsini], *broiler* > *broileri* 'small chicken', *club* > *klubi*.

The data in (76) show that epenthesis is driven by the productive *stem-level* constraint that stems must end in -V. They demonstrate in particular that epenthesis takes place even in the same phonological contexts where -V is subject to deletion at the word level in casual speech.[30]

---

[28]The underlying geminate is audible before a following vowel within the same phonological phrase, as in [joss-on] 'if is', [kunn-ei] 'when not', [nytt-on] 'now is'.

[29]I owe this observation to Daniel Karvonen.

[30]Short words like *gini* always get epenthetic *i*, obviously for the sake of satisfying prosodic minimality. In longer words, epenthesis seems to occur after CVVC- and CVVC- syllables, whose weight reflects Swedish stress. E.g. *karuselli* (Swedish [karuśell]), *pistooli* (Swedish [pistu:l]), but e.g. *bisnes, tennis*, Heinonen 1994, Anttila, p.c.

(76) a. Swedish *polis* > *poliisi*, but (casual speech) *olisi* → *olis* 'were'
b. *Paris* > *Pariisi*, but (casual speech) *parissa* → *paris* 'in the company of'

This is straightforwardly understandable as the activation of stem-level and word-level constraints with contradictory import in the overlapping domain. It is, however, incomprehensible on the view that the word is the minimal unit to which phonological constraints apply.

Allomorphy. Finnish assimilates loans to conform to the Stem Constraint by inserting a stem-final *-i* before overt case endings.

(77) a. Nom.Sg. *nailon* 'nylon' (or *nailoni*)
b. Gen.Sg. *nailoni-n*, Iness.Sg. *nailoni-ssa*, Prt.Sg. *nailoni-a (*nailon-ta*, contrast *laidun-ta)*

Since there is no general *i*-epenthesis or *i*-deletion process in Finnish, the alternation in (77) is perhaps best treated as allomorphy between an uninflectable -C stem which preserves the donor language's word form, and an inflectable -V stem which is adapted so as to conform to the Stem Constraint.

These data refute the "naive" theory that loanword adaptation is just a response to the borrowing language's word phonology. They show that (in inflected languages at least) constraints on stem phonology can also play a role.

The padding strategy. Another fact confirms this understanding of loanword adaptation. Intervocalic /s/ is subject to deletion between unstressed vowels in Finnish (cf. the *t*-Deletion process presented in 4), e.g. Gen.Sg. /kirvese-n/ *kirveen* 'axe' (cf. Nom.Sg. /kirvese/ *kirves*). In order to to satisfy the constraint that stems must end in vowels, while at the same time defeating *s*-deletion, loans in *-s* are usually borrowed with underlying /-kse/. This maintains the *s* throughout the declension while yet assimilating the lexeme to a regular inflectional pattern of the language.

(78) *kaktus* > /kaktukse/ Nom. *kaktus*, Gen. *kaktukse-n.*

If loanwords were simply modified in the minimal possible way to conform to the output shapes of Finnish words, the appearance of this /k/ would be inexplicable. One would expect something like Nom.Sg. *kaktus*, Gen.Sg. **kaktuun*, **kaktusen*, or **kaktusin*.

Thus the language goes to ingenious lengths to bring loans into line with the canonical requirements on stems without making their surface shapes too different from the foreign model. In view of these facts, there can be no question of a theory of loanword adaptation framed purely in terms of constraints on words per se. The properties of stems cannot be derived from properties of words but require a stem level subject to its own constraints.

The role of the Stem Constraint in Finnish morphophonology. The Stem Constraint, which requires stems to end in a vowel, plays an active role in the lexical phonology and morphology of Finnish. All stem-level suffixes, including case endings and the possessive suffixes in (79), require a vowel before them.

(79)

	Sg.	Pl.
1.	-ni	-mme
2.	-si	-nne
3.	-nsa, -Vn	

The possessive suffixes are attached to stems and make words. For example, in $[[\text{vete}]_\alpha\ \text{mme}]_\omega$ *vete-mme* 'our water', the stem $[\text{vete}]_\alpha$ must obey the Stem Constraint and fails to undergo word-final *-e* to *-i* raising (**ves-imme*). And since $[[\text{vete}]_\alpha\ \text{mme}]_\omega$ is a word, it does not undergo stem-level Consonant Gradation, which would give **vedemme.*[31] Note that this provides independent confirmation that case endings are stem-to-stem suffixes.

Since Finnish case endings can end both in vowels and in consonants, this is where push comes to shove. What happens when a possessive suffix is put after an inflected noun ending in -C? The violation of the Stem Constraint is avoided by a combination of three different methods, a CONSPIRACY.

(80)
a. *Phonological deletion.* Syllabic case endings (-CVC, -CVVC) lose their last consonant before possessive suffixes: (Ill. /-seen/ → *-see*, /-siin/ → *-sii*, /-hVn/ → *-hV*, Gen.Pl. /-t-ten/ → *-tte*, /-ten/) → *-de*.
b. *Morphological omission of the ending.* Structural case endings consisting of a consonant, namely Gen/Acc.Sg. /-n/ and Nom./-Acc.Pl. /-t/, are omitted before possessive suffixes. Instead, the possessive suffixes are added to the bare stem.
c. *Paradigmatic gap.* Lexical case endings consisting of a consonant, namely Instr. /-n/, simply take no possessive suffixes.

Phonological deletion. The first method is deletion of the final consonant of syllabic case endings before possessive suffixes. It is is illustrated in (81) with forms containing the illative ending *-seen* (sg.) and *-siin, hVn* (pl.) and the genitive plural ending *-den, -en, -tten* (underlying /ten/, /t-ten/).

[31] The assumption that Consonant Gradation applies at the stem level stem-level is justified by the fact that it is not fed by the word-level deletion process mentioned in (76), as in *oppisi* → *oppis* 'would learn'. This has consequences for the treatment of such alternations as *-kas* ~ *-kkaa-*, which are perhaps best treated as syllabically conditioned allomorph selection.

(81)	a.	i.	/huonee-seen/	*huonee-seen*	'room' (Ill.Sg.)
		ii.	/huonee-seen-si/	*huonee-see-si*	'your room' (Ill.Sg.)
	b.	i.	/hattu-i-hin-si/	*hattu-i-hin*	'hats' (Ill.Pl.)
		ii.	/hattu-i-hin-si/	*hattu-i-hi-ni*	'my hats' (Ill.Pl.)
	c.	i.	/talo-i-ten-si/	*talo-j-en*	'houses' (G.Pl.)
		ii.	/talo-i-ten-si/	*talo-j-e-si*	'your houses' (G.Pl.)
	d.	i.	/saare-i-ten/	*saar-i-en*	'islands' (G.Pl.)
		ii.	/saare-i-ten-si/	*saarie-si*	'your islands' (G.Pl.)
	e.	i.	/peruna-i-ten/	*peruno-i-den*	'potatoes' (G.Pl.)
		ii.	/peruna-i-ten-si/	*peruno-i-de-si*	'your potatoes' (G.Pl.)
	f.	i.	/maa-i-ten/	*ma-i-den*	'countries' (G.Pl.)
		ii.	/maa-i-ten-mme/	*ma-i-de-mme*	'our countries' (G.Pl.)

The last two pairs are especially important in showing that the deletion of the suffix-final *-n* is phonological and that Consonant Gradation applies to the stem before the possessive suffixes are added. Consonant Gradation is a process that weakens medial onsets of closed syllables; in (81e,f) the underlying /t/ of the Genitive Plural ending is weakened to [d]. The Consonant Gradation in (81e) applies in a phonetically *open* syllable. Its closed syllable conditioning environment is met only prior to deletion of the final *-n* in *perunoi-den*. The reason Consonant Gradation takes place in this form in spite of the deletion of its triggering environment is, then, that it applies to the case-inflected form prior to the addition of the possessive suffix.

(82) /peruna-i-ten/ → (C.G.) *peruno-i-den* → (affixation, -C Deletion) *peruno-i-de-si*

The example (81f) *maide-mme* makes the same point in a less obvious way. Since possessive suffixes form words, they never trigger consonant gradation in their base, *even if they are of the form -CCV*. Contrast the effect on the boldfaced root consonant of the stem-level person/number endings in (83a,c) with that of the possessive suffixes (83b,d) (which are homonymous in the 1.Pl.).

(83)	a.	/ka**t**u-mme/	→	*ka***d***umme*	'we regret'
	b.	/ka**t**u-mme/	→	*ka***t***umme*	'our street(s), our street's'
	c.	/sa**tt**u-tte/	→	*sa***t***utte*	'you happen'
	d.	/ha**tt**u-nne/	→	*ha***tt***unne*	'your hat(s), your hat's'

Because possessive suffixes do not trigger Consonant Gradation, the gradation of /t/ to *d* in *maide-mme* cannot be due to the possessive suffix /-mme/. Rather, it must be due to the underlying /-n/ of the case ending /-ten/ which is deleted before /-mme/.

Omission of endings. The phonological deletion process just illustrated applies to syllabic case endings. A similar-looking but, on closer inspection, very different "deletion" before possessive suffixes applies to the set of structural case endings which consist of just a single consonant, namely Nom./Acc.Pl. *-t* and Gen./Acc.Sg. *-n*. In this case, the endings are simply not present: the possessive suffixes are added to the bare stem without a case ending. Unlike in (81), there is no Consonant Gradation in the stem, showing that there is not even a deleted consonantal ending in the base. For example, to Nom./Acc.Pl. *hatut-t* 'hats' the corresponds the possessive *hattu-ni* (not **hatuni*) 'my hats'. This is a *morphological* gap rather than phonological deletion. The base to which the possessive suffixes are added is specifically the vocalic *stem* form, and not the nominative singular form, for, as the data in (84f,i) show, the word-final raising of /-e/ to *i* that takes place in the nominative singular does *not* show up before possessive endings.

(84)	a.	/hattu-n/	*hatun*	/hattu-si/	*hattusi*	'(your) hat' (A./G.Sg.)
	b.	/hattu-t/	*hatut*	/hattu-si/	*hattusi*	'(your) hats' (N./A.Pl.)
	c.	/hattu/	*hattu*	/hattu-si/	*hattusi*	'(your) hats' (N.Sg.)
	d.	/kaikke-n/	*kaiken*	/kaikke-si/	*kaikkeni*	'(my) all' (A./G.Sg.)
	e.	/kaikke-t/	*kaiket*	/kaikke-ni/	*kaikkeni*	'(my) all' (N./A.Pl.)
	f.	/kaikke/	*kaikki*	/kaikke-ni/	*kaikkeni*	'(my) all' (N.Sg.)
	g.	/vete-n/	*veden*	/vete-nsä/	*vetensä*	'(his) water' (A./G.Sg.)
	h.	/vete-t/	*vedet*	/vete-nsä/	*vetensä*	'(his) waters' (N./A.Pl.)
	i.	/vete/	*vesi*	/vete-nsä/	*vetensä*	'(his) water' (N.Sg.)

A paradigmatic gap: the Instructive case. The sole lexical (adverbial) case whose suffix consists of a single consonant is the "Instructive" (instrumental) case. It is always formally plural, and an Instructive NP usually but not always denotes a plural entity. It functions as a VP adverbial of means or condition, always construed with the subject:

(85)	a.	*pitkin askelin*	'with long steps'
	b.	*hartain mielin*	'with devout mind'
	c.	*paljain päin*	'with head uncovered'
	d.	*seuraavin ehdoin*	'under the following conditions'
	e.	*monin suurin ponnistuksin*	'with many great exertions'

The Instructive case displays a third method of avoiding Stem Constraint violations: in the current language, words inflected in the instructive case reject possessive suffixes.

(86)	a.	/pitkä-i-n askele-i-n/	*pitkin askelin*	'with long steps'
	b.	/pitkä-i-n askele-i-n-si/	**pitkin askelisi*	'with your long steps'
	c.	/paljase-i-n pää-i-n-mme/	**paljain päimme*	'with our bare heads'

What fills in for this gap is the Comitative case, which ends in *-ne*, and which *only* occurs with possessive suffixes.

(87) a. *pitkine askelisi* 'with your long steps'
b. *hartaine mielinenne* 'with your attentive minds'
c. *paljaine päinemme* 'with our uncovered heads'
d. *seuraavine ehtoineen* 'with its following conditions'
e. *monine suurine ponnistuksineni* 'with my many great exertions'

The meaning of the Comitative partly overlaps with that of the Instructive.

(88) a. Matti juoks-i pitk-i-n askel-i-n
Matti-Nom run-Past(3Sg) long-Pl-Instr step-Pl-Instr
'Matti ran with long steps'
b. Matti juoks-i pitk-i-ne askel-i-ne-en
Matti-Nom run-Past(3Sg) long-Pl-Instr step-Pl-Instr-3Sg
'Matti ran with his long steps'

In fact, the Instructive and the Comitative are so similar in form and function and so nearly complementary in distribution that it is tempting to unify them into a single case.[32] However, there are two strong arguments in favor of the traditional case distinction between Instructive /-n/ and Comitative /-ne/. First, *-ne* cannot be a morphophonological or allomorphic variant of *-n*. It is true that *-ne* before a possessive suffix could be derived from /-n/ by *e*-epenthesis, but that is not true of bare *-ne* on modifiers (possessive suffixes are only added to the nominal head of a phrase). From underlying /-n/ we would derive (89b) instead of (89a).

(89) a. *kaikki-ne pieni-ne lapsi-ne-si* 'with all your little children'
b. **kaiki-n pieni-n lapsi-ne-si*

Thus, if we were to combine the Instructive and Comitative into a single case (call it the Instrumental), we would still have to recognize the ending as a third prong of the conspiracy to implement the Stem Constraint. Instead of saying that the Instructive is not used with possessive suffixes and the Comitative fills in for it, we would have to say either that the Instrumental ending /-n/ gets an epenthetic *-e* before a possessive suffix (rather than deleting, as the Genitive/Accusative ending /-n/ does), or alternatively that it has a separate allomorph /-ne/ before possessive suffixes. /poika-n-si/ → *poikasi* 'your son's' (Gen.Sg.), but /poika-i-n-si/ → *poikinesi* 'with your son(s)' (Instr.). Either way, the Instrumental has its own way of satisfying the stem constraint.

---

[32]This was suggested to me by Arto Anttila, and independently in a discussion with Heli Harrikari, Tarja Heinonen, and Marja Jäämeri at the 1997 Scandinavian Summer School in Phonology, where I presented the analysis in the text. (See now Harrikari, this volume, for a very different reanalysis of the phonology of possessive suffixes.) According to Ikola 1999, some early 19th century grammarians also considered combining the Instructive and Comitative cases.

The second argument for separating the Instructive and Comitative cases is that they are functionally distinct. While the Instructive is almost always subject-oriented, the Comitative can also refer to an accompaniment of the object (see (90a)). Also, the Instructive can attach to the 2nd infinitive to form the so-called modal construction, where it still rejects a possessive suffix(see (90b)). In this function it cannot be replaced by the Comitative.

(90) a. Nä-i-t minu-t laps-i-ne-ni (*laps-i-n).
see-Past-2Sg me-Acc child-Pl-Comit-3Sg (child-Pl-Instr)
'You saw me with my children'
b. Juoks-i-n laula-e-n (*laula-e-ne-ni).
run-Past-1Sg sing-2Inf-Instr (*sing-2Inf-Instr-1Sg)
'I ran singing.'

Therefore I think that the Finnish grammarians' separation of Instructive and Comitative into two cases is well founded.

Resolving the conspiracy. Returning to the Stem Constraint and its active role in the conspiracy, we now have two more puzzles to solve. First, the conspiracy problem: why is the Stem Constraint manifested in three different ways? Secondly, the problem of opaque, anti-cyclic ordering: why does -C-deletion before possessive suffixes bleed GC in (84) but not in (81)?

Let us assume that MAX and DEP constraints give privileged status to derivational morphology over inflectional morphology, and within inflectional morphology to inherent (adverbial) case over structural case. This exploits the idea that marked categories are richer in content than the corresponding unmarked categories. In the phonological domain, this increment of richness is characterizable in substantive terms at the articulatory and perceptual level. In the morphosyntactic domain, it is characterizable by the system of features and categories that classify words and affixes into types. The category hierarchy in (91) defines three types, in decreasing order of richness of content, and, by hypothesis, of markedness. Two of them exist in both free and bound form, the third only in bound form.

(91)

	free form	*bound form*
Major Cat's	N, V, A, P	derivational affixes, adverbial cases
Funct. Cat's	D, C, Infl	Tense, Mood, Def., Number, Poss.
Licensers	—	structural case, agreement

Armed with this notion of category markedness, we posit the following constraints.

(92) a. $*\text{-C}]_\alpha$ (the Stem Constraint): stems must end in -V.
b. MAX-MORPHEME: A morpheme must be phonologically expressed.

c. DEP-MARKEDCAT: A marked category (an adverbial case, in these data) must be morphologically expressed.
d. MAX-WORD: A word must be phonologically expressed.
e. DEP-CAT: A grammatical category must be morphologically expressed.

The inputs are pairs consisting of a morphological form and the most harmonic output form corresponding to it.

The following tableau shows how these constraints adjudicate among the different ways of satisfying the Stem Constraint. We consider three candidates in each case, representing respectively phonological deletion of the final -C, addition of the possessive to the bare endingless stem, and the morphological gap in the paradigm. Each of them is optimal in a different set of cases. The phonological constraints, and outputs violating them, are omitted here; they can be can be considered undominated. The morphological constraints decide between the different outputs that satisfy these phonological constraints. For clarity, I include also the input forms, based on the plural stem, respectively with and without case inflection, with the stem phonology in place.

(93)

			MAX-MORPHEME	DEP-MARKEDCAT	MAX-WORD	DEP-CAT
Gen.Pl. ☞	$[\text{maiden}]_\alpha$-mme	$[\text{maidemme}]_\omega$				
	$[\text{mai}]_\alpha$-mme	$[\text{maimme}]_\omega$				*
		∅			*	
Gen.Sg.	$[\text{veden}]_\alpha$-si	$[\text{vedesi}]_\omega$	*			
☞	$[\text{vete}]_\alpha$-si	$[\text{vetesi}]_\omega$				*
		∅			*	
Instr.Sg.	$[\text{vesin}]_\alpha$-mme	$[\text{vesimme}]_\omega$	*			
	$[\text{vesi}]_\alpha$-mme	$[\text{vesimme}]_\omega$		*		*
☞		∅			*	

In rare cases it is possible to coerce a possessive suffix onto an instructive-marked nominal (which formally corresponds to promoting MAX-WORD). The remaining constraints then tell us that the suffix must be added directly to the stem, as in the genitive. This yields the correct output, as attested in a few fixed expressions such as *omin lupinsa* 'without permission' (lit. 'with his/her own permission'). Crucially, the possessive form is built on the bare plural stem /lupa-i-/ *lupi-*; adding it to the instructive /lupa-i-n/ *luvin* (as in the synonymous variant expression *omin luvin*, with the un-possessed noun) would predict **luvinsa*.[33]

Accounting for the direction of change. The Stem Constraint suggests a possible answer to the question why stem-level assignment of rhythmic stress is being phased out in Finnish. The stem-final bimoraic diphthongs required by secondary stress assignment clearly violate the constraint, and deferring secondary stress to the postlexical phonology makes it undominated (except for cases like *lauantai*, see (61)). *STRESS and *LAPSE are both opaque whichever way they are ranked, but the ranking *STRESS ≫ *LAPSE minimizes violations of the Stem Constraint. Suppose we assume that learners seek to maximize the transparency of constraints. Then there would be a bias in favor of this ranking, which would cause it to become increasingly favored over time.

6 Parallelist approaches

6.1 The options under parallelism

Could the inflectional patterns of Finnish nouns be accounted for under full parallelism? Four main types of solutions should be considered. One invokes analogical mechanisms that transfer properties from bases to derivatives (Output/Output constraints). Another type of analogical constraint penalizes allomorphy (e.g. Lexical Conservatism). A third approach invokes constraints that access underlying representations in one or another way (Sympathy, Extended Sympathy, Generalized Sympathy). A final alternative is to enrich output representations; Containment and Turbidity are the most important representatives of this approach. We shall consider them in turn.

Output/Output constraints. O/O constraints have the same format as other correspondence constraints, including I/O constraints. So, deriving the Finnish alternants by O/O constraints involves determining a base form from which one or more ranked O/O constraints transfer the relevant properties to the outputs. Also, the transfer has to be optional in specific contexts, which involves the complex interaction of phonological and morphological factors as explored above.

Let us consider the options. Given the two Essive Plural alternants *ullakkoina* and *ullakoina* 'attics', one is presumably derived directly by the phonological constraints, and the other by a a dominant DEP(O/O) constraint. If *ullakkoina* is the phonologically "regular" form, then *ullakoina*

[33]The example is from Penttilä 1963:122; Penttilä 1963:439 also cites two other, archaic, examples of instructives with possessive suffixes: *kaikin voimini* 'with all my powers' and *kaksin kämmenini* 'with my two hands'.

must be an "analogical" form due to a dominant DEP(O/O) constraint that refers to some degeminated Base, such as Nom.Pl. *ullakot*.[34] On the other hand, if *ullakoina* is derived directly by the phonological constraints, then *ullakkoina* must be an "analogical" form due to a dominant MAX(O/O) constraint that refers to some geminated Base, such as Ess.Sg. *ullakkona* or Nom.Sg. *ullakko*.[35]

An immediate observation to be made about these options is that *neither* of them corresponds to the historical analogical process, which uncontroversially shows the influence of the disyllabic paradigm on the polysyllabic paradigm (Itkonen 1957). The actual change thus involved interparadigmatic rather than intraparadigmatic analogy, which neither O/O nor anti-allomorphy approaches are capable of representing synchronically. The stratal OT treatment proposed here reconstructs this historical scenario, and in a sense justifies it. For it posits that polysyllables are, in fact, adopting the pattern of disyllables, albeit not so much by direct transfer of the surface pattern, as in virtue of the loss of stem-level rhythmic stress, which also captures the spread of the long illative (see 4.1).

Either way, the O/O solution faces two problems, both fatal at least under current versions of O/O theory, as far as I can tell. The first is that there is no principled way to get the paradigmatic transfer to show up in the right places. This is the problem of the *opaque conditioning* of the transfer. Disyllabic -V stems retain their geminates obligatorily, as do contracted stems. How do we retrict the analogy to a subclass of polysyllables? And how does the O/O constraint distinguish fixed polysyllables from movable polysyllables? For example, *Amerikka* and *palsternakka* have the same output stress pattern in the Nominative Singular and in the Essive Singular — in *all* prospective Base forms, in fact — yet are inflected quite differently. In the former, the transfer is optional, in the latter it is obligatory.

The second problem for O/O constraints is that they have nothing to say about the variation in the form of the suffix, for example the alternation *korjaamoita* ~ *korjaamoja*. As detailed above, suffix weakening and stem reduction are complementary, so one must be blocked by whatever triggers the

---

[34]De Chene 1975 proposes that degemination in diphthongal forms is analogical to degemination in the monophthongal forms. Consonant Gradation is transferred from the singular and present forms to the corresponding plural and past forms, e.g. from Adess.Sg. *ullakolla* to Adess.Pl. *ullakoilla*, and from 1.Pl.Present *suutumme* 'we get angry' to 1.Pl.Past *suutuimme* 'we got angry'. This is problematic for -CV endings such as Essive /-na/, and even more so for a case form like Instr. *ullakoin (*ullakkoin)*, which lacks a corresponding monophthongal form and yet obligatorily degeminates.

[35]To be sure, these choices involve problematic assumptions, such as that Nominative case has no case features, and that Singular number has no number features, or perhaps that these case and number features are somehow "included" in the Essive case and Plural number features, respectively. Let us assume for now that these problems with O/O theory can be solved somehow.

other. But no O/O constraint can apply to suffixes because they don't have Bases. Therefore O/O constraints do not provide a serious alternative.

Anti-allomorphy constraints. Several types of constraints have been devised to penalize allomorphic alternations. The most basic form is Kenstowicz's UNIFORM EXPONENCE constraint (1995), which enjoins that differences in the realization of a lexical item (morpheme, stem, affix, word) be minimized. The most intricate is LEXICAL CONSERVATISM (Steriade 1999), which defines a type of lexical relation and posits a constraint format based on it.

Since anti-allomorphy constraints can be formulated over morphemes of any type, not just stems, one might think that they could get a purchase on the suffix alternations, which escape the O/O approach, as just noted. This turns out to be not the case, for the question of minimizing allomorphy does not even arise here. All the allomorphs of stems and endings occur regardless of the variation at stake: it is just a matter of how they are distributed in the paradigm. Anti-allomorphy constraints, then, are not helpful either.

Sympathy constraints. Next let us consider the possibility that Sympathy constraints might be responsible. Sympathy constraints impose Faithfulness to a SYMPATHY CANDIDATE, the optimal candidate that obeys some Faithfulness constraint (McCarthy 1999a, 1999b). The actual outputs we are considering (such as *mellakkoja* and *mellakoita*) have stress on the third (stem-final) syllable. The Sympathy candidate, and therefore the underlying form /mellakka-i-ta/, must *not* have stress on that syllable. Intuitively put, the Sympathy constraint enables overtly stressed syllables to be treated as stressless by "borrowing" the stresslessness of the underlying representation.

In the present case, Sympathy runs into two problems. The first is that of ATOMISM. Because Stop Deletion, Consonant Gradation, secondary stress shift, vowel harmony, Illative allomorphy, and the pattern of preferences depend on opaque properties of the stem-level representation, a Sympathy analysis must in effect undo the whole word phonology in so far as it relates to stress and syllable structure. Faithfulness constraints like MAX, DEP, and IDENT can only do this in a piecemeal fashion because they are defined on specific features or segments. The generalization that the conditions governing allomorphy and stem-level phonological processes are defined on stem level representations is lost.

The second problem with Sympathy concerns Richness of the Base and Freedom of Analysis: how do we guarantee the appropriate stress and stresslessness in the underlying representation in environments where they are predictable? For example, how can we prevent underlying forms with stress on the second syllable? A hypothetical word like */samá/ will come out correctly stressed as *sáma* due to undominated *CLASH, but a Sympathy constraint can access the underlying stress to give it an impossible declension pattern, in which the Partitive Singular, for example, will be **sáma-ta* (like *si-tä*) instead of *sáma-a*. Conversely, underlying forms *without* stress on the first syllable would have to be prevented somehow. A hypothetical unstressed stem /si/ will get correctly stressed on the first syllable in the output by (6d) ALIGN-L, but by Sympathy it will be inflected like a disyllable; e.g. with Prt.Sg. **síä* instead of *sítä*.

Thus, Sympathy can replicate the effects of ordering only up to a point. The difference between the Base and the most radical Sympathy candidate (the Input) is that the Base is guaranteed to contain all the actual output properties, while the most radical Sympathy candidate, by Richness of the Base and Freedom of Analysis, need not contain any of the word's predictable properties. In stratal OT, the inflection is determined by the shape of the stem in the stem phonology, which by the principle of cyclic application is guaranteed to reflect the stem-level constraint system.

Turbidity. Finally, what if we enrich "output" representations by adding to them certain kinds of covert, unpronounced properties? This is the central idea of the "containment" approach of Prince & Smolensky 1993 and more recently of Turbidity theory (Smolensky 1998, Goldrick 1999).[36] As Goldrick explains Turbidity, "the output of the grammar will now contain unpronounced material which can influence the 'surface' — the portion of the output which is pronounced. By utilizing a single, complex output representation, we can maintain the output-oriented approach of Prince & Smolensky (1993) while extending our descriptive coverage to include opacity effects."

Turbidity enhances outputs by allowing different coexisting analyses for segmental material: in Goldrick's terms, segments can *project* one way and be *pronounced* in another. As an example, Goldrick's proposes an analysis of German in which medial consonants project (are licensed as) as codas, and are pronounced as onsets. Certain constraints (those that are "sensitive to abstract structural relations") are triggered by the projected structure, others ("lower-level constraints") by the pronunciation. This dual structure resembles ambisyllabicity in some respects, and level-ordering in others, but is nevertheless conceptually distinct from both. An ambisyllabicity analysis claims that the segment in question is simultaneously a coda and an onset in the same representation. Serial solutions claim that the 'projected' and 'pronounced' structures belong to different levels of representation which cannot be accessed together by any rule or constraint. Turbidity holds that there are two different syllabifications but that they are always *co-present* and visible

---

[36]Compare also the two-level morphology of Koskenniemi and Karttunen, where all constraints (not just faithfulness constraints as in Correspondence Theory) can refer either to input representations or to output representations.

together.

For Finnish, a Turbidity analysis would presumably say that in *úl.lak.kò.ja* 'attics' (Prt.Pl.) the penult syllable is projected as unstressed but pronounced as stressed, while in the alternative output *úl.la.kòi.ta* the penult is both projected as stressed and pronounced as stressed. In *pált.tois.sa* 'overcoats' (Iness.Pl.) *-tois-* is projected as two syllables but pronounced as one. The disparity between projection and pronunciation in the former case could be implemented by constraints equivalent to those I proposed above. Roughly speaking, the stem-level constraint system would give Turbidity's projected structure, and the word-level constraint system would give Turbidity's pronunciation structure.

Turbidity partly shares its problems with other parallel approaches to opacity, but one of its distinctive characteristics is that it apparently imposes no principled restrictions on which constraints access which representation. Constraints defined on Projection might equally well be defined on Pronunciation, and vice versa. In contrast, stratal OT entails that constraints which are stem-level by other criteria (e.g. domains, interaction with other constraints, and interaction with morphology) only apply to stem-level representations, and constraints which are word-level by other criteria only apply to word-level representations. Opacity arises only from intralevel masking; full transparency obtains *within* each level. Turbidity does not have any predictions to make on this score.

Moreover, because Turbidity posits a single representation in which possibly incompatible Projection and Pronunciation structures coexist, it predicts the possibility of structures that access *both* (for example, mutual bleeding). For stratal OT, this is an impossibility, because the stem-level and word-level representations are distinct. Turbidity also seems to allow constraints which access Pronunciation to feed or bleed constraints that access Projection. For stratal OT, this is also an impossibility, because the stem-level and word-level representations are serially related. In the Finnish case, this is what allowed us to explain the complementarity of Stop Deletion and Consonant Gradation.

The stratal OT approach is thus more restrictive than Turbidity in several respects, and therefore to be preferred to it. I conclude that stratal OT's account of opacity is superior to any currently available alternative within parallel OT.

References

Anttila, Arto. 1994. Consonant Gradation is epenthesis. Stanford Phonology Workshop, Stanford University.

Anttila, Arto. 1997. *Variation in Finnish phonology and morphology.* Ph.D. Dissertation, Stanford University.

Anttila, Arto. 1999. Derived environment effects in colloquial Helsinki Finnish. MS, BU.

Anttila, Arto. In press. Morphologically conditioned phonological alternations. *Natural Language and Linguistic Theory.* Also in `http://roa.rutgers.edu/`, `ROA-425-10100.`

Árnason, Kristján. 1992. Problems in the lexical phonology of Icelandic. *Phonologica 1988*, ed. Wolfgang U. Dressler, Hans C. Luschützky, Oskar E. Pfeiffer, and John R. Rennison. Cambridge: CUP.

de Chene, Brent. 1975. The treatment of analogy in a formal grammar. *CLS* 11.

Crowhurst, Megan. 1996. An optimal alternative to conflation. *Phonology* 13:409-424.

Elenbaas, Nine, and René Kager. 1999. Ternary rhythm and the lapse constraint. *Phonology* 16.273-329.

Goldrick, Matthew. 2000. Generalized sympathy. *NELS* 30.

Hanson, Kristin, and Paul Kiparsky. 1996. A theory of metrical choice. *Language* 72.287-335.

Harris, John. 1994. *English sound structure.* Oxford: Blackwell.

Hayes, Bruce. 1995. *Metrical stress theory: principles and case studies.* Chicago: University of Chicago Press.

Itkonen, Terho. 1957. *Mellakoihin* vai *mellakkoihin*? *Virittäjä* 61.559-286.

Keyser, S.J. and Paul Kiparsky. 1984. Syllable structure in Finnish phonology. *Language sound structure*, ed. Mark Aronoff and Richard T. Oehrle, 7-31. Cambridge, Mass: MIT Press.

Kenstowicz, Michael. 1995. Cyclic vs. noncyclic constraint evaluation. *Phonology* 12:397-436.

Kiparsky, Paul. 1973. Phonological representations. *Three dimensions of linguistic theory,* ed. Osamu Fujimura. Tokyo: TEC.

Kiparsky, Paul. To appear. *Paradigms and opacity.* Stanford: CSLI.

de Lacy, Paul. 1998. Sympathetic stress. `http://roa.rutgers.edu/`, `ROA-294`

McCarthy, John. 1999a. Sympathy and phonological opacity. *Phonology* 16.331-400.

McCarthy, John. 1999b. Serialism, OT, and the Duke-of-York Gambit. Rutgers Optimality Archive.

Paradis, Carole. 1997. Constraint effects in Gere: From cycles to derivations. *Derivations and Constraints in Phonology,* 529-550. ed. I. Roca. Oxford: OUP.

Penttilä, Aarni and Lauri Posti. 1941. Über die steigende und sog. Stossintonation im Livischen. *Finnisch-Ugrische Forschungen* 27.235-272.

Prince, Alan and Paul Smolensky. 1993. *Optimality theory: Constraint interaction in generative grammar.* Ms., Rutgers University and U. of Colorado.

Ringen, Catherine O. and Orvokki Heinämäki. 1999. Variation in Finnish vowel harmony: an OT account. *NLLT* 17.303-37.

Steriade, Donca. 1999. Lexical conservatism in French adjectival liaison. In Marc Authier, B. Bullock, and L. Reed (eds.), *Formal perspectives on Romance linguistics.* Amsterdam: Benjamins.

Välimaa-Blum, Riitta. 1999. A feature geometric description of Finnish vowel harmony covering both loans and native words. *Lingua* 108.247-268.

Wiik, Kalevi. 1967. *Suomen kielen generatiivista* fonologiaa. Turku: Turun Yliopisto.

Part II

Syntax (Case)

5

A Licensing Theory for Finnish

ASH ASUDEH

1 Introduction*

The notion of argument structure and thematic roles is by now commonplace in linguistic theory. Although the details vary, theories as diverse as Government and Binding Theory and Minimalism (Chomsky, 1981, 1986, 1995) on the one hand, and Lexical Functional Grammar (Kaplan and Bresnan, 1982; Bresnan, 2001; Dalrymple, 2001) and Head-driven Phrase Structure Grammar (Pollard and Sag, 1994; Ginzburg and Sag, 2001) on the other, posit some syntactic/semantic representation which specifies a predicate's arguments and provides equivalence classes of argument types, which I will here call thematic roles.

However, it is not enough to merely state a predicate's argument structure. An adequate theory must also explain how arguments of a predicate are syntactically realized. There must be a statement of how thematic roles are *mapped* onto grammatical functions. There is also a well-established relationship between grammatical functions and morphosyntactic case, which is realized morphologically. Therefore, a good linguistic theory should make generalizations and predictions about the relationship between thematic roles, grammatical functions, and morphosyntactic case and its morphological re-

*I would like to thank Ted Briscoe, Ann Copestake, Beth Levin, Line Mikkelsen, Diane Nelson, Chris Potts, Ivan Sag, Peter Sells, Barbara Stiebels, and the audience at my LSA 2002 presentation for comments and discussion. I owe a huge debt to Ida Toivonen for extensive discussion and help with the Finnish data, and especially to Paul Kiparsky whose work initiated this research and who provided much supervision and support. All examples are from his work or adapted and checked with Ida's help, unless otherwise noted. Lastly, I would like to thank my reviewer, who was extremely insightful and helpful. I accept full responsibility for any errors. This research was partly funded by SSHRC Doctoral Fellowship 752-98-0424.

Generative Approaches to Finnic and Saami Linguistics.
Diane C. Nelson and Satu Manninen (eds.).

alization (morphological case). Let us call a theory of the bipartite relation between argument structure and grammatical functions a *mapping theory* and a theory of the tripartite relation between argument structure, grammatical functions and case a *licensing theory*.[1]

Kiparsky (1996, 1997) presents a licensing theory based on the relational features [$\pm$ H(ighest) R(ole)] and [$\pm$ L(owest) R(ole)]. These features cross-classify thematic roles, grammatical functions, and case (morphosyntactic and morphological). This yields a simple, unified featural analysis of the various components of licensing. Kiparsky shows how this theory makes striking generalizations and predictions about typologically diverse case systems, as well as fine-grained predictions about licensing in particular languages, such as German, Finnish, and Dyirbal. But, in more recent work Kiparsky (2000, 2001) has abandoned this strictly unification-based model in favour of an Optimality Theory (OT; Prince and Smolensky 1993) formalization. This move was made in large part due to various problems with unification failure in the older model.

In this paper I present a modified version of Kiparsky's original licensing theory (Kiparsky, 1996, 1997). My modifications, in terms of Lascarides and Copestake's (1999) default logic for feature unification, result in a licensing theory which does not use the non-monotonic optimization of Optimality Theory, while avoiding unification failure where necessary. Optimization in OT is non-monotonic because, due to markedness constraints, the winner of a competition may lack information which is specified in the input. The analysis presented here makes a much more limited appeal to non-monotonic constraints: information is destroyed only as a last resort.[2] Furthermore, it is possible to view default versus non-default specification for a given feature as another aspect of typological variation, rather than merely as a formal device. I will argue that the typological space predicted by the default theory of licensing is much more restrictive than that predicted by OT, despite typology being adopted as a prime motivation for the latter style of analysis. Lastly, I will discuss the emergence of the unmarked on the default theory. This is another motivation for optimality-theoretic analyses, but I will argue that the default licensing theory presented here actually derives emergence of the unmarked while using a more restrictive and better motivated set of constraints than the OT analysis of Kiparsky (2001), which nevertheless uses only the usual type of OT constraints. Thus, the theory I present has the predictive

[1] In the original generative literature, licensing theory was typically called *linking theory* (Ostler, 1979), but the latter term is now normally taken to be a synonym for mapping (see, e.g., Butt et al., 1997).

[2] See the discussion of Conservativity in section 5.

high points of Kiparsky (1996), yet it is a largely monotonic formalization that results in a more restrictive theory than the optimality-theoretic model, although it too makes predictions regarding typology and the emergence of the unmarked. I demonstrate the modified licensing theory with an analysis of object licensing in Finnish. This was a case which Kiparsky's (1996) unification-based approach had problems with and was one motivation for the OT reformalization of the theory. I also present an analysis of Finnish subject licensing and discuss how the same analysis derives genitive-marked possessors.

Section 2 presents and motivates the licensing theory I will be modifying (Kiparsky, 1996, 2001). Then I present the salient aspects of the default unification formalism I use to modify Kiparsky's licensing theory in section 3. Finally, I present the modified licensing theory (section 4) and how it deals with the Finnish data (sections 5 and 6).

2 Kiparsky's Licensing Theory

The licensing theory presented in (Kiparsky, 1996, 2001) posits a ternary relation between thematic roles or arguments, grammatical functions (which he calls "abstract case") and morphosyntactic case. In this section I review this licensing theory, save for the optimality-theoretic analysis (Kiparsky, 2001), which I reject in favour of an analysis using default unification, which is closer in spirit to Kiparsky (1996, 1997).

2.1 Abstract Case

Kiparsky follows Bierwisch (Bierwisch, 1986; Bierwisch and Schreuder, 1992) in assuming a level of Semantic Form to represent a word's lexical semantics.[3] Semantic Form is made up of semantic constants and variables:

(1) *show*: $\lambda z \lambda y \lambda x$ [x CAUSE [CAN [y SEE z]]]

The constants in (1) are the primitives CAUSE, CAN, and SEE, while the variables are x, y, and z. The lambda-abstracted variables are equivalent to thematic roles, and their depth of embedding (starting inside out) directly encodes the thematic hierarchy. Thus, in (1), λx abstracts over the highest ranking thematic role, and λz over the lowest ranking one.

Kiparsky uses the relational features [$\pm$ H(ighest) R(ole)] and [$\pm$ L(owest) R(ole)] to define the abstract cases, with each abstract case bear-

[3] For related theories of lexical semantics, see for example Lexical Conceptual Semantics (Jackendoff, 1990), Lexical Decomposition Grammar (Joppen and Wunderlich, 1995) and the HPSG linking theory of Davis and Koenig (Davis and Koenig, 2000; Koenig and Davis, 2001).

ing a value for both features[4] (see also the work of Barbara Stiebels and Dieter Wunderlich and colleagues for a closely related approach; e.g., see Stiebels 2000 and Wunderlich and Lakämper 2001 and references therein). These are assigned to the thematic roles according to their relative position in Semantic Form. Thus, [+ HR] is assigned to the highest role and [+ LR] is assigned to the lowest role. The rest of the case matrix is filled in implicationally. Since the features are relational, a predicate can and must have one [+ HR] role and one [+ LR] role, if it has any roles that project into the syntax (unless it is listed as exceptional in the lexicon).[5] Thus, any thematic role that does not bear [+ HR] must bear [− HR] (as it is not the highest role) and any thematic role that does not bear [+ LR] must likewise bear [− LR]. For the predicate in (1) this yields the following feature matrices.

(2) *show*:

$$\lambda z \begin{bmatrix} - & \text{HR} \\ + & \text{LR} \end{bmatrix} \quad \lambda y \begin{bmatrix} - & \text{HR} \\ - & \text{LR} \end{bmatrix} \quad \lambda x \begin{bmatrix} + & \text{HR} \\ - & \text{LR} \end{bmatrix} \quad [\text{ x CAUSE [CAN [y SEE z]]]}$$

Two features with two values each yields four possible abstract cases:

(3) S [+ HR, + LR]
A [+ HR, − LR]
O [− HR, + LR]
D [− HR, − LR]

S and A are mnemonic for Dixon's (1979) pivots, where S is the subject of an intransitive and A is the subject of a transitive. Similarly, O is the object of a transitive, while D is a mnemonic for dative, the second object of a ditransitive. Thus, there are four possible abstract cases, and their featural make-up is derived automatically from assigning the two relational features to the various thematic roles in Semantic Form.

2.2 Morphosyntactic Case

The same two relational features are used to specify morphosyntactic grammatical case (as opposed to semantic case, which is not defined using these features). For example, dative case gets the feature matrix [− HR, − LR]. It therefore typically unifies with the middle thematic role in a ditransitive. Although there can be generalizations made about cases cross-linguistically

[4] The value may be underspecifi ed by leaving the case matrix blank for the underspecifi ed feature.

[5] For example, Kiparsky (1996) suggests that impersonal verbs have no thematic roles, and therefore do not get assigned these features. We will also see exceptional lexical assignment by certain atelic predicates (section 5) and VP-internal subjects (section 6).

based on these features, the grammatical case inventories of languages are specific to the language in question and can be determined by examining the syntactic distribution of the various cases. For example, Finnish has four grammatical cases: nominative, genitive, accusative, and partitive. These cases can mark various grammatical functions and certain adverbials. In section 4.2 below I motivate a particular featural make-up for these cases.

There are two essential conditions that govern the association of morphosyntactic case with case-marked thematic roles (i.e., with abstract case) (Kiparsky, 1996):

(4) a. **Unification**
Associated feature matrices must be non-distinct.
$[+\,F] \sqcup [+\,F]$
$[-\,F] \sqcup [-\,F]$
$[-\,F] \not\sqcup [+\,F]$

b. **Specificity**
Specific rules and morphemes block general rules and morphemes in shared contexts.
$[\alpha\,F_1, \alpha\,F_2]$ is more specific than $[\alpha\,F_1]$
$[\alpha\,F_1, \alpha\,F_2]$ is more specific than $[\alpha\,F_2]$
$[\alpha\,F]$ is more specific than [ ]
Every (type of) feature matrix is equally specific to itself

Thus, morphosyntactic case matrices can only be associated with abstract cases if they are not featurally distinct. And more specific morphosyntactic cases must be selected over less specific ones, where either can unify with a given abstract case. However, cases may encode information beyond the grammatical function/thematic role information specified through HR and LR. In section 6 below we will see in particular that partitive and genitive case can encode the semantics of possession and nominal partition respectively. Note that Specificity is in effect a formalization of the Elsewhere Condition (Kiparsky, 1973). We will revisit these conditions in section 3, in light of considerations from defaults.

2.3 Morphological Case

The morphosyntactic cases that are characterized in terms of [$\pm$ HR] and [$\pm$ LR] are realized as morphemes. Furthermore, zero morphemes are maximally underspecified for case features. Thus, there can only be one zero case in a language, and this case will be [ ]. This corresponds to nominative/absolutive (Kiparsky, 1996, 2001).

2.4 Positional Licensing

Lastly, the same relational features can be assigned to positions in languages with positional licensing. For Finnish, Kiparsky (2001) assigns [+ HR] to the specifier of IP and [− HR] to the complement of V. In other words, [Spec, IP] licenses subjects (S and A), while [Comp, V] in general licenses objects (O and D).

2.5 Summary and Discussion

In the licensing theory that I have just presented, two relational features, [± HR] and [± LR] are used to cross-classify abstract case (i.e., grammatical functions), morphosyntactic case and positional licensing. Furthermore, as required of a licensing theory, these case matrices are associated with thematic roles (in this case, at the level of Semantic Form).

However, since unification and specificity are the only principles governing association of abstract and morphosyntactic case, there are certain instances of case assignment in Finnish which are problematic. For example, Kiparsky (2001) motivates a case paradigm in which there is no accusative case for nouns, only for pronouns (see section 4.1 below). Singular noun objects are marked with genitive case,[6] as are subjects of nonfinite verbs. Plural noun objects are marked with nominative case, and so are subjects of finite verbs. But, subjects are [+ HR], whereas objects are [− HR]. Thus, genitive and nominative case must not be specified for HR. However, transitive subjects are [+ HR, − LR], while intransitive subjects are [+ HR, + LR]. Thus, genitive and nominative case must be unspecified for LR as well. This is a problem, though, as both cases would then have the case feature matrix [ ] and would be nondistinct. However, there is a clear difference in morphology associated with the two cases and there are syntactic generalizations which show them to be distinct.

These problems, among other considerations, motivated the move by Kiparsky (2001) to an optimality-theoretic treatment, which allows featural mismatches between input abstract cases and their morphosyntactically realized outputs. Thus, unification is abandoned. I propose instead that this move is unnecessary and that the OT analysis is less perspicuous and less well-motivated than an analysis which uses *default* unification. In the next section I very briefly review the default unification theory of Lascarides and Copestake (1999).

[6]Modulo Jahnsson's Rule. See section 5.

3 Default Unification

Lascarides and Copestake (1999) present a default logic which meets the following desiderata for default unification (Lascarides et al., 1996):

(5)
a. Nondefault information is always preserved.
b. Default unification only fails if there is conflicting nondefault information.
c. Default unification behaves like monotonic unification where monotonic unification would succeed.
d. Default unification should deterministically return a single result.
e. Default unification can be described using a binary, order-independent operation.

Although I will not go into the formal details here, the gist of default unification is that if a default is not overridden, then the default value will emerge and in a unification conflict between a default and a nondefault value, the nondefault value overrides the default value.

Default unification in this system is noted by putting a slash before the value, as in $[/+\,\mathrm{HR}]$. According to the conditions in (5), we get the following default unification patterns, as well as the nondefault unification patterns in (4a), repeated below as (7).

(6) **Default unification**

$$
\begin{array}{lcllcl}
[/+\,\mathrm{F}] & \sqcup & [-\,\mathrm{F}] & = & [-\,\mathrm{F}] \\
[-\,\mathrm{F}] & \sqcup & [/+\,\mathrm{F}] & = & [-\,\mathrm{F}] \\
[/-\,\mathrm{F}] & \sqcup & [+\,\mathrm{F}] & = & [+\,\mathrm{F}] \\
[+\,\mathrm{F}] & \sqcup & [/-\,\mathrm{F}] & = & [+\,\mathrm{F}] \\
[/+\,\mathrm{F}] & \sqcup & [/+\,\mathrm{F}] & = & [/+\,\mathrm{F}] \\
[/-\,\mathrm{F}] & \sqcup & [/-\,\mathrm{F}] & = & [/-\,\mathrm{F}] \\
[/-\,\mathrm{F}] & \sqcup & [/+\,\mathrm{F}] & = & [\pm\,\mathrm{F}]^{7}
\end{array}
$$

The reader can check that all five desiderata in (5) are met here.

In using default unification, we preserve normal unification (as used in Kiparsky's (1996; 1997) system), which I repeat here:

(7) **Unification**

$[+\,\mathrm{F}] \sqcup [+\,\mathrm{F}]$

$[-\,\mathrm{F}] \sqcup [-\,\mathrm{F}]$

$[-\,\mathrm{F}] \not\sqcup [+\,\mathrm{F}]$

---

[7] We get this because $[/-\,\mathrm{F}] \sqcup [/+\,\mathrm{F}] = [/-\,\mathrm{F}] \vee [/+\,\mathrm{F}]$ and we can move the disjunction in the result inside to get $[/-\,\mathrm{F}] \sqcup [/+\,\mathrm{F}] = [/+\vee-\,\mathrm{F}]$, which is equivalent to $[\pm\,\mathrm{F}]$ or the underspecified value [ ].

Recall from (4b) that the other ingredient in Kiparsky's original unification analysis was Specificity, or the Elsewhere Condition. First, notice that although it seems that Specificity should in some sense come for free in a default unification theory, this is a mistaken first impression. Default unification concerns the featural values in morphemes, but Specificity applies at the level of rules and whole morphemes, selecting between rules and morphemes based on their information content. Thus, defaults and Specificity apply at different loci and Specificity is an addition to the Lascarides and Copestake (1999) default unification theory, not a consequence of it. Second, we need to consider how Specificity interacts with defaults and how blocking works. In particular, does Specificity apply to the actual featural information borne by morphemes or to the amount of potential information they have specified? It seems intuitively clear that a default value for a feature is not as specific as a non-default value. That is, we might expect that [α F_1] blocks [/α F_2], [/β F_1], [/β F_2], etc. If Specificity is a relationship between morphemes, then this seems arbitrary, as the morphemes in question each have one feature with some value: the morphemes are equally informative. The basis of the intuition becomes clear if we consider Specificity as applying not to the actual featural information on a morpheme but rather to the potential information that the morpheme determines. In other words, [α F_1] is more specific than, for example, [/β F_1], because the result of unifying with [α F_1] can *only* be [α F_1], whereas the result of unifying with [/β F_1] can be either [β F_1] (maintaining the default) or [α F_1] (overriding the default). By the same token, then, [/α F_1] and even [/α F_1, /α F_2] are no more specific than [ ], because all these feature matrices allow the same results. Notice also that morphemes that encode conflicting information are no more specific than each other, since specificity is inherently a subsumption relationship, and is therefore inapplicable in situations where subsumption does not hold (i.e., when there is unification failure between any subset of morphological features borne by the morphemes in question). Third, it is worth repeating that the HR/LR information is not the only information encoded morphologically. In particular, semantic information is also encoded in this fashion: for example, in the nominal domain partitive case encodes the semantics of partition (e.g., *a piece of pie*) and genitive case encodes possession. Thus, even if two cases are equally specific with respect to HR/LR, other conflicting information can make them equally specific.

Thus, the revised version of Specificity, taking defaults into account will be:[8]

[8]Note that this is not meant to be an exhaustive list of possibilities, but it should provide the basis for extrapolating any missing combinations.

(8) **Specificity (default version)**
Specific rules and morphemes block general rules and morphemes in shared contexts.
$[\alpha\ F_1, \alpha\ F_2]$ is more specific than $[\alpha\ F_1]$
$[\alpha\ F_1, \alpha\ F_2]$ is more specific than $[\alpha\ F_2]$
$[\alpha\ F]$ is equally specific to $[\beta\ F]$
$[\alpha\ F]$ is more specific than $[\ ]$

$[\alpha\ F_1]$ is more specific than $[/\alpha\ F_1]$
$[\alpha\ F_1]$ is more specific than $[/\beta\ F_1]$
$[\alpha\ F_1]$ is more specific than $[/\alpha\ F_2]$
$[\alpha\ F_1]$ is more specific than $[/\beta\ F_2]$
$[/\alpha\ F]$ is equally specific to $[\ ]$
Every (type of) feature matrix is equally specific to itself

In the analysis that I present in the following sections, defaults are used to avoid the unification problem noted in section 2.5 above, while allowing genitive and nominative case in Finnish to be represented as featurally distinct. The instances of default unification all involve overriding a default, as in the first four cases in (6), or identical default unification, as in cases five and six.

4 Licensing in Finnish Using Defaults

4.1 Morphological Case

Finnish has four grammatical cases: nominative (-∅), accusative (*-t*), genitive (*-n*), and partitive (*-(t)a*) (Kiparsky, 2001). I assume the paradigm in (9), which is motivated extensively by Kiparsky (2001).

(9)

	'bear'		'he, they'	
	Singular	Plural	Singular	Plural
Nominative	karhu	karhu-**t**	hän	he
Accusative	—	—	häne-**t**	he-i-dä-**t**
Genitive	karhu-**n**	karhu-j-**en**	häne-**n**	he-i-dä-**n**
Partitive	karhu-**a**	karhu-j-**a**	hän-**tä**	he-i-**tä**

By contrast, the traditional paradigm posits that there is an accusative case for nouns and that it is -∅ or *-n* in the singular and *-t* in the plural.

(10)

	'bear'		'he, they'	
	Singular	Plural	Singular	Plural
Nominative	karhu	karhu-**t**	hän	he
Accusative	karhu karhu-**n**	karhu-**t**	häne-**t**	he-i-dä-**t**
Genitive	karhu-**n**	karhu-j-**en**	häne-**n**	he-i-dä-**n**
Partitive	karhu-**a**	karhu-j-**a**	hän-**tä**	he-i-**tä**

In other words, in this paradigm there is case syncretism between the accusative singular and nominative singular or genitive singular on the one hand, and between accusative plural and nominative plural on the other hand.

The paradigm in (9) treats these facts as no coincidence and instead posits that there simply is no accusative case ending for nouns. There are theoretical and empirical reasons for preferring (9) to the traditional paradigm. The theoretical reasons are as follows. First, the traditional paradigm treats -∅ and *-n* accusatives as a case of suppletive allomorphy. However, the distribution of these allomorphs is conditioned by Jahnsson's Rule (see section 5 below), which is a syntactic generalization. But, allomorphy is not normally conditioned by syntax. The paradigm in (9) treats this instead as nominative versus genitive case assignment, and case assignment can obviously be conditioned syntactically. Second, (9) eliminates the *-t*/*-n*/-∅ allomorphy entirely, which is desirable since Finnish generally lacks suppletive morphology (Kiparsky, 2001, 318). Third, the paradigm in (9) is simpler as the only case syncretism left is for the form *-t*, which marks accusative pronouns and nominative singular nouns. Fourth, as mentioned above, it avoids the suspicious fact that all accusative noun endings are exactly the same as some other case ending.

The empirical reasons for preferring (9) include 1) case identity under gapping, and 2) the behaviour of the interrogative pronoun *kuka* 'who'. A shared, gapped argument in a coordination structure must have identical abstract case:

(11) Mikko pyörty-i ja (Mikko) kanne-ttiin ulos.
Mikko.NOM faint-PAST.3SG and (Mikko.NOM) carry-PAST.3SG out
Mikko fainted and (Mikko) was carried out.

The argument of the active verb *py¨ortyi* gets nominative case, while the argument of the "passive"[9] verb *kannettiin* gets morphological nominative case if it is a noun and morphological accusative case if it is a pronoun, according to the paradigm (9). If we assume that there must be identity of abstract case

[9] Finnish only has an impersonal passive, which is not clearly a true passive (Kiparsky, 2001; Shore, 1988).

for gapping in coordination, the ungrammaticality of the following sentence with gapping follows directly, as one pronoun gets nominative case, whereas the other one gets accusative case.

(12) Hän pyörty-i ja *(häne-t) kanne-ttiin ulos.
3SG.NOM faint-PAST.3SG and (3SG.ACC) carry-PAST.3SG out
He fainted and he was carried out.

According to the traditional paradigm, the argument of *kannettiin* is accusative in both (11) and (12), and (11) would be wrongly predicted to be ungrammatical. This shows empirical support for the paradigm in (9), which treats the singular noun -∅ ending as nominative only, predicting the grammaticality of (11), but posits an accusative form for pronouns, predicting the ungrammaticality of (12) with gapping.[10]

The morphology of the interrogative pronoun *kuka* 'who' provides an empirical argument for the singular noun ending *-n* being solely genitive, rather than being syncretic between genitive and accusative singular. This interrogative pronoun has various stems and can take nominal or pronominal case inflection, in certain cases:

(13) a. Kuka näh-tiin?
who.NOM see-PASS.PAST
Who was seen?

b. Kene-t näh-tiin?
who-ACC see-PASS.PAST
Who was seen?

However, if *kuka* agrees with a noun or adjective, the accusative is excluded. Thus *kuka kumma* 'who on earth' (lit. 'what strange (one)') and *kuka muu* 'who else', but **kenet kumman* and **kenet muun*:

(14) a. Kene-n kumma-n hän näk-i?
who-GEN strange-GEN s/he see-PASS.PAST
Who on earth did s/he see?

b. *Kene-t kumma-n hän näk-i?
who-ACC strange-GEN s/he see-PASS.PAST
Who on earth did s/he see?

If, as in (9), the singular noun case ending *-n* is exclusively genitive, then (14b) is straightforwardly predicted to be ungrammatical due to lack of case concord. However, if *-n* is also accusative, as per the traditional story, the ungrammaticality of (14b) is unexplained.

[10]Note that the same empirical phenomenon could be used to establish that the *-t* ending on plural nouns (e.g., *karhut* 'bears') is a nominative rather than accusative ending.

Thus, the paradigm in (9) is well-motivated both theoretically and empirically. There is simply no accusative case ending for nouns. But, the discussion so far has focused on morphological case. Next, I turn to a consideration of the featural make-up of Finnish morphosyntactic grammatical case in terms of the features [± HR] and [± LR].

4.2 Morphosyntactic Case

I propose the following featural analysis of the four morphosyntactic grammatical cases in Finnish:

(15)

Nominative	Accusative	Genitive	Partitive
$\begin{bmatrix} \ \end{bmatrix}$	$\begin{bmatrix} - & \text{HR} \\ - & \text{LR} \end{bmatrix}$	$\begin{bmatrix} /+ & \text{HR} \end{bmatrix}$	$\begin{bmatrix} - & \text{HR} \\ + & \text{LR} \end{bmatrix}$

Genitive and nominative mark both objects and subjects, as will be spelled out in the rest of the paper. It is this fact that leads to the particular featural make-up of the Finnish nominative and genitive cases. Subjects are [+ HR], while objects are [− HR]. In addition, transitive subjects are [− LR], while intransitive subjects are [+ LR]. This means that both nominative and genitive must unify with [± HR] and [± LR]. One way that this is possible on this theory is by total underspecification, i.e., underspecification for both HR and LR. However, there can only be one totally underspecified case (see section 2.3 above). The natural choice for the underspecified case is nominative, as this also allows generalizations to be made about nominative and absolutive case together (Kiparsky, 2001). Since the genitive cannot be underspecified, it must bear some feature. The assignment of [/+ HR] allows it to appear in the right contexts, while predicting certain facts about nominative and genitive distribution due to the interaction of defaults with the three principles introduced in section 5. Thus, according to this proposal, nominative is the maximally underspecified case as discussed in section 2.3, and is not related to particular abstract cases, while genitive case is related to the S/A abstract subject cases. As for the remaining two grammatical cases, partitive is related to the abstract O case (see section 2.1), while accusative case is a realization of the D abstract case, and is thus not the primary object case. In effect partitive is what is normally called accusative, and accusative is a kind of dative. In the rest of this section I will motivate the featural assignment for these morphosyntactic cases, which departs somewhat from various versions of Kiparsky's analysis (Kiparsky, 1996, 2001).

Nominative case can appear in a multitude of contexts. It can appear on what Kiparsky (2001) refers to as 'R-objects' (resultative objects). These are the objects of aspectually bounded predicates, including all telic (i.e., resultative) ones, like *ampua* 'shoot' in (28a) below, and certain atelic predicates, such as *n¨ahd¨a* 'see'. This latter class is exceptional,[11] and I must stipulate lexically that it has no lowest role (i.e., the object argument for these predicates is assigned [– LR]). Only plural, noun R-objects get nominative case, with the *-t* case ending:[12]

(16) (Sinä) näit karhu-t.
2SG see.PAST bear-NOM.PL
You saw the bears.

The semantic form for *n¨ahd¨a* ('see') is:

(17) $\lambda y \begin{bmatrix} - & \text{HR} \\ - & \text{LR} \end{bmatrix} \quad \lambda x \begin{bmatrix} + & \text{HR} \\ - & \text{LR} \end{bmatrix} \quad [\text{ x SEE y }]$

The R-object is the lowest argument, y, which is exceptionally assigned [– HR, – LR], rather than [– HR, + LR].

The nominative also appears on certain VP-internal subjects (those without a semantically partitive interpretation; see Kiparsky, 1998), as in (18), as well as the subjects of finite intransitive verbs, as in (19), and the subjects of finite transitive verbs as in (20):

(18) Nyt tule-e uutise-t.
Now come-3SG news-NOM.PL
Now comes the news.

(19) (Sinä-∅) tulit.
2SG-NOM come.PAST
You came.

(20) (Sinä-∅) näit häne-t.
2SG-NOM see.PAST 3SG.ACC
You saw him/her.

The subject of the transitive is assigned [+ HR, – LR], as we would expect, while the subject of the intransitive receives the specification [+ HR, + LR] as the sole arguments of its predicates. Lastly, the internal subject in (18) is exceptionally assigned [– HR], giving it the case matrix [– HR, + LR]. The nominative must also be able to unify with all three feature matrices.

[11]The differences between these exceptional atelic predicates and other atelic predicates may ultimately be semantic (see Kiparsky, 1998).

[12]Recall that Finnish allows pro drop for 1st and 2nd person.

Therefore, the nominative must be able to unify with object feature matrices with form [– HR, – LR] and subject feature matrices with forms [+ HR, – LR], [+ HR, + LR], and [– HR, + LR]. In other words, it must unify with both [± HR] and [± LR]. It must either have default specifications for these features, or it must be completely underspecified. Cross-linguistic considerations force the latter choice. In the analysis of split ergativity proposed in Kiparsky (1996, 2001), absolutive and nominative cases are treated as identical. Since this nominative/absolutive case appears on both objects and subjects, it must be underspecified as [ ].

Next I turn to the accusative feature matrix. Accusative case should be specified as [– HR], because it never appears on subjects, which are always [+ HR]. Second, the accusative only appears on R-objects that are pronominal:

(21) Näit häne-t.
see.PAST.2SG 3SG-ACC
You saw him/her.

As discussed above, these objects are [– HR, – LR]. Therefore, the accusative must also be [– LR]. Thus, accusative has the feature matrix of a secondary object; primary objects, which Kiparsky (2001) calls 'I-objects' (irresultative objects), are [– HR, + LR].

In the verbal domain,[13] genitive case marks subjects of nonfinite verbs, as well as singular noun R-objects:

(22) Halus-i-n sinu-n näke-vä-n karhu-n.
want-PAST-1SG 2SG.GEN see-1PART-GEN bear-GEN
I wanted you to see a/the bear.

(23) Näit karhu-n.
see.PAST.2SG bear-GEN
You saw the bear.

Subjects can be either [+ LR] (intransitives) or [– LR] (transitives), therefore the genitive must be underspecified for [± LR]. More importantly, subjects are always [+ HR], but R-objects are [– HR]. Furthermore, the genitive only marks objects as a last resort, when Jahnsson's Rule prohibits nominative object marking, as discussed in the following section. This, together with the fact that underspecifying the genitive for both HR and LR is not possible,[14] means that it must get the feature assignment [/+ HR], which means that it

[13]This is setting aside the obvious role of the genitive as the case for possessors. See the end of section 6 below.

[14]The nominative is underspecifi ed for these features and only one case may be totally underspecifi ed; see section 2.3.

has default [+ HR] and is underspecified for LR.

Lastly, the partitive has the feature assignment [− HR, + LR]. The partitive marks I-objects and also certain internal subjects (see section 6), as in (24) and (25), which are both marked [− HR, + LR].

(24) Löit hän-tä.
hit.PAST.2SG 3SG-PART
You hit (at) him.

(25) Nyt tule-e uutis-i-a.
Now come-3SG news-PL-PART
Now comes (items of) news.

As noted by Kiparsky (2001, 327) the assignment of [− HR] captures the fact that partitive is the general complement case in Finnish, which has also been argued by Vainikka and Maling (1996), among others. On the other hand, partitive does not mark R-objects, which are [− HR, − LR]. Therefore, it gets the feature specification [− HR, + LR].

5 Licensing Finnish Objects

In this section I will illustrate how the relational theory of case specification together with default unification gives a restrictive account of the Finnish object case facts. I will be looking at three verbs, which serve to illustrate the various kinds of objects. The three verbs are: *n¨ahd¨a* 'see', which takes a [− HR, − LR] R-object only, *ly¨od¨a* 'hit (at)' which takes a [− HR, + LR] I-object only, and *ampua* 'shoot', which alternates between an unbounded (i.e., 'shoot at') reading with an I-object and a bounded (i.e., 'shoot and hit') reading with an R-object. The semantic forms for these three verbs are given here; in each case it is the λy argument which is the object.[15]

(26) *n¨ahd¨a* (exceptional atelic)

$$\lambda y \quad \lambda x \quad [\text{ x SEE y }]$$
$$\begin{bmatrix} - & \text{HR} \\ - & \text{LR} \end{bmatrix} \begin{bmatrix} + & \text{HR} \\ - & \text{LR} \end{bmatrix}$$

(27) *ly¨od¨a* (unbounded only)

$$\lambda y \quad \lambda x \quad [\text{ x HIT y }]$$
$$\begin{bmatrix} - & \text{HR} \\ + & \text{LR} \end{bmatrix} \begin{bmatrix} + & \text{HR} \\ - & \text{LR} \end{bmatrix}$$

(28) *ampua*

[15] See section 4.2 for relevant examples.

a. bounded alternant

$$\lambda z \quad \lambda y \quad \lambda x \qquad [\text{ x SHOOT y \& RESULT z }]$$
$$\begin{bmatrix} - & \text{HR} \\ + & \text{LR} \end{bmatrix} \begin{bmatrix} - & \text{HR} \\ - & \text{LR} \end{bmatrix} \begin{bmatrix} + & \text{HR} \\ - & \text{LR} \end{bmatrix}$$

b. unbounded alternant

$$\lambda y \quad \lambda x \qquad [\text{ x SHOOT y }]$$
$$\begin{bmatrix} - & \text{HR} \\ + & \text{LR} \end{bmatrix} \begin{bmatrix} + & \text{HR} \\ - & \text{LR} \end{bmatrix}$$

The assignment of HR and LR to the thematic roles in these predicates works as per usual, save for exceptional atelic predicates like *n'ähd'ä* (see above). The highest role in semantic form (which is always *x* in these examples), gets [+ HR], the lowest role gets [+ LR], and the rest of the feature matrices are derived automatically. In the bounded predicate in (28a), the lowest role is the bounding eventuality. The result role in such predicates can always be realized overtly (Kiparsky, 2001), but can also be covert and simply understood. Therefore, the role y that surfaces as the object in active sentences is [− HR, − LR] in the exceptional atelic and bounded predicates and [− HR, + LR] in the unbounded ones.

These semantic forms are as indicated (implicitly or explicitly) in Kiparsky (2001). For my analysis, I only require these forms, normal and default unification and Specificity as described in section 3 above, and the following three principles.

(29) **Jahnsson's Rule:**
If the subject is an external nominative subject,[16] then the object must have a phonologically realized (i.e., non-zero) case ending. (Jahnsson, 1871; Nelson, 1998; Kiparsky, 2001)

(30) **Realizability:**
A morphosyntactic case is only available to the syntax if it can be realized morphologically by a case ending and every argument must bear morphosyntactic case.

(31) **Conservativity:**
Override defaults only as a last resort.

These are admittedly stipulations, but each one can be motivated theoretically or empirically. Jahnsson's rule, although it surely has a deeper explanation,

[16] An "external nominative subject" is a subject that is in [Spec, IP], as opposed to VP-internal, and bears structural nominative case (Kiparsky, 2001, 333). See section 6 for a discussion of Finnish subjects and case assignment.

is a striking generalization about the distribution of nominative and genitive case in Finnish, and is one of the OT constraints used by Kiparsky (2001). Therefore, its use here loses no theoretical ground to that analysis. In particular, the formulation of Jahnsson's Rule presented here entails that if the object does not have a phonologically realized case ending (i.e., it is nominative), as in the following example from Nelson (1998, 20, (30b)), then the external subject must not bear nominative case.

(32) Naapur-ien täyty-y myy-dä talo.
neighbour-GEN.PL must-3SG sell-INF house.NOM.3SG
The neighbours must sell the house.

Notice that the verb bears default third person singular agreement and does not agree with the plural subject. The principles in (29)–(31) and the default theory of role assignment developed here will ensure that the subject in these cases gets genitive case (see section 6 below).

The principle of Realizability requires that abstract morphological information must be realized somehow. It essentially states that morphosyntactic case must be associated with some case morpheme (even the null (-∅) case). This is just a slightly revised version of the visibility condition of Kiparsky (1996). If the principle of Realizability did not hold, then the motivation for the lack of accusative case in the paradigm in (9) above would be considerably undermined. Lastly, the principle of Conservativity is a general constraint motivated by learning theoretic considerations.[17] Essentially, with respect to case assignment in particular, overriding a default creates an opaque representation, as a morphosyntactic case realized in a context that overrides its default will have a featural value that it does not have underlyingly. It is reasonable to expect languages learners to avoid positing opaque representations whenever possible,[18] and for grammars to avoid opacity as a result.[19] Thus, these three principles are simply ones that any licensing theory for Finnish that takes morphology and learnability seriously must countenance.

With all this in hand, we can now turn to the analysis of case assignment to objects. First, let us look at genitive objects as in the following sentences:

[17]Ann Copestake (p.c.) has pointed out that this principle does not stem from the default logic itself. In fact, one way to think about Conservativity is as a default principle in the metalanguage of the licensing theory proposed here, as opposed to default unifi cation which operates in objects the theory describes.

[18]Briscoe (1999) and Villavicencio (2000a,b) present models of language acquisition using Lascarides and Copestake's (1999) default logic which, for reasons related to those under discussion, minimize the amount of default overrides, based on the Minimal Description Length optimization algorithm (Rissanen, 1989).

[19]Notice that opacity is then an emergent property of language learning and the representations posited. I am not reifying the notion of opaque representation.

(33) Näit karhu-n.
see.PAST.2SG bear-GEN
You saw the bear.

(34) Ammu-i-n karhu-n.
shoot-PAST-1SG bear-GEN
I shot a/the bear.

The genitive object in both cases is an R-object (see above) and is therefore [– HR, – LR]. The object is in VP-internal object position which gets the feature [– HR] due to its position.

The charts in (35) below sum up the assignment of genitive case and lists the conditions that the other cases would violate. The selected case is outlined in the top chart, along with the abstract case and positional licensing. The bottom chart shows the cases that have been rejected and the principles responsible for their rejection.

(35) **Genitive Object**

Selected Case

Morphosyntactic Case	**Morphological Case**	**Abstract Case**	**Positional Licensing**
GEN: $\begin{bmatrix} /+\ \text{HR} \end{bmatrix}$	*-n* (gen.)	$\begin{bmatrix} -\ \text{HR} \\ -\ \text{LR} \end{bmatrix}$	$[_{\text{VP}}$ V NP] [– HR][20]

Rejected Cases

Morphosyntactic Case	**Morphological Case**	**Principle Violated**
NOM: $\begin{bmatrix} \ \end{bmatrix}$	-∅	**Jahnsson's Rule**
PART: $\begin{bmatrix} -\ \text{HR} \\ +\ \text{LR} \end{bmatrix}$	*-(t)a*	**[– LR] $\not\sqcup$ [+ LR]**
ACC: $\begin{bmatrix} -\ \text{HR} \\ -\ \text{LR} \end{bmatrix}$	—	**Realizability**

This table shows all the principles in (29)–(31) and normal and default unification at work. The nominative, although it could unify with the abstract case, is out due to Jahnsson's Rule, since there is an external nominative sub-

[20]Since [– HR] ⊔ [/+ HR] = [– HR].

ject.[21] The partitive is out because of normal unification failure on the LR feature, as indicated. The accusative is out due to Realizability: there is no accusative morphological case ending for nouns, as discussed extensively in section 4.1 above. This leaves only the genitive case, which must be selected due to Realizability. This results in opacity, but Conservativity allows this as a last resort and in this instance there is no other grammatical case that could be selected.

Next I turn to accusative case, which occurs on R-objects when they are pronominal, as in the following sentences.

(36) Näit häne-t.
see.PAST.2SG 3SG-ACC
You saw him/her.

(37) Ammu-i-n häne-t.
shoot-PAST-1SG 3SG-ACC
I shot him/her.

Notice that in these cases we have true accusative morphology as per paradigm (9). Here are the charts for accusative objects:

(38) **Accusative Object**

Selected Case			
Morphosyntactic Case	**Morphological Case**	**Abstract Case**	**Positional Licensing**
ACC: $\begin{bmatrix} - & \text{HR} \\ - & \text{LR} \end{bmatrix}$	*-t* (acc.)	$\begin{bmatrix} - & \text{HR} \\ - & \text{LR} \end{bmatrix}$	$[_{VP}\ \text{V}\ \ \text{NP}\ ]$ $[-\text{HR}]$

Rejected Cases		
Morphosyntactic Case	**Morphological Case**	**Principle(s) Violated**
NOM: $[\ \ ]$	*-∅*	**Jahnsson's Rule** **Specifi city**
PART: $\begin{bmatrix} - & \text{HR} \\ + & \text{LR} \end{bmatrix}$	*-(t)a*	**$[-\text{LR}] \not\sqcup [+\text{LR}]$**
GEN: $[/+\ \ \text{HR}]$	*-n*	**Conservativity** **Specifi city**

[21] Although the subject is not realized syntactically (i.e., sentences (33) and (34) both exemplify pro-drop), it will still get nominative case, as will be evident in section 6 below.

The nominative is again excluded by Jahnsson's Rule, as in the genitive object derivation, but is also less specific than the accusative. The partitive is out again because of unification failure for the feature LR. The accusative can be selected, since there is a morphological case ending *-t* for pronouns, and Realizability is thus satisfied in this case. Finally, the genitive is out due to Conservativity, because selecting the accusative means that the default [/+ HR] does not have to be overridden, and also due to Specificity.

The final instance of R-objects to consider is those that are marked as nominative. These are plural noun objects in bounded predicates:

(39) Sinä näit karhu-t.
2SG see.PAST bear-NOM.PL
You saw the bears.

(40) Ammu-i-n karhu-t.
shoot-PAST-1SG bear-NOM.PL
I shot the bears.

Here are the charts for nominative objects:

(41) **Nominative Object**

Selected Case

Morphosyntactic Case	**Morphological Case**	**Abstract Case**	**Positional Licensing**
NOM:$\left[\ \right]$	*-t* (nom.)	$\begin{bmatrix} - & \text{HR} \\ - & \text{LR} \end{bmatrix}$	$[_{\text{VP}}$ V NP] [− HR]

Rejected Cases

Morphosyntactic Case	**Morphological Case**	**Principle Violated**
ACC:$\begin{bmatrix} - & \text{HR} \\ - & \text{LR} \end{bmatrix}$	—	**Realizability**
PART:$\begin{bmatrix} - & \text{HR} \\ + & \text{LR} \end{bmatrix}$	*-(t)a*	**[− LR] $\not\sqcup$ [+ LR]**
GEN:$\left[/+ \ \text{HR} \right]$	*-n*	**Conservativity**

According to paradigm (1) there is no accusative case ending for nouns. Therefore, assigning accusative morphosyntactic case to the objects in (39) and (40) would violate the principle of Realizability. The partitive is again out due to unification failure on the feature LR. The nominative in this case can be selected because there is no violation of Jahnsson's Rule. That is, even though (39) and (40) have external nominative subjects (in the relevant sense), the nominative can also be selected as the object case because in the plural it does have a phonologically-realized case ending, namely *-t*. And, since we can select the nominative, selecting the genitive would not be a last resort and would result in opacity with no gain. Therefore, Conservativity rules out the genitive. Thus, these objects get nominative case.

We should also consider what happens when there is a singular nominative object, as in sentence (32) above, which demonstrated Jahnsson's Rule:

(32) Naapur-ien täyty-y myy-dä talo.
neighbour-GEN.PL must-3SG sell-INF house.NOM.3SG
The neighbours must sell the house.

Here nominative case-marking for the object is available because there is no external nominative subject and Jahnsson's Rule is therefore not violated, as discussed above. All the other cases are out for the reasons just discussed.

Having seen case assignment to genitive, accusative and nominative objects, we are now in a position to consider an alternation discussed by Vainikka (2003):[22]

(42) Uolevi-n väitetään saavan palkankorotus.
Uolevi-GEN claim.PASS get.INF raise.NOM
Uolevi is claimed to receive a raise.

(43) Uolevi-n väitetään saavan palkankorotuks-en.
Uolevi-GEN claim.PASS get.INF raise-GEN
Uolevi is claimed to receive a raise

The matrix external subject in these sentences bears genitive case: it has been raised from the external subject of the embedded nonfinite verb *saavan* (Vainikka, 2003), which bears genitive case (see section 6 below). Therefore, Jahnsson's Rule does not apply and we would expect the nominative object as in (42), but not the genitive object as in (43), because the latter violates Conservativity, given the availability of the nominative. However, Vainikka writes "this particular non-finite verb form in Finnish prefers the genitive option." At this point, I do not have an account of the availability of genitive, which is unexpected.

Vainikka (2003) goes on to note that this variation is available only for singular full NP objects. Plural full NPs must receive nominative case and

[22]I thank the reviewer for this paper for bringing these data to my attention. I have slightly modifi ed Vainikka's glosses to make them consistent with the other examples in the paper. In particular, it should be noted that she is operating with the traditional paradigm in (10), so she glosses the NOM object in (42) and (44) as ACC/NOM and the GEN object in (43) as ACC/GEN.

pronouns must receive accusative:

(44) Uolevi-n väitetään saavan palkinno-t/* palkintoj-en.
Uolevi-GEN claim.PASS get.INF awards-NOM/awards-GEN
Uolevi is claimed to receive the awards.

(45) Uolevi-n väitetään omistavan sinu-t/* sinu-n/* sinä.
Uolevi-GEN claim.PASS own.INF you-ACC/you-GEN/you-NOM
Uolevi is claimed to own you.

This is exactly what would be predicted by the default licensing theory. The nominative object is not ruled out for plurals, since it has a morphological realization; it is therefore preferred to genitive and is selected, as accusative has no morphological case, violating Realizability, and partitive has unification failure for LR. As for pronominals, there is an accusative case ending and it is selected as shown in the charts for accusative objects (38).

It may at first blush seem that examples (42)–(45) are arguments for the traditional paradigm (10), which posits that the accusative singular is syncretic with nominative, as in (42) and (44), and with genitive, as in (43). The generalization seems to be that the object is always in the accusative. However, although the accusative on this account can either be realized with no ending or a *-t* ending (nominative-like) or with an *-n* ending (genitive-like), it is not true that the forms are normally in free variation:

(46) Ammuin karhun/* karhu.
shoot bear.GEN/bear.NOM
I shot the bear.

Indeed, traditional grammar labels the two accusatives Accusative 1 and Accusative 2; they are essentially two different cases which both happen to be called "Accusative".

We have so far seen that the system described here, which uses Kiparsky's theory of grammatical case but replaces the optimality-theoretic constraints with a smaller set of well-motivated principles and default unification, gets good results for R-objects, be they genitive, accusative, or nominative. The last case to consider is I-objects, which are always partitive and occur as the objects of unbounded predicates:

(47) Löit hän-tä.
hit.PAST.2SG 3SG-PART
You hit (at) him.

(48) Ammu-i-n karhu-a.
shoot-PAST-1SG bear-PART
I shot at a/the bear.

As discussed above, these are I-objects and are thus [– HR, + LR]. This is crucial in the analysis of partitive objects, because now the partitive case can unify with the object feature matrix, as shown in the charts for partitive objects:

(49) **Partitive Object**

Selected Case

Morphosyntactic Case	**Morphological Case**	**Abstract Case**	**Positional Licensing**
PART: $\begin{bmatrix} - & \text{HR} \\ + & \text{LR} \end{bmatrix}$	*-(t)a* (part.)	$\begin{bmatrix} - & \text{HR} \\ + & \text{LR} \end{bmatrix}$	$[_{\text{VP}}$ V NP] [– HR]

Rejected Cases

Morphosyntactic Case	**Morphological Case**	**Principle(s) Violated**
NOM: [ ]	-∅ (sing.)	**Jahnsson's Rule** **Specifi city**
NOM: [ ]	*-t* (plur.)	**Specifi city**
GEN: [/+ HR]	*-en*	**Conservativity** **Specifi city**
ACC: $\begin{bmatrix} - & \text{HR} \\ - & \text{LR} \end{bmatrix}$	—	**[– LR] $\not\sqcup$ [+ LR]** **Realizability** **(nouns)**
ACC: $\begin{bmatrix} - & \text{HR} \\ - & \text{LR} \end{bmatrix}$	*-t*	**[– LR] $\not\sqcup$ [+ LR]** **(pronouns)**

In the previous charts, which were all for R-object case marking, the partitive was not selected due to unification failure for the feature LR. But, I-objects are [– HR, + LR] and the partitive can therefore unify for both the HR and LR features. When the object is singular, the zero nominative is out because of Jahnsson's Rule, as before, and also due to Specificity. When the object is plural, although the plural nominative with the *-t* ending is in principle possible as far as Jahnsson's Rule is concerned, it is blocked by Specificity. In other words, the partitive is selected because it is specified for HR and LR, whereas the nominative is underspecified. The genitive is similarly out due to Specificity, and since the partitive is available, also due to Conservativity.

For accusative case there are two scenarios to consider. First, if the object is a noun, the accusative is barred by Realizability, since there is no morphological accusative case ending, and also due to straightforward unification failure for the feature LR. And if the object is a pronoun, the accusative is again out due to unification failure, although its selection would not violate Realizability.

5.1 Summary and Discussion

In this section I have shown how we can get a restrictive theory of object case-marking in Finnish without using Optimality Theory. The analysis presented here uses only well-motivated generalizations about Finnish, morphology in general, and learnability, in addition to normal unification and a restrictive theory of default unification (Lascarides and Copestake, 1999). In addition, it only needs three principles: Jahnsson's Rule, Realizability, and Conservativity. This is in contrast to the five or more (depending on the version) constraints used in Kiparsky's OT treatments (Kiparsky, 2001).

Furthermore, the constraints used in the OT model are not so well-motivated and are not very general. Jahnsson's Rule is invoked in both analyses, and to the extent that it is a robust generalization about Finnish case-marking, it is well-motivated. However, here it is presented only as a principle governing case assignment *in Finnish*. Even though the featural space introduced by the theory makes typological predictions (see below), there is nothing in the theory that entails that each principle is universal. The other principles appealed to here, Realizability and Conservativity, are general principles that would plausibly be appealed to in any generative theory of morphology that takes language acquisition as an explanandum. Thus, Realizability and Conservativity are motivated by factors that are common to all languages, and are therefore universal; Jahnsson's Rule is a descriptive generalization about Finnish and is not universal. By contrast, in the OT model, as the constraints are universal, Jahnsson's Rule putatively exists in *all* languages. This state of affairs is clearly problematic for the OT account.

In addition, the general principles used in this analysis together with the paradigm in (9) which is also assumed in Kiparsky's analyses, clearly predict the noun/pronoun split for the accusative. In the OT analysis, though, the split is directly encoded in two constraints: MAX[−HR]/D and MAX[−LR]/N. The first constraint requires that the feature [− HR] on a thematic role in the input must be realized in the output (as morphosyntactic case), as long as the case is assigned to a pronoun. Similarly, the second constraint requires that a noun argument assigned [− LR] in the input must bear a morphosyntactic case with [− LR]. This simply reifies the split between pronouns and nouns.

Furthermore, why should it be that these case features in particular must be realized? Surely, this is a fact about Finnish. Thus, under the typological assumptions of OT these constraints are problematic and they are arbitrary in any case.

In the analysis presented here, the split is not reified: there are no principles that refer to nouns versus pronouns. Rather, the split arises naturally as a result of positing no accusative morphology for nouns, and standard unification failure for I-object pronominal accusatives. In other words, it falls out of the system proposed here that accusatives can only mark pronominal R-objects. However, there is no reason why the hierarchical scale for nouns and pronouns assumed by Kiparsky (2001) could not be used in this theory. The details would vary, but it is just as feasible to state that pronouns should have such and such a feature composition while nouns have another. The lack of such a scale in this analysis is a theoretical decision, and not a necessity of the formalism used.

Lastly, the markedness constraints *[−HR] and *[αF] are also problematic. First, why does *[−HR] exist as a more specific instance of *[αF]? There is no motivation for *[−HR] in particular: why not *[+HR], or *[+LR], or *[−LR]? Second, these two constraints are *directly* responsible for selecting every nominative object and for selecting every nominative subject in Kiparsky's (2001) analysis.

On the other hand, the present analysis treats nominative precisely as the "unmarked" case, without appealing to any constraint or principle that directly favours it. In fact, Specificity mitigates *against* it. Despite this, the nominative is selected precisely when it is a better option than picking the genitive, due to opacity. Thus, we get the *emergence of the unmarked without Optimality Theory*, but rather due to a restrictive substantive theory of morphology and learning, and to an implementation using default unification. This is equivalent to emergence of the unmarked in OT, in the sense that a normally suppressed alternative is selected in the absence of other alternatives, but I have not invoked "markedness" as a formal, explanatory device; instead I have invoked the amount of featural information that is provided by morphemes and that results from their unification with other information in the grammar. In particular, I am not making the claim that nominative is somehow more frequent or bears less semantic information than other cases; but we have seen that it is the case that surfaces when more specific cases are unavailable. This does not preclude another case being the default case in a specific position or semantic considerations from further influencing the choice of available cases.[23]

[23]Both of these factors have been discussed with respect to partitive case (Vainikka and Mal-

Beside emergence of the unmarked, another virtue of Optimality Theory is that it makes predictions about typology, as the only difference between languages arises through a factorial reranking of the constraints. Because of this property, the analysis of one language makes predictions about other languages, as the constraint set is putatively universal and thus by positing constraints we are implicitly stating facts about other languages, as these arise simply through constraint reranking. Kiparsky's OT analysis thus makes predictions about other languages, and the constraints he postulates, with the exception of the constraint concerning Jahnsson's Rule, are cross-linguistically plausible.

However, factorial reranking of constraints is not the only way to make typological predictions. In fact, the present analysis makes certain formal predictions too. Consider the feature matrices we have been using. There are two features, HR and LR. Each feature can have five values: [+],[−],[/+],[/−], and [ ]. This means we get a feature space with 5^2 possibilities out of which languages can choose case specifications. However, since defaults persist unless overridden, this is somewhat misleading. There are in actuality only nine distinct cases,[24] but each value can be default or nondefault. Even if we take the larger feature space with twenty-five possibilities as our baseline of comparison, this is roughly equivalent to an OT analysis which posits 4 constraints, with factorial ranking ($4! = 24$). Now, Kiparsky's OT analysis, and indeed *all* OT analyses of any non-toy problem, posit more than 4 constraints to describe the data. Thus, the present theory also has advantages from the perspective of typology as it makes much more restricted predictions, even though typological prediction is one of the hallmarks of Optimality Theory.

There is one last aspect of Kiparsky's OT analysis which needs to be considered. As mentioned above, the constraints *[−HR] and *[αF] are also used in deriving subject case marking. It remains to be shown that the current analysis can handle licensing of subjects. In the next section I will show that this analysis can do this successfully, providing we also bear in mind the semantics of the partitive and genitive and the role of finiteness in subject licensing.

6 Licensing Finnish Subjects

Finnish subjects can bear one of three grammatical cases: nominative, genitive, or partitive. Nominative case marks subjects of finite verbs, transitive or intransitive. It also marks internal subjects, under one possible semantic

ing, 1996; Kiparsky, 1998; Anttila and Fong, 2000).

[24]This number comes from the three non-default values for each feature: [+], [−], [ ] ($3^2 = 9$).

interpretation. Genitive case marks subjects of nonfinite verbs, transitive or intransitive. Lastly, partitive case marks internal subjects, under the other semantic interpretation. The semantic difference between nominative internal subjects and partitive ones concerns partition. Although partitive case is a structural case in Finnish, in certain contexts, such as this one, it also confers partitive semantics (i.e., reference to parts of a whole rather than the whole itself; see Kiparsky, 1998; Anttila and Fong, 2000). Here are some examples:

(50) **Nominative external subject**

a. **Finite transitive verb**
Sinä-∅ näit häne-t.
2SG-NOM see.PAST 3SG.ACC
You saw him/her.

b. **Finite intransitive verb**
Sinä-∅ tulit.
2SG-NOM come.PAST
You came.

(51) **Nominative internal subject**
Nyt tule-e uutise-t.
Now come-3SG news-NOM.PL
Now comes the news.

(52) **Genitive external subject**

a. **Nonfinite transitive verb**
Halus-i-n sinu-n näke-vä-n minu-t.
want-PAST-1SG you-GEN see-1PART-GEN 1SG-ACC
I wanted you to see me.

b. **Nonfinite intransitive verb**
Halus-i-n sinu-n lähte-vä-n.
want-PAST-1SG you-GEN leave-1PART-GEN
I wanted you to leave.

(53) **Partitive internal subject**
Nyt tule-e uutis-i-a.
Now come-3SG news-PL-PART
Now comes (items of) news.

Due to the normal assignment of HR and LR according to depth of embedding in Semantic Form, external subjects of intransitives will be [+ HR, + LR], as they are the sole arguments of their predicates. External subjects of transitives, on the other hand, will be [+ HR, – LR], as there will be a lower role for the object. Lastly, internal subject are exceptionally specified [– HR, + LR], which explains why they are licensed at all as the complement to V.

Here are the case charts for external subjects of transitives:

(54) **External Subject of Transitive**

Selected Cases

Morphosyntactic Case	**Morphological Case**	**Abstract Case**	**Positional Licensing**
NOM: $\left[\ \right]$	-∅ (nom.)	$\begin{bmatrix} + & \text{HR} \\ - & \text{LR} \end{bmatrix}$	$[_{\text{IP}}$ NP I′] [+ HR]
GEN: $\left[/+ \ \ \text{HR} \right]$	*-n*		

Rejected Cases

Morphosyntactic Case	**Morphological Case**	**Principle(s) Violated**
PART: $\begin{bmatrix} - & \text{HR} \\ + & \text{LR} \end{bmatrix}$	*-(t)a*	**[− LR] ⊔̸ [+ LR]** **[− HR] ⊔̸ [+ HR]**
ACC: $\begin{bmatrix} - & \text{HR} \\ - & \text{LR} \end{bmatrix}$	—	**[− HR] ⊔̸ [+ HR]** **Realizability** **(nouns)**
ACC: $\begin{bmatrix} - & \text{HR} \\ - & \text{LR} \end{bmatrix}$	*-t*	**[− HR] ⊔̸ [+ HR]** **(pronouns)**

Partitive case is out due to straightforward unification failure for the features HR and LR. Similarly, accusative case is out due to unification failure on the feature HR. In addition, accusative case on a full noun subject cannot be realized, further violating Realizability. This leaves nominative and genitive case, exactly as required. Specificity does not choose between these alternatives, because a default specification and no specification are equally specific (see section 3 above). I take it that there has to be a principle invoking finiteness of the verb that selects for nominative versus genitive on finite verbs' subjects and nonfinite verbs' subjects respectively. The OT analysis presented in Kiparsky (2001) must make the same assumption, as noted therein (Kiparsky, 2001, 330–331). Notice that according to this analysis, partitive and accusative are simply excluded due to unification failure. Thus, there is no recourse to constraints which prefer nominative case. Rather, the subject as an argument must get some grammatical case, as per Realizability, and the only choices are nominative and genitive.

Now let us turn to the case charts for the [+ HR, + LR] external subjects of intransitives:

(55) **External Subject of Intransitive**

Selected Cases

Morphosyntactic Case	**Morphological Case**	**Abstract Case**	**Positional Licensing**
NOM: $\begin{bmatrix} \ \end{bmatrix}$	-∅ (nom.)	$\begin{bmatrix} + & \text{HR} \\ + & \text{LR} \end{bmatrix}$	$[_{\text{IP}}\ \text{NP}\ \ \text{I}'\ ]$ [+ HR]
GEN: $\begin{bmatrix} /+ & \text{HR} \end{bmatrix}$	*-n*		

Rejected Cases

Morphosyntactic Case	**Morphological Case**	**Principle(s) Violated**
PART: $\begin{bmatrix} - & \text{HR} \\ + & \text{LR} \end{bmatrix}$	*-(t)a*	**[− HR] $\not\sqcup$ [+ HR]**
ACC: $\begin{bmatrix} - & \text{HR} \\ - & \text{LR} \end{bmatrix}$	—	**[− HR] $\not\sqcup$ [+ HR]** **[− LR] $\not\sqcup$ [+ LR]** **Realizability** **(nouns)**
ACC: $\begin{bmatrix} - & \text{HR} \\ - & \text{LR} \end{bmatrix}$	*-t*	**[− HR] $\not\sqcup$ [+ HR]** **[− LR] $\not\sqcup$ [+ LR]** **(pronouns)**

Once again, accusative case is either ruled out due to having no case ending and violating Realizability, or due to unification failure, this time for both the HR and LR features. Unlike for transitive subjects, partitive case can unify with the feature LR. However, it still fails to unify with HR. As with transitive subjects, both nominative and genitive case can unify with the abstract case, and as before the default value of [/+ HR] for the genitive is not overridden. This means there is no opacity and no violation of Conservativity. As they are equal according to Specificity, both nominative and genitive case are available, and the selection of a particular case depends on whether the verb is finite or nonfinite.

Next I turn to internal subjects, which are motivated and differentiated from objects in Kiparsky (2001). As mentioned above these subjects sit in the normal object position, which normally receives [− HR] due to positional licensing. The exceptional nature of internal subjects is captured by allowing the predicates that license these subjects to exceptionally assign [− HR] to their sole argument, rather than [+ HR]. This allows their subjects to occupy the complement of V, which receives [− HR] by positional licensing.

Another issue that arises with these subjects is that the partitive is also behaving somewhat like a semantic case, as it encodes partition of the nominal it marks. Recall (51) and (53), which are repeated here:

(56) Nyt tule-e uutise-t.
Now come-3SG news-NOM.PL
Now comes the news.

(57) Nyt tule-e uutis-i-a.
Now come-3SG news-PL-PART
Now comes (items of) news.

In this respect, the partitive is serving a semantic function that it also serves in the nominal domain, where complex factors determine whether partitive nominals are marked by the partitive or the elative (Anttila and Fong, 2000). Thus, the nominative is marking lack of partition, whereas the partitive is marking partition of the nominal. They are therefore encoding differing semantic information and as a result Specificity does not choose between them, since morphemes that encode conflicting information are not in a subsumption relation and are equally specific.

With this in mind, here are the charts for internal subjects:

(58) **Internal Subject**

Selected Cases

Morphosyntactic Case	**Morphological Case**	**Abstract Case**	**Positional Licensing**
NOM: $\begin{bmatrix} \end{bmatrix}$	-∅ (nom.)	$\begin{bmatrix} - & \text{HR} \\ + & \text{LR} \end{bmatrix}$	$[_{\text{VP}}$ V NP] [− HR]
PART: $\begin{bmatrix} - & \text{HR} \\ + & \text{LR} \end{bmatrix}$	*-(t)a*		

Rejected Cases

Morphosyntactic Case	**Morphological Case**	**Principle Violated**
GEN: $\begin{bmatrix} /+ & \text{HR} \end{bmatrix}$	*-n*	**Conservativity**
ACC: $\begin{bmatrix} - & \text{HR} \\ - & \text{LR} \end{bmatrix}$	—	**[+ LR] $\not\sqsubseteq$ [− LR] (nouns)**
ACC: $\begin{bmatrix} - & \text{HR} \\ - & \text{LR} \end{bmatrix}$	*-t*	**[+ LR] $\not\sqsubseteq$ [− LR] (pronouns)**

The accusative is out by unification failure for LR (and additionally by Realizability for nouns). Genitive, which is available on an external subject, is nonetheless blocked here by Conservativity, since internal subjects are permitted by virtue of being exceptionally marked [− HR] and the genitives default would have to be overridden to unify with [− HR]. This leaves both the nominative and the partitive, which can in fact mark internal subjects, as shown above. Due to their differing semantics, the nominative and partitive are equally specific.

Finally, note that this analysis predicts genitive possessors as well, such as:

(59) karhu-n pesä
bear-GEN den
the bear's den

(60) minu-n taloni
1SG-GEN house
my house

The possessor is assigned [+ HR], making it equivalent in this respect to a subject (S or A). Accusative and partitive case are barred for the same reasons as they were for external subjects (due to unification failure and/or Realizability). Since genitive encodes the possessor semantics, it contributes more specific information than nominative, leaving genitive as the only possible choice.

6.1 Summary

In this section, I have shown that the same principles and case specifications that license objects also license subjects, both internal and external, and possessors. Furthermore, this was accomplished without recourse to constraints which specifically target nominatives, such as *[−HR] and *[αF]. Rather, subject case marking falls out from the same general scheme, which is another desirable feature of this theory. Although subject selection depends partially on finiteness (for external subjects) and semantics (for internal subjects, also for possessors), any fully articulated theory of licensing in Finnish would have to countenance these facts.

7 Conclusion

I have presented an analysis of licensing in Finnish which uses default unification, rather than Optimality Theory. I have shown how normal and default unification permit a restrictive formulation of abstract case, morphosyntactic case, and positional licensing. Furthermore, the analysis uses only well-motivated generalizations and principles: Jahnsson's Rule, Realizability, and

Conservativity. I have shown that the same morphosyntactic case specifications and principles derive object and subject licensing, as well as genitive possessors. Subject and possessor licensing have some further constraints having to do with finiteness of the verb and partitive interpretations of internal subjects.

The use of defaults adds another locus of typological variation. Thus, languages will have an inventory of grammatical cases, which are specified using the relational features [$\pm$ HR] and [$\pm$ LR] and the value can be either default or non-default. Since case features can be underspecified, with no defaults there can be up to nine different grammatical cases. With defaults there can seemingly be up to twenty-five grammatical cases. But, as noted in section 5.1, defaults persist unless overridden. For example, if [/+ F] is not overridden, it is equivalent to [+ F]. So, another way to think about the number of grammatical cases is that there are in actuality only nine distinct cases, but each value can be default or nondefault. No language has nine grammatical cases. But, this is only specifying the space of possibilities.[25] Default specification does not expand this set of grammatical cases. Rather, it modifies the behaviour of the members. For example, partitive is a grammatical case in Finnish, but it is not in many other languages. Also, another language could have partitive case but with no default specifications; the partitive case would behave slightly differently in such a language. It remains to be seen whether default unification can provide an interesting account of typological variation. But there is no reason per se why it could not. And in fact, whether we take the space of featural differences to have nine members or twenty-five members, this is a more restrictive space of variation than that which results from factorially ranking just five OT constraints. Thus, the consideration of typology in this theory remains an interesting avenue for future work, and for the language-specific analysis of Finnish, default unification has been used here in lieu of Optimality Theory to provide a more restrictive licensing theory.

[25]There may be a cognitive/representational or learnability reason for the underutilization of structural case possibilities. Various recent treatments of case syncretization, where a phonologically ambiguous case can correspond to multiple abstract cases, have proposed complex case values such as {acc, gen} or acc&gen, depending on the theory (see, e.g. Dalrymple and Kaplan, 2000; Levine et al., 2001; Levy and Pollard, 2002). Levy and Pollard (2002) note that this leads to a proliferation of case values such that there will be $2^n - 1$ possible values, where n is the number of cases. For example, this means that a four case system like that of Finnish would have 15 case values, while a nine case system would have 511.

References

Anttila, Arto and Vivienne Fong. 2000. The partitive constraint in Optimality Theory. *Journal of Semantics* 17(4):281–314.

Bierwisch, Manfred. 1986. On the nature of semantic form in natural languages. In F. Klix and H. Hangendorf, eds., *Human Memory and Cognitive Capabilities*, pages 765–783. Amsterdam: Elsevier.

Bierwisch, Manfred and Robert Schreuder. 1992. From concepts to lexical items. *Cognition* 42:23–60.

Bresnan, Joan. 2001. *Lexical-Functional Syntax*. Oxford: Blackwell.

Briscoe, Ted. 1999. The acquisition of grammar in an evolving population of language agents. *Electronic Transactions on Artificial Intelligence* pages 47–77.

Butt, Miriam, Mary Dalrymple, and Anette Frank. 1997. An architecture for linking theory in LFG. In M. Butt and T. H. King, eds., *Proceedings of the LFG '97 conference*. Stanford, CA: CSLI Publications.

Chomsky, Noam. 1981. *Lectures on Government and Binding*. Dordrecht: Foris.

Chomsky, Noam. 1986. *Knowledge of Language: Its nature, origin, and use*. New York: Praeger.

Chomsky, Noam. 1995. *The Minimalist Program*. Cambridge, MA: MIT Press.

Dalrymple, Mary. 2001. *Lexical Functional Grammar*. San Diego, CA: Academic Press.

Dalrymple, Mary and Ron Kaplan. 2000. Feature indeterminacy and feature resolution in description-based syntax. *Language* 74(4):759–798.

Davis, Anthony and Jean-Pierre Koenig. 2000. Linking as constraints on word classes in a hierarchical lexicon. *Language* 76:56–91.

Dixon, Robert M. W. 1979. Ergativity. *Language* 55:59–138.

Ginzburg, Jonathan and Ivan Sag. 2001. *Interrogative Investigations*. Stanford, CA: CSLI Publications.

Jackendoff, Ray. 1990. *Semantic Structures*. Cambridge, MA: MIT Press.

Jahnsson, A. W. 1871. *Finska språkets satslära*. Helsingfors (Helsinki): s.n.

Joppen, Sandra and Dieter Wunderlich. 1995. Argument linking in Basque. *Lingua* 97:123–169.

Kaplan, Ronald M. and Joan Bresnan. 1982. Lexical-Functional Grammar: A formal system for grammatical representation. In J. Bresnan, ed., *The Mental Representation of Grammatical Relations*, pages 173–281. Cambridge, MA: MIT Press.

Kiparsky, Paul. 1973. Elsewhere in phonology. In S. Anderson and P. Kiparsky, eds., *A Festschrift for Morris Halle*. New York: Holt, Rinehart and Winston.

Kiparsky, Paul. 1996. Structural case. Ms., Stanford University.

Kiparsky, Paul. 1997. The rise of positional licensing. In A. van Kemenade and N. Vincent, eds., *Parameters of morphosyntactic change*. Cambridge: Cambridge University Press.

Kiparsky, Paul. 1998. Partitive case and aspect. In M. Butt and W. Geuder, eds., *The*

Projection of Arguments: Lexical and Compositional Factors, pages 265–307. Stanford, CA: CSLI Publications.

Kiparsky, Paul. 2000. Morphosyntax. Class lectures, Stanford University.

Kiparsky, Paul. 2001. Structural case in Finnish. *Lingua* 111(4–7):315–376.

Koenig, Jean-Pierre and Anthony Davis. 2001. Sublexical modality and the structure of lexical semantic representations. *Linguistics and Philosophy* 24:71–124.

Lascarides, Alex, Ted Briscoe, Nicholas Asher, and Ann Copestake. 1996. Order independent and persistent typed default unification. *Linguistics and Philosophy* 19:1–90.

Lascarides, Alex and Ann Copestake. 1999. Default representation in constraint-based frameworks. *Computational Linguistics* 25:55–105.

Levine, Robert D., Thomas E. Hukari, and Michael Calcagno. 2001. Parasitic gaps in English: Some overlooked cases and their theoretical implications. In P. W. Culicover and P. M. Postal, eds., *Parasitic Gaps*. Cambridge, MA: MIT Press.

Levy, Roger and Carl Pollard. 2002. Coordination and neutralization in HPSG. In F. van Eynde, L. Hellan, and D. Beermann, eds., *Proceedings of the 8th International HPSG Conference*, pages 221–234. Stanford, CA: CSLI Publications.

Nelson, Diane. 1998. *Grammatical Case Assignment in Finnish*. New York: Garland.

Ostler, Nicholas D. M. 1979. *Case-Linking: A Theory of Case and Verb Diathesis Applied to Classical Sanskrit*. Ph.D. thesis, MIT.

Pollard, Carl and Ivan A. Sag. 1994. *Head-driven Phrase Structure Grammar*. Chicago, IL and Stanford, CA: The University of Chicago Press and CSLI Publications.

Prince, Alan and Paul Smolensky. 1993. Optimality Theory: Constraint interaction in generative grammar. Tech. rep., RuCCS, Rutgers University, New Brunswick, NJ. Technical Report #2.

Rissanen, Jorma. 1989. *Stochastic Complexity in Statistical Inquiry*. Singapore: World Scientific.

Shore, Susanna. 1988. On the so-called Finnish passive. *Word* 39:151–176.

Stiebels, Barbara. 2000. Linker inventories, linking splits and lexical economy. In B. Stiebels and D. Wunderlich, eds., *Lexicon in focus*, pages 213–247. Berlin: Akademie Verlag.

Vainikka, Anne. 1989. *Deriving Syntactic Representations in Finnish*. Ph.D. thesis, University of Massachusetts, Amherst, MA.

Vainikka, Anne. 2003. Postverbal case realization in Finnish. This volume.

Vainikka, Anne and Joan Maling. 1996. Is partitive case inherent or structural? In J. Hoeksema, ed., *Partitives. Studies on the syntax and semantics of partitive and related constructions*. Berlin: Mouton de Gruyter.

Villavicencio, Aline. 2000a. The acquisition of a unification-based generalised categorial grammar. In *Proceedings of CLUK*. Brighton.

Villavicencio, Aline. 2000b. The acquisition of word order by a computational learning system. In *Proceedings of the 2nd Learning Logic in Language Workshop*. Lisbon.

Wunderlich, Dieter and Renate Lakämper. 2001. On the interaction of structural and semantic case. *Lingua* 111(4–7):377–418.

6

Resultatives and Depictives in Finnish

VIVIENNE FONG

1 Introduction[1]

This paper presents an analysis of the Finnish translative case *-ksi* and the essive case *-na*, with particular focus on their distribution in resultative and depictive predications. These cases are traditionally grouped with the class of Finnish semantic cases because they are associated with specific meanings (Holmberg and Nikanne 1993a), as opposed to the structural cases, nominative, genitive, accusative, and partitive (for works on Finnish structural case, see, among others, the papers in Holmberg and Nikanne 1993b). The translative is often glossed as 'change of state', and the essive is glossed 'as'. The problem is that the translative case is also found in contexts that express states with no overt change. The challenge is to come up with an analysis of the translative and essive cases that captures the full extent of their distributions, which include their canonical uses (see section 1.1), as well as these less-expected cases (see section 1.2). A crucial aspect of the analysis proposed in this paper is the identification of event structure as being relevant for the assignment of case. The internal structure of

[1] I would like to thank Arto Anttila, Tara Mohanan, and the reviewers for their comments. I am further indebted to Arto Anttila for in-depth discussions of the Finnish data, and to Satu Manninen for feedback on the data.

Generative Approaches to Finnic and Saami Linguistics.
Diane Nelson and Satu Manninen (eds.).

eventualities plays a central role in accounting for the choice of translative/essive case.

1.1 Canonical uses of the essive and translative cases

The essive predicate occurs with state verbs. As shown in (1) and (2), an essive predicate describes a state that is located at a time depicted by the tense operator on the main verb, or for the duration of the state as specified by a temporal phrase (e.g. 'three weeks', in (2)).

(1) Toini on sairaa-na.
Toini.n be.3s ill-ess
'Toini is ill.'

(2) Toini oli sairaa-na kolme viikko-a.
Toini.n be-past.3s ill-ess three week-p
'Toini was ill for three weeks.'

In depictive constructions, the essive case occurs on the predicate that expresses an attribute holding for the duration of the event/state denoted by the verb. The examples in (3) show the attribute being predicated of the object (i.e. object-oriented depictive), and the examples in (4) show the attribute being predicated of the subject (i.e. subject-oriented depictive).

(3) a. Elefantti sö-i maapähkinä-t suolattom-i-na.
elephant.n eat-past.3s peanut-pl.a unsalted-pl-ess
'A/The elephant ate the peanuts unsalted.'

b. Mei-llä ol-isi sauna lämpimä-nä.
we-ade be-cond sauna warm-ess
'We have the sauna warm.' (Vähämäki 1994)

(4) a. Hän kuol-i vanha-na.
S/he die-past.3s old-ess
'S/he died old.' (Penttilä 1963)

b. Rakennus palo-i vakuuttamattoma-na.[2]
building.n burn-past.3s uninsured-ess
'The building burned down uninsured.' (Penttilä 1963)

The translative case occurs with verbs of change of state, and is suffixed to the predicate that denotes the outcome of the change:

(5) Toini tul-i sairaa-ksi.
Toini.n become-past.3s ill-tra
'Toini became ill.'

(6) Hän muuttu-i (touka-sta) perhose-ksi.
s/he change-past.3s caterpillar-ela butterfly-tra
'S/he changed (from a caterpillar) into a butterfly.'

(7) Serkku-ni valmistu-i opettaja-ksi.
cousin-Px1s graduate-past.3s teacher-tra
'My cousin graduated to become a teacher.' (Vähämäki 1994)

The translative case also occurs with causative change of state verbs, where it is suffixed to the predicate depicting the result state.

(8) Taikuri muutt-i perhose-n touka-ksi.
magician.n change-past.3s butterfly-a caterpillar-tra
'The magician changed a/the butterfly into a caterpillar.'

(9) Taikuri muutt-i elefanti-n pienemmä-ksi.
magician.n change-past.3s elephant-a small-tra
'The magician made (lit. 'changed') a/the elephant small.'

In resultative constructions, the translative occurs on the resultative predicate:

(10) Ravist-i-n mato-n puhtaa-ksi.
shake-past-1s carpet-a clean-tra
'I shook a/the carpet clean.'

---

[2] This sentence has another reading, 'The house burned down because it was uninsured' (Satu Manninen, p.c.), which seems to be more salient if the essive predicate occurs in initial position: *Vakuuttamattomana rakennus paloi* 'Because it was uninsured, the building burned down.'

(11) Maanviljelijä ampu-i ketu-n kuoliaa-ksi.
farmer.n shoot-past.3s fox-a dead-tra
'A/The farmer shot a/the fox dead.'

(12) Tuli poltt-i talo-n tuhka-ksi.
fire.n burn-past.3s house-a ashes-tra
'Fire burnt the house to ashes.' (adapted from Penttilä 1963)

1.2 Two puzzles in secondary predication

As Halliday (1967) observes, resultative and depictive predications are attributive constructions. These two types of secondary predication contribute different semantic interpretations to event structure. The resultative element is an attribute which results from the process depicted by the verb, while the depictive element is 'an attribute which characterizes the attribuant in relation to the process, but as a concomitant, not a result, of the process' (Halliday 1967:63). Rapoport (1993) points out, however, that in English their identical surface structures give rise to ambiguity. In examples such as (13) below, not only is a resultative reading possible, but two depictive readings are available as well – an object-oriented reading, and with a little stretch of the imagination, a subject-Oriented reading.

(13) a. She cooked the fish dry. (Green 1973)
b. I boiled the lobsters sick. (Rapoport 1993)

In Finnish, on the other hand, the resultative/depictive ambiguity seems not to arise. The secondary predicates take translative case marking in resultative predication, and essive case marking in depictive predication, as shown in (14) and (15) below.

(14) a. Sointu paisto-i kala-n kuiva-ksi.
Sointu.n fry-past.3s fish-a dry-tra
'Sointu fried a/the fish dry.' [Resultative]

b. Sointu paisto-i kala-n kuiva-na.
Sointu.n fry-past.3s fish-a dry-ess
'Sointu fried a/the fish dry.' [Depictive]

(15) Elefantti sö-i maapähkinä-t suolattom-i-na / *suolattom-i-ksi.
elephant.n eat-past.3s peanut-pl unsalted-pl-ess /unsalted-pl-tra
'A/The elephant ate the peanuts unsalted.' [Depictive]

It is tempting to assume that the case morphemes *-ksi* and *-na* overtly signal the meaning differences between resultative and depictive constructions, respectively; in other words, that Finnish morphosyntax provides a perspicuous form-meaning relation for such constructions. Indeed, the essive case is traditionally described as expressing 'a (temporary) state or function, sometimes circumstances, conditions, or causes', while the translative case is described as expressing 'a state, property, function or position into which something/ someone enters, or the end point of a movement or change' (Karlsson 1987:111-112).

Based on the distribution patterns above, one might propose that the translative case encodes a meaning of change, overtly signaling how the adjectival predicate compositionally derives the change of state interpretation in resultative constructions. If change of state in (14a) is informally represented as (16) below, where the morphemes contributing elements of meaning are linked to the relevant portion of the event representation, then the translative morpheme contributes the BECOME meaning in the resultative construction.

(16) [[x ACT y] CAUSE [y BECOME STATE]]

[x ACT y]	'fry'
BECOME	TRA-
STATE	'dry'

Things are more complex, however. One puzzling fact is that a translative predicate can occur with verbs like *jättää* 'leave', where instead of encoding the result of a change of state, it encodes the state that is being maintained:

(17) Jät-i-n työ-n keskeneräise-ksi.
leave-past-1s work-a unfinished-tra
'I left the work unfinished.' (Penttilä 1963)

(18) Lasi oli tyhjä. Jäti-n lasi-n tyhjä-ksi.
glass.n be-past.3s empty. leave-past.1s glass-a empty-tra
'The glass was empty. I left it empty.'

In addition, translative predicates also occur with verbs that do not denote change, such as *jäädä* 'remain'.

(19) Toukka jä-i touka-ksi.
caterpillar.n remain-past.3s caterpillar-tra
'A/The caterpillar remained a caterpillar.'

The data in (17) – (19) bring into question whether the meanings of the translative and essive cases are as straightforward as their traditional glosses make them out to be. (17) – (19) suggest that the translative should not be associated with a BECOME meaning, since a BECOME meaning conflicts with these contexts where no change takes place. How do we reconcile the meaning of the translative as denoting the end point of a movement or a change with its occurrence in contexts that do not denote a change of state?

There is another puzzle concerning the proper interpretation of the translative case. Finnish resultative predicates can co-occur with path phrases, as shown in (20) below.

(20) Metsästäjä ampu-i karhu-n metsä-än kuoliaa-ksi.
hunter.n shoot-past.3s bear-a forest-ill dead-tra
'A/The hunter shot a/the bear dead, and the bear remained in the forest after the shooting'
(lit. A/The hunter shot the bear dead into the forest.)'

Now, it has been noted that resultatives in English cannot co-occur with path phrases (Goldberg 1991, Levin and Rappaport Hovav 1992, 1995, Rappaport Hovav and Levin 1995, Tenny 1994):

(21) a. *Sam tickled Chris silly off her chair. (Goldberg 1991)
b. *The hunter shot the bear dead into the forest.

Constraints against the co-occurrence of resultative and path predicates in English have been proposed by Goldberg (1991) and Tenny (1994), among others. More generally, these constraints fall under the rubric of what Bresnan (1982) has termed a biuniqueness condition on functional assignments, or the finiteness of predicate argument structures. Because every predicate argument must be assigned a unique grammatical function, the biuniqueness condition rules out sentences like (21a), where the adjectival and locative predicates are both interpreted as the resultative complement in the predicate argument structure of *tickle*. The Finnish example in (20) is an apparent counterexample to such a restriction. If the translative is assumed to contribute the BECOME meaning, then its co-occurrence with directional locative cases (e.g. the illative) that apparently give change of location readings would suggest a difference in the argument structure of Finnish versus English in secondary predication. This requires an explanation.

1.3 The structure of the paper

In the discussion to follow, I will first show in section 2 that Finnish resultatives and object-oriented depictives are structurally similar, and there is no obvious way to predict the choice of translative versus essive case structurally. In section 3, I pursue the idea that the case selection is semantically driven. I propose that event structure, as determined by the predicate-argument structure, is the key to understanding the assignment of translative versus essive cases. This will be the solution to the puzzle of the translative case occurring in contexts that do not denote change. In section 4, I show that the solution also applies to the directional locative predications in Finnish, thus providing an explanation for the puzzling co-occurrence of resultative and path predicates. Section 5 concludes the paper.

2 The Structure of Resultatives and Depictives

This section demonstrates that Finnish resultatives and object-oriented depictives are structurally similar, and there is no obvious way to predict the choice of translative versus essive case structurally. In section 2.1, I will consider the standard constituency tests that have been used to show the similar constituent structure of depictives and resultatives in English. In section 2.2, I apply similar tests for the equivalent constructions in Finnish.

2.1 English

In this section, I present Rothstein's (1985) tree structures that represent resultatives, subject- and object-oriented depictives in different configurations, and consider the syntactic tests that have been used to argue against such structural representations. Rothstein (1985) posits different syntactic structures for the resultative, subject-oriented depictive, and the object-oriented depictive, as illustrated in (22) – (24), respectively.

(22) Resultative (e.g., *Calvin nailed every window shut.*)

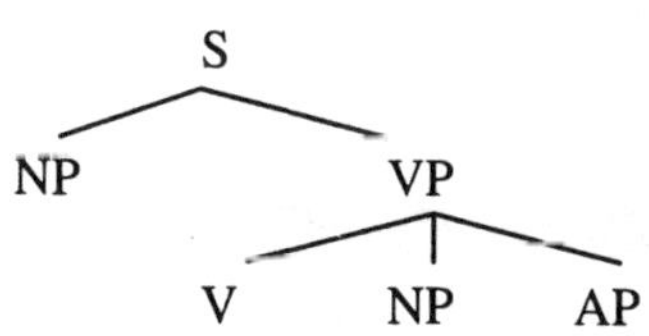

(23) Subject-oriented depictive (e.g., *The saxophonist performed the piece drunk.*)

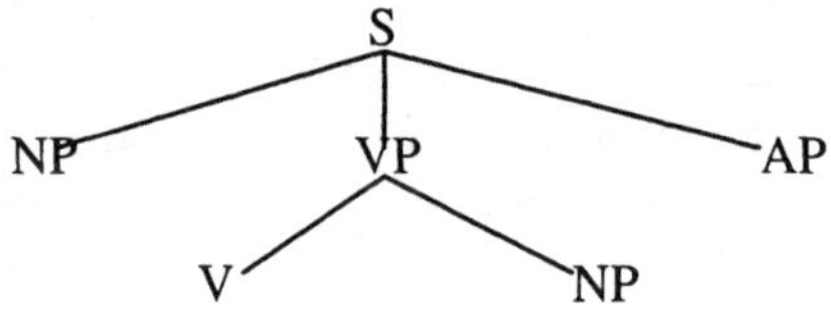

(24) Object-oriented depictive (e.g., *The student sold the book used.*)

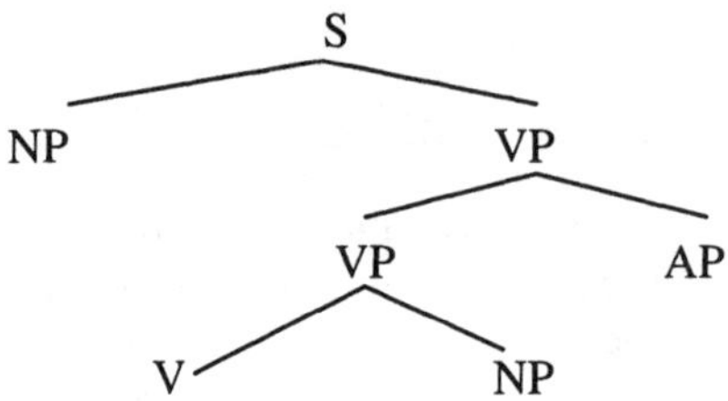

There are however problems with such a structural account of the differences between these constructions. Andrews (1982) shows that both subject-oriented depictives and resultatives have the verb, object NP, and the secondary predicate together as a unit, using constituency tests such as VP-preposing (25), *though* movement (26), and Wh-clefting of VP (27). Subject-oriented depictive (S-dep) and resultative (Res) pairs are given in the examples below.

(25) a. Little John said he would eat the meat singing, and eat the meat singing he did. [S-dep]
b. Little John said he would roast the meat black, and roast the meat black he did. [Res]

(26) a. Eat the meat singing though Little John did, nobody thought he was crazy.
b. Roast the meat black though Little John did, nobody thought he was crazy.

(27) a. What Little John did was eat the meat singing.
b. What Little John did was roast the meat black.

These tests show that both subject-oriented depictive and resultative predicates form a constituent with the verb and its object NP, and thus Rothstein's structure for the subject-oriented depictive in (23) cannot be correct.

Levin and Rappaport Hovav (1995) provide additional VP constituency tests such as *do so*-substitution (see also Green 1973) and VP-preposing (this time treating the verb and the object NP as a constituent, independent of the secondary predicate) to show that resultative phrases are attached at the same bar-level as subcategorized PPs, with a structure corresponding to (22). The data in (28) and (29) are from Levin and Rappaport Hovav (1995).

(28) a. *Jason put the book on the table, and Bill did so on the floor. [Subcat-PP]
b. *Bill fastened the shutters open, and May did so shut. [Res]
c. *The joggers ran the pavement thin, and the runners did so smooth. [Res]

(29) a. *Jason said he would put the book on the table, and put the book he did on the table.
b. *Bill said that he would fasten the shutters open, and fasten them he did open.
c. *The joggers thought that they would run the pavement thin, and run the pavement they did thin.

Compare the behavior of depictives predicated of the subject NP (examples from Levin and Rappaport Hovav 1995):

(30) a. Jason wiped the table tired [or better: dead tired] and May did so wide awake.
b. Jason said that he would even wipe the table tired, and wipe the table he did tired.

(30) shows that *do so*-substitution and VP-preposing works for subject-oriented depictives, which is a different result from the resultative (Levin and Rappaport Hovav 1995). Notice that while the tests in (25) – (27) group subject-oriented depictives with resultatives, (30) shows that they are not exactly the same: Andrews' (1982) tests in (25) – (27) indicate that at a higher level, the verb, object NP, and the subject-oriented depictive predicate form a single constituent, but (30) shows that the verb and object NP form a closer unit at a lower level. So we can conclude that the structure in

(23) for subject-oriented depictives should be rejected, and a more plausible structure is that in (24).

On the basis of (28) – (30), Levin and Rappaport Hovav (1995:49) claim that the observed difference between the resultatives in (28) and (29) and the depictives in (30) suggests that 'the state denoted by the resultative [phrase] is part of the core eventuality described in the VP', just like subcategorized PPs. However, (31) shows that object-oriented depictives behave like resultatives, and differently from their subject-oriented counterparts:

(31) a. *Fred ate the meat raw, but I did so cooked. (Simpson 1983)
 b. *The trainer ate the peanuts salted and the elephants did so unsalted.
 c. *The apprentice thought he should serve the gazpacho lukewarm, and serve the gazpacho he did lukewarm.

When depictives are predicated of the object NP as in (31), *do so*-substitution and VP-preposing of the verb and object NP produce the same effects as for resultatives (cf. (28) and (29)): the sentences are unacceptable. The parallel behavior of resultatives and object-oriented depictives suggests that object-oriented depictives must also have the structure in (22), and cannot be represented as (24).

2.2 Finnish

Similar tests in Finnish show the same patterns. An example of the Finnish equivalent of the *do so*-substitution test is given in (32).[3] Here, the verb and the object NP are treated as a unit, independent of the adjunct.

---

[3] In one of her arguments against configurationality in Finnish, Vilkuna (1989) notes that the 'do so' construction in Finnish 'is used in more restricted circumstances than the English *do* (among other things, it prefers to substitute genuine activities).' (Vilkuna 1989: 26) Nonetheless, Vilkuna acknowledges that the 'do so' test, being of the form 'V+complement', can replace V+complement sequences. I use this test to show that both resultatives and object-oriented depictives have similar V+complement sequences. I remain agnostic as to whether this particular test is sufficient evidence for the status of Finnish as a configurational language (for views contrary to Vilkuna's, see Vainikka 1989).

(32) Sointu kiillott-i hope-i-ta keittiö-ssä ja niin teki
Sointu.n polish-past.3s silver-pl-p kitchen-ine and so did
Vieno-kin olohuonee-ssa.
Vieno.n-also lounge-ine
'Sointu polished silver in the kitchen, and Vieno did so in the lounge.'

(33) shows that subject-oriented depictives can be separated from the verb and object NP, just as in English:

(33) Sointu siivos-i talo-n väsynee-nä ja niin teki
Sointu.n clean-past.3s house.a tired-ess and so did
Vieno-kin virkeä-nä.
Vieno.n-also wide.awake-ess
'Sointu cleaned the house tired and Vieno did so wide awake.'

The data in (34) below show that subcategorized locatives, resultatives, and object-oriented depictives give the same (bad) results in the substitution test:

(34) a. *Sointu heitt-i pallo-n kori-in ja niin teki
Sointu.n throw-past.3s ball-a basket-ill and so did
Vieno-kin laatikko-on.
Vieno.n-also box-ill
'Sointu threw a/the ball into a/the basket, and Vieno did so into a/the box.'

b. *Sointu pyyhk-i pöydä-n puhtaa-ksi ja niin teki
Sointu.n wipe-past.3s table-a clean-tra and so did
Vieno-kin kuiva-ksi.
Vieno.n-also dry-tra
'Sointu wiped a/the table clean and Vieno did so dry.'

c. *Kouluttaja sö-i maapähkinä-t suolattu-i-na ja niin
trainer.n eat-past.3s peanuts-pl salted-pl-ess and so
teki elefantti-kin suolattom-i-na.
did elephant.n-also unsalted-pl-ess
'The trainer ate the peanuts salted and the elephant did so unsalted.'

The Finnish *do-so* substitution test shows that resultatives and object-oriented depictives pattern alike in syntactic groupings. While the validity of this substitution test in indicating configurationality (in the sense of Hale 1983) remains controversial in Finnish (see Vilkuna 1989 and Vainikka 1989), at least this test fails to indicate any structural difference between the translative/essive case positions in resultatives and object-oriented depictives. As we will see in the following section, a semantic account of case selection is a more plausible alternative.

3 Event Structure and the Distribution of Translative and Essive Cases

In section 1.1 above, I listed some canonical uses of the essive and translative cases, and in section 1.2, I pointed out the puzzling occurrence of the translative in contexts that do not denote change, such as with verbs like *jäädä* 'remain'. In this section, I argue that the choice between essive and translative case depends on the internal structure of the events, as determined by the lexical semantics of the verb, and predicate-argument structure.

3.1 State verbs and the choice of translative/essive predicates

An interesting contrast between the translative and essive cases emerges with a pair of verbs that appear to have similar meanings, but different presuppositions.

(35) Kivi jä-i vanha-ksi-poja-ksi/ *vanha-na-poika-na.
Kivi.n remain-past.3s old-tra-boy-tra old-ess-boy-ess
'Kivi remained a bachelor.'

(36) Kivi pysy-i vanha-na-poika-na / *vanha-ksi-poja-ksi.
Kivi.n stay-past.3s old-ess-boy-ess/ old-tra-boy-tra
'Kivi stayed a bachelor.'

The verb *jäädä*, glossed as 'remain', takes a translative predicate, while the verb *pysyä*, glossed as 'stay', takes essive. (35) conveys the implication that Kivi would rather have married. That is, Kivi's current state of bachelorhood is asserted, and his hope or expectation to change from a bachelor to a non-bachelor is implied. (36), on the other hand, has no such implication.

To understand better the difference between the two verbs, consider the contrast between (37) and (38) below.

(37) Neva-n suu jä-i Täyssinä-n rauha-ssa
Neva-g mouth remain-past.3s Täyssinä-g treaty-ine
venäläis-i-lle.
Russian-pl-all
(i) 'In the treaty of Täyssinä, the mouth of the Neva remained in the possession of the Russians.' (There was no change of hands.)
(ii) 'In the treaty of Täyssinä, the mouth of the Neva went to the Russians.' (The mouth of the Neva changed hands.)

(38) Neva-n suu pysy-i Täyssinä-n rauha-ssa
Neva-g mouth stay-past.3s Täyssinä-g treaty-ine
venäläis-i-llä.
Russian-pl-ade
'In the treaty of Täyssinä, the mouth of the Neva stayed in the possession of the Russians.' (There was no change of hands.)

The verb *jäädä* is compatible with two different scenarios. One scenario could be that another country tried to capture the mouth of the Neva from the Russians, but did not succeed. In that situation, one could use (37) with reading (i). In this reading, as in (35), an expected state of affairs that is different from the present one is implied. In other words, a change of hands was expected to happen by some reference time *t*, but at *t*, it had not yet happened. Informally, this can be illustrated as (39) below, where the arrow pointing rightward is the time axis, *P* is the asserted state (i.e., the mouth of the Neva is in the Russians' possession), *not-P* the negation of that state, and *t* the time at which the state holds. Information about the time after *t* is assumed to be indeterminate (hence the dotted line), since it is unnecessary for the interpretation of the sentence that the state needs to extend beyond *t*.

(39) '*jäädä* P' under reading (i) of (37)

a. Asserted state of affairs ('The mouth of the Neva is in the Russians' possession at t'):

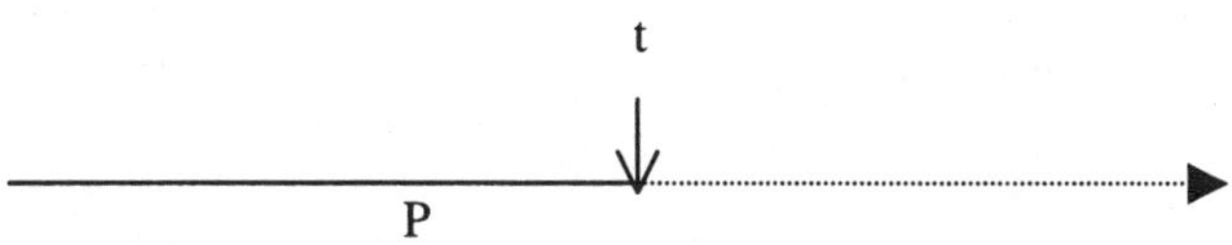

b. Implied state of affairs ('The mouth of the Neva is no longer in the Russians' possession by time t'):

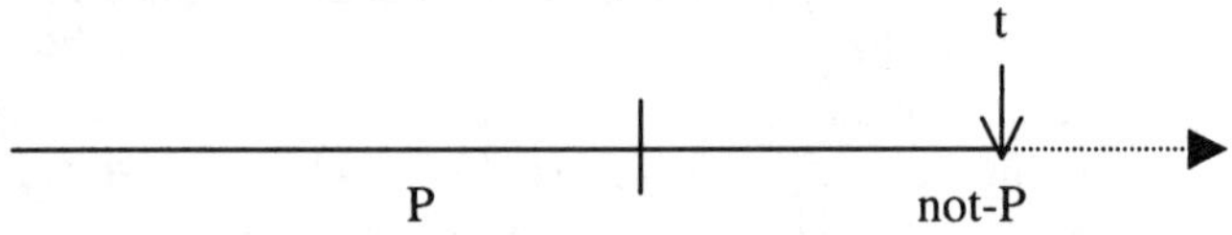

A second and very different type of scenario for (37) could be that the Russians did not have claims on the River Neva before the treaty, and after the treaty, they did (reading (ii)). Intriguingly, *jäädä* is compatible with this change of hands interpretation as well. In this reading, a change preceding the asserted state is implied. This can be represented as (40) below.

(40) '*jäädä* P' under reading (ii) of (37)

a. Asserted state of affairs ('The mouth of the Neva is in the Russians' possession at t'):

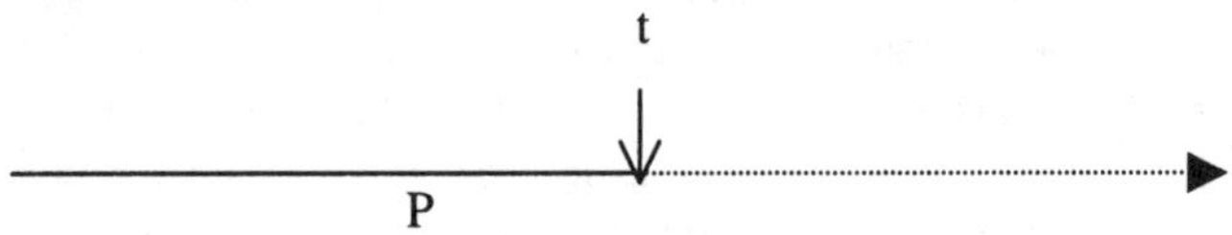

b. Implied state of affairs ('The mouth of the Neva changed hands by time t'):

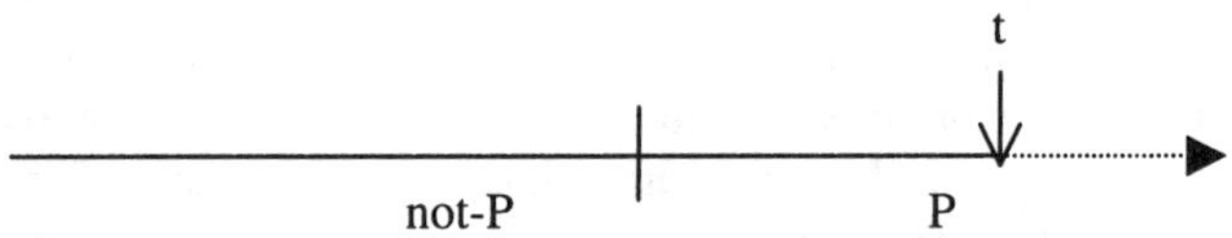

That *jäädä* can be used in both these scenarios shows that it asserts a state *P*, and in addition, implies a change. The change is either from *P* to *not-P*, or from *not-P* to *P*: note the ordering of *P*<*not-P* in (39b), and *not-P*<*P* in (40b).

I propose that the proper analysis of the verb *jäädä* 'remain' must look beyond the state *P* it asserts, to include also an opposing/alternative state *not-P*. The verb introduces an interval that must include *P* and *not-P*, with their ordering unspecified: I treat this as the presupposition triggered by *jäädä*. This treatment of *jäädä* is inspired by Löbner's (1987, 1989) analysis of the presupposition triggered by *still* and the German particles *noch* 'still' and *nicht mehr* 'no more'. Löbner claims that such particles introduce a certain perspective from which to view the truth conditions of a state *P* that is modified by such particles. For example, when modified by *noch*, the state *P* (e.g. 'on' in *Das Licht ist noch an* 'The light is still on') is viewed in relation to an alternative state *not-P* ('not on') within an interval that contains at most one change from *P* to *not-P* (Löbner 1989). But in the case of *jäädä*, the verb presents an additional twist: it does not specify the ordering of P and not-P; the ordering is determined by context. For example, (39) depicts a context where the change from *P* to *not-P* has not yet happened at the time *P* is asserted, hence the ordering *P<not-P*. In (40), the change has already happened before the time *t*, and the ordering is *not-P<P*.

Consider the negation of *jäädä*, as shown in (41).

(41)	Neva-n	suu	ei	jää-nyt	venäläis-i-lle.
	Neva-g	mouth	not	remain-past.p	Russian-pl-all

(i) 'The mouth of the Neva did not remain in the possession of the Russians.'
(ii) 'The mouth of the Neva did not go to the Russians.'

Again, two different scenarios are supported by (41). One scenario could be that the Russians lost their claim on the Neva (reading (i)). That is, the mouth of the Neva first belonged to the Russians at a time before time *t*, and at *t*, the Neva no longer belonged to the Russians. This reading, where the mouth of the Neva changed hands, can be considered the negation of (37) under reading (i), which says that there was no change of hands. Note that the implication of a change (see (39b)) does not disappear under the negation of (37). This supports the proposed analysis of *jäädä* as triggering a presupposition of change.

A different type of scenario for (41) could be that the Russians had expected to get the mouth of the Neva, but did not – the Neva did not change hands. This reading can be considered as a condition under which the reading 'there was a change of hands' ((37) reading (ii)) is false. Once again, notice that the implication triggered by *jäädä* in this context (see (40b)) does not disappear under negation. This is consistent with the proposed interpretation of *jäädä* as asserting a state and presupposing a change. In this context, the assertion is that the Neva was not in the Russians' possession at a time *t*, and the implication is that a different state of affairs – a change of hands in the Russians' favor – was expected to have happened by time *t*.

With *pysyä*, however, the sentence in (38), repeated here, is compatible with neither a change of hands, nor an expected change reading. The verb *pysyä* only asserts a state. It does not presuppose an interval containing opposing states, unlike *jäädä*.

(38) Neva-n suu pysy-i Täyssinä-n treaty-ine
Neva-g mouth stay-past.3s Täyssinä-g rauha-ssa
venäläis-i-llä.
Russian-pl-ade
'In the treaty of Täyssinä, the mouth of the Neva stayed in the possession of the Russians.' (There was no change of hands.)

That this treatment of *jäädä* and *pysyä* is on the right track is confirmed by further examples below. First, consider (42):

(42) Työ jä-i/ *pysy-i tekemä-ttä.
work remain-past.3s stay-past.3s do-inf-abe
'The work remained undone.'

In a context where one expects a piece of work to be completed by a certain time *t*, and it is still not done at time *t*, only *jäädä* can be used at time *t* to describe this state of affairs. In (43), only *jäädä* can be used to mean a failure to be promoted to a higher grade or class:

(43) Vieno jä-i luoka-lle/ #pysy-i luoka-lla.
Vieno remain-past.3s class-all stay-past.3s class-ade
'Vieno was left on the class (i.e. Vieno was not promoted to the next grade).'

Again, there is no change asserted, but the implication is that Vieno ought to have been promoted to the next grade, but failed. *Pysyä* 'stay' is felicitous in a context where staying on the same grade is a positive thing (Satu Manninen, p.c.). This supports the idea that only *jäädä* can be used with the implication that Vieno ought to have been promoted – that is, being left in the same grade is a negative thing. In cases like (42) and (43), we find *jäädä* in contexts where a change that is expected to happen has not yet happened.

Consider now a very different type of context. The verb *jäädä* can be used to describe both the state of widowhood and bachelorhood:

(44) Kuningatar jä-i leske-ksi.
queen.n remain-past.3s widow-tra
'The queen was widowed.'

(45) Kivi jä-i vanha-ksi-poja-ksi.
Kivi.n remain-past.3s old-tra-boy-tra
'Kivi remained a bachelor.'

Widowhood is a state one does not start with, but may enter into. It is the opposite of bachelorhood, which is a state one starts with, and may get out of. It is our world knowledge about the difference between widowhood and bachelorhood that gives *jäädä* the 'become' interpretation in (44) (the ordering of *not-P* before *P*), while (45), on the other hand, implies that Kivi would rather have married (the ordering of *P* before *not-P*).

In representing the meaning of sentences containing *jäädä*, I adopt a neo-Davidsonian analysis, and assume that all predicates take an extra event argument. Using (45) as the prototypical example, consider 'Kivi remained a bachelor' under the regular durative interpretation of the predicate *jäädä*.[4]

(46) 'Kivi remained a bachelor.'
a. •s [Remain(Kivi, bachelor, s) $\wedge$ $\exists t$ AT(s, t)]
b. $\exists s \exists t$ [Remain(Kivi, bachelor, s) $\wedge$ AT(s, t) $\wedge$ $t < n$]

The untensed sentence introduces a set of states in (46a). Combining this with the past tense operator we get the formula in (46b), which claims that one such state is located at a time t preceding the utterance time n. Besides expressing a state obtaining at time t, we have to take into account the presupposition introduced by *jäädä* when it takes P as its state predicate. The presupposition of the verb must be specified as a part of the verb's lexical entry. For concreteness, the presupposition and truth conditions for

---

[4] In temporal semantics, it is assumed that eventualities are grouped into aspectually different types. For this paper, we just need to assume a contrast between states versus events (non-states). It is also assumed that there exists a procedure that yields either a state or an event variable for every (untensed) sentence.

In order to deal with tense in natural language, we have to locate events in time. To do so, we need a domain T of times, which are points on the time axis, and a precedence relation $<$ that leads to a total order of T. I adopt de Swart's (1996) function AT, which is a function that maps eventualities on to their location on the time axis, also called the 'run time' of the eventuality (Krifka 1989). An eventuality e holding at a time t is represented as AT(e, t). As I will deal with only past tense sentences here, the past tense introduces the condition $t < n$, leading to the interpretation that the event holds at a time t which precedes the speech time n ('now'). (Extending this to present and future tense operators should be straightforward: the present tense introduces the condition $n \subseteq t$ and future tense (treated as non-past) introduces the condition $n \leq$ t.)

jäädä are given in construction with a constant *c*, a state predicate *P*, and the time variable *t* (see (47)).

(47) a. 'c *jäädä* P at time t' triggers the presupposition that there is a phase P starting before t, and that up to t exactly one change between P and not-P has occurred.
b. 'c *jäädä* P at time t' is true iff the presupposition in (a) is fulfilled, and P is true at t.
c. 'c *jäädä* P at time t' is false iff the presupposition in (a) is fulfilled, and P is false at t.

The analysis of *jäädä* 'remain' can be extended to the morphologically related *jättää* 'leave' that takes secondary predicates, as in (48).

(48)	Jät-i-n	työ-n	keskeneräise-ksi.
	leave-past-1s	work-a	unfinished-tra
	'I left the work unfinished.'		

(48) can be uttered when one expects a piece of work to be completed by time *t*, and it is still not done at time *t*. (49a) shows the asserted state of affairs, and (49b) the presupposition of change introduced by the verb *jättää*.

(49) a. Asserted state of affairs ('The work is unfinished'):

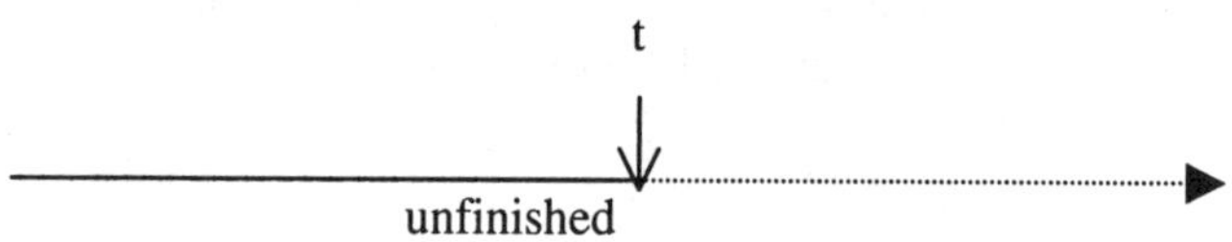

b. Implied state of affairs:

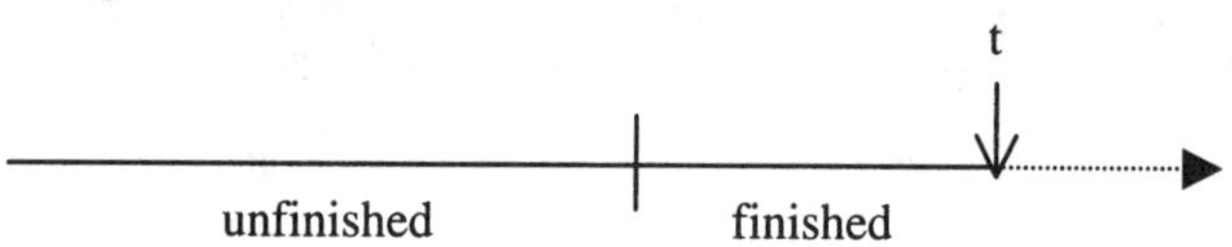

Crucially, in this treatment of *jäädä* 'remain' and *jättää* 'leave', no change of state is asserted. The change is only implied. The presupposition of change must be part of the lexical semantics of these verbs.

3.2 Event structure and the selection of translative/essive case

The translative case occurs in apparently disparate contexts. On the one hand, it occurs in constructions involving overt change (see examples (5) – (12) in section 1.1). On the other hand, it occurs with the verbs *jäädä* 're-main' and *jättää* 'leave', which have the semantic properties of asserting a state and presupposing a change. These two contexts reveal the true nature of the translative case morpheme.

Constructions involving change of state have an event structure that comprises two phases – a prior state of affairs, and a resulting state. I term these event structures as DIPHASIC (Fong 1997). A sentence like (5) (repeated here as (50)) is an event (a non-state).

(50) Toini tul-i sairaa-ksi.
Toini.n become-past.3s ill-tra
'Toini became ill.'

'Toini became ill' involves a state when Toini was not ill followed by a second state when Toini was ill. According to Kamp and Reyle (1993), only when an event's duration comes to a natural conclusion can the event be reported in the simple past tense. Such perfective sentences are therefore different from durative state sentences involving *jäädä* analysed above. In writing the formula for (50), then, the event of becoming ill is located by the tense to a time before 'now' (see (51)).

(51) 'Toini became ill.'
$\exists e \exists t$ [Become(Toini, ill, e) $\wedge$ AT(e, t) $\wedge$ $t < n$]

The truth conditions for 'c become P at t' are given below in (52).

(52) 'c become P at t' is true iff there is an interval in which exactly one change between not-P and P has occurred, and P is true at t; else false.

Similarly, in constructions involving causative change of state[5] and in resultative constructions, an entity undergoes a change of state, whether or

[5] I distinguish causative change of state verbs from causative verbs that are stative. The latter class of verbs is attested in Malayalam (Mohanan and Mohanan 1999; see also Fong 1999) and Finnish (Pylkkänen 2000). While stative causatives require a richer internal structure for states than is commonly assumed (see the authors above for details), the event structure is not diphasic in the sense that they do not comprise a prior state of affairs and a resulting state. For exam-

not the prior state is overtly expressed, so the same type of diphasic event structure applies.

We have also seen that *jäädä* and *jättää* carry with them a presupposed change of state. That is, the event structure for *jäädä/jättää* constructions is also diphasic, although this diphasic structure is not asserted, but only implied, unlike those in examples (5) – (12). However, the implied diphasic structure is also part of the lexical semantics of the verbs.

What all the constructions in (5) – (12), and the constructions with *jäädä* and *jättää* have in common is that they have diphasic event structures, whether the diphasic event structure is determined by the verb and its arguments[6] (what Verkuyl (1988) terms 'inner aspect'), or by the lexical semantics of the verb. I therefore make the following proposal: The translative case morpheme only occurs in events that have or presuppose diphasic structures. The conditions governing the distribution of the translative case are given as follows:

---

ple, the Malayalam example in (i) denotes a state; it does not involve any action that is 'performed' by Nina's eyes, and Nina in no way undergoes a change because of her eyes.

(i)	niinayuTe	kannukaL	awaLe	sundariyaakkunnu.
	Nina.g	eyes.n	she.a	beautiful-one-be-caus-present

'Nina's eyes make her beautiful.' (Mohanan and Mohanan 1999)
(Upper case letters in the Malayalam data indicate retroflex segments.)

Similarly, in Finnish, morphologically causative psych predicates such as *inhotta* 'disgust' and *suretta* 'cause to be sad' are aspectually stative (Pylkkänen 2000), and thus do not involve any change from a prior state to a result state:

(ii)	Hyttyset	inho-tta-vat	Mikko-a.
	mosquitoes.n	find.disgusting-caus-3pl	Mikko-p

'Mosquitoes disgust Mikko.' (Pylkkänen 2000)

[6] In resultative constructions, it is recognized that the resultative phrase interacts with the verb and its internal argument to derive the accomplishment event structure. But views differ on the exact nature of the interaction. Tenny (1992) describes the direct internal argument as being 'forced' by the presence of a resultative predicate into being understood as undergoing a change that delimits the event. Levin and Rappaport Hovav (1995) maintain that resultative phrases are not licensed by the lexical representation of the verb, and its addition must be licensed and integrated into the semantic representation of the sentence. Given a limited ontological typology of eventuality types, the XP denoting a state that follows an activity verb can only be interpreted as the result state of an accomplishment event. Verkuyl (1993), on the other hand, argues that the verb and the secondary predicate form a complex predicate (see also Neeleman and Weerman 1993), and together, this complex predicate assigns a theta role to the object NP to give the appropriate aspectual composition for terminative aspect.

(53) a. The translative case occurs only in events with diphasic structures involving *P* and *not-P*.
b. The translative case occurs on the predicate *P* holding at the time defined by the tense of the main verbal predicate.

In (53), the exact ordering of phases in the diphasic structure is left unspecified. The ordering of phases could be *not-P*<*P* or *P*<*not-P* (where *P* denotes the state predicate taking translative case), depending on the event structure as determined by the verb and its arguments. In events where the change is asserted, the ordering of phases has to be *not-P*<*P*, since the result predicate denotes the state holding after the change. In the case of the verb *jäädä*, where the change is implied, not asserted, we have assumed that context plays an important role in determining the possible readings for those types of sentences; the ordering of phases is determined by context and world knowledge.

The notion of a diphasic event structure is crucial in determining the translative/essive distribution in secondary predicates. We have already noted that the result predicate in resultatives holds in the second of two phases in the event structure. The translative case requires diphasic event structures, and is predicted to occur on the result predicate. In depictive constructions, the secondary predicate *P* denotes a state that is concomitant with the 'unfolding' of the event, and is not contrasted with an opposing state *not-P* within the same event. Therefore, the translative case is correctly predicted to be incompatible with depictive predicates.

In contrast to the translative case, the essive does not require a diphasic event structure to license it. As we have seen, the essive case occurs with depictive secondary predicates. Note that essive predicates can occur in diphasic event structures, but only if the essive predicate denotes a state that holds for the entire event:

(54) Toini tul-i vanha-na hajamielise-ksi.
Toini become-past.3s old-ess absent.minded-tra
'Toini became absent-minded when she was old.'

Thus, a condition like the one in (53a) does not apply to the essive. All we need to state about the essive case is this:

(55) The essive case occurs on the predicate *P* holding at the time defined by the tense of the main verbal predicate.

Finally, we are able to explain why the translative case is incompatible with *pysyä* 'stay', and only the essive case is possible. *Pysyä* does not possess any presupposition about the existence of an opposing/alternative state; in other words, it neither asserts nor presupposes a diphasic event structure. As such, the verb does not satisfy the conditions in (53) to license the translative case.

3.3 Summary

The notion of a diphasic event structure is crucial in determining the translative/essive distribution in secondary predicates. I have proposed that the translative case occurs only in events that comprise two phases (hence diphasic structures). The essive case does not have such a requirement. In other words, the difference between the translative and the essive cases is the requirement of a diphasic event structure. In this view, then, the essive case is unmarked, while the translative is marked.

4 Resultative and Path Predicates

I have argued that the translative case is licensed by event structures that are diphasic. Notice that diphasic structures are characteristic of resultative predications, which comprise a causing activity and a resultant change of state (Dowty 1979, Levin and Rappaport Hovav 1995, Parsons 1990, Pustejovsky 1991, 1995, Van Valin 1993). Levin and Rappaport Hovav (1999) have argued that bare XP resultatives like *The pot boiled dry* have no causing event (see also Van Valin and LaPolla 1997). Even without a causing event, the nature of bare XP resultatives is still diphasic, because of the change of state interpretation. In all these cases, the predicate bearing translative case depicts the final state of the entity that undergoes the change of state.

In this section, I discuss one particular result that the diphasic analysis of the translative in resultative constructions derives. The focus of the discussion is the apparent difference in the argument structures of English and Finnish in secondary predication.

4.1 The Unique Path constraint

An interesting observation about resultatives in English is that path phrases cannot co-occur with resultative predicates (Goldberg 1991, Levin and Rappaport Hovav 1992, 1995, Rappaport Hovav and Levin 1995, Tenny 1994):

(56) a. *Sam tickled Chris silly off her chair. (Goldberg 1991)
b. *The hunter shot the bear dead into the forest.

In (56), the directional phrases occurring with the verbs *tickle* and *shoot* give a caused motion reading. In (56a), the intended interpretation is that tickling causes Chris to become silly and to fall off the chair, and in (56b), the shooting causes the bear to become dead, and propels or forces the bear into the forest.

Various types of constraints on the co-occurrence of resultative and directional locative predicates have been posited for English. They are all based on the perceived semantic contributions of the directional locative and resultative predicates to event structure. According to Rappaport Hovav and Levin (1995), Accomplishments and Achievements specify an achieved state (see (57) below), and the Accomplishment semantic template associated with resultative constructions cannot be augmented further to include another achieved state or location.

(57) a. [x BECOME STATE] (Achievement)

b. [[x ACT] CAUSE [y BECOME STATE]] (Accomplishment)

In addition, Rappaport Hovav and Levin (1995) note that verbs which are inherently Achievements (e.g., *arrive*) or Accomplishments (e.g., *break*) also do not allow further template augmentation, as the sentences in (58) (from Rappaport Hovav and Levin 1995) show.

(58) a. *The travellers arrived disheveled.[7]
(Intended reading: The arrival caused the travellers to be dishevelled.)

b. *Kelly broke the dishes off the table.
(Intended reading: Kelly broke the dishes and as a result they went off the table.)

In Goldberg 1991, resultatives are seen as coding a metaphorical change of location. Goldberg proposes a 'Unique Path' constraint that applies to literal and metaphorical paths: 'If an argument X refers to a physical object, then more than one distinct path cannot be predicated of X within a single clause' (Goldberg 1991:368). The Unique Path constraint

[7] Note that this example is fine on a depictive reading.

rules out the co-occurrence of resultatives with directional phrases, since in Goldberg's account, both the resultative and the directional preposition introduce their own distinct paths.

In a similar vein, Tenny (1994:79) posits a 'Single Delimiting Constraint', where 'the event described by the verb may only have one measuring-out and be delimited only once.' By 'measuring-out', Tenny means 'the role played by the argument in marking the temporal terminus of the event', and 'delimitedness' refers to 'the property of an event's having a distinct, definite and inherent endpoint in time.' Given that resultative predicates and directional locatives can delimit the event denoted by a verb, they cannot both occur given this constraint.

What the above observations show is that given one event denoted by one verb, there are only a finite number of predicate-argument positions that can saturate the event template. For the discussion below, I will assume Goldberg's Unique Path constraint as a descriptive device, although it seems that the restriction on the co-occurrence of resultatives and directional phrases may be part of a larger phenomenon.[8]

4.2 The Unique Path constraint in Finnish

The Unique Path constraint appears to hold in Finnish as well. Observe the examples in (59).

(59) a. Joulupukki men-i savupiipu-sta ulos.
Santa Claus.n go-past.3s chimney-ela out
'Santa Claus went out of a/the chimney.'

b. Joulupukki men-i ylös savupiipu-sta.
Santa Claus.n go-past.3s up chimney-ela
'Santa Claus went up a/the chimney.'

---

[8] In other empirical domains, the factors determining the polyadicity of argument structures have been attributed to the biuniqueness condition on functional assignments or the finiteness of predicate argument structures (Bresnan 1982). The various phenomena include:

(i) No more than one instrumental phrase with a single verb:
*John escaped from prison *with dynamite with a machine gun*. (Bresnan 1982)
(ii) No more than one by-phrase in the passive:
*She was admired *by him by the President*. (Bresnan 1982)
(iii) No more than one distinct source-goal path:
*John ran *to Bill into the palace*. (Gruber 1965)

c. * Joulupukki men-i ylös savupiipu-sta ulos.
Santa Claus.n go-past.3s up chimney-ela out
'Santa Claus went up out of a/the chimney.'

(59a) and (59b) show that a single path, either going down or up the chimney, is possible. However, when the two paths occur in the same event (denoted by one verb), the Unique Path constraint rules out (59c). A second example is given in (60). (60c) shows that directional locatives and resultatives cannot co-occur.

(60) a. Vieno potkais-i matkalauku-n ulos talo-sta.
Vieno.n kick-past.3s suitcase-a out house-ela
'Vieno kicked a/the suitcase out of the house.'

b. Vieno potkais-i matkalauku-n auki.
Vieno.n kick-past.3s suitcase-a open
'Vieno kicked a/the suitcase open.'

c. *Vieno potkais-i matkalauku-n ulos talo-sta auki.
Vieno.n kick-past.3s suitcase-a out house-ela open
'Vieno kicked a/the suitcase out of the house open.'

Kim and Maling (1997) also assume that such a constraint holds in cases where the resultative is predicated of an external argument of the matrix verb. The example in (61) below (adapted from Kim and Maling 1997) shows that the object of the matrix verb is marked with the partitive case, giving an atelic reading to the activity subevent. In (62) when the object of the matrix verb is bounded, giving a telic reading, the addition of a further result state is unacceptable.

(61) Katso-i-n video-i-ta silmä-ni punais-i-ksi.
watch-past-1s video-pl-p eye-Px1s.a red-pl-tra
'I watched videos until my eyes became red (lit. I watched videos my eyes red.).'

(62) *Katso-i-n kymmenen video-ta silmä-ni punais-i-ksi.
watch-past-1s ten.a video-p eye-Px1s.a red-pl-tra
'I watched ten videos until my eyes became red.'

We can actually entertain two possible explanations for the unacceptability of (62). One, a syntactic explanation, would be that there is a prohibition against having two accusative case markers in Finnish. This is interpretable as an instance of the Case-OCP, a constraint that prohibits the same case from being assigned to adjacent elements (Mohanan 1994).[9] In fact, Finnish has no double accusative verbs (Maling 1993). However, according to Maling (1993), accusative objects and accusative adverbials can co-occur.[10] Maling argues that nominative and accusative cases form a syntactic case-tier, where only one NP can get assigned nominative case, and any remaining NPs get accusative case – so case spreading (of the accusative) is possible in Finnish. For Case-OCP to rule out (62), it must be that the object and the external argument of the verb are adjacent. Here, we are assuming that firstly, the object 'ten videos' is a quantifier phrase (Vainikka 1993), where the head of the phrase takes accusative case; and secondly, the phrase 'my eyes' is not an adverbial.

A second possibility is that the ill-formedness of (62) is not of a syntactic (case) origin, but semantic: it violates the Unique Path constraint, as suggested by Kim and Maling (1997). The partitive case marking on the object NP signals an aspectually irresultative, unbounded reading (see e.g., Hakulinen and Karlsson 1979, Heinämäki 1984, Kiparsky 1998), and in (61), only one result obtains – the result that eyes become red. In (62), 'the accusative on the thematic object would denote that the result state has already been reached' (Kim and Maling 1997:197), and adding another result phrase violates the Unique Path constraint. Whether the contrast in (61) and (62) is best explained by a syntactic (Case-OCP) or a semantic (Unique Path constraint) account is left for future research, although the semantic explanation ties in neatly with the rest of the phenomena in the present discussion.

4.3 Resultative plus 'path' predicates

Now, examples like (63) below are apparent counterexamples to the Unique Path constraint:

---

[9] In Finnish, Case-OCP emerges in at least one syntactic context: in part-whole constructions, the constraint prohibits the same case from being assigned to both the head of an NP and its NP sister: $*[N_{case\bullet}\ [NP_{case\bullet}]]_{NP}$ (Anttila and Fong to appear).

[10] Mohanan (1994) presents a similar phenomenon in Hindi. Case-OCP in Hindi is sensitive to whether the adjacent units are both 'participants' of the predicate (i.e. the syntactically required arguments of the predicate in argument structure); the constraint does not hold if one of the elements is a non-participant (i.e. an adjunct).

(63) Metsästäjä ampu-i karhu-n metsä-än kuoliaa-ksi.
hunter.n shoot-past.3s bear-a forest-ill dead-tra
'A/The hunter shot a/the bear dead, and the bear remained in the forest after the shooting (lit. A/The hunter shot the bear dead into the forest.)'

Why is (63) acceptable? The co-occurrence of translative resultative predicates with directional phrases threatens the constraint on the finiteness of predicate argument structures, and this raises the question whether the Unique Path constraint can be maintained.

The solution I propose is that directional locatives in Finnish do not denote 'paths'. The resultative reading in (63) comes from the verb *ampua* 'shoot' taking a resultative predicate *kuoliaaksi* 'dead' (see (64)).

(64) Metsästäjä ampu-i karhu-n kuoliaa-ksi.
hunter.n shoot-past.3s bear-a dead-tra
'A/The hunter shot a/the bear dead.'

When the verb *ampua* occurs with the directional locative predicate *metsään* 'into the forest', two readings are available:

(65) Metsästäjä ampu-i karhu-n metsä-än
hunter.n shoot-past.3s bear-a forest-ill
(i) 'A/the hunter shot a/the bear in (lit. 'into') a/the forest.'
(ii) 'A/the hunter shot a/the bear into a/the forest (i.e. the bear was ejected/propelled into the forest).'

On reading (i), the shooting of the bear 'into the forest' means that the bear was hit by a bullet, and it remained in the forest after the shooting. It does not imply that the bear was propelled into the forest by the shooting, or that the bear ran into the forest when it was being shot. The propulsion reading in (ii) is possible, because *ampua* 'shoot' can also encode a path meaning (akin to 'ejecting a missile from a weapon'). Reading (i) is the relevant one for our discussion here. Notice that a path reading is not what the directional locative in (63) depicts. The directional locative *metsään* 'into the forest' in (63) does not give a caused motion reading: there is no propulsion interpretation available. In fact, a propulsion cum resultative reading would be bizarre, once again showing the Unique Path constraint to be at work.

The idea that directional locatives in Finnish do not necessarily denote a change of location reading in contexts like (63) makes them different from their English counterparts. In English, directional locatives are usually associated with a change of location meaning (see Jackendoff 1990, 1996, Verkuyl and Zwarts 1992, Nam 1995, among others). This can be interpreted as a requirement that the event denoted by the verb must show a change of location as a result state. When directional locatives co-occur with resultative constructions, there are two result states – and this explains the unacceptability of the sentences in (56) above, repeated here as (66), and the English equivalent of (63), as shown in (67).

(66) a. *Sam tickled Chris silly off her chair. (Goldberg 1991)
b. *The hunter shot the bear dead into the forest.

(67) *The hunter shot the bear into the forest dead.
(To mean: The hunter caused the bear to end up in the forest by shooting, and the shooting caused the bear to become dead.)

On the other hand, as reading (i) in (65) shows, Finnish directional locatives do not require that the event denoted by the verb show a change of location as a result state; they merely require a diphasic event structure (Fong 1997, 2000). Accomplishment and Achievement verbs are inherently diphasic, and the occurrence of directional locatives with such verbs is predicted to be acceptable. As (68) and (69) show, the directional locative predicates further specify the achieved state (denoted by the verb), without introducing an additional path meaning.

(68) Karhu kuol-i metsä-än.
bear.n die-past.3s forest-ill
'A/the bear died in (lit. 'into') a/the forest.'

(69) Juna saapu-i asema-lle.
train.n arrive-past.3s station-all
'A/the train arrived at (lit. 'onto') a/the station.'

Similar examples are found in English, where resultative phrases occurring with verbs like *melt* and *freeze* are considered to provide further specification of the achieved state (see Levin and Rappaport Hovav 1995, Rappaport Hovav and Levin 1995).

(70) a. The ice melted into a puddle.
b. The swallow froze to death.

Directional locative predicates also occur in Accomplishments:

(71) Kissa rikko-i maljako-n hylly-ltä
cat.n break-past.3s vase-a shelf-abl
'A/the cat broke a/the vase off a/the shelf.'

Here, the ablative predicate denotes the location of the vase prior to the breaking event. This reading holds in a context where the broken pieces remain on the shelf after the breaking event:

(72) Hylly-ltä oli rikot-tu maljakko.
shelf-abl be.past.3s break-past.pp.pass vase

Palase-t oli-vat hylly-llä hajallaan.
piece-pl be-past.3pl shelf-ade scattered
'Off a/the shelf had been broken a vase. The pieces were scattered on the shelf.'

(72) thus shows that any change of location interpretation is an implicature that is defeasible.

Resultative constructions are also Accomplishments, and their diphasic event structure need not depict change of location. Directional locatives are thus predicted to occur in such contexts where the resultative predicate provides the result state in the diphasic event (see (63) above). But these cases do not violate the Unique Path constraint, if we make the crucial assumption that Finnish directional locative predicates are not interpreted as having path meanings here.

Thus, Finnish is in fact consistent with Rappaport Hovav and Levin's (1995) claim that Achievements and Accomplishments will not allow further augmentation with achieved location. The cases in (63), (68), and (69), which on the surface seem to be counterexamples, turn out to support the generalization, given that the directional locative predicates do not require that the event denoted by the verb show a changed location as a result state. However, this result is obtained only if we assume the diphasic event structure for the interpretation of translative and directional locative cases.

In addition, we now have a unified analysis of the occurrence of translative and directional locative cases with verbs of the same type. Verbs that yield diphasic event structures (either lexically or in combination with their arguments) can take the translative case and directional locative cases like the illative and ablative. The analysis proposed here explains why in precisely such event types, we get the otherwise puzzling effect of a translative predicate not denoting the outcome of change, and a directional locative not involving any change of location meaning.

5 Conclusion

This paper has examined the semantically driven selection of translative versus essive case in secondary predications. The translative case occurs only in events with diphasic structures, while the essive case imposes no such requirement. This accounts for the distribution of the translative case in apparently disparate contexts: contexts that express change of state, as well as contexts that express states with no overt change, but which however have implications of change. This paper shows that the internal structure of eventualities plays a crucial role in accounting not only for the choice of translative/essive case, but also in accounting for the co-occurrence of translative and directional locative cases, two classes of semantic cases whose assignment appear to be dependent on the same properties of the governing predicate.

References

Andrews, A. 1982. A Note on the Constituent Structure of Adverbials and Auxiliaries. *Linguistic Inquiry* 13:313-317.

Anttila, A. and Fong, V. to appear. The Partitive Constraint in Optimality Theory. *Journal of Semantics*. Online: ROA-416-09100, Rutgers Optimality Archive, http://ruccs.rutgers.edu/roa.html.

Bresnan, J. 1982. Polyadicity. *The Mental Representation of GrammaticalRelations*, ed. J. Bresnan, 149-172. Cambridge, Massachusetts: MIT Press.

Dowty, D.R. 1979. *Word Meaning and Montague Grammar*. Dordrecht: Reidel.

Fong, V. 1997. *The Order of Things: What Directional Locatives Denote*. PhD thesis, Stanford University.

Fong, V. 1999. Comments on Alsina. In *Grammatical Semantics: Evidence for Structure in Meaning*, ed. Tara Mohanan and Lionel Wee, 123-134. Stanford: CSLI, and Singapore: National University of Singapore.

Fong, V. 2000. 'Into Doing Something': Where is the Path in Event Predicates? Paper presented at the ESSLLI 2000 Workshop on Paths and Telicity in Event Structure.

Goldberg, A.E. 1991. It Can't Go Down the Chimney Up: Paths and the English resultative. *BLS* 17:368-378.

Green, G.M. 1973. A Syntactic Syncretism in English and French. *Issues in Linguistics*, eds. B.B. Kachru, R.B. Lees, Y. Malkiel, A. Pietrangeli, and S. Saporta, 257-278. Urbana, Illinois: University of Illinois Press.

Gruber, J.S. 1965. *Studies in Lexical Relations*. PhD thesis, MIT.

Hakulinen, A. and Karlsson, F. 1979. *Nykysuomen lauseoppia*. Helsinki: Suomalaisen Kirjallisuuden Seura.

Hale, K. 1983. Warlpiri and the Grammar of Non-configurational Languages. *Natural Language and Linguistic Theory* 1:5-47.

Halliday, M.A.K. 1967. Notes on Transitivity and Theme in English, Part 1. *Journal of Linguistics* 3:37-81.

Heinämäki, O. 1984. Aspect in Finnish. *Aspect Bound: A Voyage into the Realm of Germanic, Slavonic and Finno-Ugrian Aspectology*, ed. C. de Groot and H. Tommola, 153-177. Dordrecht: Foris.

Holmberg, A. and Nikanne, U. 1993a. Introduction. In *Case and Other Functional Categories in Finnish Syntax*, ed. A. Holmberg and U. Nikanne, 1-20. Berlin: Mouton de Gruyter.

Holmberg, A. and Nikanne, U., eds. 1993b. *Case and Other Functional Categories in Finnish Syntax*. Berlin: Mouton de Gruyter.

Jackendoff, R. 1990. *Semantic Structures*. Cambridge, Massachusetts: MIT Press.

Jackendoff, R. 1996. The Proper Treatment of Measuring Out, Telicity, and Perhaps Even Quantification in English. *Natural Language and Linguistic Theory* 14: 305-354.

Kamp, H, and Reyle, U. 1993. *From Discourse to Logic*. Dordrecht: Kluwer Academic Publishers.

Karlsson, F. 1987. *Finnish Grammar*. Porvoo: Werner Söderström Osakeyhtiö. 2nd edition.

Kim, S. and Maling, J. 1997. A Crosslinguistic Perspective on Resultative Formation. *Proceedings of the 1997 Texas Linguistics Society Conference*, 189- 204.

Kiparsky, P. 1998. Partitive case and aspect. *The Projection of Arguments: Lexical and Compositional Factors*, ed. M. Butt and W. Geuder, 265-307. Stanford: CSLI.

Krifka, M. 1989. Nominal Reference, Temporal Constitution and Quantification in Event Semantics. *Semantics and Contextual Expressions*, ed. R. Bartsch, J. van Benthem, and P.v.E. Boas, 75-115. Dordrecht: Foris.

Levin, B. and Rappaport Hovav, M. 1992. The Lexical Semantics of Verbs of Motion: The Perspective from Unaccusativity. *Thematic Structure: Its Role in Grammar*, ed. I.M. Roca, 247-269. Berlin: Foris.

Levin, B. and Rappaport Hovav, M. 1995. *Unaccusativity: At the Syntax-Lexical Semantics Interface*. Cambridge, Massachusetts: MIT Press.

Levin, B. and Rappaport Hovav, M. 1999. Two Structures for Compositionally Derived Events. *Proceedings of SALT 9*, 199-223. Ithaca, New York: Cornell Linguistics Circle Publications, Cornell University.

Löbner, S. 1987. Quantification as a Major Module of Natural Language Semantics. *Studies in Discourse Representation Theory and the Theory of Generalized*

Quantifiers, ed. J. Groenendijk, D. De Jong, and M. Stokhof, 53 -85. Dordrecht: Foris.

Löbner, S. 1989. German *schon – erst – noch:* An Integrated Analysis. *Linguistics and Philosophy* 12: 167-212.

Maling, J. 1993. Of Nominative and Accusative: The Hierarchical Assignment of Grammatical Cases in Finnish. *Case and Other Functional Categories in Finnish Syntax*, ed. A. Holmberg and U. Nikanne, 49-74. Berlin: Mouton de Gruyter.

Mohanan, T.W. 1994. Case OCP: A Constraint on Word Order in Hindi. *Theoretical Perspectives on Word Order in South Asian Languages*, ed. M. Butt, T. King, and G. Ramchand, 185-216. Stanford: CSLI.

Mohanan, T. and Mohanan, K.P. 1999. On Representations in Grammatical Semantics. In *Grammatical Semantics: Evidence for Structure in Meaning*, ed. T. Mohanan and L. Wee, 23-75. Stanford: CSLI, and Singapore: National University of Singapore.

Nam, S. 1995. *The Semantics of Locative Prepositional Phrases in English.* PhD thesis, UCLA.

Neeleman, A. and Weerman, F. 1993. The Balance Between Syntax and Morphology: Dutch Particles and Resultatives. *Natural Language and Linguistic Theory* 11: 433-475.

Parsons, T. 1990. *Events in the Semantics of English: A Study in Subatomic Semantics.* Cambridge, Massachusetts: MIT Press.

Penttilä, A. 1963. *Suomen Kielioppi.* Porvoo: Werner Söderström Osakeyhtiö. 2nd edition.

Pustejovsky, J. 1991. The Syntax of Event Structure. *Cognition* 41:47-81.

Pustejovsky, J. 1995. *The Generative Lexicon.* Cambridge, Massachusetts: MIT Press.

Pylkkänen, L. 2000. On Stativity and Causation. *Events as Grammatical Objects*, ed. C. Tenny and J. Pustejovsky, 417-445. Stanford: CSLI.

Rapoport, T.R. 1993. Verbs in Depictives and Resultatives. *Semantics and the Lexicon*, ed. J. Pustejovsky, 163-184. Dordrecht: Kluwer.

Rappaport Hovav, M. and Levin, B. 1995. The Elasticity of Verb Meaning. *IATL2: Proceedings of the tenth annual conference of the Israel Association for Theoretical Linguistics and the workshop on the syntax-semantics interface.*

Rothstein, S.D. 1985. *The Syntactic Forms of Predication.* Bloomington, Indiana: Indiana University Linguistics Club.

Simpson, J.H. 1983. *Aspects of Warlpiri Morphology and Syntax.* PhD thesis, MIT.

de Swart, H. 1996. Meaning and Use of *not...until. Journal of Semantics* 13: 221-263.

Tenny, C. 1992. The Aspectual Interface Hypothesis. *Lexical Matters*, ed. I. Sag and A. Szabolcsi, 1-27. Stanford: CSLI.

Tenny, C.L. 1994. *Aspectual Roles and the Syntax-Semantics Interface*. Dordrecht: Kluwer.

Vainikka, A.M. 1989. *Deriving Syntactic Representations in Finnish*. PhD thesis, University of Massachusetts.

Vainikka, A. 1993. The Three Structural Cases in Finnish. *Case and Other Functional Categories in Finnish Syntax*, ed. A. Holmberg and U. Nikanne, 129-159. Berlin: Mouton de Gruyter.

Van Valin, R.D., Jr. 1993. A Synopsis of Role and Reference Grammar. *Advances in Role and Reference Grammar*, ed. Robert D. Van Valin, Jr., 1-164. Amsterdam: John Benjamins.

Van Valin, R.D., Jr. and LaPolla, R.J. 1997. *Syntax: Structure, Meaning, and Function*. Cambridge: Cambridge University Press.

Verkuyl, H. 1988. Aspectual Asymmetry and Quantification. *Temporalsemantik*, ed. Veronika Ehrich and Heinz Vater, 220-259. Tübingen: Max Niemeyer Verlag.

Verkuyl, H.J. 1993. *A Theory of Aspectuality*. Cambridge: Cambridge University Press.

Verkuyl, H.J. and Zwarts, J. 1992. Time and Space in Conceptual and Logical Semantics: The Notion of Path. *Linguistics* 30: 483-511.

Vilkuna, M. 1989. *Free Word Order in Finnish: Its Syntax and Discourse Functions*. Helsinki: Suomalaisen Kirjallisuuden Seura.

Vähämäki, B. 1994. *Mastering Finnish*. New York: Hippocrene Books.

7

Postverbal Case Realization in Finnish

ANNE VAINIKKA

1 Introduction

In a number of constructions in Finnish, the element following the verb (in the unmarked word order) has some objectlike properties regardless of the syntactic category of the postverbal element (noun, adjective, or adverbial). First, in these constructions the postverbal element carries a nonagentive thematic role, as does an object NP. Secondly, none of these postverbal elements raise with the verb (to a higher functional projection), any more than an object NP does, given that all of them can be separated from the finite verb by an adverbial. Thirdly, and most importantly for the purposes of this paper, these constructions share case properties, in that each of the postverbal elements appears to allow objective case marking.

This paper attempts to cover all of the constructions in Finnish which have the properties just discussed. The four main construction types are (a) the regular object construction, (b) the predicative construction, (c) the existential construction, and (d) the possessive construction. In the final section of the paper, a further adverbial construction will be discussed, and subtypes of the four main types will be discussed along with the main construction types.

The main goal of this paper is to systematically determine which objective cases are assigned in each of the constructions of this type, since in many of the constructions it is controversial whether the postverbal element carries accusative, nominative, or genitive case, and whether the postverbal element is a subject, and object, or an adjunct. If it turns out that the post-

Generative Approaches to Finnic and Saami Linguistics.
Diane Nelson and Satu Manninen (eds.).

verbal element can occur either in the partitive or in the accusative (the cases of a regular object), but not in the nominative, it can be concluded that the case evidence points to the element occurring in the object position. Note that it is by no means straightforward to determine superficially which case has been assigned, due to the rampant homophony and ambiguity found in the Finnish grammatical case system.

The theoretical framework adopted here is loosely speaking the generative theories of Chomsky (GB, Chomsky 1981 and Minimalism, Chomsky 1993), including the assumptions made in those theories about syntactic structure and theta-role assignment. However, the versions of Case Theory developed in Chomsky's theories do not begin to account for the distribution and realization of morphosyntactic case in Finnish. Thus, one of the goals of this paper is to further develop – based on new construction types – the case model proposed in previous work (Vainikka 1989, 1992 and 1993).

Building on earlier work, it will be argued in this paper that partitive is a structurally assigned default case, while accusative is assigned based on a semantic feature (in particular, the feature [+bounded][1] potentially carried by verbs). In addition, an analysis of the postverbal nominative and a newly discovered postverbal genitive will be provided.

The four main constructions to be discussed in this paper are exemplified in (1) to (4) below. Case marking on the postverbal elements is indicated as follows: in unambiguous cases a single case name is provided *(ACC = accusative, PAR = partitive, GEN = genitive, NOM = nominative).* When the case form could be an instance of either of two cases, both are provided; for example, *ACC/GEN* means that the relevant form could be either accusative or genitive. To provide a complete picture of the homophony involved in postverbal case marking, the ambiguity is indicated even in the cases where the status of the case is uncontroversial, such as in the case of the regular thematic objects in (1):

(1) a. Kirjoitin kirjan.
I-wrote book-ACC/GEN
'I wrote (a/the) book'

b. Kirjoitin kirjaa.
I-wrote book-PAR
'I was writing (a/the) book'

Regular thematic objects of verbs are assigned either accusative or partitive case, depending on aspectual considerations, as exemplified in (1). Full NPs

---

[1] See the end of Section 2.1 for a more detailed discussion about the feature [+bounded].

in Finnish do not have a unique accusative form; singular full NPs in regular sentences with subject-verb agreement show up in the genitive (with the suffix –*n*), as in (1a).

The second main construction that will be considered here is the predicative construction formed with the copula *olla* 'be', which takes either an Adjective Phrase (AP) or a Noun Phrase (NP) postverbally:

(2) a. Kirja on vanha.
Book-NOM is old-NOM/ACC
'(The) book is old'

b. Maali on punaista.
Paint-NOM is red-PAR
'(The) paint is red'

c. Tämä mies on opettaja.
This man-NOM is teacher-NOM/ACC
'This man is (a) teacher'

Since the Finnish accusative can also be realized as nominative case (i.e. the form that carries no case suffix in Finnish) in sentences of the type in (2), the case of the postverbal element in (2a) and (2c) cannot be determined without further tests.

The third construction to be considered is the existential sentence, which reveals the same case ambiguity as the predicative construction, as shown in (3a), along with partitive case marking, as in (3b):

(3) a. Tässä on kirja.
Here is book-NOM/ACC
'Here is a book'

b. Ulkona on autoja.
Outside is car-PL-PAR
'There are cars outside'

The fourth construction under consideration is the possessive construction, which at least superficially resembles the existential sentence. The possessor occurs preverbally in an oblique case (adessive, or 'at'), and the possessed item follows the copular verb, again typically in the ambiguous form lacking a specific case suffix, as in (4a):

(4) a. Minulla on kirja.
I-ADE is book-NOM/ACC
'I have a book'

b. Minulla on kirjoja.
I-ADE is book-PL-PAR
'I have books'

Note that partitive case is found in all four constructions: as the case of an NP object in connection with incompleted aspect (1b), with the predicative AP qualifying a mass noun in (2b), and with the plural postverbal NP in the existential construction and in the possessive construction (3b and 4b). Since each construction also allows a form that is potentially an accusative form, there is substantial reason based on case assignment to suspect that all four constructions may involve the same structural configuration, namely a verb followed by the postverbal element in the object position.

Based on case distribution, it will be argued in this paper that the postverbal element in all four constructions occurs in the complement position of the verb. Three of the four constructions (the regular object construction, the possessive construction, and the existential construction) will turn out to be fully parallel, while the predicative construction involves a more complex interaction between case assignment and agreement.

2 Partitive Case as the Structural Case of the Complement Position

In traditional grammars of Finnish, the accusative[2] has been taken to be the unmarked case of object NPs, whereas the partitive is somehow semantically marked (e.g. Siro 1964, Toivainen 1979). The distinction between the two object cases has typically been taken to be a semantic one, where accusative in some sense implies 'whole' and partitive implies 'part'. For example, in an article on partitive case Larjavaara (1988:503) concludes:

> ...on the basis of its original meaning 'part of something' the partitive has developed a kind of cognitive universal sense: i.e. influenced by existential quantification, the sense 'any part or all'.

---

[2] As was seen in the above examples, the accusative may be ambiguous with the genitive or with the nominative. However, we will see that with regular NP objects it is typically easy to see whether a form is a true accusative, given the distribution of personal pronouns. Thus when we refer to 'accusative' in this section, we mean those instances of accusative which have the same distribution as accusative personal pronouns (with suffix *–t*).

In contrast to traditional grammarians, I have argued that the *partitive* must be the unmarked case of the object position, with accusative being a marked case (Vainikka 1985, 1988, 1989, 1993; see also Heinämäki 1984 and Vainikka & Maling 1996). This view has also been adopted by Kiparsky in his recent work on Finnish case marking (Kiparsky 1998, 2001:fn.9), and additional independent evidence from the DP domain for this view is presented in Anttila & Fong (2000).

2.1 The Earlier Arguments for Partitive as the Unmarked Case

The syntactic distribution of partitive and accusative in various types of complement positions reveals a striking discrepancy between the two cases: partitive case appears in the complement position of various head types, while accusative case only occurs as the complement of verbs. That is, accusative is an *object case*, while partitive is more generally a *complement case*.

Consider first the situation with prepositions. Partitive is the most common case of the complement of a preposition, as seen in the examples in (5), while accusative never occurs with prepositions.

(5) a. ilman tietokonetta
without computer-PAR
'without a computer'

b. ennen aikaista aamiaista
before early-PAR breakfast-PAR
'before an early breakfast'

c. lähellä Tamperetta
near Tampere-PAR
'close to Tampere'

In contrast, the typical case of the complement of *postpositions* (where the head follows the complement) is genitive case, as shown in the examples in (6):

(6) a. tietokoneen kanssa
computer-GEN with
'with a computer'

b. aikaisen aamiaisen jälkeen
early-GEN breakfast-GEN after
'after an early breakfast'

c. Tampereen lähistöllä
Tampere-GEN in-vicinity
'in the vicinity of Tampere'

Although one of the realizations of accusative case is homophonous with the genitive, it is clear that the case in the postposition construction is a true genitive and not an accusative. This can be seen in the examples in (7) with personal pronouns, which have unique accusative and genitive forms:

(7) a. minun/ *minut kanssani
my-GEN me-ACC with-1sgPx[3]
'with me'

b. sinun/ *sinut jälkeesi
your-GEN you-ACC after-2sgPx
'after you'

c. meidän/ *meidät tykönämme
our-GEN us-ACC near-1plPx
'at our place'

In addition to being the unmarked case of the preposition construction, the partitive is also a common case in various quantifier constructions. The accusative, on the other hand, does not occur in such constructions. Consider the following examples of what are presumably partitive complements of Q heads:

(8) a. kolme tietokonetta
three computer-PAR
'three computers'

b. pari mansikkaa
couple strawberry-PAR
'a couple of strawberries'

c. pino tyhjiä postikortteja
pile empty-PAR postcard-PAR
'a pile of empty postcards'

---

[3] The suffix –ni attached to the postposition *kanssa* 'with' is a so-called possessive suffix (glossed as 'Px' following Kanerva 1987), which is an agreement element agreeing in person and number with the genitive pronoun (in this case the 1st person singular).

d. lusikallinen lääkettä
spoonful medicine-PAR
'a spoonful of medicine'

Partitive also occurs in one of the versions of the comparative construction, presumably either as the complement of a comparative head or as the complement of the adjective (see Vilkuna's recent grammar of Finnish where she treats the NP in this construction as the complement of the adjective; Vilkuna 1996:76). It is not crucial for the present argument which element in this construction is the head, but rather that the construction provides a further context where partitive case occurs. Accusative is not possible in this particular construction:

(9) a. Niilo on Mattia nuorempi.
Niilo-NOM is Matti-PAR younger
'Niilo is younger than Matti'

b. Niilo on nuorempi Mattia.

An unusual fact about this construction is that the partitive typically precedes the comparative adjective, as in (9a); I have no explanation for this fact. Example (9b) shows that the partitive following the adjective is also possible, but it is clearly not the basic word order.

Thus, the partitive occurs in the complement position of a variety of syntactic heads, including at least V, P, Q, and possibly A. (The remaining major head type, N, does not take NP-complements at all.) The accusative, in contrast, only occurs with the V head. The most straightforward way to account for such a case distribution is to take the partitive to be the unmarked case of the complement position – equivalent of the accusative in the Indo-European languages – and to search for a different analysis of the accusative.

In previous work, I have termed partitive case "the structural default case of the complement position". The term reflects my view that a particular morphological case can be associated with a syntactic position at the level of projecting syntactic structure. That is, when the complement position is posited in the syntax (of Finnish) across all head types, this position is projected with partitive case. If no other case is assigned during the derivation of the sentence, the case that was projected with the position (i.e. the structural default case of that position) will emerge. This approach accounts for the distribution of partitive and genitive case in Finnish, the latter being the structural default case of the specifier position.

Let us now turn to the case marking of the direct object of a verb which was already exemplified above in (1). The partitive object occurs in two main sentence types: when the action is negated, or when the action is aspectually incomplete.[4] The accusative occurs in affirmative sentences which imply completed action. Consider the examples in (10):

(10) a. Riitta maalasi minut.
Riitta-NOM painted me-ACC
'Riitta painted me'

b. Riitta maalasi minua.
Riitta-NOM painted me-PAR
'Riitta was painting me'

c. Riitta ei maalannut minua/ *minut.
Riitta-NOM not painted me-PAR/me-ACC
'Riitta didn't paint me/Riitta wasn't painting me'

Under the approach that partitive is the structural default case of the complement position, the instances of partitive case in (10b) – with incompleted aspect – and in (10c) – with negation – would arise in the absence of any further case assigned during the derivation (just as it does with head types other than V).

The accusative case in (10a), however, has a very restricted distribution: it basically only occurs with V heads that imply completed action, i.e. resultative aspect. In previous work I have assumed that a (semantic) feature [+completed] is responsible for accusative case assignment in Finnish. However, although accusative assignment correlates closely with completed action, it is clear from the discussion in Kiparsky (1998) that the notion of 'boundedness' may be more appropriate, following the ideas of Heinämäki (1984) and Leino (1991), and building on aspectuality in model-theoretic semantics (Krifka 1992 and Pinon 1995). Thus, Kiparsky's [+bounded] feature will be adopted in the remainder of the paper; for a detailed discussion and definition of this feature, see Kiparsky (1998).

Whether accusative is assigned by a verb carrying the relevant feature, or whether it is assigned by a functional head such as Aspect with the same feature, is a question that will be left open here.

---

[4] In addition, partitive occurs in some situations where the NP object is partial:

(i) Näin jalkaa peiton alta.
I-saw foot-PAR blanket-GEN under
'I saw (a portion of) a foot under the blanket'

As the English gloss indicates, such NPs might involve an abstract Q-head with the meaning 'partial'.

We now turn to the four main constructions that form the topic of this paper, and consider (for the first time) the distribution of partitive case in these constructions.

2.2 The Plural Partitive

The distribution of the plural partitive case in the four main constructions discussed in this paper (the object, predicative, existential, and possessive constructions) provides both a justification for considering the four constructions to be syntactically parallel (judging by case marking), as well as providing a further argument for the unmarked, default, status of partitive case for the object position. As will be shown in what follows, the partitive can be argued to be the basic case in the plural versions of all four constructions.Plural NP objects of typical verbs occur either in the partitive or in a form that is ambiguous between the accusative and the nominative, as shown in (11). As in the singular, the case marking on the object is usually determined by aspect-related factors: the non-partitive form implies completed, or bounded, aspect (11b), while the partitive does not imply completion of the action (11a):

(11) a. Matti piirsi traktoreita.
Matti-NOM drew-3SG tractor-PL-PAR
'Matti was drawing tractors'

b. Matti piirsi nämä traktorit.
Matti-NOM drew-3SG these tractors-NOM/ACC
'Matti drew these tractors'

Following the discussion in Section 2.1, the partitive in (11a) will be considered to be the default form which emerges in the absence of the semantic feature [+bounded] responsible for accusative assignment.

The case form in (11b) is ambiguous between the nominative and the accusative, as indicated by the gloss. That is, the form *nämä traktorit* 'these tractors' is both the form used as a (nominative) subject and the form used as an (accusative) object; as in English, full NPs in Finnish do not have a unique accusative form.

Personal pronouns[5] which have a unique accusative form with the suffix *–t* in Finnish (parallel to the English situation) reveal that the relevant NP is truly an accusative object:

---

[5] Not even all personal pronouns have a unique accusative form in Finnish, but only those pronouns which bear the feature [+human]; that is, the personal pronouns *se* 'it' and *ne* 'they-inanimate' do not have an accusative form.

(12) a. Matti maalasi heitä usein.
Matti-NOM painted-3SG them-PAR often
'Matti painted them often'
(he may not have finished even one picture of them)

b. Matti maalasi heidät usein.
Matti-NOM painted-3SG them-ACC often
'Matti painted them often' (he finished several pictures)

The second construction under consideration, the predicative construction with the copula *olla* 'be',[6] reveals a similar pattern of postverbal case distribution in the plural as the regular object in (12) did:

(13) a. Nämä matot ovat uusia.
These rugs-NOM are-3PL new-PL-PAR
'These rugs are new'

b. Nämä matot ovat uudet.
These rugs-NOM are-3PL new-PL-NOM/ACC
'These rugs are new' (they are a new set of rugs)

The difference in meaning between the partitive AP in (13a) and the AP lacking a case suffix in (13b) is a subtle one. Löbel (1999) characterizes the form in constructions such as (13b) as emphasizing 'the totality of the amount referred to', while with the partitive contextually relevant additional quantities may also exist (cf. also Chesterman 1991). Vilkuna (1996:106-7) describes the form without a case suffix – what she takes to be an instance of nominative – as referring to indivisible pairs, series, or wholes, while the usual divisible plural shows up in the partitive. In any case, partitive appears to be the unmarked case in the plural of this construction, while the form in (13b) can only be used in a restricted context, e.g. when speaking of the set of rugs belonging to a particular room.

---

6 A related predicative construction in Finnish involves the verb *tulla* 'come, become', where we find a similar pattern of case marking:

(i) Matoista tuli puhtaita.
Rug-PL-ELA became-3SG clean-PL-PAR
'The rugs became clean'

(ii) Matoista tuli puhtaat.
Rug-PL-ELA became-3SG clean-PL-NOM/ACC
'The rugs became clean'

The 'subject' in this construction occurs in elative case (one of the locative cases), and the verb does not agree with the elative NP. The predicate AP in these examples occurs either in the partitive, as in (i) or in the form lacking a case suffix, as in (ii); the difference in interpretation between (i) and (ii) is subtle and difficult to grasp.

An identical pattern is attested in this construction when the postverbal element is a plural NP, as shown in (14):

(14) a. Ne ovat uusia mattoja.
They-NOM are-3PL new rugs-PL-PAR
'Those rugs are new' (lit. 'They are new rugs')

b. Ne ovat keittiön uudet matot.
They-NOM are-3PL kitchen-GEN new rugs-PL-NOM/ACC
'They are (the) new rugs for the kitchen'

Again, the partitive version in (14a) is the unmarked one in the plural, while the version *uudet matot* in (14b) can only be used in a special context of a set of rugs (e.g. belonging to the kitchen).

Thus, the partitive option in this predicative construction represents the basic option, at least in the plural, while the form lacking a case suffix (ambiguously either nominative or accusative) arises in a special semantic context. This is true whether the predicate is an AP, as in (13), or an NP, as in (14).

The two plural constructions discussed so far – the object construction and the predicative construction – are similar in that both mark the postverbal element with partitive in the unmarked case. Next we turn to the third relevant construction, the existential construction:

(15) a. Kirjastossa on mielenkiintoisia kirjoja.
Library-INE[7] is-3SG interesting books-PL-PAR
'There are interesting books at the library'
(lit. 'At the library is interesting books')

b. Kirjastossa on etsimäsi mielenkiintoiset kirjat.
Library-INE is search-PTCPL-2Px interesting books-PL-NOM/ACC
'The interesting books you were looking for are at the library'

As with the previous two constructions, the partitive form in (15a) clearly reflects the unmarked form found in the plural form of the existential construction, while the alternative form in (15b) is semantically marked, crucially involving some very specific books. However, the existential con-

7 The following abbreviations are used for locative cases in this paper: INE inessive 'in'; ELA elative 'from'; ADE adessive 'at'.

struction differs from the first two constructions in that there is no preverbal nominative subject, nor is there any subject-verb agreement (the verb occurs in the 3rd person singular regardless of the NPs in question). Traditionally, the postverbal NP in the existential construction – such as *mielenkiintoisia kirjoja* 'interesting books-PAR' in (15a) – has been treated as a partitive subject (cf. e.g. Vilkuna 1996).[8] However, given the approach to partitive and accusative assignment pursued in this paper, the postverbal NP will turn out to occupy the object position in the existential construction.

As with the three constructions discussed so far, a plural postverbal element in the possessive construction normally occurs in the partitive, although the form without a case suffix is also possible:

(16) a. Minulla on kirjoja.
I-ADE is book-PL-PAR
'I have books'

b. Minulla on ne kirjat, joita pyysit.
I-ADE is those books-NOM/ACC which-PL/PAR ask-PAST-2SG
'I have (with me) the books that you asked for'

As we have seen, the occurrence of the form without a case suffix seems to be governed by a similar semantic context both in the predicative construction (13b and 14b above), and in the existential construction (15b above), namely that the form without a case suffix occurs postverbally when the postverbal NP is in some sense specific. However, for both constructions the postverbal NP being specific represents a marked situation. In the plural possessive construction, as well, the partitive represents the unmarked case, as in (16a), while the form lacking a case suffix in (16b) emerges when the postverbal NP is in some sense specific.[9]

---

[8] Vilkuna (1996:101) also discusses a construction that appears to be a variant of the existential construction, with verbs other than *olla* 'be'; (i) is her example:

(i) Sieltä oli karannut käärme.
There-ELA had-3SG escaped snake-NOM/ACC
'A snake had escaped from there'

(ii) Kirjastosta hävisi useita kirjoja.
Library-ELA disappeared-3SG several-PL-PAR book-PL-PAR
'Several books disappeared from the library'

Example (ii) with a partitive postverbal NP shows that the postverbal element is not a nominative subject; note also lack of subject-verb agreement in (ii).

[9] It is unclear whether a single feature responsible for case assignment could somehow subsume both specificity (in the existential and possessive constructions) and indivisibility (in the predicative construction, where the notion of an indivisible set seems to be relevant). For the purposes of this paper, I will assume that such a single feature can be found, but I take it to be

The possessive construction in (16) is similar to the existential construction in (15) in that both involve a preverbal NP in oblique case, followed by a non-agreeing 3rd person singular copula. In the possessive construction, however, the preverbal NP bears some subjectlike properties, being the logical subject of possession. Thus, there is even less reason than with the existential construction to assume that the postverbal element in (16) is a postverbal subject.

All four constructions discussed so far reveal partitive case to be the unmarked case of the postverbal element, at least in the plural. This pattern supports the idea that all four constructions have a postverbal element in the complement position of the verb, and that partitive emerges in this position in the absence of a feature that would assign some other case to this position.

2.3 Partitive in the Singular

Let us now briefly turn to the status of partitive case in the singular in the four constructions. As already discussed with respect to regular object NPs, partitive case is the default case even in the singular (example (10b) above).

Recall that in the other three postverbal constructions (the predicative, the existential, and the possessive constructions), the plural NP or AP following the verb typically occurs in the partitive. However, in each of these constructions the form without a case suffix is also possible in the plural under special semantic conditions.

In the singular in these three constructions, the postverbal element typically occurs in the form without a case suffix, which is, as always, ambiguous between nominative and accusative. This is exemplified in (17):

(17) a. Tämä matto on uusi.
This rug-NOM is new-NOM/ACC
'This rug is new'

b. Tämä on uusi matto.
This is new rug-NOM/ACC
'This is a new rug'

c. Kirjastossa on mielenkiintoinen kirja.
Library-INE is interesting book-NOM/ACC
'There is an interesting book at the library'

---

beyond the scope of this paper to develop a definition for the feature. Even if two distinct features were required, this does not undermine the basic approach to case assignment advocated here.

d. Minulla on mielenkiintoinen kirja.
I-ADE is interesting book-NOM/ACC
'I have an interesting book'

Examples (17a-b) show the singular of the predicative construction, either with a predicative AP (17a) or with a predicative NP (17b).[10] Example (17c) is an instance of the existential construction,[11] while (17d) represents the possessive construction.

Unlike in the plural, where partitive was the unmarked case of the postverbal element, in the singular the form without a case suffix emerges. In all three constructions, the partitive only emerges in the singular in the case of mass nouns, as shown in (18) for the predicative construction, in (19) for the existential construction, and in (20) for the possessive construction:

(18) a. Tämä maali on uutta.
This paint-NOM is new-PAR
'This paint is new'

b. Tämä on uutta maalia.
This is new paint-PAR
'This is new paint'

c. *Tämä kirja on uutta.
This book-NOM is new-PAR
'This book is new'

d. *Tämä on uutta kirjaa.
This is new book-PAR
'This is (a) new book'

---

[10] The variant of the predicative construction discussed in footnote (6) behaves as follows in the singular:

i) Matosta tuli puhdas.
Rug-ELA became clean-NOM/ACC
'The rug became clean'

Thus, the predicative construction with *tulla* 'come, become' in (i) has the same typical case distribution as the predicative construction with *olla* 'be': in the singular, the postverbal element occurs in the form without a case suffix, and in the plural it occurs in the partitive.

[11] The variant of the existential construction discussed in footnote (8) also has the form without a case suffix in the singular:

i) Kirjastosta hävisi kirja.
Library-ELA disappeared-3SG book-NOM/ACC
'A book disappeared from the library'

(19) a. Kaupassa on maitoa.
Store-INE is milk-PAR
'There is milk at the store'

b. *Kaupassa on kirjaa.
Store-INE is book-PAR
'There is (a) book at the store'

(20) a. Minulla on maitoa.
I-ADE is milk-PAR
'I have milk'

b. *Minulla on kirjaa.
I-ADE is book-PAR
'I have (a) book'

If all four constructions were to involve the postverbal element in the object position, as suggested by the plural data, we would expect the following situation in the singular: both partitive and accusative are possible cases (as with a regular object); accusative is assigned by the verb (or a higher functional head) with the feature [+bounded]; in the absence of such a case-assigning feature, partitive emerges.

However, it appears that the feature [+bounded] cannot be responsible for the possible accusative form in the predicative, existential, and possessive constructions, since all typically involve the copula verb *olla* 'be' which does not have the possibility of a resultative interpretation. In fact, in the plural discussion it already became clear that a feature related to specificity is needed to distinguish between the partitive context and the context in which the suffixless (NOM/ACC) form occurs. Without providing a definition for such a feature (see footnote (9)), I propose that a single feature (relating to specificity, and carried either by the verb or by a functional head above the VP) is responsible for nominative/accusative assignment in both singular and plural copular constructions.[12] In the absence of this feature, partitive emerges in all four constructions, both in the plural and in the singular.

Before we consider how accusative/nominative assignment works in more detail, we need to establish whether the postverbal case form without a case suffix is nominative or accusative in the three copular constructions; this is the question we now turn to.

---

[12] This analysis was inspired by Löbel (1999) who proposes that an AP or NP in the predicative construction carries the feature [+inclusive].

3 Postverbal Nominative vs. Accusative

In the preceding sections it has been argued that the partitive case is a structurally determined unmarked case of the complement position in Finnish; this explains the distribution of partitive case with regular objects of verbs. To the extent that the three other constructions under consideration are structurally parallel to the object construction, the emergence of partitive in these other constructions is structurally explained as well.

We now turn to the question of whether the form without a case suffix in these constructions can be a true accusative, as would be expected if they all represent the verb-complement structure. The discussion in this section will be ordered here based on how object-like the postverbal element is, proceeding from the most object-like to the least object-like.

We have already seen that it is straightforward to test with regular objects of thematic verbs what the case of the object is, given the unique accusative case marking on personal pronouns. Thus, a true accusative is assigned to the object NP whenever the verb carries the feature [+bounded]; otherwise, partitive is assigned. Let us now turn to the possessive construction.

3.1 Three Tests for the Accusative and the Possessive Construction

As mentioned earlier, the possessor in the possessive construction can be thought of as a logical subject, and therefore the possessed (postverbal) NP would correspond to a logical object. There are three possible tests for the accusative that will be described here and applied to the possessive construction.[13] The first test is the pronoun test. This test straightforwardly shows that the postverbal NP in the possessive construction is a true accusative, since a (human) personal pronoun shows up in the accusative (from Vilkuna 1996:156):

(21) Onneksi minulla on sinut.
Fortunately I-ADE is-3sg you-ACC
'Fortunately I have you.'

The second potential test is based on agreement. With regular objects, a singular full NP is realized in the genitive case if a tensed verb agrees with an overt or null subject, otherwise normally in the nominative (the so-called Jansson's Law discussed in Kiparsky (2001); cf. also Timberlake (1975), Reime (1993) and Nelson (1998)):

---

[13] The first two tests, the pronoun test and the agreement test, are straightforward and belong in the traditional Finnish literature (e.g. Vilkuna 1996:126-127). The third test, the embedding test, is developed here for the first time, to my knowledge.

(22) a. Kirjoitin kirjan / *kirja.
I-wrote book-ACC/GEN / *ACC/NOM
'I wrote a/the book'

b. Kirjoita kirja / *kirjan!
Write-IMPER book-ACC/NOM / *ACC/GEN
'Write a/the book!'

Thus, only the accusative with the genitive *–n* suffix is possible with an agreeing verb in (22a), while only the nominative version of the accusative is possible with the non-agreeing imperative in (22b).

The agreement test, however, cannot be applied to the possessive construction since this construction only has a version without subject-verb agreement; the copula always occurs in the non-agreeing 3rd person singular form in the possessive construction. The postverbal form lacking a case suffix that emerges in the possessive construction is, in any case, consistent with an accusative analysis based on this test.

The third test for the accusative involves embedded constructions. What superficially looks like nominative/genitive variation occurs in certain embedded constructions (example (23b) is from Vilkuna 1996:298; the grammaticality of (23a) is implied in the text):

(23) a. Uolevin väitetään saavan palkankorotus.
Uolevi-GEN claim-PASS get-INF raise-ACC/NOM
'Uolevi is claimed to receive a raise'

b. Uolevin väitetään saavan palkankorotuksen.
Uolevi-GEN claim-PASS get-INF raise-ACC/GEN
'Uolevi is claimed to receive a raise'

No analysis of the variation is provided in Vilkuna (1996); cf. also Löbel (1999) who discusses this problematic variation without arriving at a final analysis.

I propose that the source of the nominative/genitive variation is based on the choice of the verb that is relevant for determining the form of the embedded accusative object; that is, the variation would be based on which verb has scope over the embedded object. If the matrix verb is taken as the relevant verb in the above example, the accusative object *palkankorotus* 'raise' ends up in the form without a case suffix, as in (23a), since the matrix verb is a non-agreeing one (the impersonal passive). If the embedded verb is the relevant verb, a genitive suffix emerges on the accusative object in the embedded clause, as in (23b), since this particular non-finite verb form in Finnish prefers the genitive option. (The fronted genitive phrase *Uolevin* has been raised from the embedded subject position in both examples.)

The point here, however, is not the exact source of the variation, but rather that this variation only occurs with singular full NP objects, not with plural NPs or pronouns, as shown in (24):

(24) a. Uolevin väitetään saavan palkinnot \ *palkintojen.
Uolevi-GEN claim-PASS get-INF awards-ACC/NOM \ *GEN
'Uolevi is claimed to receive the awards'

b. Uolevin väitetään omistavan sinut \ *sinun \ *sinä.
Uolevi-GEN claim-PASS own-INF you-ACC \ *GEN \ *NOM
'Uolevi is claimed to own you'

Since the embedded nominative/genitive variation only occurs with singular full NPs, as shown by the contrast between (23) and (24), there is good reason to treat the variation in (23) as involving the two variants of the accusative (which happen to be identical to the nominative and the genitive). As we have seen, the accusative has the two variants only with singular full NPs. Pronouns have a unique accusative form, and this accusative is the only possible form with pronouns in the embedded construction, as shown in (24b). Plural NPs have only a single accusative form (identical to the nominative), and this is the only possible form in the embedded construction, as shown in (24a).

We therefore have a complex argument for the presence of true accusative case wherever we find an embedded construction in which the nominative/genitive variation occurs with singular full NPs, as in (23), but no variation occurs with pronouns or plural NPs, as shown in (24).

Let us finally apply the embedding test to the possessive construction:

(25) a. Jukka väitti sinulla olevan uuden auton \ uusi auto
Jukka-NOM claimed you-ADE be-INF new car-ACC/GEN \ ACC/NOM
'Jukka claimed (that) you have a new car'

b. Jukka väitti minulla olevan sinut \ *sinun \ *sinä.
Jukka-NOM claimed I-ADE be-INF you-ACC *GEN *NOM
'Jukka claimed (that) I have you'

c. Jukka väitti sinulla olevan uudet koirat \ *uusien koirien.
Jukka-NOM claimed you-ADE be-INF new dogs-ACC/NOM \ *GEN
'Jukka claimed (that) you have new dogs'

In (25a) the source of the nominative/genitive variation would be the reverse of what was taking place in (23) above: the genitive version of the embedded accusative *uuden auton* 'new car-GEN' would arise based on the agreeing matrix verb, while the nominative version *uusi auto* must be based on the embedded clause. In any case, the variation is only possible at all with singular full NPs, providing support for the accusative analysis of the postverbal NP in the possessive construction.

There is finally a fourth test for objecthood (although not for accusative status), namely whether partitive appears under negation as it does with regular objects. For the possessive construction, partitive typically emerges under negation, as shown in (26):

(26) a. Minulla on kirja.
I-ADE is-3sg book-ACC/NOM
'I have a book'

b. Minulla ei ole kirjaa /*kirja.
I-ADE not-3sg be book-PAR / *ACC/NOM
'I do not have a book'

Thus, the possessive construction passes two of the three accusative tests (the agreement test was not applicable), as well as one further test for objecthood. We conclude that the possessed NP in the Finnish possessive construction is a true accusative object, with accusative being assigned in the context of a semantic feature related to specificity (the exact nature of which remains to be determined). In the absence of this feature (i.e. in the plural, with mass nouns, under negation) the partitive emerges, as is expected in the complement position under the present approach.

3.2 The Existential Construction and the Status of Accusative

Let us now turn to the existential construction, attempting to apply all of the accusative/object tests described in the previous section. Unlike with the possessive construction, it is difficult to determine whether accusative is involved in the existential construction. First, the pronoun test (imagine a hide-and-seek situation):

(27) Täällä oven takana on varmasti ?*sinä / *sinut / *sinun.
Here door-GENbehind is-3sg surely you- ?*NOM /
*ACC / *GEN
'There is certainly you here behind the door'

The results of the pronoun test are inconclusive, since neither the accusative nor the nominative appears to be possible, as shown in (27). This situation presumably arises from some version of the Definiteness Effect that holds for the existential construction in the Indo-European languages, according to which a definite NP (such as a personal pronoun) cannot occur in the postverbal position in the existential construction.

As with the possessive construction, the agreement test is inapplicable to the existential construction, since the construction only has a version with a non-agreeing 3rd person singular verb.

However, the third accusative test, the embedding test, suggests that accusative is involved even in the existential construction. Consider (28) (example (28a) is from Vilkuna 1996:297, where the issue is noted but not resolved); the intended context in (28b) is one of fish farming, where a new set of fish has been released in the lake:

(28) a. Luulisin järvessä olevan vielä ainakin yksi ahven \ yhden ahvenen.
I-believe in-lake be-INF yet at-least one fish-ACC/NOM \ ACC/GEN
'I believe (that) there is yet at least one fish in the lake'

b. Luulisin järvessä olevan uudet ahvenet \ *uusien ahvenien.
I-believe in-lake be-INF new fish(pl.)-ACC/NOM \ *GEN
'I believe (that) there is (a set of) new fish in the lake'

In (28a), the basis of the genitive form of the embedded accusative *yhden ahvenen* would be the agreeing verb in the matrix clause, while the nominative option would arise based on the embedded clause. Testing the variation with a postverbal pronoun is not possible, given the impossibility of a pronoun in the relevant position (cf. (27) above) in this construction. However, (28b) shows that the variation does not occur in the plural, and thus the existential construction passes this test for the accusative.[14]

---

[14] The embedding test for the accusative also seems to hold for the variant of the existential construction discussed fn.8:

(i) Uskon kaapista hävinneen uusin tarjoiluastia /uusimman tarjoiluastian.
I-believe cupboard-ELA disappear-INF newest serving.dish-NOM/ACC /newest serving dish-GEN/ACC
'I believe the newest serving dish to have disappeared from the cupboard'

Finally, we observe that the existential construction passes the fourth test for objecthood, with partitive typically emerging under negation:

(29) a. Kirjastossa on uusi patsas.
Library-INE is-3sg new statue-ACC/NOM
'There is a new statue in the library'

b. Kirjastossa ei ole uutta patsasta \ ?*uusi patsas
Library-INE not-3sg be new statue-PAR \ ?*NOM/ACC
'There isn't a new statue at the library'

Thus, the existential construction passes one of the three accusative tests; one of the tests was inapplicable, and another one (the pronoun test) gave inconclusive results. The existential construction also passes the fourth test of objecthood. We conclude that the postverbal NP in the existential construction is an accusative NP occurring in the object position in Finnish. As with the possessive construction, the accusative is assigned in the context of a feature relating to specificity, while in the absence of such feature partitive emerges.

3.3 The Predicative Construction and the Status of Accusative

We have so far argued that accusative objects occur in Finnish not only in the regular thematic object construction, but also in the possessive construction and in the existential construction. The accusative and partitive assignment mechanisms for the three constructions are identical, except for the exact nature of the feature involved in accusative assignment ([+bounded] with regular objects, a feature related to specificity in the possessive and existential constructions).[15] Let us now turn to the fourth construction, the predicative construction, where the situation is somewhat more complicated.

(ii) Uskon kaapista hävinneen uusimmat tarjoiluastiat /*uusimpien
(iii) tarjoiluastioiden
I-believe cupboard-ELA disappear-INF newest serving.
dishes-NOM/ACC /*GEN/ACC
'I believe the newest serving dishes to have disappeared from the cupboard'

[15] As pointed out by a reviewer, the three constructions may vary not only in the specific feature that is responsible for accusative assignment (say, [+bounded] or [+specific]), but may also vary in placement of the feature. Thus, [+bounded] is naturally associated with the verb, while [+specific] would more naturally be associated with the postverbal NP. One way to maintain a unified approach to the three constructions would be to assume that both features are associated with the VP. This would seem straightforward with the regular verb+object construction, but for the possessive and existential constructions it might be more difficult to assume that the copula verb is somehow involved in sharing the feature [+specific].

First the pronoun test: this test is only possible with the predicative NP, since there is no personal pronoun version of an adjective. The examples in (30) are somewhat clumsy due to the difficulty of having a personal pronoun act as the head of a relative clause; thus the question marks:

(30) a. ?Nämä pojat ovat heitä, jotka voittivat kilpailun.
These boys-NOM are they-PAR who-PL won competition
'These boys are the ones (lit. they) who won the competition'
(or, these boys belong to the ones who won the competition)

b. ?Nämä pojat ovat he, jotka voittivat kilpailun.
These boys-NOM are they-NOM who-PL won competition
'These boys are the ones (lit. they) who won the competition'

c. *Nämä pojat ovat heidät, jotka voittivat kilpailun.
These boys-NOM are they-ACC who-PL won competition

Contrary to the previous constructions, the nominative pronoun is preferred over the accusative, as shown in (30b-c). Thus, according to the pronoun test, the postverbal element in the predicative construction appears to be a true nominative; we assume that this would also extend to the predicative AP version of this construction.

The results of the personal pronoun test are supported by the agreement test, as shown in (31):

(31) a. Minä olen terve.
I am healthy-NOM
'I am healthy'

b. Sinä olet Suomen kansalainen.
You are-2SG Finland-GEN citizen-NOM
'You are a citizen of Finland'

Despite the presence of subject-verb agreement in the examples in (31), the postverbal element remains in the nominative, rather than emerging in the genitive as expected if the NP were a true accusative.

The embedding test, however, reveals a different result (example (32a) from Comrie 1997:47), and (32b) from Löbel 1999, her example (32b)):

(32) a. Tiedän kirjan olevan valkoisen \ valkoinen.
I-know book-GEN be-INF white-ACC/GEN \ ACC/NOM
'I know (that) the book is white'

b. Tiedän pallon olevan ?lelun \ lelu.
I-know ball-GEN be-INF toy-ACC/GEN \ ACC/NOM
'I know (that) a ball is a toy.'

Thus, the nominative/genitive variation is attested in both the AP and the NP versions of the predicative construction, as shown in (32). Although it is difficult to test for what happens with pronouns, the plural versions of these examples suggest that the variation is limited to singular full NPs:

(33) a. Tiedän kirjojen olevan ?*valkoisten \ valkoiset.
I-know books-GEN be-INF white(pl)-?*GEN \ ACC/NOM
'I know (that) the books are white'

b. Tiedän pallojen olevan *Maijan uusien lelujen \ Maijan uudet lelut
I-know balls-GEN be-INF Maija-GEN new toys-*GEN \ ACC/NOM
'I know (that) balls are Maija's new toys'

The results of the three accusative tests for the predicative construction are therefore contradictory: according to the first two tests the postverbal element is in the nominative, while according to the embedding test this element occurs in the accusative. Finally, the fourth (object) test gives a result different from the other constructions discussed so far, since partitive is not possible under negation:

(34) a. Kirja ei ole valkoinen \ *valkoista.
Book-NOM not-3sg be white-NOM/ACC \ *PAR
'The book is not white'

b. Pallo ei ole lelu \ *lelua.
Ball-NOM not-3sg be toy-NOM/ACC \ *PAR
'A ball is not a toy'

How to reconcile the contradictory results of the accusative tests? Since all but one of the tests support a nominative analysis of the postverbal NP or AP, I will assume that the postverbal element is normally assigned nominative case. Following in the spirit of Löbel's (1999) proposal, I assume that the nominative is assigned under agreement (via coindexation) with the nominative subject.

However, to explain the result of the embedding test, I propose that the nominative NP is located in the complement position of the copula verb, even in the predicative construction. When agreement with nominative is not possible for various reasons, object case marking takes over. Thus, in the embedded construction in (33), there is no embedded nominative subject to agree with, and the postverbal NP or AP emerges in the accusative case, undergoing nominative/genitive variation with singular full NPs (but not plural NPs).[16,17]

Instances of partitive case in the predicative construction, such as examples (13-14) and (18) above with plural and mass nouns would also involve case assignment to the object position; in the absence of the feature responsible for accusative assignment, and in the absence of agreement with the nominative subject, structurally assigned partitive emerges in the complement position, as always.

It has been argued in this section that the postverbal element in the four main constructions under consideration occupies the object position. In the regular object construction, accusative is assigned in the context of the feature [+bounded], while in the possessive and existential constructions accusative is assigned under a different feature (related to specificity). In the predicative construction, nominative typically emerges due to agreement with the nominative subject; when agreement fails, accusative is assigned (presumably in the context of a feature related to specificity). In all four constructions, partitive emerges whenever accusative is not assigned by a special semantic feature.

Now that we have established that accusative is assigned in all four constructions (even sometimes in the predicative construction), we are in a position to consider the mechanisms underlying accusative assignment in Finnish. If it can be assumed that both [+bounded] and [+specific] are features at the VP-level (see fn. 15), then we might say that the head V of such a VP carries either feature. Accusative distribution in Finnish would then be captured by the following rule:

---

[16] Note that the nominative/genitive variation in (33) could not be explained as a matter of simple agreement with the genitive embedded subject, since this is not possible in the plural; cf. example (33b).

[17] The two variants of the predicative construction discussed earlier behave as follows: Neither the pronoun test nor the agreement test are useful. Consider the embedding test:

(i) Uskon matosta tulleen puhdas/puhtaan.
I-believe rug-ELA come-INF clean-NOM/ACC / GEN/ACC
'I believe (that) the rug became clean'

(ii) Uskon matoista tulleen puhtaat/*puhtaiden
I-believe rugs-ELA come-INF clean-PL-NOM/ACC /*PL-GEN
'I believe (that) the rugs became clean'

As with the regular predicative construction, this construction passes the embedded accusative test. I will therefore assume that this construction also involves the postverbal AP in the complement position.

(35) If a verb carries the feature [+bounded] or the feature [+specific], then the verb assigns accusative to the NP (or AP) in the complement position of the verb.

The accusative rule in (35) would encompass all instances of accusative in Finnish.

4 Adverbials and Postverbal Genitive vs. Accusative

In this section we turn to a yet further construction that has a postverbal element which potentially carries object case marking, namely the adverbial construction exemplified in (36):

(36) a. Luin kirjaa vuoden.
I-read book-PAR year-GEN/ACC
'I read (the) book for a year'

b. Luin sitä kirjaa vuosia.
I-read that book-PAR year-PL-PAR
'I read that book for years'

The adverbial of duration in (36a) appears with the genitive suffix *–n*, which may be an instance of the accusative, and it has a partitive version as shown in (36b). This pattern also occurs with some other adverbials such as *Juoksin kilometrin* 'I ran a kilometer', or *Rekka painaa tonnin* 'The truck weighs a ton'.

There are four versions of the adverbial construction to consider: (i) adverbial following an intransitive verb, (ii) adverbial following an oblique argument of the verb, (iii) adverbial following a partitive object, and (iv) adverbial following an accusative object. As we will see, the first three versions all pass the accusative tests, while something different happens with the fourth version.

The pronoun test cannot be applied with any of the adverbials, due to the fact that there are no personal pronoun variants of adverbials of duration. The agreement test shows that the adverbial is a true accusative with the first three versions of the construction:

(37) a. Kävelin koko illan \ *koko ilta.
I-walked whole evening-ACC/GEN \ *ACC/NOM
'I walked the whole evening'

b. Siellä käveltiin koko ilta \ *koko illan.
There walk-PASS whole evening-ACC/NOM \ *ACC/GEN
'One walked there the whole evening'

(38) a. Viivyin kaupassa koko illan \ *koko ilta.
I-stayed store-INE whole evening-ACC/GEN \ *ACC/NOM
'I stayed at the store the whole evening'

b. Kaupassa viivyttiin koko ilta \ *koko illan.
Store-INE stay-PASS whole evening-ACC/NOM \ *ACC/GEN
'One stayed at the store for the whole evening'

(39) a. Kirjoitin kirjaa koko illan \ *koko ilta.
I-wrote book-PAR whole evening-ACC/GEN \ *ACC/NOM
'I was writing a/the book for the whole evening'

b. Kirjaa kirjoitettiin koko ilta \ *koko illan.
Book-PAR write-PASS whole evening-ACC/NOM \ *ACC/GEN
'The book was being written for the whole evening'

In the (a) version of each example, there is an agreeing verb, and the adverbial emerges with the genitive suffix. In the (b) examples, the verb is a non-agreeing impersonal passive, and only the version lacking a case suffix of the adverbial is possible, just as with regular accusative objects.

The first three versions of the adverbial constructions also pass the third accusative test, the embedding test:

(40) a. Minun väitettiin kävelleen koko ilta \ koko illan.
I-GEN claim-PASS walk-INF whole evening-ACC/NOM \ ACC/GEN
'I was claimed to have walked the whole evening'

b. Minun väitettiin viipyneen kaupassa koko ilta \ koko illan.
I-GEN claim-PASS stay-INF store-INE whole evening-ACC/NOM\ACC/GEN
'I was claimed to have stayed at the store for the whole evening'

c. Minun väitettiin kirjoittaneen kirjaa koko ilta \ koko illan.
I-GEN claim-PASS write-INF book-PAR whole evening-ACC/NOM\ACC/GEN
'I was claimed to have been writing a book for the whole evening'

Finally, these three constructions pass the fourth (object) test, in that partitive emerges under negation:

(41) a. En kävellyt koko iltaa \ ?*koko illan \ *koko ilta.
Not-1sg walk whole evening-PAR \ ACC/GEN \ ACC/NOM
'I didn't walk for the whole evening'

b. En viipynyt kaupassa koko iltaa \ ?*koko illan \ *koko ilta.
Not-1sg stay store-INE whole evening-PAR \ ACC/GEN \ ACC/NOM
'I didn't stay at the store for the whole evening'

c. En kirjoittanut kirjaa koko iltaa \ ?*koko illan \ *koko ilta.
Not-1sg write book-PAR whole evening-PAR \ ACC/GEN \ ACC/NOM
'I wasn't writing a book for the whole evening'

Thus, consistent with the reports in the traditional literature, as well as Maling (1993), the adverbial of duration has the distribution of a true accusative object. This is straightforward in the version where the verb does not have a postverbal argument, such as in (37a) above, since it might be assumed that the adverbial of duration is the direct object of the verb (with intransitive verbs).

However, the situation is more complicated when the verb has either an oblique argument, as in (38a), where the oblique postverbal argument may occupy the object position. When the verb has a partitive object, as in (39a), it is difficult to assume that the accusative adverbial also occupies the regular object position.

Given that a single object position seems not to suffice, I propose that accusative can be assigned to an adverbial in a second object position, by a verb with the [+bounded] feature. Furthermore, this second object position behaves like an object position in that even the partitive emerges under the usual conditions (see examples above in (41)).

Thus, we have the following situation: with intransitive verbs, an adverbial of duration may occupy the regular object position, and case marking obtains just as with regular objects, as shown above in (37a-b). If the verb has an oblique postverbal argument/adjunct, an adverbial of duration presumably occupies the second object position. If the verb carries the feature [+bounded], accusative is assigned to the adverbial in the second object position, as in (38a-b) above. If the verb carries no such feature, the adverbial emerges in partitive case, as e.g. in (41b).

In the third adverbial construction, where the adverbial follows a partitive object, the adverbial again occupies the second object position. In this case, if the verb carries the [+bounded] feature, accusative will be assigned to the adverbial in the second object position, as in (39a-b). The object in the regular object position remains, as if it were, without any assigned case, and emerges in the usual default case, partitive.[18]

What happens to the adverbial when the verb with [+bounded] feature has already assigned accusative to an accusative object? This is the fourth and the most interesting version of the adverbial construction. Let us now apply each of our accusative tests to the adverbial in such a construction.

As before, the pronoun test cannot be applied with adverbials. Here are the results of the agreement test (from Maling 1993:16a-c):

(42) a. Liisa muisti matkan vuoden.
Liisa-NOM remember-3SG trip-ACC/GEN year-ACC/GEN
'Liisa remembered the trip for a year'

b. Muista matka vuoden!
Remember trip-ACC/NOM year-ACC/GEN
'Remember the trip for a year!'

c. Liisan täytyy muistaa matka vuoden.
Liisa-GEN must remember-INF trip-ACC/NOM year-ACC/GEN
'Liisa must remember the trip for a year'

Thus, contrary to Maling's assumption that the adverbial in (42) is assigned accusative case, this version of the adverbial construction does not straightforwardly pass the accusative test. Regardless of the presence or absence of agreement in these sentences, the adverbial *vuoden* 'year-GEN' shows up with the genitive suffix throughout. This would suggest that the adverbial in (42) occurs in true genitive case, although we shall see that the situation is not quite as straightforward as that.

---

[18] Note that in the construction with both a partitive NP object and an accusative adverbial, there is no feature conflict involving the verb, since only accusative is assigned by a feature; partitive emerges in the absence of aspectual features, and it is not strictly speaking assigned at all (partitive emerges as a structural default case in a head-complement configuration).

Let us now apply the third accusative test, the embedding test, to this construction:

(43) Väitettiin Liisan muistaneen matka\matkan koko vuoden \ koko vuosi.
Claim-PASS GEN remember-INF trip-NOM\GEN whole year GEN \ NOM
'It was claim (that) Liisa remembered the trip for the whole year'

It appears that the nominative/genitive variation occurs under embedding even with an adverbial co-occurring with an accusative object, as in (43). However, given that we saw above in (42) that the adverbial in this construction can occur in the genitive, the genitive option even in (43) might be due to something other than accusative assignment. Strictly speaking, the embedding test is inapplicable to this version of the adverbial construction.

Thus, I conclude tentatively that when a [+bounded] verb assigns accusative to an NP object, the following adverbial somehow ends up with genitive case. However, the negation test suggests that even in this construction the postverbal adverbial occupies the second object position, given that partitive emerges under negation (although it may not have to):

(44) Liisa ei muistanut matkaa koko vuotta \ ?koko vuoden
NOM not-3sg remember trip-PAR whole year-PAR \ ?ACC/GEN
'Liisa didn't remember the trip for a whole year'

How would a postverbal adverb of duration receive genitive case? I wish to tentatively propose that the genitive emerges postverbally under agreement with the specifier position, perhaps using a similar coindexation mechanism as we needed for the nominative agreement of postverbal NPs and APs in the predicative construction.[19]

In sum, I have proposed that adverbials of duration (and other similar adverbials) may occupy either the regular object position, if one is available (as with intransitive verbs), or the second object position (with the other three variants that were discussed here). If the verb carries the [+bounded] feature, accusative can be assigned (once) in one of the two positions. Any object NP or adverbial that does not get assigned accusative case, emerges in partitive case. The only exceptions we have seen to this generalization in the whole paper are (i) nominative case assignment to the postverbal NP/AP

[19] See Vainikka (1989) and (1996) for arguments that genitive is the structural default case of the specifier position in Finnish.

in the predicative construction (agreement under coindexation with the nominative subject), and (ii) genitive case assignment to the adverbial in the second object position when accusative has been assigned to the object NP (possibly, agreement under coindexation with genitive subject).

Thus, the adverbial construction discussed here is similar in case distribution to the four main constructions discussed in the earlier sections. However, due to the differences in case distribution and word order, it was proposed that a second object position is usually involved in the adverbial construction, in which the regular two object cases occur. Furthermore, an additional mechanism was required to account for the occurrence of a previously unnoticed postverbal genitive case.

5 Conclusion

The five constructions discussed in this paper reveal the following case realization possibilities in the postverbal position in Finnish:

(46) a. Nominative is assigned postverbally to the object position under agreement with a nominative subject in the predicative construction.

b. Genitive may be assigned postverbally to the second object position, possibly under agreement with the specifier position in the adverbial construction.

c. Accusative is assigned to the object position (or the second object position) by a verb carrying the feature [+bounded], or a feature relating to specificity, in all five constructions.

d. Partitive emerges as the default case of the object position (and in the second object position) if no other case marking takes place.

The accusative rule in (45c) is a version of the rule given above in (35). The details of the nominative and genitive agreement mechanisms are a subject of further research.

References

Anttila, A. & V. Fong. 2000. The Partitive Constraint in Optimality Theory. *Journal of Semantics* 17:281-314.

Chesterman, A. 1991. *On Definiteness.* Cambridge/Sydney: Cambridge University Press.

Chomsky, N. 1981. *Lectures on Government and Binding.* Dordrecht: Foris.

Chomsky, N. 1993. A minimalist program for linguistic theory. *The View from Building 20: Essays in Linguistics in Honor of Sylvain Bromberger*, ed. K. Hale & S.K. Keyser, 1-52. Cambridge, Mass.: MIT Press.

Comrie, B. 1997. The Typology of Predicate Case Marking. *Essays on Language Function and Language Type,* ed. J. Bybee, J. Haiman & S.A. Thompson, 39-50. Amsterdam/ Philadelphia: Benjamins.

Heinämäki, O. 1984. Aspect in Finnish. *Aspect Bound. A Voyage in the Realm of Germanic, Slavonic and Finno-Ugric Aspectology,* ed. C. DeGroot & H. Tommola, 153-176. Dordrecht: Foris.

Kanerva, J. 1997. Morphological Integrity and Syntax: the Evidence from Finnish Possessive Suffixes. *Language* 63:498-521.

Kiparsky, P. 1998. Partitive Case and Aspect. *The Projection of Arguments. Lexical and Compositional Factors,* ed. M. Butt & W. Geuder, 265-307. Stanford: CSLI Publications.

Kiparsky, P. 2001. Structural Case in Finnish. *Lingua* 111:315-376,

Larjavaara, M. 1988. Kvantitatiivinen spesies. *Virittäjä* 92:469-503.

Leino, P. 1991. *Lauseet ja tilanteet.[Sentences and situations]* Helsinki: Suomalaisen Kirjallisuuden Seura.

Löbel, E. 1999. Lexicon-Theoretic Aspects of Copular Verbs: Case and Number Agreement in Finnish. Wuppertal/Köln University ms.

Maling, J. 1993. Of Nominative and Accusative: the Hierarchical Assignment of Grammatical Cases in Finnish. *Case and Other Functional Categories in Finnish Syntax,* ed. A. Holmberg & U. Nikanne, 49-74. Berlin: Mouton de Gruyter.

Nelson, D. 1998. *Grammatical Case Assignment in Finnish.* New York: Garland.

Reime, H. 1993. Accusative Marking in Finnish. *Case and Other Functional Categories in Finnish Syntax,* ed. A. Holmberg & U. Nikanne, 89-110. Berlin: Mouton de Gruyter.

Siro, P. 1964. *Suomen kielen lauseoppi [Syntax of the Finnish language]* Helsinki: Tietosanakirja OY.

Timberlake, A. 1975. The Nominative Object in Finnish. *Lingua* 35:205-230.

Toivainen, J. 1979. *Lausekielioppi [Sentence Grammar]* (Publications 12.) Oulu: University of Oulu, Department of Finnish and Lappish.

Vainikka, A. 1985. Binding *–nsa*. University of Massachusetts/Amherst ms.

Vainikka, A. 1988. The Finnish Partitive: a Reply to Belletti. University of Massachusetts/Amherst ms.

Vainikka, A. 1989. *Deriving Syntactic Representations in Finnish.* University of Massachusetts/Amherst Ph.D. dissertation. (Available from GLSA, University of Massachusetts, Amherst.)

Vainikka, A. 1992. Kieliopillisten sijojen syntaktinen kuvaus [The syntactic description of grammatical cases]. *Virittäjä* 96:295-322.

Vainikka, A. 1993. The Three Structural Cases in Finnish. *Case and Other Functional Categories in Finnish Syntax,* ed. A. Holmberg & U. Nikanne, 129-162. Berlin: Mouton de Gruyter.

Vainikka, A. & J. Maling. 1996. Is Partitive Case Inherent or Structural? *Partitives. Studies on the Syntax and Semantics of Partitive and Related Constructions,* ed. J. Hoeksema, 179-208. Berlin/New York: Mouton de Gruyter.

Vilkuna, M. 1996. *Suomen lauseopin perusteet [The foundations of Finnish syntax].* Helsinki:Edita.

Part III

Syntax (Other Topics)

8

Encoding (Non)Locality in Anaphoric Relations

ELSI KAISER

1 Introduction*

In this paper I present an analysis of the semantics of the Finnish possessive suffixes. Possession in Finnish is shown by means of a possessive suffix (Px) which, in certain contexts, co-occurs with an overt possessive/genitive pronoun (Hakulinen and Karlsson 1988, Toivonen 2000, inter alia). I argue that the presence vs. absence of the possessive pronoun is governed by a locality constraint at work in two realms of the grammar, namely in (pragmatic) discourse anaphora resolution and in (semantic) variable binding. In the latter case, I claim that the absence vs. presence of the third person possessive pronoun visibly encodes the difference between binding and covaluation (Reinhart 1997, Heim 1993). I also extend this analysis to 'regular' pronouns in Finnish, and show that they are governed by the same locality constraints.

The paper is structured as follows. Section 2 is an overview of Reinhart and Heim's work on pronoun interpretation, and also contains a brief survey

* I would like to thank Maribel Romero for invaluable comments and insights on this paper. Thanks also go to Irene Heim, Satu Manninen, Tanya Reinhart, Jeff Lidz and the audiences at the 18th Scandinavian Conference of Linguistics and the 75th LSA Annual Meeting, as well as an anonymous CSLI reviewer, for useful comments and discussion. I would also like to thank my many informants for their help. All errors are, of course, my own.

Generative Approaches to Finnic and Saami Linguistics.
Diane Nelson and Satu Manninen (eds.).

of some of the work done in pronoun resolution from a pragmatic perspective. In Section 3, I present the basics of the Finnish possessive construction and review the existing literature. My analysis and the data that motivate it are presented in Section 4. Section 5 discusses two other phenomena – ellipsis and pronoun resolution – that provide further evidence that semantic and pragmatic locality constraints guide the interpretation of null and overt forms. Section 6 is the conclusion.

2 Pronoun Interpretation

In this section, I discuss the semantics of pronoun interpretation, based on work by Reinhart (1983, 1997) and Heim (1993), and then take a closer look at the pragmatic aspects of pronoun resolution. As this section shows, locality plays an important role in semantic and pragmatic pronoun interpretation.

2.1 Binding vs. Coreference: Locality in anaphor binding in semantics

A pronoun, such as 'she' in (1b) below, can receive an interpretation in two different ways: by binding or by coreference (Reinhart 1982, 1997, Heim 1993). Before defining these two terms in more detail, we should note that sentence (1b) is ambiguous: it can mean that Lili thinks that Lucie has the flu, or that Lili thinks Lili herself has the flu.

(1a) Lucie didn't show up today.
(1b) Lili thinks **she's** got the flu.

According to Reinhart and Heim's approach, these two interpretations result from the two ways in which the pronoun 'she' can be interpreted. When the pronoun is resolved by *binding*, it is a variable that is bound by the λ-operator, as illustrated in (2a).

(2a) Binding: Lili (λx (x thinks **x** has got the flu))
(2b) Coreference: Lili (λx (x thinks **z** has got the flu) & <u>z</u> = <u>Lucie</u>)
(2c) Coreference: Lili (λx (x thinks **z** has got the flu) & <u>z</u> = <u>Lili</u>)

Under the binding construal, 'she' refers to Lili and the sentence is interpreted as meaning 'Lili thinks that she herself has the flu'. However, the pronoun can also receive its interpretation via *coreference,* in which case it is 'a free variable [that is] assigned a value from the discourse storage' (Reinhart 1997:1). This is illustrated in (2b,c). Under this interpretation, the free variable can be associated with Lucie (2b) or with Lili (2c). As a result, the coreference construal generates two possible interpretations for the sentence in (1b): Lili thinks Lili herself has the flu, or Lili thinks that Lucie has the flu.[1]

In order to understand the nature of binding and coreference more fully, and to attain a more fine-grained analysis, we need to consider a more complex configuration with an embedded predicate such as the one given below. This sentence, like the preceding examples, is ambiguous.

(3) Liisa thinks that only she respects her husband.
(adapted from Reinhart 1997:5)

On the one hand, the sentence can mean that Liisa thinks she is the only woman who respects her husband. In other words, Liisa thinks that other wives do not respect their husbands, and thus Liisa thinks she is the only 'good wife.'

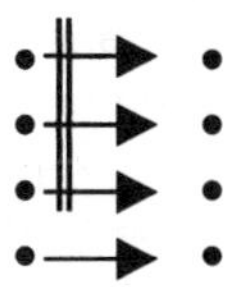

Diagram 1. 'Good wife' interpretation [Binding]

On the other hand, the sentence can also mean that Liisa thinks that she is the only one who respects *her* husband; she thinks that no other wives respect Liisa's husband. In other words, she has an 'unpopular husband'.

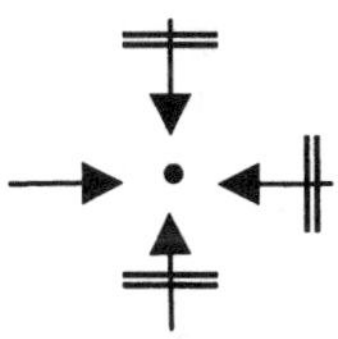

Diagram 2. 'Unpopular husband' interpretation [Coreference]

We will now consider these two interpretations in more detail to understand how they are generated. We can use the two procedures discussed above, binding and coreference, to generate the two different readings: binding for

[1] Note that the ambiguous nature of this sentence can be derived simply by the coreference construal alone. However, it would be a mistake to conclude that binding is unnecessary. Reinhart (1983) discusses cases where the effects of Binding Theory can be waived, and shows how, in order to account for these, we need both binding and coreference. See Reinhart (1983), Heim (1993) and Fox (1998) for further discussion.

the ‘good wife’ construal, and coreference for the ‘unpopular husband’ construal. The semantic λ-expressions are given below in (4a,b).

(4) Liisa thinks that only she respects her husband.
(adapted from Reinhart 1997:5)

(4a) Liisa (λx (x thinks that (only x (λy (y respects **y’s** husband)))))

(4b) Liisa (λx (x thinks that (only x (λy (y respects **her** husband)))))
& her = Liisa

First, let us consider the binding construal, as illustrated in (4a). Here, the possessive pronoun is locally *bound* by a λ-operator. The lower λ-predicate (λy (y respects y’s husband) denotes the set of individuals who respect their own husbands (Reinhart 1997:3). The sentence thus means that Liisa thinks that she is the only woman who respects her husband and that other wives do not respect their husbands (“good wife” interpretation).

Now, let us turn to the coreference interpretation, illustrated in (4b). Here, the possessive pronoun is coreferential with Liisa, an entity already in discourse storage. Thus, the lower λ-predicate in (4b) denotes the set of individuals who respect Liisa’s husband (see Reinhart 1997:3). The entire expression thus means that Liisa thinks that she is the only one who respects *her* (Liisa’s) husband (‘unpopular husband’ interpretation).

2.1.1 Coreference is not enough

In the preceding discussion, we saw evidence indicating that a pronoun can receive its interpretation in two ways: by binding or by coreference. However, on the basis of data from quantified noun phrases (QuNPs), Heim (1993) argues that these two approaches alone are not sufficient. The crucial example in favor of her argument is given in (5). Here we have simply replaced ‘Liisa’ in example (4) with the QuNP ‘Every wife’, and the sentence is still ambiguous.

(5) Every wife thinks that only she respects her husband.
(Reinhart 1997:4)

Example (5) has both the ‘good wife’ interpretation and the ‘unpopular husband’ interpretation. It can mean that every wife thinks that she is the only one who respects her husband, i.e., she thinks that other wives do not respect their husbands. As we saw above, this interpretation is generated when the possessive pronoun is interpreted by binding. In addition, (5) can also mean that every wife thinks that she is the only one who respects *her* husband, i.e. she thinks that other wives do not respect her husband. In Section 2.1, we attributed this ‘unpopular husband’ interpretation to coreference. However, the coreference construal cannot be the explanation for the ambiguity of (5), because 'every wife [and any other QuNP, *author's note*] does not have a discourse value that the pronoun can pick up' (Reinhart 1997:5). In other words, QuNPs do not permit the coreference construal.

We are thus faced with the question: What mechanism generates the second reading of (5), given that coreference is not possible with QuNPs? According to Heim (1993), the answer is covaluation (also known as 'co-binding') which, in addition to Reinhart's coreference, includes non-local binding. Example (6) below illustrates the difference between *local* binding (what we have simply been calling 'binding' in the preceding discussion), and *non-local* binding (covaluation). In (6a), the possessive pronoun y is bound by the closest λ-operator, and, as in (4a), the lower λ-predicate denotes the set of individuals who respect their own husbands (Reinhart 1997:3). As above, this results in the 'good wife' interpretation (i.e. Every wife thinks that she is the only wife who respects her husband, and thinks that other wives do not respect their husbands).

However, in the representation in (6b), the possessive pronoun x is not bound by the closest λ-operator (since it is λy). Instead, it is bound by λx, which is further away. Here, the lower λ-predicate denotes the set of people who respect x's husband (Reinhart 1997:3). The configuration shown in (6b) thus generates the 'unpopular husband' interpretation, i.e. the construal that every wife thinks that she is the only one who respects *her* husband, and that other wives do not respect her husband.

(6a)
Every wife (λx (x thinks that (only x (λy (y respects y's husband)))))
→ binding

(6b)
Every wife (λx (x thinks that (only x (λy (y respects x's husband)))))
→ covaluation

Thus, when QuNPs are involved, the only difference between binding and covaluation is the degree of locality between the binder and the bound variable. In binding, the variable is bound by the most local λ-operator, whereas in covaluation (non-local binding), the λ-operator that is capable of binding the variable is not the closest one.

In sum, in this section we saw evidence for three subtypes of anaphoric relations: (local) binding, coreference and covaluation (non-local binding). Under Reinhart's approach, coreference and covaluation are grouped together, and (local) binding is treated as another type of relation. However, as we saw in our discussion above (ex. (6)), (local) binding and covaluation are in fact similar, differing only in the degree of locality involved (see Fox 1998). This raises the question: if binding can be split into two types (local and non-local), what about (pragmatic) coreference? Does it have local and non-local subtypes as well? This is the question we will tackle in the next section, and I will suggest that the answer is yes.

2.2 A closer look at 'coreference'

In this section, we look in more detail at coreference and the constraints which guide it. I present evidence indicating that, like binding, coreference can be divided into two subtypes: (i) coreference with the local topic and (ii) coreference with something that is not the local topic.

2.2.1 Pragmatics of pronouns

To understand the process of anaphor interpretation by means of coreference, we need to take a look at the referential properties of pronouns. It has often been noted that the weakest anaphoric elements that exist in a given language (e.g. pronouns in English, null *pro* in prodrop language such as Spanish) tend to refer to the most topical/salient entities at that point in the discourse, i.e. to the entities that are at the center of attention (see e.g. Samek-Lodovici 1996:29, Walker, Joshi & Prince 1998, Centering Theory on pronouns, *inter alia*). Before turning to some examples that illustrate this, it is important to consider the notion 'topic' in more detail. In the present discussion, I follow Strawson (1964), who defines the topic of an utterance as 'what is of current interest or concern' (Strawson 1964:104), and Reinhart, who characterizes the topic of a sentence as 'the expression whose referent the sentence is about' (Reinhart 1982:5). I will thus be using the term 'topic' to refer to the entity that is at the center of attention at that point in the discourse (see Grosz, Joshi & Weinstein 1995). A large body of research has shown the subject of a sentence tends to be the most salient (most 'topical') entity in the sentence (see e.g. Brennan, Friedman & Pollard 1987, Crawley & Stevenson 1990, Grosz, Joshi & Weinstein 1995, and many others).

Now, let us return to the connection between topics and weak anaphoric elements, and consider example (7) below. 'John' is the subject of the first sentence, and thus more topical than the object, 'Bill'. The second sentence contains the pronoun 'he'. Given the claim that a weak anaphor prefers to have the most salient/topical entity as its antecedent, we would predict that 'he' refers to 'John.' And, intuitively, this is indeed the case, as noted by Hudson-D'Zmura and Tanenhaus: '[I]ntuition suggests a clear preference for *John* to be the antencedent of *he* rather than *Bill*' (Hudson-D'Zmura and Tanenhaus 1998:200). This prediction is also supported psycholinguistic studies of language processing (e.g. Hudson-D'Zmura & Tanenhaus 1998).

(7) John saw Bill walking down the street.
He$_{\text{John}}$ waved hello to him.
(Hudson-D'Zmura and Tanenhaus 1998:200).

Additional evidence for the psycholinguistic reality of the correlation between pronouns and subjects/topics comes from eye-tracking work by Arnold, Eisenband, Brown-Schmit & Trueswell (2000). By studying the eye-movements of people who were looking at a picture and listening to a short story (in English) that refers to the characters in the picture, they found that, in contexts where gender doesn't disambiguate the referent of the pronoun, people tended to interpret a pronoun as referring to the subject of the preceding sentence.

This same pattern can be shown to exist in Spanish, a prodrop language where the weakest anaphoric element is null *pro*. On the basis of the preceding discussion, we would predict that, like English pronouns, the Spanish *pro* (denoted with ø below) should display a tendency to have the most topical/salient entity as its antecedent. This is indeed the case, as illustrated by the example below (Maribel Romero, p.c.).

(8a) Juan vió a Guille en la calle.
Juan.n see-past.3s Guille.a in the street.
'Juan saw Guille in the street.'

(8b) # En cambio, **ø** no lo vió. [ø = Juan]
Instead **ø** neg he.a see-past.3s
'Instead, **he$_{\text{Juan}}$** didn't see him.'

(8c) En cambio, **él** no lo vió. [él = Guille]
Instead **he.n** neg he.a see-past.3s
'Instead, **he$_{\text{Guille}}$** didn't see him.'

The continuation shown in (8b) 'Instead, ø didn't see him' is pragmatically infelicitous in the context of Juan having seen Guille, because the null *pro* can only refer to the subject of the preceding sentence, Juan. It cannot be interpreted as referring to the object, Guille. This is exactly what we would expect if the null *pro*, the weakest anaphoric element in Spanish, is coreferential with the current topic. When the overt pronoun is used, as in (8c) 'Instead, he$_{\text{overt}}$ didn't see him', it is interpreted as referring to the object of the previous sentence, namely Guille (i.e. not the local topic), and the continuation is felicitous. Data from Turkish (Turan 1998) and Greek (Dimitriadis 1996), two other prodrop languages, pattern the same way.

These examples from English and Spanish illustrate that, from a pragmatic perspective, pronouns (or null pronouns, if the language has them) prefer to refer to the current topic, i.e. the most salient entity under discussion at each relevant point in the discourse. Finnish differs from languages of the Spanish type in that Finnish permits only partial prodrop (see Vainikka & Levy 1999). Finnish first and second person singular pronouns can be dropped freely (ex. (9a)), but third person prodrop only occurs in a limited number of contexts. It is usually not possible to have a null third person subject (so Finnish is unlike Spanish in this respect), but it is possible for a third person subject to be null if it is coreferential with a higher subject in the same sentence, as illustrated below (see Vilkuna 1996:131).

(9a) *Null first and second person pronouns (brackets indicate optionality)*
(Me) kävimme eilen ostoksilla, mutta (sinä) et ostanut mitään.
(We.n) go-past.1p yesterday shopping, but (you.n) neg.2s buy-pp.2s anything.p.
'We went shopping yesterday, but you didn't buy anything.'

(9b) **Null matrix third person subject*
Pekka tuli kotiin. *ø meni heti nukkumaan.
Pekka come-past.3s home.ill. ø go-past.3s right-away sleep-inf.
'Pekka came home. He went to sleep right away.'

(9c) *Null embedded third person subject*
Pekka tulee kun ø ehtii. (adapted from Vilkuna 1996:131)
Pekka come-pre.3s when ø have-time-pres.3s.
'Pekka will come when he has time.'

Thus, in some sense, the requirements for third-person prodrop in Finnish are more demanding than in languages such as Spanish. In Finnish, the topic of the *current* sentence (here, the matrix subject) must refer to the same entity as the null pronoun, whereas in Spanish, a subject can be null as long as it refers to the current *discourse* topic. One could interpret the Finnish third person prodrop facts as a result of binding or coreference. Perhaps the most reasonable assumption is that null pronouns with referential antecedents can be interpreted by binding, or by coreference with the topic of the current sentence (cf. ex (2)), whereas null pronouns with QuNP antecedents must be interpreted by binding. As we will see, this type of assumption enables us to explain the asymmetries that will be discussed in Sections 4 and 5 in a straightforward manner.

As we will see, the asymmetry between first/second person pronouns and third person pronouns also exists in the possessive construction, as does the requirement that a null third person pronoun be coreferential with (or bound by) the topic (subject) of the *current* sentence.

3 Finnish possessives

In this section I present the basic semantic and morphological features of the Finnish possessive construction and briefly review some of the existing literature on the topic. I will present my analysis in Section 4.

3.1 Basic description of the Finnish possessive construction

In Finnish, possession is represented by a system of possessive pronouns and possessive suffixes (Px's). In this paper we will focus on the third person possessive suffix, which surfaces as [-nsA] or [-An] (the capital letter indicates that the vowel undergoes vowel harmony and can surface as [a] or [ä]). In third person possessive constructions with pronominal possessors (e.g. 'his book'), the possessive suffix is present on the possessed noun. However, the possessive pronoun itself is null in certain contexts: According to the judgments reported in the literature, when an overt possessive pronoun is *not* present, the referent of the subject of the sentence is the possessor (Vilkuna 1996:228-230, Nelson 1998:13), as illustrated in (10a). When an overt possessive pronoun is present, the subject cannot be interpreted as the possessor (10b) (Nelson 1998:13).[2] (First and second person possessive pronouns pattern differently. Just like first and second person pronouns, they can freely occur as null elements. See Nelson (1998) for details.)

---

[2] However, in contrast to these 'standard judgments', some of my Finnish informants permit the subject to be the possessor even when the possessive pronoun is present (10b). Other sources also indicate that the interpretation of possessive constructions with an overt possessive pronoun may not be altogether straightforward. For example, in a corpus study of written Finnish, Niendorf and Peterson (1999) found examples of overt third person possessive pronouns co-occurring with the possessive suffix in contexts where the subject is the possessor. In addition, Ikola (1986:74-75) notes that overt possessive pronouns are sometimes present (in naturally-occurring language) in sentences where the subject is the possessor. In other words, violations of the standard generalization (i.e., that an overt possessive pronoun cannot be used when the subject is the possessor) are not unheard of. I will say more about this below.

As is pointed out by an anonymous reviewer, speakers' judgments about sentences such as (10b) are likely to be influenced by their knowledge of and attitudes towards the norms of Standard Finnish, as well as their dialect background (see Paunonen (1995) for more information on the sociolinguistics of the Finnish possessive suffixes).

(10a) Liisa$_j$ luki ø kirja[nsa]$_j$.
Liisa.n read-past.3s ø book-a.Px3
Liisa$_j$ read her$_j$ book.

(10b) Liisa$_j$ luki hänen$_k$ kirja[nsa]$_k$.
Liisa.n read-past.3s s/he-g book-a.Px3
Liisa$_j$ read her$_{k/*j}$ book.

When an overt possessive pronoun is absent, the *subject* is interpreted as the possessor, even when the sentence contains another semantically possible possessor, such as a direct or indirect object (see Trosterud 1993 for discussion and some exceptions). Moreover, the possessive pronoun cannot be null if it is part of the matrix subject, as illustrated below.

(10c) *(Hänen) kirjansa putosi lattialle.
s/he-g book-a.Px3 fall-past.3s floor-all
'His/her book fell to the floor.'

3.2 Previous analyses of the possessive construction

A number of analyses have been proposed concerning the Finnish possessive suffix and its relation to the possessive pronoun, and three are briefly outlined in this section. One avenue of research analyses the possessive suffix as an anaphor (e.g. Vainikka (1989), Nelson (1998)). According to this approach, third person possessive suffixes are anaphors which must be bound by the subject of the sentence or by a third person possessive pronoun (e.g. Nelson 1998:187-188; see Trosterud 1993 for a slightly different account of the role of the third person possessive pronoun). A different treatment of possessives is proposed by van Steenbergen (1991), who claims that possessive constructions without an overt possessive pronoun contain an empty element (*pro)* instead. According to van Steenbergen's analysis, *pro* is an empty anaphor which can only be bound by the subject and which occurs whenever 'it corefers with a c-commanding NP' (van Steenbergen 1991:234). She argues that the possessive suffix marks nominal inflection (van Steenbergen 1991:232).

A third approach is presented by Toivonen (2000) within Lexical Functional Grammar (LFG). She argues that the third person possessive suffix [-nsA] is 'a single phonological form [that] corresponds to two distinct sets of lexical features' (Toivonen 2000:34). She argues that when the third person possessive suffix occurs without an overt possessive pronoun in a context where the subject is the possessor, then the [-nsA] suffix is a subject-bound reflexive pronoun. According to her analysis, when the suffix occurs in the presence of an overt possessive pronoun and with a subject that is disjoint in reference, the possessive suffix is an agreement marker (Toivonen 2000:30).

The analysis I present in the present paper is, roughly speaking, compatible with most of van Steenbergen's analysis. However, my analysis represents a finer-grained account of the anaphoric nature of possessives, and is motivated by previously unnoticed data. As we will see, it seems that some of the new empirical data cannot be fully captured under existing accounts.

4 Locality and Non-Locality in Finnish Possessives

Having reviewed Reinhart and Heim's work, as well the characteristics of the Finnish possessive construction, let us now turn to the analysis I am arguing in favor of. In this section, I present data illustrating an asymmetry in the behavior of quantified NPs and referential NPs in possessive constructions with and without overt possessive pronouns. In light of the data, I argue that the distribution (presence vs. absence) of the possessive pronoun is subject to a locality constraint that operates in two domains: in the domain of (pragmatic) discourse anaphora resolution, and the domain of (semantic) variable binding.

4.1 Quantified NPs

In sentences with a QuNP subject, the distinction between binding and covaluation correlates with the absence/presence of the third person possessive pronoun. When the possessive pronoun is absent, only the binding interpretation is available (as shown in (11a)), but when the possessive pronoun is present, only the covaluation construal is possible (ex. (11b)).

(11a) *QuNP & no overt possessive pronoun*

Jokainen vaimo uskoo, että vain hän kunnioittaa ø miestään.
Every.n wife.n think-pres.3s that only s/he.n respect-pres.3s ø husband-p.Px3

'Every wife thinks that only she respects her husband.'

→ *"Unpopular husband" interpretation [Covaluation] = no*

→ *"Good wife" interpretation [Binding] = ok*

(11b) *QuNP & overt possessive pronoun*
Jokainen vaimo uskoo, että vain hän kunnioittaa **hänen** miestään.
Every.n wife.n think-pres.3s that only s/he.n respect-pres.3s s/he-g husband-p.Px3
'Every wife thinks that only she respects her husband.'
→ *"Unpopular husband" interpretation [Covaluation] = ok*
→ *"Good wife" interpretation [Binding] = no*

Example (11a), with no overt possessive pronoun, only permits the binding interpretation. It can only mean that every wife thinks that other wives do not respect their husbands. Example (11b), with a possessive pronoun, only has the covalued interpretation. It means that every wife thinks that she is the only one who respects *her* husband.

On the basis of these data, I argue that Finnish visibly encodes the distinction between variable binding and variable covaluation. When no overt possessive pronoun is used, the variable is interpreted by binding. When the overt possessive pronoun *hänen* is used, the variable is interpreted by covaluation (non-local binding).

It might seem, at first glance, that sentences such as (11b) should not be grammatical, since in (11b), an overt possessive pronoun is apparently used when the subject is the possessor. However, my informants found this sentence to be grammatical. This is actually not surprising if we take a closer look at the subject of the embedded clause, 'only she.' Semantically, 'only X' can be regarded as meaning 'no one except X' (see e.g. Rooth 1985). Thus, in a sentence such as (11b), the referent of 'only she' is not the same as the possessor. This is also illustrated by the indexing in the semantic structures below (repeated, with added indexation, from (6)). In the covaluation structure in (6b), the referent of the possessive pronoun – x_2 – is not the same as the subject of that sentence –$[\text{only } x_2]_1$ – as is illustrated by the different indices 1 and 2.

(6a) binding
$[\text{Every wife}]_2 (\lambda x_2 (x_2 \text{ thinks that } ([\text{only } x_2]_1 (\lambda y_1 (y_1 \text{ respects } y_1\text{'s husband })))))$

(6b) covaluation
$[\text{Every wife}]_2 (\lambda x_2 (x_2 \text{ thinks that } ([\text{only } x_2]_1 (\lambda y_1 (y_1 \text{ respects } x_2\text{'s husband })))))$

4.2 Referential noun phrases

In addition to functioning as bound variables with quantified antecedents, *pro* and *hänen* can also be referential, as has been suggested for English pronouns in general (e.g., Heim & Kratzer 1998). However, the correlation that we noticed in the preceding section between (a) the presence vs. absence of the possessive pronoun and (b) the availability of covaluation vs. binding seems to break down – partially – when the antecedent is a referential noun phrase. I will argue that the lack of full parallelism between QuNPs and referential noun phrases is due to the fact that the pragmatic system of anaphor resolution can be used to interpret referential noun phrases, but not QuNPs. This distinction is addressed in more detail below.

Let us turn to the examples that display the asymmetry. Unsurprisingly, example (12b), with an overt possessive pronoun, only permits the covaluation interpretation. It can only mean that Liisa thinks that other people do not respect *her* husband. This is what we would expect on the basis of the data discussed above. However, when the overt possessive pronoun is missing, as in (12a), both the covaluation interpretation and the binding interpretation are available. Example (12a) can have the binding interpretation and mean that Liisa thinks that other women do not respect their own husbands, i.e. that she is the only good wife. However, it can also have the same meaning as (12b) – i.e. the covaluation construal. This is unexpected in light of the earlier claim that an absence of an overt possessive pronoun rules out a covaluation (non-local binding) interpretation.

(12a) *No overt possessive pronoun*
Liisa uskoo, että vain hän kunnioittaa ø miestään.
Liisa.n think-pres.3s that only s/he.n respect-pres.3s ø husband-p.Px3
'Liisa thinks that only she respects her husband.'
→ *"Unpopular husband" interpretation [Covaluation] = ok*
→ *"Good wife" interpretation [Binding] = ok*

(12b) *Overt possessive pronoun*
Liisa uskoo, että vain hän kunnioittaa **hänen** miestään.
Liisa.n think-pres.3s that only s/he.n respect-pres.3s s/he-g husband-p.Px3
'Liisa thinks that only she respects her husband.'
→ *"Unpopular husband" interpretation [Covaluation] = ok*
→ *"Good wife" interpretation [Binding] = no*

In the remainder of this section, we focus on the central question raised by the data: Why is the covaluation reading ("unpopular husband" interpretation) possible in (12a) when the overt pronoun is missing, given that it is not available in (11a), with the QuNP? Recall that QuNP's, such as 'every woman' in (11a) do not permit coreference, whereas referential NP's, like 'Liisa' in (12a), *do* permit coreference (Section 2.1.1). Given this difference, it seems reasonable to conclude that the seemingly surprising availability of the 'unpopular husband' reading for (12a) is in fact due to coreference, and not covaluation. In accordance with the pragmatic tendencies noted for pro-drop in Finnish as well as other languages (e.g. Samek-Lodovici 1996, inter alia), in (12a) the null possessive pronoun is coreferential with the current topic, which is Liisa. This generates the "unpopular husband" interpretation, and thus creates the illusion of covaluation being possible.

The binding interpretation of (12b), with an overt possessive pronoun, is still unavailable because, though coreference is possible for the overt form *hänen*, locality considerations apply to pragmatic anaphora resolution as well as to bound variable interpretation. Null pronouns are used for coreference with the closest topic, and use of an overt possessive pronoun – as in (12b) – suggests that the antecedent is *not* the current topic.

Thus, on the basis of the data in (12a,b), I claim that Finnish visibly encodes the distinction between coreference with the local topic and other discourse entities, such that the null pronoun preferably refers to the local topic, and the overt pronominal form *hänen* preferably refers to something else.

4.3 Summary of proposed analysis

In my proposal, I maintain the subject-oriented nature of the null possessive pronoun, but additionally I claim that regardless of whether the pronoun is interpreted semantically or pragmatically, locality plays a crucial role. My claims are summarized in the table below. If no overt possessive pronoun is present, locality constraints apply to both semantic and pragmatic pronoun interpretation. Semantically, the variable must be interpreted by (local) binding. Pragmatically, the anaphoric element is preferably interpreted as coreferential with the current topic. If an overt possessive pronoun is present, non-locality constraints kick in. Semantically, the variable is interpreted by covaluation (non-local binding). Pragmatically, overt pronoun prefers to be coreferential with something else in the discourse, other than the current topic.[3] In sum, the null pronoun is subject to a locality requirement, whereas the overt pronoun is governed by a non-locality constraint.

---

[3] As mentioned above, for some speakers this constraint can apparently be overridden by contextual considerations. Some of my informants permit (10b), which has an overt possessive pronoun, to have the 'subject=possessor' interpretation (see also Niendorf and Peterson 1999, Ikola 1986). Overt pronouns prefer to refer to something other than the topic – however, one could explain the informants' judgments by noting that in a sentence such as (10b), there is no other entity to refer to. The only discourse entity at this point is the subject, Liisa. Perhaps the speakers permit the overt pronoun to refer to the topic as some kind of 'last resort'-type mechanism. Clearly, more research is needed to learn more about the conditions/contexts under which the 'non-topic' constraint can be overridden. In addition, it is important to note that my analysis claims that pragmatic coreference is responsible for the 'subject=possessor' readings of sentences like (10b). This approach predicts that a sentence with an overt possessive pronoun, like (10b), but with a QuNP subject, should not have the interpretation 'sub-

	Semantics	Pragmatics
No overt possessive pronoun	Binding	Coreference with current topic
overt possessive pronoun	Covaluation	Coreference preferably with something other than closest topic

5 Additional Phenomena

The claim that null possessive pronouns are subject to locality constraints and overt possessive pronouns to non-locality constraints makes a number of predictions for other phenomena in Finnish. In this section, we focus on two of these, namely (i) ellipsis, and (ii) the resolution of 'regular' pronouns. As we will see, the behavior and interpretations of these constructions provide further evidence for the analysis discussed above. Some data from Swedish will also be discussed, and we will see evidence suggesting that the distinction between null vs. overt forms (as opposed to two different overt forms) may be crucial to the locality vs. non-locality distinction.

5.1 Ellipsis data

Data from ellipsis show the same asymmetry between presence vs. absence of an overt possessive pronoun that was discussed above, and thus provide corroborating evidence for my claim concerning the role of locality in pronoun interpretation. First, let us consider (13). This sentence does not contain an overt possessive pronoun, and, according to my analysis, the null *pro* is subject to locality constraints. Thus, my analysis predicts that it could be interpreted semantically by (local) binding and pragmatically by coreference with the local topic. If the null *pro* is interpreted semantically by (local) binding, and the resulting predicate (given in (13a)) is used to resolve the ellipsis, the sloppy interpretation is generated. This reading is indeed possible, according to my informants. If the null *pro* is interpreted pragmatically by coreference with the local topic, and this predicate (given in (13b)) is used to resolve the ellipsis, then we generate the strict reading. This reading is somewhat marked, but still possible. Given that both readings are possible for the elided predicate, my analysis makes the correct prediction for (13). However, existing analyses of Finnish possessives, to the best of my understanding, predict that the strict interpretation of the el-

ject=possessor'. This is because QuNPs cannot be interpreted by coreference. Preliminary data suggest that this may indeed be the case, but further research is needed.

lipsis (given in (13b)) should be impossible, because the pronoun is null and thus should be bound by the subject *Jussi*.

(13) *No overt possessive pronoun*
Pekka puolusti ø ystäväänsä paremmin kuin Jussi ▲.
Pekka.n defend-past.3s ø friend-p.Px3 better than Jussi.n
'Pekka defended his friend better than Jussi.'
(a) ok Jussi defended Jussi's friend
[ok sloppy] ▲ = λx.x defended x's friend
(b) ? Jussi defended Pekka's friend
[? strict] ▲ = λx.x defended y's friend & <u>y=Pekka</u>

(14) *Overt possessive pronoun*
Pekka puolusti hänen ystäväänsä paremmin kuin Jussi ▲.
Pekka.n defend-past.3s s/he-g friend-p.Px3 better than Jussi.n
'Pekka defended his friend better than Jussi.'
(a) * Jussi defended Jussi's friend.
[*sloppy] ▲ = λx.x defended x's friend
(b) ok Jussi defended Pekka's friend
[ok strict] ▲ = λx.x defended y's friend & <u>y=Pekka</u>

Now let us turn to (14), which contains an overt possessive pronoun, predicted to be subject to non-locality constraints. Here, the first predicate could be interpreted as meaning that Pekka defended some unnamed third person's friend. However, some of my informants also permit the interpretation that Pekka defended his own friend.

Under the interpretation that Pekka defended someone else's friend, the overt possessive pronoun is interpreted by coreference with something other than the local topic, Pekka. We would thus expect the elided predicate to mean that Jussi also defended the unnamed third person's friend – and this interpretation is indeed possible. However, for our purposes, the more interesting interpretation is the one in which Pekka defended Pekka's friend. My approach predicts that the sloppy interpretation of the elided predicate is unavailable, because (local) binding is not possible with an overt possessive pronoun. This prediction is supported by informant judgements. What about the strict interpretation? We concluded earlier that overt pronouns can be interpreted by covaluation or by coreference with (preferably) something other than the local topic. Covaluation is not possible here, because only one λ-binder is present. Coreference with something other than the local topic generates the reading that both Pekka and Jussi defended some third person's friend. However, speakers who permit the interpretation that Pekka defended his own friend (i.e. who allow an overt possessive pronoun to be coreferential with the local topic in certain contexts) can interpret the ellipsis as meaning that Jussi defended Pekka's friend – as we would predict if the predicate shown in (14b) is used to resolve the ellipsis. Thus, we also predict the availability of the strict interpretation.[4]

5.2 Pronoun resolution in embedded clauses

The preceding discussion has focused on the distinction between null and overt *possessive* pronouns in Finnish. In this section I provide data which suggests that – as one might expect – 'regular' pronouns are also guided by the same locality constraints as possessive pronouns. First, consider a sentence such as (15), which is ambiguous.

(15) Peter thinks that only he notices that he is tired.

One of the interpretations can be described as follows. Imagine a scenario where Tom, John and Peter are hiking in the woods, and Peter suddenly starts to feel tired. However, he thinks he is the only one who notices feeling tired, i.e. he thinks that Tom and John do not notice that they are tired. This 'self-awareness' reading can be generated via variable binding. As shown in (15a) below, the subject of the predicate 'is tired' is bound by the closest λ-operator, and the lowest predicate thus denotes the set of people that notice their own tiredness.

The second interpretation of (15) is that Peter feels tired, and thinks that John and Tom do not notice that he is tired. In other words, Peter thinks his tiredness is not 'visible' to others. This 'invisible tiredness' reading is generated by covaluation, as illustrated in (15b) below. In (15b), the subject of the predicate 'is tired' is bound by the matrix λ-operator. The lowest predicate thus denotes the set of people who notice x's tiredness. As shown in (15c), this 'invisible tiredness' reading can also be generated by pragmatic coreference with the current topic (i.e. the subject of the sentence, Peter).

(15a) Peter λx (x thinks that only x (λy (y notices that y is tired)))))
→ binding ('self-awareness' reading)

(15b) Peter λx (x thinks that only x (λy (y notices that x is tired)))))
→ covaluation ('invisible tiredness' reading)

---

4 The behavior of QuNP subjects in elided contexts also needs to be examined in order to test the validity of this analysis. The crucial test sentence would be one with two QuNPs (e.g. 'Every boy defended his friend better than every man did'), but unfortunately, due to the complex semantics of this type of sentence, clear judgments concerning the availability of strict and sloppy readings are hard to obtain.

(15c) Peter λx (x thinks that only x (λy (y notices that he is tired)))))
& he = Peter
→ pragmatic coreference with current topic ('invisible tiredness' reading)

If it is the case that, in Finnish, the null vs. overt pronoun distinction is subject to semantic and pragmatic locality constraints, then the two interpretations of sentence (15) should correlate with the presence vs. absence of an overt pronoun in the lowest predicate. More specifically, we predict that in sentences where the subject of the embedded predicate 'is tired' is a null pronoun, the null pro could be interpreted semantically by (local) binding and pragmatically by coreference with the local topic. Similarly, in sentences where an overt pronoun is the subject the lowest predicate, we predict that it could be interpreted by covaluation or by coreference with (preferably) something other than the local topic.

However, it is important to note that, in sentences such as (9c) (Pekka$_i$ will come when ø$_i$ has time), pro-drop of the third person pronoun is not *required*, whereas using a null form of the possessive pronoun in sentences such as (10a) (Liisa$_i$ read ø$_i$'s book) is strongly preferred (and required, by many speakers). In other words, the requirements on pronouns are not as strict as those on possessive pronouns. This may be a result the different degrees of locality between the pronoun and its antecedent on the one hand, and the possessive pronoun and the possessor on the other hand. We might thus expect the predicted locality/non-locality requirements to be somewhat less strict for the regular pronouns.

As we will see, most of the data pattern as predicted. Let us first consider the examples with nonreferential QuNP subjects. Example (16a), with an overt pronoun in the lowest predicate, only permits the covaluation interpretation ('invisible tiredness'). It means that every boy thinks that none of the other boys notices that that particular boy is tired. However, example (16b), with a null pronoun in the lowest predicate, allows the binding interpretation ('self-awareness'), i.e. that every boy thinks that he is the only one who notices feeling tired; he thinks no one else notices any feelings of tiredness in themselves.[5]

---

[5] For some people, sentence (16b) can also have, often fairly marginally, the 'invisible tiredness' reading, which we have so far treated as being generated by covaluation or coreference. At first glance, this reading is surprising given the claim that null pronouns are interpreted either by binding (which generates the 'self-awaress' reading) or by coreference with the local topic (QuNPs do not create discourse referents that would permit coreference). The reasons for the (marginal) availability of the 'invisible tiredness' reading might be related to the double embedding structure of the sentence or/and the presence of the two verbs 'think' and 'notice.' These two verbs might create a telescoping-type effect, encouraging the reader to take the

(16a) *QuNP and overt pronoun*
Jokainen poika luulee, että vain hän huomaa, että hän on väsynyt.
Every.n boy.n think-pres.3s that only he.n notice-pres.3s that he.n be-pres.3s tired.
'Every boy thinks that only he notices that he is tired.'
→ *"Invisible tiredness" reading [Covaluation]= ok*
→ *"Self-awareness" reading [Binding]= no*

(16b) *QuNP and no overt pronoun*
Jokainen poika luulee, että vain hän huomaa, että ø on väsynyt.
Every.n boy.n think-pres.3s that only he.n notice-pres.3s that ø be-pres.3s tired.
'Every boy thinks that only he notices that he is tired.'
→ *"Invisible tiredness" reading [Covaluation]= ??(?)*
→ *"Self-awareness" reading [Binding]= ok*

Now, turning to sentences with a referential subject, we see that example (17a) below, with an overt pronoun in the lowest predicate, only permits the covaluation interpretation, i.e. it means that Pekka thinks no one else notices that Pekka is tired. However, example (17b), with a null pronoun, permits both the binding and the covaluation interpretations. This pattern is exactly like the one we saw for the examples in Section 4.2. The availability of both binding and covaluation interpretations for a sentence with a null pronoun can be explained as follows: The binding reading is due to variable binding, as expected. The covaluation reading, however, is only 'illusory', in that it is not a result of long-distance binding (covaluation), and is actually due to pragmatic coreference with the discourse topic.

(17a) *Overt pronoun*
Pekka luulee, että vain hän huomaa, että hän on väsynyt.
Pekka.n think-pres.3s that only he.n notice-pres.3s that he.n be-pres.3s tired.
'Pekka thinks that only he notices that he is tired
→ *"Invisible tiredness" reading [Covaluation]= ok*
→ *"Self-awareness" reading [Binding]= no*

---

perspective of one of the boys. This would then enable the 'invisible tiredness' interpretation to be generated via pragmatic coreference.

(17b) *No overt pronoun*
Pekka luulee, että vain hän huomaa, että ø on väsynyt.
Pekka.n think-pres.3s that only he.n notice-pres.3s that ø be-pres.3s tired.
'Pekka thinks that only he notices that he is tired
→ *"Invisible tiredness" reading [Covaluation]= ok*
→ *"Self-awareness" reading [Binding]= ok*

Thus, these examples illustrate that, for the most part, 'regular' pronouns pattern like possessive pronouns. The null forms are interpreted locally, either semantically via binding or pragmatically by coreference with the local topic. The overt forms are interpreted non-locally, by semantic variable covaluation or pragmatic coreference with something other than the local topic.

In addition to 'full' pronouns and possessive/genitive pronouns, there exists a third related environment in which we can test the overt vs. null pronoun distinction. There exists in Finnish a construction where the embedded clause surfaces as a nominalized constituent, as illustrated below. Here, the verb of the predicate 'is tired' carries nominal case marking as well as a possessive suffix, and the possessive pronoun is null.

(18a) *Referential subject*
Pekka luulee, että vain hän huomaa olevansa väsynyt.
Pekka.n think-pres.3s, that only he.n notice-pres.3s be-g.Px3 tired.
'Pekka thinks that only he notices that he is tired.'
→ *"Invisible tiredness" reading [Covaluation]= ok*
→ *"Self-awareness" reading [Binding]= ok*

(18b) *QuNO subject*
Jokainen poika luulee, että vain hän huomaa olevansa väsynyt.
Every boy thinks, that only he notices be-g.Px3 tired.
'Every boy thinks that only he notices that he is tired.'
→ *"Invisible tiredness" reading [Covaluation]= ???*
→ *"Self-awareness" reading [Binding]= ok*

My analysis predicts that a sentence such as (18a), with a referential subject, should permit the binding interpretation (since the possessive pronoun is null) and also the covaluation interpretation (via pragmatic coreference with the topic). Furthermore, sentence (18b), with a nonreferential, QuNP subject, is predicted to have only the binding interpretation, since pragmatic coreference cannot occur with QuNPs. As shown in (18), these predictions receive support from the judgements.[6]

5.3 Two types of possessive pronouns in Swedish

In this section, I present some evidence which suggests that the interpretative differences between the null and overt forms in Finnish may be related to the fact that the forms are null and overt, and is not just a consequence of their being morphologically distinct forms. The behavior of null pronouns vs. overt pronouns in prodrop languages has already provided us with some evidence that suggests that there is, in some sense, an inherent link between locality and null forms, on the one hand, and non-locality and overt forms on the other hand. However, one might still hypothesize that, in some other language, two morphologically distinct pronominal forms could play the same roles that are played by null and overt forms in Finnish.

Swedish provides an interesting test case for this hypothesis. In Swedish, the so-called reflexive pronominal forms *sin, sitt, sina* 'his/her' (showing number and gender agreement with the possessed noun) are used when the possessor is the subject of the sentence, as shown in (19a), and the non-reflexive pronominal forms *hennes, hans, dess, deras* 'her, his, its, their' are used when the possessor is not the subject of the sentence (19b). Thus, where Finnish uses a null possessive pronoun (ex. (10a)), Swedish uses a reflexive pronominal, and where Finnish uses an overt possessive pronominal (ex. (10b)), Swedish uses the non-reflexive pronominals.

(19a) Eva$_j$ älskar sin$_j$ man.
Eva.n love-pres her.refl husband.a
'Eva$_j$ loves her$_j$ husband.'
(adapted from Holmes & Hinchliffe 1994:153)

(19b) Ulla$_j$ älskar hennes$_k$ man.
Ulla.n love-pres she.g husband.a
'Ulla$_j$ loves her$_k$ husband.'
(adapted from Holmes & Hinchliffe 1994:153)

However, if we test for the difference between binding and covaluation using these two forms, the results differ from the findings for Finnish. First, let us consider examples in Swedish with referential subjects, such as (20a) and (20b) below. Sentence (20a), with the non-reflexive pronoun *hennes*,

[6] For some people, the 'invisible tiredness' interpretation seems to be very marginally available for this sentence. This might be due to the same telescoping-type mechanism that I suggested may be generating the weak 'invisible tiredness' reading for (16b).

can only mean that Lisa thinks she is the only one who respects some other woman's husband. In other words, *hennes* must be coreferential with something else in the discourse that is not the current topic. It cannot be (locally) bound or covalued (long-distance bound) by anything in the sentence. In contrast, (20b), with the reflexive form *sin,* is ambiguous and permits the binding and the covaluation interpretations. The same generalizations obtain for the examples with QuNP subjects (20c, 20d).

(20a) *Non-reflexive pronoun*
Lisa tycker att bara hon respekterar **hennes** make
Lisa.n think-pres that only she.n respect-pres she.g husband.a
'Lisa thinks that only she respects her husband.'
→ Lisa thinks that she is the only one who respects some other woman's husband

(20b) *Reflexive pronoun*
Lisa tycker att bara hon respekterar **sin** make.
Lisa.n think-pres that only she.n respects her.refl husband.a
'Lisa thinks that only she respects her husband.'
→ both binding and covaluation interpretations possible

(20c) *QuNP and non-reflexive pronoun*
Varje fru tycker att bara hon respekterar **hennes** make.
Every.n wife.n think-pres that only she.n respect-pres she.g husband.a
'Every wife thinks that only she respects her husband.'
→ Every wife thinks she is the only who respects some other woman's husband

(20d) *QuNP and reflexive pronoun*
Varje fru tycker att bara hon respekterar **sin** make.
Every.n wife.n think-pres that only she.n respect-pres her.refl husband.a
'Every wife thinks that only she respects her husband.'
→ both binding and covaluation interpretations possible

These data show that the Swedish reflexive pronouns (in (20b) and (20d)) can be bound or covalued (long-distance bound). In other words, they can be bound locally *or* non-locally. In contrast, the non-reflexive forms (shown in (20a) and (20c)) cannot be bound, and must be interpreted as being coreferential with some other entity in the discourse. Thus, the locality/non-locality distinction observed for Finnish does not map directly onto the two forms in Swedish. In Swedish, the reflexive vs. non-reflexive pronoun distinction corresponds to binding vs. non-local coreference, whereas in Finnish the null vs. overt possessive pronoun distinction corresponds to local vs. non-local interpretation (in both the pragmatic and semantic domains). These data suggest that it might be the null vs. overt difference – and not simply the existence of two morphologically different forms – that is crucially linked to the local/non-local distinction. Thus, there seems to be an inherent link between locality and null forms, on the one hand, and non-locality and overt forms on the other hand, as can also be seen in the behavior of null pronouns vs. overt pronouns in prodrop languages.

6 Conclusion

In this paper I have presented an analysis of the Finnish possessive construction, which can occur both with and without a possessive pronoun. On the basis of previously unnoticed asymmetries between the behavior of QuNPs and referential NPs, I argue that the null possessive pronoun is subject to locality constraints and the overt possessive pronoun *hänen* 'his/her' to non-locality constraints. These constraints show up in the pragmatic, referential interpretation of the two forms as well as in their use as bound variables.

More specifically, I claim that the distinction between variable binding (local binding) and variable covaluation (non-local binding) (Reinhart 1983, 1997, Heim 1993) is visibly encoded in Finnish. When no overt possessive pronoun is used, the variable is interpreted by binding. When the overt possessive pronoun *hänen* 'his/her' is used, the variable is preferably interpreted by covaluation (non-local binding). Moreover, I argue that the distinction between coreference with the local topic and other discourse entities is also overtly encoded in Finnish; the null pronoun refers to the local topic, and the overt pronominal form *hänen* 'his/her' preferably refers to something else.

In addition, I presented corroborating evidence from ellipsis and pronoun resolution in embedded contexts, as well as evidence from Swedish which suggests that the null vs. overt distinction (and not just the existence of two morphologically distinct forms) might be crucial to the local vs. non-local distinction.

References

Arnold, J. E., J. G. Eisenband, S. Brown-Schmidt and J. C. Trueswell. 2000. The rapid use of gender information: Evidence of the time course of pronoun resolution from eyetracking. *Cognition* 76:B13-B26.

Brennan, S.E., Friedman, M.A. and Pollard, C.J. 1987. A Centering approach to pronouns. *Proceedings of the 25th Annual Meeting of the Association for Computational Linguistics*, 155-162. Stanford, CA.

Crawley, R.J. and Stevenson, R.J. 1990. Reference in single sentences and in texts. *Journal of Psycholinguistic Research* 19(3):191-210.

Dimitriadis, A. 1996. When Pro-Drop Languages Don't: Overt Pronominal Subjects and Pragmatic Inference. *Proceedings of the Thirty-second Annual Meeting of the Chicago Linguistics Society.* Chicago: Chicago Linguistic Society.

Fox, D. 1998. Locality in Variable Binding. *Is the Best Good Enough? Optimality and Competition in Syntax*, ed. P. Barbosa, D. Fox, P. Hagstrom, M. McGinnis and D. Pesetsky, 129-156. Cambridge, Mass: MIT Press.

Grosz, B. J., A. K. Joshi, and S. Weinstein. 1995. Centering: a framework for modelling the local coherence of discourse. *Computational Linguistics* 21(2):203-25.

Hakulinen, A. and F. Karlsson. 1988. *Nykysuomen lauseoppia.* Helsinki: Suomalaisen Kirjallisuuden Seura.

Heim, I. 1993. *Anaphora and Semantic Interpretation: A Reinterpretation of Reinhart's approach.* Ms., MIT.

Heim, I. and A. Kratzer. 1998. *Semantics in Generative Grammar.* Oxford: Blackwell.

Holmes, P. and I. Hinchliffe. 1994. *Swedish. A Comprehensive Grammar.* New York: Routledge.

Hudson-D'Zmura, S. and M. K. Tanenhaus. 1998. Assigning Antecedents to Ambiguous Pronouns: The Role of the Center of Attention as the Default Assignment. *Centering Theory in Discourse*, ed. M. A. Walker, A. K. Joshi and E. F. Prince, 199-226. Oxford: Clarendon Press.

Ikola, O. 1986. *Nykysuomen käsikirja.* Espoo: Weilin+Göös.

Nelson, D. 1998. *Grammatical Case Assignment in Finnish.* New York: Garland.

Niendorf, M. and E. Peterson. 1999. *Variation in the Finnish Possessive: a new written standard?* Talk given at NWAVE 28, Toronto, 1999.

Paunonen, H. 1995. Puhesuomen muuttuva omistusjärjestelmä. *Virittäjä* 4/1995: 501-531.

Reinhart, T. 1997. *Strategies of Anaphora Resolution.* Paper delivered at "Interface Strategies" conference, Amsterdam, 9/97. OTS Working Paper, TL97-007.

Reinhart, T. 1983. *Anaphora and semantic interpretation.* Chicago: The University of Chicago Press.

Reinhart, T. 1982. *Pragmatics and linguistics: an analysis of sentence topics*. University of Indiana Linguistics Club. (also *Philosophica* 27:53-94).

Rooth, M. 1985. *Association with Focus.* Doctoral dissertation, University of Massachusetts.

Samek-Lodovici, V. 1996. *Constraints on Subjects: An Optimality Theoretic Analysis*. Ph.D. dissertation, Rutgers University.

van Steenbergen, M. 1991. Long-distance binding in Finnish. *Long-distance anaphora*, ed. J. Koster and E. J. Reuland, 231-244. Cambridge: Cambridge University Press.

Strawson, P. F. 1964. Identifying reference and truth-values. *Theoria* 30:96-118. Reprinted in *Semantics: An Interdisciplinary Reader in Linguistics, Philosophy and Psychology* 1972*)*, ed. D. Steinberg and L.A. Jakobovits. Cambridge: Cambridge University Press.

Toivonen, I. 2000. The Morphosyntax of Finnish Possessives. *Natural Language and Linguistic Theory* 18(3):579-609.

Trosterud, T. 1993. Anaphors and Binding Domains in Finnish. *Case and Other Functional Categories in Finnish Syntax*, ed. A. Holmberg and U. Nikanne, 225-244. Berlin: Mouton de Gruyter.

Turan, Ü. D. 1998. Ranking Forward-Looking Centers in Turkish. *Centering Theory in Discourse*, ed. M. A. Walker, A. K. Joshi and E. F. Prince, 139-160. Oxford: Clarendon Press.

Vainikka, A. 1989. *Deriving Syntactic Representations in Finnish.* Doctoral dissertation, University of Massachusetts.

Vainikka, A. & Y. Levy. 1999. Empty Subjects in Finnish and Hebrew. *Natural Language and Linguistic Theory* 17:613-671.

Vilkuna, M. 1996. *Suomen Lauseopin Perusteet*. Helsinki: Edita.

Walker, M. A., A. K. Joshi, and E. F. Prince. 1998. Centering in Naturally Occurring Discourse: An Overview. *Centering Theory in Discourse*, ed. M. A. Walker, A. K. Joshi and E. F. Prince, 1-30. Oxford: Clarendon Press.

9

Finnish PPs and the Phase Impenetrability Condition

SATU MANNINEN

1 Introduction

This paper provides a minimalist analysis of Finnish postpositional and prepositional phrases:

(1) a. talo-n edessä
house-gen in-front-of
'in front of a/the house'

b. ilman talo-a
without house-part
'without a/the house'

Within earlier generative theories of phrase structure, postpositional P heads like *edessä* always appeared to the right, while prepositional P heads like *ilman* appeared to the left, of their DP complement. The situation is illustrated in diagrams (1) and (2):

Generative Approaches to Finnic and Saami Linguistics.
Diane Nelson and Satu Manninen (eds.).

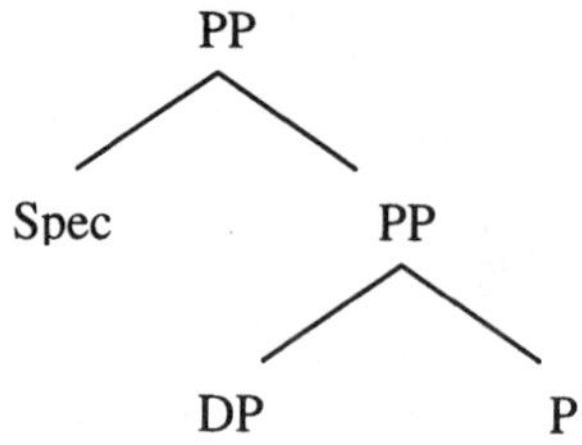

Diagram (1) Postpositional phrases

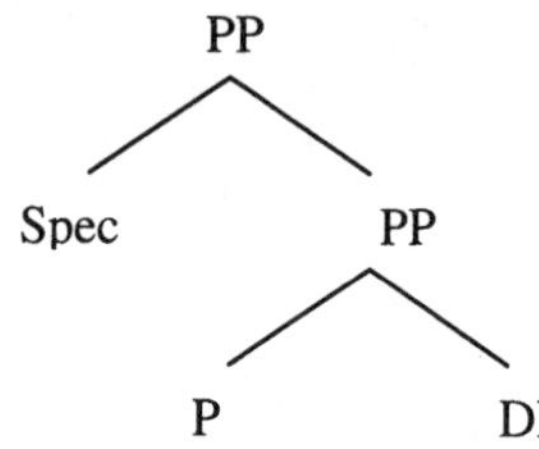

Diagram (2) Prepositional phrases

More recently, within Kayne's (1994) antisymmetry theory and the linear correspondence axiom (LCA), specifiers must asymmetrically c-command their heads, and heads must asymmetrically c-command their complements. Because the notion of asymmetric c-command is linked to linear precedence, all structures in all languages have an underlying specifier–head–complement order. On these assumptions, the structure in diagram (1) is ill-formed: the postpositional P head asymmetrically c-commands its DP complement but follows rather than precedes it in linear order.[1]

To explain the distinction between the post- and prepositional phrases, Kayne (1994, 47ff.) has proposed that, although they have similar underlying structures, in postpositional phrases the DP complement raises to the specifier of PP or of some higher functional FP. Although it is not evident from the discussion in Kayne what this higher functional FP might be and what triggers movement there, we could assume that there is a light pP on top of the PP, just as there is a light vP on top of the lexical VP. Platzack (1998, 175ff.) argues that there is a functional AgrP on top of PP, and that in postpositional phrases DP raises to Spec,AgrP. Radford (1997, 449f.) argues that there is both a light pP and AgrP on top of PP, and that DP raises to both Spec,pP and Spec,AgrP:

[1] Chomsky (1995) adopts a version of the LCA. Although he agrees with Kayne in that specifiers branch to the left, complements to the right of their c-commanding head, his system differs from Kayne's in that it allows multiple specifiers and specifier positions.

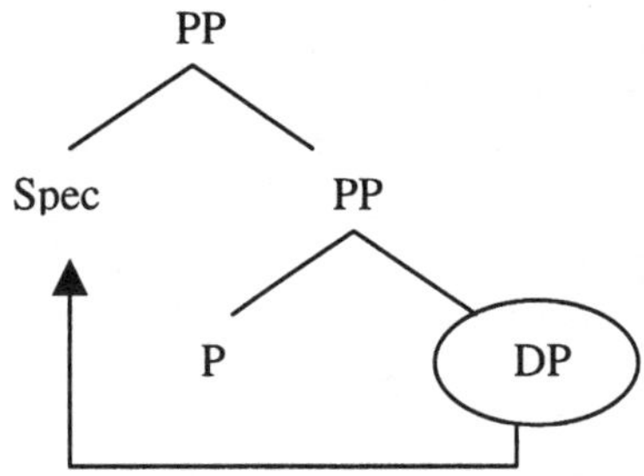

Diagram (3): movement of DP to Spec,PP

Within Minimalist frameworks, movement is allowed only if it results in the checking and deletion of uninterpretable features. One central question addressed in this paper is, therefore, what triggers the movement of DPs to Spec,PP in Finnish postpositional phrases. Another question is whether diagrams (2) and (3) really describe the correct state of affairs, so that all PPs have the same underlying structure, or whether they could have *different* underlying structures. The paper is structured as follows: in section 2 I discuss some earlier analyses of Finnish PPs which are of relevance. I also examine what counts as a PP in Finnish. In section 3 I introduce the Minimalist Inquiries framework of Chomsky (1999; 2000) and outline an analysis of Finnish PPs within this framework. In section 4 I discuss the idea that derivations proceed in phases. I look at some Finnish data, and provide arguments for analysing PPs as strong phases which are subject to the Phase Impenetrability Condition (PIC).

2 Finnish Postpositional and Prepositional Phrases

2.1 Previous Analyses

In Finnish postpositional phrases, the DP complement inflects for genetive case whereas in prepositional phrases it inflects for partitive case:

(2) a. talo-n edessä
house-gen in-front-of
'in front of a/the house'

b. silla-n alla
bridge-gen under
'under a/the bridge'

(3) a. ilman talo-a
without talo-part
'without a/the house'

b. ennen kesä-ä
before summer-part
'before summer'

Within earlier generative frameworks, post/prepositional P heads were thought to *assign* the genetive or partitive case to their complements. An alternative analysis can be found in Vainikka (1993) who argues that genetive and partitive are the structural default cases of Finnish specifier and complement positions. Rather than case *assignment,* Vainikka argues that nominal items inflect for these cases because they are base-generated in the specifier or complement position of P. On Vainikka's view, (2a) and (3a) have the underlying structures in (4):

(4) a. $[_{PP}$ [talon] $[_{P'}$ edessä]] (DP-P)
b. $[_{PP}$ $[_{P'}$ ilman [taloa]]] (P-DP)

But Vainikka's analysis raises a number of questions. First, if nominal items inflect for genetive or partitive case because they are base-generated as specifiers or complements of P, we need to adopt extra assumptions to rule out (5) – unless P has some kind of extra features determining whether the nominal item must appear in its specifier or compement position, we would expect (5) to be well-formed (i.e. the nominal item would always have the correct case):

(5) a. *edessä talo-a
in-front-of house-part

b. *talo-n ilman
house-gen without

Secondly, as shown by (6)-(7), the nominal items can sometimes either predece or follow P in linear order, without any drastic change in interpretation: (6a-b) are equally well-formed and synonymous, while (7a) is slightly better-formed than (7b). Assuming that nominal items inflect for genetive or partitive case by virtue of being merged as specifiers or complements of P, we are forced to conclude that, while (6a) and (7a) reflect the underlying structures, (6b) and (7b) have been derived by movement:

(6) a. päin seinä-ä
into wall-part
'into the wall'

b. seinää päin
'into the wall'

(7) a. tie-n yli
road-gen across
'across the road'

b. ?yli tien
'across the road'

The same conclusion is drawn by Vainikka (1993, 144) who states that examples as in (6b) "presumably involve raising the partitive NP to Spec,PP." But apart from the question of what triggers movement, examples as in (7) create a more serious problem: because the nominal item must be merged as specifier of P, it will either have to undergo *downward* movement to the complement of P position or, alternatively, the P^0 head will have to move upwards, across its own specifier position, to some higher head position.

Within Kayne's antisymmetry theory and the LCA, we have seen that post- and prepositional phrases have identical underlying structures (i.e. the complements of both post- and prepositional P heads branch to the right):

(8) a. $[_{PP}$ edessä $[_{DP}$ talon]] (P-DP)
b. $[_{PP}$ ilman $[_{DP}$ taloa]] (P-DP)

If post- and prepositional phrases have identical underlying structures, then their different linear orders must result from movement of the DP complement to Spec,PP in postpositional phrases. But as we have also seen, this raises the question of what triggers movement.

Although both Kayne's and Vainikka's analyses face the same basic question (i.e. what triggers movement), Kayne's idea of all PPs having just one and the same underlying structure clearly results in a more restrictive and economical theory. I will assume Kayne's analysis to be on the right track, and treat all PPs as having the underlying structure in (8). However, as pointed out in section 1, Kayne (1994) does not address the question of what triggers movement to Spec,PP in postpositional phrases. Within Chomsky's (1995) framework, this could be related to the types case features that the DPs have when they enter the derivation. Briefly, within Chomsky's (1995) framework nominal items are fully inflected for case when they enter the derivation: in (2)-(3) this means that, rather than being *assigned* genetive or partitive case, the DPs are already inflected for these cases when they enter the derivation. Case is then associated with case features which need checking in the course of the computation of LF. In PPs, case can be checked by raising the DP (overt movement, resulting in postpositional phrases such as (2)) or its features (covert movement, resulting in prepositional phrases such as (3)) to Spec,PP. Whether we are dealing with overt or covert movement depends crucially on feature *strength*: strong case features, such as the features for genetive case, must be checked in the overt syntax, before the derivation reaches Spell-out, while weak features, such as the features for partitive case, must wait until after Spell-out.

Although it seems possible, at least at first sight, to explain the structure and properties of Finnish PPs in a fairly unproblematic way within Chomsky's (1995) version of Minimalim, one central aim of this paper is to examine if, and how, they might be explained *better* within his (1999; 2000) Minimalist Inquiries framework. The (1999; 2000) view differs from Chomsky's earlier model in important respects: one crucial change is that case features can no longer be checked and erased via (overt or covert) movement, in an appropriate specifier-head configuration. For my purposes, this means that case feature checking can no longer be seen as the sole driving force behind movement of DPs to Spec,PP. Before discussing Chomsky's (1999; 2000) view in more detail in section 3 I determine what types of elements are (and what are not) usually classified as post/prepositional phrases in Finnish.

2.2 What do Finnish PPs Look Like?

Historically, most postpositions and prepositions in Finnish are derived from case-inflected nouns – see e.g. Hakulinen & Karlsson (1979, 153ff.), Karlsson (1981, 211ff.), Vilkuna (1996, 46f.), Jaakola (1997) and Ojutkangas (2000). Some examples of frequently used postpositions are given in (9)-(10) – as pointed out in Hakulinen & Karlsson (1979, 154), some 80% of all PPs in Finnish are postpositional:

(9) a. ede-ssä
front-iness

b. ede-stä
front-elat

c. ete-en
front-illat

d. ede-llä
front-adess

e. ede-ltä
front-ablat

f. ede-lle
front-allat

(10) a. a-lla
under-adess

b. a-lta
under-ablat

c. a-lle
under-allat

Although boundaries between the different categories are fuzzy, most contemporary linguists of Finnish agree that, rather than nouns, elements such as (9)-(10) should be classified as post/prepositions heading a PP. One reason for this is that their forms and uses are fixed to just these: *edessä* and *alla* can usually only appear in the locative case forms listed in (9)-(10). Second, they cannot appear with any nominal inflectional endings, such as the ending for plural number.[2] Third, as shown by (11)-(12), they cannot co-occur with attributive APs which show case and number agreement with them – this is expected if the elements in (9)-(10) are postpositions and

[2] Postpositional, but not prepositional, P heads can sometimes appear with possessive suffixes in Finnish. I return to this briefly in section 3.

prepositions, but unexpected if they are nouns (the hyphen in 11b indicates that it is impossible to even think of what adjectives could modify *alla*):[3]

(11) a. *iso-n talo-n välittömä-ssä ede-ssä PPs
big-gen house-gen immediate in-front-of

b. *vanha-n silla-n — a-lla
old-gen bridge-gen — under

(12) a. iso-n talo-n iso-ssa puutarha-ssa DPs
big-gen house-gen big-sg-iness garden-sg-iness
'in the big house's big garden'

b. vanha-n silla-n korkea-lla kaitee-lla
old-gen bridge-gen high-adess handrail-adess
'on the old bridge's high handrail'

On the basis of these data, I take it to be established that elements such as (9)-(10) are post/prepositions in Finnish, and turn to the question of whether inflectional endings for lexical case could also be classified as postpositions heading a PP in Finnish. This is the view taken in Kiguchi (2000) who argues that structures such as (12) (but lacking the attributive APs) be analysed as follows – according to Kiguchi (2000, 146f.) the movement of the DP complements to Spec,PP is motivated by "the suffix nature of P" (i.e. by the suffixal nature of *-ssa/-lla*):

---

[3] Finnish attributive APs agree in case and number with the noun that they modify: the APs are merged as specifiers of NP or of some DP-internal functional FP, and undergo movement inside the DP, to have their agreement features checked. The internal structure of DPs is discussed e.g. in Szabolczi (1994), Vainikka (1996), Siloni (1997), and Carstens (2000).

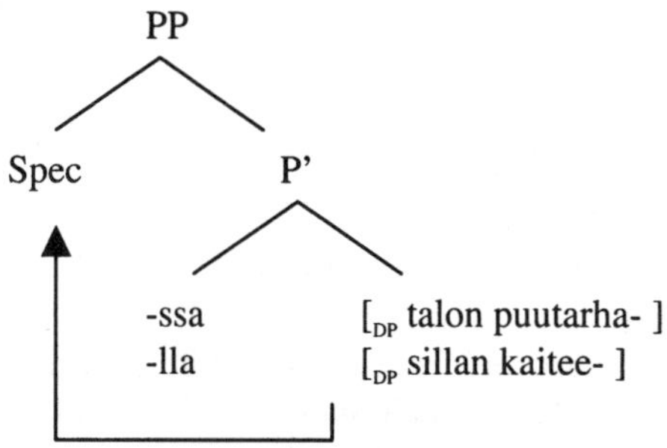

Diagram (4): PPs in Kiguchi (2000)

Although historically many lexical case endings in Finnish are indeed postpositions which have cliticized to their raised complements – see e.g. Tikka (1992), Jaakola (1997) and the references cited there – Kiguchi's analysis must be rejected for a number of reasons. First, if the suffixes *–ssa* and *–lla* are P heads in the same way as the non-suffixal *edessä* 'in-front-of' and *alla* 'under' are, then it is unclear what case they assign to their DP complements: the DPs in diagram (4) do not seem to have any case at all. However, we would *expect* the suffixes *–ssa* and *–lla* to assign case to the DPs, because otherwise we would have to conclude that Finnish has two types of P heads: suffixal P^0s which assign no case to their DP complements, and non-suffixal P^0s which assign either genetive or partitive case. By the same token, we would have to conclude that some DPs in Finnish are well-formed even though they are not assigned overt morphological case – clearly an unsatisfactory state of affairs.

A second, related problem for Kiguchi is that, because he only discusses examples which do not contain attributive APs, he overlooks the fact that in his model such APs would have to show case and number agreement with a postpositional P head: in (12), for example, this would mean that the APs *isossa* and *korkealla* do not show agreement with the nouns that they modify but rather with the postpositional *–ssa/-lla* heads. One further problem for Kiguchi is created by structures such as (13). (13) contain the DPs *kesästä* and *minuun* which inflect for lexical elative and illative case, as well as the postpositional heads *lähtien* and *nähden*. Under Kiguchi's assumptions both the elative/illative case endings *–stä* and *–uun* and the postpositions *lähtien* and *nähden* would have to appear in one and the same head of P position:

(13) a. kesä-stä lähtien
summer-elat since
'since summer'

b. min-uun nähden
I-illat with-respect-to
'with respect to/compared to me'

A uniform analysis for Finnish PPs and nominal items with lexical case is also proposed in Nikanne (1993) and Manninen (1999). Based on Larson (1985; 1987), Löbel (1994) and related work, these authors distinguish between **(i)** phonologically filled P^0s like *edessä* 'in-front-of' and *alla* 'under' which assign genetive and partitive case to their DP complements, and **(ii)** phonologically empty P^0s which assign the various lexical cases to their DP complements.[4] On this view, rather than *being* P^0s like in Kiguchi's system, the suffixes *–ssa* and *–lla* in (12) only *signal* the (inessive or adessive) case assigned to a DP by a P head – Nikanne and Manninen's view of the underlying structures of "overt" PPs like (2a)-(3a) is given in diagram (5), and of "empty" PPs like (12) in diagram (6). Note that in diagrams (5) and (6), the attributive APs are able to show case and number agreement with the noun heads that they modify – a very welcome result. Note also that, while in the "overt" PPs the DP may sometimes raise to Spec,PP, for reasons to be discussed in more detail in section 3, in "empty" PPs the most economical assumption would be for all DP complements to remain in situ:[5]

[4] Manninen (1999) labels the latter types of heads K^0s but states that P^0s and K^0s are similar types of functional heads, apart from the former being phonologically overt while the latter are phonologically empty.

[5] In Manninen (1999) it was assumed that DPs raise to Spec,PP in postpositional phrases because of feature strength. Note that, within the line of reasoning pursued here, there can be no distinction between structural and lexical case: both are assigned by a head H to a DP or, to use Chomsky's (1995) terminology, are associated with an uninterpretable case feature which needs to be checked and erased before the derivation reaches LF.

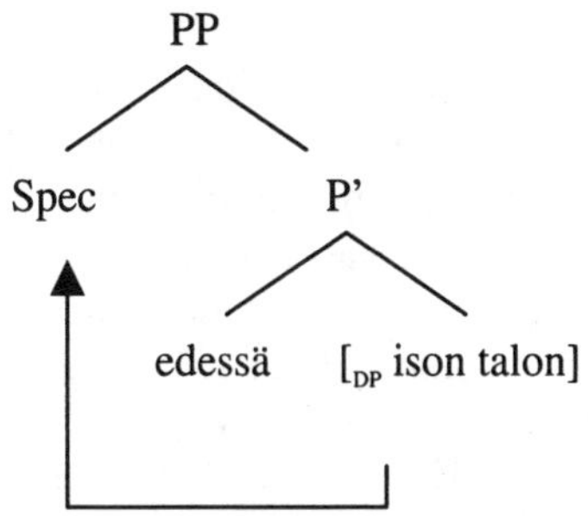

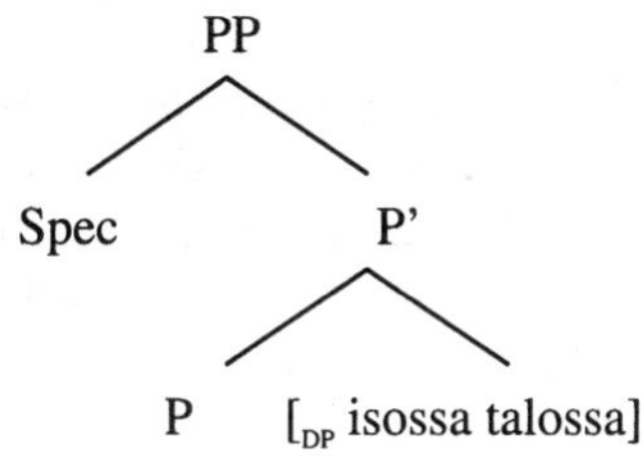

Diagram (5) "Normal" PPs **Diagram (6) Lexical case**

Summarising the discussion in this section, I have reviewed the reasons for treating elements like *edessä* 'in-front-of' and *alla* 'under' as P^0s heading a PP in Finnish. I have also discussed the idea that Finnish has phonologically empty P^0s which also head a PP, assigning the various lexical cases to their DP complements. However, as I assume, in line with Kayne (1994) and related work, that post- and prepositional phrases have one and the same underlying structure, I must address the question of what triggers the movement of DP complements to Spec,PP is postpositional phrases. Although in Manninen (1999) this movement was attributed to feature strength, we have seen that this view can no longer be maintained within Chomsky's (1999; 2000) Minimalist Inquiries framework. In section 3 I will first outline Chomsky's (1999; 2000) view of the system of case/agreement checking. I then propose a new analysis for post- and prepositional phrases which is embedded within this framework – one important goal is to determine what drives movement of DP complements to Spec,PP.

3 A Minimalist Analysis of Postpositional and Prepositional Phrases

3.1 Introduction

Let us begin by assuming that the derivation has constructed the syntactic object given in (14a). It then merges this syntactic object with a functional T^0 head, producing the larger syntactic object in (14b):

(14) a. $[_{vP}$ $[_{DP}$ The elephant$]$$[_{v'}$ v $[_{VP}$ ate $[_{DP}$ peanuts$]]]]$

b. $[_{TP}$ T $[_{vP}$ $[_{DP}$ The elephant$][_{v'}$ v $[_{VP}$ ate $[_{DP}$ peanuts$]]]]]$

T^0 heads have two kinds of uninterpretable features: their ϕ-feature set, and a selectional feature EPP. DPs have an uninterpretable structural case feature which needs to be checked and erased in the course of the computation of LF. The ϕ-set of T, Chomsky (2000, 122f.) argues, acts as a *probe* which seeks a matching *goal,* i.e. a matching set of features which establishes agreement within its local (i.e. its c-command) domain. Matching being restricted to feature identity, the nearest matching goal in (14b) is the interpretable ϕ-set of the DP *the elephant.* Having located this goal, the probe erases under matching. Taking structural case to be a reflex of an uninterpretable ϕ-set, Chomsky (2000, 122f.) argues that it, too, erases under matching with the probe (but see the discussion below).

In (14b), T also has an uninterpretable EPP-feature which requires that something be merged with the category that it heads. To satisfy the EPP of T, the DP *the elephant*, i.e. the phrase determined by the goal of T's probe, is moved to Spec,TP. Although within the Minimalist Inquiries framework the deletion of case features is dissociated from movement, Chomsky (2000, 122f.) argues that it is crucially the uninterpretable structural case feature of DP that makes the DP available for movement: uninterpretable features make a goal *active* so that it can delete a probe or determine a phrase for movement. On this view, once the structural case feature of DP has been erased, the DP is frozen in place: it cannot delete the probe of a higher head H, or move to satisfy the EPP in a higher position.[6]

3.2 Case/Agreement Checking in Finnish PPs

After the introductory remarks in section 3.1. I now turn to the structure of Finnish PPs as in (2)-(3), repeated here as (15)-(16):

(15) a. talo-n edessä
house-gen in-front-of
'in front of the house'

b. silla-n alla
brigde-gen under
'under the bridge'

[6] According to Chomsky (2000, 107) Wh-features are uninterpretable features analogous to structural case features of nouns. This allows Wh-DPs to delete the probe of a functional C and to satisfy the EPP of C by raising to Spec,CP, even after their case features have been erased.

(16) a. ilman talo-a
without house-part
'without a house'

b. ennen kesä-ä
before summer-part
'before summer'

I will assume, first, that the derivation has constructed the syntactic objects in (17), having merged a post/prepositional P^0 with DP – in line with Kayne (1994) and related work I treat the DP as P's right-branching complement:

(17) a. $[_{PP}$ edessä $[_{DP}$ talon]]
b. $[_{PP}$ alla $[_{DP}$ sillan]]

c. $[_{PP}$ ilman $[_{DP}$ taloa]]
d. $[_{PP}$ ennen $[_{DP}$ kesää]]

Second, I assume that there are three kinds of uninterpretable features in (17): the ϕ-feature set of P, the EPP-feature of P, and the structural case feature of DP. The ϕ-set of P acts as a probe that seeks a matching goal. In (17) the only choice of matching features is the interpretable ϕ-set of DP: having located this goal, the probe erases under matching. And given that structural case is a reflex of an uninterpretable ϕ-set I argue that it, too, erases under matching with the probe.

To account for the genetive-partitive contrast between Finnish post- and prepositional phrases, I adopt the idea presented in Chomsky (1999, 3ff.) that uninterpretable features enter the derivation unvalued, receiving their values under agreement. I take this to mean that the uninterpretable ϕ-features of P can be assigned a value and erased under agreement with the interpretable ϕ-set of DP. And although structural case is not a feature of probes, I propose, in line with Chomsky (1999, 4; 2000, 123f.), that the uninterpretable structural case feature of DP can be assigned a value and erased under matching with a probe which contains a complete set of ϕ-features (i.e. is ϕ-complete). As the idea that structural case features of DPs are assigned a value by an appropriate element under appropriate conditions (agreement) reminds us of the earlier view that case is assigned to DPs by an appropriate head H under appropriate conditions (government), I will continue to speak here of case *assignment*, rather than of case feature checking. This practice is adopted also elsewhere – among others, Frampton & Guttman (2000) and Frampton et al (2000) speak of case being *as-*

signed to nominal items with unvalued case features, by heads containing (a complete set of) unvalued ϕ-features.

Although the idea that P^0s have (a complete set of) ϕ-features may sound controversial, I believe it to be essentially on the right track – for a similar view, see also Haeberli (2000) and Platzack (2000). One possible argument for P^0s having ϕ-features comes from languages like German and Finnish. In German, prepositions assign either accusative or dative case to their DP complements. However, rather than merely inflecting for the correct accusative or dative case, the DPs must always inflect for the correct masculine/feminine/neuter form of that case – this is illustrated in (18). In the same way, Finnish phonologically empty P^0s can sometimes only occur with plural DPs – one example is given in (19):

(18) a. mit einer lieber Mutter
with a dear mother (dative & feminine)
'with a dear mother'

b. *mit einem lieben Mutter
with a dear mother (dative & masculine)

(19) a. vaimo-i-ne-en
wife-pl-com-Px
'with his wife'

b. *vaimo-ne-en
wife-sg-com-Px

Although the data in (18)-(19) raise a number of questions (e.g. one could argue **that einem lieben Mutter* in and **vaimoneen* are ill-formed even as DPs and that has nothing to do with the P^0) I would like to propose that (18a) and (19a) are well-formed because the interpretable ϕ-set of DP has been able to value and erase the corresponding uninterpretable ϕ-set of P^0, and P^0 has in return been able to assign the correct structural case (value) to the DP. In the ill-formed (18b) and (19b), on the other hand, there is a mismatch of features and case assignment by P^0 to DP fails. Secondly, given the way in which the system proposed by Chomsky (1999; 2000) is built up, there are also strong theoretical reasons to suppose that P^0s must be ϕ-complete: crucially, only ϕ-complete heads are able to assign case to a DP – see Chomsky (1999, 5f.). On this view, if P^0s like *mit* were not ϕ-complete, we would still expect the complete ϕ-set of DP to be able to value and erase the features of P^0. However, as the partial ϕ-set of the P^0 could not value and erase the uninterpretable structural case feature of DP, we would not expect the DPs to fail the case filter (as they would remain caseless) – for more discussion , see e.g. Frampton & Guttman (2000) and Frampton et al (2000).

Further support for an agreement relation between DP and P could come from the fact that in postpositional phrases, the P head is sometimes followed by a possessive suffix (Px). (20)-(21) show how in both DPs and PPs, a personal pronoun may either co-occur with possessive suffix or, alternatively, the first and second person suffixes may occur alone. Unlike in DPs, in PPs the third person suffixes may never occur alone:

(20) a. (minu-n/meidä-n) puutarha-ssa-ni/-mme
I/we-gen garden-iness-1sgPx
'in my/our garden'

b. Hän seisoi /He seisoivat (häne-n/heidä-n) puutarha-ssa-an
She / They stood she/they-gen garden-iness-3sgPx/3plPx
'She stood / They stood in her/their garden'

(21) a. (minu-n/meidä-n) edessä-ni/-mme
I/we-gen in-front-of-1sgPx/1plPx
'in front of me/us'

b. Hän seisoi / He seisoivat *(häne-n/heidä-n) edessä-än
She / They stood she/they-gen in-front-of-3sgPx/3plPx
'She stood / They stood in front of her/them'

Examples as in (20) are discussed in detail in Toivonen (2000) who proposes a split analysis for the Pxs: when the first and second person Pxs co-occur with a personal pronoun, they are agreement markers. When the Pxs occur alone, she analyses them as incorporated pronouns. However, as Toivonen points out, sentences such as (20b) are assigned different interpretations depending on whether the personal pronouns are present or not: when they are present, (20b) means that she/they stood in someone else's garden. But when the pronouns are absent, (20b) means that she/they stood in her/their *own* garden. This change in interpretation leads Toivonen to conclude that Finnish third person Pxs differ from the first and second person Pxs in important respects: although they can function as agreement markers in the same way as first and second person Pxs can – this explains the first readings of (20b) – they can never be incorporated pronouns. Instead, whenever a third person Px occurs alone, it functions as a reflexive pronoun which is bound by a clausal subject – this explains the second readings of (20b).

Although Toivonen does not discuss Pxs inside of PPs, her ideas can be adopted within the analysis of PPs proposed here: crucially, when the first and second person Pxs co-occur with a personal pronoun, we can analyse them as agreement markers – for a similar view, see e.g. Vainikka (1993). When the same first and second person Pxs occur alone, they are either incorporated pronouns, as suggested by Toivonen, or agreement markers agreeing with a phonologically empty pronominal element *pro*. The *pro* must then have the same set of features as the corresponding phonologically overt pronoun does. Secondly, the contrast between (21a) and (21b) shows that even in PPs, the third person Pxs differ from the first and second person Pxs: they can only function as agreement markers inside of PPs, agreeing with a phonologically overt pronoun (i.e. unlike in DPs, the third person Pxs in PPs cannot be incorporated pronouns – one reason for this could be that the complement position of Finnish P^0s must be filled by a full pronoun/DP, or by a trace of a full pronoun/DP, rather than by a weak element requiring incorporation – for some discussion see e.g. Baker (1988)).

Summarising, in this section I have discussed the system of case/agreement checking within Finnish PPs, and determined that the uninterpretable structural case features of DP can be assigned a value and erased under agreement with an appropriate ϕ-complete P^0 head. However, nothing has been said so far of how post/prepositional phrases come to have different linear word orders. This is what I will set out to do in the next section.

3.3 Word Order in PPs

To account for the linear DP-P order in postpositional phrases, one could assume that postpositional P^0 heads have an uninterpretable EPP-feature which always requires pied-piping of the phrase determined by the goal of P's probe to Spec,PP. Contrastingly, because prepositional P^0 heads *lack* an EPP-feature, dislocation cannot take place even though there is long-distance agreement between P's probe and its goal. On these assumptions, the postpositional phrases in (17a-b) would have the structures given in (22a-b), while the prepositional phrases in (17c-d) have the structures in (22c-d):

(22) a. $[_{PP}$ $[_{DP}$ ison lihavan norsun $]_i$ $[_{P'}$ edessä t_i]]
'big fat elephant in-front-of'

b. $[_{PP}$ $[_{DP}$ vanhan puisen sillan $]_i$ $[_{P'}$ alla t_i]]
'old wooden bridge under'

c. $[_{PP}$ $[_{P'}$ ilman $[_{DP}$ isoa lihavaa norsua]]]
'without big fat elephant'

d. $[_{PP}$ $[_{P'}$ ennen $[_{DP}$ pitkää kuumaa kesää]]]
'before long hot summer'

However, rather than always pied-piping the phrase determined by the goal of H's probe to Spec,HP, Chomsky (1999; 2000) has proposed that the EPP can also be satisfied by merge of an appropriate "external" element to Spec,HP. One example of this is the merge of expletives to Spec,TP:

(23) a. The elephant$_i$ seems $[_{TP}$ t$_i$ to be sad]
b. It seems that $[_{TP}$ the elephant is sad]

Let us now examine briefly what options are available for satisfying the EPP of Finnish post/prepositional P^0s. First, (24) suggest that Finnish postpositional P^0s have an EPP which must always be satisfied by pied-piping the DP, i.e. the phrase determined by the goal of P's probe, to Spec,PP. Crucially, it cannot be satisfied by merge of an external element, such as an AdvP modifier, to Spec,PP (note that in Finnish AdvPs can be merged to the specifier positions of most other heads: even the Spec,TP position, i.e. the normal subject position, can be filled by an AdvP – for some discussion see e.g. Manninen 1999):

(24) a. ??edessä talo-n
'in-front-of house'

b. ??alla silla-n
'under bridge'

c. *suoraan edessä talo-n
immediately in-front-of house-gen

d. *ihan alla silla-n
completely under bridge-gen

However, (25) suggest that, once the EPP of postpositional P^0s has been satisfied by movement of DP to Spec,PP, the P^0s could have *another* EPP-feature which allows AdvPs to be merged as specifiers of a higher Spec,PP (in line with Chomsky I allow multiple specifiers and specifier positions):

(25) a. suoraan talo-n$_i$ edessä t$_i$
immediately house-gen in-front-of
'immediately in front of the house'

b. ihan silla-n$_i$ alla t$_i$
completely brigde-gen under
'completely under the bridge'

c. *talon$_i$ suoraan edessä t$_i$
d. *sillan$_i$ ihan alla t$_i$

Second, although Finnish prepositional P^0s do not normally have an EPP requiring pied-piping of DP to Spec,PP, the data in (26) suggest they may have the second type of EPP which allows AdvP modifiers to be merged to a higher Spec,PP. In (27), we are dealing with structures which can be either postpositional or prepositional. When they are postpositional, as in (27b-c), the movement of DP to Spec,PP must take place first, before the AdvPs can be merged as specifiers of P – this suggests that the second EPP might be a property that is only available to elements which have had all their uninterpretable features valued and erased:[7]

(26) a. ilman raha-a
without money-part
'without money'

b. ennen kesä-ä
before summer-part
'before summer'

c. kokonaan ilman raha-a
totally without money-part
'totally without money'

d. juuri ennen kesä-ä
right before summer-part
'right before summer'

---

[7] Alternatively, in (25) and (27) we could be dealing with a phenomenon known as *tucking in*, i.e. the fact that movement operations insert the moved element in the specifier position closest to the attracting head. See e.g. Richards (1999) for more discussion.

(27) a. suoraan päin seinä-ä
directly into wall-part
'directly into the wall'

b. suoraan seinää$_i$ päin t$_i$
'directly into the wall'

c. *seinää$_i$ suoraan päin t$_i$

On the basis of these data and discussions, I conclude that Finnish P^{0}s have two different types of EPP features: first, there are features which force the movement of DP, i.e. the phrase determined by the goal of P's probe, to Spec,PP. Second, there are features which allow the merge of AdvP modifiers as higher specifiers of PP. I further propose that the second types of EPP features become available only after all uninterpretable features of the PP have been valued and erased. The idea that EPP features may come in different types, and that they may be satisfied in different ways and at different stages of the derivation, is not completely controversial – for further discussion, see e.g. Adger & Tsoulas (2000) and Platzack (2000).

4 PPs as Strong Phases

In the previous section, I outlined an analysis for Finnish post/prepositional phrases within Chomsky's (1999; 2000) Minimalist Inquiries framework. In this section I discuss the idea that derivations proceed in phases, and apply this system to explain some further properties of Finnish PPs. Crucially, I address the question of why even prepositional phrases must become postpositional when the DP complement is associated with a Wh-feature; consider the data in (28):[8]

(28) a. Veroilmoitus jätetään [$_{PP}$ ennen joulu-a]
Income.tax.form must be returned before Christmas-part

b. *[$_{PP}$ Ennen mitä] veroilmoitus jätetään?
Before what-part income.tax.form must be returned

c. Mitä ennen veroilmoitus jätetään?

[8] (28b) is only possible with a strong echo reading: *Before WHAT must the tax form be returned?*

To constitute a sentence Chomsky (1999, 9ff.; 2000, 106ff.) argues that a lexical array LA (i.e. a collection of lexical items, equivalent to the Numeration of Chomsky 1995) is selected from the lexicon. From this array LA a subarray LA_i is selected and used to constitute a syntactic object SO. When this is done, another subarray LA_j may be selected, constituting another syntactic object SO. The process continues in this way, step by step, until LA is exhausted. Each subarray LA_i, Chomsky argues, must determine a syntactic object that is independent with regard to interface properties. In his system, this means that each subarray LA_i must contain an occurrence of C or v, determining a clause or verb phrase. Taking *phases* of a derivation to be syntactic objects derived in this way by the choice of subarrays, Chomsky (2000, 106) concludes that a phase can be either "CP or vP, but not TP or lexical VP headed by H lacking ϕ–features and therefore not entering into case-agreement checking."

Phases are divided into *weak* and *strong* phases. Each strong phase, Chomsky (1999, 9ff.) argues, must contain a complete set of ϕ–features: this means that each strong phase must contain a ϕ-complete C or v (i.e. that strong phases are finite CPs, control CPs, and transitive vPs). Strong phases are crucially subject to the Phase Impenetrability Condition, or PIC, adapted from Chomsky (1999, 9ff.; 2000, 107ff.):

> *Phase Impenetrability Condition (PIC)*
> In $[_{ZP} \ldots Z \ldots [_{HP}\ \alpha\ [\ H\ \beta\ ]]]$, where HP is a strong phase and ZP is the next strong phase, only H and its edge are accessible to operations at ZP

Here α, a hierarchy of specifiers or elements adjoined to HP, constitutes the edge of H while β constitutes its domain: the PIC states, first, that only H and α are accessible to operations outside of HP and, second, that they are only accessible to operations within the next highest strong phase ZP. Crucially, operations at ZP cannot look into HP beyond its head H: thus, if there is a feature of Z that acts as a probe seeking a matching goal, an agreement relation can only be established between the probe and a feature of H, or the probe and a feature of α, but not between the probe and a feature of β.

On the view that phases are chunks of material that are independent with regard to interface properties, Finnish PPs can clearly be analysed as phases: all uninterpretable features of PPs are valued and erased PP-internally. The question that immediately arises is whether Finnish PPs constitute weak or strong phases. We have seen in section 3 that the uninterpretable structural case feature of DP can be valued and erased under matching with P's probe, and that this is what gives us the genetive-partitive contrast. We have also seen how postpositional P^0s have an uninterpretable EPP-feature which must be satisfied by moving DP to Spec,PP. In order to value and erase uninterpretable features of its goal, and in order to have an EPP-feature, Chomsky (1999, 4; 2000, 123f.) argues that a head H must be ϕ–complete: on this basis, it seems reasonable to conclude that at least *post*positional PPs constitute strong phases in Finnish.

In order to provide even stronger arguments for the claim that postpositional PPs constitute strong phases in Finnish, as well as to determine the status of Finnish *pre*positional phrases, let us look at the data in (29)-(31). In these examples, the uninterpretable Wh-features of C act as a probe that seeks a matching goal. C also has en EPP-feature which must be satisfied by merging the phrase determined by the goal of C's probe with the category that it heads. In (29)-(31), there is only one choice of matching features for C's probe: the interpretable Wh-features of the PP-internal DP (which, being uninterpretable, make the DP an *active* goal for C's probe). First, in (29) the PPs are headed by the postpositional P^0s *edessä* and *alla* – these P^0s have an EPP-feature which, we have seen in section 3, must be satisfied by movement of the DP to Spec,PP. Constituting now the edge of P, the moved DPs are accessible to operations outside of PP: crucially, since in (29) they are associated with a Wh-feature, they are able to delete C's probe and to satisfy its EPP-feature, by movement of PP to Spec,CP – note that, because Finnish lacks preposition stranding, when the PP-internal Wh-DP is identified as the goal of C's probe and must move to satisfy C's EPP feature, the whole PP must be pied-piped to Spec,CP:

(29) a. Minkä talo-n edessä Pulmu seiso-i?
What-gen house-gen in-front-of Pulmu-nom stood
'In front of what house did Pulmu stand?'

b. Minkä silla-n alla Pulmu asu-i?
What-gen bridge-gen under Pulmu lived
'Under what bridge did Pulmu live?'

(30)-(31) contain the *pre*positional P^0s *ilman* and *ennen*. Given that prepositional P^0s do not normally have an EPP in Finnish, the ill-formedness of (30) and well-formedness of (31) is unexpected: why must all Wh-DPs undergo movement to Spec,PP and what drives this movement, given that P^0 lacks an EPP feature?[9]

[9] (30) are possible only with a strong echo reading. The echo readings for (30) are the same as for *Pulmu ei voi elää ilman MITÄ asiaa?*

(30) a. *Ilman mitä asia-a Pulmu ei voi elää?
without what-part thing-part Pulmu not-3sg live
'Without what can Pulmu not live?'

b. *Ennen mitä päivä-ä veroilmoitus on jätettävä?
before what-past day-part income-tax.form must be filled
'Before what day must one fill in one's income tax form?'

(31) a. Mitä asiaa ilman Pulmu ei voi elää?
b. Mitä päivää ennen veroilmoitus on jätettävä?

I take the ill-formedness of (30) and well-formedness of (31) to suggest that even prepositional phrases must constitute strong phases in Finnish so that they are subject to the PIC. If they were not strong phases, we would expect the Wh-DPs in (30) to be accessible to operations at CP even though they constitute the domain of P – in particular, we would expect them to be able to delete the uninterpretable features of C even when they are in situ. But the ill-formedness of (30) strongly suggests that this is not what happens. In the well-formed (31), in turn, the Wh-DPs have been moved to the edge of the prepositional phrase – given the PIC, they can now be identified as the goal of C's probe, and they are able to delete C's probe. They can also raise to Spec,CP, pied-piping the whole PP along with them.

On the basis of these data and discussions I take it to be established that both post/prepositional phrases constitute strong phases in Finnish and are subject to the PIC. Secondly, although prepositional phrases do not ordinarily have an EPP-feature in Finnish which would force movement of the DP complement to Spec,PP, I propose that one may be optionally inserted there, to guarantee eventual convergence. The line of reasoning pursued here is in keeping with that pursued in Chomsky (2000, 109f.) who argues that, rather than just *heads* of phases, EPP might be a property of *phases*, and that an EPP-feature may be added (to a strong phase head) optionally, to guarantee eventual convergence of phases: in (30), unless no EPP was inserted in the prepositional P^0, the PP would be sent to Spell-out containing uninterpretable Wh-features which result in a crash, when the PP is evaluated at the next strong phase level. The insertion of EPP in P^0 rescues the situation as the offending element can now be extracted to the edge of PP and, when the PP is evaluated at the next strong phase level, they have already been valued and erased under matching with C's probe. A similar line of reasoning is pursued in Svenonius (2000) who discusses movement of Wh-elements out of lexical VPs. According to Svenonius, Wh-elements must always move out of the VP before the VP goes to Spell-out, or else they become inaccessible to operations outside of VP: crucially, they cannot delete C's probe or move to Spec,CP satisfy C's EPP-feature. If no strong feature triggers movement out of VP, Svenonius (2000, 5f.) argues, one can be inserted, for example, in v (i.e. since v is a strong phase, an EPP feature may be added to its head, to guarantee eventual convergence).

Let us now address briefly some remaining questions. As we have seen, the PIC crucially states that elements of a strong phase HP (i.e. H itself and its edge) are accessible only to operations within *the next highest strong phase ZP*. In the discussion so far, we have assumed the next highest strong phase to be CP, but this may not be the case. The PPs in (29)-(31) have the function of VP-adverbials (denoting place and time) which have a low position inside the lexical VP – this can be shown using a number of tests involving binding asymmetries and negative polarity items – see e.g. Stroik (1995), Alexiadou (1997), Manninen (1999) and the references cited there. However, the next highest strong phase above VP is vP, not CP. This means that the movement of PPs to Spec,CP might have to take place in short hops – first the Wh-DP is extracted to the edge of PP, and the PP as a whole is extracted to the edge of vP (possibly by inserting an EPP property to v). Only after this has been done can the Wh-DP be identified as the goal of C's probe, so that it is able to value and erase its uninterpretable features, and to raise to Spec,CP, to satisfy the EPP (an alternative would be to assume that the PPs are merged as specifiers of v projections so their original position of merge is already at the edge of vP, and the next strong phase level would be CP – but even here it is unclear how C's probe can look inside both the vP and the PP boundary).

Another question concerns universality – even if PPs constitute strong phases in Finnish, the data in (32) and (33) suggest that this may not be the case for languages like English and Swedish: in (32)-(33), the Wh-DPs seem to have been identified as the goals of C's probe, so that they can delete C's probe and satisfy C's EPP feature by raising to Spec,CP, even though they have not been extracted to the edge of P first (i.e. we would expect the Wh-DPs to extract only if PP constitutes a strong phase). This is not of course a problem for our analysis of Finnish – Raposo (2001) has argued that even within one and the same language, some PPs might constitute strong phases, others weak phases or even no phases at all:

(32) a. [At what time]$_i$ did she arrive t_i ?
b. [With which knife]$_i$ did she kill her husband t_i ?

(33) a. [På vilket sätt]$_i$ dödade hon honom t_i ?
In what way killed she him
'In what way did she kill him'

b. [I vilken stad]$_i$ bor du t_i ?

5 Conclusion

In this paper, I have proposed an analysis for Finnish postpositional and prepositional phrases, in the light of Chomsky's (1999; 2000) Minimalist Inquiries framework. We have seen that Finnish PPs can be analysed as having one and the same underlying structure, so that the DP is always a right-branching complement of P, but that they have different linear word orders because is postpositional phrases the P^0 head has an EPP feature which forces movement of DP to Spec,PP. We have also established that in both postpositional and prepositional phrases the P^0 head assigns case to its DP complement: postpositional heads assign genetive case, prepositional heads assign partitive case and phonologically empty P^0s assign the various lexical cases. In section 4 I proposed that PPs constitute strong phases in Finnish, and are subject to the Phase Impenetrability Condition of Chomsky (1999; 2000). Although there are reasons to believe that this is the correct analysis for Finnish, the status of PPs as phases in other languages is less clear and remains a topic for further research.

References

Adger, D. & Tsoulas, G. 2000. Aspect and Lower VP adverbials. *Adverbs and Adjunction*, eds. A. Alexiadou & P. Svenonius, 1-16. Linguistics in Potsdam 6.

Alexiadou, A. 1997. *Adverb Placement: a Case Study in Antisymmetric Syntax*. Amsterdam: John Benjamins.

Baker, M. 1988. *Incorporation: a Theory of Grammatical Function Changing*. Chicago: University of Chicago press.

Büring, D. & Hartmann, K. 1997 Doing the Right Thing – Extraposition as a Movement Rule. *The Linguistic Review* 14: 1-42.

Carstens, V. 2000. Concord in Minimalist Theory. *Linguistic Inquiry* 31: 319-355.

Chomsky, N. 1995. *The Minimalist Program*. Cambrisge, Mass.: The MIT Press.

Chomsky, N. 1999. Derivation by Phase. MITOPL 18.

Chomsky, N. 2000. Minimalist Inquiries: the Framework. *Step by Step: Essays on Minimalist Syntax in Honor of Howard Lasnik*, eds. R. Martin, D. Michaels, J. Uriagereka, 89-156. Cambridge, Mass.: The MIT Press.

Frampton, J. & Guttman, S. 2000a. Agreement is Feature Sharing. Ms, Northeastern University.

Frampton, J., Guttman, J. & Yang, C. 2000b. Remarks on "Derivation by Phase:" Feature Valuation, Agreement, and Intervention. Ms, Northeastern University.

Haeberli, E. 2000. Towards Deriving the EPP and Abstract Case. *GG@G* 1: 105-139.

Haegeman, L. 1994. *Introduction to Government and Binding Theory*. 2nd edition. Oxford: Blackwell.

Jaakola, M. 1997. Genetiivin kanssa esiintyvien adpositioiden kieliopillistumisesta. *Kieliopillistuminen. Tapaustutkimuksia suomesta.* eds. T. Lehtinen & L. Laitinen, 121-156. Helsinki: Helsingin yliopiston suomen kielen laitos.

Kayne, R. 1994. *The Antisymmetry of Syntax*. Cambridge, Mass.: The MIT Press.

Kiguchi, H. 2000. Syntax is Still Antisymmetric. *University of Maryland Working Papers in Linguistics*, Vol 9, eds. M. Guimarães, L. Meroni, C. Rodrigues & I. San Martin, 136-153. University of Maryland.

Larson, R. 1985. Bare NP-Adverbials. *Linguistic Inquiry* 16: 595-621.

Larson, R. 1987. 'Missing prepositions' and the Analysis of English Free Relative Clauses. *Linguistic Inquiry* 18: 239-266.

Löbel, E. 1994. KP/DP Syntax: Interaction of Case Marking with Referential and Nominal Features. *Theoretical Linguistics* 20: 37-70.

Manninen, S. 1999. Manner Adverbials and the Structure of Finnish Sentences: a Minimalist Approach. Doctoral dissertation, University of Edinburgh.

Manninen, S. 2000. Circumstantial Adverbials and the Theory of Antisymmetry. *SKY Journal of Linguistics* 13: 155-182.

Nikanne, U. 1993. On Assigning Semantic Cases in Finnish. *Case and Other Functional Categories in Finnish Syntax*, eds. A. Holmberg & U. Nikanne, 75-88. Berlin: Mouton de Gruyter.

Platzack, C. 1998. *Svenskans inre grammatik – det minimalistiska programmet.* Lund: Studentlitteratur.

Platzack, C. 2000. The Computational System as a Minimal Feature Drive Device and the Tripartite TP/VP Hypothesis of the Universal Clause. Ms. University of Lund.

Radford, A. 1997. *Syntax. A Minimalist Introduction.* Cambridge: Cambridge University Press.

Raposo, E. 1999. Towards a Minimalist Account of Nominal Anaphora in Spanish and English. Ms. USCB

Richards, N. 1999. Feature Cyclicity and the Ordering of Multiple Specifiers. *Working Minimalism,* eds. S. J. Epstein & N. Hornstein, 127-158. Cambridge, Mass: The MIT Press.

Ritter, E. 1991. Two Functional Categories in Noun Phrases: Evidence from Hebrew. *Syntax & Semantics 25*. New York: Academic Press.

Siloni, T. 1998. *Noun Phrases and Nominalisations*. Kluwer: Dordrecht.

Sportiche, D. 1988. A theory of Floating Quantifiers and its Corollaries for Constituent Structure. *Linguistic Inquiry* 19: 429-449

Stroik, T. 1995. *Minimalism, Scope and VP Structure*. Thousand Oaks: Sage Publications.

Svenonius, P. 2000. On Object Shift, Scrambling, and the PIC. MIT Working Papers in Linguistics 36.

Szabolcsi, A. 1994. The Noun Phrase. *Syntax & Semantics 27*. New York: Academic Press.

Tikka, T. 1992. Vepsän suffiksoituneet postpositiot. Doctoral dissertation, University of Uppsala.

Toivonen, I. 2000. The Morphosyntax of Finnish Possessives. *Natural Language and Linguistic Theory* 18: 579-609.

Vainikka, A. 1993. Three Structural Cases in Finnish. *Case and Other Functional Categories in Finnish Syntax*, eds. A. Holmberg & U. Nikanne, 129-162. Berlin: Mouton de Gruyter.

Vainikka, A. 1996. Head-Initial and Head-Final Constructions in Finnish. Finnsyntax.

10

Counting and the Grammar: Case and Numerals in Inari Saami

DIANE NELSON AND IDA TOIVONEN

1 Introduction

One fundamental assumption underlying most syntactic theories is that rules of the grammar cannot involve "counting"[1]. This notion originates in the earliest work in generative grammar and derives from the requirement that syntactic operations must be structure-dependent (ie sensitive to category labels) rather than sensitive to the linear order of elements in an input string. For instance, Chomsky (1965:55) argues that:

> ... grammatical transformations are necessarily "structure-dependent" in that they manipulate substrings only in terms of their assignment to categories... It is impossible, however, to formulate as a transformation such a

[1] This is a revised version of the paper that appeared in *Leeds Working Papers in Linguistics & Phonetics* 8 (2000). The authors would like to thank A. Kuuva, S. Kuuva, K. Mattus and I. Mattus for invaluable informant help. The data in this paper was collected during fieldwork during the summers of 1997-2001, and is based on information from Sammallahti & Morottaja (1993) and Sammallahti (1998). Thanks are also due to Satu Manninen, Pekka Sammallahti, Greville Corbett, Jim Hurford, and Frederick Newmeyer for valuable discussion, and to an anonymous reviewer for useful comments. All errors are the responsibility of the authors. This work was supported by British Academy research grant numbers SG-31040 and LRG-31734.

Generative Approaches to Finnic and Saami Linguistics.
Diane Nelson and Satu Manninen (eds.).

> simple operation as reflection of an arbitrary string (that is, replacement of any string $a_1 \ldots a_n$, where each a_i is a single symbol, by $a_n \ldots a_1$) or interchange of the (2*n*-1)th word with the 2*n*th word throughout a string of arbitrary length, or insertion of a symbol in the middle of a string of even length.

This prohibition on rules that "count" is taken to be a fundamental constraint on the type of syntactic rule that can be acquired. For example, it rules out the acquisition of a rule which forms a yes-no question by moving the fourth word of the input string to the front of the sentence. The human cognitive system may be capable of counting members of a set, but according to standard assumptions, UG disallows linguistic rules which manipulate elements based on assigning a numerical value to members of an input string[2].

Another, related assumption in the generative literature is that the lexicon consists of an unordered list of items, characterized by idiosyncracy and unpredictability (Chomsky 1965:84, Williams 1994). There are differences across frameworks as to how structured the lexicon is assumed to be, but there is general agreement that lexical entries are not organized in any kind of linear string.[3] If the contents of the lexicon are indeed unordered, this again excludes the possibility of "counting" for any rule that applies there. Numerals, however, pose a problem for this assumption.

Numerals are interesting for linguistic theory in many ways. For one thing, they seem to vary in syntactic category status cross-linguistically: in some languages they are determiners, in others adjectives, and in others they appear to form a category of their own. Another interesting characteristic is that they differ from other non-predicates in that they are able to assign case to the nominal they quantify. Furthermore, the formation of numerals seems to be governed by syntactic principles (Hurford 1975). Given the fact that numerals have so many interesting properties, it is surprising that they have been largely ignored in the linguistics literature.

Numerals represent an unusual set of lexical items in that they encode numerosity within a counting sequence. Current work within cognitive neuroscience (Carey 1998, Hauser, Carey & Hauser 2000) suggests that num-

---

[2] We will ignore features of the grammar which seem to involve "counting" from one to two, eg Verb Second in Germanic, the distribution of Wackernagel's clitics and the role of Bounding nodes in extraction. Many analyses of these phenomena have been proposed which derive these effects from other principles, see e.g., Halpern 1995, and the works in Halpern and Zwicky 1996.

[3] For example, in the theoretical framework of HPSG, the lexicon is often organized in hierarchies (see Pollard and Sag 1987).

ber may be built into the structure of language, but only within the limits of the 'subitizing range', from one to three or four. Although infants (and some animals) are born with the capacity to represent number in sets of objects up to about four, the ability to use linguistic symbols to count to four and beyond only appears in children later, after the acquisition of syntax (Hauser 2000:62). Importantly, the structure of natural language appears to reflect the cognitive limitations of the subitizing range: attested systems of number encode numerosity up to three or four (singular/dual/trial/plural) but not beyond, and languages may contain series of numerals at the low end of the numeral sequence which have distinct morphosyntactic properties, but not above about four (Hurford 2002). To conclude, then, the principle of structure-dependency may be related to hard-wired cognitive constraints on the ability to use linguistic symbols to denote numerosities. Natural languages may appear to invoke rules which involve "counting", but only up to three or four, because that is the maximum number of objects which can be represented without recourse to a linguistic system.

This paper discusses the case and numeral systems of Inari Saami in light of these generalisations. Inari Saami is extremely unusual in that the sequence of numerals up to 6 has different case-assigning properties to numerals 7 and above, suggesting that in this language either a syntactic counting rule is invoked or that at least a part of the lexicon is stored as an ordered string. Section 2 presents the relevant data from Inari Saami. Section 3 discusses these data in light of Case Theory and the distinction between lexical and structural case, and proposes an analysis invoking the notion of direct case. Section 4 looks at numerals in the grammar from a cross-linguistic perspective. We argue that the facts from Inari Saami show that "counting" rules, although typologically rare, do occur in numeral systems. This means that in some cases at least, the syntax does require knowledge of the value of a word in a numerical series, thus apparently violating the principles of structure-dependency and an unordered lexicon.

2 Case and Numerals in Inari Saami: The Data

In Inari Saami, one of the Saami languages spoken in the North of Finland around Lake Inari, there is a split between numerals six and seven with respect to the case marking on the following noun[4] (Sammallahti 1998:70, Olthuis 2000:191[5]). Numerals with values 2-6 assign genitive case to the

[4] Inari Saami has this in common with the other Eastern Saami languages, Skolt, Akkala, Kildin, and Ter Saami. This system differs from that of Finnish and other Finnic languages, where partitive case is assigned to numerals 2 and higher.

[5] Olthuis (2000:191) claims that numerals based on 2-6 in multiples of one hundred and one thousand (i.e. 200-600 and 2000-6000) also pattern like the core numerals 2-6 for the purposes

NPs they quantify, while those with values 7 and higher assign partitive case:

(1) a. kyehti/kulmâ/nelji /vittâ/kuttâ poccuu
two /three /four /five /six reindeer.gen.sg

b. kyehti/kulmâ/nelji /vittâ/kuttâ päärni
two /three /four /five /six child.gen.sg

(2) a. čiččâm /kávci /ovce /love /kyehtnubáloh /čyeti … poccud[6]
seven /eight /nine /ten /twelve /100… reindeer.part.sg

b. čiččâm /kávci /ovce /love / kyehtnubáloh / čyeti … pärnid
seven /eight /nine /ten /twelve /100… child.part.sg

Let us first look at the numerals 2-6. Genitive and accusative case are in fact homophonous in Inari Saami singular nouns. The only piece of evidence that the nouns carry genitive and not accusative case marking comes from judgments that most speakers are reluctant to give. The only way to tell is to try to elicit phrases like 'two fours', where 'four' is does not refer to the nominalization of the number (such as 'a number four'), but the actual numeral itself.[7] In these cases, the quantified numeral seems to be in genitive case. However, this construction does not occur in natural speech. It could therefore be argued that the noun following 2-6 is actually in accusative case. When the NP is an object, like in (3-4), it would under such an hypothesis be difficult to say whether the numeral demands an accusative noun, or whether the noun is in accusative case because accusative is the normal object case marking:

of case assignment. While this would make the Inari Saami system even more unique from a typological standpoint, the authors were unable to elicit this pattern from any other IS informant.

[6] There is an alternative partitive singular form in use for this noun: *puásujid*. This is a dialectal variant. What is important is that all speakers distinguish between genitive and partitive.

[7] Thanks to Pekka Sammallahti for pointing this out to us.

(3) Mun jiem oomâst kulmâ poccuu.
I.nom not.1sg own three reindeer.acc/gen.sg
'I don't own three reindeer.'

(4) Mun uáinám kulmâ kieδâ.
I.nom see.1sg three hand.acc/gen.sg
'I see three hands.'

However, when the NP containing a numeral is a subject, the noun still gets accusative (or genitive) case marking, although the normal subject case is nominative:

(5) a. Kulmâ kieδâ išeδii muu.
three hand.acc/gen.sg helped.3pl me.acc
'Three hands helped me.'

b. *Kulmâ kietâ išeδii muu.
three hand.nom.sg helped.3pl me.acc

(6) a. Nelji poccuu ruottii meddâl.
four reindeer.acc/gen.sg ran.3pl away
'Four reindeer ran away.'

b. *Nelji puásui ruottii meddâl.
four reindeer.nom.sg ran.3pl away

The examples in (3-6) show that nominals following the numerals two through six are assigned genitive/accusative case, regardless of the syntactic position of the NP containing them. In the rest of this paper, we will assume that these nominals are indeed in genitive case, following Sammallahti (1998).

Nominals following numerals of value 7 and higher are partitive,[8] regardless of whether the NP is a syntactic subject or object:

---

[8] Unlike in Finnish, partitive case is generally unproductive in the Saami languages and does not encode aspectual information. In Inari Saami, partitive is used after numerals, and by some speakers also in comparative expressions:

i. Sun lii muδe puárrsup.
he is I.part older
'He is older than me.'

(7) a. Čiččâm poccud láá tobbeen.
seven reindeer.part.sg are.3pl there
'Seven reindeer are there.'

b. *Čiččâm puásui láá tobbeen.
Seven reindeer.nom.sg are.3pl there

(8) a. Tun oinih kyehtnubáloh poccud.
You.nom saw.2sg twelve reindeer.part.sg
'You(sg) saw twelve reindeer.'

b. *Tun oinih kyehtnubáloh poccuu.
You.nom saw.2sg twelve reindeer.acc/gen.sg

The noun *poccud* in (7) must bear partitive case, not nominative, although it is the subject. Likewise, in (8), the object is necessarily partitive, not accusative (or genitive).

Another interesting fact illustrated by the examples above is that singular nouns in genitive and partitive case trigger plural subject agreement on the verb (5a, 6a, 7a). This suggests that the numeral, not the noun, is the syntactic head of the quantified noun phrase in Inari Saami and encodes the morphosyntactic feature NUMBER.

NumP

Num → [+CASE] NP

In contrast, in Finnish, numerals 2 and higher assign partitive singular case to nouns they quantify, but verb agreement is singular:[9]

(9) a. Yhdeksän omena-a puto-si maa-han.
nine.nom apple.part.sg fall.past.3s earth.ill
'Nine apples fell to earth.'

b *Yhdeksän omena-a puto-sivat maa-han.
nine.nom apple.part.sg fall.past.3p earth.ill

[9] Plural agreement is possible also in Finnnish, if the subject is interpreted as highly specific or definite.

In the examples in (9), the verb seems to agree with the singular partitive noun *omenaa* as if it were the phrasal head. Numerals in Finnish and Inari Saami, then, have very different properties with respect to phrasal agreement; we leave this issue open for future research.

The numeral one in Inari Saami, *ohtâ*, patterns differently from the other numerals. Firstly, nominals quantified by *ohtâ* are transparent to normal structural case marking to the phrase as a whole:

(10) Ohtâ kietâ lii tobbeen.
One.nom hand.nom.sg is.3sg there
'One hand is there.'

(11) Mun uáinám oovtâ kieδâ.
I.nom see.1sg one.acc hand.acc.sg
'I see one hand.'

In (10-11), the noun is case marked according to grammatical function; the subject is nominative and the object is accusative. Secondly, the numeral one, *ohtâ*, inflects for structural case to agree with the noun. Because *ohtâ* patterns so differently from the other numerals, the remainder of the discussion in this paper will focus on the higher value numerals.

All the examples we have seen until now concern grammatically case marked noun phrases. That is, we have only looked at canonical subjects and objects, which are normally assigned nominative and accusative case, respectively. Let us now turn to noun phrases that receive other types of case marking, for example locative. There are two possibilities: either this kind of case marking overrides the genitive case assigned by the numerals 2-6 and the partitive assigned by the numerals 7 and higher, or the case assigned by the numerals overrides the lexical and semantic case marking. We find that the first hypothesis is correct. Consider examples (12-13):

(12) a. **Muste** laa kuttâ poccuu.
I.loc are.3pl six reindeer.acc.sg
'I have three reindeer.'

b. Kuulmâ **poccust** lii ennuu purrâmâš.
Three reindeer.loc.sg is.3sg much food.nom
'Three reindeer have a lot of food.'

c. Čiččâm **poccust** lii ennuu purrâmâš.
seven reindeer.loc.sg is.3sg much food.nom
'Seven reindeer have a lot of food.'

(13) a. Mun adelim kiirjijd **almai/almaid.**
I.nom gave book.acc.pl man.ill.sg/man.ill.pl
'I gave books to the man/the men.'

b. Mun adelim kiirjijd viiδâ **almai.**
I.nom gave book.acc.pl five man.ill.sg
'I gave books to five men.'

c. Mun adelim kiirjijd käävci **almai.**
I.nom gave book.acc.pl eight man.ill.sg
'I gave books to eight men.'

The first argument of the possessive construction in (12) (literally 'on X is Y', where X is the possessor and Y is the item possessed) takes locative case, as we see in (12a). The head noun of the first NP also bears locative case, although it is preceded by a numeral which normally assigns singular genitive (12b), or partitive (12c). The indirect object of the verb *addeliđ* 'to give' in Inari Saami normally bears illative case, as illustrated by (13a). As we can see, this is not overridden by the numeral case assignments (13b-c).

Table 1 summarizes the generalizations that emerge from the data presented in this section:

	Grammatically case-marked subject	Grammatically case-marked object	Lexically or semantically case marked NP
Ns not modified by numerals; Ns modified by the number one	nominative	accusative	lexical/semantic case-marking wins
Ns modified by the numbers 2-6	genitive	genitive	"
Ns modified by the numbers 7 and higher	partitive	partitive	"

Table 1

Before we discuss why the numeral split between 6 and 7 is problematic for theories of grammar and the lexicon, we need to identify the type of case (structural, semantic or lexical) being assigned by the numeral to the noun it governs. The mechanisms underlying case assignment in Inari Saami are analysed in the next section.

3 How Numerals in Inari Saami Assign Case

We have seen in the previous section that numerals 2-6 in Inari Saami assign genitive case to the nouns they govern, while numerals 7 and above assign partitive, regardless of the structural position of the NumP. However, when the entire NumP gets locative case marking from the verb, the case assigned by the numeral gets overridden. In order to clarify the lexical properties of the numerals in question, it is necessary to work out which type of case they assign to the nouns they quantify. According to standard Case Theory, there are at least four main types:

i. semantic
ii. lexical (inherent/thematic)
iii. lexical (idiosyncratic)
iv. structural (syntactic)

Semantic case is associated with semantically transparent non-arguments (typically adverbials). Since we can assume that the numerals and nouns are in some type of head-complement relationship, this option can be ruled out.

Yip, Maling & Jackendoff (1987) distinguish between two kinds of lexical case. The first type is associated with thematic arguments of verbs, linked with particular structural positions. In addition, they argue, cases may be assigned lexically within NPs to, for example, possessors (though not in Icelandic, the main language discussed in their paper). The problem with analysing numerically-assigned genitive and partitive as lexical case is that it is unclear what sort of *thematic* role a numeral might assign to a noun it quantifies. The numeral-noun relationship within a noun phrase is distinct from more clear-cut environments for lexical case, for example possessor-noun, in which the case-marked element is linked to a well-defined thematic argument. Supposing we did want to analyse the accusative and partitive as thematic lexical cases, another problem soon arises. Why would the relationship between numerals 2-6 have a different *thematic* relationship to the nouns they quantify from numerals 7 and above, which results in the realisation of a different morphological case? It is clear then, that the partitive-genitive alternation under numerals in Inari Saami is in some sense due to special lexical properties of either numerals 2-6 or 7 and above, but this does not entail that these numerals assign thematic lexical case.

The other type of lexical case in Yip, Maling and Jackendoff's (1987) model is idiosyncratic in nature, and cannot be predicted by thematic relations. This type of case is associated with, for example, accusative and genitive "quirky" subjects in Icelandic. Since there is no evidence in Inari Saami for semantically- or thematically-based case assignment by numerals, the simplest analysis for the patterns of data presented above is that one case assigned by numerals is a structural default, and the other is an idiosyncratic lexical case.[10] Since numerals 7 and above form an infinite set, it makes sense to posit the special lexical case feature as being associated with the smaller subset of numerals 2-6, which assign genitive case. Numerals 7 and above, then, assign partitive case structurally as a default.[11]

i. numerals 2-6: assign genitive case (lexical case)
ii. numerals 7 and above: assign partitive case (structural default)

If this analysis is correct, the question remains as to what happens to these cases when quantified NPs are embedded under lexical case assigning verbs. Yip, Maling and Jackendoff's (1987:240) analysis makes the following prediction, again to capture patterns of case in Icelandic:

> Lexical case on an NP always blocks/inhibits assignment of syntactic [structural] case to that NP.

Work on "case conflict" in Free Relatives (FRs), where a single argument has the potential to get case both from the matrix verb and from the subordinate predicate, reaches similar conclusions. For instance, Vogel (2000) notes that cross-linguistically, it is structural cases that get suppressed in free relatives, not obliques. Vogel argues that case-matching facts from German and other Indo-European languages show that cross-linguistically, where two cases may potentially be assigned to a single NP, it is the structural cases (nominative and accusative) which will be overridden by oblique cases (dative, locative etc) rather than vice-versa. If a matrix verb imposes nominative or accusative case on its relative clause complement, this case will always be suppressed in favour of the case assigned by the verb inside the free relative (14). If the matrix verb imposes an oblique case on the relative pronoun, then it can only appear in free relatives where

---

[10] See Ojeda (1997) for a similar analysis of Classical Arabic.

[11] See, for example, Vainikka & Maling (1996) and Nelson (1998) for arguments that partitive is a structural case in Finnish.

the relative verb also requires an oblique case (15) (German, from Vogel 2000:3):

(14) a. Weil uns besucht, wer Maria mag. (FR verb requires nom)
because us-acc visits, who-nom Maria-acc likes
"...because whoever likes Maria is visiting us."

b. Weil uns besucht, wen Maria mag. (FR verb requires acc)
because us-acc visits, who-acc Maria-nom likes
"...because whoever Maria likes is visiting us."

c. Weil uns besucht, wem Maria vertraut. (FR requires dat)
because us-acc visits, who-dat Maria-nom trusts
"...because whoever Maria trusts is visiting us."

(15) a. Ich folge wem immer ich **vertraue**
I follow who-dat ever I trust
'I follow whomever I trust'

b. *Ich folge wen immer ich **bewundere**
I follow who-acc ever I adore
folgen 'follow'assigns dative, *bewundern* 'adore' assigns accusative

In the construction in (14), the matrix verb requires a structural case-marked complement in nominative case. However, the pronoun always receives case from the verb inside the free relative clause, whether it is nominative (14a), accusative (14b) or dative (14c). The structural case assigned by the matrix is therefore suppressed in favour of the FR verb's case. On the other hand, if the matrix verb requires an oblique dative complement (15), then this case cannot be overidden by the structural case assigned by the lower verb as in (14), as shown in (15b). Instead, the cases assigned by both verbs must match (15a). Similar patterns emerge in Modern Greek, Spanish and Romanian. This suggests that cross-linguistically, if a single argument can get case from two lexical heads, it is the structural case which gets supressed in favour of the oblique case.

Given this prediction, embedded NPs headed by numerals 7 and above pattern as expected in Inari Saami: lexical locative case assigned by the verb suppresses the structural case (partitive) assigned by the numeral. This is shown in example (13c) with the ditransitive verb *addelið*, 'to give', repeated here as (16). (Ditransitive verbs are assumed to license a case-assigning VP-shell[12] (Larson 1988)):

(16) Mun adelim kiirjijd käävci **almai**.
I.nom gave book.acc.pl eight man.ill.sg
'I gave books to eight men.'

(17)

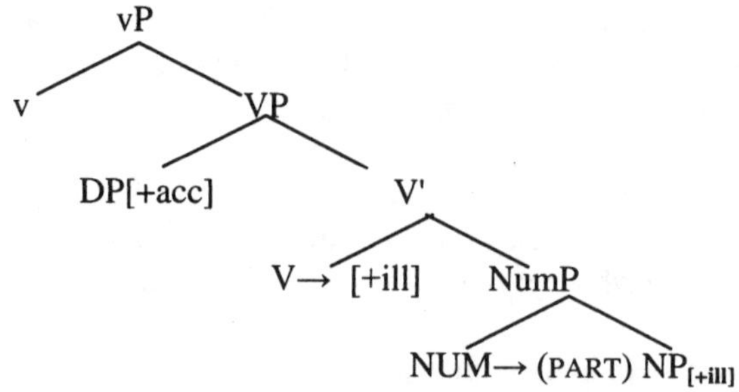

For NumPs quantified by numerals 2-6, however, a problem arises. Recall from section 2 that evidence from agreement suggests that it is the numeral, not the noun, which heads the number phrase in Inari Saami. If the head numerals 2-6 assign lexical rather than structural case to the nouns they quantify, then why does the lexical case assigned by the verb appear to suppress the more local lexical case assigned by the numeral? This is the pattern seen in (13b), repeated here as (18):

(18) Mun adelim kiirjijd viiδâ **almai**.
I.nom gave book.acc.pl five man.ill.sg
'I gave books to five men.'

(19)

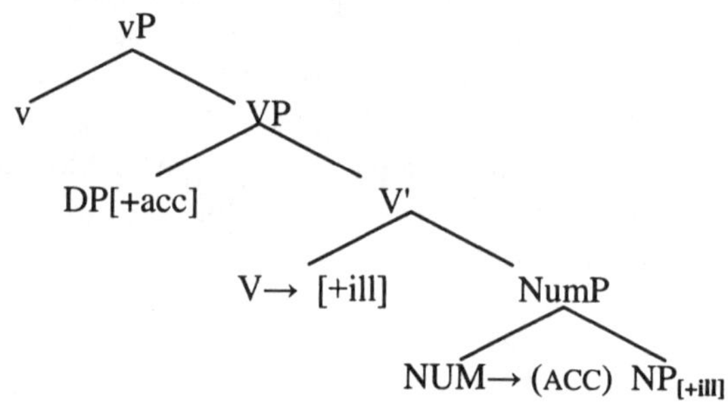

---

[12] It is not relevant for the current discussion whether case is assigned under sisterhood or checked under spec-head agreement via functional projections.

If the genitive case assigned by the numeral is genuinely lexical, then basic morphological principles dictate that case realized on the numeral should reflect the case assigned by the more local (governing) specific assigning head, ie genitive assigned by the numeral. Instead, genitive case is overridden by illative case assigned by the distal head. Genitive case behaves like a structural case here, although it is lexically assigned.

What we need, then, is an approach in which lexical genitive has different properties from lexical illative. Woolford (in press) looks at examples where more than one case is available to a given NP. For example, she notes that nominative objects in languages like Icelandic are disallowed when the subject is lexical accusative (*ACC-NOM case frame), but allowed when the subject shows lexical dative (yielding the case frame DAT-NOM): cross-linguistically, nominative objects are licensed if the subject is dative or ergative, but not if it is nominative or accusative (structural or lexical). She argues that in order to make the right generalizations, it is necessary to distinguish the type of case (direct [+s] vs oblique [-s]) from the way in which it is assigned (lexically vs structurally). Accusative case, whether structural or lexical, is always less marked than dative. Woolford (2001) invokes a constraint hierarchy in which a highly-ranked faithfulness constraint will ensures that inherent dative case assigned by verbs "wins" over accusative, regardless of whether it is lexical or structural:

nominative < accusative < dative
direct case < oblique case

This analysis can easily be extended to Inari Saami, where lexical illative patterns like dative, and genitive assigned by numerals is equivalent to accusative. In Inari Saami, Faithfulness is highly ranked, so illative case inherently assigned by verbs will suppress direct genitive. This extension of Woolford's claim seems reasonable in light of the fact that genitive is often a structural case (see, e.g., Vainikka 1989). If Inari Saami numerals assign direct genitive case, then there is no direct conflict between two lexical cases in cases like (18).

In this section, the morphosyntactic properties of the cases assigned by numerals were analysed in detail. The genitive case feature assigned by Inari Saami numerals 2-6 was argued to be distinct from other types of lexical cases, such as locative. The case assigning properties of Inari Saami numerals can thus be summarized as follows:

i. numerals 2-6: assign genitive case (lexical case)
ii. numerals 7 and above: assign partitive case (structural default)

The question remains, however, as to how a rule like (i) gets acquired if the lexicon consists of an unordered set. This issue is addressed in the next section.

4 Numerals in the Grammar and Lexicon

In the previous section, we provided an analysis of case morphology within Numeral Phrases in Inari Saami. We argued that partitive case is assigned by numerals 7 and higher as a structural default, and that numerals 2-6 are specified for a lexical feature that assigns genitive case to the quantified noun. This means that numerals 2-6 must form a special lexical subclass in Inari Saami. But if this is the case, several important questions arise about the structure of the lexicon and the grammar. If the lexicon does indeed consist of an unordered set, and if no rule of the grammar can be sensitive to the linear order of elements in a sequence or string, then:

a) How is this subset acquired? Does a child acquiring Inari Saami have to use a rule in the lexicon or grammar that counts to acquire this special subset?
b) How is information relating to lexical classes and subclasses organised in the lexicon?

The evidence from Inari Saami suggests that core numerals in the lexicon are not listed in an unordered, idiosyncratic fashion. Instead, it appears that they are listed in an ordered sequence, and lexically specified morphosyntactic properties may be acquired and stored in a way that is sensitive to this sequence.

Because numerals make up an infinite set in every language, they represent a unique class of lexical item. Hurford (1975, 1987) argues for a set of (language-specific) syntactic rules underlying the generation of higher-value *complex numerals* which draws on a core set of *lexical numerals*. Once the set of rules for forming numerals has been acquired, a speaker of a language is able to compute and generate an unlimited number of numerals; in this respect higher-level numerals behave more like phrasal categories than lexical heads (words). However, the generation of complex numerals is taken to preserve the category label, and therefore the syntactic distribution, of the input. For example, the English complex numeral *thirty-four thousand, six hundred and eighty-eight* (34,688) has the same syntactic properties as the numeral *thirty-four thousand, six hundred and eighty-seven* (34,687) because the operation that derives the new numeral has no effect on the category label of the input. Thus for every rule R that generates a new lexical item deriving the complex numeral N_2 from N_1, we can say that rule R does not affect the set of morphosyntactic properties of the input lexeme. If N_1 encodes for example the features [+N, +feminine] in a given language, N_2 should possess an identical set of features in its lexical entry. In other words, the arithmetic value of the complex numeral is predicted to have no bearing on its syntactic distribution or its morphosyntactic properties.

While this generalisation may apply to higher-level complex numerals formed by syntactic processes, the picture is less clear with the core lexical numerals of lower value which form the input to the syntactic processes mentioned above, such as 1-10, 100, and so on. Hurford (2002) notes that lexical numerals are not homogeneous with respect to morphosyntactic properties; cross-linguistically, these numerals may fall into special subclasses. For example, the numerals 1-4 in Icelandic inflect for case and gender, while 5 and above are indeclinable[13]:

(20) Icelandic accusative case-marked numerals

	1	2	3	4	5	6	...
masc	einn	tvo	þrjá	fjóra	fimm	sex	
fem	eina	tvaer	þrjár	fjórar	fimm	sex	
neut	eitt	tvö	þrjú	fjögur	fimm	sex	

In contrast to the higher-level complex numerals, then, the morphosyntactic properties of lexical numerals may vary according to their numeric value.

The simplest explanation for this type of variation among lower value numerals is that they are subject to a lexical override specification, which causes them to be exempt from a more general rule of the grammar. The default rule of the grammar of Icelandic is that numerals do not inflect for case and gender with the head noun. The lexical entries for certain numerals in Icelandic might contain an override like the following:

override: lexical entries for {1, 2, 3, 4}: inflect for case, gender

Other examples of similar lexical subsets cross-linguistically include (Hurford 2002, Muravyova 1998:530):

---

[13] In some other languages, syntactic properties of the output numeral may be determined by the final digit in the string. For example, in Icelandic the numerals 1-4 and all complex numerals ending in the digits 1-4 decline, while all other numerals are indeclinable.

Russian: 2-4 assign genitive singular to noun, 5-10 assign genitive plural
Albanian: 1-4 separate numerals for definite/indefinite
Maltese: distinct ordinals only up to 4th
Chukchee: lexical numerals 1-5 only; 6+ formed as complex compounds.

All of these patterns can be explained by appealing to the presence of lexically specified override rules. However, if we make the crucial assumption that the lexicon consists of an *unordered* list, we would expect some languages to contain special subsets of lexical numerals that are not contiguous, for example:

2, 5, 9 decline, all others indeclinable
3, 6 and 8 assign genitive case, all others assign nominative case

In fact, as the examples above suggest, rules like (4) and (5) are unattested (Greville Corbett pers comm); special subsets of lexical numerals invariably form a sequence, and always at the low value end of the numeral set.[14] In other words, it is not a coincidence that it is not the case that only the numerals 3, 6 and 8 inflect in Icelandic; children do not seem to be able to acquire this type of rule for numerals. But if this is the case, how do they acquire these sets of numerals without "counting"? How do these special subclasses arise in a lexicon without reference to the linear order of elements in a numerical sequence? It is important to note that numerals up to and including four seem to be of special significance in natural language. As mentioned above, Icelandic, Albanian and Russian all have special sets of numerals 1-4; languages grammaticalise number up to trial or perhaps quadral (four), but no attested language grammaticalises numerals above this (Corbett to appear). In an overwhelming majority of cases, any special sequence of numerals in a given language will not exceed four (Hurford 2002). From a typological standpoint, then, a clear numerical effect emerges from the cross-linguistic data.

Several explanations have been put forth to account for this cross-linguistic pattern. Hurford's (and Bloom's 2000) explanation of the special status of the lower numerals involves frequency effects: numerals up to three or four occur with much higher frequency than other numerals, so there is pressure on languages to distinguish them as a separate lexical subclass. This explanation does not challenge the basic principle of "no count-

[14] With the possible exception of Modern Greek, in which numerals 1, 3 and 4, but not 2, are morphologically marked for gender (Hurford 2002).

ing" in the grammar or lexicon: it is the higher frequency of certain numerals in the input, rather then the numeric value of the numeral per se, which allows these numerals to display morphological or syntactic properties distinct from other numerals. For higher-value numerals, however, data from language corpora challenge the frequency explanation. Although it is true that numerals 1-3 do appear to be statistically more frequent than other numerals, there is not a straightforward inverse correlation between the value of a numeral and its frequency among those of higher value. For example, a Spanish frequency dictionary (Juillard & Chang-Rodriguez 1964) lists the numeral *cinco* (five) as more frequent than *cuatro* (four), and *ocho* (eight) as more frequent than *siete* (seven). Frequency effects, therefore, may explain how children acquire special subsets of numerals to three or four, but do not provide a robust explanation for the unusual behavior of Inari Saami numerals up to the value six.[15]

Within the cognitive science literature, the relationship between number and language has been the subject of much current debate (Carey 1998, Hauser & Carey 2000, Hauser 2000, Simon 1999, Wynn 1995). What is clear from recent work in this field is that human and animal brains conceptualise number in more than one way (Hauser 2000:52-4). Number may be represented in a non-numeric 'analog' system, where ratios are important; rats, for instance, can distinguish between one and two objects and eight and sixteen objects using this system. Number may also be represented in an 'object file' system, where each object being "counted" is stored in a particuar slot in memory. Using this type of "counting", rhesus monkeys can distinguish between two apples and three apples, or three apples and four apples (Hauser et al 2000). Due to short-term memory limitations, however, number representations of this type only calculate values of up to three or four, so monkeys are unable to distinguish between five and six apples, for instance. This may be the type of representation used during subitizing, the method whereby animals and humans rapidly calculate numbers of objects up to three or four with a quick glance (Hauser et al 2000:832).

However, humans appear to be the only species that can represent number by way of the third method, a 'count sequence', in which a unique linguistic symbol is mapped onto a unique numerosity, associated with its

[15] For languages which contain special subsets for 1-5, another explanation is available. In Chukchee, for example, lexical numerals only go up to five, with higher numerals being formed as complex compounds. This system may be based on finger-counting (Muravyova 1998:530). Interestingly, there is evidence from language impairment (Gerstmann's syndrome) and brain imaging that finger counting may involve a special locus in the neural circuitry of the brain (Simon 1999). Again, however, this approach does not work for Inari Saami numerals, since very few people have six fingers on each hand.

relative value in a series. This allows human language to represent an infinite number of exact numerosities. Crucially, this fundamental distinction between object file and analog number representation on the one hand, and linguistic counting on the other, may underlie the special status of the numeral values 3-4 in natural language. Languages may invoke rules which range over special sets of numerals up to the value four precisely because the brain does not have to "count" to four. Beyond the value four, only humans may manipulate linguistic symbols to count and operate on higher value numerals.

This skill appears to be linked to linguistic development. Wynn (1995) shows that very young babies seem to have a prelinguistic awareness of numerosity: in experiments, seven-month-olds, like monkeys, are sensitive to the difference between two and three objects. At the single-word stage, experiments show that English-speaking children are aware of what number words are (ie that they are sensitive to the syntactic context of quantification), and that they refer to numerals greater than one (Bloom 2000). But it takes much longer, up to a year, for children to develop the ability to count using number words, and therefore to understand that number words refer to sets of objects of a particular numerical value. The fact that children go through a stage where they understand the concept of number, and they understand that words may refer to numbers, but they cannot attach number words to numerical values suggests that the ability to count is not an innate *linguistic* ability; instead, it may be related to the acquisition of the lexicon and syntax (Hauser 2000:62-63). However, Bloom notes that once they have developed the relevant cognitive skills to link number words up to three to particular sets of objects, children rapidly acquire higher numerals four, five, six, seven and so on, and are able to count objects using these words. This shows that higher value lexical numerals such as six and seven are acquired by mapping words onto numerical sequences; children learn the denotation of these words *as they learn to count*. If this is the case, then children must be acquiring and storing lexical items in a particular linear order, along with morphosyntactic features which are sensitive to this linear order. For the acquisition of higher value numerals, then, counting is both possible and necessary.

What is interesting from our point of view is that human languages seem to strongly disfavour rules of the grammar that invoke this advanced skill, perhaps because it is not part of the innate package of abilities a child is born with. Going back to work in early generative grammar, the question remains then as to whether human languages allow rules based on counting at all. Based on the evidence presented above, we would like to propose that the genitive case assignment feature for numerals 2-6 in Inari Saami is acquired and implemented in a way that is sensitive to the numerical value of the numeral in a sequence. A child acquiring Inari Saami, then, must be able to represent number using a count series, and count to six and seven, in order to acquire and use the case assigning rule. The importance of the data from Inari Saami is that it shows that linguistic rules that invoke counting above four, although extremely rare, can be part of the grammars of natural languages.

5 Conclusion

In this paper, we have discussed the interaction of numerals and nouns in Inari Saami, both from the point of view of theoretical syntax (specifically Case Theory) and within the context of debates about the cognitive representation and acquisition of numerals. New data was presented which showed that Inari Saami has a unique system of numerals, where a "split" occurs between numerals 6 and 7 with respect to the type of case they assign to the nouns they quantify. As we have seen, this raises important questions about the difference between lexical and structural case. The case marking system of Inari Saami numerals can be understood if we assume that the numerals 2-6 assign lexical genitive case which gets suppressed by more marked cases inherently assigned; this accounts for the patterns of interaction between numerals, nouns, and lexical cases assigned by verbs. We assume that nominals following numbers 7 and higher are assigned partitive by default, and the numbers 2-6 override this case marking lexically. However, this hypothesis leaves unexplained why the numerals with lexically specified case marking form a sequence of consecutive numbers.

In light of the data, we discuss the relationship between numerals and "counting" in the grammar. We argue that natural languages may contain rules that "count" up to about four, especially with respect to special sets of numerals, because of the essentially nonlinguistic way the brain represents smaller value numerals. The data from Inari Saami, however, suggests that languages may also contain rules that require a higher level of cognitive development: children must learn to label numerals in a count sequence *before* they acquire certain higher level numerals; and the morphosyntactic features encoded by these higher numerals are sensitive to the order of the numeral in a string.

References

Bloom, P. 2000. *How Children Learn the Meanings of Words*. Cambridge: MIT Press.

Carey, S. 1998. Knowledge of Number: Its Evolution and Ontogeny. *Science* 282(5389):641-2.

Chomsky, N. 1965. *Aspects of the Theory of Syntax*. Cambridge, MA: MIT Press.

Corbett, G. to appear. Number. *Language Typology and Linguistic Universals: An International Handbook*, eds. M. Haspelmath, E. König, W. Oestereicher and W. Raible. Berlin: de Gruyter.

Halpern, A. 1995. *On the Placement and Morphology of Clitics*. Stanford, CA: CSLI Publications.

Halpern, A. and Zwicky, A. 1996. *Approaching Second: Second Position Clitics and Related Phenomena*. Stanford, CA: CSLI Publications.

Hauser, M. 2000. *Wild Minds: What Animals Really Think*. Allen Lane, Penguin Press.

Hauser, M., Carey, S. and Hauser, L. 2000. Spontaneous Number Representation in Semi-free-ranging Rhesus Monkeys. *Proceedings of the Royal Society of London, Series B: Biological Sciences* 267(1445):829-33.

Hurford, J. 1975. *The Linguistic Theory of Numerals*. Cambridge: Cambridge University Press.

Hurford, J. 1987. *Language and Number*. Oxford: Basil Blackwell.

Hurford, J. 2002. The Interaction Between Numerals and Nouns. *Noun Phrase Structure in the Languages of Europe*, ed. F. Planck. European Science Foundation, EUROTYP project.

Juillard A. G. & Chang-Rodriguez, E. 1964. *Frequency Dictionary of Spanish Words*. The Hague: Mouton.

Larson, R. 1988. On the Double Object Construction. *Linguistic Inquiry* 19:335-392.

Muravyova, I. A. 1998. Chukchee. *The Handbook of Morphology*, eds. A. Spencer & A. Zwicky, 521-538. Oxford: Blackwell.

Nelson, D. 1998. *Grammatical Case Assignment in Finnish*. New York: Garland.

Ojeda, Almerindo 1997. How to Define Number Categories: A Lesson from Semitic. *Proceedings of CLS* 33, eds. K. Singer, R. Eggert, and G. Anderson.

Olthuis, Marja-Liisa 2000. *Kielâoppâ/ Inarinsaamenkielen Kielioppi*. Finland: Sämitigge.

Pollard, C. and Sag, I. 1987. *Information-Based Syntax and Semantics, Volume 1: Fundamentals*. CSLI Lecture Notes no. 13. Stanford, CA: CSLI Publications.

Sammallahti, P. 1998. *The Saami Languages: An Introduction*. Karasjok, Norway: Davvi Girji OS.

Sammallahti, P. & Morottaja, M. 1993. *Säämi-Suomâ Sänikirje / Inarin-saamelais-suomalainen sanakirja* [Inari Saami-Finnish Dictionary]. Ohcejohka: Girjegiisá Oy.

Simon, T. 1999. The Foundations of Numerical Thinking in a Brain Without Numbers. *Trends in Cognitive Sciences* 3(10):365-6.

Williams, E. 1994. Remarks on Lexical Knowledge. *The Acquisition of the Lexicon*, eds. L. Gleitman & B. Landau, 7-34. Cambridge, MA: MIT Press.

Vainikka, A. 1989. Deriving Syntactic Representations in Finnish. PhD Dissertation, UMass Amherst.

Vainikka, A. & Maling, J. 1996. Is Partitive Case Inherent or Structural? *Partitives. Studies on the Syntax and Semantics of Partitive and Related Constructions*, ed. J. Hoeksema, 179-208. Berlin: Mouton de Gruyter.

Woolford, E. 2001. Case Patterns. *Optimality-Theoretic Syntax*, eds. G. Legendre, J. Grimshaw, and S. Vikner. Cambridge, MA: MIT Press.

Woolford, E. in press. Burzio's Generalization, Markedness, and Locality Constraints on Nominative Objects. *New Perspectives on Case Theory*, eds. E. Brandner & H. Zinsmeister. Stanford: CSLI.

Wynn, K. 1995. Origins of Numerical Knowledge. *Mathematical Cognition* 1:35-60.

Vogel, R. 2000. Surface matters: the typology of case conflicts in free relative constructions and its implications for Case Theory. Paper presented at the Case Theory Workshop, DGfS, Marburg March 1-3 2000.

Yip, M., Maling, J. & Jackendoff, R. 1987. Case in tiers. *Language* 63. 217-50.

11

Constraints on the Morphological Causatives in the Torne Dialect of North Sámi

MIKAEL SVONNI AND MIKAEL VINKA

1 Introduction*

This paper will be concerned with some aspects of the syntax of productive morphological causatives in North Sámi, specifically the Torne dialect. (1) below illustrates a simplex transitive Torne Sámi clause, and its causativized counterpart is given in (2):

(1)	Máhtte	cuvkii	láse
	Máhtte.n	break.Past.3s	window.a
	'Máhtte broke the window.'		

*We would like to thank the editors of this volume, Diane Nelson and Satu Manninen, for comments and criticism on an earlier version of this paper. We would also like to thank an anonymous reviewer. Thanks are also due to the following people: Mark Baker, Walcir Cardoso, Chris Collins, Mario Fadda, Lotus Goldberg, Hiro Hosoi, Sônia Katsuura, Mikinari Matsuoka, Jairo Nunes, Hanna Outakoski, Charles Reiss, Pablo Ruiz, Tomokazu Takehisa, Naoko Tomioka and Lisa Travis. All remaining errors etc. are our own responsibility.

The following non-standard abbreviations are used in the glosses throughout the paper: Act=actio, O = object, Dat = dative, Tr = transitive, Intr = intransitive, FV = final vowel.

Generative Approaches to Finnic and Saami Linguistics.
Diane Nelson and Satu Manninen (eds.).

(2) Mon cuvke-*h*-in Máhte láse.
I.n break.Tr-caus-Past.1s Máhtte.a window.a
'I caused Máhtte to break the window.'

The causative is derived by adding a suffix, -h-/ahtt-,[1] to the verb stem, which has the familiar effect of introducing a causative agent, in this particular example mon 'I.n'. The Causee, i.e. the noun corresponding to the logical subject in (1), is expressed as an accusative object.[2] The original object, however, remains unchanged. Moreover, a causative sentence may also be expressed as in (3), without an overt Causee.

(3) Mon cuvke-*h*-in láse.
I.n break.Tr-caus-Past.1s window.a
'I caused someone to break the window.'

Notice that the causative agent is interpreted as the entity that causes the embedded event in (3), but it itself is not understood as the agent of that event (cf. Chomsky 1988:13). We will consistently denote this semantically implicit Causee as 'someone' in the translations.

Primia facie, there are two possible ways to treat a sentence like (3). On the one hand, the covert Causee may be phonologically null, but nonetheless syntactically realized, for instance as *pro*, in which case (2) and (3) would be syntactic equivalents. The other possibility that has been pursued in the literature is that (2) and (3) are syntactically distinct, such that the Causee in (3) is radically missing. Both possibilities exist in natural languages and given certain basic ingredients in the theory of Grammar, it is a fairly straightforward matter to tell the two apart. For instance, an overt and a null *pro* Causee should be detectable in phenomena that are sensitive to prominence relations, that is locality, whereas a radically missing Causee should act accordingly, namely not at all. In this paper we shall show, among other things, that the Torne Sámi sentences (2) and (3) are structurally distinct along these lines. However, we shall also see that the structural

[1]The causative suffix exhibits a phonologically governed allomorphy. When it attaches to vowel-final stems (corresponding to even-parity and contracted stems in Nielsen 1926-29 and Nickel 1994), as is the case in (2), the suffix is realized as -h-. However, when the stem ends in a consonant (Nielsen's 1926-29 and Nickel's 1994 odd-parity stems), the shape of the suffix is -aht(t)-; at least that is how it will be represented in this paper. It is probably more correct to say that -aht(t)- is -aht(t)V- (V=Vowel), but we will abstract away from this, for purely expository reasons.

[2]An anonymous reviewer correctly points out that other North Sámi variants marks the Causee with Illative Case (see also Nielsen 1926-9, Nickel 1994, Julien 1996). This option is however *not* available in the Torne dialect.

distinction falls out in a way that is quite different from what standard approaches to causativization in the Chomskian framework would initially beg us to expect.

This dual dichotomy goes back at least to Kayne (1975) who argued at length that causatives in some languages may appear in two distinct syntactic frames. A rich body of research in the syntax of causativization in especially various Romance languages has subsequently provided strong support for this hypothesis, e.g. Aissen (1979), Burzio (1986), Guasti (1993), to mention a few. The story goes like this. In causatives where the Causee is realized as an argument, direct or indirect object depending on case theoretic factors (cf. Baker 1988, Watanabe 1996), the causative verb is analyzed as taking a clausal complement. The Causee, in turn, is the viewed as the subject of the embedded clause. In other words, what we now have is a standard complementation structure, whose profile may be blurred by various factors, such as verb-incorporation in the sense of Baker (1988), which derives morphological causatives via V-to-V movement. In the absence of such movement, the causative is overtly periphrastic, rendering the complementation source visible to the naked eye. Kayne (1975) attaches the name *Faire Infinitive* (FI) to this kind of causative. The radically Causeeless variant, on the other hand, arises when the causative verb has the ability to take a truncated complement, specifically a bare VP. Setting aside the various VP-internal subject hypotheses that have evolved over the past decade and a half (cf. Kitagawa 1986, Kuroda 1988 and Koopman & Sportiche 1992), it follows that the complement of the causative verb does not include a subject position. Since there is no structural position where an argument Causee can originate, the complement will be subjectless and therefore the presence of an argument Causee cannot be facilitated. Following Kayne (1975), we refer to this variety of causatives as the *Faire Par* construction (FP).

According to Kayne's theory, the presence of a Causee that has unmistakable argument properties implies that the causative construction as a whole is an FI, and therefore the Causee is an embedded subject. Although we shall argue in this paper that the Causee in (2) is an argument and that (3) has no structural Causee at all, we shall also claim that *both* (2) and (3) instantiate the FP causative. This means, of course, that simply establishing whether the Causee is an argument or not, is not a sufficient criterion to diagnose FI-hood, although it is one of the necessary conditions. Therefore, the diagnostic pertaining to the realization of the Causee must be supplemented with some other, independent means to tell FIs and FPs apart. It is, for instance, generally recognized that the two causative types impose different restrictions on what kind of verb may be embedded under causation (Alsina 1992, Guasti 1993, 1996, Travis 1992). FIs are quite liberal in this regard, whereas FPs are possible only with a subset of the base verbs that are licit in the former. When this factor is incorporated in the overall picture we shall see that causatives in the Torne variant of North Sámi behave like FPs par excellence, regardless of whether the Causee is expressed or not, which sets this language apart from previously more well-studied languages such as French, Italian and Chichewa. This fact seriously limits the way (2) can be analyzed. In essence, we will be forced to the position that the Causee in (2) is syntactically distinct from the superficially similar cases in (4), which exemplify Chichewa and Italian FIs:

(4) a *Chichewa* (Alsina 1992:518)
Nungu i-na-phik-its-a kadzidzi maungu.
porcupine S-Past-cook-caus-FV owl pumpkins
'The porcupine made the owl cook the pumpkins.'

b *Italian* (Guasti 1996:295)
Ho fatto riparare la macchina a Gianni.
(I)have made repair the car Dat Gianni
'I made Gianni repair the car.'

Rather, the Torne Sámi Causee must be treated as an optional constituent, on a par with what we find in standard FPs like (5a) and (5b), where the Causee is expressed as an optional adjunct by-phrase.

(5) a *Chichewa* (Alsina 1992:518)
Nungu i-na-phik-its-a maungu (kwa kadzidzi).
porcupine S-Past-cook-caus-FV pumpkins by owl
'The porcupine had the pumpkins cooked by the owl.'

b *Italian* (Guasti 1996:295)
Ho fatto riparare la macchina (da Gianni)
(I) have made repair the car by Gianni
'I had the car repaired by Gianni.'

Specifically, we shall claim that the difference between (2) and (5) is technically related to the variable expression of, say, benefactive arguments, which may be expressed in PPs or as the first object in double object constructions. In other words, an argument Causee may be associated with syntactic properties that are distributed over various structural positions, while importantly there is no necessary derivational relation between such positions.

The paper is organized as follows. Section 2 will present some distinctions between Faire Infinitive and Faire Par causatives, focusing on issues pertaining to syntactic locality. In the process, we demonstrate that standard tests show that Torne Sámi display properties of both causative types. Section 3 deals with selectional asymmetries holding between FIs and FPs, such that FP causatives are subject to a restriction that the base verb must be agentive. From this additional perspective, we will conclude that Torne Sámi causatives must uniformly be treated as Faire Par constructions. We will also subject the agentivity restriction in the light of Kratzer's (1996) Voice Phrase hypothesis and the distribution of agent oriented rationale clauses. On these grounds we will motivate a further decomposition of the verb phrase, thus supporting work by Baker & Stewart (1999) and Pylkkänen (1999). In section 4 we address the issue of the Torne Sámi Causee, which does not immediately fit into the assumption that this language only facilitates FP causatives. We propose to assimilate the Causee, however, into a more familiar class of optional arguments, namely applied objects, thus arguing for a split between Chichewa and Romance style FPs and Torne Sámi FPs. Finally, section 5 provides some concluding remarks.

2 The Faire Infinitive and Faire Par Distinction

In this section we intend to show two things. Firstly, that the Torne Sámi accusative Causee is an argument, and secondly that the Causee is radically (i.e. syntactically) absent in the Causeeless construction. As we mentioned in the introductory section, there is a broad consensus that causative constructions may appear in at least two syntactic frames, namely what Kayne (1975) refers to as the FI and the FP. Kayne (1975) and Burzio (1986), for instance, have shown that these two causative types differ in various fine points, in ways that correlate to their different syntactic structures and therefore we will at times refer to this analysis as the Kayne-Burzio Hypothesis. We shall begin in Section 2.1 by considering some properties which has been taken to be defining of the FI and FP constructions, introducing the basic tenets of Kayne (1975) and Burzio (1986). In section 2.2. we consider the behavior of the causative types in passive contexts.

2.1 The Basic Distinctions

Recall from the introductry section that the FI causative is standardly analyzed as biclausal, along the lines shown in (6), where the causative verb takes a clausal complement, and consequently the Causee is treated as the subject of the embedded clause (Kayne 1975, Burzio 1986):

(6) *Faire Infinitive*

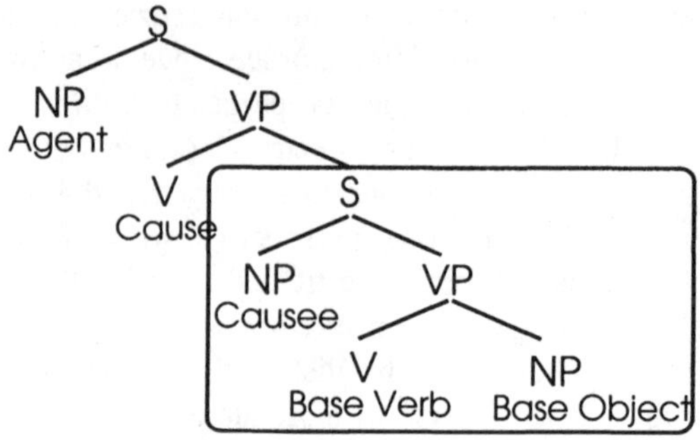

Because the Causee in (6) is an argument and a subject, and because it asymmetrically c-commands all material contained in its sister constituent, the Causee should play an active role in the formation of various A-dependencies. As is well-known, such dependencies and relations obey locality conditions that limit and constrain their applicability, harking back to Chomsky's (1973) Specified Subject Condition. A more contemporary formulation of the locality condition is found in the Minimal Link Condition (Chomsky 1995). To put it simply, the Minimal Link Condition states that in a configuration of the type [...α...β...γ...], where α asymmetrically c-commands β, and β asymmetrically c-commands γ, a relation cannot be established between α and γ. However, in such a scenario, a relation can as a matter of course be established between α and β as well as β and γ. Perhaps the most time-honored argument with this flavor in the study of causatives comes from binding phenomena (see for instance Kuno 1973 and Shibatani 1976). While the theory of binding is somewhat shrouded by uncertainties, it nontheless provides a good point of departure. Consider the sentences in (7):

(7) a *Italian* (Guasti 1996:295)

Ho fatto	riparare	la *propria*$_i$	macchina	**<u>a Gianni</u>**$_i$.
(I) have made	repair	the own	car	Dat Gianni

'I made Gianni repair his own car.'

b *Chichewa* (Alsina 1992:520)

Alimi	a-ku-lémb-éts-a	**<u>mkángó</u>**$_i$	ndakatulo	*yâke*$_i$.
farmers	S-Pres-write-caus-FV	lion	poem	his

'The farmers are making the lion$_i$ write his$_i$ poem.'

The idea is that the italicized element in each sentence can be A-bound by the underlined Causee, because the Causee is a subject. Although Italian and Chichewa exhibit some parametric differences in their case systems, which we shall return to below, the binding facts in (7) are quite in line with what one would expect under the assumption that these sentences are based on the syntactic structure (6).

As we have mentioned previously, Italian and Chichewa also have an alternative way to express causatives, namely so-called Faire Par constructions, which we encountered in (5) above. Kayne (1975) as well as Burzio (1986) propose the structure given in (8), arguing that the complement of the causative verb is a bare VP.

(8) *Faire Par*

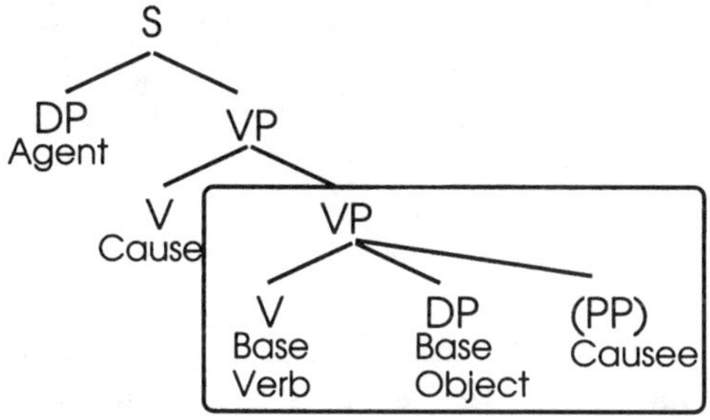

As there is no canonical subject position in the embedded domain in (8), the Causee will be either radically missing syntactically, or expressed as an adjunct. Given the absence of an embedded subject in (8), the Causee in FP-causatives plays no role in the establishment of A-dependencies. The state of affairs in this case too can be observed in binding. Consider the FPs in (9), whose only superficial difference with the sentences in (7) above lies in the expression of the Causee. While the Causee is an accessible subject in (7), neither a null nor by-phrase Causee can serve as the antecedent in the intended A-binding relations given in (9).[3]

(9) a *Italian* (Guasti 1996:295)
*Ho fatto riparare la *propria*$_i$ macchina (**da Gianni**)$_i$.
(I) have made repair the own car by Gianni
'I have had his own car repaired by Gianni.'

[3]Notice that the exact nature of the binding phenomena is not important. What is at stake in (7) and (9) is the presense versus the absense of a c-commanding A-antecedent.

b *Chichewa* (Alsina 1992:520)
*Alimi a-ku-lémb-éts-a ndakatulo *yâke*$_i$ (**kwa mkángó**)$_i$.
farmers S-Pres-write-caus-FV poem his by lion
'The farmers are having his$_i$ poem written by the lion$_i$.'

The contrast between (7) and (9) is elegantly and straightforwardly captured by the different syntactic structures (6) and (8) in conjunction with an independently required theory of syntactic locality.

Let us now consider how Torne Sámi causatives behave with regard to comparable binding phenomena, starting with cases where the Causee is overtly expressed. In the light of the discussion up to this point, it should be clear that if the Causee can occur as the most prominent link in an A-relation, then we would have a straightforward piece of evidence that we are dealing with an argument. Indeed, as shown in (10) the Causee has this ability.[4]

(10) a Mon oastti-h-in **Máreha**$_i$ biepmu *alcces-is*$_i$.
I.n buy-caus-Past.1s Máret.a food.a self.Ill-3s.Px
'I caused Máret to buy food to herself.'

b Mon loga-h-in **Máreha**$_i$ girjji *alcces-is*$_i$.
I.n read-caus-Past.1s Máret.a book.a self.Ill-3s.Px
'I caused Máret to read a book to herself.'

Here, the accusative Causee successfully antecedes the reflexive element alcces-is 'self.Ill-3sPx.' Therefore, since (10) patterns on par with (7), the indication is that the Causee is an argument.[5]

---

[4]Notice that the matrix subject may also antecede the anaphor, which not immediately expected from the Minimal Link Condition:
(i) **Mon**$_i$ oastti-h-in Máreha biepmu *alcces-an*$_i$.
I.n buy-caus-Past.1s Máret.a food.a self.Ill-1s.Px
'I caused Máret to buy food to myself.'
One way to approach (i) would be to assume that the anaphoric element (or its formal features) covertly raises to some position where it escapes at least part of the blocking effect induced by of the Causee under the MLC. However, for our purposes, the important point is the fact that the Causee has the ability to head an A-chain.

[5]For reasons not clear to us, the Causee cannot bind an accusative reflexive:
(i) *Mon basa-h-in Máhte$_i$ iežas$_i$.
I.n wash-caus-Past.1s Máhtte.a self.a.3s.Px
'I caused Máhtte to wash himself.'
(ii) Máhtte$_i$ basai iežas$_i$.

Furthermore, (11) below shows that the behavior of the Causeeless Torne Sámi causative is comparable to the Faire Par constructions in (9). In (11) the intended reading is for the reflexive alccesis 'self.Ill-3sPx' to take the semantically implicit Causee as its antecedent, which however is impossible. The fact that this interpretation fails suggests that there is no accessible antecedent for the reflexive, which in turn means that the Causee has no syntactic instantiation.

(11) a *Mon oastti-h-in biepmu *alcces-is.*
I.n buy-caus-Past.1s food.a self.Ill-3s.Px
'I caused someone to buy food to her/himself.'

b *Mon loga-h-in girjji *alcces-is*$_i$.
I.n read-caus-Past.1s book.a self.Ill-3s.Px
'I caused someone to read a book to him/herself.'

If we assume that Torne Sámi too forms causatives on the basis of structures (6) and (8), then this language is exactly like Italian and Chichewa. In other words, the Torne Sámi accusative Causee is a argument and the null Causee is not syntactically instantiated.

2.2 The Behavior of the Causative Types Under Passivization

Binding conditions A and B (Chomsky 1981, 1986ab) were at the heart of syntactic locality in classical Government and Binding Theory. However, this view has been challenged on both empirical and conceptual grounds. For instance, the existence of long-distance anaphora and logophoricity potentially refute any claims to the extent that, say, reflexive anaphors must be bound by their most local antecedent or even require a syntactic antecedent at all, as argued in Reinhart & Reuland (1993), Reuland (2001), Huang & Li (2001), among several others. These authors maintain, however, that there nevertheless is a syntactic residue to binding which rests on the familiar notion of locality, a view also maintained in Hornstein (2001). But because binding theory is a matter of controversy, it would be reassuring if the locality effects could be reproduced in other locality sensitive environments such as (A-)movement.

Máhtte.n wash.Past.3s self.a.3s.Px
'Máhtte$_i$ washed himself$_i$.'

One possible direction, suggested to us by Tomokazu Takehisa, would be to consider (ib) as some kind of antilocality effect (see e.g. Lidz 1997, McGinnis 1998), such that the Causee in some sense is too close to the Base Object for binding to obtain.

They can, although we must now be aware of a fundamental division among FIs, which we hinted at earlier. As extensively discussed in a great number of studies on causativization, the basic case licensing properties of specific languages dictate whether the Causee is realized as a direct or indirect object, for instance Baker (1988), Hoffmann (1991) and Watanabe (1996). The basic idea in both Baker (1988) and Watanabe (1996) hinges on the assumption that the base object in Italian-type languages is case licensed by the causative matrix verb, whereas the Causee may be licensed by specific rule of dative-insertion (see also Kayne 1975 and Burzio 1986). In contrast, languages like Chichewa exhibit a standard ECM-profile, where the base object is independently licensed in the embedded domain, whereas the case of the Causee is established in a relation with the causative head. This distinction gives the illusion that Chichewa-type languages respect locality, whereas Italian-type languages may violate the locality conditions.

Let us consider a few illustrations of how this simple variance in case theory forces quite different patterns to emerge in Italian and Chichewa.[6] Languages like Italian exemplify apparent cases of locality violations in that they allow long passives of causatives; that is, the base object becomes the subject in a passivized causative, raising past the Causee, as shown in the Italian example (12).

(12) *Italian* (Burzio 1986)

a Maria ha fatto riparare la macchina a Giovanni.
(I) has made repair the car Dat Giovanni
'I made Gianni repair the car.'

b La macchina fu fatta riparare a Giovanni.
the car was made repair Dat Giovanni
'The car was made to be repaired by Giovanni.'

A similar long-distance passive in a language like Chichewa (13b), on the other hand, is as expected ungrammatical, because in order to to reach the subject position, the base object must move across the higher the Causee. Hence, (13b) violates the locality condition on movement.

(13) *Chichewa* (Baker 1988:164-5)

a Catherine a-na-kolol-ets-a mwana wake chimanga
Catherine S-Past-harvest-caus-FV child her corn
'Catherine made her child harvest the corn.'

[6] This is by no means the complete picture. See e.g. Baker (1988), Marantz (1993) and Bresnan and Moshi (1990) for fuller discussions concerning these matters.

b *Chimanga chi-na-kolol-ets-edw-a mwana wake
corn S-Past-harvest-caus-Pass-FV child her
ndi Catherine
by Catherine
'The corn was made to be harvested by her child by Catherine.'

Thus Italian is the problematic case. The derivation of (12b) relies on the assumption that the base object does not move in one fell swoop from its base position to the matrix subject position. Rather, it moves cyclically via an intermediate position, which in fact is its surface position in active clauses, and from there it continues to the ultimate target position. While movement to the intermediate position is not blocked by the Causee, it nevertheless has the effect of getting the base object out of the c-command domain of the Causee, which in turn enables the base object to raise further, as shown in (14) (see Watanabe 1996, Chomsky 1995):

(14) *Italian*
[$_S$ **car$_i$** [$_{VP}$ cause-Pass [$_S$ **t$_i$'** Giovanni [$_{VP}$ repair **t$_i$**]]]]

Chichewa, on the other hand, because of case theoretic considerations, does not accomodate the possibility for the base object to raise cyclically via an intermediate position, which accounts for the ungrammaticality of (13b). Thus, (13b) has the approximate, illicit derivation given in (15), where the Causee has undergone genuine long movement (ignoring head-movement):

(15) *Chichewa*
* [$_S$ **corn$_i$** [$_{VP}$ cause-Pass [$_S$ her child [$_{VP}$ harvest **t$_i$**]]]]

Thus, in order to obtain a passive of a Chichewa causative, the Causee must be promoted to subject, as shown in (16).

(16) *Chichewa* (Baker 1988:165)
a Mnyamata a-na-kolol-ets-edw-a chimanga
boy S-Past-harvest-caus-Pass-FV corn
ndi Catherine
by Catherine
'The boy was made to harvest the corn by Catherine.'

b [$_S$ **boy$_i$**[$_{VP}$ cause-Pass [$_S$ **t$_i$** [$_{VP}$ harvest corn]]]]

In short, once we factor in the parametric differences between Italian and Chichewa regarding the way the base object is licensed, it is possible to maintain that both languages are subject to the same locality restrictions. However, because of the case theoretic particularities that hold in Italian, we do not find any surface differences in passives of FIs and FPs in that and case theoretically similar languages;[7] in both scenarios the base object becomes the subject, as revealed by a quick comparison of (12b) and (17). However, the actual derivations of the passives proceed along different lines, in that there is no need to postulate that the base object undergoes movement to an intermediate position in the FP, (17b):

(17) a La macchina fu fatta riparare (da Giovanni).
the car was made repair by Giovanni
'The car was made to be repaired by Giovanni.'

b [$_S$ **car$_i$** [$_{VP}$ cause-Pass [$_{VP}$ repair **t$_i$** (by Giovanni)]]]

What is more interesting is the fact that the asymmetries that hold between Italian and Chichewa in passivized FIs are fully neutralized in FPs. In contrast to the illformed Chichewa FI (13b) above, passivization of an FP results in the promotion of the base object to subject, as shown in (18):

[7] Also Italian exhibits a potentially movement-oriented distinction between FIs and FPs. Burzio (1986) noticed that dative clitics understood as arguments of the base verb cannot occur in Italian FIs, (i):

(i) ***Gli$_i$** faccio scrivere una lettera **t$_i$** a Maria.
to-him I will make write a letter Dat Maria
'I will make Maria write a letter to him.' (Burzio 1986:260)

Burzio attributes the ungrammaticality of (i) to reasons that are comparable to the illicit derivation of the Chichewa long passive in (15). To put it simply, due to the presence of an embedded subject, namely the Causee, the dative clitic in (i) fails to establish the right kind of relation with its trace, as shown in (ii):

(ii) *[S **gli$_i$** [VP cause [S Causee[VP V **t$_i$**]]]]

In FPs, such dative clitics are licit, which is consistent with and expected from the hypothesis that these do not involve a syntactically projection subject in the embedded domain, as shown in (iii):

(iiia) **Gli$_i$** faccio scrivere una lettera **t$_i$** (da Maria).
to-him I will make write a letter by Maria
'I will make Maria write a letter to him.' (Mario Fadda, p.c.)

(iiib) [$_S$ **gli$_i$** [$_{VP}$ cause [$_{VP}$ V **t$_i$**]]]

(18) *Faire Par* (Baker 1988:163)

a Anyani a-na-meny-ets-a ana (kwa buluzi).
baboons SP-Past-hit-caus-Asp children by lizard
'The baboon made the lizard hit the children.'

b Ana a-na-meny-ets-edw-a (kwa buluzi) (ndi anyani).
children SP-Past-hit-caus-Pass-FV by lizard by baboons
'The children were made to be hit by the lizard by the baboons.'

c $[_S$ **children$_i$** $[_{VP}$ cause-Pass $[_{VP}$ hit **t_i** (by the lizard)]]]

Because (18b) does not give rise to a locality violation of the kind detected in (13b), the indication is that there is no syntactically realized argument Causee intervening between the head and the tail of the A-chain created by Movement of the base object in (18b). Again, this is what is expected under the hypothesis that the FP causatives involves bare VP-complemenation.

Now that we have fleshed out the rough details of the behavior of the major causative types under passivization, this information can be used as a yardstick for measuring Torne Sámi causatives. This task, however, is at first sight made somewhat complicated by the fact that causatives formed from transitive base verbs where the Causee is expressed have the peculiar property that they cannot be passivized, as shown in (19).[8]

(19) a Mon cuvke-h-in Máhte láse.
I.n break.Tr-caus-Past.1s Máhtte.a window.a
'I caused Máhtte to break the window.'

b *Láse cuvke-h-uvvu-i Máhte.
window.n break.Tr-caus-Pass-Past.3s Máhtte.a
'The window was caused to be broken by Máhte (by someone).

c *Máhtte cuvke-h-uvvu-i láse.
Máhtte.n break.Tr-caus-Pass-Past.3s window.a
'Máhtte was caused to break the window.'

(19b) shows that the base object cannot become the subject in a passive, and (19c) shows that it is also impossible for the Causee to be promoted to

---

[8]This fact carries over to other North Sámi variants as well, see for instance Julien (1996).

subject. In order to make sense out of (19b) and (19c) it is important to stress that there is no inherent prohibtion against passivization of causatives. In descriptive terms, however, the underlying source that passive can apply to may not have more than one accusative object (see for instance Levin & Rappaport 1986). Thus, a causative based on an intransitive verb such as (20a) may successfully be passivized, (20b).

(20)	a	Máret	danse-h-ii	Bireha.
		Máret.n	dance-caus-Past.3s	Biret.a
		'Máret caused Biret to dance.'		
	b	Biret	danse-h-uvvu-i	
		Biret.n	dance-caus-Pass-Past.3s	
		'Biret was caused to dance.'		

Even more noteworthy, a causative sentence based on a transtive base verb may also be passivized, however with the proviso that the Causee is not expressed, as shown in (21). The result is a passive sentence whose subject corresponds to the base object of the active clause.

(21)	a	Mon	cuvke-h-in	láse.
		I.n	break.Tr-caus-Past.1s	window.a
		'I caused Máhtte to break the window.'		
	b	Láse	cuvke-h-uvvu-i.	
		window.n	break.Tr-caus-Pass-Past.3s	
		'The window was caused to be broken.'		

Recall now that sentences like (21a) behave like bona fide FPs regarding the possibilities for A-binding. (21b) further supports the hypothesis that the Causeeless causative in Torne Sámi is of the FP-variety, since the base object in fact can move to the subject position of the clause. Given that causatives *can* undergo passivization and the fact that (21b) is grammatical, (19b) above also falls into place. The ill-formedness of (19b) now straightforwardly follows from the Minimal Link Condition, on a par with the illicit long passive in Chichewa FIs, such as (13) and (15). (19a) still remains problematic, however. A possible solution is presented in McGinnis (1998) and Chomsky (1998, 1999). These authors argue that an argument that has entered a Case relation with an appropriate syntactic head is prevented from participating in further A-related operations. Let us tentatively assume passive fails to suppress the structural case that licenses the Causee in (19), and therefore it cannot raise to the matrix subject position, in accordance with

McGinnis (1998) and Chomsky (1998, 1999). At the same time, it also prevents the base object from raising, by the MLC. For the purposes of this paper, it suffices to say that a principled account is available with a minimum of stipulation, given recent advances in syntactic theory.[9] In the present context, however, the important thing to notice is that we have reached the conclusion that the Causee in (19) by necessity is an argument. At the same time, we also have accumulated substantial evidence that the Causeeless causative is radically void of a syntactic Causee.

2.3 Summary

In this section we have reviewed the basic arguments for slicing causatives into two different syntactic types. In the process, we have compared Torne Sámi against two well-known cases, namely Italian and Chichewa. In doing so, we have shown that it is beyond any reasonable doubt that the accusative Causee in Torne Sámi is an argument, and likewise, the absence of an overt Causee indicates a truncated causative of the FP-variety. It might now seem tempting to jump to the conclusion that Torne Sámi, on par with Italian and Chichewa, has access to both the FI and FP frames. However, as we shall see in the next section, such a conclusion would be premature.

3 Restrictions on the Base Verb

This section will bring up a further asymmetry between the two causative types, namely differences in the restrictions imposed on the base verb. These have far-reaching consequences for the analysis of Torne Sámi and they have repercussions for the finer details of the structure of the VP.

3.1 Preliminaries

Although the syntactic structure given in (6) and (8) above predict certain structural asymmetries to hold among FIs and FPs, there are other distinctions between the two causative types that do not immediately follow from the standard analysis (Kayne 1975, Burzio 1986), which therefore must be supplemented by some auxiliary assumption in one form or another. Let us begin by outlining the descriptive aspects of the issue. The FP variety imposes tighter selectional restrictions on the base verb than the FI, which in contrast is relatively liberal in this respect. For instance, it is a well-known fact that FIs can be based on non-agentive perception verbs like <u>see</u> and <u>hear</u>, as shown by Spanish (22a) and Chichewa (22b) (Bordelois 1988, Alsina 1992, Guasti 1993, 1996, Travis 1992).

---

[9]The reader is referred to Vinka (2002: Ch 6) for a detailed discussion of Torne Sámi in this regard.

(22) a *Spanish* (Bordelois 1988: 58)
Hicieron ver la ciudad <u>a los turistas</u>.
made.3p see the city dat the tourists
'They made the tourists see the city.'

b *Chichewa* (Alsina 1992: 528)
Chatsalira a-ku-mv-ets-a <u>ana</u> phokoso.
Chatsalira S-Pres-hear-caus-FV children noise
'Chatsalira is making the children hear the noise.'

The FP causative, on the other hand, is incompatible with embedded perception verbs, as shown in (23). Although (22) and (23) in abstract terms appear to be identical, only the former is grammatical.

(23) a *Spanish* (Bordelois 1988:58)
*Hicieron ver la ciudad (<u>por los turistas</u>).
made.3p see the city by the turistas
'They made the tourists see the city.'

b *Chichewa* (Alsina 1992: 528)
*Chatsalira a-ku-mv-ets-a phokoso (<u>kwa ana</u>).
Chatsalira S-Pres-hear-caus-FV noise by children
'Chatsalira is making the children hear the noise.'

Given the basic underpinnings of the Kayne-Burzio hypothesis, the contrast between (22) and (23) is unexpected. While the Kayne-Burzio hypothesis can be supplement by various auxiliary assumptions, there is nothing in the basic theory itself that would predict that if the verbs <u>ver</u> 'see' and <u>mv</u> 'hear' are subsituted for <u>riparare</u> 'repair' and <u>phik</u> 'cook' (see (4) and (5) above), perfectly fine FPs are produced. While this issue is problematic, it does however provides us with a further manifestation of the distinction between FIs and FPs in addition to the diagnostics reviewed in the previous section. As such it strengthens the basic idea that there are two substantively distinct causative types, while urging a refinement of the theory. For the time being, we set the problematic aspects aside and capitalize on the fact that we are now in possession of an additional piece in the cluster of properties that differentiate FIs and FPs. For instance, we now predict that any well-formed causative based on a non-agentive perception verb must be of the FI variety. This is an important point, because there are cases where the mere surface string would suggests that FPs could be based on non-agentive perception verbs. As an illustration, let us consider the Portuguese causatives in (24a) and (24b), which superficially resemble an FI and an FP respectively.

(24) *Portuguese* (Walcir Cardodo, p.c.)

a	Eu	fiz	John	consertar	o carro.
	I	made	John	repair	the car

b	Eu	fiz	consertar	o carro.
	I	made	repair	the car

As we now can observe in (25), the Causeeless causative variant is also fully grammatical even when the base verb is a non-agentive verb. Thus, (25b) is a potential counterexample to the hypothesis that the FP is selects a narrower range of base verbs than the FI:

(25) *Portuguese* (Walcir Cardodo, p.c.)

a	O professor	fez	John	conhecer	o comitê.
	the professor	made	John	know	the committee

b	O professor	fez	conhecer	o comitê.
	the professor	made	know	the committee

However, a particular characteristic of Portuguese infinitives supplies a simple but efficient means to show that (25b) does not constitute such a counterexample, but rather complies to the general pattern. As discussed in Raposo (1987), the verb in non-finite clauses in Portuguese exhibit number agreement with the subject. With this in mind, we can now notice that the infinitive verb in both (26) and (27) show such agreement.

(26) *Portuguese* (Walcir Cardodo, p.c.)

a	O general	fez	os soldados	destruirem/
	the general	made	the soldiers	destroy.p/
	*destruir	a cidade.		
	*destroy.s	the city		

b	O general	fez	destruirem/destruir	a cidade.
	the general	made	destroy.p/destroy.s	the city

(27) a	O professor	fez	John	*conherem/conhecer	o
	the professor	made	John	*know.p/know.s	the
	comitê.				
	committee				

b O professor fez conherem/conhecer o comitê.
the professor made know.p/know.s the committee

Therefore, it must be the case that the Causee is syntactically instantiated as an argument in both (a) and (b) of (24) through (27), with the phonologically empty Causee being an empty category which has the effect of concealing the underlying structural complexity of the (b)-examples. Thus the surface strings of (25b) (26b) and (27b) instantiate FIs, rather than FPs.[10]

The literature provides in essence two strategies to deal with this distinction between FIs and FPs. One view is that the base verb in the (b) sentences must be agentive (Bordelois 1988, Guasti 1990, Travis 1991, 1992), and another influential idea is that the base object must be affected (Alsina 1992, Guasti 1993, 1996). Neither of these auxiliary assumptions are necessary consequences of the hypothesis that the causative verb in the FP construction takes a VP complement rather than a larger chunk of structure, although it is also equally clear that neither assumption is incompatible with the Kayne-Burzio hypothesis. But before we consider these topics in deeper detail, let us now return our attention to our main issue, namely causativization in Torne Sámi.

3.2 Torne Sámi

The preceeding discussion has made it clear that FIs and FPs exhibit systematic differences not only with respect to the realization of arguments, but also in what range of base verbs they may occur with. Descriptively speaking, the base verb in an FI may be agentive as well as non-agentive, whereas the base base verb in an FP must be agentive. With these facts as our backdrop, we shall now subject Torne Sámi to some scrutiny, in particular how it behaves in conjunction with these selectional mismatches. Base verbs like gullat 'hear' and diehtit 'know' serves as appropriate candidates as probes into these matters. As the predictions are the most straightforward with regard to the Causeeless variant, consider the sentences in (28)

(28) a *Mon gula-h-in bajána.
I.n hear-caus-Past.1s thunder.a
'I made someone hear the thunder.'

[10] Jairo Nunes (p.c.) points out, however, that Brazilian Portuguese strongly prefers the option where the the Causee is overt.

b *Mon dieđi-*h*-in vástádussa.
I.n know-Cause-Past.1s answer.a
'I caused someone to know the answer.'

As we expect from the hypthesis we arrived at in the previous section that we're dealing with FP causatives, both sentences in (28) are ungrammatical on a par with (23) above. In conjunction with the locality effects discussed earlier, the ungrammaticality of (28) provides conclusive evidence of FP-hood. Let us now turn the examples in (29) below, which are all but identical to (28), with the exception that here the Causee is expressed. It is now important to recall that syntactic locality, both in terms of A-binding and A-movement, has shown that the accusative Causee is argument. Given a basic premise of the Kayne-Burzio hypothesis, the implication is that such causatives are FIs. All things being equal, we would now expect that (29) should be dramatically better than (28), just as the FIs in (22) are fully grammatical while the FPs (23) are not. However, contrary to expectation, (29) is as ungrammatical as (28).[11]

(29) a *Mon gula-h-in <u>máná</u> bajána.
I.n hear-caus-Past.1s child.a thunder.a
'I made the child hear the thunder.'

b *Mon dieđi-*h*-in Máreha vástádussa.
I.n know-Cause-Past.1s Máret.a answer.a
'I caused Máret to know the answer.'

The simplest option is to assume that the sentences in (29) are ungrammatical for the same reason as (23) and (28); that is, (29) too is a Faire Par construction.[12] In fact, if we subscribe to the idea that parsimony is an impor-

---

[11]Notice that if we ask any native speaker of Torne Sámi if for instance <u>gulahit</u> and <u>dieđihit</u> are possible verbs in the language, the answer is a resounding "yes." However, the verbs do not receive the compositional interpretations 'cause to hear' and 'cause to know,' but are rather assigned the idiomatic readings 'announce' and introduce' respectively. In other words, they are what is commonly referred to as lexical causatives (see Fodor 1970, Shibatani 1976, Miyagawa 1994, Harley 1995 and Marantz 1997, 2001 for discussions). As such they are plain agentive transitive verbs.

[12]The anonymous reviewer points out that (28) and (i) are fully grammatical in the eastern dialects:

(i) Mon gula-h-in <u>mánnái</u> bajána.
I.n hear-caus-Past.1s child.a thunder.a
'I made the child hear the thunder.'

The fact that these sentences are grammatical in the reviewer's dialect is a good indication of FI-hood. Notice that also (i) is gibberish ungrammatical in Torne Sámi.

tant ingredient in theory building, a basic tenet in the Chomskian enterprise, then our only option is to treat (29a) and (29b) as FPs. The problematic point is the fact that the Causee is realized as an accusative object, rather than as an adjunct. This point notwithstanding, the Torne Sámi accusative Causee shares a important property with the by-phrase Causee in Chichewa and Italian, namely its optionality. We shall return to this issue in section 4, where we shall argue that the Torne Sámi Causee, descriptively speaking, is a optional argument.

3.3 Constraining the Formation of FPs

Let us now return to the question that we raised earlier, namely how to account for the fact that perception verbs are excluded from Faire Par causatives. In essence, two different answers have been proposed in the literature. Firstly, we have the Agentivity Hypothesis, (30), which states that the causaive verb in an FP selects a bare VP complement headed by an agentive verb. This approach has been assumed in, for instance, Travis (1992).

(30) **The Agentivity Hypothesis**
The bare VP-complement in an FP must be headed by an agentive verb

The other major proposal is the Affectedness Hypothesis, stated in (31). This strategy has been pursued by among others Alsina (1992) and Guasti (1993, 1996).[13]

(31) **The Affectedness Hypothesis**
The direct object of the verb heading the bare VP-complement in an FP must be an affected argument

Both the Agentivity and the Affectedness Hypotheses are equally successful in ruling out percepton verbs from FPs. Such verbs verbs tend to be non-agentive, and therefore they are straightforwardly exluded by the Agentivity Hypothesis. It is also uncontroversial that the object of a verb like HEAR is not affected by the hearing event, and consequently sentences like (23) violate the affectedness constraint as well

---

[13]Because of space considerations we abstract away from some important differences between Alsina (1992) and Guasti (1993, 1996). For instance, Alsina's work is couched in LFG, whereas Guasti's work is done in a late GB framework. The theories presented by these two authors make subtly different predictions, which do not affect our discussion. For fuller discussions, see the original works by Alsina and Guasti respectively, as well as Svonni & Vinka (2002) and Vinka (2002).

However, they make different predictions regarding the possibility to base Faire Par causatives on unaccusative verbs. Since unaccusatives by definition are non-agentive, the Agentivity Hypothesis excludes them in the same manner as it bans perception verbs in this environment. The Affectedness Hypothesis, on the other hand, raises no principled objections against the embedding of unaccusatives under Faire Par. Since we have claimed that Torne Sámi lacks Fare Infinitives altogether, we can now test the validity of each approach. Consider now the unaccusatives in (32) and (33):

(32) a Láse cuovkanii
window.n break.Intr.Past.3s
'The window broke.'

b *Mon cuovkan-ahtt-en láse
I.n break.Intr-Cause-Past.1s window.a
'I caused the window to break.'

(33) a Fanas gopmánii.
boat.n upside down.Intr.Past.3s
'The boat flipped over.'

b *Mon gopmán-ahtt-en fatnasa.
I.n upside down.Intr-Cause-Past.1s boat.a
'I caused the boat to flip over.'

The causatives in (32b) and (33b) are ungrammatical, as predicted by the Agentivity Hypothesis.[14] The Affectedness Hypothesis, however, would incorrectly rule in these sentences. Therefore, on empirical grounds, it is clear that a constraint stated in terms of agentivity is to prefer. We should be careful to notice, however, that the exact nature of unaccusativity is not in any sense crucial for the theory presented. Rather, the important point resides in the fact that verbs that do not qualify as agentive, regardless of their argument taking abilities, cannot serve as base verbs in the FP-causative. Unaccusatives are, of course, important in this respect because (a) they often take an affected internal argument, which sets them apart from transitive perception verbs, and (b) they are non-agentive, which makes them similar to transitive perception verbs, and it is exactly this par-

[14]According to our anonymous reviewer, causativized unaccusatives of the kind given in (32) are well-formed in his/her variety of North Sámi. This would be consistent with the previously mentioned FI-characteristics exhibited by that dialect. But again, (32b) and (33b) are gibberish in Torne Sámi.

tition that makes this kind of verbs relevant in the present context. However, the Agentivity Hypothesis also raises a few questions, which we will adress in due course. However, we shall first consider some independent reasons for distinguishing between agentive and non-agentive verbs in Torne Sámi, because in the absence of such independent diagnostics, the Agentivity Hypothesis is at best speculative

3.4 Agentivity and the Structure of the Verb Phrase

The kind of evidence that we shall consider is concerned with the distribution of Sámi rationale clauses. Roberts (1987) and Roeper (1987), to mention a few, have suggested that rationale clauses are restricted to the environment of agentive verbs. We shall see that the enviroment where Sámi rationale clauses can appear all involve verbs that are good candidates for causativization; also the opposite is true, that is, environments where rationale clauses are illicit, all involve verbs that cannot be causativized. The discussion to follow will require that we pay closer attention to the internal architecture of the verb phrase, with particular focus on the finer building blocks it consists of.

Our starting point is the proposal by Kratzer (1996), that the external argument of a verb is introduced into the specifier of a functional head, which Kratzer calls Voi(ce), illustrated in (34). A similar, but subtly different proposal is found in Chomsky (1995:Ch 4). In addition to introducing the external argument, the VoiP also has a specification for agentivity, or the lack therereof. In other words, the substantive VP in (34) has no specifications pertaining to external argument or agentivity.

(34)

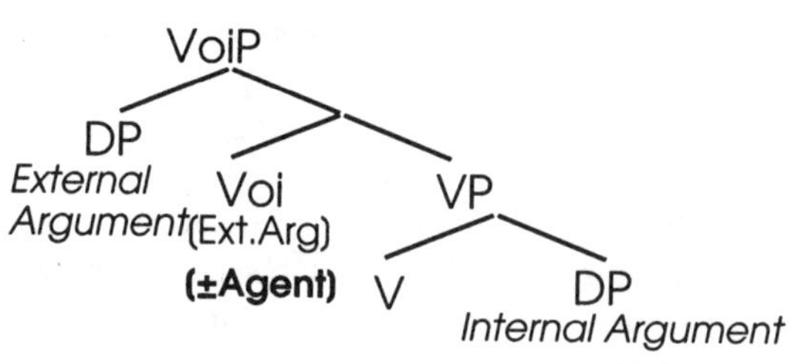

We can now formulate the idea that rationale clauses require an agentive environment in terms of Voice; specifically, they are licensed in the presence of an agentive Voice head:

(35) **Licensing of rationale clauses**
Rationale clauses are licensed in the vicinity of a [+Agentive] Voice head.

With this in mind, let's turn to (36), which illustrates a well-formed occurrence of a Torne Sámi rationale clause. Thus, the verb cuvket 'break' would involve an agentive VoiP that provides the right kind of support required by the rationale clause, in accordance with (35).

(36)

Máhtte	cuvkii	láse	
Máhtte.n	break.Tr.Past.3s	window.a	
[PRO beahttin	dihte	dáhkádussearvvi.	
cheat.Act	in-order-to	insurance company.a	

'Máhtte broke the window in order to cheat the insurance company'

Furthermore, it is a well-documented fact that rationale clauses may appear in passive environments (Manzini 1983, Roberts 1987, Roeper 1987, among others), and this is true also in Torne Sámi, as shown in (37):

(37)

Láse	cuvke-juvvu-i	
window.n	break.Tr.-Pass-Past.3s	
[PRO beahttin	dihte	dáhkádussearvvi.
cheat.Act	in-order-to	insurance company.a

'The window was broken in order to cheat the insurance company.'

In other words, a passive Voice head may be agentive, even though it does not introduce an external argument.

Let us now consider the other side of the coin that interests us, namely the interaction between rationale clauses and non-agentive verbs. As shown in (38) rationale clauses cannot occur in such environments.

(38)

*Mánná	gulai	bajána
child.n	hear.Past.3s	thunder.a
[PRO illudahttin	dihte	eatni].
make.happy.Act	in-order-to	mother.a

'The child heard the thunder, in order to make mother happy.'

This indicates that the verb gullat 'hear' is non-agentive, and that the presence of an external argument does not entail agentivity. Because VoiP is not agentive, the rationale clause cannot be supported in (38), and therefore the sentence is ruled out by (35). Finally, (39) shows that rationale clauses are also impossible with unaccusative verbs, as fully expected.

(39)

*Máhtte	heavvanii		
Máhtte.n	drown.Intr.3s		
[PRO	beahttin	dihte	dáhkádussearvvi.
	cheat.Act	in-order-to	insurance company.a

'Máhtte drowned in order to cheat the insurance company.'

In sum, those simple verbs that we have identified as agentive, exactly correspond to those that can be causativized. Hence we have independent evidence for a distinction between agentive and non-agentive verbs.

Let us now see how causatives behave together with rationale clauses. To begin with, notice that rationale clauses are perfectly fine together with causatives, regardless of whether the causee is realized or not, as shown in (40).

(40)

Máhtte_i	vuojuh-ahti-i	$(\text{Máreha})_j$	fatnasa
Máhtte.n	sink.Tr-caus-Past.3s	(Máret.a)	boat.a
$[\text{PRO}_{i/*j}$	beahttin dihte		dáhkádussearvvi.
	cheat.Act in-order-to		insurance company.a

(i) **'Máhtte**$_i$ caused Máret/ someone to sink the boat in order **PRO**$_i$ to cheat the insurance company.'

(ii) *'Máhtte caused **Máret/someone**$_j$ to sink the boat in order **PRO**$_j$ to cheat the insurance company.'

However, as indicated in (40), only the causative agent can serve as the antecedent for the understood subject of rationale clause, regardless of whether the causee is realized or not. Guasti (1993) reports that Italian Faire Par causatives behave identically to (40), whereas the Causee in Faire Infinitives can control into rationale clauses. This implies, then, that the complement in FIs is minimally a VoiP and furthermore that the complement of an FP is smaller than that. Therefore (40) supports a Faire Par analysis of Torne Sámi, and it provides a further reason for us to assimilate the Torne Sámi accusative Causee with the adjunct Causee found in Italian and Chichewa FPs.

The facts that we have just reviewed fit nicely with Kayne's and Burzio's analysis of Faire Par constructions as involving a bare VP complement, especially in conjunction with Kratzer's theory that agentivity is not a property of the substantive verb. Given the hypothesis that rationale clauses are licensed in the vicinity of an agentive Voice head, we must conclude that the complement of the causative formative in (40) does not involve a VoiP. However, this also implies that the causative verb in a Faire Par construction cannot combine with a bare VP that is headed by an agentive verb, because, as we recall, according to Kratzer such *verbs* do not exist, since agentivity is a property of Voice. Therefore, we know two things: Firstly, the causative complement in Faire Par constructions is not a VoiP, and secondly, it is not a VP. Hence, we have a problem for the Agentivity Hypothesis. In other words, the Agentivity Hypothesis as stated in (30) is but a descriptive generalzation that characterizes the set of verbs that may be embedded under the FP causative. It is no more than that, because it is silent on the behavior of those verbs when occuring in the causative context.

3.5 Implication for the Structure of the Verb Phrase

We shall now consider a way out of this dilemma. With the assumption that the external argument is introduced by a functional head such as Kratzer's Voice, it has become fairly standard to assume that this functional head may have an overt morphological exponent, as argued in for instance Harley (1995). In numerous languages, including North Sámi, morphologically related transitive and intransitive verbs appear with different overt valancy markers. While the notorius lack of systematicity in the overt distribution of these valency markers makes any attempt futile to derive one verb form from another, the ingenuity of Harley's theory is that there is no derivational relationship such that the transitive from is derived from the intransitive, or vice versa. Rather, the transitive and the intransitive is derived from a shared abstract source. For present purposes and space considerations, it suffices to simplify the discussion and assume that this common abstract source is Kratzer's substantive VP.[15] As shown (41), there are three possibilities in the morphological marking of the verb pairs manifested in Torne Sámi. (41a) illustrates that the transitive verb may appear with a suffix, while the intransitive verb seemingly does not. In (41b), the opposite pattern is found, that is, the intransitive verb exhibits a superficially higher degree of morphological complexity than the transitive member of the pair, and (41c) is a juxtaposition of the two previous patterns, with both the transitive and the intransitive verb carrying overt morphological markers of valency.

---

[15]See Harley (1995), Marantz (1997, 2001), Baker & Stewart (1999), Baker (forthcoming), among others, for pertinent discussions. See also Hale & Keyser (1993) and Levin & Rappaport (1995).

(41)		Transitive	Intransitive
	a	luvva-d-it	luvva-t
		wet-Tr-Inf	wet-Inf
		'make wet'	'get wet'
	b	cuvke-t	cuovka-n-it
		break-Inf	break-Intr-Inf
		'break.Tr'	'break.Intr'
	c	gomi-h-it	gopmá-n-it
		flip over-Tr-Inf	flip over-Intr-Inf
		'flip over.Tr'	'flip over.Intr'

The transitive verbs are in (41) (and perhaps all agentive verbs) are of a type usually called lexical causatives. Harley (1995) capitalizes on this fact and proposes that an agentive VoiP, or EventP in Harley's terms, hosts a cause-component, which implies that the verb is agentive, and that Voi introduces an external argument, as shown in (42a). The intransitive verbs in (41) are all unaccusative. These are obtained as in (42b), where VP has combined with VoiP which we tentatively specify as [inchoative], which among other things means that it is not agentive and that it does not introduce an external argument.

(42) a Transitive

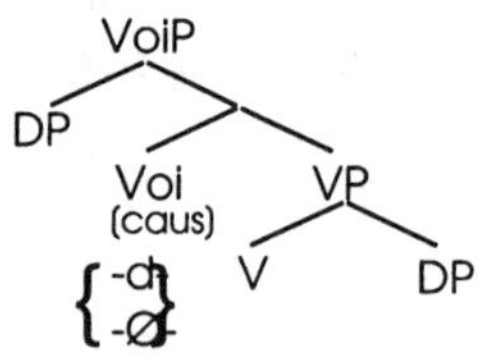

b Intransitive

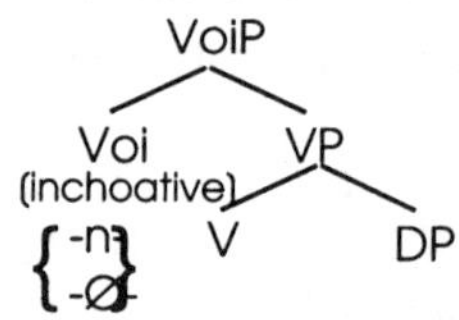

The right morphononological properies are subsequently obtained by assuming a theory of late lexical insertion, along the lines of Halle & Marantz (1993). That is, lexical insertion operates over the structures provided by the syntax, where so-called Vocabulary Items compete for insertion.[16] Harley proposes a unified account of lexical and syntactic (viz. productive) causatives, that hinges on the presence of the cause component in Voi. Productive causatives are proposed to arise when Voi selects a VoiP as its complement, as shown in (43):

[16] The details do not concern us here. See for instance Halle & Marantz (1993), Miyagawa (1994), Harley (1995), among others.

(43)

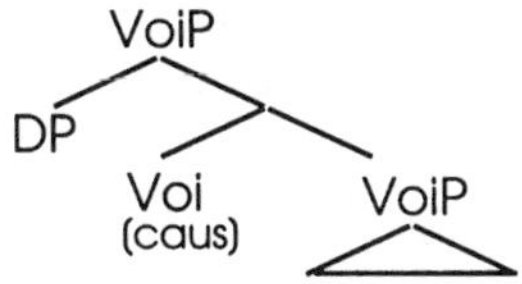

Elegant though Harley's theory is, the claim that Cause is equal to Voi, as in (42a) and (43) above, is untenable. The crucial evidence that discloses the flaw in Harley's account comes from the interaction of lexical causatives and FP-causativization. Since we showed in the previous section that the base verb in an FP causative does not involve a VoiP, Harley's proposal entails that the embedded domain in FPs could not contain any morphological pieces that relate to the valency of the base verb. Verbs like cuvket 'break.Tr.Inf' are uninformative in this regard, since the transitivizing morpheme is null. Therefore, we need to consider a verb with an overt lexical causative suffix, such as gomihit 'flip over.Tr.Inf.' According to Harley, the syntactic causative should now be homophonous with the lexical causative, which is an incorrect prediction. Rather, as shown in (44), what we get is a stacking of two causative exponents, where the innermost realization corresponds to a lexical causative head, and the outermost is an exponent of the productive causative (see Miyagawa 1984, 1989):

(44) a Mon gomi-*h*-ahtt-en (Máhte) fatnasa
I.n flip over-caus-caus-Past.1s Máhtte.a boat.a
'I caused Máhtte/someone to flip over the boat.'

b *Mon gomi-h-in (Máhte) fatnasa
I.n flip over-caus-Past.1s Máhtte.a boat.a
'I caused Máhtte/someone to flip over the boat.'

In short, if as we have argued the complement of the causative formative in an FP cannot take a VoiP complement, then it is impossible for the italicized transitivizing suffix /d/ in (44a) to be an exponent of Voice, contrary to Harley's claim. However, if we wish to maintain the main idea of Harley theory, namely that the transitivizing suffixes signify syntactic heads, then they must be found in a projection lower than Kratzer VoiP, and higher than the substantive VP, as in (45):

(45)

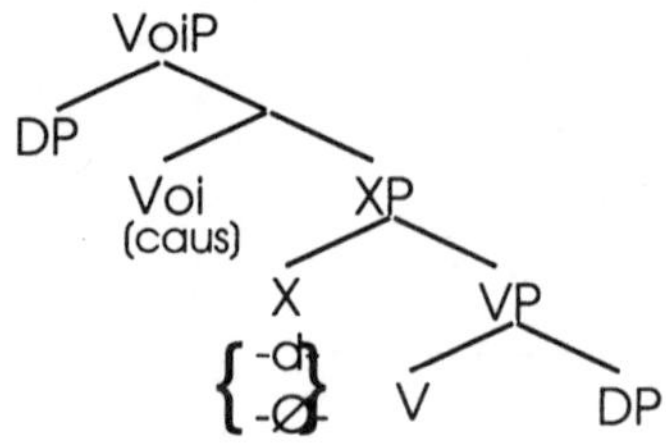

What kind of head is X in (45)? Recent studies by Baker & Stewart (1999) and Pylkkänen (1999) suggest that Kratzer's VoiP and Chomsky's (1995) vP are not two different labels for the same thing, but rather two different labels for two different things. The idea is that Chomsky's v, contra Chomsky, does not introduce an external argument, but rather in Baker & Stewart's terms, hosts a causative or process component.[17] The external argument is introduced by Kratzer's Voice, and we continue to assume that this projection is the locus of agentivity. In other words, XP in (45) is Chomsky's vP, as shown in (46).

(46) Agentive transitive

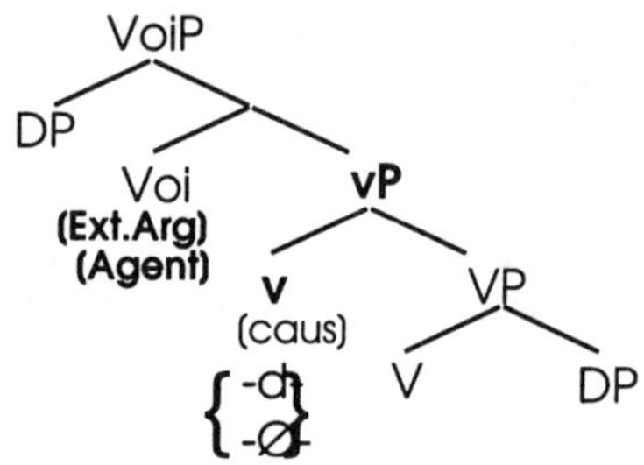

(46) depicts a "simple" agentive verb, where the agentive Voice head combines with vP. Assume further that non-agentive verbs, such as perception verbs, lack the intermediate vP, as shown in (47).

[17]In effect more true to the original proposal by Hale & Keyser (1993), that Chomsky's (1995) idea is based on.

(47) Non-agentive transitive

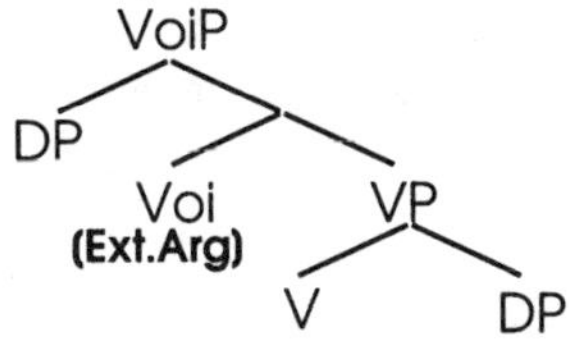

The agentivity restriction on Faire Par formation can now be viewed as a requirement that the causative verb, now viewed as v, must take a vP as it its complement, (48):

(48)

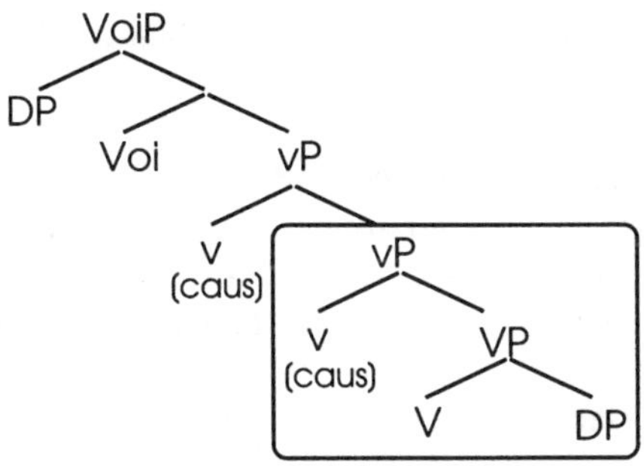

In other words, non-agentive verbs such as unaccusatives and transitive perception verbs cannot yield FPs, because their basic representations lack the intermediate v projection.[18]

3.6 Summary

In this section we have argued that FP formation is subject to an agentivity restriction on the base verb. However, we have also shown that a more careful examination of the properties of the base verb reveals that it is void agentivity when embedded under the FP causative. In conjunction with Kratzer's (1996) Voice Phrase hypothesis, it has been shown that FP formation provides an additional argument in favor of a fine-grained syntactic decomposition of the VP, along the lines of Baker & Stewart (1999) and Pylkkänen (1999). In short, the FP causative selects vP as its complement. Assuming that vP is a constituent in agentive verbs, and at the same time

---

[18]In fact, if v is merged with a VP headed by, say, a perception verb, then we obtain a lexical causative, such as gulahit' 'announce' or dieđihit 'inform.' Once such forms has been obtained, causativization may apply again, forming a perfectly grammatical FP causative, for instance, gula-h-ahtt-it 'announce-Cause-Inf' (lit. hear-Cause-Cause-Inf'= cause to announce).

letting agentivity as such be associated with VoiP, we correctly derive the descriptive effect of the Agentivity Hypothesis, and at the same time account for the fact that the lembedded verb is not associated with agentivity.

4 The Causee

This section will be devoted to the expression of the Causee in Torne Sámi causatives. The surface expression of a Torne Sámi causative like (49a) is identical to a standard FI such as the Chichewa causative in (49b). Therefore, one of the more striking claims we have made is that the two sentences in (49) are not comparable.

(49) a Mon cuvke-h-in **Máhte** láse.
I.n break.Tr-Cause-Past.1s Máhtte.a window.a
'I caused Máhtte to break the window.'

b *Chichewa* (Alsina 1992:518)
Nungu i-na-phik-its-a **kadzidzi** maungu.
porcupine S-Past-cook-Cause-FV owl pumpkins
'The porcupine made the owl cook the pumpkins.'

However, once we take into consideration such matters as selectional restrictions imposed on the base verbs, it becomes increasingly clear that the two sentences in (49) are not of a kind, as we have discussed extensively. In fact, (49a) behaves like the Faire Par causative in (50):

(50) *Chichewa* (Alsina 1992:518)
Nungu i-na-phik-its-a maungu (kwa
porcupine S-Past-cook-Cause-FV pumpkins by
kadzidzi).
owl
'The porcupine had the pumpkins cooked by the owl.'

The Torne Sámi accusative Causee and the Chichewa by-phrase share the characteristic of being entirely optional. Optionality of expression is perhaps the most prominent trademark for by-phrase such kwa kadzidzi 'by owl,' in (50). However, not the same can be said about accusative DPs such as the FI-like Causee in the Torne Sámi sentence (49a). Nevertheless, given the overall character of Torne Sámi causatives, it is clear that (49a) and (50) must be reconciled.

The obvious question to raise is if we know about any independent cases that exhibit the same kind of variation of expression as (49a) and (50).

We need not look very far to find such cases; indeed, they are rampantly occurring in natural languages. Consider (51) and (52):

(51) a Peter gave a book to Sally.
b Peter gave Sally a book.

(52) a Peter read a book for Sally.
b Peter read Sally a book.

These examples illustrate the dative- and benefactive alternations in English. The basic difference between (51) and (52) is that in the former the Goal phrase is obligatory whereas in the latter the benefactive phrase is not subcategorized for by the verb read. We also know that many languages do not permit prepositional datives at all, for instance Sesotho as illustrated in (53):

(53) *Sesotho* (Machobane 1989:113)

a Ntate o-f-a bana lijo.
father S-give-FV children food
'My father gives the children some food.'

b *Ntate o-f-a lijo ho bana.
father S-give-FV food to children
'My father gives some food to the children.'

Other languages, such as Romance, have been suggested to be the opposite of Sesotho in only allowing the prepositional dative (see for instance Baker 1988), as illustrated by Brazilian Portuguese in (54):

(54) *Brazilian Portuguese* (Sônia Katsuura .p.c.)

a Eu li um livro para Leila.
I read a book for Leila
'I read a book for Leila'

b *Eu li Leila um livro.
I read Leila a book
'I read Leila a book.'

While our concern is not the dative or the benefactive alternations, they serve as good illustrations of how something that expresses more or less the same thing can be expressed in more than one way. That is, a Goal or Benefactive DP can be either a prepositional object or a primary object. With regard to the expression of the Causee, we can now view Torne Sámi (49a) as the FP-causative counterpart to Sesotho ditransitives (53), whereas the Chichewa FP (50) is the counterpart to Romance ditransitives (54). A view that has gained considerable ground in the past decade is that double object constructions (DOC) such as (51b) and (53a) etc. base-generate the first object in an applicative phrase (Marantz 1993, Ura 1996, McGinnis 1998, among others), as schematically shown in (55a). The prepositional construction (PC) is illustrated in (55b).[19]

(55) a DOC

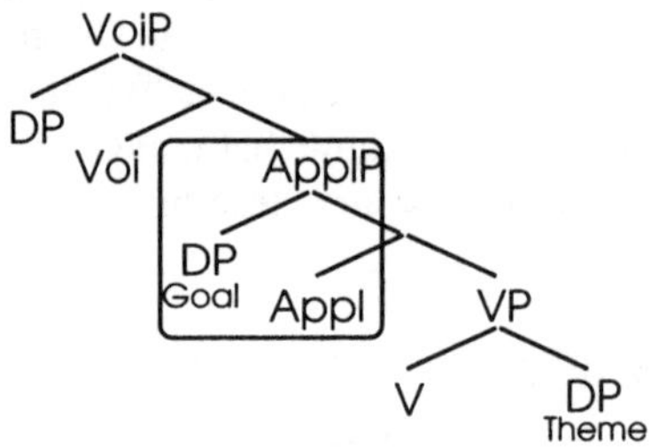

b PC

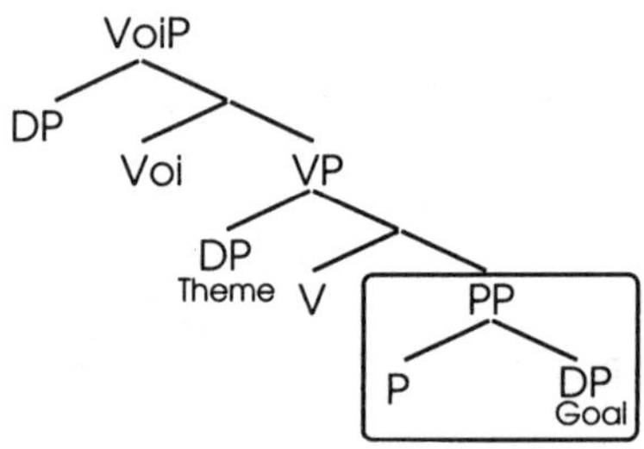

The difference in the expression of the Causee in (49a) and (50) can clearly be stated descriptively in the same terms as the DOC and the PC; in both cases a certain participant is expressed either as a primary object or as an adpositional object. The Causee is in particular similar to Benefactives in this regard, since neither is obligatory. So, if something that we descriptively call a Goal or Benefactive object can be introduced by an applied head or by an adposition, the most straightforward solution for (49a) is to adopt the essentials of the analysis in (55). In other words, in FPs where the Causee has distinct argument properties, we assume that it is introduced

[19]Of course, this is not the only option. Larson (1988) proposed that the DOC is derived from an underlying PC. This route is also taken in Baker (1995abc) and Baker & Stewart (1999).

into the specifier of an applicative phrase (56a), whereas the adjunct by-phrase Causee uncontroversially is a PP (56b).

(56) a

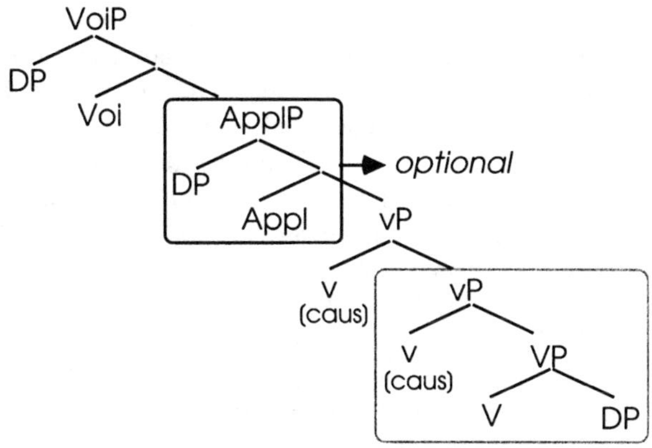

b

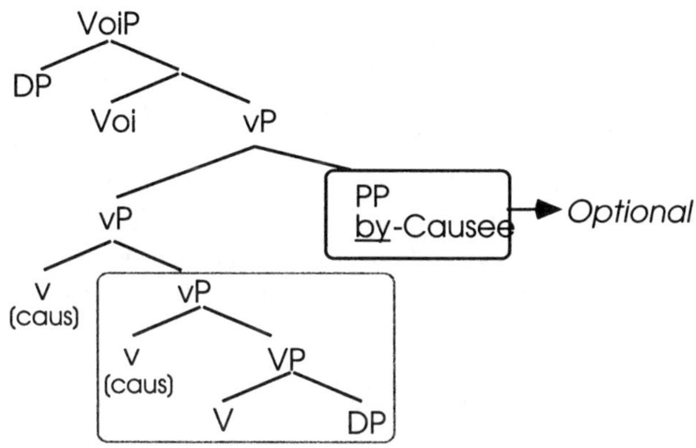

In short, the main difference between Chichewa and Torne Sámi FPs boils down to the availability of an applied head that introduces the Causee.

This idea sheds light another pertinent fact about Torne Sámi, namely that it is impossible to express the Causee as a by-phrase, as shown in (57), where we have attempted to express the Causee with illative and locative cases, in want of any kind of adposition that could do the job.[20]

---

[20]Again, (57) is fine in cerain eastern dialects (Hanna Outakoski, p.c.)

(57) Mon loga-h-in girjji (*mánnái / *mánás)
I.n read-caus-Past.1s book.a child.Ill / child.Loc)
'I made someone/the child read the book.'

In other words, just as Sesotho does not allow prepositional benefactives, Torne Sámi does not allow by-phrases in Causatives. And just like Brazilian Portuguese bans applied benefactives, Chichewa bans the applied Causee. If we treat the Torne Sámi causee as an applied object, then we have a straightforward way to account for the fact it has argument properties, as we have seen manifested in A-binding and A-movement, and at the same time we have a way to account for the fact that it is optional, and we can make sense of the fact that aside from the expresion of the Causee, Torne Sámi causatives behave like protypical FPs.

We are however still missing a piece in the paradigm, under the hypothesis that the Causee may be expressed either as a prepositional adjunct or an applied object, namely a language where both options are available. In other words, it would support the outlined theory if we found a language exhibiting the causative equivalent to the English pattern in (58):

(58) a Peter read a book for the child.
b Peter read the child a book.

In fact, Iberian Spanish fits the profile. This language has the French/Italian-style FI where the argument Causee is realized as an indirect object, (59a), and we also find the familiar FP-causative in (59b) (Aissen 1979). However, in addition to (59a) and (59b), there also a third possibility, where the Causee is realized in the preinfinitival position, (59c) (cf. Torrego 1998, López 2001).

(59) a Hicieron destruir la cuidad a los Marines.
made destroy the city Dat the Marines
'They made the Marines destroy the city.'

b Hicieron destruir la cuidad (por los Marines).
made destroy the city by the Marines
'They made the Marines destroy the city.'

c Hicieron a los Marines destruir la cuidad.
made Dat the Marines destroy the city
'They made the Marines destroy the city.' (Pablo Ruiz, p.c.)

What is interesting about the Spanish paradigm, is the fact that only sentences comparable to (59a) are grammatical when the base verb is a non-agentive perception verb, as in (60):

(60) a Hicieron ver la cuidad a los turistas.
made see the city Dat the tourists
'They made the tourists see the city.'

b *Hicieron ver la cuidad (por los turistas).
made see the city by the turistas
'The had the city seen by the tourists.'

c *Hicieron a los turistas ver la cuidad.
made Dat the tourists see the city
'They made the tourists see the city.' (Pablo Ruiz, p.c.)

Lópes (2001) argues that the post and preinfinital Causees are related by movement, however, such an analysis fails to capture the contrasts between (59) and (60). The judgments are, however, what we would expect under the thesis that the preinfinitival Causee in the Spanish (c)-examples involve an applied FP-Causee. Hence, Iberian Spanish appears to be a language that accommodates both the adpositional adjunct Causee as well as the applied Causee, and is thus abstractly comparable to the possibilities exhibited by the English examples in (58). This fact, in turn, provides additional support for our analysis of Torne Sámi.

5 Concluding Remarks

This paper has touched on a number of issues that arise in the formation of productive morphological causatives in the Torne dialect of North Sámi. We have argued that causatives in this language are uniformly of the FP variety. At first sight, this hypothesis is at odds with the fact that the Causee in Torne Sámi is expressed as an accusative object. However, once we take into consideration factors pertaining to selectional restrictions on the base verb in causativization, it is clear that Torne Sámi does not fit into the FI-profile, in spite of what the superficial surface expression of such causatives would urge us to believe. Moreover, once this additional factor is taken into the picture, we also discover that the Torne Sámi Causee does not exhibit the full range of properties allegedly found in FIs, but which are expected in FPs. On the basis of the behavior of Torne Sámi causatives, we have argued in favor of a fine-grained syntactic decomposition of the VP, and along the lines of Baker & Stewart (1999) and Pylkkänen (1999), that

Kratzer's VoiP and Chomsky's (1995) vP must be considered as two distinct syntactic heads. We have further proposed that the Causee in Torne Sámi FPs is realized as an applied object, in contrast to the PP Causee found in Chichewa and Italian. Further support for an applied analysis, we argued, comes from Iberian Spanish, which exhibits both possibilities.

References

Aissen, J. 1979. *The Syntax of Causative Constructions*. New York: Garland.

Alsina, A. 1992. On the Argument Structure of Causatives. *Linguistic Inquiry* 23: 517-555.

Baker, M. & O.T. Stewart. 1999. Double Headedness and the Anatomy of the Clause. Ms., Rutgers University.

Baker, M. 1988. *Incorporation: A Theory of Grammatical Function Changing*. Chicago: Chicago University Press.

Baker, M. 1995a. Thematic Roles and Syntactic Structure. Ms., McGill University.

Baker, M. 1995b. The Incorporation Theory of Morphosyntactic Alternations. Ms., McGill University.

Baker, M. 1995c. On the Structural Positions of Themes and Goals. Ms., McGill University.

Baker, M. Forthcoming. *On the Lexical Category Distinctions*. Cambridge: Cambridge University Press.

Bordelois, Y. 1988. Causatives: From Lexicon to Syntax. *Natural Language and Linguistic Theory* 6: 57-93.

Bresnan, J, & L. Moshi. 1990. Object Asymmetries in Comparative Bantu Syntax. *Linguistic Inquiry* 21: 147–185.

Burzio, L. 1986. *Italian Syntax: A Government-Binding approach*. Dordrecht: Reidel.

Chomsky, N. 1973. Conditions on Transformations. *A Festschrift for Morris Halle*, ed. S. Anderson and P. Kiparsky. New York: Holt, Rinehart & Winston.

Chomsky, N. 1981. *Lectures on Government and Binding*. Dordrecht: Foris.

Chomsky, N. 1986a. *Barriers*. Cambridge, Mass: The MIT Press.

Chomsky, N. 1986b. *Knowledge of Language: Its Nature, Origin and Use*. New York: Praeger.

Chomsky, N. 1988. *Language and Problems of Knowledge: the Managua Lectures*. Cambridge, Mass: The MIT Press.

Chomsky, N. 1995. *The Minimalist Program*. Cambridge, Mass: The MIT Press.

Chomsky, N. 1998. Minimalist Inquires: the Framework. *MIT Occasional Papers in Linguistics* 15.

Chomsky, N. 1999. Derivation by Phase. *MIT Occasional Papers in Linguistics* 18.

Fodor, J. 1970. Three Reasons for Not Deriving 'Kill' from 'Cause to Die'. *Linguistic Inquiry* 1: 429-438.

Guasti, M. T. 1993. *Causative and Perception Verbs*. Torino: Rosenberg & Sellier.

Guasti, M. T. 1996. Semantic Restrictions in Romance Causatives and the Incorporation Approach. *Linguistic Inquiry* 27: 294-313.

Hale, K. &. S. J. Keyser. 1993. On Argument Structure and the Lexical Expression of Syntactic Relations. *The View from Building 20,* eds. K. Hale and S.-J. Keyser. Cambridge, Mass: The MIT Press.

Halle, M. &. A. Marantz. 1993. Distributed Morphology. *The View from Building 20,* eds. K. Hale and S.-J. Keyser. Cambridge, Mass: The MIT Press.

Harley, H. 1995. Subjects, Events and Licensing. Doctoral dissertation, MIT.

Hoffman, M. 1991. The Syntax of Argument-Structure Changing Morphology. Doctoral dissertation, MIT.

Hornstein, N. 2001. *Move! A Minimalist Theory of Construal.* Oxford: Blackwell Publishers.

Julien, M. 1996. *Syntactic Word Formation in Northern Sámi.* Oslo: Novus.

Kayne, R. 1975. *French Syntax: the Transformational Cycle.* Cambridge, Mass: The MIT Press.

Kitagawa, Y. 1986. Subjects in Japanese and English. Doctoral dissertation, UMass.

Koopman, H. &. D. Sportiche. 1992. Subjects. *Lingua* 85: 211-258.

Kratzer, A. 1996. Severing the External Argument from its Verb. *Phrase Structure and the Lexicon,* eds. J. Rooryck & L. Zaring. Dordrecht: Kluwer.

Kuno, S. 1973. *Nihon bunpoo kenkyuu.* Tokyo: Taishukan Shoten.

Kuroda, S.-Y. 1988. Whether We Agree or Not: A Comparative Syntax of English and Japanese. *Lingvisticae Investigationes* 21: 1-46.

Larson, R. 1988. On the Double Object Construction. *Linguistic Inquiry* 19: 335-391.

Levin, R. &. M. Rappaport Hovav. 1995. *Unaccusativity.* Cambridge, Mass: The MIT Press.

Levin, R. &. M. Rappaport Hovav. 1986. The Formation of Adjectival Passives. *Linguistic Inquiry* 17: 623-661.

Lidz, J. 1997. Dimensions of Reflexivity. Doctoral dissertation, University of Delaware.

López, L. 2001. On the (Non)complementarity of θ-Theory and Checking Theory. *Linguistic Inquiry* 32: 694-716.

Machobane, M. 1989. Some Restrictions on the Sesotho Transitivizing Morphemes. Doctoral dissertation, McGill University.

Manzini, M. R. 1983. On Control and Control Theory. *Linguistic Inquiry* 14: 421-446.

Marantz, A. 1993. Object Asymmetries and the Chichewa Applicative Construction. *Theoretical Aspects of Bantu Grammar*, ed. S. Mchombo. Stanford: CSLI Publications.

Marantz, A. 1997. No Escape from Syntax: Don't Try Morphological Analysis in the Privacy of Your Own Lexicon. *Penn Working Papers in Linguistics.*

Marantz, A. 2001. Words. Ms., MIT.

McGinnis, M. J. 1998. Locality in A-movement. Doctoral dissertation, MIT.

Miyagawa, S. 1984. Blocking and the Japanese Causative. *Lingua* 64: 177-207.

Miyagawa, S. 1989. *Structure and Case Marking in Japanese.* New York: Academic Press.

Miyagawa, S. 1994. *Sase* as an Elsewhere Causative. In the program of *Linguistic Theory and Japanese Language Teaching, 7th Symposium on Japanese.* Tsuda Japanese Language Center.

Nickel, K. P. 1994. *Samisk grammatikk.* Karasjok: Davvi Girji.

Nielsen, C. 1926-29. *Laerebok i lappisk.* Bind 1. Oslo: Universitetsforlaget.

Pylkkänen, L. 1999. Causation and External Arguments. *MIT Working Papers in Linguistics* 35: 161-183.

Reinhart, T. & E. Reuland. 1993. Reflexivity. *Linguistic Inquiry* 24: 657-720.

Reuland, E. 2001. Primitives of Binding. *Linguistic Inquiry* 32: 439-492.

Roberts, I. 1987. *The Representation of Implicit Arguments.* Dordrecht: Foris.

Roeper, T. 1987. Implicit Arguments and the Head-Complement Relation. *Linguistic Inquiry* 18: 267-310.

Shibatani, M. 1976. Causativization. *Syntax and Semantics 5: Japanese Generative Grammar*, ed. M. Shibatani. New York: Academic Press.

Stewart, O. 1998. Serial Verb Construction Parameter. Doctoral dissertation, McGill University.

Svonni, M. & M. Vinka. 2002. North Sámi causatives as *faire par* constructions. *CLS 37: The Panels* (Papers from the 37th Meeting of the Chicago Linguistic Society, vol. 2), eds. M. Andronis, C. Ball, H. Elston and S. Neuvel. Chicago: Chicago Linguistic Society.

Travis, L. 1992. Inner Tense with NPs: the Position of Number. *Proceedings of the 1992 Annual Conference of the Canadian Linguistics Association*, 329-345.

Ura, H. 1996. Multiple Feature Checking: a Theory of Grammatical Function Splitting. Doctoral dissertation, MIT.

Vinka, M. 2002. Causativization in North Sámi. Doctoral dissertation, McGill University.

Watanabe, A. 1996. *Case Absorption and Wh-Agreement.* Dordrecht: Kluwer.

Part IV

Language Change

12

The Emergence of a Definite Article in Estonian

KATRIN HIIETAM AND KERSTI BÖRJARS

1 Introduction*

The aim of this paper is to investigate one particular aspect of the marking of definiteness in Estonian, namely the use of the element *see*, traditionally described as a demonstrative. We want to establish whether the language can be seen to be in the process of developing a dedicated definiteness marker from this demonstrative and, if so, whether the element also still retains its demonstrative function. The investigation is based on a small dataset and will only serve as an indication of what changes are taking place at present. The dataset is not big enough to form the basis for a detailed statistical analysis of the distribution of *see*. This study forms part of a bigger project to study all aspects of the expression of definiteness in Estonian (Hiietam to appear). The bigger investigation shows that case is the main way of indicating pure (non-demonstrative) definiteness in Estonian and this has indeed been the way in which Estonian and some related languages have been described in the literature. However, recent

* Some of the content of this paper was presented at the *Workshop on Circum Baltic syntax* at the *18th Scandinavian Conference on Linguistics*, Lund University, May 2000 and we are grateful to the participants for their comments. We have also benefited from the comments of anonymous referees.

Generative Approaches to Finnic and Saami Linguistics.
Diane Nelson and Satu Manninen (eds.).

studies have indicated for the closely related Finnish, that the corresponding demonstrative is showing some signs of functioning as a pure definiteness marker (Laury 1995, 1997 but see also Juvonen 2000). Similar claims have been made for Estonian (Pajusalu 1997, 1999), but based on a different type of evidence and also, to our minds, on a less systematic study.

Before we can move on to a discussion of our data from Estonian, there is some crucial groundwork to be done. In section 2, we give a very brief overview of the typological variation in the exponence of definiteness. Section 3 contains a discussion of the distinction between demonstrative meaning and pure definiteness. In order to judge whether a demonstrative element can be deemed to be developing into a pure definiteness marker, we need to define carefully the environments which are typical for noun phrases involving pure definiteness, but in which we do not expect demonstrative noun phrases to occur. In section 4, we survey general typologically-based approaches to the development of definiteness markers from demonstratives and in section 5 we evaluate previous studies of these issues in Finno-Ugric languages. In section 6 we present the data we have collected from written and spoken Estonian and in section 7 we consider what conclusions can be drawn from the data.

2 The Exponence and Development of Definiteness Markers

Definiteness as a semantic concept, i.e. as a particular way of referring to entities in the world, probably exists in some guise or other in all languages. Not all languages have explicit and dedicated exponence for this semantic concept, however. Russian, and indeed Estonian, are frequently used in the literature as examples of languages with no dedicated pure definiteness marker. In languages that do have a pure definiteness marker it may take any one of many different shapes; it may be a morphological marker or a syntactic marker; the language may require that definiteness be expressed just once in a noun phrase or that as many elements within the noun phrase as possible are marked for definiteness. English would appear to be an example of a language with "once only" syntactic marking of definiteness, as in example (1). Norwegian, on the other hand, requires more elements to be marked as definite, i.e. there is definiteness agreement within the noun phrase, but at most one of these markers is syntactic, as (2) illustrates (for an analysis of definiteness as an agreement or a non-agreement feature in Germanic, see Börjars & Donohue (2000) and Payne & Börjars (2000)). Hebrew has agreement for definiteness, involving an element that is usually analysed as a syntactic element, but Wintner (2000) provides evidence that it is, in fact, better analysed as a morphological element, data to illustrate can be found in (3).

(1) a. the big book
b. *the big the book
c. that book
d. *that the book

(2) a. den store boken[1] — Norwegian

den	store	boken[1]
DEF	big.DEF	book.DEF

'the big book'

b.

*den	store	bok
DEF	big.DEF	book

c.

*den	stor	boken
DEF	big	book

d. *denne bok

e.

denne	boken
this	book.DEF

'this book'

(3) a. — Hebrew

ha-	sepr	ha-	gadol
DEF	book	DEF	big

'the big book'

b.

*ha-	sepr	gadol	/sepr	ha-	gadol
DEF	book	big	book	DEF	big

c.

ha-	sepr	ha-	ze
DEF	book	DEF	this

'this book'

1 It is not entirely uncontroversial to gloss the adjectival form *store* as 'big.DEF'. An identical form is used in the plural for both indefinite and definite, so that the issue arises whether it should be considered one severely underspecified form. This is the view taken of Danish in Börjars and Donohue (2000). Traditionally, it is assumed that there are two different forms, one occurring in definite environments (both singular and plural) and one in indefinite environments. In this tradition, the definite form is usually referred to as weak and the indefinite as strong.

d. *sepr ha- ze / *ha- sepr ze[2]
book DEF this DEF book this

Languages can also mark definiteness outside the noun phrase, e.g on adpositions, through verb agreement markers or through word order (see Lyons 1999:86–89). Hungarian is a commonly cited example of this, where there is agreement marking on a transitive verb to indicate agreement with the subject for person and number and the object if it is definite: *olvas-ok* 'read-1SG' vs *olvas-om* 'read-1SG.DEF OBJ'. As is well-know from the literature on Finno-Ugric languages, the interaction between grammatical relations and case can also be used to indicate definiteness.[3] The data from Estonian in (4) illustrates.

(4) a. Ma sõin suppi lõunaks.
1S.N eat.PAST.1S soup.P lunch.TRANSL
'I had some soup for lunch.'

b. Ma sõin supi lõunaks.
1S.N eat.PAST.1S soup.A lunch.TRANSL
'I had the soup for lunch.'

Languages may change the way in which they mark definiteness and indeed they may change as to whether or not they mark definiteness explicitly at all. The most common historical source for a pure definiteness marker by far is a demonstrative element.[4] The change from demonstrative to pure definiteness marker is normally described as an instance of grammaticalisation, indeed, Heine, Claudi and Hünnemeyer (1991:6) refer to it as one of the 'paradigm cases of grammaticalization'. Grammaticalisation is standardly assumed to be the process whereby an element goes from being a lexical category to being a grammatical category, or, as in this case, from being a grammatical category to being a more grammatical category. In textbook cases of grammaticalisation, the element undergoes simultaneous or consecutive changes in phonology, morpho-syntax and semantics and in section 7, we will return to consequences of this assumption for the

---

[2] In Hebrew, *this book* can also be expressed as *sepr ze*, without any markers of pure definiteness, but if one marker is present, then each element must be marked (Wintner 2000:323)

[3] For a detailed analysis of the interaction between specificity definiteness and case marking, see Hiietam (to appear).

[4] For examples of other, less common sources, see Lyons (1999:331). For instance, Fraurud (To appear) has shown that there are some sign of possessive markers grammaticalising into definiteness markers in some Uralic languages.

development from demonstrative to definiteness marker.[5] Well-known examples of this change from demonstrative to pure definiteness can be found for instance in Romance where Latin *ille* provides the source for definite articles in Modern Romance, both for syntactic ones, as in French, and morphological, as in Romanian.[6] This development is also amply attested outside the Indo-European languages, Greenberg (1978) gives examples of this.

3 Definiteness and Demonstrativeness

Many attempts have been made at defining the core properties of definiteness. The most influential one is probably Hawkins (1978), but some of the ideas found there build on ideas first put forward in Christophersen (1939). A more recent impressive work in this area is Lyons (1999). Given the scope of this paper, we will need to simplify things here, but we refer to these three books for proper discussion of the subtleties involved. In this section, we will use examples from English, but with the intention of establishing criteria which are not specific to English. The characteristics we are trying to establish are not language specific syntactic restrictions, but more general semantic properties.

Consider first the examples in (5), in each case we assume that the sentence is the first one in a discourse.

(5) a. Put **the egg** in **the bowl**.
b. Put **an egg** in **a bowl**.

Both noun phrases in (5a) are definite; the hearer is assumed by the speaker to be able to identify the specific egg and the specific bowl in question. In this example the identifiability is due to the situation, i.e. the hearer is in a physical location where there is one egg and one bowl which can be identified. Note also that the use of the definite article assumes that there is a unique egg and a unique bowl which can be identified in this way. The

---

[5] Though grammaticalisation is the most commonly used term, some scholars, like Harris & Campbell (1995), do not recognise it as an independent mechanism of syntactic change, but explain the same phenomena in terms of other principles. In fact, recently, one of the core assumptions about grammaticalisation, namely unidirectionality has been called into question, see especially Campbell (2001), Janda (2001), Joseph (2001) and Newmeyer (2001), but also criticism of these views in Eythorsson, Börjars & Vincent (2002).

[6] Some authors have claimed that French *le/la/les* has developed further than a definite article, to become a marker of gender and number, to be replaced as definite article by *ce/cette/ces* without the reinforcing particle *ci/là* (Harris 1977; Harris 1980; Posner 1966). This claim is disputed by Epstein (1993).

example in (5b), on the other hand, does not refer to any specific, unique, identifiable egg or bowl, any element which fits the description will satisfy.

In the previous paragraph, we have associated three properties with the use of the definite article: identifiability, uniqueness and specificity. As we shall see shortly, not all of these properties are necessarily associated exclusively with definite reference.

(6) I've just bought **a new computer** from a company in London. ... **The computer** arrived by special delivery three days later.

The first bold noun phrase is indefinite, however, it is not the case that the reference in this case is non-specific. The speaker is clearly referring to a specific computer, but the indefinite form is used because the speaker is not assuming at this stage that the hearer is familiar with the computer in question. Specificity is then not a property associated exclusively with definite reference. The second bold noun phrase in (6) is definite and the definite reference is warranted here by the fact that the hearer can be assumed to be familiar now with the existence of the computer since it has been introduced into the discourse. So far, we have referred to this as 'identifiability', but going back to Christophersen (1939), the term 'familiarity' is used instead. The reason is that in (6), the hearer may still not to be able to identify the computer that the speaker bought, so that if there were more than one computer in the speaker's room, the hearer may not be able to identify the new one. However, the speaker is familiar with the existence of the computer. This use of the definite article to refer to something that can be assumed to be familiar by virtue of previous mention in the discourse is often referred to as anaphoric use.

The sentences in (7) could be used discourse initially even when there is no previous familiarity with the thought or the computer, either through situation or discourse. In both cases, the information that ensures familiarity is provided after the definiteness marker and the noun. This is referred to as anticipatory anaphoric reference or cataphoric reference.

(7) a. **The thought of having to do an after dinner speech** filled her with fear.

b. **The computer which I bought yesterday** doesn't have a disk drive, but it looks very nice.

Familiarity need not arise directly from the situation or a previous mention. The examples in (8) illustrate:

(8) a. Why don't you look in **the kitchen**.

b. I've just bought a new computer. I'm not that happy with **the keyboard** actually.
c. **The earth** is really just the third rock from the sun.

In (8a), the speaker need not be in a situation in which the kitchen can be directly identified. Instead, world knowledge can be used. As long as the hearer is in some sort of living quarter, the knowledge that such premises usually have a kitchen is sufficient for the speaker to assume joint familiarity. This means then that the situational familiarity can be indirect. Note, however, that uniqueness is also important here. In (8b), the use of a definite noun phrase assumes shared familiarity and this time it depends on the discourse rather than the situation, but as in (8a), it is not direct; the mention of a computer ensures familiarity with the computer and most potential hearers know that with a computer is normally associated one unique keyboard, and hence the speaker can assume the indirect familiarity which warrants the use of the definite article. In (8c), the definite article can be used since our knowledge about the universe means that we can assume familiarity with a unique entity referred to as 'earth'.

Uniqueness is also characteristic of another environment in which definite determiners typically occur, namely noun phrases containing a superlative adjective. The meaning of the superlative ensures uniqueness and, in a sense, also familiarity, which means that an indefinite determiner is infelicitous with a superlative.

(9) a. When you follow this recipe, you need to use **the biggest bowl**.
b. *When you follow this recipe, you need to use **a biggest bowl**.

A further environment in which a pure definiteness marker is frequently used, as Lyons (1999:179ff) points out, is generics. In such cases, the definiteness marker is used with a singular noun and the noun phrase can be said to refer to a prototypical entity of the kind described.[7]

(10) a. **The rat / A rat** is a surprisingly social animal.
b. **Rats** are surprisingly social animals.

We can then sum up the discussion so far and say that the two major characteristics of the use of definite reference are identifiability (or famili-

[7] We refer to Lyons (1999: 181–198) for an overview of the attempts at describing generic reference and the use of definite or indefinite markers and singular and plural nominals.

arity) and uniqueness.[8] The identifiability can be direct or indirect, it can rely on the discourse, the situation or general world knowledge. When based on discourse it can be anaphoric or anticipatory.

Turning now to demonstratives, it is clear that they share some properties with pure definiteness markers, in particular, they are both definite. Our concern here is then to establish some properties that distinguish demonstratives from dedicated definiteness markers so that we can establish for the Estonian element whether it shows characteristics associated with pure definite markers. The most obvious property of demonstratives is that they are deictic, i.e. they relate the entity to the spatio-temporal context. The English *this* and *that* are proximal and distal, respectively, which means that they locate things with respect to the speaker's here or now. However, there are demonstratives which are neutral with respect to the distal-proximal distinction, in fact, the Estonian demonstrative *see* is just such an element.[9]

Since definite articles and demonstratives share properties, it is not surprising that some of the examples we used above can be used with the demonstrative determiner as well.

(11) Put **that egg** in **that bowl.**

In this case, as in (5), identifiability is assumed, and as in (5) we can describe this as situational identifiability. As with pure definiteness, the familiarity can also arise from the discourse, in the following two examples there need not be any extra-linguistic indication:

(12)a. I bought my first computer when I left University. I never really made friends with **that computer**.

b. I decided to buy myself a PC rather than a Mac. **That decision** turned out to have been a mistake.

All the examples in (11) and (12) imply a contrast; (11) rather than (5) would be used if there were more than one egg or more than one bowl and it mattered which egg or bowl was used. To Hawkins (1978) this is a property

8 With plurals and mass nouns, uniqueness is not really an appropriate term. Instead, the crucial thing is that reference is to **all** the entities that satisfy the description. For this Hawkins (1978) used the term 'inclusiveness'. This distinction is not really required for our purposes here, however.

9 Indeed, some linguists have claimed that the spatio-temporal property is the only distinguishing feature between *this/that* and *the* (J. Lyons 1977; Sommerstein 1972). However, we will show that there are other reasons for distinguishing them and we therefore follow C. Lyons (1999:19–20) in rejecting this view.

of all demonstratives; some kind of contrast is always implied.[10] This property, of course, clashes with one of the properties of pure definiteness markers, uniqueness. If the reference is unique, then a contrast cannot be implied (or explicit) since there is nothing to contrast with. This means that the use of a demonstrative becomes infelicitous in some of the contexts in which a pure definiteness marker can be used.

(13) a. #Why don't you look in **that kitchen**.
b. #I've just bought a new computer. I'm not that happy with **that keyboard** actually.
c. #**That earth** is really just the third rock from the sun.
d. #When you follow this recipe, you need to use **that biggest bowl**.

The example in (13a) could only be used in a situation in which contrast is implied; there must be two kitchens within the relevant location. Similarly, in (13b), there must be a contrast with some other keyboard, and even then, the more likely formulation would be *the keyboard of **that** computer*, with the demonstrative associated with the entity which has been directly introduced. In fact, the use of a demonstrative with indirect familiarity is usually infelicitous. This particular distinguishing property has been analysed in different ways by different authors, but it seems clear that the use of a demonstrative demands a more direct identifiability than a pure definiteness marker (see Hawkins' matching constraint' (1978) and the notion of 'immediate accessibility' in Lyons (1999:20–21.)) The use of a demonstrative in (13c) would only be acceptable if there was another earth with which to contrast this one. Finally, the basic contrastive meaning of a demonstrative means that (13d) would not normally be acceptable; it could only be used in contexts where, say, the speaker and the hearer were arguing about which bowl was the biggest.

Just as indirect familiarity rarely permits the use of a demonstrative, neither does familiarity which arises through a description which follows the noun itself. This is what we referred to as anticipatory or cataphoric reference above.

(14) a. ***That thought of having to do an after dinner speech** fillcd her with fear.

[10] An anonymous referee objects that this is not true, since in some Finnic languages there are demonstratives which may be used where no contrast is implied. One point we want to make in this paper is that this very fact is a sign that these demonstratives are involved in a process of grammaticalisation.

b. **#That computer which I bought yesterday** doesn't have a disk drive, but it looks very nice.

The use of the demonstrative in (14b) can be acceptable if some derogatory meaning is intended, this has been described as an 'emotional distal' use (Lakoff 1974).

Finally, whereas we saw that in many languages a pure definiteness marker can be used with generic reference, both the contrast and the deictic sense inherent in a true demonstrative precludes their use with generic reference. Hence neither of the examples in (15) can be interpreted as having generic reference, but there will be assumed to be a specific instances or instances of the species to which it refers. Furthermore, the reference must be contrastive or deictic.

(15)a. That rat is a sociable animal.
b. Those rats are surprisingly sociable animals.

In terms of pinning down a distinction between definiteness and demonstrativeness, we can make the following table. Tables like this can help make things clearer, but as always, one must be aware that they are the result of simplifications.

PROPERTY	PURE DEFINITENESS	DEMONSTRATIVES
situational familiarity	√	√
familiarity through world knowledge	√	χ
discourse familiarity: direct	√	√
indirect	√	χ
anticipatory	√	χ
uniqueness / inclusiveness	√	χ
contrastiveness	χ	√
generics	√	χ

Table 1: Properties of definite articles and demonstratives

This distribution of properties then means that if a previously purely demonstrative element occurs in contexts where there is no contrast implied, or where the familiarity is indirect or anticipatory or based on world knowledge, then we would have grounds for assuming that a change to definiteness marker is in progress.

4 The Development of Definite Markers from Demonstratives

The change from a demonstrative to a definite marker can be said to involve a weakening of content, in this case from grammatical to a weaker grammatical meaning. As discussed by Greenberg (1978), the weakening frequently continues past the stage of a definiteness marker into a marker of noun class marker or case. In functional terms, it is not a surprising change; a demonstrative can be seen as an emphatic element, and emphatic elements have a tendency of losing their emphasis over time. Another example of such a change is that sketched by Givón (1976) where a pronoun occurring in an argument position where it replaces a topicalised element develops into a pure agreement marker. When the development from demonstrative to definiteness marker takes place, the demonstrative may be replaced eventually, or it may be obligatorily intensified by an adverbial demonstrative; *this here problem* or Swedish *den där boken*.[11]

Greenberg (1978:61–70) posits three stages to this development:

STAGE 0 when a demonstrative has developed from a purely deictic function to identifying elements that have been previously mentioned

STAGE I when the discourse deictic element becomes compulsory and has come to mean “identified” in general, including through context, general knowledge or because it is unique.

STAGE II when the choice of articles is largely grammaticalised, being determined by the syntactic construction and is thus redundant

In the case of Estonian *see* it is quite clear that it has not developed beyond the stage of a marker of pure definiteness, so for our purposes it is the changes involved in Stage 0 and Stage I which are of particularinterest.

---

[11] For arguments that the Swedish *den här / den där* should be seen as singular units syntactically, see Börjars (1998:20-22).

Diessel (1999; 2000) has performed a broad typological study of demonstrative elements in general and their common paths of grammaticalisation. He distinguishes between the distribution of a demonstrative and its category. There are four syntactic contexts; pronominal, adnominal, adverbial and identificational demonstratives, and there are four corresponding categories; demonstrative pronoun, demonstrative determiner, demonstrative adverb and demonstrative identifier. However, it is rare for a language to have distinct categories for each context. The only context we are interested in here is the adnominal one.[12] Diessel makes the point that the syntactic context in which a demonstrative can occur determines the path which its development may take. The most important one for us here is that adnominal demonstratives frequently develop into definite articles.[13]

On the basis of his typologically broad study, Diessel (1999:19–20) details four areas of change that frequently occur when a demonstrative element grammaticalises:

FUNCTIONAL CHANGES:

(a) grammatical items that develop from demonstratives are no longer used to focus the hearer's attention on entities in the outside world;

(b) they are usually deictically non-contrastive.

SYNTACTIC CHANGES:

(c) their occurrence is often restricted to a specific syntactic context;

---

[12] It is not absolutely clear whether Diessel would consider there to be a distinction in Estonian between a demonstrative pronoun and a demonstrative determiner. The demonstrative *see* can certainly be used both pronominally and adnominally, but Diessel's criteria for making a distinction are quite subtle. 'Adnominal demonstratives in English are, for instance, phonologically and morphologically indistinguishable from demonstrative pronouns; but I would argue that adnominal *this* and *that* do not function as independent pronouns that are joined to an appositive noun. Pronominal and adnominal demonstratives have the same form in English, but their syntax is different.' (Diessel 1999:6). The argument is then that since the adnominal demonstrative forms part of the noun phrase in much the same way as the definite determiner does, its syntax is different from a pronoun, which is in itself a noun phrase. This takes the discussion back to the debate about whether or not a distinction between determiners and pronouns is at all valid in English, or whether there is just one category which may or may not be "transitive" in the sense of being able to take a complement: *We / we students are tired of this* versus **The / The students are tired of this* or *I / *I student am tired of this*. If they are viewed as belonging to the same category, then the question arises as to whether it is a noun or a determiner. This debate can be traced back to Postal (1969) and Sommerstein (1972). However, the subtlety of this distinction, though interesting, is not relevant for our discussion here.

[13] The other categories which may result from the historical development of adnominal demonstratives in Diessel's study are; boundary markers of postnominal relative markers, determinatives and number markers.

(d) they are often obligatory to form a certain grammatical construction.

MORPHOLOGICAL CHANGES:
(e) they are usually restricted to the distal, or, less frequently, the proximal form;
(f) they may have lost their ability to inflect.

PHONOLOGICAL CHANGES:
(g) they may have undergone a process of phonological reduction;
(h) they may have coalesced with other free forms.

A point should be made with respect to (e); many linguists have commented on the fact that if a language has demonstratives marked for proximity, it is the most distal one in that system which is most likely to develop into a definiteness marker (see e.g. Harris & Campbell 1995; Harris 1980). However, unmarked demonstratives, where they occur, would also appear to be a common source of definiteness markers. In fact, Lyons (1999: 331–4), even speculates that the development from a deictically marked demonstrative to a definiteness marker would normally go through an initial stage in which the demonstrative maintains its demonstrativeness, but loses its reference to proximity. An interesting example to mention here is Swedish, where the definite article *-en* or *den* originates from an unmarked demonstrative **eno* Noreen (1923: 316–317), but where *den* still exists as a distal demonstrative, while at the same time combinations of *den* with either a distal or proximal adverbial demonstrative have grammaticalised separately: *den där* 'that' and *den här* 'this'.[14]

Diessel points out that in the early stages of grammaticalisation the morpho-syntactic and phonological properties may not be different between the grammaticalised element and the source element. We shall see in section 7 that there have been no morpho-syntactic or phonological changes in Estonian; the changes that have occurred are all functional.

Diessel points out that 'there is no clear-cut borderline between demonstratives and grammatical markers; there are only demonstratives that are more or less grammaticalized.' (Diessel 1999:20). The purpose of his criteria is then to see whether an element has started on the path of grammaticalisation, and if so, how far it has gone along that path. This is also the spirit in which Greenberg's (1978) stages should be interpreted, they are not discreet stages, but focal points along a scale. Also, it is not the case that all elements will end up at the extreme end of the scale, as noun class or case

[14] For further discussion of the development of the Scandinavian definite article, see Perridon (1989).

markers. The issue in which we are interested here is then not what the Estonian *see* should be called, but whether or not it shows any signs of having started out on the grammaticalisation path.

In this sense our paper is different in spirit from that of Cyr (1993). Montagnais, the Cree language studied by Cyr, and Cree languages more generally are traditionally described as languages which do not have a definite article, but in which the demonstrative determiner can fill some of the functions of a definite article. Her concern is that there comes a point in language development, when it is not the case that the demonstrative **functions as** a definite article, but where it **is** a definite article. Her criteria (Cyr 1993:197) for when the terminology should change are:

- if a grammatical entity X in a language A and a grammatical entity Y in a language B have similar semantico functional range of application; and
- if X represents an earlier stage of grammaticalization than Y, cross-linguistically speaking; and
- if X in the language A has reached a discourse frequency comparable to Y in the language B, then X should be said to be a Y and named as such in the grammatical description of language A.

She then shows that in a number of functions which can be assumed to be filled in other languages by an element referred to as the definite article, particularly in third and later reference to an entity within a text, the element which has been referred to as a demonstrative in Montagnais occurs and hence it should be referred to as the definite article, rather than the demonstrative functioning as a definite article. From a cross-linguistic perspective, it is, of course, helpful if elements with similar behaviour can be referred to by the same terms, but terminology is not our main concern here.

5 Previous Studies of Finnish and Estonian

Finnish, like Estonian, has traditionally been described as a language lacking a definite article, and it is certainly true that there is no element of the same status as *the* in English.[15] Definiteness distinctions are often achieved through the use of different cases, as we saw in section 2, example (4). However, as Laury (1995; 1997) points out, scholars have for a long

[15] In fact, both languages are often described as 'non-article languages', but we will not concern ourselves with the indefinite article here (Erelt 1999; Erelt *et al.* 1995; Pajusalu 1997; Pajusalu 1999). A case may be made for the numeral *üks* having some characteristics of an indefinite article.

time noticed that the demonstrative *se* takes on some article-like uses in spoken Finnish (Latvala 1895, 1899 and further references in Laury 1995, 1997), but Laury was the first linguist to perform a detailed and systematic study of this development based on a large data set.

Laury bases her study on spoken Finnish from three different periods; 1890s, 1930s-40s and 1970s-1990s. Her main claim is that '*se* has become grammaticized in spoken Finnish as a marker of identifiability' (Laury 1995:239). As we saw in section 2, identifiability is also a property of demonstratives, a demonstrative could not be used successfully unless the hearer could be expected to identify the element referred to, either through true deictic reference, or through previous mention, i.e. discourse deictic function. However, what Laury (1995; 1997) shows is that in the more recent texts, the identifiability need not be based on either the physical environment or previous mention, but can be based on indirect reference or general knowledge familiarity. This is indeed one of the criteria for grammaticalisation to definiteness marker which we listed in Table 1 in section 2.

Laury (1995:242) notices that in the three periods she studied, the proportion of lexical noun phrases with identifiable referents which are *se*-marked increases in Finnish: from 27% in the 1890s, to 35% in the 1930s-1940s, to 47% in the 1970s-1990s. The particular use of *se*-marked noun phrases also changes. In the data from 1890s, noun phrases are *se*-marked if they are assumed to be accessible to the hearer from previous discourse and particularly when they refer to some important element of the story. In the 1930s-1940s, the use of *se*-marked noun phrases had been extended to include noun phrases referring to entities which had not been previously mentioned, but which could be assumed to be familiar to the hearer though shared knowledge. One such example is given in (16) (Laury 1995:244).[16]

(16) ... sitte **se** ... **lautturin** ... **emäntä** sitten ni, se
then SE ferry.AGT.G wife.N then so SE

autto meitii sitt sinne
help.PAST 1PL.P then se.LOC-CAT
'then the ferrytender's wife then, she helped us then'

[16] In some cases, the glossing has been changed from Laury's original to fit in with the standard abbreviations of this volume. In order not to prejudge the issues of the status of *see* as a demonstrative or definiteness marker, we will gloss it as SEE in all examples and we will use this also for the Finnish examples.

In this example, there has been no previous mention of either the ferry tender or his wife, but the speaker can rely on the hearer's knowledge of a situation such as the one described to know that they involve ferry tenders and in many cases their wives. This is then a step away from the direct identifiability associated with demonstratives.

The trend of *se*-marked noun phrases indicating identifiability but not prominence in Finnish continues in the data from the 1970s-1990s, with the difference that a higher proportion of identifiable noun phrases are marked with *se*. A further interesting development is that, according to Laury, another demonstrative, *tämä* 'this' is used to indicate discourse prominence, a function filled by *se* in the texts from the 1890s. An example from a story about a confirmation service is given in (17) (Laury 1995:246).

(17)	Ja	**tää**	**miun**	**kaveri**	ni.	Me	oltii
	and	this	1S.G	friend	so	1PL	be.PAST.PASS

	siihen	**alttarille**	mänössä.
	SE.ILL	altar.ALL	go.N.INE

'And my friend, we were going to the altar.'

In this example, Laury assumes that the demonstrative in the first noun phrase is there to mark prominence, a function which the weakened *se* cannot fulfil. The second bold noun phrase shows this weakening of the use of *se*; it is used with a noun that has not been previously mentioned in the discourse, but which can be assumed to be familiar because of knowledge of churches. This is a use not associated with demonstratives.

Laury's thorough study (1995; 1997) shows that the Finnish demonstrative *se* in its adnominal use is taking on uses normally associated with the wider kind of identifiability typical of pure definiteness markers. As the proportion of *se*-marked phrases increases, they are no longer associated with discourse prominence, but with simple identifiability and they are used also when the familiarity is indirect; i.e. associative or achieved through general knowledge. According to Greenberg's (1978) classification, the Finnish *se* is at Stage I. Of course if one took a stricter approach to when an element can properly be called a definiteness marker, e.g. reserved that term for Greenberg's stage II, then *se* could be ruled out. This is, according to Pajusalu (1997) the viewpoint taken by Sundbäck (1995), who claims that the Finnish *se* should not be referred to as a definite article because it is not obligatory to express definiteness. However, the point which is important here and which is well made by Laury is that *se* has taken on functions not standardly associated with a demonstrative.

In a more recent study, Juvonen (2000) interprets the Finnish data differently and comes to a different conclusion. Her study is based on 138 retellings of a non-verbal cartoon by both monolingual and bilingual speakers of Finnish from different age groups. Her approach is a functional-typological one, hence similar to the general type of approach taken by Laury. Juvonen differs from Laury in adopting an approach to grammaticalisation in which obligatory use in specific contexts is what she refers to as the "litmus test" for grammaticalisation. Since 'not one single context could be identified in the data studied, where the absence of an adnominal determiner would have implied non-native behaviour.' (2000:193), Juvonen concludes that *se* has not grammaticalised into a definite article in spoken Finnish. She analysed the data along three different dimensions: genre, predefined groups and individual level. Only at the individual level does she find patterns that suggest grammaticalised use a demonstrative. There is, however, substantial individual variation. Whereas Laury establishes the Finnish *se* as a marker of identifiability and *tämä* as a marker of prominence, Juvonen's study shows that at the level of individual, both *se* and *tämä* are candidates for the status of definite article. Which of the two is used in this way is a matter of individual variation, with *se* being more common.

On the basis of her data, Juvonen also finds evidence of what she calls an 'optional grammatical category'. This is exactly that category which has lead other researchers to claim that spoken Finnish has a grammaticalised definiteness marker. The evidence is based on the statistical comparative method, as used for instance by Cyr (1993), and Juvonen does indeed find similar frequencies of use of the adnominal determiners in her Finnish samples as of definite article languages in an article language. She argues persuasively that the motivation for the use of this element is sociolinguistic in nature.

Comparing Laury (1995, 1997) and Juvonen (2000), then, we can say that there is some overlap between their findings, even though the terminology used is different. There are, however, also some differences in their findings, particularly with respect to the similarities and differences between the use of *se* and *tämä*.

Pajusalu (1997) reaches conclusions similar to those of Laury (1995; 1997) but for the Estonian *see*.[17] Her study is based on modern spoken Es-

[17] Pajusalu translates *see* as 'this', but does state that 'If the pronoun *see* is used to refer to some entity, then the listener generally does not know how distal that entity is.' (Pajusalu 1997:149). We assume here that for standard speakers, *see* is unmarked for proximity, both in its pronominal and its adnominal uses. The fact that the demonstrative adverbials *siin* 'here' and *seal* 'there' can accompany *see* to indicate proximal and distal reference, respectively, can be taken as evidence that *see* in itself has an interpretation which is neutral with respect to

tonian; a political discussion, an interview with an artist (both from the radio) and recorded conversations between University students. She divides the use of the adnominal *see* into a number of categories; (i) to refer to entities already mentioned in the discourse (with varying degree of directness, ranging from the same word used to a paraphrase of that word), (ii) to refer to entities identifiable by shared knowledge, (iii) to function as correlate of a relative or complement clause, (iv) "definite for the speaker" and (v) exophor (text or non-text).[18] In the category (i), the use seems frequently to be in line with discourse deictic uses of demonstratives, and the English translations do indeed use *this* or *that*. With respect to category (ii), which is of interest to us here, given the criteria established in section 3 and summarised in Table 1, Pajusalu (1997) has found 36 such uses. She gives 7 actual examples in the article, and, of these, five are examples of *see* used with the title of a play or films and come from the discussion between University students. It is not clear to us that this use, which in itself is interesting has anything to say about the article-like use of *see*. Indeed in the examples given, it is translated as a demonstrative and in English the definite article would be ungrammatical. The play or film title in some respects behaves like a proper noun. An example is given in (18) (Pajusalu 1997:1578).[19]

(18)	siis	ma	käisin	vaatamas	veel	väikeses
	then	1S	go.PAST.1S	see.SUP.INE	also	little.INE

saalis	**seda**	**"Fernando**	**Kapp**	**saatis**	**mulle**	**kirja"**
hall.INE	SEE.P	F.N	K.N	sent.3S	1S.ALL	letter.G

'and then I also went to the little hall to watch this "Fernando Kapp sent me a letter"'

In one of the other examples provided by Pajusalu (1997:159), it is not clear to us that a contrast is not intended and hence that the use is truly demonstrative. A further problem with this example is that there is indeed an immediately preceding mention of the same entity by the same linguistic expression, so that actually this example belongs in category (i). The example is given in (19).

---

proximity (cf §6.2). Pajusalu also refers to *see* as a demonstrative pronoun, but it is clear throughout that this includes the adnominal use.

[18] Pajusalu (1997:157) also briefly discusses the use of the demonstrative as a hesitation marker in Estonian, but this is not relevant to her main point, nor indeed to our discussion here.

[19] Pajusalu does not provide glossings, so in all examples taken from her article, the glossings are ours.

(19) K: Ma piinlen **selle** eluga rohkem kui
1S agonise.PRES.1SG SEE.G life.COM more than

pilditegemisega. Võibolla.
picturemaking.COM maybe

Elu mõistmisega ja maailma mõistmisega
life.G understanding.COM and world.G understanding.COM

võibolla rohkem.
maybe more

'I feel more anguish in connection with life than when painting a picture. Perhaps. Perhaps more in connection with understanding life and understanding the world.'

I: tähendab kas **selle** elu mõistmise poolega
3S.mean whether SEE.G life.G understanding.G side.COM

või siis selle niisuguse lihtsa äraelamise poolega?
or then SEE.G such.G simple.G living on sth.G side.COM

''Does it mean that in connection with understanding this life or then with simply making the ends meet?'

In category (iii), Pajusalu gives examples where the familiarity associated with the use of *see* arises from the description which follows the element, this was the use which we referred to as anticipatory in section 3, and it is indeed a usage associated with pure definiteness markers rather than demonstrative. An example is provided in (20) (Pajusalu 1997:161).

(20) … ja siis ma näen täpselt, tunnen
and then 1S see.PRES.1S exactly feel.PRES.1S

täpselt **seda fiilingut**, kuidas ma **seda pilti**
exactly SEE.P feeling.P how 1S SEE.P picture.P

pean tegema
1S.must make.SUP

'and then I see exactly, experience the feeling [lit. feel exactly the feeling], how I should paint the picture'

Pajusalu's category (iv) involves a couple of examples which are not strictly relevant to our discussion here. The final category, referred to as exophors, involves two uses; where reference is made a proposition mentioned previously in the discourse, and where reference is made either to some entity present in the speech situation or to the time of the speech situation. As Pajusalu (1997:163) points out, these are purely demonstrative uses of *see*.

Pajusalu (1997:173) concludes that the Estonian *see*, and also the adverbial demonstratives *siin* 'here' and *seal* 'there', are showing signs of being markers of definiteness since they can 'serve as indicators of the identifiable entities'.[20]

6 The Use of *See* in a Corpus of Modern Estonian

6.1 The Data

The data on which we base this study have been compiled from a number of different sources and include both spoken and written language. The spoken data consists of radio interviews recorded during the summer of 2000 from the state-owned radio station *Vikerraadio*. The written data has been taken from newspaper articles in the Estonian newspaper *Postimees* during the summer of 2001. Finally, some of the data comes from biographies which were collected as part of a project run by the *Society of Biographies* at the University of Tartu, these texts, even though written, are based on spoken versions and hence they can be said to be somewhere between written and transcribed spoken language.

6.2 Demonstrative Uses of *See*

Estonian has, in principle, two demonstratives; *see* and *too*. *Too* is a distal demonstrative which is generally not used in the standard language, but occurs mostly in Southern dialects. *See* is best described as unmarked for proximity; it may be combined with both distal and proximal adverbial demonstratives (in Diessel's (1999; 2000) terminology) *siin* 'here' and *seal* 'there'. For some speakers, *see* may, however, be used with some proximal meaning. *See* can be used adnominally or pronominally, but in the former case it clearly does not always fill the functions of a demonstrative. Like Finnish, Estonian has no other competitor for the title of definite article.[21] To make the semantic distinctions associated with definiteness in other

[20] An anonymous referee has pointed out that this can also be said for Finnish *siellä*.

[21] Though Pajusalu uses the term also for the adverbial demonstratives *siin* and *seal*, but they certainly have a weaker claim to the title than *see*.

languages, Estonian uses its well-developed case system and the lack of the indefinite *üks:* nominative case mostly indicates definiteness and partitive case indefiniteness, but there are independent factors related to verb semantics and the choice of object marking which have to be considered separately.[22]

In section 3, we established a number of properties which are characteristic of a demonstrative as opposed to a pure definiteness marker. The core of demonstrativeness lies in the ability to refer deictically and contrastively. To illustrate the deictic use, we provide the constructed example in (21), since our dataset did not contain any examples of this use.

(21)	"Ma	tahan	**seda**	**mõmmit**,"	ütles	Mari
	1S.N	want.PRES.1S	SEE.P	teddy.P	say.PAST.3S	M.N

ja	näitas	kollase	mängukaru	poole.
and	show.PAST.3S	yellow.G	teddy bear.G	toward

'I want **that teddy**, said Mari and pointed towards the yellow teddy bear.'

Examples of contrastive use can, however be found in our texts, for instance the ones in (22).

(22) a.	1999	aasta	sügisest	õpin	Marketingi
	1999.G	year.G	autumn.ELA	study.1S	marketing.G

instituudis	ettevõtlust	ning
institute.INE	enterprise management.PART	and

tahan	väga	vähemalt	**selle**	**kooli**
want.1.S	very	at least	SEE.ACC	school.ACC

kevadel	edukalt	lõpetada.	Elukooliga
spring.ADE	successfully	graduate.INF	school of life.COM

läheb	veel	ilmselt	veidi	aega.
go.3S	still	probably	little bit	time.PART

22 Klaas (1999) has studied the connection between the semantics of the Estonian verbs and its effect on the case marking of the objects. She states that there is a groups of verbs (mostly connected to feelings, emotions, experiences) which only take partitive object regardless of (in)definiteness interpretation of the entity.

'Since the autumn of 1999 I study enterprise management in the Institute of Marketing and I very much would like to graduate from at least that school in the spring. The school of life probably will still take a bit longer…'

b. **See** **aasta** oli huvitav — uus kool,
SEE.N year.N be.PAST.3 interesting new.N school.N

uued tuttavad.
new.PL.N acquaintance.PL.N
'**This year** was interesting – a new school, new acquaintances.'

In (22a), the contrast between the two schools is made explicitly in the example, whereas in (22b) the larger context makes clear that this year is being contrasted with the ones that went before it. Examples like (21) and (22) then show that *see* is still being used in its core deictic or contrastive uses in Estonian.

As Lyons (1999: 105–106, 113–115, 158–160) points out, anaphoric, i.e. discourse deictic, reference stands apart from other types of reference in that the familiarity, uniqueness or inclusiveness required is defined within the linguistic, rather than extra-linguistic context. Some languages do indeed have a separate marker for this type of reference. It is also an area where it can be difficult to distinguish between pure definiteness and demonstrativeness. Hence the use of a demonstrative as a discourse deictic with no contrastive implication can be seen as a first step in the weakening of its core deictic demonstrative properties, the deictic use has been extended from the extra-linguistic environment to the linguistic one. However, the fact that an element can have anaphoric reference cannot in itself be taken as evidence that it has taken on the function of a pure definiteness marker in such environments. We will just provide examples here which show that *see* may function anaphorically, but we will not draw any conclusions about its status from this.

(23) a.Newfoundlandi soost preili nimeks panime
Newfoundland.G breed.ELA lady.G name.TRANSL put.PAST.1PL

Sorry. Selleks, et kõik patud juba
Sorry.N SEE.TRANSL that all.N sin.PL.N already

ette saaks andeks antud. Oleks meie perest
beforehand get.COND forgive.PRTC Be.COND 1.PL.G family.ELA

vaid ükski liige teadnud, kui palju
only one.even member.N know.PRTC how many

neid **patte** saab olema, oleks kutsu
SEE.PL.P sin.PL.P get.3S be.SUP be.COND doggy.N

ilmselt mõnesse teise perre läinud
apparently some.ILL other.ILL family.ILL go.PRTC

'We named the female Newfoundland dog "Sorry", so that all sins would be forgiven already in advance. Had only a single member of our family known how many these sins were going to be, the doggy would apparently have gone to another family.'

b. Kooli tuli minna läbi **suure**
school.ILL must.PAST.3 go.INF through big.G

oru. **See** **org** oli nii mõnigi kord
valley.G SEE.N valley.N be.PAST hence some.NOM time

kasuks…
use.TRA

'To get to school you had to go through a big valley. The (this) valley was often for good use…'

In the examples in (23), no contrast is implied. As can be seen in the idiomatic translations, in this use of *see*, an English demonstrative is a possible, sometimes preferred, translation, even though, as we showed in section 3, the English *this/that* are generally not used in non-demonstrative environments.

6.3 Non-Demonstrative Uses of *See*

The main environments which we established in section 3 as being typical of pure definiteness markers rather than demonstrative ones were (i) environments where the familiarity which is a prerequisite for successful definite reference arises indirectly, (ii) is anticipatory, or (iii) is based on world knowledge and (iv) a number of different environments in which a contrastive interpretation is excluded.[23] In this sub-section, we will discuss these environments with respect to the use of *see* in our data set.

The fact that *see* can be used where the familiarity arises through indirect reference is illustrated in (24).

(24) a. Kui mingil põhjusel tuli hiljem
when some.ADE reason.ADE must.PAST.3 later

kooli minna või kehva hinde pärast
school.ILL go.INF or poor.G mark.G because of

hiljem koju **tulla** org varjas
later home.ILL come.INF valley.N disguise.PAST.3S

selle tuleku ära.
SEE.G coming.G COMP

'... when for some reason you had to go to school later or because of a poor mark to **come** home later the valley disguised **the coming**.'

b. Meil oli vana pastor ...., kelle kodu
1.PL.ADE be.PAST.3 old.N pastor.N who.G home.G

uksed olid noortele lahti. .... **See maja**
door.PL.N be.PAST.3.PL young.ALL open SEE.N house.N

õhkus külalsilahkusest.
radiate.PAST.3.S hospitality.ELA

'We had an old pastor whose **door** was always open to young people. **The house** radiated with hospitality.'

c. Ostsin just **uue arvuti**.
buy.PAST.1S just new.G computer.G

---

[23] An anonymous referee has pointed out that there is a non-deictic, non-demonstrative use of *see* which we have not said anything about, namely the affective use. The emotive use of demonstratives is a metaphorical extension which is not uncommon in languages and which exists also in English as in *That cat has forgotten where the litter tray is again*, which would normally be used non-contrastively, but with a value judgment. Whereas this development is interesting, it does not directly impinge on the issue of whether it is used as a pure definiteness marker or not. See also the comment on (14b).

Tegelikult	mulle	**see**	**klaviatuur**	väga	ei	meeldi.
actually	1S.ALL	SEE.N	keyboard.N	very	NEG	like.BASE

'I've just bought a new computer. I'm not that happy with the keyboard actually.'

In example (24a), we find a first level of indirectness, in the sense that there is a category discrepancy between the first mention and the *see* phrase. The first reference is by means of a verb, or rather two, 'come' and 'go'. The second mention is by a *see* marked noun phrase.[24]

See maja 'SEE house' in (24b) is not in a contrastive context and the familiarity implied by the use of a definite noun phrase rests on a previous indirect mention, namely 'the door of whose home'. In (24c), a constructed example, but acceptable in colloquial Estonian, the identifiability is associative as described in section 3, a type not normally expressed by pure demonstratives.

The example in (25) shows that *see* marked noun phrases can be used when familiarity with the concept can be assumed to be based of world knowledge.

(25)

Minu	arvates	**see**	**maksussüsteem**	ei	ole
1S.G	according to	SEE.N	tax system.NOM	not	be

läinud	hullemaks.
go.PRTC	bad.COMP.TRANSL

'I don't think the tax system has got worse.'

We have also found examples of *see* marked noun phrases used when the familiarity which warrants a definite reading is anticipatory, i.e. where there is no previous mention or shared knowledge assumed, but where there is postmodification.

(26) a.

Tarvitseb	lugeda	Eesti	suuremate
it is necessary	read.INF	Estonia.G	bigger.PL.G

päevalehtede	kuulutusi	et	veenduda	**selles**
daily.PL.G	advertisment.PL.P	that	convince.INF	SEE.INE

[24] It should be pointed out here that infinitivals in Estonian are not nominal; unlike verbal nouns they do not inflect for case and they are modified by adverbials rather than adjectives.

ülepakkumises,	*mis*	*praegu*	*koolitusturul*	*valitseb*.
overbidding.INE	which	now	educational market.ADE	rules

'It is necessary to read the advertisements in the bigger Estonian dailies, to become convinced of the overbidding which rules at the educational market now.'

b. … ja	**see**	**uhke**	**jaanituli**
and	SEE.N	grand.NOM	midsummer night bonfire

mis	*oli*	*sinna*	*kohe*	*sinu*	*aia*
which	be.PAST.3	there.ILL	straight	2S.G	fence.G

taha	*ehitatud*,	põles	niimoodi
behind.ILL	build.PRTC	burn.PAST.3SG	in this way

kenasti.
nicely

'and the midsummer night bonfire which was built straight behind your fence burned so nicely.'

In both examples in (26), there has been no previous mention of the entity referred to and there is certainly no contrast involved. Instead the definiteness is anticipatory, the relative clause following the nominal provides the familiarity required for successful definite reference. As pointed out in section 3, pure definite markers are expected to occur in this environment, but demonstratives are not.

We turn now to environments in which the uniqueness of the referent should make impossible the use of a demonstrative, since a true demonstrative can be assumed to retain some implication of contrast which is incompatible with the uniqueness (Cf Hawkins 1978). The data we have provide examples of *see* in such environments:

(27) a. Mul	on	alatasa	metsa	sattudes
1S.ADE	be.3	always	forest.ILL	get.PRTC

probleeme	metsas	orienteerumisega.
problem.P.PART	forest.INE	find.one's.way.COM

Kuidas	ma	leian	**selle**	**põhja**	**ja**	**lõuna**
how	1S.N	find.1S	SEE.A	north.A	and	south.A

üles,	mille	järgi,	millised	need
up	what.A	according to	which.P.N	SEE.P.N

märgid	on?
sign.P.N	be.

'I have always had problems with finding my way when I get into the forest. How do I find north and south, what are the signs?'

b.

Tead,	**see**	**kuu**	tegelikult	tiirleb
know.2s	SEE.NOM	moon.NOM	actually	circle.3s

ümber maa,	mitte	vastupidi.
aroundearth.GEN	not	the other way around

'You know, the moon actually turns around the earth and not the other way around.'

c.

Teie	eelnevate	kogemuste	põhjal,
2P.G	previous.P.G	experience.P.G	on the ground

kas	julgete	ennustada,	mis	võiks
WH	dare.2p	predict.INF	WH.N	can.COND

tänavu aasta	**selleks**	**kõige**	**populaarsemaks**
this year.ADE	SEE.TRANSL	most	popular.TRANSL
erialaks	kujuneda?		
subject.TRANSL	become.INF		

'On the basis of your previous experiences, do you dare to predict what the most popular subject could be this year?'

The *see*-phrases in (27a) and (27b), are both unlikely to involve a demonstrative interpretation, the contrast involved in the use of the demonstrative would be incompatible with the uniqueness of the concepts involved. Similarly, the superlative in (27c) implies uniqueness and since the most popular subject has not been mentioned in the previous context, there is no question of anaphoric use.

Our data also contains examples of generic use of noun phrases containing *see*. The example in (28) is from a conversation between a journalist and the admission secretary of a university; the journalist asks what documents a typical prospective university student needs to bring. Note that it is not the case that a hypothetical student has been posited to which the noun phrase refers anaphorically.

(28)

Mida	peaks	**see**	**noor**	**inimene**
WH.PART	should	SEE.NOM	young.NOM	person.NOM

meelespidama	ja	kindlasti	kaasa	võtma,	kui
keep in mind.SUP	and	definitely	with	take.INF	when

ta	tuleb	dokumente	siia
3.SG.NOM	come.3.SG	document.PL.PART	here

sisse	tooma?
in.ILL	bring.SUP

'What should a young person bear in mind and definitely bring when (s)he comes to give the documents in?'

Since reference is made here to a prototypical entity, the contrastiveness that is included in the meaning of demonstratives, is incompatible with this environment.

7 Conclusions About Estonian *See*

Returning to our Table 1, and considering the uses of *see* which we have found, we can construct Table 2, in which the occurrence of *see* is indicated.

PROPERTY	POSSIBLE USE OF *SEE*
situational familiarity	√
familiarity through world knowledge	√
discourse familiarity: direct	√
indirect	√
anticipatory	√
uniqueness / inclusiveness	√
contrastiveness	√
generics	√

Table 2: Environments in which *see* can be used

This table shows that *see* can be used in all environments, including those, like situational familiarity or direct familiarity, in which both definite articles and demonstratives can be used; including those environments characteristic of a definite article but not of a demonstrative, like indirect or anticipatory familiarity or uniqueness; and including those in which only a demonstrative can occur, like those involving a contrast.

A further environment in which we find *see*, and which is not described in the literature, is in combination with possessive pronouns. An example from our data set is provided in (29).

(29)

... siin Pärnu	kohal	taevas	on	lambakari,
here Pärnu.G	above	sky.INE	be.3	flock of sheep.N

nii armastas	**see**	**minu**	**isa**	öelda	nende
so love.PAST.3S	SEE.N	1S.G	father.N	say.INF	SEE.PL.P

säbruliste	pilvede	kohta.
curly.PL.P	cloud.PL.P	about

'... here above Pärnu is a flock of sheep in the sky, my father used to say so about curly clouds.'

In this example, which is from our spoken data, the demonstrative precedes the possessive and the noun phrase of which it is a part forms the first mention of the father in the discourse. A construction with a demonstrative followed by a possessive also exists in some marked contexts in English, as in (30).

(30) a. **This my final decision** cannot be revoked.
b. **This her final glimmer of hope** never deserted her.

In the examples in (30), the demonstrative can be said to constitute a separate intonational unit, so that the intonation would be different between *this my decision* and *this old decision*. In fact, in these cases an apposition analysis in which the demonstrative is used pronominally and forms a separate noun phrase is plausible. However, in the Estonian data, the demonstrative lacks stress and can form a prosodic word with the possessive and hence an apposition analysis does not suggest itself. We do not fully understand the environments in which noun phrases containing a combination of a demonstrative and a possessor can occur, but we want to note a few things in relation to it. Firstly, the construction type also occurs with the other demonstrative *too* as in (31).

(31)

... ta	oli	oma	õepereski	kuulnud,
3S.NOM	be.PAST.3	REFL.G	sister's family.INE	hear.PAST.3S

kui	allakäinud	ja	vastik	naisterahvas	**too**	**tema**
how	deprive.PRTC	and	nasty	woman.N	TOO.N	3S.G

kooliõde	**Viiu**	on.
schoolmate.N	Viiu.N	be.3

'... she had even heard in her sister's family how depraved and nasty woman her school mate Viiu is.'

In this example, the use of *too* has negative connotations and the combination of *too* and possessor often will have a derogatory flavour. It is clear from the context that *see* in (29) does not have any such connotations, even though it may have, as in the constructed example in (32).

(32) Mis see minu abikaasa ka söögitegemisest teab?
what SEE.N 1S.G husband.N also cooking.ELA know.3S
'What does that husband of mine also know of cooking?'

Secondly, if the order between the possessive and the demonstrative in (29) is reversed, the native native speakers we have consulted agree; an ungrammatical construction arises; **minu see isa*. However, in our sample, noun phrases with a possessives preceding SEE can be found as in (33).

(33) a. **Minu see Amnende villa** oli siiski
1S.G SEE.N Amnende villa.N be.PAST.3 yet
rahvast täis...
people.P FULL
'My Amnende villa was yet full of people...'

Native speaker judgements vary as to the grammaticality of examples of this kind and some of the small group of speakers we consulted rejected the order in (33), which actually occurred in our recordings For the majority of speakers we asked, the opposite order between the possessor and the demonstrative, *see minu Amnede villa*, was deemed to be acceptable. The uncertainty surrounding these construction types is then great and we have nothing more to say about them here. A large-scale invetsigation may reveal clearer patterns.

In terms of the changes which Diessel (1999; 2000) posits take place when a demonstrative grammaticalises, *see* has undergone the functional changes, but not the syntactic, morphological and phonological ones. We are considering only the adnominal position and the syntactic behaviour is identical for the demonstrative and the non-demonstrative uses. As far as morphology is concerned, the non-demonstrative *see* can have all the forms listed for *see* in Appendix 1, with no phonological differences, except that the demonstrative can be stressed and the non-demonstrative use cannot. However, segmentally, the non-demonstrative use does not differ from the unstressed use of the demonstrative. According to Diessel, this partial change — functional, but not formal — is common in the early stages of grammaticalisation. Considering Greenberg's categories, it is clear that *see* has passed beyond Stage 0. Some of the changes associated with Stage I are in evidence; *see* has acquired the ability to be used when the identifiability is indirect. However, *see* is obligatory in a noun phrase only if a demonstrative interpretation is intended. For a non-demonstrative definite reading, however, *see* is never obligatory. In a non-contrastive definite interpretation of *see*, the two noun phrases in (34) can yield exactly the same interpretation.

(34)	a.	Kui	sa	vaatad	**seda**	**pilti**.
		when	2S	look. PRES.2S	SEE.P	picture.P
	b.	Kui	sa	vaatad	**pilti**.	
		when	2S	look.PRES.2S	picture.P	
		'when you look at the picture.				

We can conclude then that the Estonian *see* has started to show signs of grammaticalising into a definiteness marker, but that, in Greenberg's terms, it is not yet a definite article. Comparing with Laury's (1995; 1997) results for Finnish, our impression is that the Finnish *se* has developed further than its Estonian cognate. Having said this, it is also obvious from the data studied that this grammaticalisation is limited to some speakers and some contexts. Under the strict view taken by Juvonen (2000), this would then not be true grammaticalisation, but would fit in with her notion of an optional grammatical category. Only a further in depth study of this particular construction in Estonian along the lines of her study of Finnish would reveal how the conditions of use of this optional grammatical category in Estonian compares to those established for Finnish by Juvonen (2000).

A further indication that the grammaticalisation of *see* has not proceeded that far is the fact that we have found no indication of any other demonstrative taking the place of *see*. We would speculate that were *see* to grammaticalise to the stage where it is obligatory to indicate definite reference, then some other way of indicating true demonstrativeness, like contrastiveness would be found. Obvious contenders would be obligatory use of *siin* 'here' or *seal* 'there' or the spread of the distal demonstrative *too*.

The data we have presented here is limited, but we believe that there is sufficient evidence here for the conclusion that the Estonian *see* has come some way towards becoming a marker of non-contrastive definiteness. It would appear likely that the grammaticalisation of *see* will continue, but it is impossible to say at this stage whether it will truly become a definite article in the sense of being obligatory in order for a pure definiteness interpretation to be achieved. It would be interesting to have a large scale study based on data from different age groups; Pajusalu (1997) does report that the younger speakers in her study (i.e. the University students) used *see*-marked noun phrases more with entities which are identifiable due to shared knowledge than the speakers in the other groups. It would appear then that for the younger speakers, *see* has acquired more of the characteristics of a marker of pure definiteness.

References

Börjars, K.E. 1998. *Feature distribution in Swedish noun phrases*. Oxford: Blackwell.

Börjars, K.E. & Donohue, M. 2000. Much ado about nothing – features and zeroes in Germanic noun phrases. *Studia Linguistica* 54:309–353.

Campbell, L. 2001. What's wrong with grammaticalization? *Language Sciences* 23:113–161.

Christophersen, P. 1939. *The articles : a study of their theory and use in English.* Copenhagen: Munksgaard.

Cyr, D. 1993. Cross-linguistic quantification: definite articles vs demonstratives. *Language Sciences,* 15:195–229.

Diessel, H. 1999. The morphosyntax of demonstratives in synchrony and diachrony. *Linguistic Typology,* 3: 1–49.

Diessel, H. 2000. *Demonstratives. Form, function and grammaticalization.* Amsterdam: John Benjamins.

Epstein, R. 1993. The later stages in the development of the definite article: evidence from French. *Historical linguistics 1993: selected papers from the 11th International Conference on Historical Linguistics*, ed. Henning Andersen, 159–76. Amsterdam: John Benjamins.

Erelt, M. 1999. Agreement In Estonian. In *Estonian: Typological Studies III*, ed. Matti Erelt, 47–83. Tartu: Tartu University Press.

Erelt, M. *et al.* 1995. *Eesti keele grammatika I Morfoloogia, Sõnamoodustus.* Tallinn: Eesti Teaduste Akadeemia Eesti Keele Instituut.

Eythorsson, T., Börjars, K. & Vincent, N. 2002. On defining degrammaticalization. Paper presented at *New Reflections on Grammaticalization 2*, Amsterdam, April 2002.

Fraurud, K. To appear. Possessives with extensive use: a source of definite articles? In *Dimensions of possession*, ed. Michael Herslund & Irène Baron. Amsterdam: John Benjamins.

Givón, T. 1976. Topic, pronoun and grammatical agreement. In *Subject and topic*, ed. C.N. Li, 149–88. New York: Academic Press.

Greenberg, J. H. 1978. How does a language acquire gender markers? In *Universals of human language Vol II*, eds. J. H. Greenberg, C.A. Ferguson & E.A. Moravcsik, 47–82. Stanford, Ca: Stanford University Press.

Harris, A.C. & Campbell, L. 1995. *Historical syntax in cross-linguistics perspective*. Cambridge: Cambridge University Press.

Harris, M.B. 1977. 'Demonstratives', 'articles' and 'third person pronouns' in French: changes in progress. *Zeitschrift für romanische Philologie* 93, 249–61.

Harris, M.B. 1980. The marking of definiteness: a diachronic perspective. In *Papers from the fourth International Conference on Historical Linguistics*, eds. E. Traugott, R. LaBrum & S. Shepherd, 75–86. Amsterdam: John Benjamins.

Hawkins, J. 1978. *Definiteness and indefiniteness. A study in reference and grammaticality prediction*. London: Croom Helm.

Heine, B, Claudi, U. & Hünnemeyer, F. 1991. *Grammaticalization. A conceptual framework*. Chicago: University of Chicago Press.

Hiietam, K. To appear. Definiteness in Estonian. Doctoral dissertation, Manchester University.

Janda, R.D. 2001. Beyond "pathways" and "unidirectionality": on the discontinuity of language transmission and the counterability of grammaticalization. *Language Sciences* 23:265–340.

Joseph, B.D. 2001. Is there such a thing as "grammaticalization"? *Language Sciences* 23:163–186.

Juvonen, P. 2000. Grammaticalizing the dfinite article. A study of definite adnominal determiners in a genre of spoken Finnish. Doctoral dissertation, Stockholm University.

Klaas, B. 1999. Dependence of the object case on the semantics of the verb in Estonian, Finnish, and Lithuanian. *Estonian: Typological Studies III*, ed M. Erelt, 47-83. Tartu Ülikooli Eesti keele Õppetooli toimetised. 11. Publications of the Department of Estonian of the University of Tartu. 11. Tartu: Tartu University Press.

Lakoff, R. 1974. Remarks on *this* and *that*. *Papers from the 10th regional meeting of the Chicago Linguistic Society*, eds. M. La Galy, R. Fox & A. Bruck, 345–56. Chicago: Chicago Linguistic Society.

Latvala, S. 1895. Lauseopillisia havaintoja Luoteis-Satakunnan kansankielestä. *Suomi* 12:1–89.

Latvala, S. 1899. Lauseopillisia muistiinpanoja Pohjois-Savon murteesta. *Suomi* 17:1–90.

Laury, R. 1995. On the grammaticalization of the definite article *se* in spoken Finnish. *Historical linguistics 1993: selected papers from the 11th International Conference on Historical Linguistics*, ed. H. Andersen, 239–50. Amsterdam: John Benjamins.

Laury, R. 1997. *Demonstratives in interaction : the emergence of a definite article in Finnish*. Amsterdam: John Benjamins.

Lyons, C. 1999. *Definiteness*. Cambridge: CUP.

Lyons, J. 1977. *Semantics 1-2*. Cambridge: Cambridge University Press.

Newmeyer, F.J. 2001. Deconstructing grammaticalization. *Language Sciences* 23:187–229.

Noreen, A. 1923. *Altisländische und altnorwegische Grammatik* (4th ed). Halle: Max Niemeyer.

Pajusalu, R. 1997. Is there an article in (spoken) Estonian? *Estonian Typological Studies II*, ed. M. Erelt, 146–77. Tartu: Tartu University Press.

Pajusalu, R. 1999. Deiktikud Eesti keeles. PhD thesis, Tartu Ülikooli Kirjastus.

Payne, J.R & Börjars, K.E. 2000. The exponence of definiteness in the noun-phrase: an LFG account. *Proceedings of the LFG'00 conference*, eds. M. Butt & T. Holloway King, Stanford: CSLI. Online proceedings: http://cslipublications. stanford.edu/LFG/5/lfg00.html.

Perridon, H. 1989. Reference, definiteness and the noun phrase in Swedish. Doctoral dissertation, University of Amsterdam.

Posner, R. 1966. *The Romance languages: a linguistic introduction*. Garden City, Ny: Anchor Books.

Postal, P.M. 1969. On so-called "pronouns" in English. In *Modern studies in English. Readings in transformational grammar*, eds. D A Reibel & S A Schane, 201-24. Englewood Cliff, NJ: Prentice-Hall.

Sommerstein, A.H. 1972. On the so-called definite article in English. *Linguistic Inquiry* 3:197-209.

Sundbäck, I. 1995. Suomen kielessäkö artikkeli?. *Kielikello*. 2: 25–8.

Wintner, S. 2000. Definiteness in the Hebrew noun phrase. *Journal of Linguistics* 36: 319-363.

Appendix: The Estonian case system

The plural marker comes prior to the case marker. Case marker in **Bold**, plural marker in *Italics*. The Estonian partitive case = accusative in other languages (Latin, German). Illative, inessive and elative are interior local cases. Allative, adessive and ablative are exterior local cases.

	Singular		Meaning
1. **Nominative**	See	See puu	**(the/this/that) tree**
2. **Genitive**	Selle	Selle puu	**Of the tree**
3. **Partitive**	Se-**da**	Se-**da** puu-**d**	**tree (as a partial subject or partial object)**
4. **Illative**	Selle-**sse**	Selle-**sse** puu-**sse**	**Into the tree**
5. **Inessive**	Selle-**s**	Selle-**s** puu-**s**	**In the tree**
6. **Elative**	Selle-**st**	Selle-**st** puu-**st**	**From, of, out of the tree**
7. **Allative**	Selle-**le**	Selle-**le** puu-**le**	**To the tree**
8. **Adessive**	Selle-**l**	Selle-**l** puu-**l**	**Upon, on, at the book, tree**
9. **Ablative**	Selle-**lt**	Selle-**lt** puu-**lt**	**From, off the tree**
10. **Translative**	Selle-**ks**	Selle-**ks** puu-**ks**	**For, as the tree**
11. **Termina-tive**	Selle-**ni**	Selle puu-**ni**	**Up to, to, (till, until) the tree**
12. **Essive**	Selle-**na**	Selle puu-**na**	**As the tree**
13. **Abessive**	Selle-**ta**	Selle puu-**ta**	**Without the tree**
14. **Comitative**	Selle-**ga**	Selle puu-**ta**	**With the tree**

13

On the Negated Past in Finnic and Saami

MARIT JULIEN

1 Introduction*

In many Finnic and Saami languages, the past participle shows up not only in perfect tense constructions, as in (1a), but also in the negated past, as in (1b). In the affirmative past, on the other hand, as in (1c), the tense marker is different from the participle. The examples given here are from Northern Saami, but a similar pattern is found in Inari Saami, Skolt Saami, Kildin Saami, Finnish, Karelian, Northern Estonian, Votian, and Ingrian (Korhonen 1973, Trosterud 1994).

(1) a. Moai letne jearra-n Bireh-is.
1d.n be.2d ask-pp Biret-loc
'We (two) have asked Biret.'

* The research for this paper was financially supported by the Research Council of Norway, grant no. 110928/520. The final version has benefited greatly from the editors' comments to an earlier version as well as from the suggestions of an anonymous reader. I also wish to thank Biret Anne Bals and Harald Gaski for helping me with some of the data.

Generative Approaches to Finnic and Saami Linguistics.
Diane Nelson and Satu Manninen (eds.).

b. Moai ean jearra-n Bireh-is.
   1d.n neg.2d ask-pp Biret-loc
   'We (two) did not ask Biret.'

c. Moai jeara-i-me Bireh-is.
   1.d.n ask-past-2d Biret-loc
   'We (two) asked Biret.'

While the occurrence of the participle in (1a) is in line with the use of the participle in other languages that have one, the construction in (1b) is somewhat surprising, given that the verb form that appears in the affirmative past bears no likeness to the participle, and moreover, a negated past like (1b) clearly does not have a perfect reading.

In this paper, I will argue that past participles in general are the nonfinite realisations of tense heads with a [+Past] feature. This means that in the so-called 'perfect' constructions, where the participle is combined with a tense-marked auxiliary, there are at least two occurrences of tense. Where the past participle is used in the negated past, on the other hand, the participle is the only tense-marked element of the construction. The reason why the past tense is spelled out as a participial ending in constructions like (1b) is that the tense head here has not moved to the Finite head—only the negation has. Because of this, the nonfinite, participial past tense marker shows up. That is, the markers on the main verbs in (1a) and (1b) are not only formally identical; they represent exactly the same underlying set of features.

I start the discussion, in section 2, by giving a sketch of the diachronic development of the negated past, as described in Korhonen (1973, 1981). In section 3 I consider the analysis of this development given by Trosterud (1994). I show that Trosterud's analysis, according to which the use of the participle appeared in the negated past is a consequence of paradigm economy, is not empirically adequate.

In section 4 I turn to Holmberg et al. (1993), who suggest that the distribution of the Finnish participle is due to the participle having a variable feature specification, which allows it to appear under two different functional heads. Their analysis will be contrasted with the one I present here, according to which the participle has the same feature specification in all its occurrences.

In section 5, I deal with the claim that participles represent tense and not aspect. In section 6 follows my analysis of the past participles in Saami and Finnic, and of the development of the use of participles in the negated past. In section 7 I add a comment on the Northern Saami verb *leat* 'be', which is exceptional in that the form that appears in the perfect is not identical to the form that appears in the negated past. Finally, my conclusions are summed up in section 8.

2 The Diachrony of the Negated Past

According to Korhonen (1973, 1981) the construction that is now the negated past in Finnish, Northern Saami, and several related languages, was originally the negative of the perfect construction. In (2) I list a selection of verb forms from the reconstructed Proto-Finnic. Since what we are interested in here is the distribution of individual markers and not their form as such, I follow Korhonen (1973) and use modern Finnish word forms.

(2) *Proto-Finnic verb forms (Korhonen 1973:181)*

	AFFIRMATIVE		NEGATIVE		
PRESENT	minä	kuule-n	minä	e-n	kuule
	I	hear-1s	I	neg-1s	hear
PAST	minä	kuul-i-n	minä	e-si-n	kuule
	I	hear-past-1s	I	neg-past-1s	hear
PRESENT	minä	kuul-lut	minä	e-n	kuul-lut
PERFECT	I	hear-pp	I	neg-1s	hear-pp

The construction with the negation carrying the tense marker is still preserved in Southern Saami, Livonian, Southern Estonian, and in the Mordvin, Mari, Permic, and Samoyed languages (Korhonen 1973, Trosterud 1994). The examples in (3) and (4) are Southern Saami (from Bergsland 1994).

(3) a. Manne guarka-m.
I understand-1s
'I understand.'

b. I-m guarkah.
neg-1s understand
'I don't understand.'

(4) a. Manne guarka-ji-m.
I understand-past-1s
'I understood.'

b. I-dtji-m guarkah.
neg-past-1s understand
'I didn't understand.'

The example in (5) shows that the copula is optional in the Southern Saami perfect.

(5) Manne {(lea-m/li-m} guarke-me.
I be.pres-1s/be.past-1s understand-pp
'I have/had understood.'

Strikingly, there is a strong positive correlation between the presence of a past tense form of the negation and the absence of an obligatory copula. Korhonen (1973) suggests that there is a causal relation between these two properties: Historically, the introduction of the copula led to the construction that used to be the negated present perfect taking over the function of the negated past.

After the copula was introduced, the old present perfect constructions were replaced by constructions containing a copula. But as Korhonen (1973) points out, the old negated form of the present perfect was not dropped from the language immediately. Hence, there was a stage where the following forms all coexisted:

(6) *Verb forms at the intermediate stage (Korhonen 1973:182)*

	AFFIRMATIVE			NEGATIVE			
PRESENT	minä	kuule-n		minä	e-n		kuule
	I	hear-1s			I		neg-1s
	hear						
PAST	minä	kuul-i-n		minä	e-si-n		kuule
	I	hear-past-1s		I	neg-past-1s		hear
??				minä	e-n		kuul-lut
				I	neg-1s		hear-pp
PRESENT	minä	ole-n	kuul-lut	minä	e-n	ole	kuul-lut
PERFECT	I	be-1s	hear-pp	I	neg-1s	be	hear-pp

Korhonen (1973) suggests that the reason why the old negative present perfect was retained better than the old affirmative present perfect had to do with finiteness: after the introduction of the copula, every verbal construction includes a finite verbal element. In the affirmative present perfect, this can only be the copula. In the negative, on the other hand, the finite element is always the negation. Accordingly, if the copula appears in the affirmative because the grammar now requires finiteness to be overtly realised, it follows that the copula is not needed in the same way in negated clauses.

Korhonen also suggests that since *minä en ole kuullut* is an indisputable perfect form, *minä en kuullut* was left competing with *minä esin kuule* as the realisation of the negated past. In Finnish, Northern Saami and several other languages the former negated perfect has won out, and is now the only means of expressing the negated past. At present, Ume Saami, Pite Saami, and Lule Saami form a transitional zone between the conservative Southern Saami, shown in (3)–(5), and the innovative Northern Saami, shown in (1): In these languages, the copula has been introduced into the perfect construction, but the tense-marking of the negation in the negated past is still retained (Trosterud 1994). The Lule Saami examples in (7)–(9), from Spiik (1989), will serve as an illustration.

(7) a. Mån tjálá-v.
I write-1s
'I write.'

b. I-v tjále.
neg-1s write
'I don't write.'

(8) a. Mån tjáll-i-v.
I write-past-1s
'I wrote.'

b. I-ttji-v tjále.
neg-past-1s write
'I didn't write.'

(9) a. Mån la-v tjáll-ám.
I be-1s write-pp
'I have written.'

b. Mån lidji-v tjáll-ám.
I be.past-1s write-pp
'I had written.'

It is also worth noting that for Lule Saami, which is the northernmost of the transitional languages, it is reported that the innovative negated past is often heard, although it has not yet replaced the traditional construction completely (Korhonen 1973).

3 Trosterud's Explanation

According to Trosterud (1994), the reason why the participle construction became the preferred realisation of the negated past after the introduction of the copula had to do with paradigm economy. He argues that after the introduction of the copula, the perfectivity of the perfect construction is marked by the copula. Since the participle still appears in the perfect construction, however, it is more economic to have it do service as a past tense marker in the negated past as well, since the total number of formatives used in the negated past and the negated perfect will then be lower than if the old negated past is retained. He sketches the two alternatives in the following way:

(10) A. e-n kuul-**lut** 2 formatives (preferred)
e-n **ole** kuul-**lut**

	B.	e-**si**-n kuule e-n **ole** kuul-**lut**	3 formatives (disfavoured)

But notably, here Trosterud takes into consideration only the negated forms of the past and the (present) perfect. If we also include the affirmative forms in the calculation, the two alternatives are in fact equally economic. This is because in the affirmative past, the nonparticipial past marker is in any case retained. Hence, with the affirmative forms included, the comparison between a language with the innovated negated past (A) and a language with the traditional negated past (B) is as shown in (11).

(11)	A.	kuul-**i**-n e-n kuul-**lut** **ole**-n kuul-**lut** e-n **ole** kuul-**lut**	3 formatives
	B.	kuul-**i**-n e-**si**-n kuule **ole**-n kuul-**lut** e-n **ole** kuul-**lut**	3 formatives

Note that I assume that the past marker that combines with the negation (*-si-* in the example) is essentially identical to the past marker that goes with full verbs (*-i-* in the example). This is in fact also claimed by Trosterud himself (Trosterud 1994:176–177):

> In all the languages with a past tense negation verb, the past tense is expressed with exactly the same suffix as the past tense of other verbs, whereas in all languages with past tense expressed on the main verb, the past tense is identical with the participle suffix.

Thus, regardless of which form is used for the negated simple past, the tense of that construction is always expressed by a formative that is also employed elsewhere in the paradigm. This means that the counting of formatives in (11) is in accordance with Trosterud's view. It follows that there is no longer any support for Trosterud's proposal that the change in the negated past was due to paradigm economy.

4 The Participle According to Holmberg et al.

Holmberg et al. (1993) take the maximal expansion of the finite Finnish clause to be as shown in (12), where Fin is Finite, Neg is Negation, TM is Tense/Mood, Aux is Auxiliary, T is Tense, and Pass is Passive.

(12)

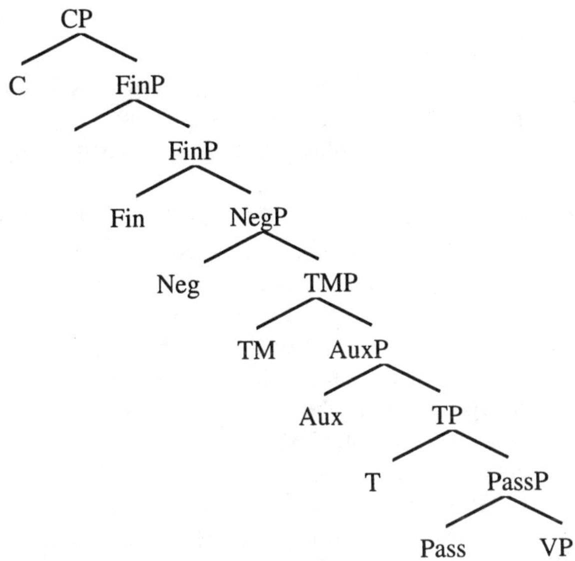

They further assume that subject agreement markers are generated in the Fin head. The TM head is where the tense and mood markers are inserted. The choice of marker is determined by the feature combination of the TM head, in the following manner:

(13)

FEATURES	–Mood –Past	–Mood +Past	+Mood –Past	+Mood +Past
MARKER	-C (present)	*-i* (past)	*-ne* (potential)	*-isi* (conditional)

The T head is where the past participial suffix, or alternatively, the nonpast participial suffix, is inserted, in constructions with the auxiliary *ole* 'be', as in (1a) above and in (14) below.

(14) a. Sinä ol-i-t osta-nut sen kirjan.
you.n be-past-2s buy-pp that.a book.a
'You had bought that book.'

b. Sinä ole-t osta-va sen kirjan.
you.n be-2s buy-nonpast that.a book.a
'You are to buy that book.'

Note that since the tense markers -C and *-i* are both specified as [–Mood], they may not be inserted in the T head, which has no mood features at all. There is thus a crucial difference, on the approach of Holmberg et al., between realising a tense feature plus [–Mood] and realising just a tense feature.

As for the fact that the past participle also shows up in the negated past, where there is no auxiliary *ole*, Holmberg et al. ascribe it to a morphological property of the past marker *-i*. They propose that *-i* is specified to occur only in finite verb forms. In negated forms, only the negation is finite. Technically, they see this as the result of the Neg head having undergone head movement to the Fin head, so that the negation ends up being finite and carrying subject agreement. In this case, the TM head cannot be realised as *-i*. If, in a negated clause, the TM head has the feature combination [–Mood +Past], the past participle marker *-nut* is inserted instead of *-i*. Holmberg et al. (1993) assume that this is possible because the participial marker has the variable feature specification [(–Mood) +Past]. Hence, it can be used as an allomorph of [–Mood +Past] and also as the participial past.

The insight that the past suffix *-i* is connected to finiteness will be retained in the alternative analysis that I will outline below. However, I will argue that the variability that Holmberg et al. (1993) refer to as the 'dual nature' of the past participle is not a necessary feature of the theory.

5 The Tense of Past Participles

Traditionally, the past participle is taken to have aspectual content. In Julien (2001) I contested the traditional view, arguing that the past participle is universally a realisation of nonfinite past tense, not of aspect. This is also how I am going to analyse the past participle in Finnic and Saami. However, in this section I will give a more general account of the syntax and semantics of the past participle before I return to the discussion of Finnic and Saami in the next section.

Let us begin by considering the 'perfect' construction in English, as exemplified in (15).

(15) a. I have read that book.
b. I had read that book.

On my analysis, the constructions in (15a) and (15b) are biclausal, as proposed earlier by Kayne (1993) and also argued for by Taraldsen (1995). That is, they are made up of a finite matrix clause, with a VP headed by the auxiliary and with a T head spelled out by the tense suffix that appears on the auxiliary, and of a nonfinite embedded clause, with a VP headed by the main verb and with a T head spelled out by the participial suffix.

According to the influential analysis of Reichenbach (1947), the perfect, just like other tenses, specifies a certain ordering of three temporal primitives: the speech time (S), the predicate event time (E), and a reference time (R). In more recent analyses, however, the ordering of temporal primitives is broken down into two relations, one between S and R and one between E and R (Comrie 1985, Hornstein 1990). This makes it possible to associate each relation with a separate tense element in syntax, and claim that each tense element relates exactly two temporal primitives. The temporal primitives themselves can be identified as times (Stowell 1995, 1996, Zagona 1995), as time intervals (Demirdache & Uribe-Etxebarria 2000), or as events (Giorgi & Pianesi 1997).

I will follow Giorgi & Pianesi (1997) and assume that a tense element relates two *events*. That is, it has two events as its arguments, and it specifies a temporal relation between these events. The advantage of postulating events as the arguments of tense elements is that one then avoids imposing any particular extension in time on these arguments: the events may be punctual or nonpunctual, open or closed (see Giorgi & Pianesi 1997).

As for the question of how the events are represented in the syntax, I will not go into details here (some proposals are found in Zagona 1995, Stowell 1995, 1996, and Julien 2001); I will merely note that VPs headed by full lexical verbs represent predicate events, and that the speech event must be higher than any other event that is represented in a given construction. For each tense element, an event that is higher in the structure will be its first argument while an event that is lower in the structure will be its second argument. Further, with Stowell (1996) and Demirdache & Uribe-Etxebarria (2000) I take the meaning of the past tense to be 'after', the meaning of the future tense to be 'before', and the meaning of the present tense to be 'simultaneous with'. Thus, if a higher event X and a lower event Y are the arguments of a tense element T, the relation between X and Y will be specified as 'X after Y' if T is past, as 'X before Y' if T is future, and as 'X simultaneous with Y' if T is present.

Now if a given tense element is the highest tense element of the construction, it will normally have the speech event S as one of its arguments, since S is higher than any other relevant event.[1] The lowest tense element of a construction must have the predicate event E as one of its arguments. It follows that if a construction contains only one tense element, it must have both S and E as arguments, and accordingly, it relates S directly to E, so that no R is involved. In constructions with two tense elements, by contrast, the higher head relates S to an R while the lower head relates that R to E, so that the relation between S and E is an indirect one, mediated by R.

It should be noted that a similar idea is expressed by Stowell (1996). He proposes that temporal heads always relate an event time to a reference time, and that the reference time has the interpretation of speech time only if it is not controlled by another temporal argument higher up in the syntactic structure. This gives the effect that the highest temporal argument must be construed as speech time, and that in simple tenses, E is directly related to S.

My proposal builds more directly, though, on the analysis given by Demirdache & Uribe-Etxebarria (2000). Although Demirdache & Uribe-Etxebarria take the past participle to represent aspect and not tense, they nevertheless argue, following Klein (1995), that tense and aspect belong to one and the same system, in that tenses as well as aspects are predicates which relate two time intervals. For example, they analyse both the past and the perfect as having the meaning 'after'. That is, on their approach both the past and the perfect relate two time intervals x and y such that x is after y. Replacing Demirdache & Uribe-Etxebarria's terms Utterance Time and Assertion time with S and R, the meaning of the past perfect can be shown schematically as in (16).

---

[1] The use of narrative present is an exception to the generalisation that the highest tense element has S as one of its arguments. One could perhaps argue, though, that the narrative present relates to a fictious speech time. Also note that an embedded finite tense does not necessarily have the speech event as one of its arguments. This is shown in the following Northern Saami example, from Nickel (1990:448):

(i) De gula-i-met, go unna billo-š gilkkah-a.
then hear-past-1p as little bell-dim sound-pres.3s
'Then we heard a/the little bell sounding.'

Here the past tense of the matrix clause relates the speech event to the event denoted by the matrix predicate, i.e. to the event of hearing. The (finite) present tense of the embedded clause relates the event denoted by the embedded predicate, i.e. the event of sounding, not to the speech event but to the matrix predicate event, which serves as an R for the embedded tense.

(16) I had(PAST) read(PERFECT) that book. PAST: S after R
PERFECT: R after E

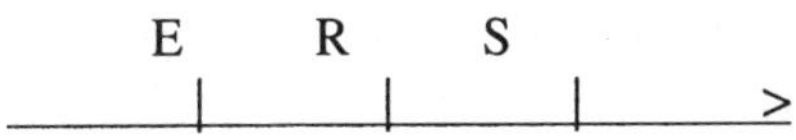

On this view, the difference between the ordinary past tense and the past participle is that the former typically relates R to S, whereas the latter establishes a relation between R and E. According to Demirdache & Uribe-Etxebarria (and Klein 1995), this is what distinguishes tenses from aspects. In other words, the ordinary past tense has an absolute function while the past participle has a relative function (cf. Comrie 1976).

However, I will argue that it does not follow that the past participle is not also a tense. The morphological distinction between the ordinary past and the past participle does not necessarily reflect a contrast between tense and aspect. It could simply be that the realisation of a tense head with the feature [+Past] depends on whether or not that tense head appears in a finite or in a nonfinite context. My proposal is that in English and many other languages, such a head is realised as a nonparticipial past tense marker in finite contexts, while in nonfinite contexts, it is realised as a past participle.

Normally, the ordinary past marker will represent an absolute past tense, while the past participle will represent a relative past tense. But the absolute function of the non-participial past and the relative function of the participial past are not necessarily intrinsic properties of the respective markers. Rather, their different functions follow from the different syntactic positions of the markers. A non-participial, finite past marker can be the highest tense element of a construction, and accordingly, it can have the speech event as its first argument. Hence, finiteness tends to be associated with absolute tense. A participial past marker, on the other hand, will always be embedded under some finite verbal element. Normally, it is also embedded under a finite tense element, and it is then the finite tense element which has the speech event as its first argument, while the participial past has some R as its first argument. Because of this, the participial past is associated with relative tense.

The fact that in many languages the past participle can never have an absolute function is probably the reason why the participle is seen as crucially different from the ordinary past. But note that there are quite a few languages where absolute, finite tenses have the same realisations as relative, nonfinite tenses (see Julien 2001). In fact, even in English and other Germanic languages the nonparticipial past is often similar to the participial past.[2] And consider the following examples from Kituba, a Bantu-based creole language of Zaire, where one and the same marker, glossed as 'anterior' by Mufwene (1990), expresses an absolute past if it is the highest tense marker of the construction but a relative past elsewhere (examples from Mufwene 1990:99f.):

(17) a. Béto mé(ne) di-**á(k)a**.
we finish eat-ant
'We ate a long time ago.'

b. Ntángu ya María kwis-**á(k)a**, múna béto méne di-**á(k)a**.
time C Maria come-ant, then we finish eat-ant
'When Maria came, we had already eaten.'

c. Ntángu ya María ata kwisa, múna béto méne di-**á(k)a**.
time C Maria fut come, then we finish eat-ant
'When Maria comes, we will have eaten.'

A similar situation is found in Northern Sotho. While (18a) is an example of a simple past tense, relative tenses are shown in (18b) and (18c) (examples from Louwrens, Kosch, & Kotzé 1995:51ff).

(18) a. Mosadi o-rêk-**ilê** nama.
woman sagr-buy-past meat
'The woman bought meat.'

b. Mosadi o-bê a-rêk-**ilê** nama.
woman sagr-aux.past sagr-buy-past meat
'The woman had bought meat.'

c. Mosadi o-tlô-ba a-rêk-**ilê** nama.
woman sagr-fut-aux sagr-buy-past meat
'The woman will have bought meat.'

Strikingly, the only morphological difference between the verb in (18a) and the embedded verb in (18b) and (18c) is the shape of the subject agreement prefix, which is *o-* in the former but *a-* in the latter. According to Louwrens, Kosch, & Kotzé (1995) the *o-* agreement marker is used in the indicative positive, for this class of subjects, and the *a-* marker elsewhere.

---

[2] Comrie (1985) also points out that absolute tense is not always formally different from relative tense.

They do not comment on the appearance of the *a-* marker on the embedded verb in (18bd), which also seems to be a positive indicative form. One might guess, though, that the *o-* only appears on finite verbs, so that a non-finite verb must carry the *a-* marker instead.

However that is, the past tense marker has the same shape in both environments. In fact the only difference between the past tense in (18a) on the one hand and the past tense in (18bc) on the other is that the former makes reference to the speech event whereas the latter does not. In the model I am proposing here, we would take all these occurrences of past tense to be realisations of a T head with the feature [+Past], and the absolute or relative reading to follow from the position of the head in the construction as a whole.

I will now show that the readings of the perfect constructions can be derived under the assumption that both the auxiliary and the main verb are tensed. Since there are two tense elements present, it cannot be the case that the speech time S is directly related to the predicate event time. The relation must be mediated through a reference time R, such that the higher tense element relates S to R while the lower tense element relates R to E. This is illustrated in (19) for the present perfect and in (20) for the past perfect (*sim* is short for 'simultaneous with').

(19) I had(PRES) read(PAST) that book. PRES: S sim R
PAST: R after E

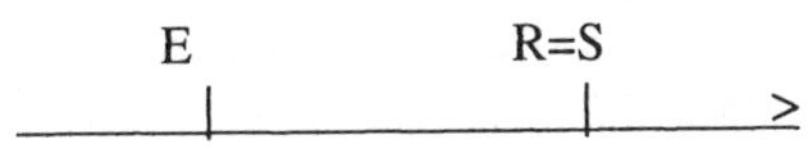

(20) I had(PAST1) read(PAST2) that book. PAST1: S after R
PAST2: R after E

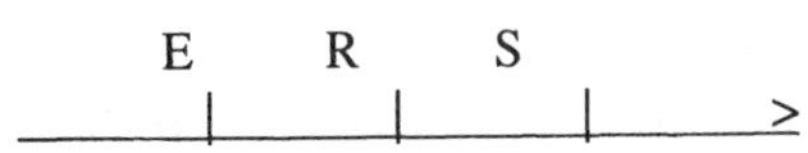

Notably, R is not a real event; it is an eventlike entity, or a dummy event, which only appears in the computation of temporal relations. I will assume that every R must have some specific function; otherwise it would not be licit at LF. This is comparable to the constraint prohibiting *vacuous application of viewpoint* shifting in the approach of Demirdache & Uribe-Etxebarria 2000, which ensures that every R enters into a temporal relation that is different from other temporal relations in the construction. As for the function of R, R can be characterised as representing a *perspective* time, i.

e. a time from which another event is viewed, or as representing a *topic* time, i.e. as a time about which a particular claim is made (Klein 1992, Giorgi & Pianesi 1997).

The function of R is seen clearly in (20), where R does not coincide with neither of the events S and E. In this case, R can be specified by a temporal adverbial, as in *When Thelma arrived, I had read that book.* This indicates that R here represents a time about which it is stated that the predicate event precedes this time.

In (19), R coincides with the speech event S. In this case, any claim about R can also be made about S, so it is not immediately obvious what function R has. It has been noted, though, that even if the predicate event precedes the speech time both in the present perfect and in the simple past, the time of the predicate event can be specified by an adverbial in the simple past but not in the present perfect (see e.g. Klein 1992). In the present perfect, an adverbial denoting some specific time will modify S or R. Since S and R coincide, it is hard to say which one. This is illustrated in (21).

(21) a. I read that book yesterday.
b. *I have read that book yesterday.
c. I have read that book now.

My proposal is that when R coincides with S, R is focused. This proposal is inspired by Klein's (1992) notion of *topic time contrast*, which means that the topic time (R in my framework) may be contrasted with other times where what is asserted for the topic time does not hold. It is also related to the idea put forth by Demirdache & Uribe-Etxebarria (2000) that the assertion time (i.e. R) is the time interval that the aspect puts in focus.[3] I will take this to mean that when R coincides with S, the attention is drawn to R and thereby to S. Because of this, the interpretation is not only that the predicate event is in the past, as implied by the past participle, but also, because of the presence of R, that it is viewed from the time of speech. This is then what lies behind the 'current relevance' perceived with the present perfect which has so often been noted.

On the present approach, simple tenses involve no R; there is only one tense element which relates S directly to E. Perfect constructions, by contrast, contain two tense elements, and accordingly, also an R with the functions just mentioned. If this is the correct analysis, so that in (20), both the auxiliary and the main verb realise a T with the feature [+Past], it follows that perfect constructions are biclausal. Even if we assume that there are

---

[3] This is based on the theory of the focus function of aspect found in Smith (1991).

more than one tense head per clause (Cinque 1999), there cannot be more than one past tense head in one single clause. Hence, (20) must contain two IP layers and two VPs, as suggested by Kayne (1993).

The main point that I wanted to make in this section was, however, that the participle does indeed represent a past tense which is like any other past tense except that it is nonfinite.

6 Finnic and Saami Again

In this section we shall see that analysing the past participle as a realisation of tense paves the way for a rather simple analysis of the appearance of the past participle in the negated simple past in many Finnic and Saami languages, and of the diachronic development of this construction. But first I will point to some data that give an even stronger indication that the past participle, at least in Northern Saami, does have temporal content.

In each of the Northern Saami constructions given in (22), there is an embedded non-finite clause. In (22a) the verb of the non-finite clause has the past participial form, whereas in (22b) it appears in the so-called 'aktio essive' form, which also could be termed progressive, and in (22c), the embedded verb shows up as an infinitive.

(22) a. Elle lohká/logai Máhte boaht-án.
Elle says/said Máhtte.a come-pp
'Elle says/said that Máhtte has/had come.'

b. Elle lohká/logai Máhte boahti-me.
Elle says/said Máhtte.a come-prog
'Elle says/said that Máhtte is/was coming.'

c. Elle lohká/logai Máhte boahti-t.
Elle says/said Máhtte.a come-inf
'Elle says/said that Máhtte will/would come.'

We see that the meanings of these nonfinite verb forms can be rendered by tensed verbs. More precisely, the past participle in (22a) corresponds to a relative past tense, since it places the coming event in the past with respect to the event denoted by the matrix verb, which coincides with the speech time if the matrix verb has present tense but precedes the speech time if the matrix verb is in the past tense. The progressive in (22b) indicates that the coming event is simultaneous with the matrix event, regardless of whether the latter coincides with the speech time (when the matrix verb is in the present tense) or precedes it (when the matrix verb is in the past tense). Finally, the embedded infinitive in (22c) places the coming event in the future with respect to the matrix event.

Although both the past participle and the progressive (or aktio essive) in Saami are traditionally taken to represent aspectual categories, the readings that we get in (22) are no different from what we would get from a relative past tense, a relative present tense, and a relative future tense, respectively. This is one reason why I take the past participle to represent a nonfinite past tense and the progressive to represent a nonfinite present tense, in Finnic, in Saami and in other languages (see Julien 2001 for more detailed discussion). As for the infinitive, it clearly gives a future reading in (22c). In other cases, it has no effect on the temporal semantics at all.[4] Hence, I will follow Wurmbrand (2001) and assume that infinitives are sometimes tensed and sometimes not.

A consequence of what I have just said is that perfect constructions in Finnic and Saami are analysed in the same way as English perfect constructions. That is, I take them to be biclausal, such that the tense of the auxiliary represents a T head in the matrix clause while the participial suffix represents a T head in the embedded clause.

Now recall that in the analysis of the perfect construction given by Holmberg et al. (1993), the tense marker of the auxiliary and the participial suffix are realisations of two different functional heads within one single clause, as indicated in (12). The former represents the TM head while the latter represents the T head. But when the participle appears in the negated past, it is taken to spell out the TM head, which is otherwise spelled out by one of the non-participial tense markers. Similar ideas are expressed by Trosterud (1994). On this view, it follows that the use of the participle in the negated past requires that the participle must be able to spell out either of these heads.

However, on my analysis the Aux and T proposed by Holmberg et al. (1993) and shown in (12) are replaced by the matrix V and the embedded T, respectively. It is the possible to say that the participle represents a TM head both in the negated past and in the perfect, the only difference being that in the former case this tense head belongs to the matrix clause, while in the latter case it belongs to the embedded clause. As we shall see, this leads

---

[4] The following is an example of a seemingly tenseless Northern Saami infinitive:

(i)	Elle	liik-o	dáns-ut.
	Elle	like-pres.3s	dance-inf
	'Elle likes to dance.'		

to an alternative explanation of the change that has taken place in the negated past in many Finnic and Saami languages.

If the present perfect always is the result of combining a matrix present tense with an embedded past tense, as in (19), the Proto-Finnic present perfect, which is expressed by just the participle (see (2)), must include a present tense which is phonologically null. This is not a very radical proposal as the present tense is arguably phonologically null also in the affirmative and negative simple present forms. But since the only overt verbal inflection in the present perfect is that of the participle, it is only the participle that shows that we have a perfect and not a simple past. That is, only the presence of the participle indicates that the construction also contains a finite tense which is phonologically null. Whenever the participle appears, it signals that there is also a higher tense element in the construction. Accordingly, the past participle suffix in Proto-Finnic must be analysed as the realisation of a non-finite *relative* past tense.

At the later historical stage where the copula has been introduced into the perfect constructions, it is the presence of the copula which shows that the perfect is a complex tense. The reasons for the introduction of the copula into the language are outside the scope of the present discussion. What will concern us here is the consequences this must have had for the grammars that new language learners construct. I am assuming here a theory of grammatical change like that of Lightfoot (1991), according to which each language learner constructs one and only one grammar on the basis of the positive evidence that is robustly present in her linguistic environment. This means that changes in grammar are in principle abrupt, occurring from one generation to the next.

Now whereas a child exposed to constructions of the form *minä kuullut* would have to assume that the past participle suffix represents a non-finite *relative* past tense, a child hearing constructions of the form *minä olen kuullut* will conclude differently. In the latter case, the past participle suffix need no longer be specified as the realisation of a relative tense. Its relative function is clearly indicated by the fact that it is preceded by an auxiliary in the present tense. Thus, in the new grammar, it suffices to characterise the past participle suffix as the realisation of a non-finite past tense, more precisely, as the realisation of [+Past] tense head that has not undergone head movement to a Fin head with a [+Finite] feature.[5] This is probably a simplification of the grammar, since having a marker which specifically represents a relative tense appears to be very marked universally.

[5] If the tense head spelled out by the participle suffix in perfect constructions has moved to Fin at all, which is an issue I will not go into here, it has certainly not moved to a Fin head with a [+Finite] feature.

With everything else unchanged, the reanalysis of the participial suffix still does not allow it to show up in the negated past. In the negated past in (2), the past tense marker is attached to the negation, which also bears agreement. As noted by Holmberg et al. (1993), the agreement markers seem to be the realisations of the Fin head in Finnish and related languages. This means that inflected negations like *idtjim* in (4b) and *ittjiv* in (8b), which correspond to *esin* in (2) and (3), are formed from an underlying syntactic structure as shown in (23a) by movement of the Neg head to TM and of Neg+TM to Fin. Note that at this stage, the TM head is higher than the Neg head (cf. Trosterud 1994), which is the opposite of the order proposed by Holmberg et al. for Finnish. The configuration after movement is shown in (23b).

(23)a.

b.

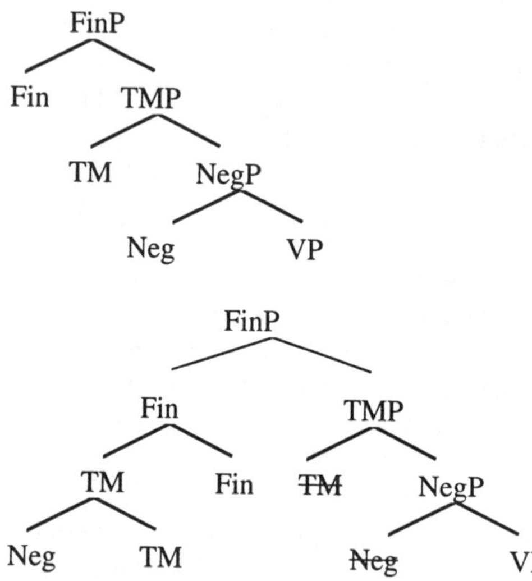

A [+Past] feature in the TM head in (23b) is included in a complex head with the [+Finite] feature of the Fin head. Hence, the [+Past] feature will be spelled out by the finite past marker *-(s)i*. (Here and in the following I use the forms from modern Finnish, which were given in (2) and (6), to represent schematically the various forms found in the different languages.)

As noted in section 2, Korhonen (1973) suggested that the use of the participle in the negated past was a consequence of the copula having become obligatory. This can now be explained in the following way. Even in those Finnic and Saami languages where the copula is not obligatory, the copula appears in perfect constructions if the tense (or polarity) is emphasised (see Bergsland 1994). That is, *minä olen kuullut* is heard alongside *minä kuullut*. At some historical stage in the development of the languages that now have an obligatory copula and use the participle in the negated past, there must have been a generation of language learners who decided that *minä olen kuullut* is the only grammatical alternative. Suppose now that for these speakers, the copula appears in *minä olen kuullut* because their grammar requires that *finiteness* must always be spelled out, as suggested by Korhonen (1973). This means that they can still have *minä en kuullut* as the negated present perfect, since the finiteness is here realised on the negation.

At an even later stage, there are speakers who take the copula itself, and not just the overt realisation of finiteness, to be obligatory. Hence, the negated present perfect must be *minä en ole kuullut*. The older generation, however, still produce forms like *minä en kuullut*, without a copula. For a speaker in whose grammar the copula is obligatorily spelled out, there is only one possible analysis for such forms; namely, one where *minä en kuullut* is in opposition to *minä en kuule*, the negated simple present, so that the participial past tense marking in *en kuullut* is taken to contrast minimally with the present tense in *en kuule*. In other words, constructions like *en kuullut* are now analysed as representing the negated simple past.

The new negated past differs from the old negated past in the organisation of morphemes. While in the old negated past the tense marker was suffixed to the negation, it is suffixed to the verb in the new negated past. This means that the negation now moves to Fin without picking up T. Accordingly, T must now be situated below Neg (cf. Trosterud 1994). The new ordering of functional heads is shown in (24a), and the configuration after head movement of the negation and of the verb is shown in (24b).

(24)a.

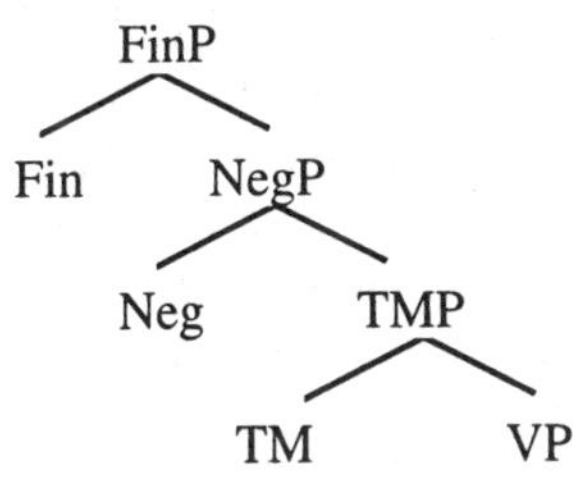

b.

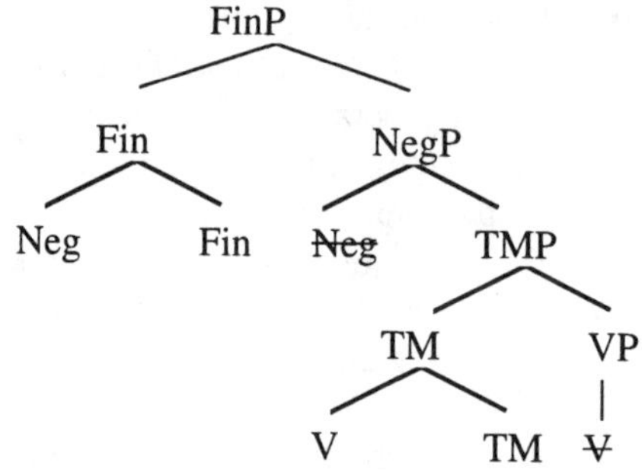

What made the reanalysis of the clause structure possible must have been the fact that the present tense marker was phonologically null. Hence, a negated present tense construction like *en tule* was compatible with (23a) as well as with (24a): It could be analysed as having the present tense marker suffixed to the negation (*e+Ø+n*), in contrast with *esin tule*, or suffixed to the main verb (*tule+Ø*), in contrast with *en tullut*.

When the latter option is chosen, negated clauses are assigned the structure shown in (24b). Here the negation has moved to Fin while the verb has moved to TM. The TM head is not included in a complex head with the Fin head, and accordingly, if the TM head has the features [–Mood +Past], it will be spelled out by the past participial suffix. Recall that in the grammar with an obligatory copula, the past participial suffix is no longer specified as the representation of a *relative* tense. Hence, it may appear in perfect constructions, where it spells out the non-finite past tense of a clausal projection that is embedded under a finite auxiliary, and also in the negated past.

But as already noted, the participial suffix can only be inserted in the TM head if that head has the feature specification [–Mood +Past]—in this respect, all the languages under discussion are similar. In the present model, this can be captured by saying that the participial suffix also has this feature specification. The embedded TM in perfect constructions never shows any mood distinctions, so it could be taken to have the features [–Mood +Past], just like the TM head in the simple past.

Alternatively, if individual markers are allowed to be underspecified, as in the Distributed Morphology theory of Halle & Marantz (1993, 1994), we could say that the participial suffix only marks [+Past]. Underspecification means that a given marker need not be specified for every feature that is present in the syntactic terminal node that the marker spells out. Hence, a marker specified as [+Past] can be chosen as the spellout of a TM head with the features [–Mood +Past] or [+Mood +Past], as long as there is no marker that is better suited to spell out this head. Now if the mood markers that compete with the participial for insertion in the TM head are specified as [+Mood], they cannot be inserted in a TM head specified as [–Mood]. Hence, it will be the participial suffix and not the mood markers that is inserted if the TM node is [–Mood +Past].

It is now clear why the use of the past participle in the negated past was contingent on the introduction of the copula. We can also see why those Uralic languages that lack an obligatory copula have past tense forms of the negation (Trosterud 1994). If tense were not marked on the negation in a language where the copula is normally absent from the perfect construction, the verb in the negated past would have to be a non-finite *absolute* past tense form, so that it could be distinguished from the negated perfect, where the participle is a non-finite *relative* past tense. This hypothetical situation is shown schematically in (25).

(25) negated present: en kuule
negated past: en kuul+X
negated perfect: en kuullut

As long as the ordinary past suffix *-i* is idiosyncratically barred from appearing in non-finite verb forms, there is no marker available for the position of X in (25b). But if tense is marked on the negation, there is no problem—then the ordinary, finite, absolute past marker can be used in the negated past as well as in the affirmative past, and it will contrast only with the relative, participial past. Hence, as long as *-i* is a finite past, and no non-finite absolute past is introduced, the tense-marked negator is retained until the copula is made obligatory.

7 A Note on Verbs Meaning 'Be'

In Northern Saami there is one verb that does not conform to the generalisation that the past participle as used in perfective tense constructions is identical to the past connegative form, that is, the form that appears in the negated past. The deviant verb is *leat* 'be'. In (26a) I show a finite past form of *leat*, in (26b) and (26c) follow two examples with the past connegative of *leat*, and in (26d) and (26e) I show the past participle of *leat*.

(26) a. Mii le-i-mmet doppe.
we be-past-1p there
'We were there.'

b. Mii eat lea-n doppe.
we neg.1p be-past there
'We were not there.'

c. Mii eat lea-n lohk-an ollu.
we neg-1p be-past read-pp much
'We had not read much.'

d. Mii lea-t lea-maš doppe.
we be.pres-1p be-pp there
'We have been there.'

e. Mii lea-t lea-maš vuošš-an teaja.
we be.pres-1p be-pp boil-pp tea.a
'We have sort of boiled tea.'

As we see, after the negation we get the form *lean*, whether or not *leat* is followed by another verb. That is, *lean* is the past connegative form of the auxiliary *leat* as well as of the main verb *leat*. In perfect tense constructions, on the other hand, we invariably find *leamaš* as the past participial form of *leat*.

The verb meaning 'be' is also exceptional in Lule Saami. We have already seen, in section 2, that tense is normally marked on the negation in the negated past in this variety. Another example is given in (27a).[6] But recall that the innovative negated past is also possible in Lule Saami. Then in (27b) I show the negated past of *liehket* 'be'. If we compare this to the negated present of *liehket* in (27c), we see that in (27b), the past tense is marked on *liehket*, which appears in the form *lim*. Thus, the innovative negated past has become obligatory with #, while it is optional with other verbs in Lule Saami.

The example in (27d) serves to demonstrate that the past connegative *lim* is also used when *liehket* is an auxiliary. In (27e) is the present perfect of *liehket*. As we see, the past participle that appears here is not identical to the past connegative. Finally, (27f) shows that the finite past form of *liehket* is different from the past connegative as well as from the past participle.

(27) a. Mån i-ttji-v barga.
I neg-past-1s work
'I did not work.'

[6] The examples in (27) are constructed with the aid of Spiik (1989) and Tjihkkom (1992).

b. Mån i-v l-im moaren.
I neg-1s be-past angry
'I was not angry.'

c. Mån i-v l-a moaren.
I neg-1s be-pres angry
'I am not angry.'

d. Mån i-v l-im bargga-m.
I neg-1s be-past work-pp
'I had not worked.'

e. Mån la-v læhká-m moaren.
I be.pres-1s be-pp angry
'I have been angry.'

f. Mån l-idji-v moaren.
I be-past-1s angry
'I was angry.'

The generalisation that can be formulated on the basis of the data in (26) and (27) is that nonfinite 'be' plus an *absolute* past tense is realised as *lean/lim*, while nonfinite 'be' plus a relative past tense is realised as *lea maš/læhkám.*[7]

---

[7] After verbs in the conditional mood, both *lean* and *leamaš* can sometimes be used in Northern Saami. The examples in (i) illustrate this (cf. Nickel 1990:64).

(i)a. Munnje livččii lea-maš ávki.
me.ill be.cond.3s be-pp use.n.s
'To me it would have been of use.'

b. Munnje livččii lea-n ávki.
me.ill be.cond.3s be-past use.n.s
'To me it would have been of use.'

There is also some variation after modal verbs in the past tense. Thus, while Nickel (1990:473) says that *leamaš* is used after *sáhtii* 'could', Harald Gaski (p.c.) tells me that *lean* is more natural for him. The two options are shown in (ii).

(ii)a. Munnje sáht-ii lea-maš ávki.
me.ill can-past.3s be-pp use.n.s
'To me it could have been of use.'

That *leamaš* always involves a relative past tense can be seen even more clearly if (26b) is compared to (27a). While the sequence *eat lean* in (26) means 'were not', *eat leamaš* in (27a) must be rendered as 'have not been'. And strikingly, (27b) is semantically equivalent to (27a).

(27) a. Mii eat lea-maš doppe.
we neg-1p be-pp there
'We have not been there.'

---

b. Munnje sáht-ii lea-n ávki.
me.ill can-past.3s be-past use.n.s
'To me it could have been of use.'

A possible explanation of the alternation between *leamaš* and *lean* observed here is that the morphological marking of the finite verb might be ambiguous. In particular, the –*ii* ending of the conditional form *livččii* could be seen as an integral part of the conditional marking or as past tense marking. In the former case, the finite verb is not tense-marked, which means that the non-finite verb represents an absolute tense. In the latter case, the non-finite verb represents a relative tense. If *leamaš* is the realisation of a relative past tense while *lean* is the realisation of an absolute past tense, it is expected that either form should be able to follow after a finite verb in the conditional.

Similarly, the morphological marking on the finite verb *sáhtii* in (ii) does not necessarily represent tense. As Iatridou (2000) demonstrates, in many languages what is formally past tense marking can be used to express either past tense or counterfactual mood. It might be that this also applies in (ii) — note that the meaning of *sáhtii* here corresponds closely to the meaning of English *could*, which clearly need not be interpreted as past tense. But if the morphological marking of *sáhtii* can represent either tense or mood, it follows again that both *lean* and *leamaš* can show up here, if the distribution of these forms is as I have suggested.

In addition, it seems that *leamaš* in itself can convey a marked modal meaning. My informants tell me that after a conditional, *leamaš* is preferred over *lean* if another verb follows, as in (iii).

(iii) a. Doppe livččii lea-maš somá lea-t.
there be.cond.3s be-pp fun be-inf
'It would have been fun to be there.'

b. Doppe livččii somá lea-t.
me.ill can-past.3s fun be-inf
'It would be fun to be there.'

If we compare (iiia) to (iiib), we see that *leamaš* in (iiia) provides an additional layer of modality between the basic predication and the conditional *livččii*, or in other words, it adds more distance between the basic predication and the actual world. It is possible that this is another factor that is relevant to the distribution of *lean* and *leamaš*.

b. Mii eat lea-t lea-maš doppe.
we neg-1p be-pres be-pp there
'We have not been there.'

This fact suggests that there is an empty *leat* preceding *leamaš* in (27a). The reason why this *leat* need not be realised phonologically must be that its presence is in any case indicated by *leamaš*, which unambiguously represents a relative past tense.

Consider also the following, where the nonfinite *leamaš* appears to be coordinated with the finite *lea*:

(28) Oktavuohta leamaš ja lea ain min stuorámus fápmu.
unity been and is still our biggest strength
'Unity has been and still is our biggest strength.'

Again, I would like to postulate a phonologically empty *leat* with present tense in front of *leamaš*. Note that the present tense is phonologically zero in Northern Saami anyway. Leaving out a present tense *leat* therefore in reality only means leaving out the copula itself, which is not a very drastic move.

Hence, in Northern Saami and Lule Saami there is a three-way distinction in the past tense forms of 'be': There is a finite past form, a non-finite absolute past form and a relative past form. Still, the dominant pattern in these languages, as well as in many other Finnic and Saami languages, is that the past connegative form is identical to the past participle that we find in perfect tense constructions. This was the problem that I set out to explain. I concluded that the only semantic difference between the past connegative and the past participle is that the former has an absolute function while the latter has a relative function. In most cases, this distinction is not marked. The fact that in some varieties the distinction *is* marked on the verb 'be' does not affect my analysis of the cases where it is not. Note that it is the identity in form between the connegative and the participle that a priori is unexpected and that appears to require an explanation.

One might also note in this connection that the paradigm of *leat* 'be' in Northern Saami shows another distinction that is not seen in other verbs. While the form that follows the negated imperative is normally identical to the form that follows the negated indicative—see (29), *leat* has a special form for the negated imperative—see (30).

(29)a. I-t jeara.
neg-2s ask
'You do not ask.'

b. Ale jeara!
neg.imp.2s ask
'Do not ask!'

(30)a. I-t leat suhtus.
neg-2s be angry
'You are not angry.'

b. Ale leage suhtus!
neg.imp.2s be angry
'Do not be angry!'

However, the fact that there is a distinction between *leat* in (30a) and *leage* in (30b) does not prevent as from characterising *jeara* in (29) as the present tense connegative form of *jearrat* 'ask', without any mention of the indicative imperative distinction. On my view, giving the past connegative/past participle a unified treatment, when the two are identical, is no less justified.

8 Conclusion

In this paper, I have given a new account of the historical change that has taken place in several Saami and Finnic languages, whereby the traditional Uralic negated past construction, with tense marked on the negation, has been replaced by the construction that was formerly the negated perfect. I have showed that this replacement can be explained as the result of reanalysing the past participle, a process that was triggered by the introduction of the obligatory copula into the perfect constructions. In the new grammar, the past participle invariably represents a nonfinite past tense, and no distinction is made between a nonfinite past tense with an absolute function and a nonfinite past tense with a relative function. Contrary to Holmberg et al. (1993) and Trosterud (1994), I claim that there is no question of syncretism or of paradigm economy; the past participle represents exactly the same feature combination regardless of whether it appears in the negated past or in perfect tense constructions.

References

Bergsland, K. 1994. *Sydsamisk grammatikk.* Kárášjohka: Davvi Girji.

Cinque, G. 1999. *Adverbs and Functional Heads.* Oxford: Oxford University Press.

Comrie, B. 1976. *Aspect.* Cambridge: Cambridge University Press.

Comrie, B. 1985. *Tense.* Cambridge: Cambridge University Press.

Demirdache, H. and M. Uribe-Etxebarria. 2000. The Primitives of Temporal Relations. In *Step by Step*, ed. Roger Martin, David Michaels, and Juan Uriagereka, 157–186. Cambridge, Mass.: MIT Press.

Giorgi, A. and F. Pianesi. 1997. *Tense and Aspect: From Semantics to Morphosyntax*. Oxford: Oxford University Press.

Halle, M. and A. Marantz. 1993. Distributed Morphology and the Pieces of Inflection. In *The View from Building 20*, ed. Kenneth Hale & Samuel Jay Keyser, 111–176. Cambridge, Mass.: MIT Press.

Halle, M. and A. Marantz. 1994. Some Key Features of Distributed Morphology. *MIT Working Papers in Linguistics* 21:275–288.

Holmberg, A., U. Nikanne, I. Oraviita, H. Reime, and T. Trosterud. 1993. The Structure of INFL and the Finite Clause in Finnish. In *Case and Other Functional Categories in Finnish*, ed. Anders Holmberg and Urpo Nikanne, 177–206. Berlin: Mouton de Gruyter.

Hornstein, N. 1990. *As Time Goes By: Tense and Universal Grammar*. Cambridge, Mass.: MIT Press.

Iatridou, Sabine. 2000. The grammatical ingredients of counterfactuality. *Linguistic Inquiry* 31:231–270.

Julien, M. 2001. The Syntax of Complex Tenses. *The Linguistic Review* 18:125–167.

Kayne, R. S. 1993. Toward a Modular Theory of Auxiliary Selection. *Studia Linguistica* 47:3–31.

Klein, W. 1992. The Present Perfect Puzzle. *Language* 68:525–552.

Klein, W. 1995. A Time Relational Analysis of Russian Aspect. *Language* 71:669–695.

Korhonen, M. 1973. Zur Geschichte des negativen Präteritums und Perfekts im Ostseefinnischen und Lappischen. In *Commentationes Fenno-Ugricae in Honorem Erkki Itkonen*, 174–184. Helsinki: Suomalais-Ugrilainen Seura.

Korhonen, M. 1981. *Johdatus lapin kielen historiaan*. Helsinki: SKS.

Lightfoot, D. 1991. *How to Set Parameters: Arguments from Language Change*. Cambridge, Mass.: MIT Press.

Louwrens, L. J., I. M. Kosch, and A. E. Kotzé. 1995. *Northern Sotho*. München: Lincom Europa.

Mufwene, S. S. 1990. Time Reference in Kikongo-Kituba. In *Pidgin and Creole Tense-Mood-Aspect Systems*, ed. Jon Victor Singler, 97–117. Amsterdam: John Benjamins.

Nickel, K. P. 1990. *Samisk grammatikk*. Universitetsforlaget, Oslo.

Reichenbach, H. 1947. *Elements of Symbolic Logic*. New York: Macmillan.

Smith, C. S. 1991. *The Parameter of Aspect*. Dordrecht: Kluwer.

Spiik, N. E. 1989. *Lulesamisk grammatik*. Sameskolstyrelsen.

Stowell, T. 1995. What do the Present and Past Tenses Mean? In *Temporal Reference, Aspect and Actionality, vol. 1: Semantic and Syntactic Perspectives*, ed. Pier Marco Bertinetto, Valentina Bianchi, James Higginbotham, and Mario Squartini, 381–396. Torino: Rosenberg & Sellier.

Stowell, T. 1996. The Phrase Structure of Tense. In *Phrase Structure and the Lexicon*, ed. Johan Rooryck and Laurie Zaring, 277–291. Dordrecht: Kluwer.

Taraldsen, K. T. 1995. Participle-based Small Clause Complements of *få* 'get' in Norwegian. In *Small Clauses (Syntax and Semantics 28)*, ed. Anna Cardinaletti and Maria Teresa Guasti, 207–233. San Diego, Calif.: Academic Press.

Tjihkkom, K. 1992. Lulesamisk grammatikk. Sáme åhpadusráde, Guovdageaidnu.

Trosterud, T. 1994. Auxiliaries, Negative Verbs and Word Order in the Sami and Finnic Languages. In *Minor Uralic languages: structure and development*, ed. Ago Künnap, 173–181. Tartu: University of Tartu.

Wurmbrand, S. 2001. *Infinitives. Restructuring and Clause Structure.* Berlin: Mouton de Gruyter.

Zagona, K. 1995. Temporal Argument Structure: Configurational Elements of Construal. In *Temporal Reference, Aspect and Actionality, vol. 1: Semantic and Syntactic Perspectives*, ed. Pier Marco Bertinetto, Valentina Bianchi, James Higginbotham, and Mario Squartini, 397–410. Torino: Rosenberg & Sellier.

Language Index

Subject Index